D0551598

SECOND EDITION

A HISTORY OF MODERN GERMANY

1800 TO THE PRESENT

MARTIN KITCHEN

WILEY-BLACKWELL

A John Wiley & Sons, Ltd., Publication

This edition first published 2012
© 2012 Martin Kitchen

Edition History: Blackwell Publishing Ltd (1e, 2006)

Wiley-Blackwell is an imprint of John Wiley & Sons, formed by the merger of Wiley's global Scientific, Technical and Medical business with Blackwell Publishing.

Registered Office
John Wiley & Sons Ltd, The Atrium, Southern Gate, Chichester, West Sussex, PO19 8SQ, United Kingdom

Editorial Offices
350 Main Street, Malden, MA 02148-5020, USA
9600 Garsington Road, Oxford, OX4 2DQ, UK
The Atrium, Southern Gate, Chichester, West Sussex, PO19 8SQ, UK

For details of our global editorial offices, for customer services, and for information about how to apply for permission to reuse the copyright material in this book please see our website at www.wiley.com/wiley-blackwell.

Library of Congress Cataloging-in-Publication Data
Kitchen, Martin.
  A history of modern Germany, 1800 to the present / Martin Kitchen. – 2nd ed.
    p. cm.
  Rev. ed. of A history of modern Germany, 1800 to 2000.
  Includes bibliographical references and index.
  ISBN 978-0-470-65581-8 (pbk. : alk. paper) 1. Germany–History–1789–1900. 2. Germany–History–20th century. 3. Germany–History–1990– I. Kitchen, Martin. History of modern Germany, 1800 to 2000. II. Title.
  DD203.K58 2012
  943.087–dc22

                          2010043502

A catalogue record for this book is available from the British Library.

This book is published in the following electronic formats: ePDFs [ISBN 9781444396881]; ePub [ISBN 9781444396898]

Set in 10/12.5 Minion by Toppan Best-set Premedia Limited
Printed in Malaysia by Ho Printing (M) Sdn Bhd

1   2012

Contents

Illustrations

Maps

Figures

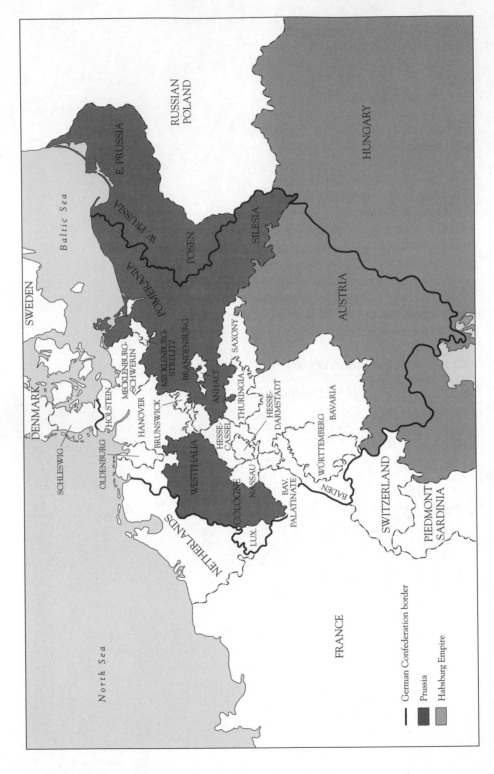

North Sea

Baltic Sea

SWEDEN

DENMARK

SCHLESWIG

HOLSTEIN

OLDENBURG

MECKLENBURG-
SCHWERIN

MECKLENBURG-
STRELITZ

POMERANIA

W. PRUSSIA

E. PRUSSIA

RUSSIAN
POLAND

POSEN

BRANDENBURG

SILESIA

AUSTRIA

HUNGARY

HANOVER

BRUNSWICK

ANHALT

SAXONY

THURINGIA

HESSE-
CASSEL

HESSE-
DARMSTADT

WÜRTTEMBERG

BAVARIA

WESTPHALIA

COLOGNE

NASSAU

BAV.
PALATINATE

BADEN

SWITZERLAND

PIEDMONT
SARDINIA

LUX.

NETHERLANDS

FRANCE

German Confederation border
Prussia
Habsburg Empire

MAP 1 Germany, 1815

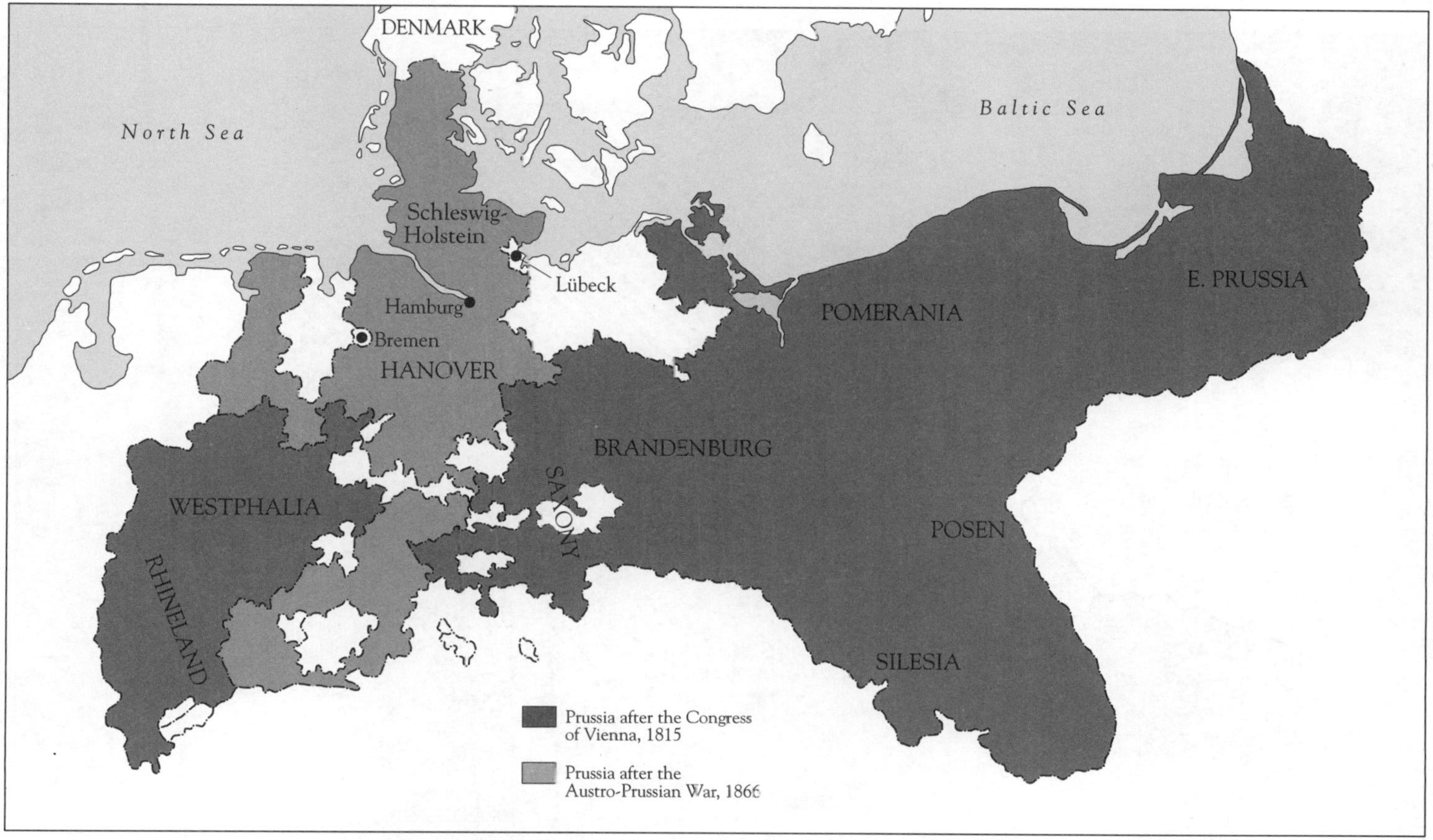
DENMARK
North Sea
Baltic Sea
Schleswig-Holstein
Lübeck
Hamburg
Bremen
HANOVER
POMERANIA
E. PRUSSIA
BRANDENBURG
SAXONY
WESTPHALIA
RHINELAND
POSEN
SILESIA
Prussia after the Congress of Vienna, 1815
Prussia after the Austro-Prussian War, 1866

MAP 2 Prussia before and after the Austro-Prussian War

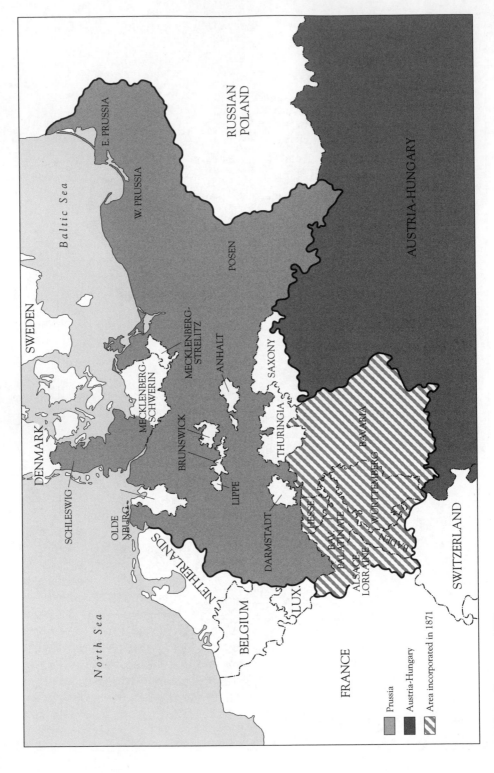

MAP 3   Germany, 1871

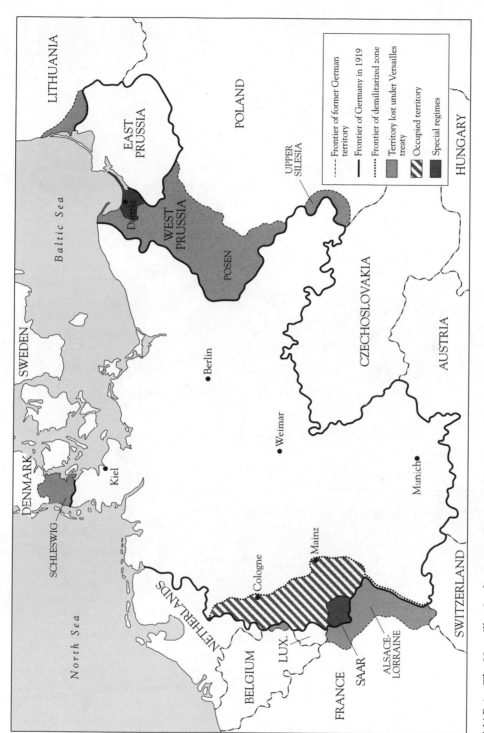

MAP 4   The Versailles Settlement, 1919

Frontier of former German territory
Frontier of Germany in 1919
Frontier of demilitarized zone
Territory lost under Versailles treaty
Occupied territory
Special regimes

MAP 5   The division of Germany at Potsdam, 1945

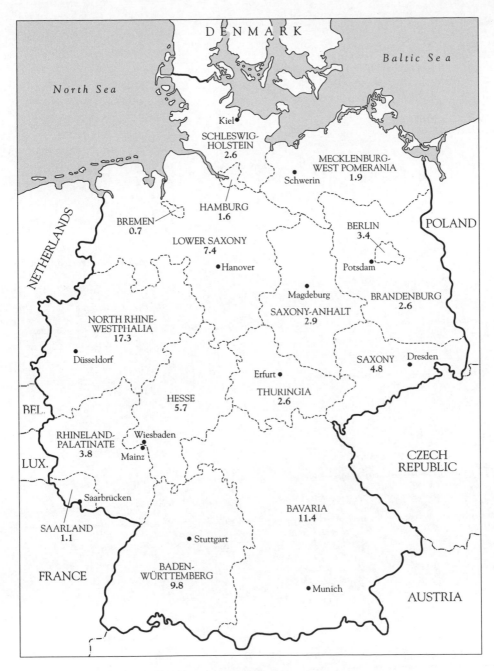

MAP 6   Germany, 1993

Introduction

In 1800 Germany was a ramshackle empire, made up of hundreds of petty principalities, free cities, and ecclesiastical and aristocratic estates, which ever since 1512 had borne the impressive title of the Holy Roman Empire of the German Nation. Voltaire caustically remarked that it was neither holy nor Roman, and certainly not much of an empire. As for German – the word really did not mean much at that time.

Among the German states only Austria and Brandenburg-Prussia counted for much, and Prussia was not even part of the empire. The empire nonetheless had many virtues, its federal structure providing a model for the founding fathers of the United States, but it was in a state of relentless decline and was impervious to reform. It was overrun by the armies of revolutionary France and reorganized under Napoleon. The historian Thomas Nipperdey begins his monumental history of nineteenth-century Germany with the catchy phrase: "In the beginning was Napoleon." Like most such aphorisms it is a half-truth. This was no second creation, but it did mark the end of the empire and a significant transformation of Germany's political geography. Napoleon forced sixteen of what the great reformer Baron vom Stein contemptuously called "petty sultanates" into the Confederation of the Rhine, thereby greatly enhancing Bavaria, Württemberg, and Baden in the hope of creating a third Germany to offset Austria and Prussia. The Confederation was reformed along French lines, adopting the progressive Napoleonic code of law, whereas in Prussia the reforms were designed to strengthen the state so as eventually to free those provinces that were under French occupation. These reforms and the struggle against France were to lay the foundations of Prussian strength in the new century, and to lead to the formation of a new Germany in 1871. In the process the progressive liberalism of the early decades of the century was gradually transformed into an increasingly reactionary nationalism.

A somewhat vague notion of a German national identity was first articulated in the eighteenth century. It was centered on the linguistic and cultural peculiarities of the German-speaking world. It was abstract, humanistic, cosmopolitan, philosophically rarefied and apolitical. The intense hatred of the French, caused by the revolutionary and Napoleonic wars, along with the unacceptable behavior of the French occupying troops soured this early nationalism. Cosmopolitanism turned into an arrogant feeling of cultural superiority. The apolitical became a reactionary obsession with a mythological German past. The rarefied was distilled into an impenetrable but intoxicating obscurity. The new nationalists hoped that when the wars were over a powerful and united Germany would emerge, but their hopes were dashed at the Congress of Vienna, where they were overridden by the imperatives of the great European powers.

Britain and France preferred to accept the changes made by Napoleon and completed his work by creating a German Confederation comprising the 39 remaining states. There was

A History of Modern Germany: 1800 to the Present, Second Edition. Martin Kitchen.
© 2012 Martin Kitchen. Published 2012 by Blackwell Publishing Ltd.

neither a head of state nor a government, but simply a federal assembly to which the member states sent their representatives, with Austria providing the chairman. The solution was acceptable to the Austrians, for they were the senior partners, and Metternich appeared to be firmly in charge as he imposed his reactionary and repressive policies on the Confederation.

Outward appearances were deceptive. Whereas Austria failed to set its house in order by tackling the serious problems of a multinational empire at a time when national sentiments were becoming inflamed, Prussia was laying the foundations of its future economic strength. The Rhineland, which Prussia had been awarded at the Congress of Vienna much against its will, since it was a backward and Catholic area, became the centre of Germany's industrial might. The Customs Union (Zollverein), founded in 1834 under Prussian leadership, made many of the German states economically dependent on Prussia, and created a market that was soon to challenge British supremacy. Capital moved northwards as Austria declined. All that was needed was some form of unification for Germany to be the most powerful nation on the Continent. But what form was this unification to take? Would it be a Greater Germany that included Austria, or a Little Germany under Prussian domination?

Metternich introduced a number of repressive measures, but he was unable to contain the various groups that clamored for constitutional reform, liberal nationalism, and radical change. Following the example of the French there was revolutionary upheaval in Germany in 1848. A national assembly met in Frankfurt that was immediately confronted with the fundamental and perplexing questions, "Who is a German?" and "Where is Germany?" There was at first general agreement that Germans were people who spoke German and, in the words of the patriotic poet and historian Ernst Moritz Arndt, who was born a serf and was thus a personification of the fundamental changes in the social fabric, Germany was "Wherever German is spoken." On second thoughts this raised more questions than it solved. Were the proudly independent German-speaking Swiss really Germans? What about the Alsatians who spoke German but had French citizenship? Then there were the hundreds of thousands of Polish-speaking Prussians. Were they honorary Germans simply because there was no Polish state? A similar question was raised about the Czechs in the Austrian provinces of Bohemia and Moravia. Then there was some discussion whether Jews should be treated as equal citizens, or whether the German people needed to be protected against these threatening outsiders.

Most of the delegates to the Prussian parliament wanted a greater German solution that would include Austria. Such a Germany would, they hoped, be strong enough to protect and later absorb the German minorities on its borders in Holland, Luxemburg, Schleswig, Switzerland, and Alsace-Lorraine. Such ideas came up against the national aspirations of Poles and Czechs in the east, and were hastily dropped in the west for fear of confronting France. Whereas German liberals had traditionally championed the Polish struggle against Russian autocracy, they suddenly changed their tune, denouncing any suggestion that the German minority in Poland should be absorbed in a backward and uncultured nation. Similar accusations of treason were levied during the discussions over the Czech lands, northern Italy, and Schleswig. Healthy national egotism triumphed over any concern for other peoples' rights to national self-determination. Precious few liberals realized that the denial of the rights of others undermined their own claims, and that victory over insurgents in Italy, Hungary, Bohemia, and Poland greatly strengthened the forces of reaction. It was a fatal flaw of this new form of nationalism that it was based on ethnicity rather than the acceptance of a shared set of values and respect for common legal system. One hundred and fifty years after the revolution of 1848 a Russian who could not speak a word of

German, but who was born of parents who claimed to be of German descent, had an automatic right to German citizenship, whereas a German-speaking child born of Turkish parents in Germany had no such claim. In spite of recent reforms of the immigration laws a residue of this heritage is still painfully apparent.

The men of 1848 were only free to deliberate and decide by majority vote as long as Austria and Prussia were busy dealing with their own immediate problems. Once the reaction had triumphed in both states the parliamentarians were ordered to pack their bags and returned to their respective states. In the years that followed, Austria and Prussia jockeyed for position within the Confederation, until Bismarck was appointed Prussian chancellor. He immediately set about settling the German question with "blood and iron."

Very few people realized the dangers of national unification by such violent means; prominent among them was Friedrich Nietzsche. After all, Greece, Serbia, and Italy were all founded in violence, while most nations were forged in civil wars. Later historians were to endorse Nietzsche's reservations, claiming that German history traveled down a unique path (*Sonderweg*), but this was soon shown to be an exaggerated case of self-immolation and an inadequate explanation for the phenomenon of National Socialism. The German empire of 1871 had a parliament elected by universal manhood suffrage, which was much more than the "fig-leaf of absolutism" that the socialist leader, August Bebel, claimed. Bismarck, its founding father, pronounced Germany to be "saturated." Once his great gambling streak was over, knowing full well that the other European powers were ever watchful of this prosperous and powerful newcomer, he was anxious to keep the peace.

The "Second Reich," much like that which it had replaced, was a loose confederation of states, but it was dominated by Prussia. The military had always played a dominant role in Prussian society, and the Prussian army, having won three wars in quick succession virtually unaided, was admired, adulated, and emulated. It was virtually free from parliamentary control since the war minister was not answerable to parliament and the budget only came up for approval every seven years. The kaiser jealously guarded his power of command and protected the army from outside influences. Such was the social prestige of the army that Bismarck remarked that "human beings start at the rank of lieutenant."

Bismarck, often painted as a diplomatist of genius, left a fatal legacy. He permanently alienated France by agreeing to the annexation of Alsace and Lorraine and then earned the hostility of Russia, first by his alliance with Austria-Hungary and then by triggering a trade war. His ill-considered dabbling in imperialism made the British increasingly wary of the new Germany. When his successors began to build a battle fleet, Britain, humiliated by the Boer War, sought continental partners and joined the Franco-Russian alliance, thus realizing Bismarck's "nightmare of coalitions."

Bismarck's domestic policies were as divisive as his foreign policy was hazardous. He painted a lurid picture of the Reich's putative enemies, foremost among whom were the Social Democrats, but which also included Catholics, the French, Poles, Alsatians, Danes, and, whenever politically expedient, the Jews. With such a comprehensive catalogue of opponents a majority of citizens were considered to be aliens, while only Protestant conservatives were deemed to be true Germans. The system began to fall apart when powerful liberal and democratic forces confronted a hidebound conservatism, backed by racist anti-Semitic populism. When war began in 1914 these social and political tensions were temporarily overcome in a remarkable display of national unity, but as the war dragged on the nation fell apart. When the Western Front collapsed in 1918, soon after the spectacularly successful spring offensive, most Germans were shocked and taken by surprise. The army

high command had concealed the true picture, and accused the democratic forces of stabbing the army in the back, thus causing the country's downfall.

Germany was left truculently defiant of the Treaty of Versailles and was determined to
undo a peace settlement that was harsh enough for everyone to feel that it was grossly
unfair, but too feeble to be enforceable. Germany's determination to undo the peace settlement was partly concealed by the Treaty of Locarno in 1925 and its subsequent admission to the League of Nations. Then a severe economic crisis combined with a complete
breakdown of the political system enabled Adolf Hitler and his National Socialists to agitate
to increasing effect. Resistance to the Nazi menace was weakened by the inability of the
democratic forces to settled their acute differences in order to reach a workable compromise in the face of a common danger, and by the folly of conservatives who imagined that
they could use Hitler to serve their own purposes.

As soon as he was appointed chancellor, Hitler rapidly established a one-party dictatorship and his opponents were terrorized into submission. Once he was firmly in command
he began systematically to tear up the Treaty of Versailles. Military service was introduced
in 1935; the Rhineland was occupied in 1936, Austria and the Sudetenland in 1938, Memel
in 1939.

The Nazis provided a radical and horrific answer to the perennial question "Who is a
German?" Bismarck's old enemies – the Social Democrats, the politicized Christians, the
left-leaning liberals – were forced into exile or locked away in concentration camps. The
Polish elite was systematically murdered, millions of others enslaved. The much-vaunted
"racial community" was purged of all elements considered to be dangerous and debilitat-
ing, such as the mentally and physically handicapped, habitual criminals, homosexuals,
Gypsies, and Jews. They were segregated, sterilized, or murdered.

Hitler's appalling vision could not be realized without a major war, which at first looked
as if he might win, in spite of the warnings of his more level-headed generals. Through a
deadly combination of ideological frenzy and bureaucratic efficiency, Hitler perpetrated a
crime of unimaginable horror, which he believed to be his greatest achievement and legacy
for which succeeding generations would be grateful. It left a world in ruins, with tens of
millions dead, among them 6 million Jews.

In 1945 Germany was a pile of rubble with a starving population. It was a little Germany
between Rhine and Oder, once again a power vacuum, divided into four occupation zones.
As a result of the imperatives of the Cold War the country was divided into a democratic
and capitalist state in the west and a Stalinist planned economy in the east. Western
Germany was treated leniently – some would argue far too leniently – encouraged by the
Western powers in its efforts to develop a parliamentary democracy and a liberal market
economy. Although the crimes of a great many former Nazis were all too often overlooked,
an extraordinary effort was made to confront the past. No country had ever made such an
effort to atone for its crimes.

Whereas the economy of the western Federal Republic (FRG) grew at an astonishing rate
thanks to the exceptional efforts of a generation determined to start anew, the eastern
German Democratic Republic (GDR) was mismanaged so as to be virtually bankrupt by
the 1980s. As the Soviet empire crumbled the GDR was left isolated as a post-Stalinist
dictatorship. Abandoned by the Soviet leadership, the regime collapsed and, as a result of
the first free election for 57 years, the country opted to unite with the Federal Republic.
On October 3, 1990 Germany was thus reunited, but the gulf between the two Germanys
remained alarmingly wide. Few had realized the hopeless state of the East German economy,

the antiquated infrastructure, the appalling state of public health and housing, to say nothing of the psychological effects of almost 60 years of dictatorship, snooping, censorship, and repression. The staggering cost of reconstruction placed a heavy burden on the West German taxpayers, who regarded the easterners as indigent, surly, and ungrateful. Easterners in turn resented this arrogance, and felt that they had been colonized by a selfish bunch of greedy materialists.

The process of unification is still far from complete. The walls that have been built in people's heads and hearts have to be broken down and the disparities between East and West overcome. But the prospect of a democratic and dynamic Germany, fully integrated into the European community, free from any dangerous ambitions, is a reassuring reminder that the country has learnt from its past mistakes and is determined to build on the democratic traditions that are also part of its troubled past.

German history is also the story of German historians, for they have shaped the way we see the German past. Leopold von Ranke, who established history as a professional discipline, was born in 1795 and died in 1886. Having witnessed the transformation of a ramshackle confederation into the most powerful state in Europe it is hardly surprising that he saw the state, its origins, its development, and its interaction with other states as the prime object of historical study. Ranke's epigones thus asserted the "primacy of foreign policy." With the reunification of Germany in 1990 the whole question of the German state was again on the agenda, prompting some remarkable neo-Rankean scholarship such as Heinrich August Winkler's "The Long Road West" (*Der lange Weg nach Westen*).

It was not until the 1960s that the younger generation of German historians began to reject the Rankean approach to the study of history. Very few were influenced by the dominant Annales school with its sociological approach, its emphasis on mentalities, and, later, the linguistic turn – resulting from a rejection of political and diplomatic history as well as a hostility towards Marxist class analysis. Instead they rediscovered the works of a number of highly talented émigré historians such as Eckart Kehr, Arthur and Hans Rosenberg, Georg Hallgarten, and Alfred Vagts. They were politically engaged on the left, strongly influenced by Marx and Weber as reworked by the Frankfurt school into critical theory. Their self-proclaimed aim was to create a "historical science beyond historicism" (*Geschichtswissenschaft jenseits des Historismus*). Above all they saw history as a critical and emancipatory discipline. Theirs is a therapeutic model of historical discourse, based on the conviction that the historian has a grave moral responsibility to shoulder the burden of guilt for Germany's recent unfortunate past. The result was a mirror image of the old nationalist historical legacy, which saw a glorious tradition stretching from Luther to Frederick the Great to Bismarck and reaching its apotheosis with the foundation of the Reich in 1871. Now the legacy was that of the anti-Semitic and reactionary Luther, of the militaristic Great Elector, the authoritarian Frederick the Great, and the Bonapartist Bismarck, coupled with the disjuncture between economic modernity and political backwardness in the Kaiserreich, and the traditions of dreamy inwardness and deference to authority, all of which culminated in the bestiality of National Socialism.

It is hardly surprising that since 1945 German historians have concentrated on the question how a highly civilized country, which vaunted its moral and cultural superiority, seeing itself as the "land of writers and thinkers" (*Dichter und Denker*), could sink into the deepest depths of fanaticized barbarism. The initial explanation, served up in an easily digestible form by the historian A. J. P. Taylor and the journalist William Shirer, was that there was a long tradition of aggressive nationalism, anti-Semitism, authoritarianism, hero-worshiping, and slavish obedience to authority that made something like National Socialism almost inevitable. This explanation was soon shown to be a very facile one. What seemed in retrospect to be inevitable was the result of an almost infinite number of contingent variables. National Socialism may not have been the inevitable outcome of German history, but Hitler did not descend from the clouds as he does in Leni Riefenstahl's remarkable documentary on the Nuremberg Rally of 1934, *Triumph of the Will*. The heavy burden of the past resulted in an astonishing lack of resistance to a regime that trampled on all the positive traditions that Goebbels dubbed "the ideas of 1789." There is some truth in the argument that National Socialism was the fruit of certain trends that were common to all of Europe. It is also true that at least in part it was a response to Russian communism. But none of this implies that Germany was not fully responsible for what happened between 1933 and 1945, or that National Socialism was not fully grounded on some unfortunate traditions in Germany's past. Above all, National Socialism was certainly not an "accident" as some historians have argued.

The debate became further confused by a debate between "functionalists" and "intentionalists." The first argued that the extremism of the Nazi regime resulted from the state's structure, with its internal divisions and rivalries, its confusing decision-making process, and the unpredictability of charismatic leadership. The latter insisted that it was all essentially the result of Hitler's obsessive designs. After much acrimonious discussion both sides made concessions, and calmer heads suggested that the truth lay in a combination of the two approaches.

Fortunately there is much more to German history than the search for the origins of National Socialism and the analysis of the twelve years during which it was in power, half of which were largely determined by the exigencies of war. There is also a strong and vibrant liberal and democratic tradition to which this book pays tribute, and which makes nonsense of the claim that National Socialism was the result of some fatal flaw in the German character. Such an idea is unable to account for the fact that the "horrid Huns," with their ghastly atavistic inheritance and murderous anti-Semitic intent, now live in what is, for all its many faults and shortcomings, an exemplary democracy, securely integrated with Europe, and free from any territorial ambitions.

When we talk of Germany we tend to think of it as a powerful monolith, when in fact for most of the period under discussion it was a loose federation of widely different states. Even the Wilhelmine empire comprised four separate kingdoms with four separate armies, and a number of semi-autonomous entities. It was only during the mercifully brief Third Reich that the country was a centralized state. Regional differences were, and still are, extremely strong. Protestant Prussia was very different from and antagonistic toward Catholic Bavaria. Rhinelanders had precious little in common with Pomeranians or Holsteiners. Local loyalties, summed up in the uniquely German concept of *Heimat*, whether to proudly independent cities like Hamburg or Frankfurt, or to a particular town or village, remain powerful and are reinforced by local customs and practices.

The great nationalist historians concentrated on Prussia, for it was the driving force behind unification, and they glorified Bismarck's Germany, which was dominated by Prussia. Subsequent historians continued to write as if the history of Germany was the history of Prussia writ large. Some of Karl Lamprecht's acolytes, who concentrated on cultural history, studied local history and customs as part of the National Socialist *völkisch* project, but it was not until after the Second World War that serious regional and local histories were written which give us an inkling of the complexities and richness of German history. Detailed studies provide a timely reminder that different Germans experienced the history of their country in widely different ways. A miner in the Ruhr, a university-educated lawyer in Berlin, a Bavarian farmer, and a Frisian fisherman lived in worlds that were poles apart. The set of relationships between men and women underwent a sea change in the period under review. It is difficult to imagine that from such widely differing circumstances something as all-encompassing as a national character of the "German mind" could ever be constructed.

I make no apologies for writing a narrative history. History, as the word suggests, is essentially about telling a story. It is, with all due respect to the dwindling band of post-modernists, about a series of real events set in chronological order so as to show how one thing led, subject to however many eventualities, to another. For many years this approach has been dismissed by those who attempted to apply rigorously theoretical approaches derived from the social sciences to the study of history. In recent years historians have returned to a narrative approach, without which 200 years of German history would make little sense, and would dissolve into a series of unconnected events, trends, and data. On the other hand I am well aware that events occur within and are shaped by social structures, economic factors, and cultural attitudes. This new edition places greater emphasis on such issues. It also contains a much more detailed discussion of the peculiarities of the German Democratic Republic and brings the story more up to date.

The Oxford philosopher J. L. Austin, well known for his sardonic wit, once said that one might be tempted to call oversimplification the occupational disease of historians if it were not their occupation. I am all too aware of the many oversimplifications, omissions, and oversights in this book. Some are inevitable, others excusable, a few have been avoided in this new edition; the remainder are entirely my fault. My one wish is that readers will find the story I have to tell of interest, and that reading it will inspire them to look elsewhere for further insights. To this end I have appended a short bibliography of works in English.

CHAPTER ONE
GERMANY UNDER NAPOLEON

CHAPTER CONTENTS

A History of Modern Germany: 1800 to the Present, Second Edition. Martin Kitchen.
© 2012 Martin Kitchen. Published 2012 by Blackwell Publishing Ltd.

Writing at the turn of the eighteenth to the nineteenth century the whimsical German writer Jean Paul commented that providence had given the French the empire of the land, the English that of the sea and the Germans that of the air. He would have been at a loss to define what exactly he meant by the "Germans" and most likely would have found the question pointless. It could hardly have been confined to those who lived in the territory of the Holy Roman Empire of the German Nation, for that would have excluded a large number of German speakers, including the Prussians. Nor would he have included all those areas where German was spoken. The German empire indeed existed in the air. It was a threadbare patchwork of innumerable political entities, from the European states of Austria and Prussia to the fiefdoms of the imperial knights, imperial monasteries, independent towns, and even villages.

All this was to change under the impact of the French revolutionary wars and above all of Napoleon. The French seized the territory on the left bank of the Rhine and in 1803 the map of Germany was redrawn as a result of the lengthy deliberations of an Imperial Deputation which did little more than add its seal of approval to a plan presented by the French and Russians. The deputation's Conclusions (*Reichsdeputationshauptschluss*) of February 25, 1803, resulted in the secularization of the territorial possessions of the Catholic Church including those of the Prince Bishops of Mainz, Cologne, and Trier. Archbishop Dalberg of Mainz, a crafty politician, retained his princely estates and his electoral title, was made grand duke of Frankfurt and continued in office as chancellor of an empire that was soon to vanish. A host of smaller units were annexed (mediatized) and absorbed by the larger states under the guise of compensation for territory lost to the west of the Rhine. The remains of once influential states such as the Electoral Palatinate vanished overnight. More than 3 million Germans were given new identities, and most of the "petty sultanates" that had been the butt of Jean Paul's mordant wit disappeared.

The southern and southwestern states profited the most from these changes. Bavaria, Baden, and Württemberg were greatly strengthened as a counterweight to Prussia and Austria, but such power as they had resulted from their dependence on France. Clearly the empire was now doomed, and Dalberg's efforts at reform proved to no avail.

Shortly after the publication of the Conclusions, France and England once again went to war. The French promptly occupied Hanover, which was in personal union with England and now directly threatened Prussia, in spite of the provisions of the Treaty of Basel of April 1795 that guaranteed the neutrality of northern Germany. The southern German states, determined opponents of the empire that constrained their sovereignty, joined in with their French masters in an attack on Austria in 1805. On October 17 Napoleon scored a great victory over the Austrians at Ulm, but four days later Nelson destroyed the French fleet at Trafalgar in the most decisive naval victory in history. Britain now had absolute command of the seas, leaving Napoleon no alternative to a land war on the Continent.

The southern German states were rewarded with spoils from the Habsburg empire. Bavaria and Württemberg became kingdoms, Baden and Hesse-Darmstadt grand duchies. Napoleon's adopted daughter, Stephanie Beauharnais, was married off to the odious Karl, grand duke of Baden. The Holy Roman Empire was formally dissolved in 1806, and in July of that year the south German states were reorganized in the Confederation of the Rhine, a military alliance with the Emperor Napoleon in the self-appointed role of protector. The majority of the tiny states, which had remained independent after the Conclusions, were now absorbed by their larger neighbors.

Brandenburg-Prussia remained quixotically defiant in its isolation, its army a pathetic shadow of Frederick the Great's, its leadership decrepit and incompetent. The French made short shrift of them at the twin battles of Jena and Auerstedt in October. The once powerful Prussian state collapsed, Berlin's chief of police announcing that: "The king has lost a *bataille* and it is the responsibility of all citizens to remain calm." The phrase "Ruhe ist die erste Bürgerpflicht" (a citizen's prime responsibility is to remain calm) and the clear distinction made between the king and his subjects were classic expressions of the spirit of Brandenburg-Prussia.

After an indecisive battle against the Russians at Preussisch-Eylau in early 1807, Napoleon smashed the tsar's army at Friedland in June and peace was concluded at Tilsit. Prussia nearly vanished from the map of Europe. It only survived because of the intervention of the tsar and Napoleon's calculation that a buffer state between France and Russia might be desirable. Prussia lost all its territory west of the river Elbe, much of which went to make up the kingdom of Westphalia for Napoleon's worthless brother Jérôme. The smaller duchy of Berg was awarded to his brother-in-law Murat. Prussia was stripped of its recent acquisitions of Polish territory. They became part of the new Grand Duchy of Warsaw. It was obliged to pay horrendous reparations and was subjected to French occupation until such a time as they were paid in full.

The map of Germany had thus been radically redrawn and Prussia reduced to insignificance. In 1802 Hegel wrote:

All component parts would benefit from Germany becoming a state, but such will never come about as a result of deliberations, but only of force that is in tune with the general level of education and combined with a deeply and clearly felt desire for the need for unification. The common mass of the German people along with the estates, who only know of the separation of the various regions and who think of unification as something quite foreign to them, must be brought together by a conqueror's power. They must be coerced into regarding themselves as belonging to Germany.

Napoleon, Hegel's "world spirit on horseback," destroyed the old empire and inaugurated a new period in German history. Small wonder that Hegel stood in awe of the French emperor, as did so many of his contemporaries, but his admiration remained on a lofty philosophical plane. There were only a few opportunists and disgruntled ideologues who came to terms with the sordid reality of French domination.

The empire was a ramshackle affair, but it had many virtues. Most found it far more congenial than revolutionary France. Benjamin Franklin admired its federal structure and argued that it should be used as a model for the constitution of the United States. The old empire was destroyed by blood and iron, just as some seventy years later the new empire was to be created by the use of force. Germany was subjected to Napoleon's will, and his empire was now greater than that of Charlemagne. Only an uneasy Austria remained semi-independent.

The Continental System

The German economy was seriously disrupted by Napoleon's continental blockade that in 1806 banned imports from and exports to Britain. It also applied to neutral countries, thus representing a fateful step towards a total war in which there was no distinction between combatants and non-combatants. The blockade proved hard to enforce. It was tightened in 1807, but it was still far from effective. German smugglers were so successful that the French felt obliged to occupy Holland and the German coast as far as Lübeck in 1810; but British goods still found their way in. The French took draconian measures against those found in possession of such contraband. This only served to fuel resistance to the occupiers, thus strengthening national self-consciousness. The situation was further exacerbated by the "Continental System" that subordinated the German economy to French needs. German goods could not be exported to French-controlled Europe, while French goods could be freely imported into Germany.

The traditional export of wood, wool, grain, and linen to England was now rendered virtually impossible, but some manufacturers seized the opportunities afforded by the exclusion of British competition. They were ruined after 1815 when British goods once again flooded the German market. All Germans were affected by sharply rising prices, by heavy taxes, and by frequent controls by the French authorities.

By 1808 the Confederation of the Rhine was forced to provide Napoleon with 119,000 soldiers, thus placing a further burden on the unfortunate Germans. French officials supervised the minutest details of each state's administration, a rigorous censorship was applied, and the nationalist opposition hunted down. In such circumstances it is hardly surprising that attempts to give the Confederation of the Rhine a federal constitution failed. The southern German states, on whom the obligation to provide troops fell hardest, jealously guarded what remained of their sovereignty. The French did not wish to risk further alienating their German vassals for fear that they might emulate the Spanish by rising up against a despotism that proclaimed itself to be a harbinger of liberty, equality, and fraternity.

Resistance to Napoleon

The uprising in Spain was an inspiration to many Germans, particularly in Prussia, which although it had not been forced to become a member of the Confederation of the Rhine was suffering terribly under the burden of reparations. It had been confidently assumed that the French would not demand more than a grand total of 20 million francs. The final bill was for 154 million. The end of the occupation, the staggering cost of which the Prussians were obliged to pay, was thus postponed indefinitely. The first minister, Baron vom Stein, at first had argued in favor of trying to meet the French demands, but once he heard of events in Spain he argued in favor of a popular revolt against French rule. He was a singularly poor conspirator; the French got wind of his schemes and secured his instant dismissal. Stein's property was seized, but he managed to escape to Bohemia having been tipped off by a friendly French official. Henceforth he was a major figure in the European struggle against Napoleon. Leading military reformers such as Scharnhorst and Gneisenau also discussed a comprehensive reform plan to be coupled with a revolt against French rule.

Although the Prussian government would not entertain such schemes, Napoleon felt obliged to make some concessions to ease this mounting tension. In the Treaty of Paris of September 1808 reparations were somewhat reduced and the occupation was ended, but some 10,000 French troops remained to guard military roads and to man the fortresses on the Oder. The costs were borne by Prussia. They were more than the state could bear. Prussia's finances were in a parlous condition and not even Hardenberg, who was appointed chancellor in June 1810, was able to improve the situation significantly, for all his considerable administrative talents. Frederick William III, never the most decisive of monarchs, relapsed into a torpor on the death of his resourceful and immensely popular queen, Luise, in 1810. She was to become the object of a romantic cult, with poets such as Novalis as its priests. She was transformed into an idealized daughter, wife, and mother and Gottfried Schadow's erotically charged statue of the young Luise with her sister Friederike was withheld from public view until the revolution of 1848 heralded the beginning of a less prudish age. This masterpiece of German classicism suggests that there was much more to Luise than a prototypical bourgeois Hausfrau.

The poetic notion that the people would arise and a storm would be unleashed was hopelessly unrealistic. The regular army was no match for Napoleon's, the new Territorial Army (Landwehr) was militarily worthless. This fact was somewhat obscured when the Austrians defeated Napoleon at Aspern in May 1809 as he attempted to cross the Danube. Jubilation at this surprising victory was premature. Support from the other German states was minimal. Some adventurers, such as the Prussian Major Schill, joined the fray. Frederick William III closed his ears to entreaties from the military reformers to do the same. There was a poorly organized peasants' revolt in Westphalia, but most Germans remained passive bystanders. Napoleon crossed the Danube at night, exploited the division between the two Austrian armies, and confronted the Archduke Charles' army at Wagram on June 5. Charles fought well, and the first day was indecisive, but on the second Napoleon's brilliant use of artillery resulted in a crushing defeat. Shortly afterwards Napoleon entered Vienna.

The only successful revolt was in the Tyrol, which had been annexed by Bavaria in 1805. Andreas Hofer, supported by the Archduke John, lead a brilliant guerrilla campaign in the mountains, defeating the French and Bavarian forces in a rapid series of engagements. But this was a traditional, Catholic, and regional movement at odds with the spirit of the age. Hofer was eventually captured and executed in Mantua. Major Schill and the patriotic publisher Palm shared a similar fate, to become the first three martyrs of the German cause, whose memory was recalled in the 22-year-old Ludwig Uhland's "Ich hatt' einen Kamaraden" ("I had a comrade") which became an immensely popular patriotic anthem later to be appropriated by the nationalist and militaristic right.

In the Peace of Schönbrunn Austria ceded further territories and was obliged to pay crippling reparations. Most of Europe was under Napoleon's sway. Only Spain offered fierce resistance to the French in a guerrilla war, the ferocity and brutality of which were immortalized in Goya's shattering etchings. Austria sought to appease and accommodate Napoleon, who became the emperor's son-in-law, having been rebuffed by the tsar, whose sister he had hoped to marry. Metternich, who always put security above legitimacy, encouraged Napoleon's social climbing in the hope that the marriage would spare Austria from further depravation.

Russia was always an uneasy partner for Napoleon. There were so many points of conflict between the two states that conflict seemed increasingly likely. Austria and Prussia now had to choose between the two sides. Metternich, assuming that Russia was unlikely to be able to withstand an invasion, proposed giving France limited support so as to come out on the winning side. In Prussia Gneisenau pleaded for an alliance with Russia combined with a popular uprising. The king dismissed such romantic notions as "mere poetry." Napoleon demanded the right to march his forces across Prussia and insisted that 20,000 men from the Prussian army, which had been reduced to a mere 42,000, should take part in the campaign. Hardenberg saw no alternative but to accept these humiliating conditions.

The reaction among the patriots was instant. About one-quarter of the officer corps resigned their commissions, among them Clausewitz and Boyen, both of whom went to Russia. The chief of police offered his services to the tsar. Frederick William III thus no longer enjoyed the loyalty of many of his most prominent officials, who now saw themselves as serving the nation and the people rather than the monarch. Such was the force of revolutionary ideas that they affected even those who were the most ardent opponents of their Bonapartist manifestation.

The Prussian Reform Movement

Although outwardly Prussia seemed weak and feeble, its government aimless, the period from 1806 to 1811 was one of astonishing and rapid reform. Drastic changes were needed were the state ever to free itself from French domination. But it was not simply a matter of power politics. The French Revolution had swept aside the old aristocratic society based on the estates and replaced it with the bourgeois concepts of freedom and equality. These were notions fraught with contradictions, as critics never tired of pointing out, but there was a general recognition that a state could only survive if the people identified with it to some degree. Subjects had to become citizens were the gulf between the state and society to be bridged.

These were revolutionary ideas, as conservative reformers like Hardenberg knew full well. For this reason they were determined that it should be a revolution from above, controlled and channeled by the bureaucracy, so that the state could be immunized against a revolution from below. It was to be a revolution based on the rule of law, the application of logical reasoning, and concern for the good of the state. A monarchical government was to be given a degree of popular legitimacy in order to avoid the horrors of revolutionary democracy and a reign of terror.

Although there had been some efforts at reform before 1806, it was the virtual collapse of the Prussian state in that fateful year that convinced all but the most purblind of conservatives that drastic changes were needed. The Prussia of Frederick the Great had been an exemplary absolutist state, an example to the rest of Germany, a European power of consequence. But by 1806 Prussia was lagging behind the southern German states, its sclerotic social order hopelessly out of tune with the times. For years reformers had been calling for major changes, but they had been blocked by an aristocracy determined to defend its privileges and by a reluctant monarchy. Now they seized their opportunity.

The reformers were inspired by Kant's lofty concept of individual rights, obligations, and reasoned self-interest that was taken up by such influential figures as Fichte and Pestalozzi. The individual citizen was to come of age, be self-actualizing, free from the restraints of a hierarchical society, free to develop his own talents and abilities, free to contribute to the common good. The enlightened absolutism of the old regime was to be replaced by the enlightened absolutism of the self, which lay at the heart of the liberal humanism of the bourgeois epoch. Obligations were emphasized at the expense of rights. For many this vision of the new man was exciting, but for others it was terrifying. When combined with the economic theories of Adam Smith it was to condemn the old order to extinction. Since the motive force behind the reforms was to free Prussia from the French, the reforms aimed to strengthen patriotic and nationalistic sentiments, thus further subordinating individual liberties to a common cause.

It was an ambitious program aimed at a thorough overhaul of the state. The administration was to be rationalized and careers open to the talents. The economy was to be released from the shackles of the past, and *Manchesterismus* was to be its guiding principle. The army was to be reformed, with promotions based on talent rather than on social status. Society was to be freed from the restrictions and inequalities of the old order. There was to be full equality before the law. The creative power of the people was to be devoted to a common cause.

So much for the lofty ideals – the reality was somewhat different. There was considerable resistance to reform in some quarters, particularly at court and among conservative aristocrats. There were also many differences between the reformers themselves. Baron vom Stein, who was principal minister from 1807 until his dismissal at Napoleon's command in the following year, was the initiator of the reform movement. As an imperial knight with an impeccable aristocratic lineage he detested the absolutist state and urged the devolution of power, thereby strengthening traditional rights and privileges. He was also suspicious of economic liberalism, which he felt would lead to the sacrifice of individual rights to the exigencies of the market.

By contrast Hardenberg, who became chancellor in 1810 and remained in office until his death in 1822, believed in the centralization of state power and a liberal economic policy. Less troubled by moral and philosophical concerns, he argued that, with the guarantee of property rights, equality before the law, and fair taxation, the individual should be able to fend for himself, while recognizing the need for the firm guiding hand of an autocratic state.

The first priority was the reorganization of the administration. The late absolutist state was a shambolic affair with no identifiable areas of competence, a myriad of conflicting interests and institutions, and no clearly defined order of government. The chaotic old cabinet system was swept aside and the king could now only act through his ministers. The absolutist state gave way to bureaucratic governance.

Under Stein the ministers were treated as equals in a collegial system. He had hoped to create a council of state, composed of a wide range of prominent people, to act as a kind of surrogate parliament, keeping a watchful eye on overly ambitious ministers. Hardenberg had no sympathy for such ideas. He created the office of chancellor, who controlled the access of subordinate ministers to the king.

At the local level Prussia was divided into districts (*Regierungsbezirke*) each with an administration (*Regierung*) in which the district president (*Regierungspräsident*) was treated as first among equals. Prussia was thus a federal state with each district enjoying a degree of autonomy, and the president was responsible to the local diets (*Landtage*), which were introduced in 1823/4. They were based on the estates and thus dominated by the aristocracy. Only those who had owned property for many years were eligible to vote. Many highly educated men were thereby disenfranchised. Church affairs, education, health, and road-building were among the presidents' other responsibilities. At Stein's insistence there was a strict division of powers between the judiciary and the executive.

Beneath the districts were the circles (*Kreise*) which were supervised and controlled by the district president. At this level Hardenberg hoped to realize his centralizing vision. A state-appointed director was to take the place of the *Landrat* ("District Commissioner" or "District Officer") who was elected by the local aristocracy. He was to be assisted by an administration elected by the aristocracy, the towns, and the peasantry in equal parts, and by a state-appointed judge. Gendarmes were to take over the function of local policing, thus putting an end to the aristocracy's right to police their own estates. Aristocratic resistance to these proposals was so strong that they were shelved, leaving the old order entrenched on the land, the *Landrat* remaining as an organ of a patriarchal-feudal order. Given that there were only 1,300 policemen in all of Prussia, policing rights of the aristocracy further strengthened the old order. Members of the bourgeoisie who purchased aristocratic estates were denied all the special privileges that went with them. In the Rhineland aristocratic rights that had been abolished were reinstated, causing much bitterness among the bourgeoisie. Tensions between the aspiring middle class and the aristocracy were more noticeable in Prussia than elsewhere in Germany.

Stein's notion of self-government as a counterweight to an all-powerful state was best realized in the towns. Ancient rights and outmoded privileges were abolished, leaving the administration of justice in the hands of the state. Towns became self-governing. A college of electors was chosen by districts rather than by estates. Passive voting rights were given to all who met certain minimal requirements of property, profession, and length of residence. Active voting rights were more restrictive. The propertyless, soldiers, and Jews were not regarded as burghers and were excluded from participation at either level. Councilors were elected for a term of twelve years, honorary councilors for six years. Both the mayor and the salaried councilors had to meet state approval.

The reform of municipal government resulted in the creation of a highly professional class of civic administrators and served as a model for similar reforms in other European states. But it was not an unmitigated success. The reforms were ordered from on high, they were not a response to pressure from below. Their emancipatory effect was thus of little consequence. Furthermore, since they did not coincide with similar reforms in the countryside, the divisions between town and country were further accentuated.

The most radical of the reforms in Prussia was the liberation of the peasantry from the remnants of the feudal order. Serfdom was repugnant to enlightened bureaucrats, its abolition seen as a blow at the very foundations of the absolutist, aristocratic social order. Stein entertained the Romantic notion that the brutish and enslaved peasantry would become proud yeomen who would form the backbone of a revitalized nation. Added to this mixture of Kantian morality and Rousseau's Romanticism came of a large dose of Adam Smith's economic liberalism. It was argued that only if property and labor were freely brought to market could an economy flourish. Aristocratic estates henceforth could be freely bought and sold so that wealthy bourgeois could invest in the land. Serfs would become wage laborers. A traditional, aristocratic, semi-feudal society was to give way to capitalist agriculture.

Once again the impetus for reform came from above, from the liberal bureaucracy, and not from below. There were precious few instances of peasant protest prior to the reform – indeed some peasants regretted the passing of a familiar patriarchal order. Similarly, few aristocratic landowners realized the opportunities that a free market economy offered. Resistance to reform was so strong that it was only after the collapse of Prussia in 1806, when the state was faced with a crippling economic burden, that Stein was able to sweep all objections aside. On October 9, 1807, ten days after his appointment as minister, he issued the "October Edict" that announced the abolition of serfdom in Prussia by St. Martin's Day (November 11) 1810.

The peasants were now free subjects before the law, able to own property, to marry as they wished, and free to move and to practice any trade or profession. Aristocrats were also free to sell their estates and to enter professions that had previously been reserved for the bourgeoisie. In theory a society based on the estates was replaced by a class society that allowed for a high degree of social mobility. In practice there were many remnants of the old regime. No edict could ever fundamentally alter the habits, customs, and mentalities that had been ingrained over generations. Nevertheless this was a radical step forward that changed Prussia in a number of ways. Many aristocrats sold their estates to bourgeois entrepreneurs, and the close association of the aristocracy with the land was now little more than a Romantic myth. By mid-century about half of the aristocratic estates had passed into bourgeois hands. As elsewhere in Europe, wealthy entrepreneurs longed to become country gentlemen, but although some were subsequently ennobled, unlike in England, where titles did not pass on to younger sons, a strict segregation of classes was maintained and intermarriage between aristocrats and bourgeois were extremely rare.

The peasantry was no longer protected by the obligations owed by lords to their serfs so that the pressure of population caused widespread poverty on the land. Conservative opponents of reform argued that capitalism resulted in benevolent feudal lords being replaced by rapacious creditors who bled their wretched victims white. They were well organized with their exclusive representative bodies and their own banking system, to say nothing of their close ties to the court and to the upper echelons of government. They prepared to fight back as soon as the state of emergency had passed.

Many concessions were made to the aristocracy. Cheap credit was made available to landowners who were suffering the consequences of drastically falling prices for agricultural produce. The law of 1810 governing the treatment of servants and laborers (*Gesindeordnung*) was hardly in the spirit of the reformers. Landlords kept their manorial courts that meted out corporal punishment. They could thus demand unquestioning obedience from their underlings. They kept their exclusive hunting rights, were given many tax exemptions, and appointed the local minister and schoolmaster. The law turned a blind eye when aristocrats fought duels, a way of settling disputes denied to lesser breeds. The entrenched powers of the aristocracy were such that there were strict limits to the reform.

A particularly intractable question was that of appropriate compensation for the loss of feudal obligations. This could hardly be in the form of immediate money payments since the peasantry was miserably poor and the state overburdened with debt. Compensation in land was even harder to determine. A decision was therefore postponed. It was not until 1821, when the reaction was winning the upper hand, that a commutation was finally put into effect. Landowners were compensated either by the transfer of land or by the payment of rents. They further profited from the conversion of common lands into private property and by a land settlement designed to bring about a more rational allocation of acreage. Stein and Hardenberg's vision of a proud yeomanry was thus never realized. Few liberated peasants were able to survive as independent farmers. In Prussia east of the Elbe the Junker estates profited considerably as a result of the liberation of the serfs. It remained an area of large estates rather than modest farms. This was to have far-reaching social and political consequences. In the Prussian provinces west of the Rhine, where the Napoleonic code had been applied, the smaller farmers were in a far more favorable position.

For all its shortcomings and injustices the reform on the land was a vital step forward in the process of modernization. Agricultural capitalism replaced a feudal cooperative mode of production. Custom, habit, and tradition gave way to scientific farming and double-entry bookkeeping. The larger estates were reorganized into effective productive units that swallowed up many a small farm unable to compete. But the reform was incomplete. The manorial estates retained many of their ancient rights and privileges within the context of a modern economic order.

The reformers placed economic freedom above individual freedom. The power of the guilds was broken by the Trade Edict (Gewerbeordnung) of 1810. The legal distinctions between town and country were abolished. Church lands were secularized, and much of the royal demesne placed on the market. Hardenberg's determined efforts to reform the tax system so as to make it both equitable and even-handed were only partially successful. A purchase tax on selected items met with fierce resistance and was later abandoned. Taxes on businesses were applied in both town and country, but the opposition of the Junkers was so strong that an attempt to make them pay equal land taxes failed. In 1811 and 1812 a one-time income tax with a marginal rate of 5 percent was introduced, but this occasioned frantic protest by the wealthy against the violation of the private sphere by the state and the assault on private property rights. In 1820 a "class tax" was introduced which combined a poll tax with a sort of income tax. This, combined with the remaining forms of indirect taxation, was a particularly heavy burden on the poor and contributed to the growing disparities of wealth and income.

Prussian Military Reforms

There was one issue on which the reformers and the conservatives could agree. Prussia could never be liberated without fundamental improvements in the army. The Prussian army, once the finest in Europe, had failed to keep pace with fundamental changes both in military science and in society at large. It had failed miserably in 1806. Its tactics were outmoded, commissions in its superannuated officer corps were given on the basis of birth rather than ability, and the men were subjected to brutal discipline. Foreign mercenaries made up at least one-third of its personnel. It existed as an institution separated at every level from the society around it. The reformers, with Scharnhorst at their head, were determined to bridge the gap between the army and society and convert the downtrodden and mindless soldiers into self-actualizing patriots to whom the highest ranks and honors were open.

For this to be possible soldiers had to be respected as autonomous subjects, equal before the law, no longer subjected to inhuman punishment. The fact that the French drastically reduced the army gave the reformers a golden opportunity to cut out much of the dead wood from the officer corps. Henceforth commissions were to be awarded by competitive examination, and promotions likewise were no longer to be based almost exclusively on length of service. Gneisenau waxed poetic on the genius that slumbered in the lap of the nation that would soar on eagle's wings once the fetters of custom and class were removed. The arch-conservative Yorck, although a modernizer of the army with his mastery of light infantry tactics, was appalled. He argued that an attack on the privileges of the aristocracy would lead to an attack on the legitimacy of the monarchy and smacked of Jacobinism. His objections were swept aside, his fears soon proven unfounded. A conservative institution like the Prussian officer corps could never be so radically reformed. Old prejudices in favor of the traditional aristocratic families who had served the state for generations were too deeply entrenched. Many young aristocrats were men of considerable talent and had little difficulty in passing the rigorous examinations required to gain a commission and climb the ladder of promotion. Scharnhorst and Gneisenau might have been bourgeois, but Clausewitz and Boyen came from distinguished old families.

These reforms were all based on the liberal and democratic principle of universal military service, which was designed to create a people's army in contrast to the standing army of the autocratic state. Predictably the idea of a nation in arms was anathema to the conservatives, but many bourgeois reformers also felt that this was going too far along the road to equality and marked a general leveling down of society to its lowest common denominator. The king, fearing the reaction of the French should universal military service be put into effect, had little sympathy for the Romantic notion of a people's war. It was thus not until 1813, when Prussia was again at war, that all men of age were called up to serve the nation in arms.

A territorial army (*Landwehr*) was formed with a solidly bourgeois officer corps, unlike the regular army in which the aristocracy still predominated. The ideals of the reformers were most fully realized in the *Landwehr*. It was passionately supported by the liberals and equally intensely detested by conservatives for decades to come.

The proposal to arm all remaining males between the ages of 15 and 60 in a *levée en masse*, without uniforms and with elected officers, appalled most respectable citizens. They denounced the guerrilla bands foreseen in this *Landsturm* as Jacobins who posed a greater danger to Prussia than they did to its enemies. The suggestion was hastily dropped. The reformers concentrated on the *Landwehr* as the realization of their vision of a people's army. Under Boyen's army bill of September 1814 all those eligible for military service were to serve three years in regiments of the line and then two years in the reserve. They were then obliged to serve in the first division of the *Landwehr* until the age of 32 and the second until the age of 50. All those who did not serve in the regular army had to join the *Landwehr* at the age of 20. The educated bourgeois could serve one year in the regular army, after which he became an officer in the *Landwehr*. There was thus a clear distinction between an aristocratic and conservative regular officer corps and a bourgeois and liberal *Landwehr*. Conflict between the two was thus almost inevitable.

The practical military results of these measures did not meet the reformers' expectations. Admittedly Prussia was able to field an army of over a quarter of a million men: it was better trained, and its staff work greatly improved. Some units, particularly in the *Landwehr*, were fired by an idealistic and patriotic spirit. On the other hand such enthusiasm was by no means general. There were large numbers of desertions. The regular officer corps remained intransigent in their opposition to universal military service. The notion that in 1813 "a people arose, a storm burst forth" is a romantic myth. Amid widespread indifference the conservative forces braced themselves to undo the work of the reformers. They were largely successful; but the bourgeoisie had made important inroads into the old order. The outcome of this struggle was no foregone conclusion.

Educational Reform

The reformers insisted that a society of free citizens with careers open to the talents had to be well educated. Throughout Germany the educational system was in disarray. Most university professors were tedious pedants, hopelessly out of touch with the times. The student body was indolent, debauched, and given to outbursts of mindless violence against the unfortunate townsfolk. Schooling was equally abysmal, without supervision, organization, or control from central authority. Ill-qualified and miserably paid teachers used brutal discipline to drill a few vestiges of an elementary education into their hapless pupils. The great educational reformers such as Fichte, Pestalozzi, and Wilhelm von Humboldt took up Kant's ideal of the autonomous self-actualizing individual and argued that education should not be directed towards fulfilling the demands of the state, the market, or tradition, but should be an end in itself. The development of a spontaneous, critical, and imaginative subject was more important than training for a profession or trade. The practical objectives of the Enlightenment were to give way to the subjective ideals of neo-humanism. Education was not to be the preserve of a small elite but was to be universal. Only thus could the many-sided talents that slumbered within the nation be awoken. Even the king, who could hardly be described as an intellectual, was captivated by such ideas and announced that: "The state must make up in the intellectual sphere for what it has lost in physical power."

The University of Berlin, founded in 1810, was based on these principles. Knowledge was to be pursued for its own sake regardless of any practical application. An inter-disciplinary education in the humanities was designed to create well-rounded individuals rather than narrow specialists. In his inaugural address as rector, Fichte announced: "The true life-giving breath of the university ... the heavenly ether is without doubt academic freedom." This was an expression of the all too often derided German notion of freedom as inward, subjective, and metapolitical. In fact the reformers who espoused these lofty ideas were eminently political. Horror-struck by the enormities committed in the name of freedom, they insisted that a people could only be genuinely free by thoroughgoing individualization.

Tuition was free, there was no fixed curriculum, and no set number of years of study. Dialogue between teacher and pupil and the common pursuit of pure knowledge was the sole requirement. For all the protestations to the contrary it was an elitist concept that aimed to replace the old aristocracy of birth by a highly educated meritocracy. Setting the gentleman scholar as an ideal, it largely ignored the exigencies of the nascent industrial age. All depended on state support. The reformers argued that the state had a moral obliga-tion to educate its citizens according to their precepts. In return for this hands-off policy the state would be strengthened by the optimum development of individual capabilities. It was a lofty ideal, a dream of the higher bureaucracy and professoriate, who worked closely together. It ignored the fact that changes in the structure of the state would neces-sarily lead to changes in its attitude to education. The age of reform was to be of limited duration. The state was soon to reassert its authority by using the educational system to strengthen its hold over the citizenry.

The Prussian school system was also reformed with two levels. The preparatory school (*Elementarschule*) led to the grammar school (*Gymnasium*). The latter were self-consciously elite institutions that, like the universities, emphasized the humanities, particularly Greek and Latin. All teachers were required to have a university degree. A school-leaving certificate known as the *Arbitur*, which soon became the prerequisite for entry to university, was introduced in 1812.

Teachers in the elementary schools (*Volksschule*) were also required to have a diploma from a teacher-training college (*Normalschule*) where they absorbed a modified version of the teachings of the great Swiss educational reformer Pestalozzi. Reform of these schools, in which retired Prussian NCOs had flogged a rudimentary education into their unfortunate charges took much longer, but at least a step had been taken in a promising direction. A separate ministry of education was established in 1817 which kept a close eye on the schools.

The aim of all these reforms was the creation of a modern bourgeois state free from the privileges of the estates and provincial particularism. This could not be created overnight, and the reforms ran far ahead of social reality. For this reason they only went half-way. Only when society changed could there be any serious discussion of a modern constitution. The state was still dependent for money on the institutions of the old regime in which the privileges of the estates were anchored, and this proved an effective barrier to thoroughgoing reform. An aristocracy jealous of its privileges thus had effective means of frustrating the centralizing and modernizing intentions of the bureaucracy.

The Confederation of the Rhine

For all the limitations, the reforms were the most ambitious and comprehensive in Prussia. In the Confederation of the Rhine the contradictions and frictions were even more severe. On the one hand Napoleon hoped to consolidate the modernizing achievements of the revolution, but he also set out to exploit these subject states and reward his followers with estates carved out of them. The south German states were faced with the additional problem of integrating the many disparate territories they had absorbed under a centralized administration and under a common set of laws. Baden had increased fourfold and Bavaria had doubled in size as a consequence of the Napoleonic reordering of Germany. They set about this task in the traditional manner of the absolutist state: by administrative control and rational planning. Here there was hardly a whiff of Kantian humanism, while the democratic notions of the French Revolution met with little response in the upper echelons. Governments were reorganized, but rather than create collegial systems the powers of absolutist ministers such as Montgelas in Bavaria and Reizenstein in Baden were greatly enhanced.

In the course of the territorial changes in southern Germany, Catholic Bavaria absorbed large numbers of Protestants, whereas Protestant Baden now had a Catholic majority. True to enlightened absolutist traditions the state maintained strict control over the churches, mounting a campaign against religious excesses. In both Bavaria and Württemberg pilgrimages were forbidden, miracles were not to be mentioned in homilies, and even the public display of Christmas cribs was outlawed as part of the campaign against superstition and fanaticism. In Württemberg pietism was similarly outlawed as a pernicious form of mysticism. But at least full religious equality was recognized in these states. The often excessive struggle against religious enthusiasm was matched with an admirable degree of interdenominational tolerance.

The first priority was the ordering and organization of the new territories. Local privileges and exemptions were abolished, and central control tightened. Given the heavy burden of debt that rested on all of the states in the Confederation of the Rhine a fundamental reform of the fiscal system was essential. Educational reform lagged far behind that in Prussia. The military authorities had no truck with notions of a people in arms, preferring lengthy terms of service in conscript armies.

The most dramatic and far-reaching changes in southern Germany resulted from the secularization of church lands. In Bavaria half of the land was in the hands of monastic orders. This was taken over by the state and sold off at rock-bottom prices to the peasantry. Only the forests remained largely under state control. Unlike in Prussia, where the liberation of the serfs had benefited the large estates, land reform resulted in the creation of a large number of small farms and modest peasant holdings. There were other equally significant consequences of secularization. This was a major step forward in the creation of a modern secular state, and the impact on the church was equally dramatic. Higher eccle-siastical offices were no longer the preserve of the aristocracy. The church, which was now supported financially by the state, turned away from worldly affairs and concentrated on its spiritual mission.

As in Prussia, the aristocracy lost some, but by no means all, of its ancient privileges. With the collapse of the old empire the mediatized imperial aristocracy retained a special status within the sovereign state. The thoroughgoing reform of property rights was blocked by the determined rearguard action of the privileged. Even in states such as Westphalia and Berg, where the Code Napoléon was imposed, compensation was demanded for the aboli-tion of feudal rights. Since neither the state nor the peasantry had the money to meet such requirements these rights remained in force.

The great jurist Anselm von Feuerbach, the moving spirit behind the Bavarian penal code of 1813, a model of progressive legislation, argued that the logical consequence of these reforms was that the state should have a constitution. But Feuerbach was ahead of his times, soon to be pushed aside in the reaction that followed Napoleon's defeat. The Bavarian constitution of 1808 allowed for the indirect election of a National Assembly by a highly restrictive franchise. It guaranteed the independence of the judiciary and guaran-teed certain individual rights. But the National Assembly never met. A similar institution, provided by the Westphalian constitution of 1807, met only twice.

Thus in the Confederation of the Rhine many ancient privileges were abolished, par-ticularism was largely overcome, bourgeois freedoms were strengthened, and the rule of law was asserted. The individual was partially freed within the context of a centralized bureaucratic state that was reinforced by a vigilant police force. The old order of the estates was gradually being replaced by a class society. Although the principle of equality before the law was still largely theoretical, at least it was placed on the agenda.

The Prussian reform movement was inspired by the desire to bridge the gap between the state and society, to involve the citizens directly or indirectly in the affairs of state. The centralized states of southern Germany, although determined to overcome the outmoded rights of the estates and to modernize society, were deeply suspicious of the dangerous potential of popular sovereignty. The consequences of these differences were somewhat surprising. The tradition of the reforming state lived on in southern Germany and provided a congenial atmosphere for the liberal bourgeoisie. In Prussia the old order found it far easier to reassert itself after 1815.

Germany and the Defeat of Napoleon

Of the 600,000 men in Napoleon's Grande Armée that marched against Russia in 1812 about one-third were Germans. By the end of the year there was only a demoralized remnant of some 100,000 men able to stagger back to Poland. The tsar, against the advice of his generals, decided to continue the fight westwards and finally rid Europe of the Napoleonic menace. On December 30 the Prussian general, Yorck, signed the Convention of Tauroggen with the Russians, by which the troops under his command no longer accepted orders from the French.

Yorck, an ultra-conservative opponent of reform, was a glowing patriot. He had acted without the knowledge of the king and with the intent of joining the Russians to drive the French out of Germany. Frederick William III, outraged at this act of mutinous insubordination, cashiered the general. Yorck took no notice and cooperated with Stein in recruiting soldiers in East Prussia to fight the French.

The king continued to dither, negotiating first with the French then, urged on by the patriotic forces, with Austria and Russia. Finally, at the end of February 1813, he signed an alliance with Russia whereby he agreed to cede part of Prussia's Polish provinces to Russia in return for territorial compensation elsewhere in Germany. He responded to a wave of patriotic enthusiasm by announcing a people's war in his appeal "To My People." Universal military service was introduced that included volunteer units known as the Free Corps, made up largely of the urban middle class. The poorly trained and ill-equipped *Landwehr* proved to be an ineffective fighting force. A new medal for valor, the iron cross, was struck as a symbol of the struggle for king and fatherland.

Patriotic enthusiasm was confined almost exclusively to the eastern provinces of Prussia that were not occupied by the French. Elsewhere there was a general indifference, although there were protests in Westphalia and Berg, both states under direct French domination. Some of the northern ports, which had suffered badly under the Continental System, also witnessed some unrest. The states of the Confederation of the Rhine remained passive. In Vienna Metternich prudently arrested demonstrators calling for a popular uprising against the French.

For the Prussian patriots the war was now a struggle of the German people against a foreign tyranny. The German princes who had allied with Napoleon were regarded as traitors to the national cause. The tsar, who combined woolly-headed notions of national liberation with a careful calculation of Russia's interests, was much taken by these ideas. He was encouraged by Stein, who became his unofficial advisor on German affairs. It was Stein who drafted the text of the Proclamation of Kalisch that outlined allied war aims. They included the restoration of a reformed German empire with a constitution that reflected the "quintessential spirit of the German people," along with freedom for the German princes and their subjects. Russia as guarantor of the New Germany would be in a powerful position to determine its future, but with a notoriously unpredictable tsar it was unclear what lay in store.

The first engagements of the campaign did not go well for the new allies. They were defeated at the battles of Grossgörschen and Bautzen and driven out of Saxony. Napoleon, having failed to follow up on these successes, agreed to an armistice in order to build up his forces. Meanwhile a number of states joined Britain in the Great Coalition, but Russia and Prussia remained undecided. Metternich was still hesitant to commit Austria to the allied cause. Although suspicious of the heady nationalist and popular spirit among some of the coalition partners, he gradually eased away from France. In June 1813 he finally joined the coalition, which now included both Russia and Prussia. The war aims with respect to Germany were agreed upon at Teplitz in September. They included the restoration of the 1803 frontiers in northwestern Germany and of the Rhine frontier. Metternich's concept of a war to restore the balance of power in Europe had triumphed over notions of liberation, freedom, and nationalism.

After some initial engagements the Saxon army was left demoralized. Bavaria withdrew from the Confederation of the Rhine, its territorial integrity guaranteed by Metternich in the Treaty of Ried, a treaty that was later to be denounced by nationalist historians as blocking the way to national unification. The two armies finally clashed at Leipzig from 16 to 19 October 1813. Napoleon suffered a crushing defeat in this "Battle of the Nations," but it was something of a pyrrhic victory, with both sides losing about 60,000 men. The coalition armies failed to follow up their success, thus allowing Napoleon to escape.

The question now was whether the war should continue. After the Treaty of Ried with Bavaria similar arrangements were made with Baden, Württemberg, and the other member states of the Confederation of the Rhine. The Confederation thus ceased to exist, but the Napoleonic territorial settlement in southern Germany remained in force. Once again Metternich had managed to ensure that the exigencies of security took precedence over legitimacy. This was enough for Metternich, who now hoped to treat with the French, but the slogan "The Rhine is a German River and not Germany's Frontier" met with fervent popular response, and Prussian hawks demanded an all-out war to destroy the tyrant.

Napoleon rejected Metternich's peace feelers so that the immediate problem was solved, but the debate as to how the war should be pursued caused severe strains within the coalition. Thanks to the energetic engagement of Castlereagh and Metternich the coalition was stitched together and once again agreed upon a set of war aims. France should withdraw to its 1792 frontiers, and Germany should have a federal structure. Allied troops entered Paris at the end of March 1814. Napoleon abdicated. The Treaty of Paris of May 30, 1814 was free from vindictiveness. It left France within its 1792 borders, still a major player within the European balance of power.

The Congress of Vienna

The future of Europe was to be decided at the Congress of Vienna, a glittering assembly of crowned heads, diplomatists, adventurers, and beauties. The aim was above all to create a stable Europe based on a broad interpretation of the principle of legitimacy. No one thought it possible to turn the clock back to pre-revolutionary times and there was general agreement that the Napoleonic territorial settlement in southern Germany should be accepted. Where stability seemed threatened, legitimacy had to give way.

There was general agreement between Britain and Austria that a strong and independent central Europe was desirable as a bulwark against both France and Russia. Prussia was clearly to play a critical role within this constellation. Prussia would have to be compensated in the west, given Russia's claims on its Polish provinces. Prussia's main aim was to annex Saxony, a state that had remained faithful to its alliance with Napoleon. Castlereagh and Metternich favored this idea because of their concern about the tsar's ambitions in Poland. The Russians were adamantly opposed. Frederick William III, anxious not to antagonize his ally, ordered Hardenberg to distance himself from Castlereagh and Metternich.

After much acrimonious debate Prussia lost most of its Polish territory to "Congress Poland" and was awarded approximately half of Saxony. Prussia's gains in the west were even more significant. In order that Prussia should protect Germany's western frontiers it was given the Rhineland as far as the Saar and the Nahe. This resulted in fundamental changes in Prussia. The country was now divided between its western and eastern portions with their widely different cultures, traditions, and religions. Were these differences overcome, Prussia would achieve hegemony in northern Germany. There were further far-reaching consequences of this settlement. The Rhineland was soon to become the most valuable piece of industrial real estate in Europe, the foundation of Prussia's economic might. That Prussia was given the task of defending Germany's borders against any revival of French military might further underlined the importance of the army. The unequal development at every level between the Prussian homeland and its newly won western provinces was to cause many severe problems in the years ahead.

Prussia's role in Germany was thus strengthened, while Austria concentrated more on the Tyrol and Italy. Bavaria was unable to find any support for its attempt to become a third force in Germany by absorbing Frankfurt and Mainz. Prussia thus emerged as the big winner, although this was not apparent at the time. Austria's political influence was far greater. Austria, with England's support, had limited Russia's influence in Europe and Prussia's in Germany. The Federal Act of June 8, 1815, signed only ten days before the battle of Waterloo, created a loose confederation of states rather than a federal state. It had no federal army and not even a federal court. There was only one federal institution, the Federal Council (Bundestag), where delegates from the member states met to discuss matters of internal security. Austria's dominant position was emphasized in that it provided its permanent president.

Apart from repressing its critics the Confederation was a toothless affair. It did nothing to overcome the economic divisions within Germany, failed to take the initiative in transport policy, and did not create a common currency. It was equally passive in legal matters. When the people of Hesse appealed to it against their grotesque prince, who had swept aside all the French reforms and restored the *ancien régime* to the point of insisting that wigs should once again be worn, the Confederation did nothing.

The Vienna settlement asserted the rights of the states and their legitimacy against the demands of liberals and nationalists. In the short term it provided stability, but the seeds for future conflict were already sown. It brought a long period of peace, but it could not contain the democratic and nationalist forces that threatened it. Combined with the territorial changes in Prussia, which resulted in further contradictions and discord, these were ultimately to severely limit the conservative restoration.

CHAPTER TWO
GERMAN SOCIETY IN TRANSITION

CHAPTER CONTENTS

A History of Modern Germany: 1800 to the Present, Second Edition. Martin Kitchen.
© 2012 Martin Kitchen. Published 2012 by Blackwell Publishing Ltd.

The period from the Congress of Vienna in 1815 to the revolutions of 1848 is known as the "pre-March," the month in which the revolutions began. Its spirit is that of "Biedermeier." The word is a composite of the protagonists in two satirical poems, Biedermann and Bummelmaier. "Bieder" signifies conventional, restrained, and somewhat dull, with more than a whiff of smug parochialism. "Maier" is the average Joe, Smith, or Jones. It was a reflection of an atmosphere of the peace and quiet of the restoration after the heady days of the revolution. Jean Paul summed up the spirit of Biedermeier when he spoke of the "absolute happiness to be found in restraint." It was an attitude that permeated all aspects of life, society, and the arts. The undemonstrative simplicity of an essentially bourgeois style was echoed in the literature of the time in the works of Franz Grillparzer, Adalbert Stifter, Theodor Storm, Annette von Droste-Hülshoff, Ludwig Uhland, and Eduard Mörike. The emphasis here was on detailed, objective, awe-inspiring descriptions of the otherness of nature, which was far removed from the earlier Romantic view of nature as a sentimental reflection of the self. The Biedermeier ideology served to hide from view the profound changes that were happening within society as a result of the "dual revolution": the democratic and emancipatory forces unleashed in 1776 and 1789, coupled with the radical social consequences of the industrial revolution. Whereas the Biedermeier writers were conservatives, the radical authors in the "Young Germany" group such as Ludwig Börne, Georg Büchner, Karl Gutzkow, Heinrich Heine, and Georg Herwegh belong to the pre-March.

PLATE I   A Biedermeier interior. © BPK

PLATE 2   The Biedermeier family. © BPK

One fundamental change was apparent to all and could not be disregarded in however complacent an age. Hegel, in his *Elements of the Philosophy of Right* (1820), spoke of a population explosion that resulted in "a great mass of people falling below the subsistence level." He regretted that in spite of the "excessive wealth" of bourgeois society, there was still not enough to control the "extreme poverty and reproductive vigor of the rabble." Hegel was certainly not alone in noticing this problem, but he clearly saw the connection between population expansion, poverty, and society's ability to act. Germany shared in the dramatic Europe-wide population expansion, which began in the latter part of the eighteenth century, with Germany's population roughly doubling between 1750 and 1850. As in almost everything else, there were considerable regional differences. Whereas in eastern Prussia the population increased by 120 percent in the pre-March, in most of Bavaria the figure was a mere 20 percent. There were a number of causal factors for the population explosion. The removal of traditional impediments to marriage not only resulted in a marked reduction of the number of bachelors and spinsters, but also allowed couples to marry somewhat younger, thus increasing the wife's period of socially condoned fecundity. In spite of the harsh punishments meted out to unwed mothers, in the hope thereby of addressing the problem of overpopulation, bastardy rates were astonishingly high. Ten percent of births in Protestant Berlin at the beginning of our period were illegitimate. In Catholic Munich the figure was as high as 20 percent. Other factors played a role. There were no great epidemics during this period and the outbreaks of cholera in the nineteenth century did not cause anything like the same number of deaths as in the past. It was not until mid-century that physicians like Rudolf Virchow began a serious examination of the social causes of disease. Nutrition improved, as did the weather. There were significant medical improvements including vaccination, which was made compulsory for smallpox in Bavaria in 1807, and in Prussia in 1817. There was a higher standard of personal hygiene coupled with a drop in infant mortality, both contributing to a slight decline in the death rate. But the most important factor of all was that couples made a conscious decision to have large families. Demographers have come up with all manner of ingenious explanations for this, but none is convincing. Perhaps it is appropriate that the motives behind this most personal of decisions should remain a mystery.

It has been estimated that the population of the German Confederation in 1816 was just under 33 million. By 1865 it had risen by 60 percent. During this period about 3 million Germans emigrated, most of them to the United States. Although there are considerable regional differences in all these figures, the average expectation of life was terribly low in spite of many improvements. In the old Prussian provinces it hovered around 25 during the first half of the century. In the Rhineland provinces it was about 30. Only in the latter part of the century was there an increase in life expectancy, to 35.6 for men and 38.5 for women between 1871 and 1880. It was therefore a very young society with at least one-third of the population under the age of 15.

Given the high rates of infant and adolescent mortality the average age at death is somewhat misleading and subject to wide deviations. Thus in 1800 the average marriage lasted for twenty years and ended with the death of one of the partners. Most households consisted of husband and wife and underage children. In the wealthier classes there would be a number of servants. In artisan families there would also be an apprentice or two. Extended families of three generations were exceptionally rare, even in rural areas, although peasant households were considerably larger than urban ones. Children left the home early to learn a trade or enter service, thus becoming part of another household.

The household performed many functions. As a farm or artisanal enterprise it was a place of work. It was obliged to perform many of the functions that are now taken over by the state. It did its best to look after the health of its members, stood by them when times were bad, and tended them in their old age. As the peasant or the artisan grew more prosperous the division between the core family and those who worked for it became more clearly defined. Servants were now summoned to their masters and mistresses by a tug on a bell-rope. But in rural areas society was still open and transparent, social control oppressive, and the private sphere severely restricted. In the towns the ideal of bourgeois privacy were more easily realized.

In such circumstances it is hardly surprising that romantic love played precious little role in the choice of a partner. One sought a spouse of appropriate social standing and of impeccable reputation who was known to be reliable, hardworking, and honest. Mutual respect and a sense of obligation were the foundations on which the family rested. This could turn into genuine affection, but familial relations were mostly stiff, formal, and rigid. In urban areas there was a slight loosening of convention among the petite bourgeoisie. Some even went as far as to address their spouses by their first names.

The wealthier bourgeois families followed the example of their English counterparts in separating the family as far as possible from the outside world of work, society, and even the wider family. Within this secure and propertied class there was slightly more room for romantic love, for affection and personal fulfillment. This more often than not was the stuff of romantic novels, but it was an ideal that, partly because there were so many obstacles in its way, had a wide appeal. Gradually the purely pragmatic reasons for the choice of a partner were replaced by subjective and emotional considerations. The public was giving way to the private, and marriage as an institution was slowly undermined. Hegel pointed out the dual nature of the family. It is partly based on subjective and personal considerations, but it is also an institution hallowed by custom. Since the subjective and personal is exposed to the vagaries of change, the greater these elements become the more the permanence of the institution is challenged. The highly respectable Biedermeier family thus had within it the seeds of its own destruction.

The privacy of the family was also emphasized in changing attitudes towards death. Formalized acceptance of a natural event, sweetened by a Christian eschatology that took the sting from death and denied the grave its victory, was replaced by informal and subjective expressions of grief. The deceased hardly mattered for, as Schopenhauer remarked with characteristic irony, after one's death one returned to what one was before one's birth. The family that was left behind had a deep sense of loss, privation, and abandonment. They planted their family totem in the graveyard on which the names of succeeding generations were inscribed. Ritualistic visits to the family grave, with their overtones of ancestor worship, provided some solace in an age when religious convictions were waning, thereby strengthening a sense of family identity. Hopes for a life after death were gradually replaced by projection onto the children and grandchildren, thus further emphasizing the central importance of the family.

Women and Children

The new emphasis on the individual and the subjective resulted in a modest change in women's role within the family. Schiller's ideal of the conscientious "Haus-Frau" in his poem "The Song of the Bell" gave way to a grotesque idealization of an ethereal womanhood by the Romantics. The Biedermeier ideal was that of an educated, intelligent, and impeccably mannered wife, devoted to the family, providing comfort and affection for its members, while avoiding any conflict with her spouse. The patriarch's role was to go out into the wider world to provide for the family. His wife's duty was to ensure that the family was an island of peace and harmony amid the stressful world of the marketplace, politics, and work.

As more and more families began to enjoy a relatively prosperous bourgeois existence, women no longer had to do onerous physical work around the house. They could devote more time to cultivating their literary, musical, and artistic tastes and talents. This resulted in a revival of the Romantic version of the feminized woman. She was seen as weak, hypersensitive, a bundle of nerves, given to fainting fits and sudden headaches, to be revived by smelling salts and liberal doses of laudanum.

Yet for all this, the very fact that husbands left the house to go to work meant that women effectively ran the household and were responsible for the upbringing of the children, thus gaining a measure of independence. Many used this position of power and influence to undermine patriarchal structures. The henpecked husband was as much a feature of the age as was the stern paterfamilias. Many a man of substance was driven to distraction by a wife who used her feminine weakness as a powerful weapon. The ideal of partnership and the division of labor within the harmonious family was all too often shattered by the caprices and intractability of human nature.

Some women led astonishingly independent lives in spite of all these social constraints. There were a number of remarkable women who ran brilliant salons. Prominent among them were Henriette Herz, Dorothea Mendelssohn, Sarah Levy, and Amalie Beer, all of whom came from Jewish backgrounds. This was not the result of the emancipation and integration of German Jews – quite the contrary. It was precisely because they were outsiders that they were able to provide the neutral ground on which people from different stations in life could meet as equals.

The most prominent of these salons was that of Rahel Levin. Her marriage to the equally charming and intelligent Prussian diplomat Varnhagen von Ense was one in which the ideals of mutual love, openness, and understanding were fully realized. After a year of marriage she wrote to a friend: "My great joy is that I don't even notice that I am married! In everything, big and small, I am free to live and feel as I will. I can tell Varnhagen everything and be completely truthful. That fills him with happiness and joy. I make him happy too – I alone." Unlike the luxurious salons in Paris with their lavish receptions and carefully selected guest-lists these were positively austere. Tea was served in very modest surroundings. The door was open to all comers. The bourgeois salon thus replaced the court as a center of intellectual discourse, the bourgeoisie thereby scoring yet another success over the old order.

Actresses, singers, and female writers guarded their independence, and widows, such as Arthur Schopenhauer's extraordinary mother Joanna, enjoyed an exceptional degree of freedom. Respectable bourgeois women played important and fulfilling roles outside the family in education, charity organizations, and the Protestant church. It was not until the 1830s that women were permitted to work as nurses in men's wards. Here again Catholic nuns and Protestant deaconesses were at the forefront in breaking down old prejudices and conventions.

Ideas of female emancipation, which originated in France, did not reach Germany until the 1830s and were eagerly espoused by the writers of the Young Germany movement, who were enthusiastic advocates of free love. Some, like Ferdinand Lassalle's lover the Countess Sophie Hatzfeld, followed the example of George Sand by donning male attire and ostentatiously smoking cigars in public while indulging in vigorously heterosexual affairs in semi-private.

The women's movement in Germany began in 1849 when Louise Otto-Peters founded Germany's first magazine specifically for women. The first national women's conference was held in 1865, at which the General German Women's Association was founded. These were modest beginnings, somewhat late in the day, but the long-term effects were to be truly revolutionary.

Biedermeier Germany viewed emotionalized sexuality with deep suspicion. The aristocratic libertines of earlier times were seen as monsters. The sexual adventures of the Young German writers were viewed with disgust. Karl Gutzkow's novel *Wally the Skeptic*, published in 1835, was a polemic in favor of sexual freedom which landed the author in jail for its "despicable representation of the faith of the Christian community." Protests at this judgment resulted in a number of writers being sent into exile, among them Heinrich Heine. Girls were kept in total sexual ignorance while boys were simply warned of the dire consequences of masturbation. Joanna Schopenhauer was horrified at the way in which highly regarded married men in France openly flaunted their delicious mistresses. As in Victorian England, the bourgeoisie viewed extramarital sex as the distasteful habit of a degenerate aristocracy or as the result of the crude animal lusts of the lower classes. Prostitution thrived, since men with an overwhelming desire to do bad things chose to do them with bad women. Wilhelm von Humboldt, who preached and practiced a marriage based on love, partnership, and mutual respect, was a regular visitor to houses of ill fame.

Childhood was a construction of the eighteenth century with Jean-Jacques Rousseau its impassioned advocate. His appeal to women to breastfeed their infants and his insistence that children had rights and specific needs met with a wide response. It was generally recognized that children needed affection, consideration, and encouragement. Relations between parents and children became gradually more relaxed and informal, the familiar *Du* form was now more widely used, discipline was less rigid, and punishments were less harsh. Books were now written specifically for children, but as Heinrich Hoffmann, the brilliant psychologist and author of *Struwwelpeter*, pointed out, they were mostly "altogether too enlightened and rational, falsely naive, un-childlike, untruthful and artificial." In 1816 Friedrich Froebel opened a school in Griesheim near Darmstadt, which aimed at the spontaneous and natural development of a child's talents. These ideas were expounded in his major work *Human Education* published in 1826. In spite of fierce opposition, particularly from the Catholic Church, he opened the first "Kindergarten" in 1836.

Critics felt that children were being pampered and smothered by motherly love. Although they were by nature selfish, rebellious, and vicious, they were absurdly idealized as little angels. The desire to express love, affection, and concern conflicted with the need to educate, discipline, and, where necessary, punish. This led to increasing tensions between parents and children, which by the end of the century provoked Sigmund Freud to make some wild speculations about the human psyche.

The Household

Bourgeois households were attended by a number of servants, as were those of the wealthier tradesmen. Servants lived in their own quarters separated from the core family. They were underpaid and overworked, without rights or legal protection. In the Biedermeier period a large percentage of the population was employed in domestic service. It has been estimated that about 45 percent of the citizens of Vienna were servants in the 1820s. Later on in the century this number declined considerably as the number of servants employed per household dropped and industrialization provided opportunities to earn higher wages. Many of these servants were young girls from the countryside, who learnt respectable bourgeois ways during their period of service, becoming in turn respectable wives and mothers. In this way much of the working class was gentrified to a certain degree. Bourgeois attitudes were also strengthened in that children were used from an early age to be waited upon and to give orders.

The vast majority of Germans lived in conditions far removed from the comforts of the bourgeois household. There was precious little room for self-fulfillment, emotional development, and even basic privacy in poverty-stricken and overworked lower-class families. Children were put to work as early as possible and left home at an early age. Bourgeois reformers like Wilhelm Heinrich Riehl looked at these families with horror. They wrote of drunken and heartless husbands who brutalized their wives and children; of women working long and crippling hours in addition to their household duties, whose children received little besides abuse. By mid-century about one-quarter of German women were gainfully employed, about half as domestic servants, and most of the rest as factory workers or on the land. Women's wages were roughly half those of men. Although the situation was never as appalling as it was in Britain, child labor was widespread. By 1840 some 17 percent of the factory workers in Chemnitz were children. Although no accurate figures are available, it is safe to assume that the percentage of children working on the land was still higher.

This was a period of fundamental transformation in social life. The dramatic changes in the mode of production occasioned by the industrial revolution resulted in equally remarkable changes in social life. The most obvious was the separation of domicile and place of work. With the exception of all but the most genteel of farmers and a dwindling number of handloom weavers, there was a clear distinction between the two. Life in the home was rendered more pleasant by technical advances such as the invention of the cooking stove that replaced the open fire, gas lighting, and linoleum. "Lucifers" or safety matches, which first appeared in 1829, as Hoffmann pointed out in the true story of "Paulinchen" in *Struwwelpeter*, were a frequent cause of accidents. Flush toilets did not appear on any great scale until the 1860s and then almost exclusively in bourgeois homes in urban areas. The greater mobility of labor meant that the vast majority of people no longer owned their own house or cottage but rented apartments in the cities and towns.

Housing conditions for the majority of the population were appalling. Single agricultural laborers lived like animals in barns and lofts, their married workmates in filthy two-room hovels. Workers in the towns lived in dreadful conditions, packed into tiny apartments or squalid row houses, in attics and cellars. Only in the 1860s did some industrialists such as Alfred Krupp, the "Cannon King," begin to build model housing so as to ensure a steady supply of reliable workers.

The bourgeois lifestyle was comfortable but restrained. There were fewer rooms designed for lavish entertainments, and the center of the house was now the living room, which was aped by the petite bourgeoisie with their "front rooms" used only on special occasions. The elaborate Louis Seize style of furniture, as made by the Roentgens father and son and the Spindler brothers, was no longer in favor. The Biedermeier style was discreet, lacking in decoration, well proportioned, light, and practical. By the 1830s it began to give way to a more ornate style in the gothic revival or neo-Renaissance manner, with plenty of plush and heavy dark woods. A similar change can be seen in architecture from the restraint of the Biedermeier to the flamboyance of the historicist style.

It was not until the 1830s that the delightfully feminine Empire fashions with a pronounced décolleté, seductive draping, and a glimpse of ankle gave way to a more prudish style in which the body was hidden away in yards of material and a tiny waist and wide hips were accentuated. By mid-century the crinoline swept all before it, providing rich material for caricaturists and satirists. Men's fashions went through less of a transformation. They favored a simple cut and dark colors. Elegance was expressed in the quality of the cloth and tailoring. Artists and radicals donned somewhat outlandish outfits and nationalists set about designing the folk costumes of a mythical past.

Town and Country

The combination of industrialization and rapid population growth transformed the cities and towns. The population of Berlin rose from 172,000 in 1800 to 419,000 by 1850. Stuttgart increased from 18,000 to 47,000 in the same period, and Düsseldorf from 10,000 to 27,000. As the towns expanded the old city walls disappeared, thus ending the abrupt distinction between town and country. Towns were now clearly divided into districts according to social status, usually the rich and powerful in the west, the poor workers in the east, the lower middle class to the north and south. The towns were soon also to be divided by railway lines, the poor living on the wrong side of the tracks.

Towns were also transformed by the increasing number of public buildings, from ministries to museums, railway stations to schools, universities to law courts. Shopping arcades and, later, department stores revolutionized the retail trade. There was precious little planning or control. Traditional restrictions on the sale and transfer of land were removed; now market forces were only curbed by health and safety regulations. Banks made handsome profits as the demand for mortgages grew. It was not until mid-century that the towns began to take over responsibility for public utilities, although Vienna had placed the water supply under civic control as early as 1803. The great fire in Hamburg in 1842 gave Gottfried Semper, an architect of genius, an opportunity to put aesthetic considerations above cost effectiveness in his plans for the reconstruction of the inner city. Munich was also fortunate to have monarchs who wished to beautify their capital and ministers like Montgelas who could realize their vision. The Maximilian and Ludwig streets are their lasting monuments. In most German cities the city fathers imposed a rigorous and unimaginative geometric uniformity that saved money but was dull and lifeless.

Agriculture

Germany was still an overwhelmingly agricultural land, thus vulnerable to the frightful effects of a poor harvest, which were far worse than anything experienced even in the most severe crises of industrial society. The famine of 1816/17 was a major catastrophe in Germany, as it was throughout Europe. The effects of the potato blight of 1845/7 were as horrific as they were in Ireland, awakening the conscience of the nation to the sufferings of the poor and providing a background to the revolutions of 1848. In both cases prices were inelastic, in that according to Engel's law, when the price of foodstuffs rises the poor are forced to spend a greater proportion of their income on them. As incomes rise so does elasticity and they spend a smaller proportion. Taking the price of grain as 100 in 1913 it was 161.4 in 1817 and 124.6 in 1847. In a good year, such as 1824, it fell as low as 38.6.

Agricultural production increased markedly due to improved methods and rising prices, caused in large part by the Continental System. Then a series of excellent harvests between 1819 and 1824 caused supply to outstrip demand. The British Corn Laws blocked exports from the enterprising large estates east of the river Elbe. They were now obliged to sell on the domestic market. The fall in prices resulted in many farmers failing to meet costs. It also meant that the price of agricultural land fell to half and even one-third of its taxable value. Hundreds of aristocratic estates were put up for sale. Credit was hard to find, and bankruptcies were frequent. Many smallholders lost their land and were forced to seek employment as agricultural laborers. Population pressure increased demand, giving farmers some relief until by the mid-1840s there was once again a serious hunger crisis. An excellent harvest in 1847 reversed the process, but it came too late to defuse the social tensions that had mounted in the years of dearth.

There were sharp regional differences in agriculture, from the large Junker estates in East Elbia to vintners in the Rhineland, sugar-beet farmers in Saxony and cattle-breeders in East Frisia, tenant farmers in Westphalia and the alpine farmhouses of Bavaria. But all of them had to confront the reality of agricultural capitalism: of modernization and increased output, of double-entry bookkeeping and market exigencies. The old days of subsistence farming were over. There were precious few remnants of feudalism. Again regional differences were substantial. In Bavaria, Baden, and Württemberg there was still a vast number of holdings so small that the farmer was obliged to earn extra money in some proto-industrial enterprise in order to make ends meet. Similarly a number of aristocratic landowners preferred to put their money in state bonds rather than use it to modernize their estates. The situation was quite different in Saxony, Hanover, northwest Germany, and eastern Prussia. Here the percentage of smallholdings, although still significant, was much smaller. In Prussia by 1848 there were 12,000 aristocratic estates (*Rittergüte*) and 6,000 farms of more than 600 hectares (1,500 acres). The great aristocratic estates, held by the noble families for generations and almost all subject to entailment, were now traded on a flourishing real-estate market. In East Prussia by 1885 only 12.8 percent of aristocratic estates had been in the possession of same family for more than fifty years. The aristocratic estates in Prussia organized themselves in cooperatives (*Landschaften*) which gave them easy access to capital at low rates of interest. The ordinary farmer found it exceedingly hard to rake up sufficient capital to improve his holding. He had lost the use of common land, and was highly taxed and strapped by interest payments.

That there were major improvements in agriculture in this period is in large part due to the efforts of Albrecht von Thaer, a Hanoverian doctor who studied English scientific agriculture. He popularized these theories in his model farm in Mödlin in Prussia and with the publication of his four-volume study *The Principles of Rational Agriculture*, published between 1809 and 1812. In the introduction to his magnum opus he gave a clear definition of his intent. Agriculture was in his view "a profession the purpose of which is to make a profit or to earn money by the production and sometimes the processing of vegetable and animal substances." This thoroughly capitalist aim was to be achieved by scientific breeding, an improved system of the rotation of crops, and double-entry bookkeeping. Thaer's ideas were reinforced by the economist Johann Heinrich von Thünen, whose influential work *The Isolated State* (1826) extended Adam Smith's ideas to spatial economics and the theory of rent. The farmer was to become as much an entrepreneur as the industrialist. Conservatives were horrified. They felt that the farmer was part of God's order, bound by moral obligation, the backbone of society – not a mere tradesman.

The great chemist Justus Liebig discovered the process whereby plants extracted nourishment from the earth, and realized that this nourishment had to be replaced. Plants had to be fed just like animals. In this sense plants were "made" in much the same way as industrial goods. Thaer's rotation of crops led inevitably to a decline in productivity if the phosphoric acid, potash, and lime absorbed by successive crops were not replaced. Liebig was blind to many factors such as the importance of climate, crop rotation, and the need to add nitrogen to the soil. Some argued that he was merely echoing the earlier work of Karl Sprengel, but he was a scientist of genius who counted among his discoveries chloroform and the three basic organic compounds – fats, carbohydrates, and proteins – to say nothing of Liebig's Meat Extract. He was the founding father of the fertilizer industry, in which Germany was to be pre-eminent.

Rapid improvements in agricultural machinery, much of which came from England, along with further refinements in breeding stock and a significant increase in the amount of land under cultivation, all contributed to a steadily increasing output. The amount of land lying fallow was greatly reduced. By mid-century it was only 1 percent in Saxony and 3 percent in the Rhineland, but in Bavaria it was still 19 percent. The number of people working on the land increased from 9.53 million in 1816 to 11.48 million in 1849. There was a corresponding increase in labor productivity. Agriculture thus provided employment for an expanding population, thereby relieving rural poverty before industry provided alternative employment. Agriculture was dependent on climatic conditions and was highly vulnerable to disease so that this favorable trend could easily be brutally reversed. Nevertheless, contrary to the teachings of the Reverend Thomas Malthus, agricultural production increased more rapidly than did the population in the first half of the century.

The state played an active role in spreading these new ideas by the foundation of a number of agricultural colleges, as well creating model farms, combating the spread of animal diseases, improving drainage, redistributing land, and encouraging agricultural associations and fairs such as Munich's Oktoberfest, founded in 1810. Eager to keep up to date with the latest discoveries and theories, farmers joined these organizations and subscribed to a host of agricultural journals. Smaller producers sought to keep pace by forming cooperatives, which were given financial support by the local savings banks based on the cooperative principles of Friedrich Wilhelm Raiffeisen, whose work began in response to the appalling agricultural crisis of 1845/7. German farmers thus embraced modern capitalist methods of farming and estate management, but their mentality was rooted in an earlier age, thereby acting as a brake on the development of fully fledged bourgeois-capitalist agriculture that would have resulted in an even more impressive rate of growth. There was thus a curious dissonance between ideology and praxis that intrigued Max Weber but would have stumped Karl Marx.

The vast majority of the rural population was made up of poverty-stricken agricultural workers. Although for most people life on the land had always been wretched, their lot had worsened since, but not necessarily because of, the reforms. Their numbers had increased disproportionately to the rest of the population, thus debasing the value of their labor, and their ranks were swollen by heavily indebted peasant farmers who were unable to survive in a more competitive and capital-intensive environment. Enclosures forced them to resort to poaching and the illegal collection of firewood, for which they were severely punished. In southern Germany sympathetic gamekeepers were often known to turn a blind eye to these miscreants. It was not until much later in the century that job opportunities in the industrial sector, improved transportation, and emigration offered major relief to the pressing problem of rural poverty. This was partly offset in Prussia by the law (*Gesindeordnung*) which restricted the farm workers' freedom of movement and their right to organize, as well as permitting outrageously long working hours. Only the more prosperous small farmers could afford a scrap of meat, and then certainly not more than once a week. Most peasants lived on potatoes without salt, bread, soup, and milk. It is small wonder that tensions mounted on the land and exploded in widespread violence in the revolutionary years of 1848/9.

Peasant demands were quite different from those of urban radicals. They protested against concrete abuses, against the remnants of feudal injustices as well as against new injustices resulting from the reforms. They demanded the restoration of ancient rights. They had no sympathy for the liberal and democratic ideas of the townsfolk, who in turn despised the peasantry for their reactionary conservatism, their anti-capitalism, their clericalism, and their profound distrust of the state and its bureaucracy.

In much of Germany there was thus a sharp distinction between town and country. There were deep cleavages of status, class, and wealth in rural areas but they were partly transcended by a way of life in which there were certain shared values and a feeling of community. The countryside was conservative. Liberal townsfolk were never able, and were often even unwilling, to win support for their ideas in rural areas. The strength of agrarian conservatism was such that it profoundly affected the development of Germany towards a modern democratic state.

Industrialization

It is hardly surprising that the industrial revolution came to Germany decades later than in England. Most of the states of the German Confederation protected their domestic markets with high duties and tariffs. The larger states had a number of internal customs barriers. The transportation network was inadequate, thus further protecting inefficient markets. Germany was constantly plagued by war. It lacked the stimulus of overseas colonies. It had inadequate natural resources. Conservatives looked on the English experience with horror, seeing industrialization as the direct cause of poverty, urban squalor, crime, and social unrest. It spawned a vulgar, pushy, and enormously wealthy class of industrialists, bankers, and speculators. A new word entered the German language, *Pauperismus*, and years later Friedrich Engels' classic study of the condition of the working class in England was to find high praise in conservative circles. Conservatives did all they could to stave off the day when Germany would follow the English example, blaming widespread poverty on a rapacious bourgeoisie. Liberals held the remnants of feudalism and aristocratic landowners responsible for present miseries. They argued that the state had failed in its obligations towards the disadvantaged.

In spite of this aristocratic-conservative opposition to industrial society, some aristocrats seized the opportunities offered by new techniques and machinery. This was particularly true of Silesia, where magnates such as Count Henckel zu Donnersmarck and Prince Hohenlohe founded industrial enterprises without concern for loss of caste by soiling their hands with trade. Although technically they lagged far behind the English and were quite unable to meet the domestic demand, they were decades ahead of the bourgeois entrepreneurs in the west.

The Ruhr was soon to overtake Silesia as an industrial center. With ample coal resources, a greatly improved transportation network, and a liberal economic atmosphere it was congenial to innovative entrepreneurship. With its solid traditions of craftsmanship it was well equipped to meet the demands of the machine age. On the west bank of the Rhine, where French law had been imposed, it was relatively easy to form a limited liability company. Elsewhere the authorities viewed such methods of capital accumulation with the deepest suspicion. They felt that they encouraged wild speculation, favored irresponsible management, and channeled capital away from government bonds and investment in agriculture. Conservatives did what they could to curb the stock markets, which they accused of draining capital away from the aristocratic *Landschaften* and depressing the bond market. When the stock market soared with the railway boom the government responded with a series of regulatory measures, beginning in 1844, that brought it virtually to a standstill by 1850. The result was a serious shortage of investment capital, thanks to the old regime's selfish refusal to acknowledge the needs of a modern economy.

The first joint-stock bank in Germany based on the model of the French Crédit Mobilier, the Schaffhausensche Bankverein, was founded on the initiative of the Camphausen–Hansemann ministry in 1848 to bail out the Schaffhausen Bank which had failed due to a series of bad investments in the Rhineland. Until then entrepreneurs could only borrow modest sums from private banks or foreign investors, but most enterprises were self-financing and thus under-capitalized and highly vulnerable. Private banks and individuals, loath to act as venture capitalists, preferred safer investments in government bonds and real estate. Railways and inland shipping needed such large amounts of capital that they could only be financed by joint-stock companies, in which large numbers of small investors risked their money. The success of many such ventures gradually wore down resistance to the notion of limited liability.

A number of major banks were founded along the same lines. They included Gustav Mevissen's Darmstädter Bank and the Rothschilds' Österreichsiche Kreditanstalt, both founded in 1855. The Discontogesellschaft opened in the following year. These new banks handled all manner of business from small individual accounts to long-term investments in industry. The ties between big banks and big industry were very close, and there was soon a complex web of interlocking directorships and investments which ensured that the two sectors would work closely together for their mutual benefit.

The insurance industry also provided an increasingly significant amount of capital, as the banks were quick to realize. In an ever more complex market, businesses needed where possible to be protected from risk. As the number of policyholders grew, so premiums could be lowered. Skillful investment of funds brought further benefits to clients, attracting even more to cover their risks. By the 1840s Hansemann's fire insurance company and Mevissen's joint-stock transport insurance were flourishing concerns. There were also a number of life insurance companies based on Ernst-Wilhelm Arnoldi's Gothaer Versicherung, founded in 1820. Today it is one of Germany's largest insurance companies.

One important source of credit is often overlooked. Throughout Germany there were a number of small local savings banks, sponsored by the state or commune, in which money could be deposited and which were ready to extend loans to small businesses. They were encouraged in the pre-March because they were seen as a vital palliative to the problem of poverty and social unrest, in that they gave people with enterprise and initiative the possibility of moving ahead, thereby opening up new employment opportunities. These *Sparkassen* still play an immensely important and stabilizing role in German banking.

The reforms of the Napoleonic era not only led to a revolution in agriculture but also did much to break down the social, political, and legal restraints on industrialization. The drastic reduction in the number of petty states reduced the number of internal trade barriers. The Continental System protected German industrialists against British competition, and western Germany profited from its close ties to the French market. But this was outweighed by the negative effects of war, the disruption of traditional trade patterns, widespread poverty, and shortage of capital. Once the wars were over, English manufactured goods again flooded the market. German firms, which had mushroomed in recent years, went under. States pursued rigorously deflationary policies and no changes were made in a tax structure that favored the larger landowners. Precious little encouragement was given to industry, apart from removing customs barriers and spending money on roads and waterways. Railways were initially private companies, but the state soon began to see the need to become involved in this revolutionary form of transportation. Liberal civil servants managed to persuade governments that Germany could only hope to catch up with Britain if technical education was made widely available in technical universities and polytechnics. This initiative was only really to bear fruit much later when, in the second industrial revolution, Germany was to overtake Britain as an industrial nation. In western Germany the French started chambers of commerce, the success of which resulted in the formation of similar institutions elsewhere.

The first steam engine in Germany was used on August 23, 1785. It was the result of industrial espionage by a Prussian official who had been sent to England to examine the Watt engine, and it was operated by an English mechanic, Mr. Richards. This soon became the pattern. Expensive English machinery was imported and was operated by highly paid English mechanics. High costs, shortage of capital, and an ample supply of cheap labor meant that the mechanization of industry was painfully slow. In 1846, 97.8 percent of looms were still operated by hand. In such conditions the German textile industry could not possibly hope to compete with Britain.

The iron industry also limped behind that of Britain. As late as 1837 less than 10 percent of Prussia's iron was produced in coke-fired furnaces, when the process had been in widespread use in England for decades. The puddling process, which was in wide use in England from the 1780s, reached Silesia in 1828. It was not until the 1840s that large-scale modern ironworks were founded, such as those of Stumm on the Saar, Hoesch at Eschweiler, and the Friedrich-Wilhelm Hütte in the Ruhr. Krupp astonished visitors to the Great Exhibition in London in 1851 with his display of a block of steel weighing two tons, a technical marvel that wounded the pride of British industrialists. The railway boom, which began in the late 1830s, created a tremendous demand for iron and steel that German producers were soon able to meet. Coal production also increased dramatically to meet the greatly increased demand from industry. In the first half of the century the number of workers in the iron, steel, and coal industries trebled. Demand from the railway sector in Germany played the role of the cotton industry in England in stimulating the industrial revolution.

The first railway in Germany between Nuremberg and Fürth was opened in 1835. It was a mere 6-kilometer stretch, but it made a handsome profit. Four years later a line was opened from Leipzig to Dresden. A rash of similar links between major urban centers followed in a frantic and somewhat haphazard attempt to turn a quick profit. The state intervened in an effort to bring some order into this chaos by building those linking stretches that were essential but unprofitable. Some lines were proposed in order to stimulate economic activity in remote areas, the best known of which was the Eastern Railway (Ostbahn), the debate over which played an important role in the political crisis of 1848.

The transportation revolution in Germany was not confined to the railways. Enormous efforts were made to improve the navigability of the great rivers, the most remarkable of which was the widening of the Rhine at Bingen from 9 meters to up to 30 meters, thus allowing ships to sail from Rotterdam to Basel. Similar improvements were made to the Danube, Isar, and Ruhr. New inland ports such as Duisburg-Ruhrort and the Bavarian town of Ludwigshafen, built across the river from the rival port of Mannheim, became major centers. Canals were also built, the most important of which was the Ludwigskanal that linked the Main to the Danube.

The relatively modest progress of the German economy in the first half of the century provided the preconditions for the great leap forward in the third quarter. In almost every sector there was a spectacular increase in output during this period. Germany led the world in the industrial application of major discoveries in organic chemistry. The 1860s saw the creation of companies that were soon to conquer world markets, such as Bayer, the Badische Anilin- und Sodafabrik (BASF), and Hoechst.

This was not merely an advance in terms of output figures and profits; the industrial revolution marked a significant step forward for society as a whole. There remained areas of underdevelopment, there were still vast disparities and injustices, and many lagged behind. But the standard of living of the vast mass of the population improved significantly. The problems of pauperism, mass unemployment, chronic food shortages, and the pressure of population growth, if not overcome, were at least significantly reduced. The gloomy prognostications of the Malthusians gave way to a somewhat starry-eyed faith in technical progress.

Class Structure

Industrialization also created new problems, injustices, and forms of domination: wild fluctuations in the business cycle, overcrowded towns, the creation of an industrial proletariat with all its problems, socialism and the class struggle, relative impoverishment and alienation, a problem first skillfully dissected by Hegel. It also created a whole new class of white-collar workers as management became more complex and clear distinctions were made between production, research, and administration. By the 1860s 10 percent of the workers at the Siemens factory were clerks. At the same time the distance between management and workers became greater, ownership was remote from the workplace, and patriarchal relationships were replaced by a cold and impersonal bureaucracy. Alienation was thus the result not merely of a rapidly changing society in which old certainties were destroyed, or of the division of labor within the factory. The depersonalization of the worker that resulted from the new concept of time dictated by the machine, the anonymity of the worker on the production line, the widespread practice of piecework, the regimentation of work, and the permanent threat of instant dismissal resulted in feelings of helplessness and anxiety.

Poverty was still a major concern and many remedies were put forward. Baron vom Stein spoke of the threat posed by "a rootless immoral rabble," whose growing numbers would likely make increasing demands. Would there be a repeat performance of "la grande peur" in the summer of 1789? In 1836 the arch-conservative General von der Marwitz, who bitterly opposed Stein's reforms, which he claimed had turned Prussia into "a newfangled Jewish state," spoke of "a completely new and unknown class" of "deracinated people, for whom a pleasingly foreign neologism has been found: the proletariat." In the following year the Freiburg Professor Buss spoke in the Baden parliament of the "helots" and "factory-serfs" as a "terrible weapon" that could well lead to "subversion" were their wretched conditions not addressed. Solutions to this mounting problem ranged from encouraging emigration to stringent birth control, from a suspension of the freedom to practice a trade to a belief that industrial growth would provide the wealth that could then be more evenly distributed. While some argued for wide-ranging social legislation banning child labor, shortening the working week, and guaranteeing a minimum wage, others felt that charitable organizations were sufficient to relieve most of these problems. It was not only socialists like Karl Marx who thought in terms of the class struggle. Lorenz Stein believed that only a socially conscious monarchy could mediate the conflicting interests of bourgeoisie and proletariat. Amid all the many different recipes for solving what was to become known as the "social question" there was a general agreement that the state should keep its distance, letting Adam Smith's "invisible hand" work its magic. Thereby they blissfully forgot that Smith did not believe that the market could solve social problems. Later in the century this central tenet of liberalism became increasingly open to question as the economy manifestly failed to meet the pressing needs of the indigent.

The liberal southern Germans Karl von Rotteck and Robert von Mohl addressed the fundamental problem of why it was that the richer a society became the greater the problem of poverty. They saw this as a problem of the distribution of wealth for which solutions had to be found. But what was the root cause of pauperism? Was it a necessary consequence of industrial capitalism, as Engels suggested, or was it due to the inability of an outmoded agricultural system to meet the requirements of a rapidly increasing population? Neither explanation was satisfactory. The fundamental problem was caused by the "demographic revolution" that began in the mid-eighteenth century. There were a number of reasons why the economy did not grow sufficiently to absorb the mounting pressure of those seeking work. Reforms in the agricultural sector had provided fresh opportunities for employment, but by the late 1830s the labor market was saturated. Trades and crafts were declining, and proto-industry, confronted with English imports and the products of native industry, was rapidly collapsing. The most dramatic example of this was the revolt of the Silesian weavers in 1844. It was not until the 1850s that industrial expansion began to offer significant employment opportunities, not only in the factories but also in the building trades and transport. In such conditions emigration was the only safety valve. There were 21,500 registered emigrants in the 1820s, 145,100 in the 1830s, and 585,400 in the 1840s. But these were mostly artisans and craftsmen: paupers could not afford the fare.

During the pre-March the bulk of production was artisanal. Craftsmen who were the backbone of the old middle class became demoted by industrialization to what was to be labeled the petite bourgeoisie, or *Kleinbürger*. By the 1830s there was a dramatic increase in the number of artisans living barely above the subsistence level, who struggled on in frantic competition with mechanized industrial production. By the mid-1840s they had become the tragic scavengers on the garbage heap of economic history. In 1844 the Silesian handloom weavers, driven to desperation by a catastrophic fall in prices that led directly to mass starvation and a typhus epidemic, rose up in revolt, to be brutally crushed by the army. It was a horrific series of events that awoke the conscience of the nation and inspired generations of socially critical artists. Heinrich Heine's passionate poem "The Silesian Weavers," Gerhardt Hautpmann's play *The Weavers*, and Käthe Kollwitz's harrowing series of prints are moving testimony to the lasting impact of this tragedy. There were similar uprisings elsewhere in Germany in the 1840s albeit on a smaller scale, such as the "Potato Revolution" in Berlin in 1847.

PLATE 3   The suffering of the Silesian weavers. © BPK

At the beginning of the century artisans and craftsmen were organized in guilds, but in many parts of Germany the French or the reformers ended their monopolistic control and introduced complete freedom in the trades. Guilds continued to exist in parts of northern Germany, in the south, and in Austria, but they were greatly weakened by removing industrial production from their control, and many craftsmen and artisans were no longer members of these guilds. In some trades, such as building, the state demanded certificates of competence. Guilds continued informally in states such as Prussia as voluntary associations. This confusing patchwork of the old and the new was typical of a transition period between modes of production.

The guilds were to win back some of their privileges in the period of reaction after 1848, but given the industrial boom that followed, this policy was bound to fail. In many trades the once proud artisans were unable to compete with industrial production and were forced to join the ranks of the industrial proletariat. With the triumph of industrial production there came a certain revival of craftsmanship in the luxury trades. A handful of tailors now made immaculate clothes for the rich. Artisans and craftsmen certainly faced a severe crisis, but after a fairly rapid period of adjustment they were soon able to recover. Many became highly skilled industrial workers, forming a working-class elite. Others found profitable niches in the new age of industrial capitalism. Indeed, Germany's rapid industrialization could never have occurred had there not been an adequate reserve of skilled labor, of inventiveness and experience, which this class provided.

Politically the artisans were arch-conservatives. They stood in determined opposition to capitalism, to free trade, and the liberal reformers. They hoped to put the clock back to the golden age of the Meistersingers of Nuremberg when the likes of Hans Sachs were proudly independent, with a secure place in the social order. The artisans thus made common cause with the reactionaries in 1848.

Their apprentices had no sympathy for such ideas. Feeling exploited and stifled by the formal and informal authority of their masters, they saw little chance in the existing economic climate of ever becoming master craftsmen themselves. They gave vent to their protest by joining the ranks of the radicals and socialists. August Bebel, the founding father of German social democracy, came from such a background, and even as party leader was obliged to eke out a modest living by making well-crafted doorknobs which he sold door to door. Their anti-capitalism was strongly flavored with the reactionary anti-capitalism of their masters and they had little sympathy with Karl Marx's belief that industrial capitalism was a necessary and progressive stage of historical development.

This large petite bourgeoisie was thus unable to ally with the liberals in their struggle for constitutional and democratic reform. They were in certain respects progressive in their dislike of the aristocracy, the bureaucracy, the rich and the powerful. They demanded more rights for ordinary people and the devolution of power, but in economic matters they were hopelessly reactionary. They felt menaced by liberal demands for free trade and modernization as well as by an industrial proletariat into whose ranks they felt threatened to fall.

It would be meaningless to talk of a "working class" in the first half of the century. Differences in status and in income were so vast as to make the concept meaningless. A skilled mechanic in a factory could make up to fifty times more than someone plying a rural trade. The turnover of unskilled factory workers was extremely high as rural workers would move to the towns to work for a few months in a factory and them return to their previous pursuits. Industrial workers still made up a very small fraction of manual laborers. On the whole they enjoyed a higher standard of living than a handloom weaver or an agricultural laborer. Although there were wide fluctuations, as competition from industrial goods from England and the pressure from lower wages in the cottage industries began to diminish, real wages for factory workers began to rise by mid-century. Life was still extremely hard, but it was a great improvement on the wretched conditions in the earlier part of the century. Nor were the living conditions of industrial workers quite as frightful as they were in England. A strong tradition of patriarchal concern for one's workers, the result of a mixture of Christian charity and calculated concern to maintain a reliable and loyal work-force, alleviated many of the worst social consequences of industrialization. But theirs was still a precarious existence. Working staggeringly long hours in wretched conditions, they lived under the constant threat of industrial accidents, disease, early death, or impoverished old age. In 1870 factory workers averaged seventy-eight hours of work in a six-day week. It was not until the 1880s that the state intervened to offer some protection in the form of insurance benefits. Industrial workers were torn out of a network of traditional relationships which had not yet been replaced by a new set by means of political parties, trades unions, and associations. It was to be some time before a specifically working-class consciousness began to form. It played no role by mid-century, for all Karl Marx's fond hopes.

The new class of industrial magnates came from a variety of backgrounds. There were industrialists from the higher nobility in Silesia and Bohemia, but elsewhere they came from humbler stock. The iron and steel barons such as Krupp, Stumm, and Hoesch had begun as artisans, as had the great engineers Borsig and Henschel. Mannesmann and Stinnes had been merchants, and so had Camphausen and Mevissen. David Hansemann the banker, entrepreneur, and jack of all trades was born in the manse. George von Siemens' father was a civil servant who heartily disapproved of his son's banking profession, which in his view entailed a loss of caste. He contemptuously referred to his son, a director of the Deutsche Bank, as a "clerk."

As they grew in wealth and confidence the industrialists, merchants, and bankers began to see themselves as men of distinction and rank. They contrasted their bourgeois virtues, their sense of obligation, and their unflagging diligence with the aristocracy's absurd emphasis on social status, snobbish exclusivity, and pretentiousness. Disliking the officer corps with its aristocratic values, they made sure that their sons avoided military service. They were unable to marry off their daughters to aristocrats without royal permission since, in an effort to preserve their estate, aristocrats were only permitted to marry within their own ranks. A few exceptions were made. Krupp and Stumm obtained royal consent for their daughters' marriages to a von Bohlen and a von Kühlmann respectively, but insisted that their lowly family names be hyphenated with those of these illustrious aris-tocrats. In the process of what has been called "the feudalization of the bourgeoisie" men like Krupp, who had made immense fortunes, built palaces and gave magnificent recep-tions; but rather than aping the aristocracy they were in fierce competition with it and refused to be ennobled. Some, like Thyssen, maintained the earlier, more frugal lifestyle, but later generations could not resist the temptation to keep up with the Krupps.

In the pre-March these men were liberals, opponents of aristocratic privilege, and demanded a constitution. They resented all the bureaucratic hindrances to the freedom of the market, especially the resistance to the formation of joint-stock companies. They were also acutely aware of the social dangers posed by poverty and employed young Dr. Karl Marx to address this problem in the pages of their *Rheinische Zeitung*. But precious few of them were active in politics. They left that time-consuming business to the well-educated members of the professions.

The upper echelons of the civil service formed a privileged class that was intensely conscious of its superiority over those its members regarded as mere tradesmen and mechanics, however wealthy they might be. Wealth had yet to become the measure of social prestige. They were close to the sources of power, could marry into the aristocracy virtually without hindrance, enjoyed handsome tax relief, and, with their own courts of honor, were clearly distinguished from the ordinary bourgeois. The aristocracy, the officer corps, and the higher civil servants formed the pinnacle of society in the pre-March. Some of the residual privileges of the civil servants are still enjoyed in Germany today.

Within the bourgeoisie those who had a university education, known then and now as *Akademiker*, also enjoyed certain privileges that came from their educational qualifications. They formed an educated middle class – the *Bildungsbürger* – who regarded themselves as the standard-bearers of German culture and who looked down on the *Besitzbürger*, who had little to show for themselves besides property. Lawyers, doctors, apothecaries, and evangelical ministers were *ex officio* members of this exclusive group. Education was the key to social advancement. Since there were precious few scholarships it was virtually impossible for those without means to enter the ranks of the educated middle class.

Germany was a patchwork of small states with striking regional differences and was divided along religious lines. The process of creating a unified German nation was thus complex, lengthy, and incomplete. The *Bildungsbürger* played a key role in this process in that they accepted a common culture and a common set of values, which was given political expression in liberalism. The industrial proletariat was also to have a certain sense of solidarity that transcended the regional and the religious. It later became the driving force behind the socialist movement.

The vast majority of the population of Germany possessed little beyond their labor power. They were agricultural laborers, servants, factory workers, and the like living on wretched wages in squalid conditions. Having no property, they had no civil rights. In Frankfurt am Main in 1811 only one-third of the population were classified as "burghers." Below them was a substantial class of beggars and vagabonds whose ranks grew alarmingly due to the pressure of population. It was only in the second half of the century that industrialization provided steady employment for much of this surplus population. Workers were strictly forbidden to form associations in an attempt to redress their grievances, but gradually many conservatives, Bismarck among them, felt that granting workers the right to form associations would win them over to the monarchy, thereby clipping the wings of an increasingly arrogant and pushy bourgeoisie. But it was not until 1869 that a limited right of association was permitted in Prussia.

Jews

One of the great achievements of the French Revolution was to grant equal civil rights to Jews. They were emancipated in Germany west of the Rhine and in the states under French control. Archbishop Dalberg of Mainz followed suit in the Duchy of Frankfurt. Most of the German states considered that this was far too radical a step. They felt that Jews should be integrated into society by a gradual process of education and enlightenment. The Prussian reformers had no sympathy for such reservations. They argued that all citizens should have equal rights as well as equal obligations. Hardenberg and Humboldt managed to secure full civil rights for Jews in Prussia in 1812, the only major exception being that they were still unable to obtain positions in the civil service, except as teachers. The Prussian delegation joined with Metternich at the Congress of Vienna in an attempt emancipate all the Jews within the German Confederation, but this radical step was strongly opposed by many of the smaller states.

Prejudice and discrimination remained firmly entrenched in German society. Jews were widely seen as the representatives of a new and threatening age and there were a number of anti-Semitic riots in which peasants and the petite bourgeoisie gave vent to their discontents. The emancipatory edicts of 1812 were not applied in the new Prussian provinces, so that a number of crippling restrictions remained. Almost 40 percent of Prussian Jews were still without civil rights. Jews were excluded from the student fraternities and from the officer corps. They were unable to teach in the universities, and it became increasingly difficult for them to become schoolteachers.

Many factors stood in the way of emancipation. Governments feared the reaction of the mob to anything that seemed to favor the Jews. In Prussia the ideology of the Christian state made no provision for Jews. In southern Germany the objections were economic rather than religious. Only in Electoral Hesse did the process of emancipation continue. By the 1840s, well-educated Germans felt that the continued discrimination against Jews was intolerable. Most of the remaining formal injustices, inequalities, and restrictions were removed in 1848, virtually without debate. Peasants and artisans once again expressed their fury in isolated instances of atavistic violence, but they were hopelessly out of touch with the times, relics of an older form of anti-Semitism and not harbingers of the new racial anti-Semitism.

In spite of many hardships and injustices, and although many chose to emigrate to the United States, the number of Jews in Germany grew in the course of the nineteenth century. In 1820 there were about 270,000 Jews in the territory that was to become the German empire, half of whom lived in Prussia, mainly in Posen, West Prussia, and Upper Silesia. By 1850 the number had risen to 400,000 and by 1869 to 512,000. During this period there was a steady movement of Jews away from the country into towns such as Berlin, Vienna, Frankfurt, Prague, and Cologne. In Frankfurt and Prague about 10 percent of the population was Jewish.

At the beginning of our period the majority of German Jews were desperately poor, eking out a wretched existence as peddlers, cattle-dealers, and moneylenders in the countryside, or as tailors, pawnbrokers, and shopkeepers in the towns. Very few Jews enjoyed a comfortable bourgeois lifestyle; the Rothschilds were an extremely rare breed. By 1871 there had been a remarkable change in the fortunes of German Jewry. In spite of many restrictions and obstacles the vast majority now enjoyed a comfortable and secure living in the professions, in banking and commerce, and as respected shopkeepers and craftsmen. Only a small number were still living at the margin.

Social Change

The evolution of a full-blown capitalist market economy in the pre-March necessarily led to a profound social change that was reflected in a wholly different class structure. This was not lost on contemporaries such as the conservative economist and sociologist Lorenz von Stein, who spoke of the proletariat and the class struggle before these issues were taken up by the revolutionary Karl Marx and which were later analyzed by the liberal Max Weber. In the pre-March everyone openly admitted that they lived in a sharply divided class society.

They did so in a manner that might seem shocking in an age that tends to deny the existence of class and where everyone, except billionaires and the poverty-stricken, apparently belongs to an amorphous middle class.

The aristocracy had formed an estate, but was it now a class? The restoration appeared to reinforce the status of the aristocracy, but they were obliged to turn their estates into capitalist enterprises and were challenged by an increasingly rich and influential middle class that was evolving a distinct political agenda. Conservatives saw a self-conscious aristocracy as the best guarantee against the revolutionary concepts of "liberty, equality and fraternity," of which the second was thought to be not only subversive, but also unnatural. The aristocracy was divided within itself between the exalted princes at the top of the pile and the clodhopping country squires at the bottom. In between which were the sub-castes in the military and the civil service. These latter had lost ground in the reforms, which opened up opportunities for talent, regardless of birth. In Bavaria, Montgelas put an abrupt end to the aristocratic monopoly over the more important offices and created a professional civil service, entrance to which was by competitive examination. There were similar reforms in Baden and Württemberg. Members of the aristocracy were not thereby excluded from high office and still possessed important advantages based on birth and status, but they were curbed by state regulation. The aristocracy fought bitterly in Prussia to preserve their privileges against the incursions of the bureaucracy and they came to terms with agrarian capitalism, in certain areas even with industry. The large estates profited greatly from the reforms by enclosures, by incorporating tenant farms, and by compensation payments from freed serfs. Many were unable to make these payments and sank into the ranks of the rural proletariat. All smallholders and most medium-sized farmers had to augment their income by some form of proto-industrial craft, such as weaving.

Like the landed aristocracy, the urban bourgeoisie jealously guarded its privileges. Two-thirds of the population was denied the vote. A vast gap existed between the small group of dignitaries at the top and the vast mass of the population, between which was a variegated petite bourgeoisie, regarded with barely disguised contempt from above and resentful distrust from below. This was a world far removed from the reformers' ideal of self-actualizing "citizens" (Staatsbürger).

The old-fashioned elite was soon challenged by the entrepreneurs, merchants, and bankers, who seized the opportunities offered by the new economic environment to form a self-conscious bourgeoisie. This new class was determined to assert its political rights against a haughty aristocracy, condescending urban patricians, meddlesome bureaucrats, and the menace from the "dangerous class" below. Some were envious of the aristocracy, aped its ways, and did all they could to join its ranks. Others were proud of their station, regarded the very idea of an aristocracy as an anachronism, and set out to create a class-specific culture. But in the pre-March the bourgeoisie was still in the process of formation, consisting merely of a few hundred families.

The group known by the admirable German term of Bildungsbürger, roughly translatable as "clerisy" or "educated middle class," greatly expanded in these years. It included senior civil servants, schoolteachers, university professors, and the clergy, along with professionals such as doctors and lawyers. They reinforced the distinction between the educated and the unlearned. They accumulated cultural capital that proved to be a key to political power. They articulated the bourgeois attack on aristocratic privilege and its defense against the threat posed by what they deemed to be a primitive rabble, thereby formulating liberal ideology as the basis of a political program for a coherent bourgeoisie.

There were just as many distinctions within the working classes as there were within the aristocracy and middle classes. Skilled and unskilled workers, women and children, apprentices and journeymen, workers in factories and workshops, land laborers and fishermen lived in very different worlds. Almost all existed precariously on the edge of destitution. They were faced with a multitude of proposals for a solution to their problems. Varieties of socialism vied with Catholic appeals to Christian solidarity; liberal self-help organizations were challenged by conservatives, who felt that welfare measures for the poor and needy would meet with the loyal gratitude of the masses. It was not until the end of the pre-March that various versions of socialism and communism had the greatest appeal. Karl Marx and Friedrich Engels' transformation of left Hegelianism and political economy into historical materialism had yet to provide the socialist movement with the powerful weapon of "scientific socialism." At this time Dr. Marx was just one of many outsiders, although undoubtedly the most brilliant and forceful of them, who dreamt of revolution. That such dreams could be entertained was largely due to the exceptionally precarious position of the working classes. Precious few had regular employment. At least half of them lived a marginal existence. By the late 1840s the problem of mass poverty, the direct consequence of fundamental changes in the economic order, resulted in a heightening of social tensions to the point that Germany was on the brink of revolution.

CHAPTER THREE
RESTORATION AND REFORM
· 1815–1840 ·

CHAPTER CONTENTS

A History of Modern Germany: 1800 to the Present, Second Edition. Martin Kitchen.
© 2012 Martin Kitchen. Published 2012 by Blackwell Publishing Ltd.

The war years had aroused great hopes for change and equally intense fears. There were those who hoped that the reforms would continue in peacetime, and those who felt that they had already gone too far. Although the vast mass of the population of Germany was indifferent to the outcome of the struggle between these two factions of reform and restoration, the outcome was to have a profound effect on the course of German history.

At the Congress of Vienna it was agreed that each of the German states should have provincial diets. The wording of the act was extremely obscure. It spoke of "constitutions based on the estates," but quite what that involved and precisely what role the Confederation was to play in the constitutional question was left vague. Metternich's secretary, Friedrich Gentz, produced a powerful memorandum in 1819 in which he drew a clear distinction between "provincial diets" and "representative constitutions" and insisted that the latter were incommensurate with the Federal Act. The Federal Council (Bundestag) in Frankfurt disagreed. It decided that it had no business interfering with the constitutional arrangements of the member states. The states, wishing to assert their independence from the Confederation, got to work drawing up constitutions before one was imposed on them from above. This proved to be only a temporary setback for Metternich. Student unrest provided an excellent excuse to call a halt to further constitutional reform.

In spite of these difficulties constitutional progress was made in southern Germany, particularly in Bavaria, Baden, and Württemberg, all of which had gained considerable amounts of new territory which needed to be integrated into the state, a process that could best be realized by means of a constitution. Many states gave in to the mounting pressure for constitutional reform because most faced severe financial problems in the immediate post-war years, and some form of representative body was felt to be an expedient means of collecting new taxes. Civil servants also wanted to protect the administration of the state from the capricious whims of absolutist princes, while the princes not infrequently supported the notion of constitutional reform as a means of preserving their sovereign rights against the encroachments of the Confederation.

The country that more than any other was in dire need of a constitution was Prussia, which was now a patchwork of disparate territories stretching from Memel to Aachen, sharply divided culturally, religiously, and economically between the western and eastern provinces. Protestant Prussia was now two-fifths Catholic, of whom about half were Poles. The great reforms since 1806 were incomplete. The restorative forces that were concentrated around the crown prince were gradually gaining the upper hand. Frederick William III, never the man to give strong leadership, shunned a confrontation with his son and the powerful ministers who surrounded him.

The reformers managed to secure the creation of a council of state, an idea that had been vigorously supported by Stein, but they did not succeed in their ambition to create some form of representative body for the entire state. Some even doubted whether it would be possible in such a heterogeneous state as Prussia. The demands for constitutional reform were strongest among the liberal bourgeoisie of the Rhineland, with Joseph Görres as their outstanding spokesman, but the reform movement was seriously hampered by the inability of the various factions to settle their differences over what form the constitution should eventually take.

Demagogues and Radicals

Foremost among the demagogues and radicals who supported the movement for constitutional reform were the intensely nationalist student fraternities and the equally passionate gymnastic clubs founded by Friedrich Ludwig Jahn and Friedrich Friesen. These radical nationalists affected an absurdly "Germanic" appearance with distinctive hats and clothes, straggly beards, and a dreamy gaze towards distant horizons. Lonely figures so attired populate the paintings of the masterly Romantic artist Caspar David Friedrich. They were often boorish, were unattractively contemptuous of all foreigners, and prone to a virulent anti-Semitism.

The first student fraternity (*Burschenschaft*) was founded in Jena in 1815. Like their epigones in the 1968 generation they demanded drastic reform of the stuffy universities with their outmoded curricula. They were inspired by a vision of a democratic and free community, but they were also fiercely nationalistic and rejected the cosmopolitanism of an earlier generation of students. Although precious few of them had actually fought in the wars of liberation, they adopted the black, red, and gold colors of the Lützow Free Corps, as well as their motto: "Honor, Freedom and Fatherland."

In October 1817 the *Burschenschaften* organized a festival at the Wartburg in Eisenach to mark the third centenary of the reformation as well as to celebrate the battle of Leipzig of 1813. It was attended by some 500 students from various universities, along with a handful of sympathetic professors. On the first evening some of Jahn's more radical followers built a bonfire, onto which were thrown various items symbolic of militarism and feudalism such as a corporal's swagger stick, a wig, and a pair of corsets, along with the works of certain writers deemed to be "un-German."

A year later the various fraternities joined together to form a national organization with a somewhat confused program combining the ideals of the French Revolution, such as freedom, national unity, and representative government, with an intensely Romantic hankering after an idealized vision of the medieval empire. At the universities of Jena and Giessen there were small groups of German Jacobins who were devoted followers of one Karl Follen. They called for a centralized republic that would be the expression of the people's general will, to be created if needs be by violence.

Metternich was horrified when he received reports of the Wartburg Festival and was convinced that the *Burschenschaften* were a serious threat that had to be eliminated. At the European Congress of Aachen in 1818 he requested that the universities should be placed under close supervision, but he met with stiff opposition from Wilhelm von Humboldt, who held academic freedom to be sacrosanct. In March the following year one of Karl Follen's fanatical followers, the theology student Karl Sand, stabbed the reactionary author and tsarist informant Kotzebue to death at his home in Mannheim. Shortly afterwards a senior civil servant in Nassau was murdered by an apothecary known to be close to the radical student circle at Jena, known as "The Blacks."

There was much sympathy among liberals for Sand's actions. As is so often the case, the victim was blamed for the crime. Görres announced that "despotism" was the root cause. A distinguished theology professor felt that Sand had acted out of conviction and pureness of heart. Sand died as a martyr to the national cause and his wily executioner, a man of democratic convictions, built a garden shed in a vineyard outside Heidelberg out of the timber from the scaffold. It became a popular place of pilgrimage.

PLATE 4 *Burschenschaftler* attending the Wartburg Festival 1817. © BPK

Metternich decided to take firm action against the universities and the radical press, which he held to be a serious threat to the Confederation, but he came up against a certain resistance from a number of the member states to any encroachments on their sovereignty that such a step would inevitably involve. The Prussian authorities made a number of arrests, among them Jahn and Ernst Moritz Arndt. The great theologian and philosopher Friedrich Schleiermacher, who had expressed his sympathy for the radical students, was placed under close police observation.

Metternich met the Prussian king at Teplitz to discuss the situation and then called a meeting of the heads of the major German states at Carlsbad in August. They agreed upon a program to crush the radical movement, which was rushed through the Bundestag in an extremely dubious and hasty manner. It was promulgated on September 20, 1819 as the Carlsbad Decrees.

The universities were now under close police surveillance. Any professor found expounding views deemed to threaten the institutions of the state or the public order was to be dismissed. The *Burschenschaften* were banned. All members were disbarred from the civil service. Newspapers and pamphlets were all to be censored. Books longer than 320 pages were felt to be too expensive for general consumption and were not subject to

PLATE 5   Student representatives burning reactionary books and symbols. © BPK

pre-publication censorship until 1842. A commission was established in Mainz to unearth revolutionary activities. The Confederation could intervene in any state that refused to enforce these measures or which was threatened by revolution. Virtually the sole function of the German Confederation was now to crush radical dissent.

Metternich tried to go one step further by stopping the movement for constitutional reform and revoking some of the more progressive constitutions. Here he was frustrated by resistance from Württemberg, Bavaria, and Saxony-Weimar, but he was able to push through measures that made constitutional changes exceedingly difficult. The implementation of the Carlsbad Decrees varied in severity from state to state. They were rigorously enforced in Prussia and in Austria. Radical students were given lengthy prison sentences. Many prominent professors were rusticated. Gymnastics were strictly forbidden. Fichte's fiercely nationalistic *Speeches to the German Nation* was not permitted to be reprinted. In 1827 the Mainz commission released a report that was greeted with hoots of derision. Schleiermacher, Arndt, and Fichte were said to have inspired the "demagogues," who had also been encouraged by Stein, Hardenberg, and the other great reformers.

Life in Germany in the 1820s was repressive and dreary, but Metternich's attempt to turn the Confederation into a police state was only partly successful. The system was inefficient, somewhat absurd, and the loose federal structure offered areas of relative freedom. The German tendency to look inward was further enhanced in the Biedermeier period and an atmosphere of apolitical resignation and philistine domesticity prevailed. This in turn exasperated those who could not make their peace with existing conditions, and gave rise to a fresh wave of radicalism.

Bourgeois Discontent

The most serious challenge to the Metternichian system came not from radical students and fanatical Jacobins, but from liberalism. The German version of liberalism was heavily influenced by Kant in that it stressed the rights and obligations of the autonomous individual and the need to work towards emancipation from the imperatives of the state, the bureaucracy, and one's station in society. This was seen as a duty and obligation, a lengthy process towards an unspecified future where each would realize his own vision of reason and of freedom, a consensus reached through rational discourse. Most liberals, particularly in southern Germany, had serious reservations about a liberal capitalist economy with its concomitant social problems that could so clearly be observed in England. Feeling that stability and social harmony were far more important than economic growth, they hankered after a cozy pre-industrial society. Germany's foremost political economist, Friedrich List, took the opposite view. He argued that only a modern industrial society could provide the wealth that alone could provide the means to relieve the problems of poverty and want. The great entrepreneurs of the Rhineland, such as Ludolf Camphausen and David Hansemann, Gustav Mevissen and Hermann von Beckerath, were in full agreement. As Karl Marx was to comment, German liberalism, with its ambivalence about modernity, was very long on theory and very short on practice. It was a state of mind rather than a political program. As Kant had argued, freedom existed for them in the realm of ideals and obligations, in contrast to the real world of politics and society.

In more practical terms this involved a demand for restricted popular sovereignty, the strict limitation of state intervention, the rule of law before which all were equal, guarantees for basic individual rights, the right of association, and the separation of powers. A system whereby that which was not expressly permitted was forbidden had to be replaced by one in which everything was permitted except that which was expressly forbidden. The franchise was to be limited to the educated and the propertied, not frivolously wasted on those who were unable to form an intelligent opinion or who had no material stake in society. Even then there could be no agreement on whether or not the democratic rights of a majority could be reconciled with individual rights. From the very outset this was to be a fundamental problem at the very center of the liberal worldview. There was the uneasy feeling that liberty and equality were irreconcilable, but whereas conservatives believed that these twin ideals led inevitably to a reign of terror, liberals hoped that with reason, moderation, and compromise this horror could be avoided. They remained, however, extremely cautious and rejected utopian blueprints in favor of modest and gradual reform.

German liberals faced another dilemma. They were for a lean state that intervened as little as possible in the daily lives of its citizens; but the state was in most instances run by liberal bureaucrats bent on the destruction of the last vestiges of an autocratic system. The state also stifled free speech, trampled on academic freedom, and violated the fundamental rights of its opponents. The state, part ally part foe, was viewed with the utmost suspicion since liberals realized that they alone, not the state, could realize their vision of a free society. Gradually the conviction grew among liberals that society should free itself, not wait to be liberated by enlightened civil servants. Opposed to a revolution from above and alarmed at the prospect of a revolution from below, they wanted gradual reform in the interests of the educated, propertied, and politically aware middle classes. State and society were now on a collision course.

Nationalism

As a bourgeois society was formed, with its market economy, its rationalism, its pluralism, and its individualism, old social ties were sundered and social cohesion was threatened. Religion no longer provided helpful signposts on life's journey. The marketplace was alarmingly free and unforgiving. New social divisions became increasingly threatening. Society was no longer held together by tradition, by a clearly defined social hierarchy or by divine sanction, but increasingly by the use of a common language and a sense of belonging to a common culture. Such a society provided fertile ground for the new religion of nationalism, which offered a fresh and exhilarating sense of community.

Nationalism implied a real or imaginary nation. A nation can be based on consent, on the right of citizens to choose their nationality and by implication their right to govern; or on a common ethnicity, language, or culture. Germany was not a nation in the former sense since one could not become a German by obtaining a German passport; one could only be German if one was a member of the German people (*Volk*).

German nationalism was fueled by the wars against France, and by the French occupation of the western states. It was also driven by the desire to create a new and freer society. It was directed against the French outside and the despots within. The struggle against foreign domination did not of necessity go hand in hand with a liberal vision of a free people. The contradiction between the two positions, partly obscured during the wars of liberation, was to become glaringly apparent. Although there was considerable sympathy for the French and their struggle for freedom, almost all opposed Napoleon. Goethe admired his genius and Hegel managed to convince himself that he was the world spirit on horseback, an instrument of historical change that could no more be condemned than an earthquake or a volcanic eruption. But they were isolated figures. Beethoven crossed out the dedication of his "Eroica" symphony. Görres, who had been a Jacobin, now took solace in contemplation of Germany's medieval greatness. Fichte, the erstwhile ultra-radical, became a rabid nationalist and the outpourings of this great philosopher of nationalism descended to the level of crude and apocalyptic rantings that have a vile foretaste of things to come. The idea of the organic state to which the individual citizens were subservient and in which alone they could fully realize themselves had widespread appeal. Arndt, to whom nationalism was the "religion of our time" and the teutonomane Jahn trumpeted this message. Even such level-headed men as Stein and Humboldt were swept away on this wave of nationalism. Schleiermacher managed to convince himself that since the German *Volk* was God's creation, to serve it was to serve its maker. Kleist, who had suffered an acute identity crisis on reading Kant, temporarily overcame his ontological anxieties by wallowing in an ecstatic nationalism and indulging in an orgy of hatred of the French in his play *Hermannschlacht*.

As memories of the "national awakening" of 1813 began to fade, a search began for a national identity. Architects built in the "German" style, but there was some uncertainty whether this was gothic or Romanesque. Painters churned out canvases of Germany's heroic past, writers produced historical novels. Monuments were erected to all manner of figures, from Hermann to Gutenberg and Mozart. Luther was seen as a uniquely German figure, with Protestants claiming that their religion was the only one appropriate for a true German. Ludwig I of Bavaria built Walhalla as a Germanic pantheon of the great figures of the past. In 1842 Frederick William IV ordered a magnificent celebration to mark the beginning of the final phase of the building of Cologne cathedral, one of the great monuments to Germany's former glory.

Opinions were divided as to what form the new Germany should take. Goethe, who remained true to the cosmopolitanism of the eighteenth century, thought that it should be a cultural community based on the model of ancient Greece that did not require the formation of a nation-state. Local patriotism and regionalism were deeply entrenched, and had been strengthened in the southern German states that had profited from the Napoleonic reordering of Germany. But there were countervailing forces. The remarkable number of national associations and festivals, the mushrooming of the national press, lively communication between the great universities, reforms of primary and secondary education, and a much greater mobility all served to strengthen a sense of supra-regional belonging.

Virtually all liberals were nationalists. They sharply criticized the smaller German states and demanded a united Germany. Freedom and unity was their rallying cry, although there was some disagreement as which of the two was the more important. They attacked the Confederation for its failure to create a common currency and common weights and measures, for not removing the plethora of customs and tariff barriers, and for not developing a rational transportation policy. There was also general agreement that the new Germany would be a federal state, but there were only vague notions of how it would be organized and what would be the relative roles of Austria and Prussia. That Austria was part of Germany was indisputable.

Liberals stood for the principles of the French Revolution, at least in its earlier and moderate phase, and were sympathetic towards the Greeks in the 1820s, the Poles in 1830/1, and the Swiss in 1847/8. Conservatives argued that the liberal call for freedom led inevitably to chaos and terror. Order and stability were, in their view, the essential preconditions for real freedom. The alternative to order and stability was revolution. There could be no middle way. In the place of the endless squabbles and the clash of irreconcilable points of view that liberals were pleased to call democracy there had to be a traditional and legitimate authority that existed by the grace of God. "Authority not majority" was their rallying call. The notion of progress was seen as a vain illusion. That one could slice off heads in the name of reason showed that society needed to be guided by a religiously sanctioned authority that was impervious to utopian hubris. German conservatism was poles apart from the progressive conservatism of Edmund Burke and much closer to the black reactionary fulminations of de Maistre and Bonald.

For conservatives the urban middle class was the greatest danger. Capitalists, intellectuals, and liberal civil servants with their dangerous talk of the rule of reason and their calls for a constitution were at odds with the mass of the people who simply wanted peace and quiet in an ordered, hierarchical community in which everyone knew their place in what Karl Ludwig von Haller dubbed the "patrimonial state." This attack on the bourgeoisie won conservatives considerable support from artisans and peasants who were losing ground as Germany rapidly became an industrial society. Conservatives denounced economic liberalism for bringing with it alienation, the separation of capital and labor, the breakdown of traditional ties, and the creation of a hydra-headed and soulless bureaucratic state. It is fascinating to observe how closely many of their attacks on bourgeois society resemble those of later socialists. For the likes of Adam Müller, Friedrich Schlegel, and Görres in his final incarnation, to call this bleak and inhuman society "free" was a cruel mockery. Conservatives were every bit as vehement in their denunciation of nationalism. For them it was a flagrant violation of legitimate, time-honored, and sovereign rights, the brainchild of a godless bourgeoisie. They were particularists, supporters of the German Confederation dominated by Metternich and of the Europe of the Holy Alliance.

Prussia in the pre-March had no constitution, was authoritarian, penny-pinching, and efficient, but it was not a police state nor was it subject to the whims of its rulers. Even if its legal codes limped behind those of its more progressive neighbors, at least the rule of law prevailed. It was a state that was run by an honest, hardworking, and capable civil service, but it was no longer in tune with middle-class aspirations as it had been in the period of reform In the southern German states, where the constitutional movement had gone furthest, the pace of reform slowed down markedly. Precious little was done to modernize the economies of these states, so that the disparity between Prussia and southern Germany grew ever greater. The south had constitutions, conservative governments, and a stagnant economy. Prussia had antiquated political institutions but a more modern social structure and a thriving economy.

The southern German states developed what came to be known as "constitutional patriotism." The states, the frontiers of which had been radically redrawn during the Napoleonic era, were defined by constitutions. These constitutions limited the power and the sovereignty of the princes. Laws could not be enacted without the consent of representative bodies. The franchise for the *Landtage*, or diets, was indirect, limited, and unequal. A largely hereditary upper chamber ensured the predominant role of the aristocracy. The diets' powers were circumscribed and they met infrequently. Yet in spite of all these limitations parliamentary life in southern Germany flourished to the point that the lower houses became vigorous advocates of middle-class aspirations. A peculiarity of these bodies was that about half their members were civil servants, who became some of the most outspoken critics of the state which they continued loyally to serve.

There were strict limits to the powers of the southern German parliaments. The governments could dismiss them, could influence elections, and could take disciplinary action against deputies; but they preferred to avoid confrontation with elected representatives. Parliamentary control over taxation was a factor that could not be ignored. Attempts to circumvent it, as in Baden in the 1820s, created so many difficulties that the government eventually had to give way. Once the crisis was over, the *Landtag* in Baden made passing the budget dependent on the abolition of censorship. The Bundestag promptly demanded that this move be revoked. This convinced liberals that significant changes could only be made at the federal level, not in the individual states. Liberal nationalism was thereby further strengthened.

A series of dramatic conflicts between governments and parliaments had a profound effect on German liberalism. The relationship between government and parliament became the central constitutional question, with liberals seeing themselves in a controlling rather than a governing role. They formed a permanent opposition keeping a watchful eye on governments to make sure that the people's rights were respected. Governments and parliaments were in permanent conflict, so that no progress could be made towards a liberal constitution. This left liberals increasingly frustrated.

The Zollverein

The only positive political event in Germany during the pre-March was the formation of the Customs Union (Zollverein) in 1832. At the Congress of Vienna the proposal that the Bundestag should be given the task of determining a common customs policy had not been accepted because of objections, principally from Bavaria, that this would be a violation of the sovereignty of the member states. The Zollverein was the work of Prussian economic reformers who enthusiastically accepted the idea put forward by, among others, Stein, the economist Friedrich List, and the sugar baron Johann Friedrich Benzenberg that Germany could only develop economically if it formed a common market. An ugly customs war between Austria and the other German states following the catastrophic crop failure in 1816 made this argument very persuasive.

The arduous process of forming a German customs union began in 1818 when all customs barriers between the various Prussian provinces were abolished. The Prussians were hardly innovators in this respect. The Bavarians had removed internal customs barriers as early as 1807, Württemberg in 1808, and Baden in 1812, but the Prussian officials were determined that their customs union should be extended to include as many of the other German states as possible.

The law of 1818 created a free market for 10.5 million Germans, but it also imposed crippling transit duties. The General German Association for Trade and Industry, the first all-German association of this sort, with Friedrich List as its very capable spokesman, began to agitate for a German customs union on the Prussian model. The Confederation felt that such an institution was dangerously liberal and some of the German states were also opposed to the idea, so an alternative solution had to be found.

Largely on the initiative of Baron Karl August von Wangenheim, the Württemberg delegate to the Bundestag, a southern German customs treaty was signed in May 1820 by Württemberg, Baden, Bavaria, Hesse-Darmstadt, and most of the Thuringian states. This did not amount to much, because the signatories were deadlocked for years with Bavaria demanding protective tariffs while Baden wanted free trade.

Prussia, under the exceptionally able leadership of the minister of finance, Friedrich von Motz, and the economics expert in the foreign office, Albrecht Eichhorn, was determined to extend the Prussian customs union to northern and central Germany. Motz's vision went far beyond the purely economic. He believed that the smaller German states were doomed to backwardness if Germany remained divided. Austria, burdened with all the problems of a multi-national empire, was quite incapable of taking a leadership role in this respect; therefore Germany had to be united under Prussia by means of a customs union. Motz argued that customs dues were symbolic of political division. Political unity would necessarily follow upon their abolition. Not all Prussian officials agreed with Motz's liberal vision, but they all saw the necessity of bringing the two halves of the Prussian state together in one free-trading zone and to abolish all the enclaves within this patchwork of provinces.

This proved to be a long and difficult task. It was not until 1828 that Anhalt finally admitted defeat in a customs war and joined the Prussian union. Electoral Hesse and Hanover, which stood between Brandenburg-Prussia and the western provinces, fiercely resisted all attempts to win them over. The Prussians now looked south. Later in the same year they managed to convince Hesse-Darmstadt to join, thus establishing a foothold south of the river Main. Austria and many of the other German states were determined to resist the Prussians. Egged on by Austria and France, a middle German customs union was formed comprising Saxony, some of the Thuringian states, Electoral Hesse, Hanover and Brunswick, Nassau, and Bremen. In southern Germany Bavaria and Württemberg formed a customs union, also in 1828.

Prussia won over two of the Thuringian states with a generous offer to improve the roads, then in 1829 signed a trade treaty with the southern German union. Two years later Hesse-Cassel finally gave way so that the bridge was built between the eastern and western provinces. In 1833 negotiations between the Prussian and southern German unions were finally concluded, Prussia having made substantial concessions. The resulting union was named the Deutscher Zollverein. Saxony and the Thuringian states joined the party shortly thereafter, and the Zollverein was formally inaugurated at midnight on New Year's Eve 1834. In the following years some of the smaller states joined in, so that by 1842 of the thirty-nine German states twenty-eight were members. Hanover, Brunswick, and Oldenburg remained aloof.

The Zollverein greatly strengthened Prussia's position in Germany, but it did not make a little German solution under Prussian leadership inevitable. It was organized on federal lines much like the European Community is today. Members had the right of veto and were free to leave at will. The Zollverein states could always appeal to Austria for help, and most of them were to support Austria against Prussia in the war of 1866. On the other hand Prussia's rapidly growing industrial might gave it a preponderance of power within the customs union and eventually in Germany.

Germany Under Metternich

Germany was an important diplomatic arena in which most of the powers had a direct interest: Russia as guarantor of the Vienna settlement, Britain because of the personal union with Hanover; Holland and Denmark also had a stake in the Confederation. From time to time France would cast a greedy eye on the Rhine frontier. The German Confederation itself counted for nothing on the international stage. It had no foreign ministry and no foreign policy. Of the German states only Austria really counted so that in as much as Germany had a foreign policy it was that of Metternich and of Austria. Prussia's prestige paled by comparison.

The principles of Metternich's foreign policy were straightforward. He wanted to maintain the conservative order, ensure stability, and preserve Austria's position as a great power. The problem was that it became increasingly difficult to pursue all three aims at once, and ultimately the enterprise was doomed to failure. Metternich was shrewd enough to know that his system's days were numbered, but he was not statesman enough to adjust to meet the challenges of a rapidly changing society. All he could hope to do was to hang on for as long as possible and put off the evil day when the system would collapse. The events of 1848 came as no great surprise to him, and he congratulated himself that the revolution had come so late in the day.

Metternich was a firm believer in summit diplomacy. After the Congress of Vienna a series of congresses were held regularly to strengthen cooperation between the European powers and to discuss common security problems. But the powers had divergent interests. Britain was less concerned with questions of legitimacy and conservative restoration, was sympathetic to the national aspirations of subject peoples, and concentrated on maintaining the balance of power in Europe. Principles were not to be allowed to get in the way of achieving this aim. Tsar Alexander I was wildly unpredictable with his half-baked mystical views about a new order for Europe. The British were determined to keep the Russians in check, and Metternich was anxious to maintain good relations with Britain to this end. At the same time Austria was Russia's neighbor and Metternich hoped that, by convincing the tsar to pursue more levelheaded and conservative policies, conflict could be avoided. Russia and Austria might agree on armed intervention against revolutionary movements in Italy, Spain, and Portugal, but the British government would have nothing to do with this. Britain withdrew from the Congress system and from 1822 merely sent observers. Castlereagh committed suicide that year and the new foreign secretary, Canning, was strongly opposed to the Holy Alliance. He enthusiastically endorsed revolutionary national movements in South America, and in 1826 "called the New World into existence to redress the balance of the old."

Given their conflicting national interests Austria and Russia could hardly remain close allies. Nicholas I, who succeeded his elder brother in 1825 and who was married to Frederick William III of Prussia's daughter, was an appalling despot who resolutely followed what he considered to be the national interests of Russia. Along with the British he supported the struggle for Greek independence. The British wanted to stop Greece from becoming a Russian protectorate; the Russians wanted to weaken the Ottoman empire, whereas Metternich supported the sultan for reasons of legitimacy. With Britain and Russia on opposite sides over the Eastern Question and his system in ruins, Metternich's influence over foreign affairs was minimal.

The revolution now came closer to home. The July revolution in France triggered off a series of uprisings throughout Europe. Belgium broke away from the Netherlands. There were numerous revolts in Italy. In Poland there was a major uprising against Russian rule. England and France let it be known that they would not tolerate any intervention in Belgium, and in any case the Austrians had their hands full in Italy, and the Russians were preoccupied in Poland. The creation of an independent Belgium was another major setback for Metternich. It had proved possible to stop the formation of a Belgian republic, and French aspirations to turn Belgium into a quasi-protectorate had been frustrated, but the principle of legitimacy had been thwarted and others could well be tempted to follow the Belgian example.

The impact of the July revolution was also felt in Germany. In Brunswick there were protests against the heavy-handed absolutist regime of Duke Karl, who had taken away the consultative rights of the estates in 1827. The duke refused to make any concessions; a mob of artisans, workers, and youths set the palace on fire, and the duke fled. The *Landtag* declared him incapable of ruling and his brother was appointed regent. The duke attempted to return but was stopped by army units supported by the militia. After a peasant revolt in 1832 a constitution was promulgated which strengthened the representation of the middle classes and peasants and lessened the influence of the aristocracy.

William II, the Elector of Hesse, was one of the worst despots in Germany, who outraged the bourgeoisie by aping the ancien régime and by flaunting his mistress. Demonstrations were held in Kassel, Hanau, and Fulda calling for a diet. A volunteer militia was formed, and there were widespread protests against all manner of abuses. As in Brunswick, artisans and workers were the most active, and the bourgeoisie used this fact to argue that a constitution was essential in order avoid a civil war between haves and have-nots. The elector gave way and appointed a *Landtag*, which promptly demanded that he abdicate. The crown prince was made co-regent and a constitution was adopted which was by far the most progressive in all of Germany. There was a single chamber elected by a reasonably wide franchise and dominated by the bourgeoisie and peasantry. It was the only parliamentary body in Germany that had the right to initiate laws and to veto emergency decrees.

The protest movement in Saxony was multifaceted. Most agreed that the antiquated system of government needed to be drastically overhauled and society modernized, but this was mixed with confessional squabbles and artisanal protests against industrialization. After a series of protests a reform ministry was appointed, but it was soon under pressure to get on with the job. The result was a new constitution in 1831 which, although not nearly as progressive as that in Electoral Hesse, was a significant step forward.

Hanover also was the scene of violent demonstrations against the reactionary regime of Count Münster. In the university town of Göttingen the tutors (*Privatdozenten*) led a rebellion that had to be suppressed by the army. The government decided to act. Münster was dismissed and discussions were begun with the diet over a constitution that came into effect in 1833. It made few concessions to the urban liberals, but they took some comfort in the fact that taxes had been reduced and the peasantry finally freed from their feudal obligations.

There were no such dramatic upheavals in southern Germany in 1830, but the liberal opposition was encouraged to take a bolder stand and there were a number of demonstrations in favor of Polish independence, the largest of which, in Munich, was broken up by the army. Radical groups were emboldened by these events in 1830, and in 1832 a huge meeting was held at Hambach in the Palatinate, organized by the recently formed "Press and Fatherland Association." Between 20,000 and 30,000 attended, making this the largest political demonstration to date in Germany. They waved the black, red, and yellow German flag along with the white eagle of Poland. They were mostly artisans and peasants, but a number of students attended, along with some representatives from France and Poland. They listened to a series of rousing speeches calling for a democratic "legal revolution" that went far beyond liberal constitutional reform, for the emancipation of women, and for the formation of a German nation-state. The tone of these speeches was cosmopolitan and far removed from the rabid German nationalism of the Wartburg Festival. A number of smaller demonstrations were held elsewhere in Germany, and there were isolated instances of violence.

Even moderate reformers such as Heinrich von Gagern and Karl Rotteck agreed with the authorities that this was all the work of misguided demagogues. At Metternich's prompting Bavaria declared a state of emergency and an ancient field marshal was sent to the Palatinate to round up radicals and uproot the many liberty trees, which had been provocatively planted throughout the region. Most of the ringleaders of the Hambach Festival managed to escape arrest. One month later the Bundestag passed the "Six Articles," which drastically limited the rights of the diets and established a Control Commission to ensure that these provisions were rigorously enforced. A federal law was proclaimed which tightened censorship and banned all political associations and meetings.

The protest movement continued in spite of these measures. In the following year there were celebrations in the Palatinate to mark the anniversary of the Hambach Festival. In Frankfurt am Main a group of students from Heidelberg led an attack on the main guardhouse. It was a dramatic gesture designed to trigger off a general revolt in which the Bundestag building would be seized, the delegates arrested, and a revolutionary council formed. As is so often the case, the citizenry wrote the whole episode off as a student prank and regarded it with amused detachment.

The authorities did not share this indifference. The army was sent in and six soldiers were killed, along with one student. Metternich then pressed through further repressive legislation. The Central Office for Political Investigation was formed, which began work at once tracking down radicals. Within ten years 2,000 investigations had been conducted. The Prussian authorities took drastic measures: 204 students were arrested, most of whom were given lengthy jail sentences; thirty-nine were condemned to death. Membership of a student fraternity was now regarded as high treason.

In 1835 the police unearthed a network of radical intellectuals and artisans from Giessen, Marburg, and Frankfurt who called for a violent overthrow of the existing order, the creation of a republic based on popular sovereignty, and genuine equality. The brilliant young dramatist Georg Büchner was the outstanding spokesman of this group and in his *Hessian Courier* of 1834, which he co-authored with Friedrich Ludwig Weidig, he coined a slogan that was to become an overworn cliché in left-wing circles: "Peace to the cottages! War on the palaces!" Büchner managed to escape arrest and fled to Zurich, where he died of typhoid in 1837 at the age of 24.

The liberal bourgeoisie who lived neither in cottages nor in palaces were horrified at these inflammatory notions and sympathized with the authorities in their determined pursuit of dangerous radicals. Had they read Büchner's masterly study of the complexities and moral ambiguities of the French Revolution in his drama *Danton's Death* or his harrowing analysis of the structures of social control and psychological dependency in *Wozzeck*, to say nothing of his gentle mockery of the old order in his comedy *Leonce and Lena*, they would have been less indignant.

Büchner was one of a number of gifted radical writers in the 1830s which included Heinrich Heine, whose political verse expressed his love-hate relationship with Germany, and who gave vent to his ironic wit in language of unparalleled brilliance and clarity. Heine and Ludwig Börne were the leading figures of a literary movement known as Young Germany, the writings of whose adherents were banned by the Bundestag in 1835 for immorality and blasphemy. The immediate cause of this drastic action was the publication of a novel by Karl Gutzow, *Wally the Skeptic*, which attacked the hypocrisy of the churches and preached free love and the emancipation of women.

The "Young Germans" were politically naive and few their literary works are of much value. Only Heine combined literary genius with an astonishing ability to analyze the malaise of his times. History more often than not has proved him right. Heine and Börne were the most prominent of the German exiles in Paris. They were among the founding members of the German People's Association (Deutsche Volksverein) formed in Paris as a branch of the Press Association. It was disbanded by the police in 1834 and a hard core of radicals formed the Union of Outlaws (Bund der Geächteten); a few years later a splinter group called the Union of the Just (Bund der Gerechten) was formed, which espoused an inchoate communism and with which the young Karl Marx was soon in contact. Its most prominent figure was Wilhelm Weitling, a journeyman tailor living in exile in France and Switzerland, who in a series of books propounded his version of utopian socialism. It was a pre-industrial vision in which the industrial proletariat played no role. His messianic vision, in which property and money would be abolished and which cast Jesus as the original communist, was to be realized through social revolution. It is through the Young Germans that the Hambach Festival can be seen within the context of the European socialist movement.

Prussia and Austria remained remarkably quiet during these troubled years, but attempts in Electoral Hesse to turn back the clock were strongly resisted and there was permanent tension between the government and the *Landtag*. Popular pressure forced the regent to dismiss the fiercely reactionary first minister Ludwig Hassenpflug, the brother-in-law of the Brothers Grimm of fairy-tale fame, but succeeding ministries were no great improvement, and Electoral Hesse remained high on the list of states deserving of liberal opprobrium.

Hanover's personal union with England ended in 1837 when Queen Victoria became Queen of England and the arch-reactionary Ernst August of Cumberland ascended the Hanoverian throne. He refused to take an oath of loyalty to the constitution, dismissed the diet, and declared the constitution null and void. Shortly afterwards seven prominent professors at Göttingen proclaimed their loyalty to the constitution, whereupon they were instantly dismissed. When warned of the possible consequences of removing such distinguished scholars as the Brothers Grimm and the historians Dahlmann and Gervinus, the king made the disturbingly perceptive remark that professors, like whores, could always be had for money. The "Göttingen Seven" were now the heroes of German liberalism. They were feted as men of principle who upheld constitutional rights against princely caprice. These were no stone-throwing rowdies or fervid demagogues, but largely apolitical professors who had the courage to denounce the king's willful action. Baden and Bavaria supported the Hanoverian opposition's appeal to the Bundestag to right these wrongs, but the majority of the German states supported Metternich, who sympathized with Ernst August's coup which was thus sanctioned by the Confederation. A new constitution was introduced in 1840, but it was a far less liberal document than the earlier version in that it greatly reduced the powers of the diet, to which ministers were no longer responsible.

For all the repression the intellectual and political life in Germany was far from being stifled. The very fact that Germany was a Confederation meant that the atmosphere in the various states varied widely. The Göttingen Seven might be dismissed in Hanover, but those who so wished had no difficulty in finding a chair at another university. It was also in the period of the Carlsbad Decrees and the Six Articles that the main political movements in Germany became clearly delineated: conservatives, Catholics, liberals, democrats, and socialists. Conservatives were anti-nationalist, felt that the Confederation should exercise its full powers against liberals and radicals, and argued that Austria and Prussia should work closely together against the forces of change. The Prussian statesman Joseph Maria von Radowitz was the first to see that conservatism could indeed be reconciled with nationalism and was to argue that Prussia should assert itself within a reformed Confederation.

Catholicism

Catholics, unlike Protestants, also began to be seen as a distinct party. The relative roles of church and state had been redefined by the French Revolution and by secularization. The church wanted to be free from state interference but at the same time to have a decisive influence over such central issues as education and the family. Catholics thus opposed the secular and authoritarian state, but also anti-clerical liberals with their individualism and their vain belief in the unlimited power of reason. This argument was to continue throughout the century and was to be brilliantly recreated in the debates between Naphta and Settembrini in Thomas Mann's masterpiece *The Magic Mountain*.

Catholics came into direct conflict with the state in Prussia when in 1803 the government required that, east of the river Elbe, children of mixed marriages should be brought up in the religion of the father. According to Tridentine practice, children of marriages between Catholics and Protestants had to be brought up as Catholics. In 1825 the government requirement was extended to all of Prussia, including the predominantly Catholic Rhineland. Although the Pope urged restraint there was widespread resistance to the law, and in 1837 the bishop of Cologne was arrested for publicly denouncing it. He and a number of other bishops became heroes in the eyes of all their co-religionists. In 1840, at the beginning of his reign, Frederick William IV gave way to his Catholic subjects and the church won a major victory over the state, thus giving political Catholicism a major boost. A number of Catholic associations were formed, and pilgrimages, attracting large numbers, had distinct political overtones. Joseph Görres published another brilliant pamphlet, *Athanasius*, which provided a program for political Catholicism. He argued that since parties were an essential part of the modern constitutional state Catholics should organize themselves to struggle for their rights. These ideas were developed in a new journal, *Historisch-politische Blätter für das katholische Deutschland*, published in Munich. Görres and his friends waged war on the bureaucratic and authoritarian state, on the liberal heirs of the French Revolution out to destroy all in their wake, on godless socialism, and above all on the Reformation, which lay at the root of all modern evil. Görres the one-time radical was now firmly in the camp of Catholic conservatism, dreaming of reconstituting a corporate society of a long-gone age.

The majority of German Catholics were little concerned about the philosophical questions of individualism and rationalism which separated the ultra-conservatives from the liberals. They sympathized with Catholics in Poland and Ireland who were struggling for national independence. They supported the liberal demands for freedom of expression, freedom of association, and a diminution of state power. Some went even further and sharply criticized industrial society as the direct cause of poverty, deprivation, and alienation. They demanded state intervention to protect the working class from the grosser forms of exploitation, encouraged the working class to organize to further its interests, and played an active part in workers' education. Adolf Kolping founded the Catholic Journeymen's Association in 1845 to provide for the needs of working men on their travels. Later in the century Bishop Ketteler of Mainz was to develop social Catholicism into a major political movement.

On the national question the vast majority of Catholics were federalists, anti-Prussian, and for a greater Germany that included Catholic Austria. They all agreed that the interests of the church were their paramount concern and refused to allow differences between conservatives and liberals to compromise their position on this cardinal issue. Political Catholicism laid the foundations for a genuine people's party in which Catholic princes and Catholic workers, Catholic conservatives and Catholic liberals, Prussians and Bavarians could work together towards common goals. Conservatives represented the interests of the old elite, liberals those of the new, but the Catholic movement transcended this division and had no clearly defined class bias. Here were the beginnings of the Christian Democratic movement that was to play such an important role in European politics. Unfortunately this division between Catholic and Protestant liberals greatly weakened the liberal movement in Germany and thus strengthened the conservative camp, and put a brake on the development of parliamentary democracy.

Liberalism

The liberals distanced themselves ever more from the radicals. They were deeply suspicious of the radical call for equality. While accepting that equality was the essential precondition of freedom they were keenly aware that it could also destroy freedom. They had before them the example of the French Revolution, which had clearly demonstrated the totalitarian aspects of egalitarianism, and de Tocqueville's study of American democracy, published in 1835, was widely read in liberal circles. Liberals had a horror of revolution and of the rabble whom the radicals aroused with their fiery rhetoric.

As liberalism moved to the right it ceased to be a purely bourgeois movement and appealed to a number of aristocrats such as Heinrich von Gagern, Prince Karl zu Leiningen, and Anton von Schmerling, who were to play important roles in the revolution of 1848. All agreed that that the existing state of affairs needed to be drastically changed, that Germany should become a nation-state with a liberal constitution, but there was considerable disagreement as to how the new Germany should look.

Liberalism was also given a boost by what the great nationalist historian Heinrich von Treitschke called the "intellectual diets" – the national meetings of intellectuals and scientists, doctors and schoolteachers, lawyers and linguists, singers and gymnasts. These occasions were highly politicized and laden with national pathos, in particular the meetings of "Germanisten," who reveled in ancient Germanic language and lore. By the 1840s there were regular meetings of a purely political nature in which liberals from all over Germany met to discuss matters of common concern, but it was not until late in the decade that a national newspaper, the *Deutsche Zeitung*, was founded in Heidelberg.

Radicalism

Whereas liberals argued that a natural state of inequality resulted from an unequal distribution of intelligence and talent, radicals insisted that this resulted from an unequal distribution of power. They called for popular sovereignty, a republic, and a parliament elected by direct and universal suffrage and without the division of powers with its checks and balances. If necessary these goals should be attained by violent revolution.

The intellectual standard bearers of this radicalism were the Young Hegelians who used the powerful tool of Hegelian dialectic to criticize existing conditions and to demonstrate how the real diverged from the rational. David Friedrich Strauss and Ludwig Feuerbach mounted a massive attack against organized Christianity. Strauss' *Life of Jesus* (1835) presented Christ as a purely mythical figure whose existence as a human being was largely irrelevant. Feuerbach went one step further and proclaimed that God was a creation of man, rather than the other way round. This idea was taken up by two Young Hegelians, Karl Marx and Friedrich Engels, who in their *German Ideology*, which they wrote in 1845 but which remained unpublished, took Feuerbach one step further and argued that his materialism was an "ideology" in that it failed to see that the need for religious self-mystification could only be relieved by a social revolution necessitated by the contradictions within society. Moses Hess and Karl Grün presented their version of "true socialism" in direct contrast to Wilhelm Weitling's mystical vision of a future society, but it also existed purely in the realm of ideas. Karl Marx savaged all these unfortunate utopians in a series of brilliant essays. Philosophy of this ilk, he proclaimed, bore the same relationship to social change as masturbation did to sexual intercourse. Marx and Engels, with their catchy phrase with which the *Communist Manifesto* begins, that "the history of all hitherto existing society is the history of class struggle," and proclaiming the proletariat as the universal class, were far ahead of their times. In 1848 such a class barely existed in Germany.

Radical poets were every bit as influential as the philosophers. They included Hoffmann von Fallersleben, the author of "Deutschland über Alles," published in his ironically titled *Unpolitical Songs* of 1841; Ferdinand Freiligrath, who loudly proclaimed the revolution in such verses as "Ça ira" of 1846; and the ubiquitous Georg Herwegh, who counted among his friends Turgenev and Bakunin, Herzen and Belinsky, Marx and Heine, and finally Richard Wagner, whose mother-in-law was one of his many mistresses. Frederick William IV was so intrigued with Herwegh that he invited him to an audience in 1840, but on reflection thought it prudent to exile him. Herwegh then moved to Paris, where he entranced his wide circle of brilliant friends and admirers.

For all these glittering figures and occasional upheavals, the pre-March was outwardly a dull and repressive period of restoration and reaction. Only a few keen minds realized that underneath this apparent stagnation revolutionary changes were taking place. No government, however oppressive and reactionary, could stop the profound socio-economic and cultural transformation that was under way. A period often seen in terms of stolid Biedermeier complacency, a quiet and untroubled idyll of sober simplicity, reflected in Karl Spitzweg's paintings of dotty little men, was in fact the complex starting point of a process that would fundamentally alter society. In 1848/9 the last vestiges of feudalism disappeared and Germany entered the age of industrialization and constitutional rule.

CHAPTER FOUR
THE REVOLUTIONS OF 1848

CHAPTER CONTENTS

A History of Modern Germany: 1800 to the Present, Second Edition. Martin Kitchen.
© 2012 Martin Kitchen. Published 2012 by Blackwell Publishing Ltd.

The year 1840 was a turning point in Germany in two respects. Fredrick William IV ascended the Prussian throne and the Orient crisis of that year marked the beginning of a new phase in German nationalism. High hopes were pinned on the new Prussian king. He was known to be a pleasant person with a lively intelligence, who was highly critical of the bureaucratic and authoritarian Prussian state of the Frederician tradition. He thought in somewhat romanticized German national rather than Prussian terms. He was a man of compromise who sought to heal the political divisions within the country.

To this end he began his reign by pardoning Jahn and Arndt, the "demagogues" of 1819, and appointed three of the Göttingen Seven to chairs at Berlin University. The great reforming war minister of the Napoleonic era Hermann von Boyen was reappointed at the ripe old age of 70. Censorship was relaxed, the policing powers of the Confederation reduced, the Germanizing policy towards the Poles in Posen was relaxed, and an accommodation was reached with the Catholic Church. A series of amazing speeches, which were remarkably short in substance, gave rise to no end of misunderstandings. They contained memorable rhetorical flourishes that articulated many of the leading ideas of the time in a manner that was pleasing to almost all except Metternich and the tsar. Unlike his father, Frederick enjoyed genuine and widespread popularity. In these early years of his reign it seemed to go almost unnoticed that he was a staunch conservative who deeply distrusted the liberal bourgeoisie with their demands for a constitution.

The year 1840 was also a critical one for the German Confederation. Cooperation between Prussia, Austria, and Russia against Polish nationalism in 1830 had resulted in the formation of an alliance of the three states aimed at crushing revolutionary movements and also with an eye to dividing up the European spoils of the Ottoman empire. But within a few years the situation once again changed dramatically. In 1839 Mehemet Ali, an Albanian warlord who was master of Egypt and Syria, won yet another decisive victory over the Ottomans at Nezib. It seemed that Constantinople might well fall. England, Russia, and Austria now found themselves united in support of the Ottomans against Mehemet Ali and his French allies. Acre fell to the British in 1840, Mehemet Ali lost Syria, and the French suffered a major diplomatic setback.

The French prime minister Adolphe Thiers, a Marseillais and historian of the French Revolution, in an ill-considered moment of frustration, demanded a revision of the 1815 settlement and the Rhine frontier. Germany prepared for war, France was forced to back down in a "diplomatic Waterloo," forcing Thiers to resign. His successor Guizot, another historian and politician, announced that he intended to seek "reconciliation with Europe" and urged his fellow-countrymen to concentrate on making money.

The crisis triggered a wave of German nationalism the likes of which had never been seen before. Poets churned out reams of patriotic verse, which was rapturously received by an excited public. The most famous of was Nikolaus Becker's "Song of the Rhine," which warned the French to keep their hands off this sacred German river. It was set to music by countless composers and enthusiastically sung by glee clubs throughout Germany. Hoffmann von Fallersleben's "Deutschlandlied" with its strident nationalism, which was to become Germany's national anthem when set to Haydn's music, was also written at this time. Equally popular was Max Schneckenberger's "Watch on the Rhine" with music by Karl Williams.

Thus 1840 marks a decisive point in the development of German national consciousness. Germany saw itself as the country of the future that would defend itself against the "Romanism" of France and the "Slavism" of Russia by becoming an industrial giant with an invincible army and a superior culture. Germany was united in a wave of anti-French nationalism that momentarily covered over all major political differences. Many liberals and some radicals reconsidered their cosmopolitanism. The year marks a new stage in the development of the tensions between national sentiment and liberal demands. The political landscape of Germany was changed forever.

Frederick William IV was also swept along by this wave of nationalism. He enthusiastically supported the movement to complete Cologne cathedral, the building of which had ceased in 1559. Here he saw an opportunity to reconcile the Catholic Church with the Prussian state, the monarchy, and the people, Prussians and Rhinelanders. It was to be a dramatic demonstration of the unity of the German princes in defense of the German Rhine. He and Archduke John of Austria, whose patriotic credentials were impeccable, were the principal speakers at a massive rally in September 1842 to mark the laying of the foundation stone. Frederick William IV gave a typically rousing speech and was followed by the archduke, who announced: "As long as Prussia and Austria along with the rest of Germany, wherever German is spoken, are united, we shall be as strong as the rocks of our mountains." This was reported in the press as: "No longer Prussia and Austria, but one Germany, as solid as our mountains." The archduke was a remarkable man. He had led an army against Napoleon at the age of 18, when he showed both courage and skill. A lifelong admirer of Rousseau, he detested Metternich and all that he stood for. He had married a postman's daughter and was happiest living the simple life in the mountains. He showed wisdom and justice as a provincial governor and was loved and respected for his intelligence and even-handedness. The faulty reporting of his speech made the already popular archduke into a national hero.

Frederick William IV saw himself as somehow mediating between God and the people, but there was no place within this mystical relationship for what he dismissed as "principles scribbled on parchment." At the beginning of his reign both the East and West Prussian diets, which were dominated by the liberal aristocracy, respectfully requested the completion of the constitutional process that had begun in 1815. The king turned this request down. Liberal demands became more strident, and liberal publications were censored, but charges of lèse-majesté and high treason were dismissed by sympathetic magistrates.

Frederick William was shrewd enough to realize that the constitutional question would not simply fade away; besides, he needed money in order to finance a national railway network. In 1842 the "United Committees" were convened, made up of representatives from the provincial diets. The new body agreed that a comprehensive plan for the railways was necessary, but felt that it was not an appropriate body to vote on the financing of such a huge project. The provincial diets saw this as the golden opportunity to secure some sort of national parliament. After years of agitation during which demands for freedom of the press, legal reform, and budgetary control had become ever louder, the king ignored Metternich's and the tsar's objections and called a "United Diet" in February 1847. All the members of the provincial diets came to Berlin to discuss the budget. They were assured that they would meet on a regular basis and that a smaller body known as the "United Committee" would be periodically consulted about future legislation. The liberals did not think that this was going nearly far enough, but they accepted it as being at least a step in the right direction.

More than 600 delegates met in Berlin. All were men of substance, more than half of them were aristocrats, seventy from the very highest ranks of the nobility. Yet in spite of all this blue blood it was a remarkably liberal body. It agreed wholeheartedly with the government's schemes to build the Ostbahn, a railway from Berlin to Königsberg, and to the proposal to create credit institutions to help the peasantry free themselves from their remaining debts resulting from compensatory payments at the time of the emancipation. But they demanded a high price. By a two-thirds majority they demanded of the abolition the United Committee, to be replaced by a United Diet, meeting on a regular basis. As the liberal Rhinelander David Hansemann phrased it: "Once money is involved amicability disappears." The king promptly sent the United Diet packing. In doing so he strengthened the determination of the united front of aristocrats, bourgeois, and farmers to push for constitutional change. The constitutional question was thus a pressing issue, even in somewhat anachronistic and conservative Prussia.

An increasingly self-confident bourgeoisie was the standard bearer of the new industrial society that was developing in Germany. It set the tone in the years between 1815 and 1848. It faced the intractable forces of the old order, the harsh repression of the Metternichian system, and the irksome supervision of the bureaucratic and authoritarian state. The dynamism of the new clashed with immobility of the old, giving rise to frustration and radicalism on both sides. There was little pragmatism on either side, wide divisions within the ranks, and a latent tendency towards the impractical and the doctrinaire.

By 1845 the economic and social problems of a society in transition had reached crisis dimensions. Bad harvests resulted in a sharp rise in the price of food, followed by famine and disease. Incomes dropped and unemployment rose at an alarming rate. Charitable institutions, whether state or local, church or secular, were unable or unwilling to help. Thousands were forced to beg or resorted to petty crime. Typhus and cholera were rampant. In 1846 it was estimated that between 50 and 60 percent of Prussians lived a life described as "wretched and endangered." Whereas historians have all too easily assumed that industrialization was the root cause of this widespread misery, contemporaries such as Gustav Mevissen, the industrialist and owner of the *Rheinische Zeitung* of which Karl Marx was the editor, the historian and liberal politician Heinrich von Sybel, the Catholic jurist Peter Reichensperger, and the economist Friedrich List insisted that industrialization would provide a solution. They could point to the simple fact that in areas where there was no "modern industry" the problem of pauperism was most severe. But such voices were rare, and the solutions they offered were mostly abstract and political. Small wonder then that many grew impatient with the liberals' self-absorbed legalism and sought a radical and even revolutionary solution.

Revolution

As in 1830, it was events in Paris that triggered a series of uprisings in Germany in 1848. Louis Philippe lost his throne on February 24, and three days later there was a mass meeting in Mannheim addressed by the radical Friedrich Hecker and the liberal Karl Mathy. They demanded freedom of the press, freedom of assembly, trial by jury, a militia, and a German national parliament. On March 1 a deputation went to Karlsruhe to present these demands, accompanied by a vast crowd, some of whom were armed. The grand duke of Baden at first refused to negotiate, at the same time turning down an offer of military assistance from Prussia. He then formed a new ministry, which included the liberal leaders. They began to implement most of their original demands.

Similar pressure was exerted on many of the German states, in most instances with a similar outcome. Elections were held, liberal ministries appointed, constitutional changes set in train, the remnants of the old feudal order abolished. There was very little violence. The mob stormed the town halls in Frankfurt and Munich, but it was only in Prussia and Austria that there were serious confrontations between the people and the military.

There was Jacobin or, in the widely used phrase of the day, "communist" agitation in the Prussian Rhineland. In Cologne the prominent radical doctor Andreas Gottschalk, cheered on by an enthusiastic crowd of some 5,000, called for the establishment of a revolutionary committee. The demonstration was broken up by the army, much to the relief of the liberals. After a series of smaller demonstrations in Berlin involving clashes with the military, Frederick William IV decided to make a conciliatory gesture. He abolished censorship, and promised that the United Diet would reconvene and that Prussia would at last be given a constitution. A large crowd gathered outside the royal palace Berlin on March 18 to express their appreciation and to urge that these measures be implemented as soon as possible. The crowd demanded that the troops guarding the palace be withdrawn. The garrison commander, General von Prittwitz, regarding this as a menacing attack on the king's power of command and on the very foundations of the Prussian military state, ordered his men to break up the demonstration. Only two shots were fired, it was unclear by whom, but that was enough to start a bloody street battle. Barricades were erected, and by the next day more than 230 people lay dead.

Conventional military wisdom was that if the army was unable to storm the barricades within twenty-four hours it should be withdrawn and lay siege to the town. Prittwitz accordingly requested that the fighting in Berlin be stopped. Although hardliners, led by the king's brother William, regarded this as craven submission to the mob, Frederick William was appalled at the heavy death toll and was determined to defuse this highly explosive situation. On March 19 he attended the funeral of those who had died on the barricades. He then took part in a ceremony in which the palace guard was handed over to units of the citizens' militia. Prince William, the leader of the military party, joined Metternich and Guizot in exile in England.

On March 21 the king rode through the streets of Berlin with the gold, red, and black armband of the liberal nationalists. Although he refused to be addressed as "emperor of Germany," he gave his most famous and typically gnomic speech in which he announced to an enraptured crowd that "Prussia dissolves into Germany." One week later he appointed a new ministry under two prominent liberals from the Rhineland – Ludolf Camphausen and David Hansemann. The Prussian ultra-conservatives, Bismarck prominent among them, appalled at the triumph of the western liberals, laid plans for a counter-revolution. The revolutionaries had won the first round, but they were divided amongst themselves, and the king, on whose support they depended, was uncertain, hesitant, and under constant pressure from the army and the royalists.

In Prussia the revolution was largely urban, but in many parts of Germany, particularly in the southwest and in Thuringia, there were peasant uprisings. They were directed against the great landowners, the administrators of the demesne lands as well as Jewish moneylenders and cattle dealers. Deeds were burnt, taxes were left unpaid, poachers had a field day, and committees of public safety were formed. In Wiesbaden thousands of peasants demanded that noble estates be taken over by the state and divided up among the people. These peasant uprisings had precious little in common with the urban revolts. Their social composition, their aims, and their choice of methods were quite different. Urban liberals

PLATE 6   Street fighting in Berlin on the Night of March 18/19, 1848. © BPK

were appalled by this violence in the countryside and condemned the peasants' lack of respect for private property. In some instances liberal governments sent in the troops to restrain the peasantry. On the other hand they sympathized with the demand that aristocratic privileges be abolished and that the last vestiges of feudalism be removed. Once that was achieved, peace and quiet was restored and the peasantry, and thus the vast majority of Germans, had no further interest in the revolution. Constitutional reform and the national question were of little consequence to them, and only in very rare cases were urban radicals able to mobilize rural discontents to win support for their cause.

The proletariat, on whose behalf Marx and Engels wrote the *Communist Manifesto* in 1848, failed to live up to their high and wholly unrealistic expectations. Far from forming the vanguard of a socialist revolution, workers indulged in an orgy of Luddism. In some industrial centers machines were smashed, and steamships and railways were taken over by the workers. They participated in the demonstrations in the larger towns and fought on the barricades in Berlin, but in other areas the workers remained remarkably passive. The artisans and their apprentices were far more active. They shared the proletariat's passionate hatred of industrialization to such an extent that the two groups are virtually indistinguishable.

In a complex dialectic the violent protests and political demands of the peasantry, industrial workers, and artisans lent weight to the peaceful demands of the urban notabilities. But at the same time there was a wide divergence over both aims and methods. Furthermore there was not one revolution in Germany in 1848 but several. The revolutionary movement was decentralized, thus weakening the movement for fundamental change in the Confederation. In each of the states liberals were sorely afraid of being overtaken by radicals and socialists, anxious that the movement for constitutional reform and national reconstruction might be swept aside by a social revolution. The very fact that governments had given way so easily and quickly to their initial demands raised the question where power resided. Was it in the studies of the urban intelligentsia or in the street? The liberal ministries were determined to halt the social revolution, but they were also keenly aware that it was popular violence that had brought them to power. The old regime having capitulated, they now had more to fear from the radicals as the revolution entered a new phase in which the national question began to be addressed.

The Frankfurt Parliament

On March 5 a diverse group of mainly southwestern politicians met in Heidelberg to discuss the next move. They included the radical republicans Hecker and Struve and the moderate liberal monarchist Heinrich von Gagern. They were able to agree on little else than that a "pre-parliament" should be formed from representatives from the various diets to meet in Frankfurt to set the ground rules for an all-German election. Shortly afterwards the Bundestag in Frankfurt appointed a seventeen-man committee to discuss federal reform.

The pre-parliament began its discussions on March 31. The 574 delegates, mainly from southern and western Germany, with only two from Austria, were soon divided into two hostile camps. The liberals wanted to create a parliamentary monarchy in close consultation with the Bundestag. The radicals demanded a republic with executive and legislative powers invested in a revolutionary convention. There was general agreement, however, that the decision as to the form of the future Germany should be decided by a new body elected on a broad franchise. The moderates shied away from outright confrontation, hoping that it would be possible to create a united and free Germany in consultation with the existing governments.

Hecker and Struve would have none of this. On April 12 they proclaimed a provisional republican government in Constance then marched on Freiburg with some 6,000 armed supporters. Federal troops had little difficulty in crushing this ill-organized rebellion on April 20. Hecker fled the country. Robert Blum, the leader of the moderate left, denounced the rebels for betraying the republican cause by robbing it of its democratic legitimacy. Marx and Engels were even stronger in their condemnation of this ill-considered putsch.

The elections for a national assembly were organized by the individual states so that the number of those eligible to vote varied widely. Nevertheless by the standards of the day a remarkably large number of men, somewhere between 75 and 90 percent depending on the state, were able to go to the polls. Since there were no political parties that could articulate sectional interests, most of those elected were prominent figures in the local community. The parliament, which met in the Paul's Church in Frankfurt, was made up largely of civil servants, lawyers, and university graduates. Of the almost 800 members there were only four artisans and one peasant. Ten percent were aristocratic and forty-nine professors played a prominent role in the debates. The social composition of the parliament did not result from bias in the electoral system but reflected the social esteem in which the academic professions were held. Members of state parliaments, such as the Prussian *Landtag*, tended to come from slightly lower down the social scale, largely because the more prominent citizens preferred to go the Frankfurt. Women were not represented in either the national

PLATE 7   A meeting of the National Assembly in the Paul's Church in Frankfurt, September 16, 1848. © BPK

or state parliaments but they played an active role in 1848 by participating in demonstrations and by organizing a number of women's groups. This in turn provoked a misogynist reaction with widespread complaints that women were getting out of hand.

Ultra-conservatives and ultra-radicals were scarcely represented and there was a small Catholic faction relative to the strength of political Catholicism in the March days. The various political factions were named after the inns where they met: conservatives in the Café Milani, moderate liberals in the Casino, left liberals in the Württemberger Hof, Robert Blum and the democrats in the Deutsche Hof, and Hecker's radicals in the Donnersberg. Of these the Casino faction was by far the largest with about 130 members, including most of the distinguished professors such as the historians Droysen, Dahlmann, and Waitz. When the debate centered on whether Germany should include or exclude Austria – the *großdeutsche/kleindeutsche* question – the Greater German faction met in the Mainlust, the Little Germans in the Weidenbusch.

The Frankfurt parliament set about creating a new Germany with an appropriate constitution, but there was wide disagreement as to how this could or should be done. A functioning executive was obviously essential, but it was unclear whether the new parliament had sovereign powers and what its relationship with existing federal institutions, as well as with the member states of the Confederation, should be. Heinrich von Gagern offered a compromise solution between the conservative call for consultation with the states and the radical republican demand for a sovereign parliamentary executive committee. He suggested that the widely popular Archduke John of Austria should be appointed

"Reich Administrator," thus giving the parliamentary system a monarchical coping. Hopefully this would reconcile the radical demand for parliamentary sovereignty with conservative dynastic concerns.

Gagern's proposal was accepted by the overwhelming majority of the delegates in the Paul's Church, including a number of prominent radicals. The states having accepted the decision, the Bundestag handed over its powers to the archduke. He promptly appointed Prince Karl Leiningen, Queen Victoria's half-brother and a prominent German Whig, as minister president with the like-minded Austrian Anton von Schmerling as minister of the interior and the strong man in the new government.

The new government had widespread popular support, but it was virtually powerless. It had no money, no offices, no civil service, and no army. It was wholly dependent on the goodwill of the member states of the Confederation, which was highly questionable. When the new minister of war, the Prussian General von Peucker, ordered the various armies to swear an oath of allegiance to the archduke and salute the national flag, Austria, Prussia, Bavaria, and Hanover promptly refused. An attempt to build a German navy was an equally embarrassing flop.

For the moment the Frankfurt parliament filled a power vacuum in Germany. Austria was wholly absorbed in suppressing uprisings throughout its multi-national empire. Prussia was still reeling after the March days. But the worthy parliamentarians failed to realize that they had to act expeditiously before the counter-revolution recovered from the initial shock. As Bismarck was later to remark, the men of 1848 spent far too much time with resolutions and majority votes. They debated the constitutional question for six months. At the beginning of July, in what one is tempted to call a typically German fashion, they began discussing highly theoretical questions of fundamental rights. It was only at the end of October that they at last addressed practical issues such as where the frontiers of the new Germany would be, and how the state should be organized. Without a state, questions of fundamental rights, however important they might be, were of little consequence.

The question "Where is Germany?" was almost impossible to answer. Linguistic, cultural, geographical, and historical boundaries did not coincide and there were many enclaves with significant minorities. In the Habsburg empire the Germans were a tiny minority. The problem became acute when on March 21 the Danes annexed the Duchy of Schleswig. The Germans in the duchy resisted, claiming that by ancient law that the duchies of Schleswig and Holstein could not be separated. They formed their own government, which was recognized by the Frankfurt parliament and which invited the Prussians to send troops to protect them. The Prussians readily obliged. The Frankfurt parliament announced that Germany was now at war with Denmark and that the Prussian army was acting on its behalf.

At this point the British government intervened. It persuaded the Prussians to withdraw from Schleswig, whereupon the Frankfurt parliament denounced Berlin for betraying the German people and the German national cause. Under pressure from England and Russia and with a Danish naval blockade, Prussia signed the Peace of Malmö at the end of August, which established a new government in the duchy with Danish participation. The peace was denounced in Frankfurt, particularly by the left, as a dastardly breach of faith by Prussia. By a vote of 238 to 221 the parliament refused to ratify the treaty, thus forcing the Leiningen government to resign. Some radicals, Marx among them, dreamed of a revolutionary war against Denmark, Prussia, and Russia, along the lines of the French revolutionary war of 1792. This was hopelessly unrealistic given Germany's precarious position both internally and internationally. The Frankfurt parliament reconsidered the vote, finally ratifying the treaty by a narrow majority.

Another pressing problem was that of Poland. The new Prussian government promised to reorganize the Prussian province of Posen in favor of the Poles. They also favored an independent Polish state. Before any changes could be put into effect the two nationalist movements were in conflict with Polish militia units clashing with the Prussian army. Posen was now divided into Prussian and Polish regions.

The Polish issue was debated in Frankfurt, where there was precious little sympathy for the Poles. The democrat William Jordan spoke for many when he spoke of the "empty-headed sentimentality" of the pro-Polish faction and argued that Germans should think in terms of "healthy national egotism" since cultural superiority gave them every right over the backward Poles. Karl Marx and the radical left were in full agreement with this denunciation of a melodramatic cosmopolitanism. By a vote of 342 to 31 parliament voted that the bulk of Posen should be considered part of the new Germany.

The Frankfurt parliament took a similarly robust attitude towards Czech national aspirations. The Czech leader, yet another historian Franz (František) Palacky, turned down the suggestion that Bohemia should be part of Germany and argued that Czechs were better served by remaining within the multi-national Habsburg empire. The Frankfurt parliament would have none of this. Bohemia had been part of the Holy Roman Empire of the German Nation and was within the Confederation; therefore it was clearly German. The same attitude was taken towards South Tyrol when a delegate from the Trentino suggested that it too should break away from Germany.

The acerbic nationalism and arrogant feeling of cultural superiority of the Frankfurt parliament is singularly unattractive, but is far removed from later manifestations of German national sentiment. No claim was made for Alsace or for areas in the Baltic outside the bounds of the Confederation, where there were substantial German populations. Furthermore, the Frankfurt parliament was mindful that minority rights within the new Germany should be respected. On the other hand there was a lot of heady talk of Germany as the future European superpower that would turn its mighty army against the barbarous Slavs as the newborn nation had its baptism of fire. Much of this was little more than hot air, over-compensation for Germany's pathetic weakness; but it betrayed a disturbing cast of mind. Monsters were slumbering in Germany that only the keenest of minds such as the poet Heinrich Heine and the novelist Gottfried Keller were able to detect.

The Frankfurt parliament was plagued not only by the national question but also by the social problems of a society in the process of fundamental change. An artisans' congress was held in Frankfurt in an attempt to put pressure on the parliament. Politically the artisans were mostly liberal democrats, but economically they were arch-conservatives. They were anti-capitalist and anti-industrial. They hankered after the pre-industrial society of guilds and proud master craftsmen. They called for an ordered brotherhood under a protective and interventionist state.

The working classes were also active in 1848. Workers' associations (*Arbeitervereine*) sprang up all over Germany. At the end of August a national congress organized by Stefan Born, at that time a disciple of Karl Marx, was held in Berlin at which an umbrella organization called the Workers' Brotherhood (Allgemeine Deutsche Arbeiterverbrüderung) was formed. It was a reformist rather than a revolutionary organization, which stood for working-class solidarity, the formation of unions and cooperatives, and, above all, for education. It called for "social democracy," by which was meant fair wages and justice for all in a humane and caring society. Obviously there were widely differing views on how these ideals could be realized, but there was general agreement when Born denounced "dreamers who foam with rage" and urged a moderate and pragmatic approach. The intellectual giants of the socialist movement, Karl Marx and Friedrich Engels, ignored the workers' associations, and their Communist League played no role in the revolution. They had precious few followers and their articles in the *Rheinische Zeitung* failed to resonate among the nascent working class.

Meanwhile, the forces of the counter-revolution prepared to strike back. In Prussia the "camarilla" around the crown prince was tirelessly active. The Gerlach brothers, Ernst and Leopold, founded an ultra-conservative newspaper soon to be known as the "Iron Cross" (*Kreuzzeitung*) because of the medal printed above its title: *Neue Preußische Zeitung*. This was to become the authoritative voice of Prussian conservatism. The Junkers formed an association to further their interests, meeting in what came to be known as the Junker parliament, to discuss matters of common concern. The army was solidly behind the counter-revolution and longed to seek revenge for the humiliation it had suffered in March. Its attitude was succinctly expressed in the title of an influential pamphlet: *Soldiers Are the Only Remedy for Democrats*.

The radicals had been crushed in April in Baden, but they were still active in the Paul's Church, where they continued to demand the creation of a republic based on popular sovereignty. They railed against the conservatives and the liberals, issuing jeremiads about the horrors of the counter-revolution. Disillusioned with parliamentary procedures, they hoped to push the revolution forward by extra-parliamentary activism. They called for a second and more radical revolution in which the will of the people would be directly expressed by means of a Jacobin dictatorship. Some 200 delegates representing radical associations from throughout Germany as well as some delegates to the Paul's Church, met in Frankfurt in mid-June under the chairmanship of Julius Fröbel, the nephew of the founder of the kindergarten movement. They decided to form a national republican movement with a distinctly totalitarian flavor based in Berlin. They gained considerable support from the disaffected lower orders, who were yet to feel the effects of an economic upturn. But it was the acceptance of the Malmö armistice by the Frankfurt parliament that brought matters to a head. On September 18 a radical mob stormed the Paul's Church, which was defended by Austrian, Prussian, and Hessian troops. Eighty people were killed on both sides, including the conservative deputies General von Auerswald and Prince Lichnowsky, whereupon the Archduke John placed the city under martial law. It was a richly significant scene: the Frankfurt parliament could only continue to exist as long as it was still tolerated by Austria and Prussia.

The violence in Frankfurt, particularly the brutal murder of two deputies, discredited the radicals in the eyes of most Germans. The subsequent uprising in Baden, led once again by Hecker and Struve, who blamed the rich and the Jews for the failure of the revolution, had precious little popular support. It was quickly suppressed by the minuscule Baden army. Elsewhere in the southwest there were murmurs of discontent, but little violence.

Moderate liberals, terrified by the prospect of further violence, felt obliged to join forces with the conservatives to combat the radicals. They thus stopped the revolution in its tracks. The vast majority of Germans agreed with them in prioritizing law and order at the expense of freedom and due process. The radicals refused to give up the struggle. At the second Democratic Congress, held in Berlin at the end of October, they pronounced the Frankfurt parliament illegitimate and demanded new elections. But by this time the counter-revolution was virtually complete in Vienna and in Berlin, leaving the radicals hopelessly divided among rival factions.

Frederick William IV hoped to reach some compromise agreement with the National Assembly over the constitutional question. By insisting on its sovereign rights, the Berlin parliament, a somewhat more radical body than the Paul's Church, was in direct conflict with the king. There was constant pressure from the radical democratic working classes and the unemployed leading to frequent clashes with the bourgeois citizens' militia. Prince William, the "Grapeshot Prince," returned to Berlin in June as a delegate to the National Assembly, thus rendering the atmosphere increasingly tense. On June 14 the mob stormed the Berlin arsenal, the citizens' militia was unable to control the situation and the army had to be called in from Potsdam. The reactionaries called for the dismissal of the National Assembly, but the king felt this would be too drastic a move.

On July 26 the National Assembly published a draft constitution. It was a moderate liberal document but one that was unacceptable to conservatives and the left alike. It called for the army to be bound by the constitution. In the struggle over this central issue the moderates in the Assembly found themselves caught between the reactionaries and the radicals. The king took a step in the direction of the reactionaries and then a step back in the direction of compromise. The Assembly's position began to harden as it called for parliamentary control over the judiciary and police, the abolition of aristocratic titles along with all orders and titles, plus the ending of the king's claim to rule by the grace of God. There were sporadic outbursts of violence as the mob grew restless. The moderate reforming minister president, General Pfuel, seeing his hopes for compromise dashed, resigned at the end of October. His place was taken by Count von Brandenburg, who favored a little Germany with the Prussian king as emperor. The arch-reactionary Otto von Manteuffel was minister of the interior. The National Assembly was promptly adjourned but refused to move. General Wrangel marched his troops into Berlin and proclaimed martial law. The National Assembly and the citizens' militia were disbanded. The reaction was in full command. Not a shot was fired, not a drop of blood spilt. On December 5 the king granted a constitution which, to the extreme annoyance of the conservatives, bore a distinct resemblance to that proposed by the National Assembly. It was a shrewd move. It eased the tensions and bought time. The line to Frankfurt was not broken, the German question left open.

Although the counter-revolution was near complete, discussions continued in Frankfurt over the constitution. It was finally voted upon on December 20, but the cardinal issues of whether Germany should include Austria and who should be the head of the new nation-state were left open. It was a moderate liberal document that upheld principles of equality before the law, civil rights, and the abolition of all remaining vestiges of the feudal system. It was resolutely liberal on economic issues. Radicals were disappointed that it did not address the social question, that it was not more robustly democratic, that the influence of the churches was not to be curbed, and, a favorite demand, that the Jesuits were not to be turfed out of Germany. The new Germany was to be a federal state, but the framers of the constitution could find no solution to the problem of overcoming the disparities between the component states. Should the smaller entities be annexed or the large states like Prussia be divided up into smaller federations? Although the existing situation was highly unsatisfactory, it was decided to leave things as they were and hope for the best. There were to be two houses of parliament, a House of the People (Volkshaus) which would be democratically elected and a House of the States (Staatenhaus) in which the individual states would be represented. The suffrage question was not settled until the beginning of March 1849. Many liberals voted for universal direct manhood suffrage in the confident hope that this would make it impossible for the Prussian king to accept the imperial crown.

There were few republicans in the Frankfurt parliament, and even those who inclined towards a republican solution realized that it would be impossible to abolish all the existing monarchies within the Confederation. They favored what came to be called a "republican monarchy." Monarchs should exist by the grace of the people represented in parliament, not by the grace of God. Their model was the Glorious Revolution of 1688. But who was to be emperor? Should he be elected as in the old empire? Should parliament elect an emperor who would then establish a hereditary dynasty? Should Austria and Prussia takes turns in appointing an emperor, or should one or other ruling house rule in perpetuity? All this was highly theoretical, as was most of the discussion in the Paul's Church. In the last resort the answer to the German question lay in the outcome of the struggle within and between Prussia and Austria.

The majority of delegates to the Paul's Church assumed that the Habsburg empire was on the point of disintegration and that therefore German Austria and Bohemia would willingly join in the new Germany. Austria would then work out some form of personal union with what was left of the multi-national empire. This was a hopelessly unrealistic position. Austria could not possibly be both part of a German great power and remain a great power outside the new Reich. A greater Germany would have necessitated the dismemberment of the Habsburg empire. With the counter-revolution in Austria nearly complete on November 27, 1848, Metternich's protégé and successor, Prince Schwarzenberg, proclaimed the indivisibility of the empire, thus putting paid to any hopes for a greater German solution. In March the following year he proposed that the entire Austrian empire should be included in the new Germany. This was totally unacceptable since Germany would then be dominated by Austria, a state in which the vast majority of the population was not even German.

The *kleindeutsche* solution was now the only possible answer to the dilemma. Its leading advocate was Heinrich von Gagern, who became minister president in mid-December, but the liberal Austrian Schmerling and his *großdeutsche* supporters were still numerous and hopeful that the Austrians might be persuaded to change their minds. German nationalists, among them many on the left, felt that Austria could not possibly be excluded. They imagined that it could well do without its non-German provinces. South German Catholics detested Protestant Prussia and identified with their Austrian co-religionists. Many feared that a Little Germany would provoke Russia and Austria to intervene, leaving the country under the knout.

Prussia, on the other hand, might be reactionary and militaristic, but at least it was a thoroughly German state and had gone through an impressive series of reforms. It was a rational state, at least in the Hegelian sense, the architect of the Zollverein, soberly Protestant, certainly not a threat, even prepared it seemed to "dissolve into Germany." Schwarzenberg's intransigence led to a mass desertion from the *großdeutsche* cause, and even Schmerling defected in March. By now it was a case of either a Little Germany or none at all. On the 28th of that month Frederick William IV of Prussia was elected emperor of the Germans, with 290 votes in favor of the motion and 248 abstentions.

The ruling elite in Prussia favored acceptance, provided that the franchise was changed, provision made for an absolute veto, and the election accepted by the princes; but Frederick

William was adamantly opposed. He saw himself as a king by the grace of God and refused to accept a crown that was made of "muck and mire," a "dog collar with which they want to chain me to the revolution of 1848." It was an unthinking and intensely emotional response, but subsequent events make it seem unlikely that even a compromise solution would have had much of a chance of success.

Heinrich von Gagern still hoped that a compromise was possible, but it was rejected both by Frederick William and the majority in the Paul's Church. The Frankfurt parliament now began a gradual process of dissolution. Austria and Prussia withdrew their delegations, Saxony and Hanover followed suit. A rump parliament of intransigent radicals moved to Stuttgart, where they were soon chased away by a contingent of the Württemberg army. There were isolated outbursts of violence in protest against the reactionary course. Barricades were erected in Dresden and were graced with the presence of such luminaries as the anarchist Mikhail Bakunin, Richard Wagner, who was in Dresden as director of the Semper Oper and had just finished his opera *Lohengrin*, the great architect Gottfried Semper, whose magnificent opera house had been opened in 1841, and the socialist Stefan Born. Prussian troops were called in to crush the uprising, and fierce fighting ensued. Rebels managed to install a temporary government in the Palatinate. A colorful assortment of radicals from all over central Europe rushed to its support. Once again the disorganized and ill-disciplined radicals were no match for the Prussian army, and the uprising was soon suppressed. In the Rhineland Friedrich Engels was able to put the relationship between theory and praxis to the test in a series of riots that were soon mastered by the citizens' militia. Defeated barricade fighters, mercenaries, and idealists now rushed to Baden for a last-ditch stand. Here the Prussian army took somewhat longer to repress the revolt, but the final outcome was never in any doubt. There followed a series of treason trials and summary executions. Every tenth man captured in the fortress town of Rastatt was shot. The brutality of the Prussians in Baden left a lasting trauma and bitter hatred and there was a fresh wave of emigration, mainly to the United States.

Olmütz

Frederick William having turned down the imperial crown, the Prussia minister president Radowitz now proposed a Little German union. Agreement was reached at the end of May, with Saxony and Hanover to create a federal Little Germany, and in the following weeks most of the other German states approved this scheme. Bavaria was adamantly opposed to the idea of excluding Austria, and Württemberg did not relish the idea of a Germany dominated by Prussia. Saxony and Hanover had made their agreement contingent on the approval of all the other German states and thus now withdrew their support.

The Prussians went ahead regardless, and elections were held on a strictly limited suffrage in January 1850 for a parliament that met in Erfurt. The Erfurt Union had precious little support and Schwarzenberg was determined to destroy it. He put forward a proposal for a greater German union in which Prussia would have special status, but would still be subordinate to Austria. Radowitz turned this down, so that Austria and Prussia were now on a collision course.

The Austrians sponsored a congress to restore the German Confederation but it was boycotted by Prussia. Electoral Hesse, which was in a state of turmoil with the diet, the judiciary, the bulk of the civil service, and the officer corps in adamant opposition to a series of unconstitutional and reactionary measures proposed by the government, appealed to the Bundestag for help. The Danish government also asked for federal assistance against an intransigent and revolutionary local government in Holstein. Austria and Bavaria agreed to send troops to assist both governments. Prussia saw this as a direct threat to its western provinces and mobilized its army.

Frederick William was never enthusiastic about the Erfurt Union, had no desire to antagonize Austria, and was under massive pressure from the tsar to back down. He therefore dismissed Radowitz but still insisted that Austrian troops should be withdrawn from Electoral Hesse. After several weeks of tension the Prussians suddenly capitulated, signing at Olmütz on November 29, 1850, a treaty with Austria in which they agreed to disband the Erfurt Union. On the other hand Schwarzenberg had to agree to a fresh round of negotiations for the reformation of the Confederation and was thus unable to push through his scheme for an Austrian-dominated Germany.

For most Prussians Olmütz was an ignominious humiliation, but there was one notable exception. Otto von Bismarck poured scorn on the armchair warriors who were prepared to go to war for an absurd little state like Electoral Hesse and for the Erfurt Union which subordinated Prussian interests to those of the member states. He argued that Prussia's national interests would be far better served in a revived Confederation. Bismarck, in this savagely witty speech, clearly articulated his belief that Prussian policy should be based on *Realpolitik* rather than party politics. It was a belief to which he was to hold true for the rest of his remarkable career.

CHAPTER FIVE
THE STRUGGLE FOR MASTERY
·1850–1866·

CHAPTER CONTENTS

A History of Modern Germany: 1800 to the Present, Second Edition. Martin Kitchen.
© 2012 Martin Kitchen. Published 2012 by Blackwell Publishing Ltd.

As after 1815, the German Confederation now set about undoing most of the liberal achievements of 1848. Constitutional reforms were revoked. In many instances new constitutions were promulgated that were far less liberal than those in effect before 1848. In Württemberg and Electoral Hesse, this was done by a coup and the proclamation of martial law. Only in Baden was a liberal regime able to continue unchanged, but even here the heavy hand of the Confederation could still be felt. A federal law in 1854 placed severe restrictions on the freedom of the press and of assembly throughout Germany. In Catholic states, particularly in Austria, the reaction negotiated concordats with the church that strengthened the church's hand in matters such as education, marriage, and the family. Protestant states followed Prussia's example by strengthening to role of the church in the daily life of the citizenry.

The attempt to put the clock back was only partially successful. The last vestiges of feudalism had been removed. The formation of the first joint-stock bank was the lasting achievement of the revolution in Prussia. Attempts to revive elements of the guild system by protecting artisans against the challenge of industrial capitalism were bound to fail in the long run due to the harsh realities of the market. Constitutions were still in place, however much they might have been modified. Many influential figures were determined to win back their lost freedoms and rights. The concordats provoked a strong liberal reaction. In Protestant states there was a wave of anti-clericalism that obliged the states to give way. Liberals were most active in the smaller German states. Reactionary authoritarianism was at least partially tolerable in a strong and efficient state like Prussia with a booming economy, but was insufferable in insignificant, incompetent, and minuscule political entities such as Brunswick, Oldenburg, or Hesse-Darmstadt.

Prussia at last had a constitution with universal manhood suffrage, although it was singularly unequal and indirect since voters were divided into three classes according to the amount of taxes they paid. In 1849, 4.7 percent of voters chose one-third of the electors, the next third were elected by 12.6 percent of those eligible to vote, and the remaining third by 82.7 percent. Fewer than 22 percent of those eligible to vote actually bothered to do so in 1852. The upper house (Herrenhaus) was the preserve of the landowning aristocracy. The army was outside the constitution and could proclaim martial law at will. It was directly responsible to the king, who also had the power of veto and the right to rule by decree.

Prussia in the years of reaction was a police state, its symbolic figure the chief of Berlin's police, Carl von Hinkeldey. An army of snoopers and informers rooted out communists and democrats, the press was muzzled, and liberally minded civil servants were dismissed. On the other hand the reactionary government enacted a considerable amount of social legislation, including the control of child labor, factory inspection, and sanitation measures. Hinkeldey was known to be on the side of the poor and was immensely popular. He did much to stop rack-renting and to enforce health regulations. Thousands attended his funeral in 1856. Otto von Manteuffel's government with its pliant diet of docile civil servants, an independent executive that could count on the support of the bureaucracy and the army, and his conscious efforts to win popular support was typically Bonapartist. It was thus never a full-blown reactionary government and did not set out to undo all the achievements of 1848.

Austro-Prussian Rivalry

The year 1848 marked the end of the cooperation between Austria and Prussia in the German question that had characterized the Metternichian era. Otto von Bismarck, as

Prussia's representative to the Bundestag, was determined to resist Schwarzenberg's attempts to bring the entire Habsburg empire into the Confederation, for this would mean a Germany dominated by 70 million Austrians. The Prussian-controlled Zollverein was a powerful counterweight to Austrian pretensions, and Bismarck was able to frustrate Austria's attempts to dominate the Bundestag, thereby strengthening its authority over the member states.

In 1853 Britain, France, and Piedmont went to war with Russia and landed a joint force in the Crimea. Both sides in the conflict were eager to recruit Austria and Prussia. Prussian opinion was divided. Arch-conservatives wanted an alliance with Russia. Manteuffel was for strict neutrality because Prussia had no interest in the Eastern Question. Prince Frederick, second in line to the throne, and his supporters, known as the Wochenblattpartei after their newspaper, wanted to join the Western powers. A member of this group, the Prussian diplomat Count Albert von Pourtalès, suggested to the British government that Prussia would join the coalition if Britain would lend its support to Prussian efforts to exclude Austria from Germany. Britain turned this proposal down for it still hoped to get Austrian support. The Prussian ambassador, Baron von Bunsen, also hoped that by joining the coalition Russian hegemony in eastern Europe would end, Poland would be restored, and Prussia's position in Germany enhanced. Once again the British government did not want to risk alienating Austria. The Wochenblattpartei lost the king's favor. Bunsen was recalled. The war minister Eduard von Bonin, another prominent figure among the westerners, lost his job. Prince Frederick protested vigorously against Bonin's dismissal. The king promptly took away his nephew's commission, whereupon Frederick's wife, one of Queen Victoria's daughters, fled back home to England. Clearly there could be no question now of Prussia joining the coalition, but there was little enthusiasm for joining the war on Russia's side. Prussia therefore remained neutral. In December 1854 Austria called upon the Confederation to mobilize, but Bismarck had little difficulty in frustrating this move. He argued that Austria's interests in the Balkans were not a German concern. Prussia by contrast had no interests outside Germany. Austria was left isolated, and Prussia scored a major victory that partly overcame the shame of Olmütz. Austria had succeeded in alienating both sides in the Crimean conflict and thus played no role in the peace conference in Paris. Prussia was also ignored, but was considered weak rather than devious.

The Crimean War resulted in a marked decline in Russia's power and influence in Europe. The France of Napoleon III now took center stage, soon to be eclipsed by a Prussian-dominated Europe. Austria had alienated Russia without earning any gratitude from France and was left isolated. Prussia managed to preserve the conservative under-standing with Russia and had given the Confederation forceful leadership during the December crisis.

Austria was soon to suffer another severe setback, this time in Italy. In 1858 Napoleon III signed a treaty with Piedmont-Sardinia with the intent of driving Austria out of north-ern Italy and uniting the country. The Piedmontese premier Cavour skillfully provoked Austria into a declaration of war in April 1859. The Austrian army, under-financed and ineptly led, was defeated at the battles of Magenta and Solferino by a French army whose senior commanders were equally incompetent, but whose troops and subordinate officers showed considerable courage and dash.

Austria's defeat in Lombardy placed Germany in a precarious position. Friedrich Engels spoke for many when he asked whether Napoleon III would make a bid for the Rhine now that France was firmly established on the Po. Austria called for support from the Confederation. Prussia was willing to go part of the way to meet Austria's request, but demanded a high price. Prussian support was made dependent on being given an equal voice to Austria in the Bundestag, command over the troops on the Rhine, and hegemony in northern Germany. Austria, believing that the Confederation was obliged both constitutionally and through sheer self-interest to become involved, was unwilling to make any such concessions.

Napoleon III, anxious not to become involved in a lengthy war, quickly negotiated a preliminary peace at Villafranca in July. Prussia was thus saved from the awkward choices of whether and how to intervene. Austria ceded Lombardy to the French, but kept Venetia. Napoleon then gave Lombardy to Piedmont-Sardinia and received Savoy and Nice in compensation. In Germany there were some who argued that Prussia should now seize the opportunity to create a little Germany. They ranged from Bismarck, who had been sent as ambassador to St. Petersburg to cool his heels, to the socialist leader Lassalle, from the Wochenblattpartei, to radicals such as Ludwig Bamberger and Arnold Ruge. But the vast majority of Germans were anti-French and sympathized with Austria. They argued that all Germans should stick together and resist the French. For Marx and Engels Napoleon III was the arch-villain. Ultra-conservatives like Ernst Ludwig von Gerlach and Friedrich Julius Stahl heartily agreed.

It was thus a confusing situation made all the more complex by Napoleon III's baffling policies. German nationalists admired Cavour and hoped to emulate the Italians, but the process of Italian unification greatly strengthened France, thereby threatening Germany. They were angered by both Prussia and Austria. Prussia, they felt, had demanded too high a price and had left Austria in the lurch. Austria had given in to France too precipitately and should have waited for the Prussians to come to their aid. This latter charge overlooked the fact that Austria could not have afforded to be saved in Italy by Prussia, for this would have further enhanced Prussia's standing in Germany.

The "New Era"

The Crimean and Italian wars gave fresh impetus to liberals and nationalists. Their hopes were also raised when Crown Prince William became regent in October 1858, his unfortunate brother, who was always somewhat unbalanced, having become completely deranged. William was a conservative, the "grapeshot prince" of 1848, but he was a fervent Little German nationalist, opposed to the arch-conservatives and even prepared to swear by the constitution. His government was liberal-conservative, bent on healing the differences among the elites and determined to preserve their status by judicious reform and a generous social policy. William had spent all his life as an army officer and was determined to reform the army so as to lend weight to an active and independent Prussian foreign policy. Education was to be reformed and the churches ordered to stay out of politics. This was a program that was broadly attractive. Conservatives were delighted; liberal hopes ran unrealistically high since they overlooked some of William's more conservative utterances. Bismarck urged the regent to open up to the liberals so as to create a broad consensus that would greatly strengthen Prussia in the eyes of liberal Germans. The regent took note, but felt it prudent to move Bismarck from the Bundestag to St. Petersburg lest he cause too much trouble with Austria in the midst of the Italian crisis.

The "New Era" began cautiously. Moderate reforms were passed. Pressure was placed on the appalling regime in Electoral Hesse to reinstate the constitution of 1831. Reforms in Austria under Schmerling, a leading figure in 1848, greatly strengthened the role of the German urban middle class, who were fervently Greater German and anti-Prussian. Liberal governments were installed in Bavaria and Baden. Elsewhere in Germany conservative regimes became more relaxed. Prussia was thus in no way unique. A new generation was coming to power, which agreed with Bismarck that a conservative regime could no longer do without popular support. It was also a reflection of the social changes that had taken place in Germany as a liberal bourgeoisie grew in strength only to find that it was soon to be faced with the threat of an organized working class. The social question was being redefined in the industrial age and could not be answered in terms of ultra-conservative nostalgia for a bygone age.

The "New Era" was a period of dramatic economic change. This was the take-off period of industrialization in Germany during which, in spite of sharp fluctuations and even crises, there was a general improvement in living standards. The truly appalling problems of poverty that marked the early part of the century had been overcome. Industrialization absorbed large-scale unemployment, the crisis of the late 1840s was overcome, and from the 1860s the situation of the industrial working class improved. Artisans and craftsmen adapted to the industrial age by forming cooperatives, by greater specialization, or by becoming highly skilled industrial workers. The peasantry also profited from this general prosperity and from improved agricultural methods. But it was the bourgeoisie that really began to thrive with the wide range of job opportunities offered by an industrial society and by the handsome profits to be made on the stock exchange.

Changes in the Social Structure

It would be a serious error to imagine that the process whereby society was being transformed from being agricultural and rural to becoming modern, urban, industrial, and commercial was not fraught with problems and subject to serious disjuncture. New and sharper class distinctions were apparent as the artisan class slowly eroded. Some became entrepreneurs and entered the ranks of the bourgeoisie; others sank into the anonymity of the urban proletariat. Industry was seriously under-capitalized, bankruptcies were frequent, and the stock market collapsed in 1858. The process of modernization was fraught with difficulties as traditional mentalities and structures struggled to adapt to alarmingly new conditions. Many were left by the wayside, but there was remarkable growth between 1850 and the early1870s from which most profited. It was a society on the move, but not one in which social revolution was incubated.

By 1866 the word "estate" was no longer in common currency. Further developments in a capitalist market economy swept away the last vestiges of the old social order and reinforced the class structure. All sectors of the economy were affected by the impetus of market forces, which in turn resulted in profound changes in social configurations. Agriculture was now entirely market-oriented, the maximization of returns the principal concern, the application of scientific methods and the practice of double-entry bookkeeping now the norm. The rural population was divided into two main groups. At the top were some 25,000 large-scale farmers, both aristocratic and bourgeois. At the bottom, a vast army of day laborers toiled. In northern Germany and east of the Elbe river the

PLATE 8   German industrial might: a rolling mill in Saarbrücken c. 1870. © BPK

landowning aristocracy successfully adjusted to a new market reality, while managing to preserve their social exclusivity, prestige, and political power to the point that they formed a distinct class, which is often misleadingly described as "feudal." The day laborers formed a kind of rural proletariat.

In the 1840s there was an inchoate middle class in urban areas, made up of entrepreneurs and professionals. This class grew rapidly in size and self-consciousness as industrial capitalism expanded briskly until 1873, when the rate of growth slowed down dramatically for almost a quarter of a century. The result was the formation of a class of industrial entrepreneurs of considerable wealth and increasing prestige, determined to share in the exercise of political power. They presented a challenge to the status and self-image of the aristocracy, the traditional urban patricians and the *Bildungsbürger*. But industrial capitalism soon began to erode the divisions within the middle classes. The traditional urban elites initially resisted the pushy newcomers, but they soon realized that this was a hopeless struggle. They were quick to realize that there were golden opportunities for their sons in the new world of investment banking, industry, mining, and the railways. Their daughters could be assured of a future of material comfort by marriage into the new class. Thus rivals amalgamated and parvenus were transformed into town worthies. In much the same manner the *Bildungsbürger* lost their separate identity and were absorbed into the new bourgeoisie. The doctor, the apothecary, the lawyer, and the pastor were readily accepted, not least because a higher education was a mark of distinction in the eyes of a successful entrepreneur. Marrying off a daughter to a doctor was thus a shrewd move that gave the family a touch of culture and learning. Industrial entrepreneurs had earlier met with stiff opposition from a conservative bureaucracy, which looked askance at their risk-taking and innovative élan; but this also changed. The bureaucracy ceased to behave like disapproving guardians of what they imagined to be the public interest and were increasingly willing to cooperate, as they had in the case of the Zollverein and with their concessions to economic liberalism in the 1860s. Rivalry within the middle classes was also overcome by the challenge from below as those in possession of capital found themselves in an ever-intensifying conflict situation with those whose only capital was their labor. Initially a relatively small and homogenous entrepreneurial elite confronted a heterogeneous mass of laborers, which was gradually coalescing into a distinct working class. Even before the 1848 revolution Friedrich Bassermann, a successful businessman and liberal politician from Baden, had said that the "disproportionateness between owners of property and the proletariat" was a matter of serious concern throughout Europe. The revolution had come as a profound shock in that it was a dramatic illustration of deep-rooted social divisions and antagonisms. Pre-March dreams of a classless society of autonomous citizens were shown to be a pious illusion. The bourgeoisie turned to the reactionary state for protection and closed its ranks to meet the threat from below. The working classes came to believe that they could not rely on help from well-meaning liberals or a benign bureaucracy and would have to defend their class interests themselves. Rural areas had also been in turmoil during the revolution, with landowners petrified at the prospect of a peasants' revolt, of jacquerie, or of a movement analogous to the "Captain Swing" riots in England. But the rural proletariat as well as the mass of smallholders were slow to develop specific class identities and thereby a feeling of solidarity. The big landowners by contrast were strengthened in their determination to protect their interests.

Relations between the bourgeoisie and the aristocracy were complex. Many self-made entrepreneurs, proud of their achievements, regarded with contempt a class that owed its privileges solely to the accident of birth. Others bought landed estates and aped the ways of their social superiors. Industrialists, bankers, and lawyers thought it good for business to have an aristocrat on the board or in the firm. An exalted name on a brass plate by the entrance door of a lawyer's office, or in an annual report for shareholders, helped to inspire confidence. Many a bourgeois was eager to add a touch of distinction to the family name by a daughter's marriage to an aristocrat. One Berlin banker managed to find a noble spouse for each of his five daughters.

The concept of class is reflected in official language, but in this transitional period it was necessarily somewhat vague. Zollverein statistics speak of a "merchant class," "professional class," "business class," "the working classes," and "the lower classes." At the same time the notions of a "working class" and "proletariat" were becoming increasingly common in specialist literature. Similarly, older terms such "the educated classes" or "the propertied classes" were giving way to the broader ideas of "the middle classes" or a "bourgeoisie." Conflicts of interest were implicit in the notion of class, and it was not only revolutionaries who spoke of the class struggle. Conservatives in the historical school of political economy, such as Wilhelm Roscher, realized that the division of society into classes and the tendency of industrial society to create a small group of the very rich pitched against a vast mass of the impoverished meant that the traditional conservative ideology of a balanced society with estates living in harmony was an illusion. The publicist and sociologist Wilhelm Riehl, who was one of the first to realize the threat that industrial and agricultural capitalism posed to the environment, saw in the urban working class a "fertile environment for the socialist spirit of egalitarianism."

As society changed so did politics. The old equation of liberal change versus conservative status quo, the people and the crown, "us" and "them," no longer held good. The complexities of a modern class society were such that alliances had now to be made that crossed traditional lines of class and ideology. Napoleon III and Bismarck gave vivid examples of how revolutionary means could be used to achieve conservative ends, much to the bewilderment of contemporaries and to the bafflement of many a historian.

Liberalism and Conservatism

It took some time for the liberals to recover from their crushing defeat in 1848. It is perhaps surprising that the term *Realpolitik*, which is usually associated with Bismarck, its greatest practitioner, was actually coined by a liberal, August Ludwig von Rochau, in 1853. He insisted that the greatest weakness of the liberals in 1848 was that they were out of touch with the real world: they were dreamers, idealists, and doctrinaire theoreticians. They had to abandon their idealist and romantic notions of the German past and get in tune with the new philosophy of positivism, empiricism, and materialism. Politics for Rochau was all about power, for without power no ideals or political goals could be realized. Liberalism was the political expression of the aspirations of an increasingly self-confident bourgeoisie, determined to become the dominant political class. That demanded a concentration on economic concerns rather than ideals and moral issues.

The bourgeois world of the New Era was infused with liberalism. Professors and civil servants, schoolteachers and Protestant pastors, businessmen and lawyers joined the great national liberal associations, and subscribed to liberal journals such a the Heinrich von Sybel's *Historischer Zeitschrift*, Heinrich von Treitschke's *Preußischer Jahrbücher*, and Gustav Freitag's *Grenzboten*. Most of the disillusioned radicals who remained in Germany also joined the liberal ranks. The liberals won wide support from ordinary people in the many national associations that still flourished in Germany: the glee singers, gymnasts, and marksmen. For all the divergences of opinion and social status the liberals formed a coherent and influential force that no politician could afford to ignore.

Wherever there were elected diets the liberals formed a majority. Even Prussia, with its three-class electoral system, actually gave an advantage to the well-established bourgeois. Most liberal politicians came from the bourgeois elite and were deeply suspicious of the masses. They needed their support, but were acutely aware of the dangers of rabble-rousing and demagogy. They hoped to educate the masses to become responsible citizens, thereby closing their ears to the siren calls of popular democracy and socialism. Some left-wing liberals put their faith in the people, but they too denounced those democrats who sought to mobilize the masses. But for the moment such concerns were hardly pressing. There was a general political apathy with precious few bothering to make use of their franchise, so that politics was the concern of a small elite. Prosperous businessmen lent their support to the movement and, as in 1848, the politicians themselves for the most part were university-educated professionals, most of them civil servants and lawyers.

Liberals were traumatized by the experience of 1848 when it appeared that parliamentary democracy could easily descend into Jacobin terror. In the New Era they were less concerned with strengthening parliament than with ending the dominant influence of the aristocracy and the military over the government. Most liberals had abandoned their dislike and distrust of the state. A state that was free from all antiquated absolutist tendencies, in which enlightened liberals had an ascendant influence by means of a liberal constitution, could be a force for the good, a guarantor of law, order, and individual freedom. Now it was not only the right-wing liberals who doubted that parliaments were sufficient to overcome social and political conflicts and who feared that too much freedom could well result in anarchy.

Left-wing liberals still argued in favor of universal suffrage and insisted that the masses could be trusted to vote for men of substance and culture. The right had less faith in the common man and pointed to France, where a plebiscitary democracy had resulted in a Bonapartist autocracy. Bourgeois values were seen as universal values. The vast majority of liberals distinguished themselves sharply from the lower orders, whom it was hoped would benefit from general prosperity gradually to reach a cultural level that would enable them to join the universal class. There was also disagreement over the role of the state in the economy. Most wanted to leave everything to Adam Smith's "invisible hand," but some intellectuals such as Treitschke felt that the state would have to intervene in order to ensure a degree of social justice. There was one thing on which both wings could agree – national unity was the absolute priority. Without unity there could be no real freedom.

As Rochau had preached, nothing could be achieved without gaining power. The liberals of the New Era mostly took the approach of the liberals of 1848: power could only be won by cooperation and compromise, not by confrontation and demanding all or nothing. Left liberals argued that they represented the people, that governments could no longer ignore the will of the people. Therefore they should act as a pressure group without unleashing the unpredictable and perilous forces of radical democracy.

The divisions within the liberal movement were a reflection of the heterogeneity of Germany in a transitional phase of social development, its lack of a common political culture, regional and religious differences, and the still unsolved German question. Liberals could circle their wagons when they came under attack, as in Prussia under Bismarck, or Bavaria and Baden when faced with clerical and conservative reaction. Once the pressure was off they were too divided over the questions of a Little or Greater Germany and the awkward issue of which was to be privileged: freedom or unity. They thus found that they were obliged to ally themselves with either Prussian or Greater German conservatives if they were not to be condemned to utter powerlessness. It was that extraordinary outsider Bismarck who was to decide the two major questions that faced the liberals, and in doing so split the movement irrevocably.

Changes in conservative attitudes were far less dramatic. There was a gradual awareness that throne, altar, and landed estate were not sufficiently strong to preserve the social order. Many conservatives argued that that they should reach out to the peasantry and artisans as well as to all those in opposition to the rapaciously modernizing bourgeoisie and their academic hangers-on. Lorenz Stein, with his idea of a "social monarchy," and Hermann Wagener, the proponent of an energetic social policy, were to have a profound effect on later developments: Stein on William II and Wagener on Bismarck. Such ideas rendered the period of reaction after 1848 far less grim than it has often been painted, for conservatives began to realize that they had to have a degree of popular support. Bismarck more than any other conservative knew that the bourgeois-liberal modern world was a reality that could not be wished away. He took a leaf out of Napoleon III's book and with ruthless realism achieved conservative ends by means that were far from conservative.

Social Democracy

A new factor in the social equation was the rise of an industrial working class – an army of the propertyless possessing nothing but their labor. In 1848 the proletariat scarcely existed outside the brilliant imagination of Karl Marx. Even by the 1860s, when an independent labor movement began, there was still no class-conscious proletariat as society was in the final stages of the long transitional phase from artisanal to industrial production. Communist groups and workers' associations had been ruthlessly suppressed after 1848, but in the New Era liberals began to organize workers' educational associations in an effort to win the support of craftsmen and workers to their struggle against the established powers.

Liberals believed that education would provide the answer to the social question by providing workers with the skills needed to succeed, an understanding of the broad issues of the day, and access to the riches of higher culture. Education would inoculate them against socialist ideas and help them understand the community of interests between capital and labor. Some liberals went further, arguing that workers should be taught to think critically, to challenge established authority and to become active participants in the democratic movement for change. Socialists were to take up these ideas, and workers' education was to play a central role in the labor movement.

The left-liberal Hermann Schulze-Delitzsch, the leading figure behind this liberal approach to the working class, believed that bourgeoisie and proletariat had a common interest in an economy unshackled from state control since the benefits from increased national wealth within a liberal nation-state would be shared. He believed that any friction between capital and labor could be overcome by cooperatives both for production and retail. These ideas were imported from England, where Robert Owen's ideas had been disseminated by the London Co-operative Society and put into practice by the Rochdale Pioneers in the 1840s.

These were utopian ideas, but they had a powerful resonance among socialists in spite of Karl Marx's stern disapproval. Ferdinand Lassalle, the founding father of German Social Democracy, launched a ferocious attack on Schulze-Delitzsch, but he still argued that cooperative labor was the answer to all economic and social evils. Even Bismarck, with his distaste for capitalist entrepreneurs, was favorably disposed towards cooperatives. Most of these schemes proved unworkable, but some success was achieved with cooperative savings banks that provided modest loans for working people.

Liberals took a patronizing attitude towards the working classes and argued that they should be educated up to their level before being regarded as equal partners. Workers were excluded from the National Association by a hefty annual subscription. Suggestions that concessions should be made to enable workers to join were bluntly rejected. On the other hand the Association sponsored a workers' delegation to go to London for the World Exhibition. It was decided that the delegation should report back to a workers' congress. A committee was convened in Leipzig to discuss the form this congress should take, but its conclusions were alarming to liberals. It called for an independent labor movement and appealed to Ferdinand Lassalle to write a reply to Schulze-Delitzsch's denunciations of a labor movement cut loose from the liberals. Lassalle was a radical democrat and intellectual, a flamboyant bon vivant and dandy, a captivating orator, and a charismatic and dictatorial leader. His "Open Response" of March 1, 1863, is one of the key texts of Social Democracy.

Lassalle's central contention was that his somewhat vague vision of socialism could only be achieved by universal suffrage. The ballot box and not revolution was the only way forward. Since 1848 liberals of all shades had no longer been the driving force behind the national revolution; differences between capital and labor were irreconcilable. According to his "iron law of wages" – a notion upon which Karl Marx poured vitriolic scorn – the

PLATE 9   The founders of German Social Democracy. © Friedrich Ebert Stiftung

working class was condemned never to rise above a minimum subsistence level. Only when society was organized into productive cooperative associations of the workers themselves, financed by the state, could this misery be overcome. Lassalle believed that the working class should take its destiny in its own hands, and argued that the nation-state had a vital role to play in the creation of a just society. Lassalle's state socialism was thus an odd mixture of radical democracy, authoritarianism, and fervent nationalism. His important contribution to the labor movement was his insistence that the liberation of the working class should be the task of the working class itself and that all links to Schulze-Delitzsch's liberals should be severed.

The Leipzig committee accepted Lassalle's report, which became the program of the General German Workers' Association (ADAV) with Lassalle as its president. This was not only the first independent national working-class political organization; it was also the first modern political party in Germany. Many workers' associations were not prepared to make such a radical break with the progressives. They were suspicious of state power, especially in its Prussian manifestation. They remained Greater Germans in the tradition of 1848 and were understandably confused by Lassalle's inchoate ideas. When he was killed in the following year following an absurd affront to a crack marksman over his fiancée, ending in a duel which was little more than a suicide, the party, now numbering some 3,000 members,

PLATE 10   August Bebel. © Friedrich Ebert Stiftung

began to fall apart. But Lassalle's influence on the labor movement in Germany was profound.

A number of trade unions were formed in the 1860s and a series of strikes marked a further radicalization of the working class. Lassalleans with their "iron law of wages" felt that trade unions were a futile waste of time and effort. Liberals who were anxious to lure workers away from ADAV were more sympathetic, but this in turn threatened the liberal alliance with business interests. The Social Democratic Workers' Party (SDAP), founded by August Bebel and Wilhelm Liebknecht at a congress in Eisenach in 1869, was formed in staunch opposition to ADAV. The Eisenachers' largely Marxist program appealed to radical workers, to trade unionists, and to Greater German radicals who could not stomach the Lassalleans' Little German and pro-Prussian policies.

Even as late as 1869 the socialist movement was hardly the "specter that is haunting Europe" as Marx and Engels had claimed it to be as early as 1848. There were some 3,000 Lassalleans, while Bebel and Liebknecht had even fewer followers. During the New Era the central issues were the national question and army reform in Prussia.

Prussian Army Reforms

On becoming regent in 1858 William had made it clear that he was determined to make some drastic changes in the Prussian army. Nothing had been done to improve the army since the great reforms of the Napoleonic era. In spite of a dramatic increase in population from 11 to 18 million, its size had remained the same. The army was minute when compared to those of Russia, France, and Austria. Mobilization during the Crimean War had shown up some serious deficiencies. Above all the Landwehr needed a complete overhaul. It had proved thoroughly unreliable in 1848, some units having sided with the rebels. Its officers were poorly trained and elderly, the men ill-disciplined. It needed to be better integrated into the regular army. William also believed that service in the army should be increased from two to three years. Three years were needed to turn citizens into soldiers, to convert disgruntled liberals into loyal subjects, to make a clear distinction between the civil and the military and to professionalize an army that was based on the liberal principle of universal military service. The largely aristocratic officer corps saw itself as the monarchy's Praetorian Guard, standing outside the constitution, ever ready to strike back against revolution, modernity, and liberalism.

There was general agreement that the army needed to be reformed and its size increased, but there was considerable disagreement over the thorny issue of its social role. William's first minister of war, Bonin, whom he had instantly reappointed, wanting to avoid confrontation with the House of Deputies (Abgeordnetenhaus) over the Landwehr, argued that a relatively independent territorial army was essential in order to reconcile civilians with the regular army. William would have none of this and promptly replaced Bonin with Count Albrecht von Roon, a man known not to shy away from confrontation. Roon proposed increasing army service from two to three years and the size of the army from 150,000 to 220,000. The Landwehr was to be reduced in size and significance and henceforth given regular, reserve, or retired officers. In short it should virtually cease to exist as a force independent from the regular army.

The liberals welcomed the proposed increase to the size of the army, for they were concerned about Prussia's security and also wanted a strong army to support a vigorous

German policy. The cost of Roon's proposals was far from exorbitant. The great stumbling block for left liberals was the Landwehr, about which they harbored fond romantic illusions. For them the Landwehr was a true citizens' army, the guarantee of liberal freedoms against the reactionary and aristocratic regular army. The right-wing liberals were less concerned about the Landwehr. They were far more worried about the three-year service, which they saw as a dangerous step towards the militarization of bourgeois society. They were determined to resist William and Roon's ambition to turn the army into the "school of the nation" intent on transforming citizens into mindless robots to be sent back to civilian life as loyal, pliant, and obedient subjects. Above all, the liberals were determined that the House of Deputies should have a say in military affairs and should not simply rubber-stamp the government's proposals. Step by step the army should be brought under the constitution.

The liberals were prepared to provide the money for the increases in the army, but would not agree to the proposed administrative reforms or to the three-year service. The government counter-attacked, claiming that parliament had no authority to determine the size or organization of the army. Such matters came under the king's "power of command" (*Kommandogewalt*). The question of army reform thus now became an outright power struggle between the throne and parliament. Ultra-conservatives around the head of the military cabinet, Edwin von Manteuffel, hoped that this would lead to a coup d'état and the overthrow of the constitution. Most conservatives did not want to go quite so far, but they were determined to use the crisis to clip parliament's wings and move sharply to the right. Even though liberal objections to the proposed army reforms were exceedingly modest, Roon announced that Prussia was "rotting in the sewer of doctrinaire liberalism." He welcomed the prospect of settling accounts with the liberals once and for all.

Roon took the money, reorganized the army, established the new units, and paraded them before a humiliated public. Left-wing liberals were outraged both by Roon's provocative actions and by the supine attitude of the Old Liberals (as the faction was known) to the right. A group which included Hermann Schultze-Delitzsch, the historian Theodor Mommsen, and the pathologist Rudolf Virchow formed a new party know as the Progressives (Fortschrittspartei), which called for major liberal constitutional reforms. In the elections in December 1861 the new party won 109 seats, the Old Liberals 91, and the conservatives were reduced to a mere 14 seats. Manteuffel called for a military dictatorship, the army rattled its swords, but William remained calm. He was determined to keep the army out of parliamentary control, but he knew that the liberals were not a serious revolutionary danger. Encouraged by their resounding success at the polls the liberals now fought back by demanding exactly how the money they had granted for the army had been spent, whereupon the king dissolved the House of Deputies and appointed a new conservative government.

A fresh round of elections returned a comfortable liberal majority to the House. The opposition was now willing to reach a compromise, but insisted on the two-year service. William would not budge on this issue, insisting that parliament should have no say in the way that the army was organized. The conflict was now one of principle. Which side would be obliged to give way – the crown or parliament? The outcome of this struggle would be of fundamental significance to Prussia's constitutional development. Would the crown bow to parliament, or strengthen its authority in a bloodless coup?

The House now refused to vote on the budget on the assumption that the government would be unable to govern without a budget and would be forced to concede. The king and the ultra-conservatives did not for a moment intend to capitulate. They came up with the ingenious idea that there was a "hole" in the constitution since there was no provision made therein for what should happen when the House and the government were deadlocked. Most of the ministers were horrified at the proposal that they should govern without a budget and insisted that this was blatantly unconstitutional. They knew that another election would bring no relief and therefore begged William to give way. The king thought of abdicating in favor of his son Frederick. The crown prince, who was sympathetic towards the liberals, begged his father not to take this drastic step and the crisis deepened.

Bismarck

At this point Roon urged his friend Bismarck, who was at this time Prussian ambassador in Paris, to come to Berlin by sending a famous telegram: "Periculum in mora. Dépêchez-vous" ("There is danger in delay – get a move on!"). Bismarck, knowing that his hour had come, hastened to the capital. This was one of the decisive moments in Prussian, German, and European history. It determined that Prussia would not become a parliamentary democracy on British lines, but would remain an autocratic military monarchy with a parliamentary appendage.

William had serious reservations about Bismarck. He was a rogue elephant, an extremist with a brutal streak, a political gambler and adventurer, an unpredictable and highly strung opportunist. In addition Queen Augusta detested the man. But at the height of the crisis in 1862 he saw no alternative to the mad Junker if he wanted to govern without a budget and push through the army reforms in their original form. Bismarck pulled out all the histrionic stops and swore that he would serve the monarch "as an Electoral-Brandenburg vassal," not as a "constitutional minister," thereby preserving the full authority of the crown. At the same time he insisted that he would act as he saw fit and that he was not the creature of any man or any party. From the outset Bismarck was thus vested with virtually dictatorial powers able at last, as he put it, to make his own music.

Bismarck appeared as minister president before the budgetary committee on September 30, bearing an olive branch as a symbol of his willingness to reach an accommodation with the liberals to whom he had already offered three ministerial positions. But he cautioned the deputies that he intended to govern without a budget. In the most famous of his many pithy phrases he told his horrified audience that: "The great questions of the day are not settled by speeches and majority votes, that was the mistake of the men of 1848, but by blood and iron." The liberal historian Heinrich von Treitschke, who was later to become a starry-eyed admirer of Bismarck, spoke for many when he said: "it seems to me that when I hear a simple Junker like this Bismarck fellow talk of the blood and iron with which he intends to lord it over Germany, the blackguardly is only outdone by the ridiculous."

Bismarck ruled without a budget. Civil servants who raised any objections were instantly dismissed, denied a pension, and stripped of their civil rights. Prosecutors who demurred when called upon to proceed against the government's critics were given similar treatment. The press was muzzled and parliament dissolved. The elections returned the liberals with a two-thirds majority. Bismarck continued to ignore parliament and it was dissolved once again in May 1866, shortly before the war against Austria.

The heated rhetoric on both sides disguised the fact that liberal ambitions were far from revolutionary, and that Bismarck knew that he could not tackle the "great questions of the day" without substantial parliamentary support. He began to do so by stealing the liberals' thunder. His attitude towards the German problem was, as we shall shortly see, very close to that of the Progressives, his most outspoken critics in the House of Representatives (Abgeordnetenhaus). He was strongly opposed to Manteuffel's proposal for a coup d'état but thought it prudent to hide his intention to win over the liberals by lashing them in public. Bismarck told Ferdinand Lassalle, with whom he got along famously, that he intended to introduce universal manhood suffrage at some future date. This was clearly no ordinary conservative, but a Bonapartist who set out to break the political deadlock by a foreign political success that would win over the liberal nationalists. This in turn was to place the liberals in an awkward predicament. They wanted both national unity and liberal freedom. Some felt that these two principles were dialectically linked and that Prussia as part of a united Little Germany would cease to be autocratic and militaristic. Others doubted that unity under a Bismarck could ever bring freedom.

The German Question

For the time being the German question was submerged by the constitutional crisis. In the early 1860s there had been general agreement that it could not be settled by revolution. Precious few wanted a repeat performance of 1848. "Blood and iron" was not yet on the agenda, with Austria humiliated after Villafranca and the tiny Prussian army in a wretched state. Reform of the Confederation seemed to be the only possible way forward.

There was no shortage of suggestions as to how the Confederation should be changed. Prussia wanted equality with Austria with hegemony north of the river Main plus the right to call the shots in Schleswig-Holstein and Electoral Hesse. Given the threat to Germany posed by Napoleon III, the Prussians were prepared to cooperate with Austria. Austria was in an awkward position. It did not wish to give up its dominant position in Germany, but it also needed a strong Confederation to help strengthen its position in Venetia. It was anxious to frustrate Prussia's reform plans, but also realized that it might need Prussian support. The Austrians therefore could not decide whether to tackle the Prussians head on, or to agree to an Austro-Prussian dualism.

The Third Germany (Trias) was determined to resist an Austro-Prussian duumvirate, and was equally appalled by the idea of a Germany dominated by Prussia and excluding Austria. The Saxon minister president Count Friedrich von Beust put forward a comprehensive plan in 1861 that called for a triumvirate, a strengthened federal executive, and a federal parliament. The weakness of this scheme was that the Trias was a fissiparous collection of states, which Bavaria sought to dominate. Beust's ambitious scheme therefore came to nothing.

Since the Austrians were unable to agree with the Prussians they now turned towards the Third Germany but it was too late. Little German sentiment was growing. The government of Baden approached Prussia suggesting a dramatic reform of the Confederation that would include a constitution, a federal parliament, and the exclusion of Austria, which in turn would be given the assurance of military support and would be closely associated with the new Germany. Bismarck was already thinking along much the same lines, but the Prussian government disliked the idea of a federal parliament and still shied away from a confrontation with Austria.

Austria could mobilize considerable support against this Little German solution. Most of the Third German states now supported the idea of a common code of law and a conference of parliamentary delegates. It was even suggested that Prussia should be obliged to submit to the majority decisions of the Bundesrat, whereupon Bismarck threatened to withdraw from the Confederation. He then threatened the Austrians with war if they did not agree to parity in Germany along with Prussian hegemony in the north. Knowing that this would be totally unacceptable to Austria he then proposed a German parliament with direct elections. The suggestion was met with a mixture of amazement, derision, and alarm.

In 1863 the Austrians mounted their counter-attack. They proposed a strengthening of the federal executive with a five- or six-man directory, the creation of a chamber of princes, and supported the idea of a conference of parliamentary delegates. They further suggested that a new Little German Confederation could be formed without them if the Prussians did not agree. The Emperor Francis Joseph invited the German princes to discuss these plans in Frankfurt in August. In a stormy scene Bismarck forced William to refuse the invitation, for this was transparently a scheme to reduce Prussia to having only one voice in the directory.

The Austrian plan floundered and died due to determined Prussian opposition, but the German question still remained a burning issue. Popular opinion had been mobilized by the National Association (Nationalverein) founded in 1859 at the height of the Italian crisis. Its members were moderate liberals who supported the federal constitution of 1849 and called for the creation of a Little German nation-state with a parliament elected by universal manhood suffrage. They saw Prussia as Germany's Piedmont, but a Prussia with Bismarck as minister president promising "blood and iron" and trampling on Prussia's constitutional rights was something that no liberal could stomach. From 1862 the National Association's project had to be put on hold, but this did not mean that the Greater Germans with their German Reform Association (Deutsche Reformverein) won any converts. Their vision of a Germany in which Austria and Prussia could live together in harmony was hopelessly unrealistic. Liberal democrats who longed for a German parliament also knew that this was impossible in a Germany that included Austria. Bismarck might have proposed a parliament out of cynical considerations of *Realpolitik*, but Bismarck would not be there forever and Prussia could change.

In 1860 Richard Cobden, the radical "apostle of free trade" and president of the board of trade in Palmerston's cabinet, negotiated a trade treaty between Britain and France which for Prussia was both a threat and an opportunity. The "revolutionary" France of Napoleon III allied to Britain was an alarming prospect to Prussian conservatives. But almost simultaneously Prussia was approached by France for a trade treaty and by Austria proposing a defensive agreement as well as entry into the Zollverein. The Prussians saw a golden opportunity to exclude Austria from the Zollverein, thus delivering Austria an economic Villafranca. A trade agreement was reached with France in 1862 opening up the French market to German industrial goods, thus helping the economy to climb out of a severe recession. Austrian attempts to wean the southern German states away from the Zollverein came to naught, in spite of strong anti-Prussian sentiments in the region. Bismarck threatened to dissolve the Zollverein unless there was unanimous consent of all its members to the treaty with France. Faced with such a prospect even the most staunchly anti-Prussian governments meekly agreed. This did not make a Little German solution under Prussian leadership inevitable, but it certainly made it more than likely. The new Germany might have been made by blood and iron, but coal and iron were its foundations.

The uprising in the Polish provinces in Russia gave Bismarck his first opportunity to strengthen Prussia's diplomatic standing. He was determined that Napoleon III should not be allowed to "form a French bridgehead on the Vistula" by helping the Poles as he had the Italians, but even more important was the opportunity to discredit the Russian foreign minister Gorchakov with his pro-Polish and pro-French policies. The Prussian army was mobilized and help offered to Russia in the Alvensleben Convention of February, 8, 1863.

There were howls of protest in Paris against Prussia. The Empress Eugénie suggested to the Austrians that they should give Venetia to Italy and in return Buol's old idea of annexing Silesia could be put into effect. France would then move up to the Rhine, and Prussia would be given some modest compensation in the north. Napoleon had overplayed his hand. He had lost the understanding with Russia, which now turned towards Prussia. Bismarck was freed from pressure on two sides, and by guaranteeing Belgium was now in England's good books. Public opinion was outraged that Prussia was now on the best of terms with Asiatic despotism and had alienated France.

The Schleswig-Holstein Question

It was thus in a most uneasy situation that the Schleswig-Holstein question was once more on the agenda. In November 1863 the new Danish king, Christian IX, formally divided the duchies and incorporated Schleswig into the Danish state. German nationalists were outraged at this flagrant violation of international treaties. They demanded that both duchies should be independent from Denmark and when the son of the duke of Augustenburg, who had renounced his claim in the previous crisis, claimed the duchies he overnight became the darling of the liberal nationalists in Germany. Schleswig-Holstein Associations sprang up throughout Germany in the first mass political movement in Germany since 1849.

Bismarck had no sympathy for the baying hordes of Augustenburgers. He did not want to see a new state formed on Prussia's borders. He was fearful that the powers would intervene as they had done in 1848 and that the Russians and French would patch up their differences. He therefore insisted that the London Protocols of 1852 should be respected and that Christian IX be recognized as the legitimate king of Denmark and duke of Schleswig-Holstein, although the duchies should remain united. In taking this position he was denounced by the German nationalists as a vile traitor, but he could afford to ignore their emotional protests. The new Austrian foreign minister, Rechberg, was anxious to cooperate with Prussia and agreed that international treaties had to be respected. Bismarck exploited this situation to the full and dragged Austria into blindly supporting his policy in Schleswig-Holstein, even though it resulted in the loss of all support from the Trias and forced Austria into an untenable position. This was truly a bravura piece of diplomatic wizardry.

The smaller German states wanted the Confederation to go to war with Denmark, but Austria and Prussia threatened to dissolve the Confederation if their policy was not accepted. The Bundestag agreed by a majority of only one vote to an "Execution" against Christian IX's illegal annexation of Schleswig. Federal troops now marched into Holstein and in February 1864 Austrian and Prussian forces occupied Schleswig. They were soon in Jutland, and on April 8 Prussian troops stormed the Danish fortifications at Düppel in a dramatic and widely publicized action that won the grudging admiration of many a German nationalist.

These events were of considerable concern to the powers. Russia suspected that Napoleon III would soon become involved in the reordering of northern Europe. Palmerston was pro-Danish, but like the Russians was anxious to keep the French in check. Queen Victoria did not want to get involved. Napoleon III was determined to use the crisis to his advantage. A conference was held in London in April but proved fruitless. The Danes were under the illusion that they had widespread support and refused any compromise. Palmerston wanted to intervene, but since public opinion, most of the establishment, and the queen were all deeply suspicious of Napoleon III and thus strongly opposed, he was obliged to give way. Napoleon III shied away from unleashing a European war without any allies. Russia was determined to preserve the alliance with Prussia, and Bismarck skillfully used the threat of an understanding with France to strengthen these ties. The London conference having thus failed, the war continued, Denmark was defeated, and Schleswig-Holstein became an Austro-Prussian condominium.

The Danish war was an old-fashioned, limited, cabinet war but it caused a diplomatic revolution. Britain and Russia both now made it plain that they had no immediate interests in Germany. They stood aloof in 1866 and left France isolated in 1870. The effects within Germany were equally significant. There were complaints that Augustenburg had been betrayed and that the rights of the people of Schleswig-Holstein to national self-determination had been ignored, but there was widespread delight at a German victory. Liberals, both right and left, began to revise their opinion of Bismarck. Treitschke no longer thought him absurd and Sybel, Mommsen, and Droysen, his colleagues in the historians' guild, joined him in endorsing Prussian policies.

The condominium was clearly only a temporary solution, with Bismarck determined that the duchies should be firmly under Prussian control. To this end he suggested to Rechberg that Prussia and Austria should go to war with France so that Austria could win back Lombardy and Prussia would annex the duchies as compensation. It is difficult to know how serious this proposal was, but Francis Joseph had no desire to add a large number of disgruntled Italians to his empire, while William still thought that the annexation of the duchies was altogether too risky a business.

At this point Austria was finally excluded from the Zollverein and Rechberg, the man of compromise with Prussia, was dismissed. Austria now went over to a policy of confrontation with Prussia. It did so from a singularly weak position. It had no allies. Russia was at daggers drawn over Romania, France would demand Venetia as the price of friendship, in Germany the Trias was alienated and Greater Germany a dead letter. In Schleswig-Holstein the Austrians now supported the claims of the duke of Augustenburg. It was a popular move in the smaller German states, with their strong aversion to power-hungry Prussia. On May 25 a Prussian crown council decided to aim for outright annexation of the duchies, even at the risk of war. Bismarck now set about preparing the diplomatic ground. Public opinion in Germany was still far too enamored of Augustenburg and an arrangement had to be made with France.

Tensions between Prussia and Austria were temporarily relieved with the Treaty of Gastein in August 1865, whereby Schleswig was to be administered by Prussia and Holstein by Austria. This left Austria in an untenable position, with Holstein sandwiched between Prussian territory and with Prussia enjoying a number of special rights in the duchy. Austria, tottering on the verge of bankruptcy, had no alternative but to give way, but Gastein was clearly only a temporary arrangement.

The Austro-Prussian War

Austria was denounced in the Trias states for having betrayed Augustenburg and for apparently agreeing to divide the duchies, which according to the Treaty of Ripen of 1460 were to be joined together in perpetuity. The Prussians found every possible excuse to denounce the Austrians for violations of the terms of the treaty. By early 1866 both sides came to the conclusion that war was almost inevitable: Austria out of desperation, Bismarck for power-political reasons. Determined to win the support of liberal nationalists for Prussia's war against Austria he put forward a proposal for federal reform in April 1866. This was truly revolutionary. Bismarck the conservative was seeking an alliance with the nationalists, calling for a German parliament with universal manhood suffrage and the expulsion of Austria from the Confederation. It was a cunning move, for it also made it unlikely that the powers would intervene. As Bismarck phrased it later, the offer of universal manhood suffrage was designed to stop other countries from "sticking their fingers into our national omelette."

The problem was that the Augustenburgers and southern German liberals thought this was disingenuous villainy, while Greater Germans and conservatives were equally appalled. Bismarck had more success in foreign politics. On April 8, the day before he presented his reform proposals to the Confederation, he concluded an offensive alliance with Italy. It was agreed that Prussia should provoke a war with Austria within three months and Italy would join in so as to complete the process of national unification.

Everything now depended on Napoleon III. He wanted to finish off the job in Italy, but he also wanted substantial compensation from Germany. He did not want to see Prussia replace France as united Italy's midwife, and many of his advisors argued that France had more immediate interest in the Rhine than in the Po. At the very last moment he reached an agreement with Austria. Austria agreed to hand over Venetia to Italy; Napoleon III agreed to remain neutral. Austria was to be compensated in southern Germany. A Rhineland state would be formed outside the Confederation and closely tied to France.

Austria brought war closer by bringing the Schleswig-Holstein question before the Bundestag and by convening the estates in Holstein. Prussia responded by marching into Holstein on June 9 – a flagrant breach of federal law. Austria called upon the Confederation to mobilize against Prussia. Bavaria, Württemberg, Saxony, and Hanover, and a number of smaller states, including the two Hesses, voted in favor. Baden abstained. The remainder sided with Prussia. Prussia declared the Confederation dissolved and issued an ultimatum to Saxony, Hanover, and Electoral Hesse. When all three states refused to bend, Prussia attacked on June 15.

The war was immensely unpopular in Germany and it was bitterly ironic that virtually the only support for Bismarck came from the socialist ADAV because of his promise to introduce universal manhood suffrage. Bismarck released Lassalle's successor Johann Baptist von Schweizer from jail and arranged to subsidize his newspaper, *Der Sozialdemokrat*. The outcome was uncertain and most people, Napoleon III among them, imagined that it would be a long war, possibly lasting several years. Bismarck also thought this a distinct possibility and preparations were made to stir up national revolts in the Habsburg empire which included a plan to bring Garibaldi first to Dalmatia and then to Hungary.

Thanks to Helmuth von Moltke's operational genius the war was staggeringly short. Within three weeks the Austrian army was smashed at Königgrätz in Bohemia on July 3, when three Prussian armies marching separately came together on the battlefield, but only in the nick of time. The Austrians lost 45,000 in the battle including 20,000 prisoners, the Prussians 9,000. It was a decisive victory, but not a rout. The bulk of the Austrian army escaped. Austria scored victories over the Italians on land at Custozza on June 24 and at sea at Lissa on July 20, but it was obvious that The Austrians were no match for the Prussians. The Prussian army was equipped with a needle gun that could release seven rounds a minute and could be fired lying down. The Austrian muzzle-loading rifle could barely fire two rounds a minute and had to be fired standing up. Austria got precious little help from its coalition partners and Benedek was no match for Moltke, the greatest military genius since Napoleon. He had made full use of the railways to ensure rapid mobility and controlled his dispersed forces by telegraph.

Prussia's swift victory caught Europe by surprise. Napoleon III acted as mediator, and an armistice was quickly concluded. Bismarck had no desire to humiliate Austria and the French agreed to his moderate terms: the creation of a north German Confederation under Prussia; the annexation of Schleswig-Holstein, Hanover, Electoral Hesse, Nassau, and Frankfurt; plus the creation of an independent southern German federation excluding Austria. Once Napoleon III agreed to this arrangement the Austrians were left with no alternative but to treat with Prussia. The strongest opposition to Bismarck's plan came from the king. He wanted to teach Austria a lesson and had serious reservations about trampling on the legitimate sovereign rights of the north German states. Bismarck did not want Austria to harbor thoughts of revenge and saw it as a potential future ally. North of the river Main he favored a revolutionary solution analogous to what had happened in Italy. After a series of heated exchanges with Bismarck, William gave way.

Napoleon III tried to get some reward for his efforts, but Bismarck, who was appealing to German national sentiments, categorically refused to cede an inch of German soil. Napoleon III was without allies and had to give way, much to the disgust of his nationalist critics like Thiers. Russia, distressed about the national-revolutionary implications of the settlement, called for an international conference to discuss the German question. The British government was opposed to this suggestion, as was Bismarck. The French also showed little interest and the Russians backed down. The European powers were now reconciled to the new situation in Germany. The provisions of the preliminary Peace of Nikolsburg were finalized in Prague on August 23, 1866. Bismarck also negotiated a series of defensive alliances with the southern German states guaranteeing their territorial integrity. In the event of war their forces were to be placed under a Prussian supreme commander, thus surrendering a significant part of their sovereignty. This was a clear warning to Napoleon III to keep his hands off Germany.

Europe was radically changed in the summer of 1866. Austria was now excluded from the Germany of which it had been a vital part for a thousand years. The German Austrians soon shared power in the Habsburg empire with the Magyars in the new political construction of Austria–Hungary. The Slavs were still denied an equal voice. Germany was now well on the way to becoming a nation-state, since the new order was clearly only temporary.

CHAPTER SIX

THE UNIFICATION OF GERMANY
· 1866–1871 ·

CHAPTER CONTENTS

A History of Modern Germany: 1800 to the Present, Second Edition. Martin Kitchen.
© 2012 Martin Kitchen. Published 2012 by Blackwell Publishing Ltd.

The Prussian victory at Königgrätz left many contemporaries dazed and confused. The arch-reactionary, militaristic Junker Bismarck, who had trampled on the Prussian constitution, had begun the war with a call for a national parliament based on universal suffrage, thus partially realizing the ambitions of the Little German bourgeoisie. But elections held in Prussia on the same day as this decisive battle resulted in a crushing defeat for the liberals. There was considerable amazement when Bismarck asked the *Landtag* for an indemnity for the expenditure that it had refused to sanction during the constitutional crisis. It was a masterly move. Most conservatives were delighted that he had made no apology for what he had done, thereby implying that he would do it again if necessary. Many liberals found some comfort in that he thus acknowledged that he had ignored parliamentary rights. The indemnity made an alliance between moderate conservatives and (the newly formed) National Liberals possible.

The "Old Conservatives" (as the ultra-conservatives styled themselves) were appalled that Bismarck was swimming with the tide of nationalism, constitutionalism, and parliamentarianism. They remained adamant in their opposition to his domestic *Realpolitik*. On the other side a number of liberals found it equally impossible to swallow Bismarck's Bonapartist strategy and the cynicism of the indemnity. They disagreed with the National Liberals that a Germany formed under his leadership could ever become an acceptable constitutional state. Liberals in the Progressive Party voted by a fairly narrow majority against the Indemnity Bill. The left center voted by a two-thirds majority in favor. Only a few of those who were to join the pro-Bismarck National Liberals voted against.

Germany north of the river Main was reorganized as the North German Confederation. The princes and governments formed an upper house (Bundesrat) with a presidential committee (Praesidium) appointed by Bismarck as chancellor forming a government. The lower house (Reichstag) was elected by universal and secret manhood suffrage. In an attempt to exclude such dangerous elements as the "educated proletariat" and "demagogues," members were not paid. The states to the south did not form a southern German equivalent, largely due to the opposition of Baden and Württemberg. For all the economic, cultural, and confessional differences between north and south it was clear that these arrangements were temporary, and the "Main line" along the river Main provisional. After Königgrätz the Greater German solution was no longer on the agenda. The big question was not whether a Little Germany should be created, but under what circumstances. Should unity take priority over freedom, or vice versa? Should a united Germany under Bismarck's Prussia be accepted as the unavoidable first step towards the creation of a constitutional state, or should unity only be accepted on the basis of a liberal constitution? The second major question was how the southern German states should be linked to the North German Confederation. Should this be the concern of governments or of parliaments? Should unity be achieved at one fell swoop, or piecemeal? Were an international crisis and the resort to "blood and iron" unavoidable?

Anti-Prussian sentiments resulted in strange bedfellows. Socialists and radicals were enthusiastic supporters of the idea of a nation-state, but were determined to resist its domination by a conservative and militaristic Prussia. Conservative particularists and ultramontane Catholics joined in the anti-Prussian chorus; but cocking snooks at the "Borussians" was all that united them. Arch-conservatives and revolutionary socialists could never agree on a solution to the national problem. Anti-Prussianism was naturally strongest in the south, but it was also prevalent elsewhere, particularly in Hamburg, Hanover, and Saxony. On the other side were the National Liberals, who argued that first Germany should be united, and only then could the constitutional question be resolved.

Amid all this confusion no one had a master plan, least of all Bismarck. His main concern was the power vacuum south of the Main. He could not allow southern Germany to fall under the sway of Napoleon III or of Austrian revisionists. At the same time he knew that the German question could only be solved by cooperation and consent, not by coercion. He knew he had to move cautiously and was careful not to neglect public opinion. Above all he was determined to preserve the Prussian monarchy and the authoritarian state in this radically new capitalist, bourgeois, national liberal, and constitutional world in which the relations between the European states had been drastically altered.

Military reforms in southern Germany on the Prussian model were a small step forward in the direction of a federal Germany under Prussian leadership. So too was the creation of a Customs Parliament, first with an upper house (Zollbundesrat) and then a lower house (Zollparlament). Elections for the Customs Parliament were a disappointment for those who had hoped for a popular demonstration in favor of national unity. The particularists won a resounding victory in southern Germany. It was a vote against Prussia and a major setback for Bismarck. The National Liberals had hoped that the Zollverein would be the motor for national unification. They were bitterly disillusioned. Bismarck was less pessimistic. He knew that the southern German states could not afford to leave the Zollverein. He could therefore write off the election results as a temporary setback. The southern German states were tied to the north economically through the Zollverein and militarily by a series of defensive alliances. Sharp differences between the different states, confusion, and lack of firm leadership, meant that a south German Confederation was never a serious option. The solution of 1871 was not inevitable, but for most contemporaries, whether they liked it or not, it seemed to be the most probable outcome of Prussia's victory over Austria in 1866.

Austria's exclusion from Germany and Prussia's dominant position in central Europe was viewed by the powers with relative equanimity. The British government was far from enthusiastic about Bismarck's conservatism, but it welcomed a counterweight to the unpredictable and ambitious France of Napoleon III. Russia could find comfort in the assurance that in Prussia it had a reliable conservative partner against Austria. The Austrians were absorbed with the problem of negotiating the "Compromise" with Hungary of 1867, and with dealing with the subject nationalities. These problems were so pressing that they could not possibly think of seeking revenge for Königgrätz.

For Bismarck 1866 had only brought a temporary solution to the German problem. Having once conjured up the support of liberal nationalists, nothing short of the creation of a nation-state would suffice to integrate them in a monarchical and conservative system dominated by Prussia. Bismarck had no idea how or when this national policy could be realized and he was confident enough to wait upon events. He was ready to seize any opportunity to secure this ultimate goal. Above all he was determined to maintain firm control and not allow liberal nationalists or public opinion undue influence. His was a revolutionary policy designed to overthrow the power-political balance of Europe, but it was to be a revolution from above that could not be allowed to slip out of his hands.

The France of Napoleon III was an unstable power that sought to overcome its chronic domestic political tensions by a dramatically adventurous foreign policy. It was thus highly unpredictable. Napoleon III was determined to assert France's hegemony over western Europe, but at the same time, in line with his policy of undoing the decisions of 1815, he showed great sympathy for nationalist movements in Italy, Poland, and central Europe. Yet for all that, he could hardly risk the establishment of a powerful Germany that would dominate Europe east of the Rhine. He could either try to contain Prussia north of the river Main, or support a German nation-state in return for major territorial concessions. Alternatively he could enter on a confrontation course with Prussia and try to stop any further accretion of power.

Napoleon lost the first round against Bismarck. He had hoped to purchase Luxembourg, which had been part of the now defunct German Confederation, from the king of Holland, who was short of cash and had no interest in the duchy. German nationalists were outraged at the proposed sale. Bismarck could not afford to alienate the nationalists and therefore made the defensive treaties public, whereupon the Dutch king announced that he would only agree to the sale if his Prussian counterpart agreed. Bismarck wanted to avoid a direct conflict with France and therefore put the question before the north German parliament, which threw up its hands in predictable horror. Bismarck then used this reaction as an excuse to turn down the French bid but since, unlike Moltke, he did not think that the Luxembourg question was a convincing reason to go to war with France, he agreed to withdraw the Prussian garrison from the duchy and guaranteed its neutrality. Luxembourg thus ceased to be part of Germany although it remained in the Zollverein. France was spared from total humiliation, Europe from war.

The Luxembourg crisis spelt the end of any hopes that Prussia might agree to be France's junior partner in Europe, leaving Napoleon III determined to frustrate Bismarck's territorial ambitions. Austria was the only viable partner for such a policy, but with its internal problems and its rivalry with Russia in the Balkans it was in no position to play an active anti-Prussian role. On the other hand negotiations between Paris and Vienna, coupled with Britain's and Russia's preference for the maintenance of the status quo in Germany, obliged Bismarck to move cautiously. Thus between 1867 and 1870 there was something of a foreign political stalemate over the German question and no opportunity arose that Bismarck could exploit.

Liberalism, Nationalism, and Particularism

Elections for the north German Reichstag were held in February 1867. Bismarck's supporters won 180 of the 297 seats: the National Liberals, Free Conservatives, a smattering of Independents and "Old Liberals." The opposition was made up of 59 Old Conservatives, 13 Poles, 19 left liberals, and 18 "Guelphs" – Hanoverian nationalists and federalists. Once the constitution had been agreed upon fresh elections were held in August that year, resulting in little change in the relative position of the parties.

Bismarck now set Rudolf Delbrück to work modernizing the economy. As a thorough-going economic liberal he removed all remaining trade barriers in the North German Confederation, established uniform weights and measures, abolished all restrictive practices, and the Trade Bill of 1869 completed the emancipation of the Jews. Finally in 1870 a common code of law was introduced. The Reichstag played a vital role in this crucial series of fundamental reforms.

Prussia remained staunchly conservative and the Free Conservative and National Liberal alliance that dominated the Reichstag was seldom in the majority. The grotesquely reactionary ministers of justice and economics were replaced by men of a slightly more liberal cast of mind, but otherwise Prussia was unaffected by the liberal climate of the Confederation. The conservative, monarchical, and Borrusian tone did nothing to help the process of integrating the territories that had been absorbed by Prussia in 1866. Those who had been in opposition to the repressive regimes in Electoral Hesse and Hanover saw this as a welcome change and mostly joined the National Liberals. In Hanover the deposed king still had his supporters in the Guelph party that won the support of a number of other disaffected anti-Prussians. The proudly independent Frankfurters bitterly resented being absorbed by the new state of Hesse-Nassau. Schleswig-Holstein, faithful to the Augustenburgs, remained aloof.

The Prussian administration, anxious not to offend the sensibilities of the new provinces, allowed them a considerable degree of autonomy. The princes were given ample compensation for their losses. The major exception was Hanover, where King George V protested against the loss of his throne and formed an anti-Prussian "Guelph Legion." Bismarck made use of an emergency decree to seize the king's considerable private fortune, the interest on which was supposed to be used to combat the Guelphs. In fact Bismarck used this "Guelph fund" as a secret slush fund for all manner of nefarious activities, including bribing the press, politicians, and princes.

Liberal reforms in the economy, education, and the law were also carried out in most of the German states south of the Main in the late 1860s. Reforms in the economy through the Zollverein and the Customs Parliament, along with military reforms on Prussian lines, had liberal and national implications, thus furthering the Little German cause. On the other side of the political divide were conservative Catholics, opponents of economic liberalism, Greater Germans, and particularists. The "patriotic" majority in Bavaria was determined to preserve the country's independence. In Baden a vociferous minority held similar views. The Württembergers were anti-Prussian and Greater German, but parliament was virtually deadlocked over the German question, the government paralyzed. The situation was further complicated by fierce debates over the Vatican Council, which was to lead to a serious split within the Catholic Church in Germany. The Bavarian king refused to cave in to the anti-Prussian ultramontanes. Württemberg was determined to resist the anti-Prussian democrats. Both governments thus needed an alliance with Prussia in order not to give in to parliamentary majorities. In Baden there was a general agreement on the desirability of joining the North German Confederation. Bismarck viewed the southern Germans with ill-concealed contempt. He compared Bavaria, whose natives he described as a cross between human beings and Austrians, as Germany's Calabria: a primitive and backward area that he could well do without.

The Franco-Prussian War

The gridlock over German unification was broken by events outside its borders. In 1868 the Spanish army deposed the absolutist queen and sought to establish a constitutional monarchy. The favored candidate was the German Prince Leopold of Hohenzollern-Sigmaringen, the south German and Catholic branch of the Prussian ruling house. At first Bismarck paid little attention to the Hohenzollern candidature, but by the winter of 1869, when it was clear that the Spanish were anxious to go ahead, he lent it his full support. Napoleon III used the prospect of a Hohenzollern on the throne of Spain as an opportunity to denounce Prussia's German policy as reactionary and selfish land-grabbing, rather than an expression of the genuine nationalism that he wholeheartedly supported in Italy and Poland. Bismarck hoped to gain support in the south for his German policy by confronting France, thereby mobilizing German national sentiment.

In April 1870 Leopold, having been cautioned by the Prussian king who wanted to avoid a showdown with the French, turned down the Spanish offer and the affair seemed to be over. Then, one month later, Napoleon III moved the ambitious and hawkish Gramont from the embassy in Vienna to the foreign ministry. He hoped to strengthen Napoleon's position at home by a resounding victory over Prussia. Bismarck welcomed the challenge. He persuaded William to drop his objections to Leopold's candidature and the prince agreed to put his name forward. On July 5 Gramont denounced Prussia for attempting to revive the empire of Charles V (an argument that Bismarck had used when trying to win William's support for the candidature) and warned that should the Hohenzollerns persist France would go to war. Both Britain and Russia expressed sympathy for the French point of view. Bismarck beat a hasty retreat, and the candidature was once again withdrawn.

The French government, emboldened by this victory, now went for the kill. The French envoy Benedetti was sent to Bad Ems where the Prussian king was taking the waters to demand what amounted to an apology and a guarantee that the Hohenzollern candidature would never again be revived. William found this deeply insulting and, although he had no intention of further supporting Leopold's aspirations to the Spanish crown, flatly refused.

The king sent a telegram to Bismarck reporting on this exchange. Bismarck published a slightly shortened but not significantly altered version in the press. Contrary to Bismarck's assertion in his memoirs that he so radically altered the tone of the "Ems telegram" that he provoked France into declaring war, the French government had already decided to go to war before the telegram was published. The "Ems telegram" did, however, mobilize public opinion throughout Germany and the country was united in its determination to resist the overbearing French.

France formally declared war on July 19. The defensive treaties with the south German states came into immediate effect. Napoleon III thus caused what he had tried at all costs to avoid: a Germany united under Prussian leadership. The Franco-Prussian war thus became a Franco-German war to which the south German states, including the Bavarian patriots, gave their full and enthusiastic support.

The planned French offensive came to nothing due to poor planning and organizational chaos. After a number of bloody engagements in Lorraine, part of the French army under Marshal Bazaine was trapped in the fortress town of Metz, prompting the commanding officer to remark: "We are in a chamber pot and are about to be shat upon!" The French commander Marshal MacMahon wanted to withdraw towards Paris, but he was ordered to relieve Metz. Moltke saw his chance, halted his advance towards the French capital, and encircled the bulk of the French army at Sedan. The French capitulated. Napoleon III was captured, along with 100,000 other prisoners of war. The republic was declared in Paris, and on September 6 the new government announced that it would agree to a peace provided that the territorial integrity of France was respected. This the Prussians refused.

The French Republic under Gambetta created a partisan army that fought a bitter and brutal guerrilla war, harrowingly described in Guy de Maupassant's stories, in a desperate attempt to stop the cessation of Alsace and Lorraine. By mid-September the Germans laid siege to Paris, and by the end of January the republican government agreed to an armistice.

PLATE 11   The Battle of Sedan. © BPK

A preliminary peace was signed on February 26, in which France was to lose Alsace and Lorraine and pay an indemnity of five thousand million francs.

Bismarck was anxious to end the war as soon as possible for fear of the reaction of the powers. This brought him into direct conflict with the military, who wanted to annihilate the French army and to reduce France to total subjection for at least the next hundred years. The international constellation was favorable to Prussia. Britain had sympathized initially with France over the Hohenzollern candidature, but had lost patience with its increasingly bellicose policy. Austria could hardly intervene with the whole of Germany resolutely in support of Prussia. Italy resented the presence of French troops in Rome left to guard the Pope. Russia's deep resentments about Napoleon III's support for the Poles far outweighed fears of a united Germany. Although Bismarck was heartily disliked throughout most of Europe, the prospect of a French victory and consequent hegemony was far more alarming than the extension of Prussian power and influence south of the Main.

The annexation of Alsace and Lorraine was demanded by the military, applauded by the majority of Germans, and supported by Bismarck. It permanently poisoned relations between Germany and France, although Bismarck insisted they would have been every bit as strained even without these annexations. The powers saw this as an alarming sign that a defensive war had become a brutal war of conquest and that Bismarck was not only aiming at uniting Germany but striving for hegemony in Europe. His critics at home and abroad were loud in their condemnation of this policy, with Karl Marx shrewdly arguing that he had thus sown the seeds of a European catastrophe. This unease at a new nation founded by blood and iron, seemingly intoxicated by victory, and gorged with conquest, was shared by many intellectuals from the extremes of left and right.

The German Empire

It was clear to all that this Germany, swept away on a wave of national euphoria, would form a nation-state, but it was uncertain what form it would take. The south German states were anxious to retain their identity and their sovereignty. Bismarck, wanting to negotiate with the princes and governments, was determined to resist the blandishments of popular nationalism. National unity would be achieved from above, not from below; as a federation of monarchical states, not a unitary parliamentary government.

Bismarck hoped that the south German states would join the North German Confederation. In October 1870 Hesse-Darmstadt and Baden requested membership. Bismarck hoped that he could persuade Bavaria and Württemberg to follow suit. Faced with Bavarian resistance, Bismarck negotiated separately in Versailles with the other states in the course of November, leaving Bavaria increasingly isolated. At the end of November the Bavarians finally gave way. Württemberg, which at the last minute had tried to win a privileged position in the new state, just as Bavaria had done, capitulated two days later.

The Prussian chancellor had made very few concessions. The Bundesrat was somewhat strengthened, thus giving the member states slightly more say in federal affairs. Bavaria retained an independent peacetime army, as well as a separate postal service and railway. It was also permitted to send an ambassador to the Vatican, have a separate say in the negotiation of peace treaties, and an independent right to tax beer – the national tipple.

In order to assert Prussia's supremacy over the new Germany, Bismarck was determined that the king of Prussia should be made emperor, and that the title should be offered to him by the princes, not come "from the gutter" as had been proposed by the Bundestag in 1849. King Ludwig of Bavaria was given a massive bribe from the "Guelph fund" to persuade him to offer the imperial crown to William on behalf of the German princes. William was most unhappy about the proposed title of "German emperor," which he felt had an empty ring about it, and wanted to be known the "emperor of Germany," but Bismarck argued that this would cause offense among the princes, who would feel subordinated to the Prussian king. Both agreed that the other suggested title – "emperor of the Germans" – smacked of popular nationalism and was unacceptable.

The new German empire was formally created on January 1, 1871, when the various treaties were concluded. The real foundation of the Second Reich was on January 18, when William was formally proclaimed kaiser. That was the traditional coronation day of the Prussian kings since 1701, when the Elector of Brandenburg was crowned king "in" Prussia. Held in the Hall of Mirrors at Versailles, it was not quite the magnificent ceremony represented in Anton von Werner's famous painting, commissioned fourteen years later. There were many reservations and much foreboding. Most noticeable was the absence of parliamentarians and civilians. The Reich of blood and iron was proclaimed by the military, by the princes, and by the old elite, all squeezed into military uniforms festooned with the medals of a victorious army.

The German empire of 1871 was a curious affair destined to last a mere forty-seven years. It was a national constitutional state with a parliament elected by universal manhood suffrage, comprising a loose federation of quasi-independent states, the whole dominated by the Prussian military state. It was the result of a series of uneasy compromises: between the federal and the particular, monarchy and democracy, aristocracy and bourgeoisie. There was no national flag and no national anthem. It was sharply criticized by many and won the undivided devotion of precious few. The states had wide-ranging areas of competence, including a monopoly of direct taxation and most indirect taxes, education, church affairs, and transportation. Each state had its own constitution and administration. As it was a federal state, federal law took precedence over state law, but the states differed widely in matters of jurisprudence.

The Reich was responsible for foreign policy, the military, economic, and social policy, and federal law. Sovereign power was said to reside in the "allied governments" represented in the Bundesrat with the kaiser as its hereditary president. Bismarck as chancellor served as chairman. Prussia, which made up two-thirds of the territory of the Reich and a similar proportion of the population, only had one-third of the votes in the Bundesrat, although it had a right of veto over military and constitutional matters. In practice Prussia dominated the Bundesrat since it could easily force the smaller states to toe the line.

In theory the Bundesrat had a number of significant executive powers. It had the same right to initiate legislation as the Reichstag, and no legislation could pass without its approval. The kaiser and the Bundesrat had the right to dismiss parliament and to declare war, although in practice such decisions were taken by the kaiser and the chancellor. Fundamentally it was an administrative body, made up of delegates and plenipotentiaries from the states. It did not have its own building, but was housed anonymously in the chancellery. It had virtually no staff and played no public role. Bills were prepared in the Reich ministries, or by the Prussian government, and presented to the Bundesrat at the last moment. Its inexperienced and ill-prepared members were little more than rubber stamps, since Bismarck preferred to negotiate with the states individually before launching any legislative initiative.

But it was not completely powerless. It stood as a guarantee of state rights and was determined to resist any attempt to strengthen Prussia's already excessive power within the Reich. Furthermore it was designed to hold the Reichstag in check. The chancellor, the secretaries of state, and the Prussian ministers stood before the Reichstag as representatives of the Bundesrat and were not answerable to parliament. No member of the Reichstag could be simultaneously a member of the Bundesrat, and thus could not be chancellor, secretary of state, or a Prussian minister. With Prussia's right of veto over any constitutional changes this was a formidable barrier to the growth of parliamentary government as well as a means of further strengthening Prussia's domination over the empire. Federalism thus stunted parliamentary government. Those who wanted to hold the Reichstag in check were obliged to support states' rights. The states were united in their determination to resist any attempts by the Reichstag to increase its powers, since it would mean a diminution of their own rights. This determination gave a degree of coherence to this exceedingly complex and confusing constitutional structure. It also helped reconcile the states to Prussia's unique position within the Reich.

Prussian and imperial institutions were so intimately intertwined that they could hardly be distinguished. Since the king of Prussia was also president of the Bundesrat, all bills put forward in that body were first discussed by the Prussian parliament. Bismarck was both Prussian minister president and chancellor of the Reich. When these two offices were separated under his successor, Leo von Caprivi, the system proved unworkable so that when the Bavarian Prince Hohenlohe was appointed chancellor he was simultaneously made minister president of Prussia. Bismarck as Prussian foreign minister "instructed" the Bundesrat's plenipotentiary for foreign affairs – an office held by a Bavarian appointee – but in reality was in absolute command of imperial foreign policy. The Prussian minister of war also functioned as an imperial minister. Imperial secretaries of state worked closely with the Prussian ministries and were appointed ministers without portfolio.

In these early years Prussia clearly dominated the Reich; but Prussian influence was slowly undermined by the need to make concessions to the states, by the influence of imperial secretaries of state on Prussia, by the development of a distinct federal identity, and by the need for Prussia to stand together with the states to uphold the status quo and to resist the inroads of parliamentary democracy. The dominant position of Prussia within the empire was the most important factor hindering the development of parliamentary democracy. Prussia, with its House of Peers (Herrenhaus) and a parliament elected by a three-class system, was dominated by the aristocracy, the military, and an ultra-conservative civil service.

It would be a mistake, however, to imagine that the Reich was simply Prussia writ large. A distinct national identity developed that transcended the member states. This is most clearly seen in the emergence of the kaiser as a metapolitical symbol of national unity, and in the celebration of such national triumphs as the annual "Sedan Day." At the imperial level the monarchy was constitutional, and it was often forgotten that the kaiser was also an absolutist king of Prussia, pursuing a quite different agenda. As matters of national concern became increasingly important so too did the Reichstag.

The national parliament was much more than the "fig-leaf of despotism" that the socialist leader August Bebel claimed it to be, or the powerless institution of many later historians. Although no legislation could pass without the approval of the Bundesrat – and thus in effect without that of the kaiser, the chancellor, or Prussia – no bill could become law unless it passed the Reichstag. The newly founded empire needed a vast number of new laws. Laws had to be approved by the Reichstag. The government had to ensure that this approval was forthcoming. Deals had to be negotiated and concessions granted.

The government also needed money and needed it in ever-increasing amounts. The approval of the Reichstag was required for the annual budget and for additional increases in revenue. Military expenditure, which accounted for the bulk of the national budget, was excepted. It was covered first by seven-year bills (*Septennate*) and then by five-year bills (*Quinquennate*) which virtually excluded parliamentary debates over the military budget. Similarly the bulk of federal revenue came through indirect taxation and customs duties, which were issues that seldom came up for debate. Parliament could not of its own initiative either increase or decrease taxation. Nor could the Reichstag seriously consider refusing the budget for fear of disastrous reactions from an electorate that was becoming increasingly reliant on the largesse of the state. Since the Reichstag was virtually excluded from government its role was largely negative. Riven with party strife, it could never present a determined opposition, and was further weakened by the fact that it could be dismissed at any time. Bismarck would call snap elections and turn them into Bonapartist plebiscites, thus strengthening his own position and painting the Reichstag as an unpatriotic collection of impractical prattlers, the opposition members as enemies of the state.

Yet for all this the Reichstag was still an open forum for debate in which members enjoyed parliamentary immunity. Chancellors and ministers of state could be questioned, exposed, and embarrassed, but they could not be obliged to resign. With universal and equal manhood suffrage, no parliament in the world was elected on a broader franchise. Its meetings were open to the public, the debates widely reported in the press. It was thus an essential part of the public sphere, the focus of hopes for a more open society, an important counterweight to Prussian–German autocracy.

Bismarck had forged an uneasy compromise between liberal nationalism and the authoritarian state. He was determined to fashion a functioning modern state. He knew that he could not do this without the support of bourgeois society and of informed public opinion. The ultra-conservative Prussian monarchy could not be strengthened without making concessions to the modern world. This he did by creating something radically new: a German nation-state. The Reichstag was an integral part of this new structure, with Bismarck imagining that it would be a grateful, pliable, and conservative institution. This proved to be a serious miscalculation. With the dramatic changes in the social structure of Germany and the consequent rise of democratic socialism, the number of "enemies of the state" within the Reichstag grew rapidly, soon to become the largest faction. The consequent marginalization and denigration of the Reichstag was to have disastrous consequences for the development of democracy in Germany.

The Reich had no government as such. The chancellor held the only federal executive office. The Reich chancellery in the Wilhelmstraße, with its ever-expanding staff, was thus the center of power. Until 1876 this office was run by Rudolf Delbrück, whom Bismarck made responsible for all economic and financial questions. Legislation was drafted in the chancellery, thus gradually eclipsing the Bundesrat in this regard. Federal offices were needed to deal with the increasing amount of federal legislation and to administer such matters of federal concern as the post, railways, the treasury, and the administration of justice. A federal administration for Alsace and Lorraine was established, along with a health office, a statistical bureau, and a host of other institutions, the most important of which was the High Court (Reichsgericht). It took years to build up a complex federal administration with extensive executive powers that was to overshadow the states and render the Bundesrat virtually powerless.

There was still no imperial government, no cabinet, and no ministries. The secretaries of state were appointed by the kaiser and were the chancellor's subordinates. Only the chancellor was "responsible" in that he was answerable to the Reichstag, although parliament could only censor him, not secure his dismissal. Bismarck dominated the secretaries of state and made sure that they did not confer with the kaiser without his permission. His successors were more lax, preferring a collegial system which allowed the secretaries of state a considerable degree of independence. As a result something resembling a federal government developed. This in turn created new frictions between the Reich and Prussia and the dialectical process continued whereby the Reich became more Prussian, Prussia more federal.

Bonapartism

It was not long before Bismarck's critics, both liberal and conservative, began to speak of the chancellor as a dictator, a tyrant, an autocrat, or a usurper until they settled on the powerfully descriptive neologism *Kanzlerdiktatur*. They did not mean thereby that the chancellor was a dictator in the precise sense of the term, for they could read the constitution and knew that there were strict limitations on his power. It was used in the general sense that Bismarck misused the power allotted to him, interpreting the constitution as he saw fit. It was therefore little more than an imprecise term of abuse that does precious little to explain the exact nature of Bismarck's rule. Constitutional lawyers hastened to his defense, insisting that Germany was a constitutional monarchy to which the chancellor was subservient. Although this might have been true on paper, it does not correspond with reality.

The concept of "Bonapartism" provides a useful explanatory model between the extremes of dictatorship and constitutional monarchy. It was first coined by Karl Marx in his brilliant analysis of Napoleon III's rule in his pamphlet of 1852 entitled *The Eighteenth Brumaire of Louis Bonaparte*. He argued that Bonapartism was a form of government characteristic of an industrial society in a relatively early stage of development. France had gone through a bourgeois revolution in 1789 that had removed the remaining obstacles to the development of industrial capitalism, but it faced an increasing threat from the radical left, manifest in the revolutions of 1830 and 1848. Marx saw this as the origins of the clash between bourgeoisie and proletariat, the outcome of which he believed would be a communist society. The bourgeoisie, frightened by the increasing threat from below, looked for protection and imagined that they had found it in a dictatorship. Napoleon III skillfully exploited this unstable situation. Legitimized by universal manhood suffrage, he freed the executive from all traditional restraints. The result was a kind of plebiscitary dictatorship, acclaimed by the bulk of the peasantry, an anxious petite bourgeoisie and an uneasy bourgeoisie, while the army stood by loyally.

The system offered both carrots and sticks. The press was muzzled, the law rigorously enforced, working-class political organizations suppressed, the opposition silenced. But the working class was given generous welfare provisions, the middle classes were subsidized, and assistance was given to cooperatives. This paternalistic system was both progressive and repressive, in some sense almost revolutionary, thus quite distinct from traditional conservatism. Bonapartism exploited nationalism, using it to paper over domestic conflicts by pursuing an adventurous foreign policy. The regime was further legitimized by military victories and overseas expansion in a political strategy later to be termed "social imperialism." It was, however, an inherently unstable system. Military defeat would cause it to collapse. It could only last as long as the bourgeoisie lacked the confidence to take charge and the working class could be excluded from a share in political power.

At first sight it would seem that the situation in Germany was analogous that in France. It was a rapidly industrializing country that was traumatized by memories of revolution in 1848. The bourgeoisie was all too conscious of the threat from the working class. The peasantry was supportive, the army steadfast. Bismarck's initially liberal economic policy favored the bourgeoisie, but they were largely excluded from political power. His hazardous foreign policy resulted in three successful wars. The resulting "Little German" empire reconciled all but a handful of arch-conservative grandees to his rule. He also combined progressive with repressive policies. He granted universal manhood suffrage, laid the foundations of the welfare state, and used innovative methods to stimulate the economy. But he came down hard on his opponents: the Social Democrats were suppressed by the anti-socialist laws and political Catholicism was attacked in the *Kulturkampf*. He fanned national resentments against England, France, and Russia, while cynically dabbling in colonialism for domestic political reasons. Yet, for all these similarities with the France of Napoleon III, the analogy does not quite fit.

First and foremost, the German uprisings in 1848 were in no sense on the same scale of importance as the French Revolution. Germany in 1850 did not have the balance between the classes that existed in France. Tensions between the classes were not nearly as acute as they were in France. Most important of all, Bismarck's rule was not designed to protect the bourgeoisie from a threatening working class, but rather to strengthen the king's power in Prussia and Prussian influence in Germany, thereby strengthening the old regime. His mass support did not come from a royalist peasantry – a class that was far less numerous in Germany. The bourgeoisie was divided between those who supported Bismarck and those in opposition to him, the various alliances and groupings changing throughout the course of his chancellorship. Nevertheless, Bismarck learnt from Napoleon III that political power could be reinforced by a plebiscitary dimension and that conservative fears of universal manhood suffrage were unfounded. Bismarck was certainly not a usurper or mountebank dictator like Napoleon III. He was brought to office by an ultra-conservative clique, appointed by a king, and dismissed by an emperor. Although he accumulated vast power, ultimately he relied on the approval and sanction of the king-emperor. He fell from office once he had lost this support.

The regimes of Napoleon III and Bismarck were not identical, nor could they be. France and Germany were at different stages of development, had undergone diverse historical experiences, and had distinct political cultures. The two men were poles apart in character, ability, and intellect. There is altogether too little room within a theory such as Bonapartism for individual agency. A personality as powerful as Bismarck refuses to disappear behind structural schemata. But nonetheless there is a manifest affinity between the two regimes, as Bismarck himself readily admitted. The Bonapartist model therefore, although not fitting exactly, helps when modified to explain some of the peculiarities of Bismarck's rule.

The Military and Militarism

The military had always played a key role in Prussia, and in a Reich forged by blood and iron it was the central institution. The German Reich was a military state, German society permeated by the military. "Human beings," Bismarck said "begin at the rank of lieutenant." The Prussian army was by far the largest of the four armies, and although the three other "contingents" owed allegiance to the kings of Bavaria, Württemberg, and Saxony respectively, they all came under the kaiser's command in time of war. Only the Bavarian army remained independent in peacetime. The three contingents followed the Prussian lead in organization, instruction, and weaponry. The military budget and questions such as those of the size of the army and length of service were settled at the federal level. The army was thus Prussian rather than German, the Prussian minister of war, as chairman of the Bundesrat's Military Commission, served as a de facto federal minister. The military thus played an essential role in strengthening Prussia's domination over the Reich.

The military was outside the constitution, beyond parliamentary control, answerable only to the Prussian king and kaiser with his absolute power of command (*Kommandogewalt*). It was every bit as concerned with the enemy within as it was with its enemies beyond the borders of the Reich. It was ready to crush a revolution, break a strike, and disperse a demonstration, and even to instigate a putsch. It was not bound to consult the civil authorities before acting.

All matters pertaining to personnel were dealt with by the Military Cabinet, which worked closely with the kaiser. William II was to surround himself with a number of military cronies who formed an informal *maison militaire* of considerable power and influence that served further to strengthen his power of command. Mere civilians, who were deemed to have no understanding of military arcana, had no place within these circles.

The Prussian minister of war had responsibility for the budget, administration, and military justice. Inevitably there was enduring friction between the ministry and the military cabinet. Since the latter was a direct expression of the kaiser's power of command, the minister answerable to the Reichstag, a number of important responsibilities were shifted from the ministry to the military cabinet. At the same time the spiraling cost of the military, particularly after 1898 when Germany began to build a high seas fleet, meant that the Reichstag had a far greater say in military affairs. It held the purse strings and could determine how the funds were allocated. The war minister could no longer afford to hide behind the sacrosanct power of command and had to submit to rigorous questioning by parliamentarians. This in turn alienated the war minister from the kaiser and his entourage, who were alarmed by the prospect of the army becoming subordinated to parliament. Any concession to the Reichstag was taken as a sign of weakness, so that both the war minister and the chancellor were caught between the need to appease the monarch's obsession with his power of command and the necessity for a degree of cooperation with the Reichstag. The slightest hint of a compromise with parliament caused an immediate hardening of the military front, so that by 1914 the Reichstag was only able to make very modest gains. The army remained arrogantly aloof, intensely hostile to parliament, a state within the state.

Although the kaiser, with his power of command, had absolute control over the military, it was hopelessly divided and lacking in any sense of direction. The war ministry, the general staff, the Military Cabinet, and the *maison militaire* incessantly wrangled over areas of competence. This was compounded by inter-service rivalry with the navy, which in turn was riven with internal strife between different offices. There was no coherent military planning, no consistency in armaments procurement, no serious preparation for a war which most people in responsible positions felt was both inevitable and desirable.

Nowhere was this more blatantly obvious that in the general staff, whose carmine-striped demigods planned and plotted in splendid isolation and consequently to disastrous effect. The war was hardly over before the general staff began planning for a preventive war, first against France, then also against Russia. As long as Bismarck was chancellor the preventive war enthusiasts in the general staff were held in check. He found political solutions to the crises of 1874/5 and 1886/7 when the general staff was raring to go. Moltke's successor, Count Alfred von Waldersee, argued in favor of a war against Russia, combined with a coup d'état against the Social Democrats, during his tenure from 1887 to 1891. He too was frustrated, first by Bismarck then by Caprivi.

Bismarck fought long and hard to keep the military under political control. His successors had to deal with William II, a saber-rattling poseur who lacked the strength of character to stand up to an increasingly influential military. The kaiser bypassed the foreign office and relied on the reports from the military and naval attachés, who painted a grim picture of the bellicose intentions of Germany's neighbors. The chancellor and the civilians were never consulted when the general staff drew up its war plans, and were excluded from the "War Council" of 1912.

Waldersee's successor, Count Alfred von Schlieffen, turned Clausewitz on his head by arguing that war was far too serious a business for politicians to have any say in its conduct. The eponymous plan on which he worked throughout his term of office envisaged an invasion of France through neutral Belgium and Holland. The plan was shown in its various versions to three chancellors – Hohenlohe, Bülow, and Bethmann Hollweg – but none of these men saw fit to examine its fateful political consequences. They felt it was inappropriate for mere civilians to question the expertise of a man who was widely regarded as a strategist of genius, a worthy successor to the great Moltke. Apart from a vague plan for an offensive in the east, the *Ostaufmarschplan*, which was never seriously considered and was dropped entirely in 1913, the German army had only one war plan: an attack on France that was almost bound to involve Britain, because of the invasion of neutral Belgium, compounded by Germany's naval ambitions. The proposal to invade neutral Holland was later dropped by Schlieffen's successor, the younger Moltke.

It was not only the civilians who were excluded from discussions about the details of military planning. Germany's ally Austria-Hungary was kept completely in the dark. It was only in 1909 during the Bosnian crisis that hints were dropped that they were planning an offensive in the west. At the same time Moltke promised his Austrian counterpart, Conrad von Hötzendorf, that Germany would stand by Austria under any circumstances should it become involved in a war in the Balkans. The chief of the general staff was here clearly exceeding his remit, and was making a political commitment of incalculable consequence. The defensive Dual Alliance of 1879 was thus converted into a blank check for Austria to attack Serbia, even at the risk of Russian intervention, at which point Germany would join in by attacking France through Belgium. Britain would then probably be involved and Europe plunged into a terrible war the length and outcome of which many experts were hesitant to predict.

The army never consulted the navy, which in turn cooked up a series of harebrained plans which a number of naval strategists felt were bound to fail. Neither branch of the military bothered to contemplate the consequence of failing to break the British blockade. A number of far-sighted soldiers thought that the Schlieffen Plan was at best a highly risky gamble. The military Cassandras who warned that the war was likely to be very lengthy were ignored. No preparations were made for such an eventuality.

The military was determined to remain outside the constitution by insisting that the power of command was sacrosanct. It separated itself from civilians by the exclusivity of its officer corps, its code of honor, and its separate code of law. This was to lead to a series of clashes with the civilians: over the reform of military law, over the size and social composition of the army, and over its relations with the civil authorities. Every such confrontation put the role of the military in question, thereby whittling away at its exclusive rights. As the foundations of the military monarchy were gradually undermined the fronts began to harden and the temptation to risk a war in the hope of overcoming these tensions became ever harder to resist.

In the 1860s two-thirds of the Prussian officer corps was aristocratic. In the general staff and the smarter regiments the proportion was far higher. As the army expanded, the percentage of aristocrats naturally declined, thus precipitating a lengthy debate as to whether further expansion would change the whole character of the army, water it down, and render it unreliable in the event of domestic unrest and revolution. Was "character" more important than "brains"? Could an army with a high percentage of liberal bourgeois officers and Social Democratic proletarian other ranks maintain law and order at home and pull off another Sedan? The Schlieffen Plan called for a mass army and the plan had no chance of success without one; but the larger the army the greater the importance of the Reichstag, thereby blurring the sharp division between civil and military. General Keim's Army League, with its raucous populist clamor for substantial army increases, thus was viewed with horror by the kaiser's military entourage. That the Navy League, Admiral Tirpitz's child that took on a willful life of its own, had a similar plebiscitary moment was lost on the kaiser, with his obsession with battleships.

The distinction between aristocratic and bourgeois officers has often been exaggerated, and the distinction between technically minded modernizing bourgeois and conservative traditionalist aristocrat is inadmissible. The aristocracy, which still made up more than half the officers of the rank of colonel and above in the Prussian army in 1913, set the tone. Officers were selected not by competitive examination, but by regimental commanders. They picked men of like mind and background. Only the sons of "respectable" bourgeois with sound views were selected. Pay was so wretched that a lieutenant in the more highly regarded regiments needed a private income. Jews were excluded. As in the British army the tradesman's entrance was tightly shut. Bourgeois officers aped the ways of their aristocratic brothers-in-arms and subscribed to a common code of honor, resolutely refusing to be outdone in overbearing arrogance and contempt for mere civilians with their vulgar materialism. The appalling young subalterns who were so brilliantly and savagely caricatured in the satirical magazine *Simplizissimus* were unfortunately all too common. The naval officer corps was slightly less exclusive, but here too the aristocracy was over-represented. For all the increasing importance of technical skills and training, both officer corps remained a caste rather than a profession. But it was a caste that was widely admired and emulated in a process of "double militarism" whereby civilian society panegyrized military virtues, relished the prospect of war, enthusiastically supported the Army and Navy Leagues and forced its children into miniature military uniforms. The special status of the military and its widespread acceptance was a serious impediment to the modernization of the political system and the development of civil society.

Nationalism

Bismarck continually insisted that Germany was satiated and that war had to be avoided at all costs. It was only after his fall from power in 1890 that Germany was seized by the deadly hurrah-patriotism of the imperialist age, when many influential figures put forward the preposterous argument, later to be parroted by Adolf Hitler, that the country would either become a world power or face extinction. In 1871 there was a wave of patriotic bombast, but there was no call for Germany's frontiers to coincide with linguistic borders as Hoffmann von Fallersleben's "Deutschlandlied" of 1841 had demanded. Greater Germany was a dead letter. Only a few isolated intellectuals, such as the orientalist, cultural philosopher, and anti-Semite Paul de Lagarde, worried about the fate of Germans living beyond the borders of the new Reich. Irredentist ideas first came to the fore with the formation of the Pan-German League (Alldeutscher Verein) in 1891, but even they did not think in terms of an *Anschluss* with Austria.

German nationalism underwent a dramatic change in 1871. Where nationalism had once been a progressive force aimed at sweeping away the old regime and furthering the cause of constitutional liberties, it was now conservative, bent on maintaining the status quo in a militarized Prussian Germany. The nation was now identified with the state, any criticism of which was denounced as unpatriotic. Political parties that demanded reform were thus condemned as enemies of the Reich. The Social Democrats were denounced as "fellows without a fatherland" and parliamentary democracy seen as un-German.

Bismarck had appealed to liberal nationalists in his bid to create a united Germany. The Reichstag was their reward, and the Reichstag was an essential part of the nation. Many conservatives, with their distrust of the newfangled and their misgivings about Bismarck's politics, took a great deal of time to reconcile themselves to this new nationalism, in part because the heritage of the democratic nationalism of an earlier age was never completely extirpated. A Reichstag elected by universal manhood suffrage remained its lasting monument. It stood out like a sore thumb, a provocation to the new breed of nationalists. Its supporters – Social Democrats, the Catholic Center Party, and some of the Independents – were marginalized and condemned as unpatriotic. Nevertheless, for most Germans the Reichstag, and not the kaiser, was the focus of national attention, the only truly representative body of the nation with all it shortcomings, deficiencies, and divisions.

There were considerable problems involved in finding suitable occasions for national holidays. January 18, the day on which William was proclaimed emperor, only found resonance in Prussia. The "Sedantag" celebrating the victory over France soon degenerated into an unpleasant demonstration of anti-French and anti-Catholic prejudices and was consequently boycotted by Catholics. The kaiser's birthday soon became a popular excuse for national jollification. There was no official national anthem. The "Wacht am Rhein" and "Heil dir im Siegerkranz" (sung to the same tune as "God Save the King"), both with martial and anti-French overtones, were unofficial anthems. The "Deutschlandlied," set to Haydn's tune from the "Kaiser" quartet, became increasingly popular in the 1890s, by which time "Deutschland über Alles" had taken on a singularly unpleasant imperialist and irredentist flavor.

There were similar problems with a flag. The revolutionary red, gold, and black tricolor of 1848 was unacceptable. The red from this flag was added to the black and white of Prussia and used as a flag for the merchant marine. It was then adopted by Tirpitz's navy and as such became a symbol of Germany's imperial might. Germany did not have either an officially recognized national anthem or a flag until the Weimar Republic, by which time neither was treated with much respect or affection.

Modern nationalism is by its very nature exclusive. Herder's admonition to rejoice in the unique features of a culture as a contribution to humanity's rich multiplicity had long since been ignored; the cultural relativism of the postmodern was still in the distant future. The French were now seen as the "hereditary enemy," inferior but potentially dangerous. What were seen as the indolent, drunken, uncultured, and Catholic Poles could only be tolerated as helots. Their co-religionists in the Reich were condemned as ultramontane and thus un-German. Social Democrats similarly had no fatherland. Jews, as outsiders, were increasingly seen as an insidious threat to this divided, threatened, and incomplete nation. The rest of the world could only offer sordidly materialistic "civilization" and cold "intellect," whereas the Germans had the boundless riches of "culture" and the deep insights of the "soul." An open, pluralistic civil society had little chance of emerging when raucous imperialism became a component part of a project of national integration and homogeneity in which state and society were to become one.

The German Jewish Community

There were just over half a million Jews living in Germany in 1871. The Jewish community was now by and large urban, bourgeois, and prosperous. By 1910 their number had grown to just over 600,000, a much slower rate of population growth than that of the community at large. Jews now formed less than 1 percent of the total population. This was due to two principal factors. Like other well-situated and highly educated middle-class people they limited their families. Secondly, marriages with non-Jews were frequent. In about 75 percent of such cases the children were not brought up in the Jewish faith. Precious few Jews, other than the offspring of mixed marriages, were baptized. Those that took this step almost invariably joined the Evangelical Church.

The diminution of the Jewish community caused by a low birth rate and mixed marriages was partially offset by the arrival of large numbers of poor Orthodox Jews from Russian Poland and Galicia. These *Ostjuden* mostly had large families and followed the general pattern of emigration from the country to the smaller towns, thence to the cities. Thus the Jewish population of Greater Berlin grew from just under 40,000 in 1871 to over 140,000 by 1910. Other cities, such as Frankfurt, Cologne, Munich, and Breslau, witnessed similar increases.

There were still some poverty-stricken Jewish tinkers and craftsmen, most of whom were recent immigrants from the east, but a large proportion of Jews were involved in trade and banking. About 60 percent were classified as upper-middle-class, and a further 25 percent were middle-class. Of the hundred richest men in Prussia in 1910, twenty-nine were Jewish. In 1908 ten of the eleven greatest fortunes in Berlin were Jewish. Only a small proportion of Jews were rich, but there was a disproportionate number of Jews among the super-rich.

Jews were also prominent in the professions and in education. From 1886 to 1914 about 8 percent of students in Prussian universities were Jewish. In Berlin they constituted up to 25 percent of the pupils in the exclusive and highly competitive grammar schools (*Gymnasien*). Jewish girls won an even higher percentage of places in such schools and made up 14 percent of female university students by 1911. In 1907, 6 percent of doctors, 15 percent of lawyers, and 8 percent of journalists were Jewish. Three years later at Berlin University Jews made up 12 percent of university instructors (*Privatdozenten*), 8.8 percent of assistant professors (*Extraordinarien*), and 2.5 percent of professors (*Ordinarien*). About half were in the medical faculty. Clearly it was exceedingly difficult for Jews to climb the promotional ladder, but they were still "over-represented" at the top by 150 percent.

In spite of the removal of all legal discrimination against Jews, many barriers to their social advancement remained. With the exception of Bavaria they were excluded from the officer corps of the army, which was an essential precondition of social acceptance. Far fewer Jews were admitted into the civil service than had the necessary qualifications and none reached the top positions. The same was true of the teaching profession. Precious few were admitted into the foreign office, but the judiciary proved to be an exception. Four percent of the judges in Prussia were Jewish, and there were two Jews on the imperial High Court (Reichsgericht). Its president was a baptized Jew.

Jews were excluded from most clubs and associations, including university fraternities. Even rich and influential men like Bismarck's friend and banker Gerson Bleichröder, unquestionably a member of the elite, were not universally welcome. The police chief of Lübeck argued that the nouveau riche provoked socialism so that there was little to choose between Bleichröder and Bebel. Liberals waited for Jews to assimilate, to rid themselves of their minority consciousness, to shed their "otherness," but there were too many closed doors for this to be possible.

The vast majority of Jews embraced German culture wholeheartedly. They dressed like Germans, ate the same food, and embraced the ideals of the *Bildungsbürgertum*. Reform Jews were relaxed in their Sabbath observances, broke dietary laws, brought organs into their synagogues, and gave richly bound copies of Goethe and Schiller as bar mitzvah presents. Their bible was Leo Baeck's *The Nature of Judaism*, that adumbrated the principles of a tolerant, open, and modern approach to this ancient faith. Heine remarked that "Jews are like the people among whom they live, only more so." This was certainly true of Germany, where Jews saw themselves as Germans rather than Prussians, Bavarians, or Saxons; but the fervent patriotism of German Jews was unrequited.

The assimilated Reform Jewish bourgeois family was far more modern in its attitudes than its Gentile counterpart, and was frequently criticized on this account. There were fewer children, it was less authoritarian and patriarchal, women enjoyed far greater freedom, and it championed culture and *Bildung*.

Assimilation was never complete because Jews were never fully accepted as equals. They remained outsiders, and as such had a unique perspective on a society and culture that in spite of everything they loved and respected. It is thus hardly surprising that Jews played a prominent role as critics and satirists, as journalists, and in the new disciplines of sociology and psychology. The desire to assimilate and the lack of acceptance resulted in an unfortunate dichotomy between self-satisfied arrogance and self-hatred in the German Jewish psyche. Proud of their exceptional achievements, they were convinced of their superiority; but attributing their failure to fully assimilate to their Jewishness, they overcompensated by an exaggerated attachment to things German. The pride and touchiness of the rejected was often combined with a self-induced antipathy, resulting from a feeling of frustration and inadequacy.

The vast majority of German Jews wanted to be fully accepted as Germans while at the same time remaining true to their faith. The Central Association of German Citizens of Jewish Belief (Centralverein deutscher Staatsbürger jüdischen Glaubens), founded in 1893, fought against all forms of discrimination and anti-Semitism and stood, as the name of the organization made clear, for the reconciliation of German Jews and Gentiles within the Reich. The result of this desire to belong while preserving a high degree of specificity was a negative symbiosis, the outcome of which depended on the attitude of the wider community. What for some Jews was assimilation for others was acculturation. The more the Jewish community wrestled with the problem of its identity the greater became the distance from those who had no such difficulties. Very few were attracted to Zionism, which both assimilated and Orthodox Jews saw as an absurd youthful revolt. By 1914 the German Zionist Association had only 10,000 members, most of whom were German nationalists who had no desire to emigrate. For them Zionism was a promising solution to the problem of the *Ostjuden* whose presence in Germany they found embarrassing. Youthful Zionists, however, rejected the stuffy philistine atmosphere of imperial Germany and dreamt of building a new and freer society in Palestine.

Throughout the first part of the nineteenth century the lot of Jews in Germany had improved greatly. Anti-Semitism was still widespread, but it was relatively muted and was far from intellectually respectable. In the 1870s a new and even more pernicious form of pseudo-scientific and racial anti-Semitism developed. Earlier anti-Semitism was rooted in the traditional animosities between Christians and Jews, in criticism of religious orthodoxy with its emphasis on living in accordance with a complex set of immutable laws and injunctions, or in the discomfort and even hatred resulting from a confrontation with otherness. Religious bigotry and fanaticism were on the wane, German Jews were emancipated and to a considerable degree assimilated, so that these older prejudices lost their potency. The new anti-Semitism was based on the belief that the Jewish people posed a biological threat to other races.

The problem lies with the anti-Semites and not with the Jews. Anti-Semites projected their fears, anxieties, and insecurities onto the constructed figure of "the Jew." The Jewish community was highly successful and prosperous, and thus the object of envy. It was also in many respects modern and thus representative of all the problems of the modern age. It was a distinct and remote community, thus alien and threatening. Germany in the 1870s experienced in an acute form the crisis of the modern. Society was in a state of social and economic upheaval, values were changing rapidly, as a brief period of boom was followed by a lengthy depression. Many regretted the passing of a simpler, less hectic age. In such circumstances "the Jew" was a convenient scapegoat. With a widespread disillusionment with the individualism, rationalism, and liberalism of industrial society, which left so many disillusioned, frustrated, and resentful people struggling behind, anti-Semitism found widespread support.

But it was not merely the illiberal, irrational, and resentful wannabes who fanned the flames of anti-Semitism. There was an intolerant and totalitarian moment within liberalism itself that allowed no space for those that did not subscribe to the liberal, Protestant, and national code. There was precious little room here for pluralism and openness. The other, whether Catholic, socialist, Pole, or Jew, was excluded.

The new, virulent, and secular anti-Semitism became widespread when the speculative bubble that began in 1871 burst three years later. The *Gartenlaube* (*The Arbor*), a popular journal aimed at the petite bourgeoisie, published a series of articles blaming the stock exchange crash on Jewish speculators. But at the same time the remarkably courageous and liberal popular novelist Eugenie Marlitt drew sensitive and affectionate portraits of Jews in stories published in the same magazine. Many a ribald comment was made based on the fact that the Berlin stock exchange was on the Jerusalemer Straße. The conservative *Kreuzzeitung* ascribed the responsibility for the crash to an unsavory alliance of Jews, Bismarck, and liberals. Such sentiments were echoed in the gutter press and in hundreds of pseudo-scientific works. The most notable of the latter was Eugen Dühring's *The Jewish Question as a Racial, Moral and Cultural Problem*, published in 1881. The author was something of an academic star, best known to posterity because of Engels' robust attack on his half-baked socialist ideas. He argued that since Jewish identity was racially determined assimilation was impossible. No amount of baptismal water could wash away this biological stigma. The only answer to the Jewish question was expulsion.

Anti-Semitism was also part of the new nationalist creed and was expounded in intoxicating prose by the historian Heinrich von Treitschke in the pages of the *Preußische Jahrbücher*, a quality journal of which he was an editor. He demanded that Jews should become assimilated to the point that to all intents and purposes they ceased to be Jews. He distanced himself from the rabble-rousing popular anti-Semitism of the day, but in doing so made his brand of anti-Semitism acceptable in "respectable" society. He admired the Jewish community for its industriousness, its culture, and its sense of tradition, but he rejected what he felt was its increasing materialism, vulgarity, and scrambling ambition. He expressed his frustration in the poisonous phrase "The Jews are our misfortune," which was to become the motto of Julius Streicher's obscene publication *Der Stürmer*. Treitschke would have been appalled to find himself in the unsavory company of the Nazis' chief Jew-baiter, but he cannot be absolved from responsibility.

The anti-modernist, anti-capitalist, chauvinistic anti-Semitism of these new "racial" anti-Semites was often combined with the older forms of religious anti-Semitism to make a particularly heady brew. Such was the case with the Christian Social (Workers') Party

PLATE 12   The Berlin Stock Exchange. This 1889 drawing by E. Thiel was published in *Illustrierte Zeitung*, a widely circulated periodical; many of the traders have stereotypical Semitic features

formed by the Protestant court preacher Adolf Stoecker in 1878. He was an electrifying demagogue who hoped to woo the working class away from the Social Democrats with a mixture of rugged Protestantism and social reform. The present malaise was blamed on Jewish speculative capitalism. Stoecker also denounced Social Democracy as a Jewish movement, and henceforth anti-Semitism became a twin-pronged attack on socialism and capitalism, both seen as part of a worldwide Jewish conspiracy.

Stoecker was closely associated with William II, whose notions of becoming a "social kaiser" owed much to his ideas. But there were many misgivings at court about Stoecker the demagogue who courted the racial anti-Semitic riff-raff. As the economy pulled out of a recession, his brand of radical anti-Semitism began to lose its appeal, and rumors that he kept a Jewish mistress damaged his reputation both as a principled anti-Semite and as a man of God. Other smaller anti-Semitic parties also withered on the vine. So ended the first round of political anti-Semitism, and the Jewish community breathed a sigh of relief.

Anti-Semitism was no longer a major issue in election campaigns but it had not disappeared. It was no longer a pressing concern for the political parties, but it was deeply ingrained in a number of the associations that played such an important role in Wilhelmine Germany. The General German Craftsmen's Association (Allgemeine Deutsche Handwerkerbund), founded in 1882, represented the interests of a large group that was becoming increasingly marginalized by the victory march of industrial capitalism. This was a group that had sided with the reactionaries in 1848 for fear that the liberal market economy would result in these proud independent producers being reduced to the ranks of the proletariat. Now they seized upon the idea that industrial capitalism was "Jewish." They lent their support to Stoecker's Christian Social Party, and after its demise they trumpeted their anti-Semitism in the pages of their newspapers and at their national conventions.

The Farmers' League (Bund der Landwirte) was the largest and most influential of these associations which, from its inception in 1893, adopted a harshly anti-Semitic tone. Jews were expressly excluded from membership. Capitalism, liberalism, socialism, interest payments, and cattle-dealing were all denounced as "Jewish." Dairy farmers coined the popular phrase "Jew tallow" for margarine. Anti-Semitism was deliberately used to whip up popular support for the League and for the Conservative Party which was its organized political wing.

Relations between the League and the Conservatives were often strained. The party reluctantly realized the need to win electoral support as the Reichstag grew in importance, but it had severe reservations about the League's demagogic tactics. The League also threw its support behind anti-Semitic candidates who ran against conservatives, and the marriage of convenience between the League and party was never particularly harmonious.

Anti-Semitism was widespread in a number of other national associations and student fraternities but it was still not considered quite respectable to be openly anti-Semitic. Fontane's Dubslav von Stechlin, the hero of his masterly novel *Der Stechlin*, felt that his honest and trustworthy Jewish moneylender has been corrupted by the vulgar materialism of the times and had grown a "cloven hoof." The sympathetic pastor Lorenzen expresses a nuanced version of Stoecker's views, with which the author clearly identifies. In Fontane's *Effi Briest* Instetten's enthusiasm for Wagner's music is said to have been due to the maestro's position on the Jewish question coupled with his own nervous condition. Fontane as theater critic had little patience for Lessing's plea for tolerance towards Jews in *Nathan the Wise*. It would be going too far to charge Fontane, the mildest and most open-minded of men, with anti-Semitism. He deplored the vulgarity and materialism of the new Germany in such novels as *Frau Jenny Treibel*, and hankered after the good old days when life was simpler, people knew their station, and God was in his heaven. He, like his character Wüllersdorff in *Effi Briest*, resigned himself to an acceptance of the world as it was, for all the absurd conventions and customs to which society paid homage. Fontane was a liberal, certainly no reactionary, deeply suspicious of all ideologies, but the very fact that such an admirable person could even toy with the anti-Semitic camp is an indication of the insidious undertow of anti-Semitism in the Germany of his day. Not all craftsmen, shopkeepers and shop assistants, farmers, and students were anti-Semites; in fact relatively few were in any meaningful sense of the term. The Social Democratic leader August Bebel, who was himself a typical craftsman, spoke for many when he denounced anti-Semitism as the socialism of fools. France, Russia, and Austria-Hungary far outbid Germany as centers of anti-Semitism, and the sneaky, underhand English brand of anti-Semitism was probably even more pernicious. But anti-Semitism was on the political agenda, was to take root, and was to have an unimaginably horrific outcome. For this reason it needs to be discussed in detail.

Germany did indeed produce more than its fair share of hair-raising anti-Semitic theories. They combined the culturally pessimistic notions of the degeneration of civilization to a level of brutish mediocrity, the result of a racial struggle in which the creative Aryan Germans were undermined and enfeebled by parasitic Jews, with highly compatible social Darwinist notions. Anti-Semites embraced race theorists; the result was a devil's brew that Max Weber was to describe as "zoological nationalism." A people and the nation were formed not as the result of a historical process, as even an anti-Semite like Treitschke argued, but by blood. Hence all traces of Jewish and other non-German elements must be extirpated, Christianity must be rid of all traces of Judaism, the Germans must become more German, and racial purity must be restored. The Jew represented everything that was alien to the *Volk*, and un-German. Good and creative Germans were locked in battle with evil and parasitic Jews. This was the basic idea behind the works of such writers as Julius Langbehn and Paul Lagarde. Its most detailed expression was in the best-selling *The Foundations of the Nineteenth Century* by Houston Stewart Chamberlain, an Englishman turned more German than the Germans, son-in-law of another prominent anti-Semite: Richard Wagner.

Traditional anti-Semitism among Catholics was reinforced by the widespread belief that the new German empire, with which they had yet to become reconciled, was the work of liberals and Jews. This prejudice was reinforced with Bismarck's persecution of the Catholic Church in the *Kulturkampf* in which the Jews were also felt to have had a hand. It is greatly to the credit of Ludwig Windthorst and the leadership of the Center Party that they convinced their followers that as a persecuted minority they should respect the rights of other minorities. As a result the Center Party soon earned the anathema of the anti-Semites.

Whereas German Catholics thus turned their backs on political anti-Semitism, conservatives instrumentalized it by means of the Farmers' League in order to win mass support. In doing so they let the genie out of the bottle. Conservative anti-Semitism, based on a snobbish attachment to rural values and Protestantism, a dislike of industrial society, socialism, modernism, and intellectuals, never sat well with rabble-rousing popular anti-Semitism. But by tolerating it and using it they nurtured a plant that was to produce poisonous fruit.

Liberals, who were ideologically opposed to anti-Semitism, founded the Association for Defense Against Anti-Semitism (Verein zur Abwehr des Antisemitismus) in 1891. On the other hand, liberals felt no compunction in making electoral pacts with anti-Semites in order to block the election of Social Democrats. Of all the parties these last were the most principled opponents of anti-Semitism. Decried as the Jewish and un-German "Red International" they had little choice in the matter; but there were elements of anti-Semitism even among socialists. As anti-capitalists they could not always desist from joining in the chorus denouncing the "Yellow International," and even Karl Marx could not overcome the temptation to make snobbish anti-Semitic jibes remarkably similar in tone to those of Treitschke.

By the 1890s the German Jewish community had grounds for optimism: political anti-Semitism was on the wane; there were only isolated instances of violence against Jews. Their rights were guaranteed by the law, upheld by the government, and supported by most political parties. They had achieved positions of great distinction in all walks of life. There was still widespread discrimination and prejudice, but there was no other country where they had done so well. They looked confidently towards the future when the last remainders of the atavistic bigotry that had plagued them for millennia would fade away and there would be no Jewish question, no Jewish problem. German Jews were proud and even grateful to be German. They went enthusiastically to war in August 1914 and fought valiantly for kaiser and Fatherland. Then things began to go sour. Denunciations of Jewish war profiteers and skrimshankers were combined with attacks on Jewish doves and pacifists. Jews were seen as a particularly sinister section of the "enemy within," bearing heavy responsibility for the "stab in the back" of 1918. The hopes of the pre-war years were dashed, the future uncertain.

CHAPTER SEVEN
BISMARCK'S GERMANY

CHAPTER CONTENTS

A History of Modern Germany: 1800 to the Present, Second Edition. Martin Kitchen.
© 2012 Martin Kitchen. Published 2012 by Blackwell Publishing Ltd.

The construction of the German empire was brought about by complex series of often contradictory alliances. Liberals were wholeheartedly behind Bismarck's efforts to modernize the economy by removing all remaining barriers to the freedom of trade and commerce, to establish a uniform code of law, and to eliminate the last vestiges of feudalism from the administration. The Center Party stood for states' rights and opposed all efforts to strengthen the federal government. Liberals in turn were violently anti-Catholic and denounced the ultramontane church as hostile the national interest, a foreign body, a nest of superstition and backwardness. Many conservatives were strongly opposed to Bismarck's enthusiasm for a capitalist market economy, particularly in the form personified by his Jewish friend and banker Gerson Bleichröder, who became the subject of vicious attacks in the conservative *Kreuzzeitung*. They vigorously resisted his efforts to reform the administration, particularly at the local level. They had serious reservations about his attack on the Catholic Church, for in their Protestant eyes even Catholicism was preferable to godlessness. Above all they were appalled that a man whom they had thought was one of their own should be allied with the liberals.

Bismarck's closest associates in the early and critical years were liberals. Prominent among them were Rudolph von Delbrück, the head of his chancellery, known as the "chief of general staff of the free traders," the banker Otto von Camphausen as Prussian finance minister, and the fanatically anti-Catholic Adalbert Falk, the Prussian minister of education. His alliance with the liberals was sealed in the common attack on the Catholic Church known as the "Battle of Cultures" (*Kulturkampf*). The Center Party, the Catholic Church's political wing, resisted all Bismarck's parliamentary initiatives, thus binding him closer to the liberals. The closer he came to the liberals the deeper the rift between him and the conservatives. The black reactionary Prussian of 1848, the scourge of the liberals and nationalists, now appeared as the figurehead of the National Liberals.

The German empire of 1871 was a secular state, and although the majority of the ruling elite was Protestant it had no specific denominational affiliation. As a modern secular state it was involved in far more issues involving the individual than its absolutist predecessor had been; indeed it was legitimized by the very fact that it intervened in the personal lives of it subjects. It demanded that they sacrifice their lives in war, set the parameters within which the economy functioned, took over responsibility for the education of the young, and for the welfare of the elderly and the disadvantaged. It alone had the legal right to join couples together in matrimony. Modernity involved more state, with the gradual elimination of institutions that mediated between the individual and the state. This is the reverse of the situation today when modernization implies less state, deregulation, and the growth of civil society. The new German empire thus inevitably became involved in a renewed conflict between church and state, often represented as a renewal of the struggle between pope and emperor, so that "Canossa" soon became an overworked cliché.

The *Kulturkampf*

The Catholic Church emerged from the First Vatican Council in 1870 as anti-modern, anti-national, integralist, ultramontane, authoritarian; it was fiercely opposed to liberalism and democracy in all its forms. The Franco-Prussian War broke out the day after the doctrine of papal infallibility was pushed through the Vatican Council despite the reasoned objections of the majority of the German bishops. The papacy might be infallible, but it had lost the last vestiges of its temporal power in the process of Italian unification. One leading cleric greeted the news of Prussia's victory over France with the horrified exclamation that the world was falling apart. The enemy was now liberal nationalism, along with the secular society for which it stood. "Progress, liberalism and modern civilization" had already been roundly condemned as among the eighty iniquities listed in Pius IX's encyclical, the *Syllabus of Errors* of 1864.

The churches in Germany, then and now, were in a unique relationship with the state. Catholics and Protestants paid, and still pay today, a portion of their taxes towards the upkeep of the church. Theological faculties of universities in which priests and ministers were prepared for ordination were state funded. The state had a say in the appointment of bishops and kept a close watch on their activities. In return the churches demanded influence over education and matrimonial law. The situation was further complicated by the divisions between Catholics and Protestants. About one-third of the population was Catholic, and most of the rest were Protestant.

Liberals, whether nominally Catholic or Protestant, set out to liberate the Catholic faithful from a hidebound, reactionary, and irrational clergy. Thus they stood for secular education and for secular marriages. They were determined to reduce the influence of ultramontane priests and bishops over the church. They declared all-out war against the Jesuits, whom they saw as the storm troopers of ultramontanism. They won a number of significant victories in the 1860s in Bavaria and Baden, where there were a number of anti-clerical riots. The secularization trend intensified with the foundation of the German empire. The promulgation of the doctrine of papal infallibility was a clear indication of Rome's siege mentality. In spite of this hardening of the fronts, the majority of German bishops were moderate, anxious to avoid a confrontation with the new state. Their spokesman, Archbishop Ketteler of Mainz, called for cooperation between church and state. Even Pius IX, the "prisoner" in the Vatican, reluctantly accepted the new Germany when the French troops were obliged to withdraw.

That the role of the Catholic Church became such a pressing political issue is largely due to Bismarck's reaction to the Center Party. The party was founded in 1870 to look after the interests of Catholics in northern Germany. It then joined forces with southern German particularists and anti-Prussians, along with Poles, Guelphs, and the disaffected citizenry of Alsace and Lorraine. The party, with its serious reservations about the Reich, was open to the charge of being ultramontane and even un-German. Its great strength lay in the fact that it was the only genuine people's party in Germany. Its supporters ranged from lofty aristocrats to peasants, from industrial magnates to industrial workers, from prosperous professionals to lowly craftsmen. Furthermore it drew its support from all over the Reich, wherever there were Catholics.

In the first Reichstag debate in 1871 the Center Party requested that the government should support the pope's efforts to restore his temporal power, in other words openly to confront the Kingdom of Italy. Their second motion was that the fundamental rights of the church guaranteed in the Prussian constitution should be applied throughout the Reich. Bismarck, who believed that such rights should be within the jurisdiction of the states, seized the opportunity to denounce the Center Party as being solely interested in the sectional interests of the church, not in matters of national concern.

Bismarck the Protestant Junker shared many of the anti-Catholic prejudices of his estate and his co-religionists, but his antipathy towards the Center Party was based more on its opposition to the strong federal government and to the dominant role of Prussia, both of

PLATE 13   Bismarck by Franz von Lembach, c.1880. © BPK

which were central to his vision of the new empire. Since it was in his nature to seek con-frontation with his political opponents he decided to launch a "preventive war" against the Catholic "enemies of the Reich."

The time was propitious. The church was in turmoil after the Vatican Council. "Old Catholics" who refused to accept the dogma of papal infallibility were excommunicated, whereupon the Prussian state refused to dismiss those among them who held teaching positions in universities, seminaries, and schools, or as chaplains in the military. This was combined with a ban on priests holding administrative positions in schools in the Polish-speaking provinces, in an attempt to end their baneful influence over a basically loyal and docile population. Elsewhere in Germany the states adopted a less heavy-handed approach.

The next phase in the *Kulturkampf* came somewhat surprisingly from Catholic Bavaria, which introduced legislation at the federal level in 1871 banning priests from making subversive statements in their sermons. In addition to this "pulpit paragraph" the proposal by the Reichstag majority that the Jesuit order be banned was accepted by the Bundesrat in the following year.

Thenceforth the *Kulturkampf* was carried on at the state level. Adalbert Falk, the Prussian minister of education, was its most aggressive champion. He significantly reduced the influence of the Catholic Church over education and interfered in the curricula of theological faculties and seminaries while seeking greater influence over church appointments. When the church fought back the state cut off funds, closed down seminaries, and seized church property. Bishops were dismissed, imprisoned, or exiled. Catholic associations and their press were subjected to constant harassment by the police. In 1875 virtually all religious orders were banned in Prussia with the exception of those involved in nursing and the instruction of young girls. The "Bread Basket Law" meant that funds were denied to all dioceses that resisted. Parishes could now elect their own priests, the administration entrusted to lay councils. Civil marriages were made compulsory in Prussia in 1874 and in the Reich one year later. In the German states there were similar moves to secularize education, limit the activities of the religious orders, and interfere in the administration of the church. But with the possible exception of Baden these measures were nowhere enforced with the same rigor and brutality as in Prussia.

Pius IX fought back. In 1875 he threatened to excommunicate all those who obeyed these oppressive laws. Bishops and priests became popular martyrs. In Prussia almost one-quarter of the parishes no longer had a priest, and eight of the twelve dioceses were without a bishop. The longer the church came under attack the more determined was the will to resist. Similarly the Center Party, which was made up of so many conflicting interests, stood firmly united in opposition. Gradually the forces of the *Kulturkampf* began to crumble. Conservatives became increasingly concerned that the whole affair was bringing discredit upon both Prussia and the Reich. On the left the likes of Eduard Lasker were appalled at the violation of fundamental civil rights and freedom of conscience. The Center Party leader Ludwig Windthorst skillfully played upon misgivings in the government camp. He appealed to conservatives to uphold traditional Christian values, and warned liberals of the dangers of excessive state power and the left of the importance of civil liberties.

Resistance was also growing at the grassroots level. Secularization was seen as a vicious attack on a customary way of life. The almighty state tried to sweep away traditional holidays and festivities. Haughtily arrogant officials looked down upon ordinary folk as mired in a backward, superstitious, ignorant world of miracles, pilgrimages, and idolatry. They were determined to defend their little universe against the ravages of the modern. Political Catholicism thus became more radical, more populist, and paradoxically, given its constituency, more modern.

With their support waning, both on the left and on the right, the liberals became even more intransigent. The *Kulturkampf* for them was a life and death struggle for freedom, enlightenment, modernity, the economy, the state, and the nation against the "Black International." It was indeed for them a struggle for culture in which no quarter could be given. They became so obsessed with this fight that they overlooked the far more important question of changing the power structure of the Reich. They had abandoned themselves to Bismarck, on whom they were now totally dependent.

Bismarck and the Liberals

Bismarck and the liberals made a curious alliance. They could march shoulder to shoulder in the *Kulturkampf*, but the old issue of the army had not been laid to rest with the indemnity vote. It reappeared in 1874 when Bismarck, at the urging of the military, wanted a guarantee of permanent funding for army. This proposal for an "Eternal Law" (*Aeternat*) met with the unyielding resistance of the liberals, who wanted to retain the system of annual budgets. The struggle was bitter, but in the final resort Bismarck still needed the liberals, while they did not want to run the risk of an election. The result was a compromise whereby the army estimates were guaranteed for seven years (*Septennat*). The liberals lost a number of rounds with the chancellor over legal reform, but at least they were able to frustrate his attempt to broaden the concept of political offenses, punishable by law. The brilliant rhetorician and left-wing liberal Eduard Lasker denounced these proposals as "rubber paragraphs," since they were open to a very wide range of interpretations.

The liberals had no choice but to put up with Bismarck, stand up to his bullying tactics, try to extend the powers of the Reichstag, and wait for more propitious times. The crown prince, with his English wife, was known to have liberal sympathies. Liberals therefore nurtured the reversionary interest, much to Bismarck's anger and disgust. Bismarck in turn detested Lasker, his outstanding opponent in the Reichstag, who opened the liberals up to the left. He therefore began to mend his bridges with the conservatives as a counterweight to the left-wing liberals. The liberals had played a significant part in molding the Reich, but now their influence was waning as Bismarck decided upon a radical change of course in economic and fiscal policy and turned his attention to the struggle against Social Democracy.

Social Democracy

The socialist movement in Germany was still in its infancy, but it was growing apace. Rapid industrialization swelled the ranks of the proletariat, the movement's natural constituency. Bismarck had calculated that universal manhood suffrage would enfranchise a conservative peasantry as had been the case in Napoleon III's France, but as Germany gradually changed from being an agricultural to an industrial society the urban working-class vote steadily increased. In 1871 Germany had only eight towns with a population over 100,000; by 1910 there were forty-eight. In 1871 a mere 4.9 percent of the population lived in urban areas; by 1910 this had risen to 21.3 percent. An increasing number of workers who lived in small rural communities used the ever-expanding railway network to commute to their workplaces in industrial centers. For them the clear distinction between rural and urban was rapidly eroding. The appeal of socialism grew as boom turned to bust and the depression set in. Furthermore the socialists, although in practice moderate and reformist, adopted a revolutionary Marxist rhetoric, which terrified the respectable bourgeoisie. Talk of the class struggle, the public ownership of the means of production and exchange, and the dictatorship of the proletariat seemed even more threatening after the experience of the Paris Commune and with the "machines infernelles" of wild-eyed Russian, Italian, and Spanish anarchists. Such fears were deliberately fanned by Bismarck, but they were very real and understandable. The "Red Menace" was much more than an electoral ploy or a rhetorical stratagem.

There were two prescriptions for dealing with socialism. Bismarck, who always saw everything in terms of black and white, friend and foe, argued in favor of repression and had wide support in Prussian government circles. The old slogan of 1848, "only soldiers help against democrats," now read "only soldiers help against Social Democrats." An alternative approach was suggested by Hermann Wagener, an editor of the *Kreuzzeitung*, a progressive conservative who wanted to open up the Conservative Party to become a genuine people's party. He argued that repression would simply strengthen the socialists. The only solution was a comprehensive program of social reform that would do away with the grievances on which the socialists thrived. Bismarck however wanted first to crush the socialist movement before considering social reform.

The socialist leaders and Reichstag deputies Bebel and Liebknecht were arrested in 1872 and charged with treason for remarks they had made about the conduct of the war and the Paris Commune. They were very well treated in a minimum-security prison: Bebel welcomed the opportunity to at last have time to read *Das Kapital* and took great pride in the prize radishes he grew in the prison garden. After their release the two socialist parties, the Lassalleans and the Eisenachers, were united at the Gotha conference of 1875 to form the Socialist Workers' Party of Germany (SAPD). The party's program was essentially Marxist, although Karl Marx vented his ire at the Lassallean deviations contained therein in his powerful pamphlet: "Critique of the Gotha Program." In 1890 the party was renamed the Social Democratic Party of Germany (SPD).

From Free Trade to Protectionism

Liberal concerns about the violation of basic civil liberties implied in Bismarck's proposals to combat Social Democracy further estranged the chancellor from the party at a time when the Reich was in increasing financial difficulties. The French had paid their reparations in full, and income from customs duties and indirect taxes was dwindling as the depression set in, so the federal government had to go cap in hand to the states and ask for an increase in their supplementary payments known as "matriculatory contributions." The tax system was inefficient and grossly unfair, weighed heavily on the poor, and was desperately in need of reform. Bismarck's aim was to increase the revenues of the Reich, thereby reducing the dependence of the federal government on the states. At the same time he hoped that the states, particularly Prussia, could alleviate the burden of local taxation, especially the disproportionate taxes on agriculture, which were the direct cause of so much social unrest. This implied shifting the burden of taxation from direct taxes (such as income tax), which went to the states, to indirect taxes (such as sales tax or customs duties), which went to the Reich. He focused exclusively on strengthening the Reich against the states and seems to have overlooked the fact that the poor would be hardest hit by increases in indirect taxation, and that this would lead to further unrest and consequently to an increase in the appeal of Social Democracy.

In a further attempt to bolster federal revenue, Bismarck proposed nationalizing the railways and establishing a tobacco monopoly as in France and Austria-Hungary. Such interventionist initiatives were anathema to many liberals, as were proposals to increase customs duties, the proceeds of which would go directly to the Reich. The depression which began in 1873 was the first major crisis of industrial society and had all the concomitant side-effects: a stock-exchange crash, rising unemployment, falling demand, bankruptcies, and widespread uncertainty, fear, and discontent. Many, both from the left and from the right, felt that the culprit was unbridled liberal capitalism, which the Germans labeled *Manchesterismus*. Liberalism was now discredited in the eyes of many. For them hope for the future lay either in state intervention or in socialism.

The agrarians had long been enthusiastic free traders. They exported in large quantities, mainly to England, in return importing British agricultural machinery. Now facing competition from cheap grain from Russia and North America, they began to clamor for protection. The same was true in the iron and steel industries, where the market was swamped with imports. Textile manufacturers were also insistent that they could not survive without a helping hand from the state. Powerful interest groups lent their enthusiastic support to Bismarck's proposals for tariff increases, chief among them the Central Association of German Industrialists (Zentralverband Deutscher Industrieller), founded in 1876. Economic historians have shown that the situation was far from being as grim as contemporaries imagined, giving rise to talk of the "myth" of the great depression. But the difficulties arising from a marked slowdown of the rate of growth were unevenly distributed, causing increasing misery in certain sectors. For many, times were bad and getting worse.

Tariff increases provided Bismarck with an ideal issue to help him in his change of course. They had widespread popular support, would reduce the federal government's reliance on the matriculatory contributions, strengthen the central government, and help him distance himself still further from the free-trading liberals around Lasker. The increasing importance of interest groups resulted in a corresponding diminution of the importance of the political parties. Indeed the National Liberal Party, which represented a plurality of interests, was destined to fall apart. In order to create a new political alignment Bismarck had to end the *Kulturkampf* and thus finally end his reliance on liberal support. The election in 1878 of a new pope, the moderate and conciliatory Leo XIII, provided an opportunity to end this unfortunate and profoundly damaging episode.

Anti-Catholic measures were toned down, but they did not disappear. The "pulpit paragraph" remained in force, civil marriages were still compulsory, and the ban on the Jesuits was not lifted. Bismarck now drove a wedge between the pope and the Center Party. The pope, who had severe reservations about political Catholicism, at times intervened, forcing the party to toe the chancellor's line. Bismarck hoped that the resulting tensions between the pope and the party would result in Catholic voters turning their backs on the party. But the party was exceedingly reluctant to take its marching orders from Rome and the voters remained faithful. In 1886 and 1887 the Prussian government made peace with the Catholic Church in a series of measures whereby the *Kulturkampf* was officially buried. The wounds took a long time to heal. Catholics saw themselves as an endangered minority, still subject to discrimination, not yet fully integrated into German society. It was not until after the Second World War that Catholics were fully integrated into the political process. This was another of Konrad Adenauer's great achievements

The change of course was slow and hesitant. The first sign was the dismissal of the free-trader Delbrück in 1876. The National Liberals lost a number of seats in the elections in the following year. The Lasker wing's influence was greatly diminished. Bismarck negotiated for months on end with the National Liberal leader, Bennigsen, suggesting that he become a de facto vice chancellor, but he felt that such a position would leave him seriously compromised. Bismarck's renewed attack on free trade and his proposal for a tobacco monopoly in 1878 finally convinced Bennigsen to end these interminable and fruitless discussions. A number of free-trading Prussian ministers resigned that year, among them Camphausen from finance, Aschenbach from industry, and Friedrich Eulenburg from the interior. But Bismarck was still not totally convinced of the need for and expediency of higher tariffs, or for an alliance with the Center Party. He still hoped that he could bully the National Liberals into compliance with his wishes.

The political deadlock was broken when a mentally deranged journeyman plumber took a pot shot at the kaiser on May 11, 1878. The would-be assassin, Max Hödel, had briefly been a member of SDAP but had been expelled for dipping his hands into the party's coffers, whereupon he had joined Stoecker's Christian Socialists. Bismarck claimed that the socialists had masterminded the affair, and an anti-socialist law was placed before the Reichstag. The predictable result was another setback for Bismarck. The majority of the Reichstag refused to support this ill-considered bill which, by aiming at the curtailment of essential civil liberties, amounted in Bennigsen's words to a "war against the Reichstag." Bismarck had hoped that the liberals would abandon their few remaining principles, but he had made a serious miscalculation.

The Anti-Socialist Laws

Less than a month after the first assassination attempt, another crackpot managed to seriously wound the kaiser. The perpetrator, Dr. Nobiling, an unemployed scholar and anarchist, promptly committed suicide. Bismarck seized the opportunity to deal the liberals a crushing blow. By pulling out all the stops he bullied the Bundesrat into agreeing to dissolve the Reichstag. Bismarck fought the election campaign on a platform of anti-socialist laws and economic and financial reform, in the hope of securing a majority made up of conservatives and sympathetic National Liberals, possibly with Center Party support.

There was widespread discontent over the state of the economy. An assassination attempt on a popular kaiser lent credence to the chancellor's insistence that there was a very real revolutionary threat. Combined with massive support from powerful interests groups, the campaign was successful. The National Liberals dropped from 128 to 99 seats. The Lasker liberals and the Progressives also lost seats. The two conservative parties made substantial gains. The Center Party held its own. The result was a majority of deputies who supported the proposed tariffs, drawn from the conservatives, the Center Party, and about a quarter of the National Liberals.

Using British legislation against Irish nationalists as a model, Bismarck now had little difficulty in securing a majority for his anti-socialist laws. The National Liberals, even those on the extreme left of the party, gritted their teeth and voted in favor, fearing that otherwise Bismarck would call another round of elections in which they would suffer further humiliation.

The anti-socialist laws declared Social Democracy, and any other "revolutionary" movement, to be enemies of the state, of society, and the constitution. All public activities by the party were forbidden. Its press was banned, and party activists could be denied a means of earning a living and could even be exiled. It was a draconian measure, but there were a number of loopholes. Party members could still sit in the Reichstag. They could stand for election and could conduct electoral campaigns. Implementation of the laws was left to the individual states and they were thus applied with widely varying degrees of severity. They were to apply for twelve years, and the debate over their renewal was to contribute to Bismarck's downfall. The laws were bound to fail, just as the *Kulturkampf* had failed. Catholics stood together against a common threat; likewise, the socialist working class showed admirable solidarity with their party. The *Kulturkampf* strengthened the Center Party and support for the SAPD increased significantly between 1878 and 1890.

Bismarck's New Course

Bismarck now had a majority in the Reichstag for tariff reform. After lengthy debates and many unsatisfactory compromises a general agreement was reached to increase tariffs. They were very modest in the agricultural sector. Nowhere could they be called protective, but they brought in substantial additional revenue while causing a marked increase in the cost of living at a time when the depression was beginning to really hurt. Increased revenues implied a reduction in the Reichstag's budgetary control. It also meant that the Reich would no longer have to request matriculatory payments from states, so their influence over federal affairs would also diminish. The Center Party and the pro-government National Liberals, whose votes Bismarck needed to pass the legislation, were determined to frustrate his attempt to further weaken the Reichstag and the Bundesrat. The Bavarian Center Party deputy Count Georg von und zu Franckenstein put forward an ingenious scheme to overcome this problem. All revenues coming to the federal government in excess of 130 million marks was to be divided up among the states, and would then be returned as part of the matriculatory contributions. Thanks to the "Franckenstein Clause" budgetary rights of the Reichstag and of the state parliaments (*Landtage*) would thus be preserved. Bismarck thus suffered yet another defeat. He had tried to secure the financial independence of the Reich, but was unable to get increased tariffs without agreeing to the Franckenstein Clause.

The chancellor saw one positive result from the change of course. The National Liberal Party now split apart. In the final debate over tariff reform Lasker charged Bismarck with pitching the countryside against the towns, the haves against the have-nots, the producers against the consumers. He accused the chancellor of breaking the alliance of 1867 between the forces of the old and the new and of now trying to destroy the bourgeoisie with its liberal vision. The few remaining liberal ministers in Prussia now resigned. The left liberals around Lasker, Ludwig Bamberger, and Max von Forckenbeck formed a separate party in 1880 known as the "Secession" and longed for the liberal crown prince to succeed. The Progressives, led by Eugen Richter, were also heavy losers in the election. They hoped that the Secession would join forces with them, but this did not happen, largely due to Richter's authoritarian style of leadership. Although most liberals were singularly pessimistic about their prospects, the chronically apprehensive Bismarck feared that his nightmare vision of a German "Gladstone government" was a step closer to becoming reality.

In the elections of 1881 there were thus three liberal parties. Although the aggregate vote for the liberals increased, the National Liberals lost a substantial number of seats. Their losses were the left liberals' gain. In 1884 the two left-liberal parties amalgamated to form the German Independent Party under Richter's forceful leadership. It was against both "reaction" and socialism, against the increased tariffs and Bismarck's social legislation. It stood for the rights of the Reichstag, and for annual military budgets. This was hardly an inspiring program, and the party was still divided over a number of issues. The new party did poorly in the 1884 election in which the call for colonies played an important role. In the run-off elections National Liberals tended to support Free Conservative candidates rather than Independents. In urban areas the Social Democrats made substantial gains at their expense.

The Independents lost more than half their seats in the elections of 1887, in which Bismarck pulled out all the nationalistic stops, but won almost all of them back again in 1890 in the uncertain political atmosphere after Bismarck's departure from office. Meanwhile the National Liberals leaned increasingly towards the right. They were no longer a party of the middle, but were now closely allied with the Free Conservatives, united in opposition against the Center Party, the Independents, and the Social Democrats. It was a gradual process that was not completed until Bennigsen resigned the leadership in 1883. In the following year Johannes Miquel, a former Social Democrat, friend of Karl Marx, and mayor of Frankfurt, drafted the party's Heidelberg Program, which placed the party solidly behind Bismarck's social policy and endorsed his anti-socialism and colonialism, as well as his position on tariffs and agricultural protection. In calling for a strong and interventionist state it distanced the party from the Independents and turned it into a faction of conservative democrats. It was a popular move. The party doubled its number of seats in the 1887 election as part of the "cartel" with the two conservative parties, but German liberalism was marching resolutely down a dead-end street. Miquel could not persuade his partners in the cartel of the need for extensive social reform, and both liberal parties were losing out to the Social Democrats as the party of change. This was not a uniquely German phenomenon. In all parliamentary democracies the fundamental choice was between conservative democracy and Social Democracy in whatever guise. This shift was most pronounced in Germany because of the dramatic growth of support for the SAPD. Elsewhere, as in England, liberal parties tried to revive their fortunes by an injection of Social Democratic ideas, but this could only postpone their final demise.

In 1879 Bismarck's hopes for a cartel were frustrated by Bennigsen's intransigence. Memories of the *Kulturkampf* were still too vivid for it to be possible for the Center Party to ally with the two conservative parties. Bismarck therefore decided to ignore the Reichstag where possible, thereby weakening the political parties. He now turned to the interest groups as a counterweight to the parties, linking them closely to various ministries and involving them in drafting legislation. The parties fought back fiercely, denounced this attempt to create a "chancellor dictatorship," and warned the interest groups of the dire consequences of their support for Bismarck's efforts to undermine the constitution.

The unpopularity of the tariff increases and the persisting depression resulted in Bismarck suffering a severe setback at the polls in 1881, and he was left without a parliamentary majority. The Center Party, the left-liberal Secessionists and Independents, the Social Democrats, and a number of National Liberals were strongly opposed to Bismarck and his anti-parliamentary chicanery, but they could agree on precious little else. The chancellor had no working majority, but neither did he have to face a united opposition. Having secured his change of course he could now afford to bide his time, and continue with his plans to find ways around the Reichstag and bully the parliamentarians with threats of dissolution and even a coup d'état.

The Reichstag turned down his proposals for a tobacco monopoly in 1882 and for a spirits monopoly in 1887; both attempts were designed to make the federal government financially independent. Similarly the Center Party made its support for an increased tariff on agricultural goods dependent on increasing the revenue transferred to the states from customs duties. Other schemes for a tax on capital gains and for the nationalization of the railways met with determined resistance and had to be shelved.

Social Policy

Bismarck's major achievement in the 1880s was in the field of social legislation. The inspiration came from reform-minded officials, but had he not championed these ideas they would never have been put into effect. He was determined to legislate against the "subversive agitation" of the Social Democrats, but he also felt that the state should meet "the justified wishes of the working classes." He also learnt from Napoleon III that social stability could be greatly strengthened by making people dependent on the state. A nation of *rentiers* was unlikely to find much that was attractive in Social Democracy. As he told the Reichstag: "I have lived long enough in France to know that the dependence of most Frenchmen on the government has mainly to do with the fact that most of them are recipients of government pensions and subsidies." The wind would be taken out of the socialists' sails, the working class rendered passive, the state strengthened by what one historian has described as "massive bribery." As Bismarck said: "The state will have to get used to a bit more socialism." In response to horrified conservative reaction to this taboo word, he replied that "state socialism" was merely a continuation of the Stein–Hardenberg reforms.

A group of social conservative reformers, among them Hermann Wagener, Theodor Lohmann, and Karl Rodbertus, took up Lorenz von Stein's notion of a "social kingdom" and urged the chancellor to lay the foundations of a welfare state. Lohmann argued that the empire, founded in 1871, was now in need of a second, domestic, foundation. There were many opponents to such a scheme. The Social Democrats were understandably suspicious of Bismarck's motives. Entrepreneurs favored private insurance schemes. Liberals rejected it out of hand as a sinister attempt to strengthen an already far too powerful state. Catholics, with the notable exception of reformers such as Wilhelm von Ketteler, the archbishop of Mainz, feared that it would mean the end of Christian charity. Conservatives thought that with the anti-socialist laws there was no need to buy domestic peace at so high a cost.

Bismarck, convinced of the political desirability of these measures, made them a central component of his version of the Prussian tradition of a "revolution from above"; but faced with such stiff opposition he was obliged to make a series of compromises. Initially he did not want workers to pay towards benefits, because this would mean a reduction in their wages and their consequent opposition, thus making the entire operation pointless. He therefore proposed that a state tobacco monopoly should bear the entire cost of his proposed health insurance bill. Opposition was such that he had to agree to workers paying two-thirds of the contributions in the bill which was finally passed by the Reichstag in 1883. It provided benefits after the third day of sickness up to a maximum of thirteen weeks. But only 4.3 million workers were covered, equivalent to 10 percent of the population. Agricultural laborers were excluded from the scheme, leaving them dependent on the paternalistic largesse of their employers. After three years of rancorous debates this measure was eventually followed in 1884 by the introduction of accident insurance. Benefits amounted to two-thirds of average earnings, beginning in the fourteenth week, when the sickness benefit ceased. The scheme was administered by cooperative associations of employers (*Berufsgenossenschaften*), which Bismarck encouraged as a corporate alternative to parliament. In 1889 the Disability and Old Age Pension Act became law. Here Bismarck managed to secure substantial state subsidies. Pensions were extremely modest, averaging a mere 152 marks per year in 1914 at a time when the average annual industrial wage was slightly more than 1,000 marks. Old-age pensions were only paid to men over 70. In 1900 only 27 percent of men lived that long.

Germany trailed far behind Britain in legislation controlling labor conditions, and France's social security system was far more advanced. Bismarck was bitterly disappointed that his social welfare measures had not resulted in the working class adopting a "loyal attitude towards the state," but for all their many shortcomings, the foundations of the welfare state had been laid. In the long run Bismarck's calculations proved correct. All European states were eventually to become legitimized and thereby strengthened by welfare systems on a scale unimaginable to the reformers of the 1880s.

The Social Structure of Imperial Germany

Imperial Germany was a society marked by stark differentiations of wealth, social status, and privilege. It was, in other words, a class society and as such reflected the European norm. It was far removed from the relative egalitarianism of prosperous present-day Germany, but it was also quite distinct from the earlier agrarian, pre-industrial society based on the estates. The extent to which distinctions between the haves and the have-nots increased under the impact of industrialization has been hotly debated, and although no accurate statistics are available the evidence points to an increasing inequality of wealth, education, working conditions, housing, and health. These inequalities were gradually diminished over time, thanks to an astonishing level of economic growth; but in the 1890s this was still in the distant future. Inequalities existed not only between distinct classes, but also within them, making the very concept of class a kind of shorthand which, although generally accepted and fully comprehensible, does not do justice to the complexity of an advanced industrial society. Within the working class there were sharp distinctions between the skilled and the unskilled, as well as between urban and rural workers. The bourgeoisie included fabulously rich industrialists and the village doctor struggling to make a respectable living. How should the mason with his small construction firm be categorized? Should he be distinguished from a tailor in his tiny workshop? Where did the growing number of white-collar workers fit into this scheme? Did they form a sub-section of the bourgeoisie, known as the "petite bourgeoisie," or were they part of the "respectable" working class? Where were the dividing lines between the prosperous farmer and the smallholding peasant?

"Class" is a word loaded with ideological freight, but it is fundamentally an economic concept, applicable only in a developed capitalist economy. It relates to wealth, to relationships to the means of production and to the resulting way of life. This could lead to wide distinctions within a specific class. A successful farmer, although he increasingly aped the fashions of the urban bourgeois, lived in a milieu that was distinct from that of a city lawyer. A further complication was that in Germany education afforded additional status. The "educated middle class" (*Bildungsbürgertum*) comprised the very small percentage of the population with a university education, thereby forming a distinct caste that included senior civil servants, prosperous professionals, and impoverished grammar school teachers. There were 18,000 university students in 1869, when the population was about 45 million, rising to 79,000 by 1914 when the population was roughly 67 million. This is but one example of the tradition of an estate living on in a class society. The market determined the rough outlines of class, but certain groups were privileged in a manner that had precious little to do with economic status. The aristocracy was still an estate, looking down on those who successfully played the capitalist market as upstarts and parvenus. Professionals regarded those "in trade" as grossly inferior and unacceptable as in-laws. In a Prussian-dominated Germany the army played a unique role, its officer corps open to a select few.

The state acted as a brake on the development of a modern class society. The aristocracy enjoyed all manner of privileges, from special tax provisions and access to political power to a monopoly of the upper echelons of the civil service and the military. Unlike the British aristocracy, which had no compunctions about restoring family fortunes by a judicious marriage with the daughter of a wealthy entrepreneur, or even an American heiress, the Germany aristocracy, with precious few exceptions for which royal assent was required, only married their own, thus condemning many to lives of genteel and snobbish poverty. The aristocracy set the tone in certain circles, with bourgeois estate owners, army officers, senior civil servants, and students in the more exclusive fraternities often adopting their characteristic behavior, frequently to exceedingly unattractive and boorish effect. Most bourgeois, viewing this behavior with disgust, developed a distinctly middle-class culture in which a sense of social obligation, moderation, and restraint was coupled with a life of solid comfort. This was to be the model for the future. Max Weber, who placed freedom above order, regretted that this did not go far enough. He complained that the bourgeoisie was far too much influenced by the collective values of the civil service, rather than the marketplace with its individualism.

Perhaps, as in so much else, Max Weber was overly pessimistic. The aristocracy certainly set the tone in glittering court ceremonies, in the officer corps, and in key positions in the civil service. It enjoyed many political and economic privileges, but it was the bourgeoisie that was culturally dominant. For all the talk of the "feudalization of the bourgeoisie" there was a corresponding "embourgeoisement of the aristocracy." The bourgeoisie dominated the economy, set cultural norms, determined urban life, and propagated the values of rationalism, hard work, and individualism to the point that the old concept of community was giving way to the new notion of society. In spite of all this, the bourgeoisie had no time for complacency. Its position was challenged by farmers hurt by the agrarian crisis, by artisans and craftsmen unable to meet the challenge of industrial capitalism, and by an organized working class with its vision of a new socialist order. The uncomfortable feeling arose that it might perhaps be expedient to seek a defensive alliance with the aristocracy in order to resist these challenges. In part this was due to the relative lack of opportunity for upward social mobility. It was possible to improve one's status within a class by learning a trade or getting a university degree, but it was exceedingly difficult to cross the class barriers. There were of course exceptions, such as the great art historian Richard Hamann, whose father was a postman and who was appointed professor at the age of 34, but such cases were exceedingly rare. Here education and training were of fundamental importance as the demand grew for skilled labor, technicians, scientists, engineers, and managers. A major expansion of the universities and polytechnics in the 1890s offered further opportunity for social advancement, as did the steady increase in the need for management skills. Within the bourgeoisie this resulted in a dramatic percentage increase of entrants to the *Bildungsbürgertum* from the petite bourgeoisie in terms of percentages, but it must be remembered that this was a small and exclusive group, so that the aggregate number of the upwardly mobile was still very small. There were also increasing opportunities for advancement from the ranks of the blue-collar workers into white-collar jobs, or for peasants to become elementary school teachers.

Class distinctions were emphasized by a conservative mentality that resisted any aspiration to better one's status or that of one's children. "What's good enough for me is good enough for you" was a widespread view. The socially ambitious were condemned for having ideas above their station. Those who succeeded in social advancement were often snobbishly dismissive of the milieu from which they had risen, thus reinforcing class prejudice. Although the "respectable" working class began to adopt the manners, dress, eating habits, and furniture of the bourgeoisie, class distinctions remained as rigid as ever. A greater emphasis was now placed on the finer distinctions of comportment, dress, and speech between the classes and sub-classes that made up this complex, heterogeneous society that defies precise statistical analysis or sociological definition.

Food and Drink

For all the many problems, inequalities and setbacks, imperial Germany witnessed a marked increase in the general standard of living. The first half of the nineteenth century had been haunted by widespread undernourishment and famine, but this was now a thing of the past. There were still individual cases of appalling deprivation, but the mass of peasantry and the industrial proletariat was adequately fed and their daily calorific intake steadily increased until the outbreak of the First World War. Bread, legumes, and potatoes remained the basic foodstuffs, but there was a marked increase in the consumption of meat. First there came a noticeable drop in the consumption of legumes, then of potatoes. Sugar was no longer a luxury, thanks to the widespread domestic cultivation of sugar beet. Consumption grew fourfold between 1870 and 1910. Meat consumption, mainly of pork, rose from 22 kilos per capita per annum in 1850 to 27.6 kilos in 1879, and had risen to 44.9 kilos by 1913.

These improvements were in part due to rising real wages, since the purchase of food accounted for a sizeable part of the family budget. In 1907 it was calculated that the average working-class family spent 60 percent of the family income on food. Even more important was the revolution in the food industry and in transportation. There were significant improvements in farming techniques and livestock breeding. The provision of milk to urban areas was rationalized, and condensed milk was introduced in 1884. Pasteurization began two years later. Margarine was invented in 1870, providing a cheap source of fat for the poorer sections of society. Refrigeration revolutionized the preservation of foods so that fresh fish gradually replaced salted. The discovery of chemical preservatives greatly increased the shelf-life of many foodstuffs. Tinned vegetables first appeared in the shops in the 1870s, to be followed by meat and fish in the 1880s. Knorr and Maggi introduced their powdered soups in the 1880s. In bourgeois circles food became richer and more varied, regional dietary peculiarities became less marked, and closer attention was paid to a healthy diet. By 1900 it was considered desirable to preserve a slim figure as a new and sporting feminine image was constructed. Rural areas resisted such changing fashions, while the working class remained stolidly conservative when it came to their victuals. Diet had improved, but there was still a marked lack of vitamins and minerals, of fruit and vegetables, of milk products and fish that were later to be considered essential for health.

There were of course class-based differences in diets, but the working-class diet was gradually approximating that of the middle-class. It was healthier, more nutritious, and more varied, and by 1900 bore a closer resemblance to today's diet than it did to that of 1850. Canteens now provided food for the destitute, and free school meals were given to the children of the poor. By contrast, factory canteens were mostly appalling. The lukewarm swill supplied to workers was all too often washed down with excessive quantities of beer. A major problem in the working-class household was that the patriarchal family structure resulted in the husband getting the lion's share of the food. Wives were often ignorant of basic notions of hygiene and diet; but here too bourgeois notions seeped down, partly because many of these women had been in domestic service, and also because of the well-meaning if often intrusive efforts of various middle-class women's groups.

As the middle class prospered the eating habits of the courts and the wealthy were imitated in luxury hotels and the finer restaurants, which provided gargantuan meals with as many as twelve courses. Such feasting was simplified and rendered more specifically bourgeois by the end of the century, by which time half the number of courses were served in "restaurants" most of which, as the name suggests, followed the French example, often with an elaborate menu in French. Those who were unable to afford such luxury went to a modest guesthouse that provided homely, bourgeois food.

Germany was a country of trenchermen, but also of tipplers. Martin Luther had said that every country has its own devil and that "our German devil lurks in a wineskin and is called drunkard." In general the bourgeoisie moderated its drinking habits as tea and coffee replaced beer. All forms of excess were frowned upon. Alcohol consumption in the working class increased significantly with the industrial production of cheap schnapps distilled from potatoes. Considerable amounts of beer were also consumed in the workplace. Getting blind drunk on payday was a widely practiced and socially acceptable ritual. Blue-collar workers spent on average twice as much on drink as white-collar clerks. In 1850 the per capita annual consumption of pure alcohol (contained in beer and spirits) was 6.4 liters. This increased to 10.5 liters in 1874. It then remained steady, possibly as a result of the long depression, began to drop in the new century, and by 1913 had fallen to 7 liters. The major reason for this remarkable change was that the consumption of schnapps fell by about one-third between the 1860s and 1913, whereas that of beer, with its low alcohol content, rose threefold, all because of increases in the tax on spirits. Drinking habits were also regionally determined, with Rhinelanders holding the record for wine consumption, and Bavarians the unrivaled champions in the beer stakes.

Drinking was the principal leisure-time activity for a wide section of the population, the local inn or tavern the favored site of social interaction and cultural exchange. Inns and taverns were also the only places available for political meetings. The various factions in the Frankfurt parliament of 1848 were named after the bars where they met, and Social Democrats made the tavern the locus of a specifically working-class culture. Although there was a general disapproval of excessive drunkenness, the temperance movement made little headway. Drinking was primarily a male vice that was indulged at the expense of women and children. It all too often led to domestic violence and unbridled sexuality. Gradually alcoholism came to be seen as a major social problem rather than as a sin, as a disease rather than as a moral transgression. By 1912 there were forty-eight detoxification centers and 158 centers offering help and advice on drinking. The increasing availability of cheap, alcohol-free drinks helped to relieve the problem of excessive drinking, as did the gradual acceptance of coffee by the working class, even if it was of a poor quality and often made from some form of substitute. Tea was seldom drunk outside genteel circles.

Like that of alcohol, the consumption of tobacco increased sharply between 1870 and 1913, from 1 kilo per capita per annum to 1.6 kilos. The middle class smoked cigars while the working man gradually replaced his pipe with cheap cigars and cigarillos. Cigarettes first became readily available in urban areas in the late 1870s and grew in popularity, particularly among the working class. Less time-consuming than the cigar, it was an ideal accompaniment to a short break from work. The cigarette was later adopted by fashionable youth and also, much to the horror of the traditionally minded, by a very small number of women. Cigarettes were at first hand-made, but gradually mass-production techniques were applied so that cigarette-making became a major industry supported by vigorous advertising campaigns.

Fashion

Diet was class-specific with a tendency towards a certain democratization of consumption. Much the same was true of clothing. People were clothed according to their social status, their occupation, and their age and marital status, as well as their geographical location. With the invention of the sewing machine, and the subsequent mass production of ready-made clothing, the movement towards the standardization of clothing was given additional impetus. This was particularly true in rural areas, where the more prosperous farmers and their wives gradually abandoned their regional dress in favor of the styles of the urban bourgeoisie. In this case the distinction between the wealthier and the poorer farmers and peasants became more clearly demarcated. The working class copied the bourgeoisie with their "Sunday best" clothes, but a clear distinction remained in quality and cut.

The bourgeoisie set the style. The simplification of male attire, which was already apparent in the Biedermeier period, continued. Color was restrained and uniform, the simple tie replaced by fanciful cravats. Looser-fitting jackets replaced wasp-waisted tailcoats, but collars were still starched and detachable, although the folded collar gradually replaced the high wing collar. Edward VII as Prince of Wales set the tone for the impeccably dressed male, a role later played by his successors Edward VIII and Prince Charles. It was he who sanctioned the replacement of tails by the dinner jacket on less formal occasions and of the top hat by the homburg. Trousers were first pressed around the turn of the century, but the Prince of Wales' curious habit of having the crease on the side found few followers. Men's hair was cut shorter, and although beards were widespread an increasing number of fashionable men were clean-shaven.

Women's clothes were far more subject to the whims of fashion. The crinoline, the object of much badinage, gave way to the *cul de sac*, which greatly exaggerated the buttocks, an effect enhanced by a tightly corseted waist. Skirts were long so as to cover the ankle, but the décolleté was accentuated. The dress was sleeveless, but hands were covered, often with elbow-length gloves. By the 1870s daytime dresses were cut shorter and had sleeves, but the ankles were covered with high, laced boots. Women's dress also became increasingly informal, relaxed, and sporting. The skirt and blouse had replaced the more formal dress by the 1880s. As women took up hiking, skating, and sports such as tennis their clothing had to adapt. The emphasis was now on the new concept of "figure." That figure was the "S" form which dressmakers sought to enhance by the skillful drape of the cloth. Hair was long, but piled high. Makeup was for the exclusive use of actresses and prostitutes.

Women

The changes in women's fashions were a reflection of changes in women's role in society. The romantic notion of marriage as a partnership between self-actualizing equals was short-lived, with patriarchy quick to recover the lost ground. A bourgeois woman's aim in life was to get married and have a family. This necessarily involved obligations and self-sacrifice, but it did not stifle the desire for elegance, refinement, and a lively social life. A woman's life was determined by her father, her brothers, and her husband. Men and women were unequal before the law. They were educated separately and differently. Women could not go to university and thus were unable to enter the professions. The one exception was teaching, but this only applied to unmarried women: a woman was required to relinquish her teaching post on marriage. Women were first admitted to university in Heidelberg in 1891. In 1905 there were still only 137 women students in the universities, but by 1914 there were 4,057. A growing number of women from the petite bourgeoisie took clerical positions as the need for white-collar workers increased greatly due to the exigencies of advanced industrial capitalism. But the revolutionary change was the increasing number of women factory workers. Their plight awoke the sympathies of social reformers, who saw them as an essential part of the social problem.

The women's movement was essentially a bourgeois phenomenon. It called for equality before the law, equal educational rights, and access to the professions and emancipation from patriarchal control. It accepted the notions that there were essential differences between the sexes and that a woman's principal role was to be a wife and mother. It demanded equality within the context of an incontrovertible otherness. Men were seen not as enemies, but as potential partners in a common cultural endeavor. To be a wife and mother, thus fulfilling the bourgeois ideal, was all very well, but what about the increasing number of unmarried women? Without access to further education or to an appropriate profession they led an essentially parasitic and pointless life. Small wonder then that a large number of the early feminists came from their ranks, and they soon came to champion the cause of women factory workers, whose predicament was paradigmatic of the multiple problems that beset women's fate.

There were still relatively few women working in factories – just over half a million in 1882 and fewer than 2 million by 1913, the vast majority in unskilled routine jobs. Their wages averaged about 60 percent of those of male workers. They were mostly young and unmarried. Married women gradually ceased to work as their families grew, for there were precious few day-care centers and there was a stigma attached to a married woman having to work, since it was a reflection on her husband's ability to earn a living wage. Women's work was strictly regulated. They were forbidden to work at night, their working hours were limited, and they were excluded from activities that demanded considerable physical strength. Maternity leave, granted in 1911, was covered by insurance payments. There has been a robust effort by feminist historians to demonstrate that all this was part of a male effort to combat the challenge presented by women in the workplace, but there is not the slightest evidence that this was indeed the case. Men feared the challenge from lower-paid female labor, but these fears were largely unfounded since industrial expansion provided a sufficiency of employment. Furthermore, these laws had nothing remotely to do with initiatives from the factory floor.

The organized women's movement began in 1865 when Louise Otto-Peters, who had first captured public attention in 1849 when she founded Germany's first magazine specifically for women, founded the General German Women's Association (ADF). It was a middle-class organization calling for equal educational opportunities, for the right to enter the professions, and for improvements in family law. It did not demand voting rights. A number of women's groups sprang up in subsequent years, the most important of which was Helene Lange's association of female teachers, founded in 1890. In 1894 many of these groups were brought under the umbrella of the League of German Women's Associations (BDF). It was still a solidly bourgeois organization, but there were some more radical

elements within it, including the Association of Progressive Women's Groups, with its own
newspaper *Die Frauenbewegung* (*The Women's Movement*). This group sought contact with
the Social Democratic Party, but its often strident tone did not appeal to the comrades.
Radicals concentrated on three contentious issues. They demanded an end to police control
over prostitution and their places of work, along with legal sanctions against their clients.
They demanded votes for women, but did so in a moderate manner far removed from that
of the British suffragettes. Lastly they called for a drastic rethinking of sexual morality.
Helene Stöcker took up some of Nietzsche's notions on liberation and the freeing of the
creative spirit to call for emancipation from a duplicitous morality and the emancipation
of sexuality. A host of ancillary issues were addressed, including a relaxing of divorce law,
improvements in the status of unwed mothers, sex education, and family planning. There
were widespread differences about what form these should take, and some controversial
issues such as eugenics were widely discussed. Although the differences between radicals
and conservatives within the women's movement can all too easily be exaggerated, it was
greatly weakened by the disparity of views and by frequently cantankerous debate. The
radicals gradually gained the upper hand until 1908, when a fierce argument raged over
the contentious issue of abortion. A special committee presented a motion calling for the
abolition of paragraph 218 of the criminal code that made abortion illegal, but this was
voted down by the general assembly. The arguments over a woman's right to choose versus
the rights of the unborn are a familiar theme, but the argument that abortion undermined
the "racial health" of the nation was a distasteful novelty. The defeat of the motion was a
major setback for the radicals, causing the BDF to go on a conservative course.

The new leadership of Gertrud Bäumer, who had been Helene Lange's private secretary,
and Marianne Weber insisted on the difference between men and women. For them men
were coldly intellectual and objective, with an abstractly mechanical view of the world that
was at the root of their egotistical search for dominance. Women stood for femininity,
motherhood, service, affection, and selfless concern for others. In short they embodied the
life principle. Emancipation thus would not involve equality with men, for that would
involve loss of these vital feminine characteristics. Women's cultural mission was to infuse
society with feminine values, which in turn implied that women should enter the teaching
and healing professions on an equal basis. This triggered yet another fierce debate. Should
married women continue to work? Could work outside the home be reconciled with a
woman's obligations as a mother? Was there any essential difference between housework
and work outside the home? How should housework be assessed? Should it be rewarded?

There was a socialist women's pressure group alongside this bourgeois women's movement. However woefully deficient he might have been in practice, Marx championed the
equality of the sexes in theory, and Engels devoted part of one of his least satisfactory
pamphlets to women's role in society. Socialists were in favor of the emancipation of
women, but the question was for them of secondary importance, since they insisted that
it could only be achieved within the context of a social revolution and the liberation of
mankind. Class was of far greater importance than gender. Only proletarian women were
objects of concern. August Bebel, a champion of women's rights, in 1879 published a hugely
successful book on the subject entitled *Women and Socialism*, in which he argued that
proletarian women were doubly exploited, first as workers and secondly as women. They
therefore could only be liberated when both forms of exploitation were ended. For him all
social evils that beset women, such as prostitution, abortion, illegitimate births, sexually
transmitted diseases, and the decline in the birth-rate, were due to the capitalist system.

They could only be overcome in a socialist society. Under socialism love and sexuality, no longer commodities, would be free to develop. The bogus and hypocritical bourgeois family would be replaced by one based on love and freedom of choice. The divorce laws would be relaxed should that choice prove to have been mistaken.

Clara Zetkin was the outstanding figure in the socialist women's movement. She was a feisty character, born in a solid bourgeois family and trained as a schoolteacher. She insisted that women could only be freed by work outside the home, because only in that way could they directly experience the full horror of capitalist exploitation. For this reason, like many later feminists she objected strongly to any special legislation that protected women in the workplace. Since she was convinced that socialism took priority over the immediate concerns of women she refused to cooperate in any way with the bourgeois women's movement. August Bebel heartily endorsed this view. As Clara Zetkin moved steadily to the left (she was to become a founder member of the German Communist Party in 1919) she became somewhat isolated within the party, but she remained editor of the Social Democratic women's magazine *Gleichheit* ("Equality") which increased its circulation from 30,000 in 1908 to 175,000 by 1914.

The SPD's attitude towards certain important issues on the women's agenda was often problematic. The party naturally supported women's right to vote, but with little enthusiasm, since it knew that it stood to lose by such a move. Socialist feminists did not call for equality within the family, but for partnership. They felt that married women should stay at home rather than go out to work. They were very dubious about birth control, since they flatly rejected the neo-Malthusian argument that the social problems of the day were due to the unbridled lust of the lower orders, as well as the eugenicists' arguments that rigorous birth control was essential to improve the race. The abolition of paragraph 218 was also not part of the party program.

Attitudes Towards Sexuality

There were no revolutionary changes in the status of women in the course of the nineteenth century, but there were significant improvements in their legal status, educational and occupational opportunities, in their political influence, and in the organizational forms of their debates and demands. Attitudes towards sexuality took a somewhat different course. Here there was a gradual imposition of what came to be known as "Victorian" attitudes. Sex ceased to be seen as something natural and enjoyable to become a taboo subject, something that regrettably had to be accepted. The suppression of sexuality was an essential component of a bourgeois morality that was based on notions of obligation, duty, selflessness, altruism, and playing one's appropriate role in society. The ideal now was abstinence before marriage followed by absolute fidelity towards one's partner. In an age when morality was all too often confused with sexual morality, the three cardinal sins were masturbation, pre-marital sex, and adultery. Whereas men had a bestial drive to commit all three of these sins, women as guardians of morality were transformed from innocent virgins into protective mothers and guarantors of respectability within the family. Women were no longer the Jezebels and temptresses who led men astray, but were seen as having a minimal sexual drive that was just sufficient for the satisfaction of their maternal instincts. Women had to be excessively feminine, men demonstrably masculine. Boyish women and effeminate men were viewed with horror; homosexuality was an unspeakable deviance. These ideals were also seen as specifically German. The "Deutschlandlied," later to become the national anthem, spoke of "German women, German fidelity." Deviations from the ideal were seen as distinctly un-German: casual attitudes towards one's marriage vows were seen as typically French, while an excessive sex-drive was characteristically Jewish. The consequence of breaking the rules of respectability was at best a guilty conscience, at worst social ostracism, as in the case of Fontane's heroine Effi Briest, a superb study of the problems here addressed. Yet for all the oppressive prudery and woeful ignorance, many people managed to enjoy sexually fulfilling partnerships. Queen Victoria thoroughly enjoyed a vigorous sex life within the context of a happy and fulfilling marriage. She only regretted that her lovemaking was frequently interrupted by the birth of yet another child. Medical men knew that the vision of frustrated men and frigid women was largely mythical, at least within the confines of marriage.

Possibly the worst aspect of this unsatisfactory situation was the fact that the normative and the actual were so widely separated, resulting in a double morality. Bourgeois women were to remain pure and virginal until marriage and bourgeois men, who would never dream of marrying a woman with a "past," respected this convention. Women of lesser station were fair game, were they domestic servants, peasants, factory girls, or prostitutes. There were thus two types of women: the chaste and worshipful mothers, sisters, and wives, and the hetaera: the whore and the servant girl, both of greatly inferior class, an incitement to delightful adventures, but sordid. Such women, by relieving men's sexual desires, helped preserve bourgeois women's virginity, thereby playing a useful role. Gladstone, a dedicated rescuer of fallen women, forcefully summed up this view when he praised the Greece of his beloved Homer on the grounds that "the society of that period did not avail itself of … the professional corruption of a part of womankind in order to relieve the virtue of the residue from assault." Young men from the bourgeoisie graduated from guilt-ridden adolescent onanism to spend the often lengthy years of bachelorhood in the brothel or with a mistress from the lower orders. As a result there was an appalling incidence of venereal disease among university students, of whom Nietzsche is the best-known example, combined with an exceptionally high bastardy rate in university towns, with Marburg at the top of the list with 37 percent. All this served to accentuate the unhealthy separation of sex and love. Sex might be pleasurable, but it was also dangerous, dirty, and evil. It was thus something one did with bad women, even after marriage to an idealized virgin. Whereas in Paris and Vienna it was common practice to keep a mistress, married Germans favored the brothel rather than the *chambre séparé*, although by the turn of the century it had become a status symbol in Berlin to subsidize the careers of successful actresses and variety artistes.

Statistics on the number of prostitutes are little more than wild guesstimates; suffice it to say that there were a large number of professionals in brothels or on the streets along with the semi-professional *belles du jour*. Although living off immoral earnings and public indecency were illegal, prostitutes were tolerated by the police. Some were regularly supervised by the medical authorities. The johns were largely, though not exclusively, middle-class. A fierce debate raged over the question of prostitution, which although it was often superficial and misguided, at least raised the veil from a taboo subject. Feminists denounced the double morality of the bourgeoisie and demanded that all controls over their sisters in the sex trade be lifted. The medical profession insisted on rigorous measures to stop the spread of sexually transmitted diseases, which was then as great a problem as that of AIDs is in our day. Law enforcement agencies called for a crackdown on criminality within the demi-monde. Moralists denounced prostitution as yet another glaring example of the evils of the Babylon of modernity.

The peasantry was restrained by religious sanction, by tradition, and by a concept of honor, but did not share the double morality of the bourgeoisie. It was far more open and tolerant in sexual matters. Much the same was true of the urban working class, where inhibitions and sexual repression undoubtedly existed, but the consequences of the transgression of the social norms in matters sexual were seen as misfortunes rather than as contraventions of the moral code. This in turn was all part of the secularization of society in the course of which the rules of sexual behavior were determined not by priests and ministers, but by the medical profession.

Whereas men of the cloth had laid down what was sinful, doctors now determined what was normal. Homosexuality was clearly abnormal and a positive danger to state and society, since it was a characteristic of the effeminate, weak, and feeble. Male homosexuality was a criminal offense in Prussia and remained so under paragraph 175 of the criminal code of a united German Reich. It remained in force in the German Democratic Republic until 1968 and in the Federal Republic until the following year. The paragraph originally only covered anal intercourse. It was not until the Third Reich that all forms of male homosexual activity, however widely interpreted, were rendered illegal. Gradually experts in the new "sexual science" began to challenge this view of homosexuality. Iwan Bloch, the author of a highly successful study *Sex Today* (*Das Sexualleben unserer Zeit*, 1907), saw homosexuality either as a by-product of modern civilization – a view that greatly appealed to the cultural pessimists – or as an inborn trait that often affected highly intelligent and creative people, who therefore deserved sympathy. Other prominent researchers, such as Havelock Ellis and Magnus Hirschfeld, lent their support to those who demanded the decriminalization of homosexuality, while the homosexual community mounted a vigorous campaign for the recognition of their rights. The result was a slight shift towards an acceptance of homosexuality, but homosexuals were still ostracized, marginalized, and regarded as perverts and liable to prosecution. Whereas active homosexuality was unsafe in Germany, in Italy one was out of danger and there were plenty of beautiful peasant boys and fisher lads who appeared to be happy to oblige. Taormina became a gay paradise, preserved for posterity in Wilhelm von Gloeden's photographs of naked local youths, crowned with laurels and posed in a vaguely classical manner. These titillating pictures were enormously popular in certain circles and further stimulated the tourist trade. Artists also saw homosexuality as a useful weapon with which to mount an attack on hypocritical bourgeois morality. Wedekind's *Lulu*, with its lesbian Countess Geschwitz, Thomas Mann's *Death in Venice*, Robert Müsil's *Young Törless*, and the poetry of Stefan George and his gay acolytes are cases in point, but it is doubtful whether they did much to change public attitudes.

An even more important factor in the gradually changing attitudes towards sexuality was what may be described as a rediscovery of the body. Throughout the nineteenth century the Greek ideal of nudity had been revered and widely consumed, whether in the form of public monuments or as soft porn for tired businessmen. The expressionlessness, the absence of soul, and the lack of individual character in Greek sculpture appealed to contemporary notions of sexuality. It was remote and depersonalized, even though a vital and alluring force. By the turn of the century there was an increased emphasis on naturalness, health, and sports. Clothes became looser and more informal, sun and water were regarded as health-giving, mixed bathing in increasingly revealing costumes became commonplace. The human body was seen as something natural, vital, and even beautiful.

Germans were in the vanguard of the nudist movement, which was part of a protest against modern civilization and a Rousseauesque return to nature. The nudists were far from being sexual revolutionaries. They propagated a desexualized nudity free from false shame and lubricity. They were most upset that their magazine *Die Schönheit* ("Beauty"), with its nude photographs, had considerable appeal to peeping Toms. The celebration of the human body further emphasized the difference between masculine and feminine. The cult of the male, often with a distinctly homoerotic flavor, particularly in the youth movement, was matched by a cult of the female as a healthy and fecund beauty. Coupled, they would build a healthy, strong, and vital nation, acting as a counterforce to the destructive nervousness, concupiscence, and brutish materialism of modern civilization.

CHAPTER EIGHT
GERMANY AND EUROPE
1871–1890

CHAPTER CONTENTS

A History of Modern Germany: 1800 to the Present, Second Edition. Martin Kitchen.
© 2012 Martin Kitchen. Published 2012 by Blackwell Publishing Ltd.

The creation of a united Germany in the course of three wars caused a revolution in the European balance of power. As Disraeli told the House of Commons: "This war represents the German revolution, a greater political event than the French. There is not a single diplomatic tradition that has not been swept away." The new state was the dominant power in Europe, but it was surrounded by envious, resentful, and anxious neighbors, who found it difficult to adjust to these new power-political realities. European statesmen puzzled over the question whether Prussia-Germany would attempt further expansion or rest content within its new borders. Would the Reich threaten the peace of Europe, or would it concentrate on the pressing problems of state-building? Whatever the answer, Germany was no longer a patchwork of insignificant states forming a buffer between France and Russia, a deployment area for Europe's armies, but a major power likely to harbor hegemonic aspirations.

In such a situation Bismarck chose the only possible course. He had to convince the European powers that Germany was satiated, that it had no further territorial ambitions and wanted only to live in peace with its neighbors. The German Reich had to prove that it was an acceptable newcomer among European nations. This was an immensely difficult problem, made virtually insoluble by the annexation of Alsace-Lorraine, which destroyed the balance of power and ensured the lasting enmity of France. It proved to be a disastrous legacy.

Bismarck was less perspicacious than Disraeli. He felt that he had good reason to believe that Germany could live in freedom and peace for the foreseeable future. Republican France was crippled by reparation payments, riven with internal dissent, and was an unacceptable partner for tsarist Russia. The Habsburg empire harbored many resentments after its humiliation in 1866, but it badly needed support against Russia in the Balkans. Bismarck was at first determined to resist Andrássy's proposal for an anti-Russian alliance, fearing that this might serve to overcome Russia's antipathy towards republican France. At the same time he did everything he could to hinder any attempt at reconciliation between Russia and Austria-Hungary, for that would seriously inhibit Germany's freedom of action.

Russia had dynastic ties to Germany and Bismarck was always concerned to keep the line to St. Petersburg open. Prussia and Russia had sealed their determination to stand together against recalcitrant Poles in the Alvensleben Convention of 1863. Russia had remained benevolently neutral over the question of German unification. On the other hand Russia was in decline, the Pan-Slavs gaining in influence and the new Germany presented both a challenge and a threat.

It is small wonder that Bismarck suffered from a "nightmare of coalitions." It was only safe provided none of the powers in the wings allied against it. It could only guarantee its security with Britain as an ally, but this would never happen because such an alliance would render Germany too powerful. Denied the possibility of such an alliance, Bismarck had no choice but to try to improve relations with both Austria-Hungary and Russia. This proved exceedingly difficult because both powers wanted Germany's exclusive support. This Bismarck could not risk for fear that the other party would turn towards France. For all its high-flown rhetoric the League of the Three Emperors of October 1873 was thus basically inconsequential. There was an affirmation of common conservative principles and a basic agreement on the dangers posed by socialism, but differences between Russia and Austria-Hungary in the Balkans were irreconcilable. Russia wanted to improve relations with France and offered support after its humiliating defeat. Bismarck had little to offer Russia for fear of alienating Britain. France would clearly soon be once again a major player.

France recovered astonishingly quickly. It paid off the indemnity far more quickly than anyone expected, obliging the Germans to withdraw their troops. In 1875 the French set about reorganizing and enlarging the army. The Prussian general staff promptly drew up plans for a preventive war. Bismarck, who rejected the idea of such a war out of hand, thought in terms of a counter-attack. Constantin Rössler, a journalist known to serve as the chancellor's mouthpiece, published an article in the *Post* on April 8, 1875, under the headline "Is War in Sight?" It was designed to convince the French not to go ahead with their plans for fear that they might lead to war. The "War in Sight" crisis backfired. Britain and Russia, at France's behest, denounced Bismarck's provocative behavior. There was widespread sympathy for France, and Germany's bully-boy tactics were not appreciated. The crisis left France even more determined to improve the army. Britain and Russia had shown that their common determination to preserve the balance of power in Europe far outweighed their many differences elsewhere. Bismarck had been taught a lesson, which he took to heart. Any attempt by Germany to assert its hegemony was bound to meet with immediate and determined resistance.

Chastened by the experience of the "War in Sight" crisis Bismarck put his thoughts on paper while taking the waters at Bad Kissingen in the summer of 1877. Given the rivalries between Britain and Russia, exacerbated by Disraeli's purchase of the Suez Canal shares in 1875, between Russia and Austria-Hungary over the Balkans, and between France and Britain because of their colonial rivalry, Germany enjoyed a high degree of freedom as the "middle empire" in Europe. Bismarck concluded that: "All the powers with the exception of France need us and in the foreseeable future will be prevented from forming coalitions against us as a result of their relations one with another."

The Congress of Berlin

While Bismarck was drafting this Kissingen Memorandum the Balkans were once again in a state of turmoil, and his optimism over Germany's security steadily eroded, soon to turn to panic. Russia, allied with Romania, had already declared war on the Ottoman empire in April, soon driving the Turks out of Europe in spite of suffering heavy losses at Plevna in 1877. This was a battle that clearly showed the folly of attempting mass attacks against modern weaponry, a lesson that precious few officers took to heart. A greater Bulgaria stretching to the Aegean was created at the Treaty of San Stefano in March 1878. Since Bulgaria was little more than a Russian satellite, both Britain and Austria-Hungary were determined to stop this extension of Russian power and influence in a region in which they both had vital interests. The British fleet headed for the Straits to protect Constantinople while Austria-Hungary threatened to join in an anti-Russian alliance. Europe drew back from the brink, and a conference was convened in Berlin.

Bismarck had no direct interests in the Balkans and dreaded being dragged into the conflict. As early as 1876 the tsar had asked him on which side he would stand in the event of a war between Russia and Austria-Hungary over the Balkans, but he had refused to be tied down. He insisted that the preservation of the integrity of the Habsburg empire was in Germany's vital interest and did all he could to avoid a Balkan war.

Realizing that the Treaty of San Stefano was unacceptable to Austria-Hungary, Bismarck refused to encourage them to accept its terms. At the same time he was anxious not to offend the Russians. In the long run this was an untenable position. He did all he could to remain neutral. He refused to be used either by the British against the Russians, or by the Russians against the Austrians. But when Russian ambitions were thwarted and the Eastern Question was put before the Congress of Berlin, it seemed to the Russians that Germany was clearly biased in favor of Austria-Hungary. Bismarck as chairman of the conference announced that he intended to act as an "honest broker." This was treated by the Russians with skepticism. Gerson Bleichröder concurred, remarking that in all his years as a banker he had never come across such a creature.

The Congress of Berlin was a magnificent affair, the last old-style diplomatic meeting on the grand scale, with Bismarck, Disraeli, and Gorchakov as its star performers. Bismarck's skills were widely admired, but it was inevitable that Russia would feel humiliated and frustrated. The Congress could do little more than confirm the deal that had already been struck between Britain and Russia. Anything less than San Stefano would be perceived by the Russians as a loss of face. They were therefore bitter that the Germans had done nothing to further Russia's Balkan ambitions. The German chancellor was now a convenient scape-goat for all Russia's disappointments. Through no fault of his own, Bismarck had perma-nently alienated Russia, and the way was open for the Franco-Russian alliance that was the worst of all his nightmares. Russia continued to demand Germany's support against Austria-Hungary and against Britain. Bismarck realized that with its precarious position in the middle of Europe Germany could not afford to take sides. That one of the powers should insist that it do just that showed up the faulty logic of the Kissingen Memorandum.

The Dual and Triple Alliances

Relations between Germany and Russia worsened in the months after the Congress of Berlin. The Pan-Slavs mounted a ferocious campaign against Germany and the ever-watchful censors allowed a number of scurrilous attacks on the chancellor to appear in the Russian press. Tariff increases in 1879 aimed at protecting German agriculture against Russian exports were a further source of grievance. On August 15, 1879, one month after the new tariffs were put into effect, the tsar sent the kaiser a "slap in the face" letter with a harshly worded demand that Germany come clean over its future attitude towards Russia. The tsar blamed Bismarck for the present deplorable state of relations between the two countries, ascribing it to his personal and unfounded animosity towards his former friend, Prince Gorchakov. He reminded William of the singular services Russia had offered Prussia in 1870 and warned that if Germany persisted in showing such ingratitude the conse-quences would be "disastrous."

Both the kaiser and his chancellor were deeply shocked by both the tone and the content of this letter with its threats of war. William, smarting under the tsar's charges, was anxious to mend fences with a conservative power for which he had much affection. Bismarck panicked, envisioning an alliance between Russia, Austria-Hungary, and France that would lead to Germany's destruction. The Kissingen Memorandum was now shown to have been mere wishful thinking. Germany needed an ally against Russia, and that ally could only be Austria-Hungary. The result was the Dual Alliance of October 1879. The signatories agreed actively to support each other in the event of an attack by Russia and to remain benevo-lently neutral in other circumstances. The treaty was to be reviewed after five years

William was strongly opposed to Bismarck's radical break with the pro-Russian tradi-tions of Prussian and German foreign policy. He perceptively warned that it could well lead to an alliance between Russia and France. He asked to meet the tsar in Alexandrovo at the beginning of September in an attempt at personal diplomacy, which Bismarck promptly condemned as an "embryonic Olmütz." This initiative did nothing to improve the situation. The kaiser finally agreed to the Dual Alliance after yet another threat by Bismarck that he would resign. William caustically remarked that it would appear that the chancellor was more important than the emperor.

Bismarck presented the Dual Alliance as a revival of the German Confederation in "an appropriate contemporary form." This was putting a brave face on what he was soon to realize was a move made in haste and with possibly fatal consequences. The master diplomat had tied his hands behind his back and spent much of his remaining time in office in Houdini-like efforts to untie them. The ink was hardly dry before he realized that a defensive treaty could be used offensively. Austria-Hungary could provoke Russia and then appeal to Germany for help. Bismarck therefore sent numerous notes to the Vienna embassy warning that any attempts to alter the spirit of the treaty in this manner should be resisted at all costs. Bismarck's successors ignored these strictures. The Dual Alliance was reinterpreted to mean a solemn undertaking to stand together whatever the circumstances in a poignant demonstration of "Nibelungen fealty."

In opting for Austria-Hungary, Germany increased the likelihood of Russia turning towards France. Bismarck knew that without Russian support France would never attack Germany. From 1871 the Prussian general staff assumed that the next war would be on two fronts. His remarks to the effect that the Dual Alliance would oblige Russia to approach Germany were once again mere wishful thinking. In September 1871 he had sounded out the British government as to its attitude in the event of a war with Russia. Disraeli had been noncommittal. Now the liberals were back in power so that Bismarck, with his horror of Gladstonian liberalism, did not pursue the matter. He saw no need for the moment to make a decisive choice between Russia and Britain.

The League of the Three Emperors was revived in 1881, but secretly so as not to incense the Pan-Slavs. It still had precious little substance. Russia promised to stay neutral in the event of a war between France and Germany. Germany undertook to stay out of any conflict between Russia and Britain. For Bismarck the object was to avoid conflict between Russia and Austria-Hungary in the Balkans and to counteract the Pan-Slav demand for closer ties between Russia and France. He imagined that he was now once again the "honest broker" between Austria-Hungary and Russia, thereby closing his eyes to the clouds on the horizon. While the Prussian military pondered the problems of a two-front war against Russia and France, Bismarck secured the renewal of the tripartite agreement in 1884 for another three years.

Meanwhile in 1882 the Dual Alliance became the Triple Alliance with the inclusion of Italy. Italy had been irritated by France's annexation of Tunis in 1881 and by its exclusion from Egypt. Italy approached the Dual Alliance in an attempt to improve its position in Libya and Albania. Given the differences between Italy and Austria-Hungary in the Balkans and the problem of South Tyrol the treaty was of dubious value. In 1883 Romania joined the alliance, hoping for protection against Russia. With the perennial problem of Transylvania poisoning relations between Austria-Hungary and Romania this also hardly strengthened the alliance; nor did the tacit support of the Ottoman empire and Spain.

Germany was now at the center of two alliances with contradictory aims: an expanding system of alliances based on the Dual Alliance and the League of the Three Emperors: the first anti-Russian and pro-British, the second pro-Russian and anti-British. Bismarck called this oddity a "game with five balls." Germany appeared to be on reasonably good terms with all the powers, with the exception of France, without making any firm commitments. It was a singularly unstable situation. Even a master diplomatist like Bismarck was unlikely to be able to keep all five balls up in the air for much longer.

Colonialism

In 1881 Bismarck announced: "There will be no colonial policy as long as I am chancellor." In 1871 Bismarck had treated the French suggestion that Germany take Indo-China in lieu of Alsace-Lorraine with derisory laughter. Yet in 1884–5 Germany established colonies in Southwest Africa, East Africa, Togo and Cameroon, New Guinea, the Bismarck Archipelago, the Solomons, and the Marshalls.

Bismarck's motives for entering the race for colonies were many and varied. He knew that colonies were expensive, tiresome, and potential sources of conflict, but they offered certain advantages. Some of the hardship caused by the depression might be offset by providing fresh markets for German goods, assuring supplies of raw materials, and creating an autarchic trading area protected from the exigencies of world trade. The attention of disgruntled Germans could be diverted away from concerns over domestic politics by exciting them with a vision of an overseas mission. Similarly Germany's dangerously exposed position in central Europe might be overlooked by drawing attention to its overseas empire. The chancellor therefore decided to use the colonial question as a platform in the 1884 election. He denounced his opponents for lacking both patriotism and vision. By making colonialism the central issue he hoped to undermine the position of the pro-British and liberal crown prince. This too was somewhat dubious. Frederick was an enthusiastic supporter of the Samoa project and shared much of the popular enthusiasm for colonies. Perhaps this anti-English colonial policy might open the way to improved relations with France, as seemed to be the case during the Congo Conference held in Berlin in the winter of 1884/5.

This was the heyday of European imperialism: the scramble for Africa was becoming increasingly frantic and imperialism captured the popular imagination. Colonies were seen as an appropriate signification of Great Power status. The German Colonial Association (Deutsche Kolonialverein) was founded in 1882 with Miquel and Prince Hohenlohe-Langenburg as its most prominent members. The Society for German Colonization (Gesellschaft für deutsche Kolonisation) had a far less exalted membership. It was led by Dr. Carl Peters, a youthful psychopath, adventurer, and rapist, who set about carving out colonies in East Africa. In 1885 the two organizations were amalgamated as the German Colonial Society (Deutsche Kolonialgesellschaft). Colonialism was an immensely popular cause, and the society soon had some 10,000 members.

Initially Bismarck hoped to involve the state as little as possible in colonial affairs. Most colonies started when the Reich guaranteed protection to merchants and adventurers who set up shop in Africa and the South Seas. Carl Peters was an extreme and unattractive example of the breed. His example was followed by Adolf Lüderitz in Southwest Africa, Adolf Woermann in Togo and Cameroon, and Adolph von Hansemann of the Diskonto-Gesellschaft in New Guinea, among a host of others.

These protectorates soon ran up against the representatives of other imperialist powers and appealed for support. As a result colonialists were often calling the shots in Berlin.

Bismarck was content to encourage the resulting tensions with Britain, but he resented the fact that the tail was all too often wagging the dog. Gradually the informal protectorates became formal colonies, with Bismarck soon losing what little enthusiasm he had for the colonial enterprise.

In 1885 the colonialist Ferry government fell in France and the country turned its mind to revenge under the war minister Boulanger, a blustering and somewhat absurd figure known as "Général Revanche." As France and Russia drew closer, tensions between Germany and France were intensified with the Schnaebelé espionage affair. Meanwhile an election in Britain returned the Conservatives under Lord Salisbury, who was felt to be well disposed towards Germany. Boulanger was sacked in 1887, but "the man on the white horse" still enjoyed enormous popular support and plotted a coup d'état. This turned out to be a damp squib, and he fled the country in 1889. By this time Bismarck had had lost his taste for colonial exploits. Pointing at a map of Europe he told a visitor that Germany was in the center between France and Russia. "That," he said "is my map of Africa." In 1890 he laid the groundwork for the exchange with Britain of Helgoland for Zanzibar, thus indicating his desire to turn his back on the colonial empire and concentrate once more on European affairs.

Almost all the assumptions behind Bismarck's colonial policy proved to be false. Germany's position as the "empire in the middle" was weakened by colonies, which could not be defended without building a vast fleet, which in turn inevitably led to further complications. Economically the colonies brought precious little relief. Only 0.1 percent of German exports went to the colonies. Likewise only 0.1 percent of imports came thence. By 1905 only 2 percent of German capital was invested in the colonies, which in turn were inhabited by a mere 6,000 Germans, most of them civil servants and soldiers. Even in the short run the returns were disappointing for the chancellor. He did not even get a majority in the 1884 elections. In the long run the colonial episode unleashed the vicious forces of nationalism, racism, and imperialism, coupled with an intensification of anti-British sentiment, all of which was to be a major part of Bismarck's disastrous legacy. The way was opened for the hubris of "world politics."

The Collapse of Bismarck's System of Alliances

Bismarck's elaborate and contradictory system of alliances began to unravel. In 1885 the German prince Alexander von Battenberg, who had been chosen as prince of Bulgaria in 1879, was egged on by the British to annex Eastern Rumelia, thus asserting his independence from Russia. Austria supported Alexander, thereby acting against both the spirit and the letter of the League of the Three Emperors. Alexander was kidnapped, released and, under extreme pressure from Russia, abdicated in September. He then returned home to Darmstadt. In the following year another German prince, Ferdinand of Saxe-Coburg-Gotha, an officer in the Austro-Hungarian army, was elected prince of Bulgaria. Russia refused to recognize the new prince. The League of the Three Emperors was now in ruins, the break between Austria-Hungary and Russia final.

Bismarck had tried to broker a deal between Austria-Hungary and Russia, and had warned his ally that Germany had no obligations towards them under the terms of the Dual Alliance in this instance. He tended to sympathize with Russia's position, in spite of massive popular support in Germany for Ferdinand. This brought him no dividends in

St. Petersburg. The Russians blamed Germany rather than Austria-Hungary for their losing control over Bulgaria and for thus suffering a humiliating defeat in the Balkans. For the Pan-Slavs this was a repeat performance of what they had perceived to be Bismarck's anti-Russian policies at the Congress of Berlin. Once again their Balkan ambitions had been dashed thanks to lack of support from Berlin. Those Slavophiles and Westernizers who had been arguing in favor of an alliance with France were now gaining the upper hand.

Russia was not quite ready to embrace republican France, a country that welcomed Russian revolutionaries and sympathized with Poland. The foreign minister Giers was eager to maintain friendly relations with Berlin, but the enormously influential Pan-Slav journalist Mikhail Katkov, the champion of an alliance with France, was a powerful influence. In the end it was economic forces that finally brought the two countries together. Germany's protective tariffs of 1879 had adversely affected trade with Russia. Previously 34 percent of Russian exports had gone to Germany, whence came 44 percent of its imports. The situation was exacerbated by two further tariff increases by Germany and the inevitable responses by Russia. As a result grain exports from Russia declined while the Russians were less able to import the vital industrial goods that were essential for the modernization of the economy. Between 1879 and 1885 Germany's agricultural tariffs had trebled. This was seen in Russia as a deliberately unfriendly series of punitive measures, designed to hamstring their efforts to generate the capital needed in order to industrialize. Furthermore, up to 80 percent of Russia's sources of foreign capital came from loans traded on the Berlin stock exchange. There were powerful voices in Germany protesting against Russian counter-measures and demanding that the export of capital to Russia should cease.

Italy had reached an agreement with Britain over the Mediterranean that was later endorsed by Austria. This enabled Bismarck to negotiate a renewal of the Triple Alliance in February 1887. He now hoped to bring Britain closer to the Triple Alliance, thereby forming a front against an increasingly hostile Russia. The Mediterranean agreement formed the basis of the informal and secret Oriental Triple Alliance in December between Austria-Hungary, Italy, and Britain, and guaranteed the status quo in the Balkans and the Ottoman empire. It was designed to frustrate Russian ambitions in the area. The army increases of 1886/7, ostensibly aimed at revanchist France, were also a response to closer ties between St. Petersburg and Paris, marked by discussions between the general staffs of Russia and France in 1886.

In June that year Bismarck signed the "Reinsurance Treaty" with Russia. He had always been anxious to keep the line to St. Petersburg open, and was horrified by the widespread popular enthusiasm for a preventive strike against Russia, which was advocated by Moltke and Waldersee in the general staff and by Holstein in the foreign office. He was now determined to calm things down. The initiative came from the Russians and Bismarck jumped at the suggestion. Russia and Germany agreed that they would remain neutral in the event of an unprovoked attack by France or Austria on either signatory. Germany accepted that Bulgaria was in the Russian sphere of influence and promised diplomatic support should Russia find it necessary to occupy the Straits.

The Reinsurance Treaty was a very ambiguous affair that did not sit well with Germany's other commitments. It was against the spirit of the Triple Alliance and the letter of the Oriental agreement. It was left open to the signatories to decide whether an attack was "unprovoked." It gave Germany no protection against Russia. At best, as Herbert von Bismarck remarked, it would keep the Russians off their backs for six to eight weeks. It did nothing to solve the problem of the rivalry between Austria-Hungary and Russia in the

Balkans. It was very doubtful whether it would prevent an alliance between Russia and France. At best Bismarck had kept the line open to St. Petersburg and bought a little time, but Holstein had some justification in denouncing the treaty as "political bigamy."

Relations between Germany and Russia steadily worsened. Enthusiasts for a preventive war mounted a massive campaign in the German press. At the foreign office Holstein worked behind Bismarck's back by encouraging Austria-Hungary to take a firmer line against Russia. Bankers and industrialists demanded stronger retaliatory measures against Russia. Grain tariffs were raised again in 1887, so that they were now five times higher than in 1879. Further restrictions were placed on the import of meat and livestock. The Reichsbank was forbidden to make advances against Russian securities thus precipitating the panic sale of Russian bonds. Numerous Russian nationals were expelled from the Reich. The Russians responded by increasing the tariffs on industrial goods, and foreigners were forbidden to buy or transfer real estate in Russia, a measure that affected a large number of German property owners in the western provinces. Pan-Slavs lashed out against Germany and called for closer ties with France. The government, in its desperate search for capital, turned first to Amsterdam and then to Paris. The French responded by investing heavily in Russia, only to lose all in 1917.

Bismarck was clearly beginning to lose his grip. He might have imagined that he was appeasing the anti-Russian preventive war enthusiasts by increasing the pressure on Russia; but at the same time he was using these measures as a means to convince St. Petersburg of the desirability of improving relations with Germany. He failed to realize that the times had passed when Germany could act alone. Tied to Austria, he could not opt for Russia. An alliance with France was unthinkable. An approach to Britain in 1889 failed because Bismarck would not agree to give support to Britain against Russia in return for British support against France. In any case Britain had no need for Germany and Salisbury had no desire to be tied down by a formal alliance. Relations between the two countries remained good in spite of the failure of these talks.

German diplomacy under Bismarck was a one-man affair even if at times he had to fight tooth and nail with the kaiser in order to get his way. In domestic politics he took advice, listened to suggestions, and seized upon the ideas of others. In foreign policy he acted alone according to a set of assumptions that were rapidly becoming outdated in an age of imperialism and rabid nationalism. The principles of the Kissingen Memorandum no longer applied, five balls could not be kept up in the air, and the "saturated" empire in the middle was no longer secure.

CHAPTER NINE
WILHELMINE GERMANY
1890–1914

CHAPTER CONTENTS

A History of Modern Germany: 1800 to the Present, Second Edition. Martin Kitchen.
© 2012 Martin Kitchen. Published 2012 by Blackwell Publishing Ltd.

The kaiser might have been little more than the hereditary president of the Bundesrat, a monarch among many, a *primus inter pares*, but he was the lynchpin of the entire system. Bismarck had carved out a position of exceptional power to the point that there was much talk of a "chancellor dictatorship," "Caesarism," and "Bonapartism" but, as he knew full well, he was nothing without the full support of kaiser and king. For this reason he was dreading the day when William I would die and his dangerously liberal son succeed. The kaiser was an unimaginative and reactionary professional soldier of limited intelligence but with a strong sense of the obligations, responsibilities, and duties of his high station. This earned him the respect, but hardly the love, of his people. Over the years Bismarck bullied him into submission so that he faded into the background.

He died in 1888, the critical "Year of Three Kaisers," aged 90. His son Frederick III was married to Queen Victoria's eldest daughter, a strong-willed woman with liberal leanings with which her husband was much in sympathy. It was doubtful whether Bismarck's nightmare vision of a "German Gladstone ministry" would ever have been realized. Frederick's candidate for the role, Admiral Stosch, was hardly built of Gladstonian timber, and German liberalism had already run its course. In any case the unfortunate new kaiser, who was suffering from cancer of the larynx, died after a reign of ninety-nine days. Nietzsche, certainly no liberal, proclaimed Frederick III's death to be a great and decisive misfortune for Germany. In as much as his son, William II, was indisputably a great and decisive misfortune not only for Germany, but also for the rest of Europe, history was to prove this to be a sound judgment. It was a view shared by another great contemporary – Max Weber.

Described by his English uncle Edward VII as "the most brilliant failure in history," the 29-year-old William II was highly talented but superficial, a neurotic braggart and romantic dreamer, a militaristic poseur and passionate slaughterer of wild animals, a father of seven children who was happiest in the exclusive circle of his homosexual and transvestite intimates. Bismarck said of him that he wanted every day to be his birthday. Another wit remarked that he wanted to be the bride at every wedding, the stag at every hunt, and the corpse at every funeral. His abiding hatred of England was dictated by a feeling of inferiority and his pathological hatred of his English mother, whom he placed under house arrest as soon as his father died, charging her with pilfering state papers. He attributed his withered arm, which caused him much distress, to the sinister machinations of his mother's gynecologist. This contradictory, blustering, over-theatrical, arrogant yet profoundly insecure figure embodied many of the contradictions of the Germany of his day. His yearning for popularity and love of bombastic show were far from typically Prussian, but a manifestation of the new German pushiness, bluster, and aggression. The young kaiser was an exceptionally bad judge of character and ability who surrounded himself with a deplorable bunch of advisors. The result was a standstill in domestic affairs combined with an increasingly ill-considered, unrestrained, and aggressive foreign policy. It was a recipe for disaster.

The young emperor had long made it perfectly clear that he wished to escape from under the shadow of a chancellor who was forty-four years his senior and who had long outlived his popularity. He told his cronies: "I'll let the old boy potter along for another six months, then I'll rule myself." The first bone of contention with the chancellor was over how to deal with the Social Democrats. The kaiser was temporarily much taken by the court preacher Adolf Stoecker's currently fashionable ideas. Seeing that the anti-socialist laws were a miserable failure, he announced his intention to become a "social kaiser," who would win the love of his proletarian subjects by a menu of social reforms spiced with a healthy dose of

PLATE 14   William II "The Kaiser." © BPK

anti-Semitism. Bismarck thought this absurd and wanted to continue with his repressive policies.

In 1889 there was a massive strike of miners in the Ruhr. At its height about 140,000 miners downed tools. The army longed to have a crack at the strikers, but Bismarck held it back, hoping that the crisis would deepen and the complacent bourgeoisie get a real shock. William II decided to demonstrate his newfound affection for the laboring masses and received a delegation of strikers. This surprising gesture worked wonders. The mine owners expressed their readiness to negotiate and the strike was called off.

Bismarck's draft proposal for a limitless anti-socialist law was rejected by a solid majority of Reichstag deputies, including the German conservatives, whereupon the kaiser agreed to call a fresh round of elections. The result was a crushing defeat for Bismarck's cartel. Although Bismarck had lost his parliamentary majority he proposed to reintroduce the anti-socialist measures, coupled with a bill banning strikes along with a demand for a substantial army increase. The Reichstag was to be cowed into submission by a threat to call further elections and even the possibility of a coup d'état. In desperation he turned to his old enemy, Windthorst, proposing a coalition with the Center Party, but it was too late. The kaiser refused to begin his reign on a confrontational course with the labor movement. On March 17, 1890, he requested Bismarck's resignation. This he received the following day.

William II's System of Government

The new kaiser was determined to be his own chancellor and the ministers would be his "dogsbodies." In a public address in 1891 he announced: "Only one person can be master in the Reich, I cannot tolerate anyone else!" Dismissing the Reichstag as the "imperial monkey house," he surrounded himself with a number of advisors and cronies who bolstered his neo-absolutist ambitions. Chief among them were the heads of the Civil, Military, and Navy Cabinets, who were responsible for all promotions and appointments in their respective services. Then there were the adjutants and liaison officers who acted well beyond their constitutional remit. Equally important was the circle of his intimate friends around the epicene Philipp Eulenburg, whom his friends addressed as "she," and through whom Holstein and Bülow were to gain the kaiser's ear.

The precise nature of Wilhelmine Germany has been the subject of much heated debate. Erich Eyck spoke of William II's "personal rule," but he soon came under attack from historians who argued that this was all smoke and mirrors and that there was precious little behind the blustering rhetoric. That he had influential friends was hardly surprising or unique. After all Bismarck too had had his problems counteracting the Empress Augusta's influence on William I. Furthermore William II was incapable of ruling. He blew hot and cold, frequently changed his mind, and his impetuosity earned him the sobriquet "William the Sudden." He was unable to work systematically, passing six months in the year traveling, rising late in the day, and spending most of his waking hours at table, taking a stroll, or enjoying the social whirl. It is small wonder that his generals were determined to do everything possible to stop this militarily incompetent "supreme warlord" leading them into battle.

Structuralist historians such as Hans-Ulrich Wehler developed this theme to the point of calling William II a "shadow kaiser." In this version the political life of Wilhelmine Germany was determined by the economy, by an anonymous power structure and by class conflicts that were played out by interest groups, the bureaucracy, and the military. The personality of the kaiser was thus irrelevant. Within the given structural determinants another figurehead would have made no difference. John Röhl has led a robust assault on this widely held interpretation, has withstood charges of writing "personified" history, and has done much to restore credence in "personal rule" albeit in a largely negative sense.

As is so often the case in such debates the truth lies somewhere in the middle. There was indeed much tub-thumping bombast at court. The kaiser was a loud-mouthed poseur with absolutist pretensions, but there was little of substance behind all this. On the other hand he was more than a shadow kaiser: his power and influence were considerable, but only when he chose to intervene. He had certain pet projects that he pushed through, and he intervened, usually to disastrous effect, in foreign policy. Most important of all, unlike his grandfather who left most such decisions to Bismarck, he paid considerable attention to key appointments. Bülow and Tirpitz were the kaiser's men, essential ingredients of his "personal rule." Two great crises in his reign served to clip his wings. The first was the press campaign against the court "camarilla" led by the acerbic journalist Maximilian Harden, who exposed the kaiser's intimate and influential friends Philipp zu Eulenburg and Kuno von Moltke as homosexuals. The second was the kaiser's humiliation over the *Daily Telegraph* affair of 1908, which led to Bülow's resignation. His successor Bethmann Hollweg was a bureaucrat who had worked his way up through the Prussian administration. He was neither courtier nor toady and certainly not an instrument of the kaiser's personal rule.

Nevertheless, careers depended on royal favor. This in turn encouraged an atmosphere of lick-spitting opportunism at court, a groveling search for the favor of the All Highest. The kaiser's men, from the chancellor Bülow down, did their outmost to shield him from criticism and unpleasant reality, and were able to influence and even manipulate him. Temperamentally he was a modernizer and a technophile who had a horror of war; but his entourage managed to influence him to the point of making him more conservative and belligerent. Thus he was given to making grotesquely reactionary statements and to swearing that at the next crisis he would not cave in, but would lead the nation into war – all this in a pathetic attempt to show his entourage that he was a real man.

William II's sins of commission were trivial compared to his sins of omission. Germany would almost certainly have built a high seas fleet without him, the army would have played a devastatingly reactionary role in spite of his interventions, imperialism would have been just as raucously racist had he not been on the throne. He might have emphasized these trends in his outrageous speeches and public utterances as well as in his choice of advisors and his direct interventions in the political process; but in all this he was very much a product of his times. His disastrous legacy was that he failed to provide the coordination that the system desperately needed. Nowhere was this more evident than in military affairs. The Schlieffen Plan tied the hands of the politicians. There was no proper consultation between the army and the navy, or between the Prussian army and the Bavarian, Saxon, and Württemberg armies. There was similar confusion in foreign policy. Holstein and Marschall felt that Britain would eventually realize that it needed Germany's support. Bülow favored a closer relationship with Russia. William II wavered between these two positions. His might thus have been a negative personal rule, but it set the tone of the age as well as being the reflection of a society that was fundamentally unstable. It is not for nothing that this is called the "Wilhelmine era."

Bismarck's immediate successor, General Leo von Caprivi, afforded the secretaries of state far greater freedom of action, allowing them access to audiences with the kaiser which he did not bother to attend. This tendency became even more pronounced when he felt obliged to resign as Prussian minister president in 1892. His successor, Hohenlohe, was a weak and elderly aristocrat chosen in 1894 to bolster the kaiser's personal rule. The secretaries of state grew ever more independent from the chancellor and closer to the kaiser. Given the rivalries between the secretaries of state, both in Prussia and in the Reich, along with the simultaneous independence of the imperial and Prussian bureaucracies, and the kaiser's inability to provide decisive leadership, the system became extremely erratic and unpredictable. Bülow, who became chancellor in 1900, brought back some order and method by partially restoring the collegial structure. This course was continued under Bethmann Hollweg.

At the root of the problem was that whereas under Bismarck Prussia dominated the Reich, the system began to fall apart under his successors. Imperial secretaries of state had been mostly Prussian ministers, and those who were not had had attended meetings of the Prussian ministry of state. Now Prussia and the Reich began to part company. Prussia stuck to its conservative course, while the Reichstag pushed for reform. The imperial secretaries of state were now fully independent from the Prussian government. Their ministries, rather than their Prussian counterparts, prepared the drafts of legislation prior to presentation to the Bundesrat. Bills were still vetted by the Prussian ministry of state, but the Reich was now gaining the initiative. The great issues of the day – armaments and social policy – were matters for the Reich and the Reichstag, a fact that further strengthened the federal agencies.

Prussia still enjoyed hegemonic power in Germany. Power was centered on the kaiser and his chancellor. The Prussian army was the most powerful institution in the land. The Reich's bureaucracy was largely recruited from the Prussian administration. The importance of the federal ministries grew to the point that one spoke of a "Reich administration" (*Reichsleitung*) by the end of the century and of an "imperial government" (*Reichsregierung*) under Bethmann Hollweg. There was a corresponding decline in the influence of the Bundesrat, which had been the epicenter of Bismarck's system. The federal government frequently failed to consult the states, presenting bills directly to the Reichstag. The kaiser echoed this trend by insisting that, as German emperor, he was not the first among equals. The other monarchs were liege lords and vassals.

The Reichstag

The greater the importance of the federal government, the greater the power of the Reichstag. The government needed a Reichstag majority in order to push through its legislation. The budgetary rights of the Reichstag were strengthened as the fiscal burden increased. The Reichstag proved to be a reliable partner for the government, resulting in an increasing number of bills being first discussed by the parties and then introduced in the Reichstag rather than in the Bundesrat. Even as convinced an anti-parliamentarian as Admiral Tirpitz, with his dream of an "eternal law" for the navy, came to realize that there was no way round the Reichstag if he wanted to build his battleships. Individual states that were unable to get their way in the Bundesrat could always try again in the Reichstag. Similarly, when the government failed to get its way in the Bundesrat, it could always appeal to the Reichstag.

A big step forward was taken in 1906 when Reichstag deputies were paid a modest emolument. This opened the way for the creation of a professional political class, but it also furthered the process of political bureaucratization: a process brilliantly analyzed by the German sociologist Robert Michels. This had a profound effect on the Social Democratic Party (SPD), the most highly organized and modern of all the political parties, which was to become the largest parliamentary party in 1912. Should it use the Reichstag merely as a propaganda forum and wait for the eagerly expected revolution as the party's chief ideologue Karl Kautsky argued, or should it try to use the Reichstag as an instrument of social reform as the revisionist Eduard Bernstein proposed? Should it remain intransigently in opposition under the old slogan: "Not a single man, not a single Pfennig for this system"; or should it follow the example of Millerand and the French socialists and support certain proposals of the bourgeois government? The party's discourse remained resolutely revolutionary. Marxist platitudes raised the hackles of respectable bourgeois. But in practice the party was becoming increasingly reformist. In 1913 the SPD voted for the army estimates, and in August 1914 the "fellows without a fatherland" supported the war effort with patriotic enthusiasm, in spite of all the anti-war resolutions of the Socialist International, in which it was the largest party.

Germany was still far from having a parliamentary system with government by a parliamentary majority and ministers responsible to parliament. The Social Democrats were still regarded as pariahs. After the elections of 1912, when the Reichstag was no longer dominated by an alliance between conservatives and the Center Party, the SPD became a possible coalition partner. This was a frightful prospect for conservatives, but it was one that some members of the Center Party and the National Liberals viewed with equanimity. The time was not yet ripe for a coalition stretching from Bassermann and the National Liberals to Bebel and the SPD. It was not until the First World War that a center-left coalition developed that was to form the basis of Germany's first parliamentary regime.

Caprivi and the "New Course"

Bismarck's successor Caprivi was a man who, in spite of his army rank, had for many years been secretary of state for the navy. He was an Austrian by birth, level-headed, decent, conscientious, and with liberal leanings. Lacking a landed estate and many of the other trappings and characteristics of the aristocracy, he was despised by the Junkers as the "chancellor without an acre or a blade of grass." Although he was determined to uphold the authority of the monarchy and of the state as well as being a sworn enemy of the Social Democrats, he was a man of compromise and of moderate reform.

His task was not an easy one. Bismarck had far outlived his popularity, but he was a very hard act to follow. The old man in Friedrichsruh mounted a vicious campaign against the kaiser and his chancellor and became the center of a conservative opposition. Bismarck's attacks were dismissed at court as the senile drivel of a feeble-minded old man. His memoirs, published shortly after his death in 1898, became an instant bestseller. This mendacious work was both a literary masterpiece and a massive attack on the policies of his successors. It misled generations of historians and was used as a weapon against the kaiser's personal rule, as were the numerous monuments to Bismarck that sprouted up throughout Protestant Germany, the largest and most hideous of which was built by the proudly independent burghers of Hamburg. But Bismarck's was a voice from the past. Society had changed so dramatically since 1871 that the political structure he had given to the Reich was no longer either appropriate or workable.

Caprivi was favorably disposed towards William II's momentary enthusiasm for social reform and his desire to be seen as the "social kaiser." A certain amount was done to improve the lot of the working class, to give it a voice in the workplace, and to create an effective means of arbitrating disputes between management and labor, but the SPD continued to gain support and there was a wave of strikes. By 1893 William II had lost interest in these social programs and went on a diametrically opposite course by supporting the ideas of Baron Carl von Stumm-Halberg. "King Stumm" demanded that his fellow industrialists should be masters in their own house, stern patriarchs who could demand and expect absolute obedience from the workforce, in return for which employers should ensure the wellbeing of their employees. The confrontational politics of the "Stumm era" overlooked the fact that in 1894 the Bavarian Social Democrats voted for the budget, thus marking the beginning of reformist politics in the party. A showdown between capital and labor as proposed by Stumm would clearly be counterproductive.

Caprivi was open to the ideas of those who argued that Germany, as a rapidly expanding industrial nation, was hurt by high tariffs. With the clear trend towards what now would be called globalization and which was then in certain circles described as imperialism, Germany could not afford to indulge in a neo-mercantilist policy of autarchy under the slogan of "protection of national labor," nor could it afford to featherbed the agricultural

PLATE 15   Bismarck dead and surrounded by the ghosts of the past. © Deutsches Historisches Museum

sector. Caprivi summed up the situation with the slogan: "Either we export goods, or we export people!" The problem took on greater urgency as economic relations between Russia and France grew ever closer.

The chancellor set about negotiating long-term trade agreements that would stimulate industrial exports. This in turn necessitated lowering agricultural tariffs, which was bound to upset the powerful agrarians and turn the conservatives against the government. In the winter of 1892 trade agreements were signed with Austria-Hungary, Italy, and Belgium and ratified by the Reichstag, in spite of opposition from the majority of the conservatives.

Conservatism, once a powerful political ideology, was rapidly becoming an expression of the special interests of the agrarians. German agriculture was becoming increasingly uncompetitive. Prices were forced downwards by as much as 50 percent due to intense foreign competition, leaving many farmers in dire straits. There were loud cries for help and a frantic search for scapegoats. The Social Democrats, with their egalitarian demands for cheaper foodstuffs, and Jewish dealers were singled out for special blame. In 1893 the

Farmers League (Bund der Landwirte) was formed, a populist, anti-Semitic, rabble-rousing movement that gained widespread support, particularly in the eastern provinces. The Junkers had conjured up a spirit that soon got out of hand. Conservatives were dabbling with mass politics and associating with outspoken demagogues who launched violent attacks on the chancellor. Many an old-style but far-sighted conservative civil servant began to worry that the sorcerer's apprentice might eventually threaten the master.

The debate on the critical treaty with Russia in March 1894 amounted to a vote of confidence in the chancellor and his policy of encouraging industry, reducing the cost of basic foods, and putting the agrarians in their place. The result was a resounding victory for Caprivi. The conservatives fought back, promising a struggle to the death against liberal capitalism and demanding a state trading monopoly for agricultural produce combined with guaranteed minimum prices. These proposals were rejected by the Reichstag majority.

The conservatives were losing ground in the Reichstag, but they held their own in Prussia. They won major concessions in a comprehensive tax reform. The proposal to introduce death duties was rejected. Real estate was far less heavily taxed than movable capital. The three-class electoral system based on the amount of taxes paid became even more inequitable after these reforms, thus further strengthening the parties on the right.

Educational reform proved to be Caprivi's greatest headache. The conservative Prussian minister of education, Count Robert von Zedlitz-Trützschler, proposed a bill that would mark a return to confessional schools. The object behind this move was to win the support of the Center Party, which was needed in the Reichstag to ensure the passage of the trade treaties as well as the army estimates. The proposal was met with a storm of protest from the liberals and freethinking intellectuals who regretted the end of the *Kulturkampf*. The kaiser, strongly supported by Miquel, fearing the end of the cartel in Prussia, refused to accept the idea of an educational reform that was not supported by the National Liberals, whereupon both Caprivi and Zedlitz-Trützschler resigned. Caprivi was now no longer Prussian minister president, but remained chancellor and also Prussian foreign minister, so as to be able to instruct the Prussian delegation to the Bundesrat. His place in Prussia was taken by the ultra-conservative Count Botho zu Eulenburg.

The conservatives stepped up their attacks on the government with the populist and anti-Semitic Tivoli Program of December 1892. The Center Party attacked the government from the left. Caprivi dissolved the Reichstag when it rejected a 72,000-man increase in the army. The elections returned a majority of National Liberals and populists. The aristocratic conservatives suffered a severe defeat. The Social Democrats, with 23.3 percent, won the largest share of the popular vote, but the Center Party gained the largest number of seats.

With considerable skill Caprivi, having pushed through the army estimates, won an impressive majority for the Russian trade treaty, but he had lost the confidence of the kaiser. William II disliked the chancellor's schoolmasterly tone, was irritated by the debacle over confessional schools, and was furious that Caprivi had reduced the period of compulsory service in the army from three to two years. Inspired by Stumm to take a firm stand against Social Democracy and alarmed by a wave of anarchist attacks which culminated in the stabbing to death in Lyons of the French president Sadi Carnot by an Italian revolutionary in June 1894, the kaiser demanded immediate legislative action against the forces of revolution.

Caprivi pointed out that any such legislation was the province of the individual states, but Botho zu Eulenburg and Miquel wanted a federal law. Knowing perfectly well that the proposed "anti-revolutionary bill" (*Umsturzvorlage*) would never pass the Reichstag, they plotted a coup d'état to abolish universal manhood suffrage. The kaiser's call for action was widely popular, prompting him to make yet another outrageous public address in Königsberg calling for the forces of order to stand together against the subversives and revolutionaries. Caprivi stood firm. William II backed down, largely because of the likely reaction abroad to such an outlandish course of action; but the chancellor's days in office were now numbered.

The kaiser used an unfortunate press release, which implied that the chancellor had put him in his place, as an excuse to dismiss both Caprivi and Eulenburg at the end of October 1894. Thus ended Caprivi's "New Course," an imaginative and promising attempt to reform a country that was in an awkward transitional period between the overbearing and ossified late Bismarckian era and the arrogant hubris of the Wilhelminian epoch. It failed because of the kaiser's fickleness, the stubbornly doctrinaire attitude of the main political parties, the excessive influence of interest groups, the alarming growth of radical populism, and the inherent structural problem of relations between Prussia and the Reich. It is exceedingly doubtful whether under such trying circumstances another chancellor would have done any better.

Hohenlohe

Caprivi's successor as chancellor was the elderly Prince Chlodwig zu Hohenlohe-Schillingsfürst, a lofty Catholic magnate from Baden with wide administrative experience and of liberal conservative views. At 75, deaf and forgetful, he was certainly not the man to restrain the young kaiser; but as a man of the old school, with the typical anti-Prussian sentiments of a southern German and with the dismissive attitude of a *grand seigneur* towards Prussia's "cabbage Junkers," he was not going to be content to play the role of the kaiser's man.

The kaiser was determined to continue with his anti-socialist and confrontational program in spite of the chancellor's reservations. The "anti-revolutionary bill" was reintroduced in the Reichstag at the end of 1894. It was rejected out of hand. The kaiser's intimates now talked wildly of a coup d'état to be led by the former chief of the general staff, General Waldersee. Nothing came of this, but all social legislation was put on hold. An attempt at anti-socialist legislation in Prussia failed by a narrow margin. The fronts hardened still further over a major strike in the Hamburg docks in the winter of 1896/7. Prominent social reformers such as the sociologist Ferdinand Tönnies and the evangelical pastor Friedrich Naumann expressed their sympathy for the strikers. Waldersee, as corps commander in Hamburg Altona, wanted to use force to break the strike. William II sympathized, and in a public speech announced that any means, however drastic, were justified in the struggle against the forces of subversion and revolution. In further speeches he called for stern measures against picket lines. A further attempt at anti-socialist legislation was made in 1899 with the "Prison Bill" (*Zuchthausvorlage*) but it suffered an ignominious defeat, leaving the conservatives isolated in their extreme position. This was the end of the "Stumm era" and Hohenlohe's days were numbered. Bülow , whom the kaiser was grooming as his replacement, waited in the wings.

Tirpitz, the Navy, and "World Politics"

Relations with Britain had taken a turn for the worse when the kaiser sent a telegram in January 1896 congratulating President Krüger on repulsing Dr. Jameson's raid on the Transvaal. This dramatic expression of solidarity with the Boers in their struggle against the British was greeted with violently anti-German tirades in the British press, but it was Tirpitz's naval building program that was really to poison relations between the two countries.

The high seas fleet was the key element in the "world politics" (*Weltpolitik*), which enjoyed widespread public support. Germany wanted to join the ranks of the imperialist powers, but the newcomer had precious little room for maneuver. It could push its claims for a few marginal areas in Africa and demand equal rights in China, Morocco, or the Ottoman empire, but at every turn it came up against the established imperialist powers of Britain, France, and Russia. When Bülow was appointed secretary of state for foreign affairs in 1897 he announced in the Reichstag: "The days when the Germans left the land to one of their neighbors and the sea to the other, keeping only the sky for themselves and when pure theory reigned are now over … We do not wish to put anyone in the shade, but we also demand a place in the sun." Nevertheless, any increase in Germany's colonial empire necessarily diminished the relative strength of other empires. This was a particularly sensitive issue for the British, whose empire already showed marked signs of decline.

Anglo-German relations were bedeviled by the contradictions between Germany's position in the center of Europe and as an aspiring imperialist power. Germany needed Britain's support in Europe against the threat from Russia and France, but its imperial aspirations made this hard to achieve. Germany wanted to ensure its security in Europe while pursuing a forceful *Weltpolitik*. Very few in positions of authority realized that these were contradictory ambitions. Most fondly imagined that the Anglo-Russian and Anglo-French antagonisms were immutable factors in international relations, so that Britain would never join the ranks of Germany's opponents.

This contradiction was deeply embedded in the strategic thinking behind Tirpitz's battle fleet. On the one hand it was designed to protect the coastline against the Russian and French fleets, so as to break any close blockade. But it was also intended to guard Germany's overseas empire and commercial interests. For that to be possible naval bases were needed in remote parts of the globe. Tirpitz argued that cruisers were inadequate for either role. A fleet of battleships was needed that was powerful enough not only to break a blockade and protect the colonies, but also to act as a deterrent. The fleet was to be so powerful that neither Russia nor France would dare risk a confrontation and on the principle of "if you can't beat 'em, join 'em" Germany would become a attractive potential partner.

Tirpitz's ideas differed very little from those of sailors such as Sir John Fisher, who had absorbed Alfred Thayer Mahan's theory that Great Power status depended on sea power. The problem lay in the political consequences of naval building. From the outset Tirpitz saw his battle fleet as a direct challenge to Britannia's claim to rule the waves. His "risk theory" was primarily designed to ensure British neutrality in the event of a continental war. Even before the first naval bill was debated, the admiralty envisaged Britain as a potential enemy. Anglo-German naval rivalry was soon to become the central issue. All the other arguments in favor of a high seas fleet soon became mere propagandistic rhetoric, designed to disguise the real thrust of Tirpitz's strategy. At times Tirpitz entertained the fantastic idea that Germany could take on the Royal Navy and replace Britain as a naval power, at others he imagined that Britain would be obliged to make major concessions and accept Germany as an equal partner. At the very least the fleet would guarantee that Britain would stay out of any future European conflict. Germany did not have the financial resources or, in spite of the widespread enthusiasm among the bourgeois parties for the naval building program, the political will to build a fleet that was large enough to fulfill any of these three roles. Moreover it never entered Tirpitz's mind that Britain might look for support elsewhere. As a result all three of Tirpitz's scenarios were to prove to be pure fantasy.

Another fatal weakness was the failure to coordinate military and naval strategy with foreign policy. Whereas the diplomats thought, however ambivalently, in terms of some kind of arrangement with Britain, the army under Schlieffen worked on plans for a western offensive involving the violation of Belgian neutrality that was likely to involve Britain in a continental war. Tirpitz's anti-British strategy was worked out independently from the army while the chancellor was kept in virtual ignorance of strategic matters. They were never discussed with politicians.

Economic factors also played an important role in the burgeoning Anglo-German rivalry. Thanks in large part to Germany's spectacular achievements in the second industrial revolution, particularly in the chemical and electrical industries, Germany's share of world trade was only fractionally less than Britain's on the eve of the Great War. Britain, no longer the workshop of the world, felt humiliated by an aggressive newcomer with whom it now had a negative trade balance. Germany in return feared that the British might be tempted to erect a protective tariff wall around the empire. The call for a place in the sun, providing safe markets for German goods, became ever more insistent. In the overly dramatic discourse of the day, Germany had to become the hammer or it would be merely the anvil.

As elsewhere in the developed nations, the relationship between economic interests and foreign policy were complex and often contradictory. A consortium under the Deutsche Bank was initially enthusiastically supportive of the government's sponsorship of the Baghdad railway, a grandiose plan to link Constantinople with Basra, but soon began to lose interest when faced with foreign competition, higher risks, and spiraling costs. Similarly, the government was unable to work up much enthusiasm for investment in the perennially dubious China market. Mannesmann's mining interests in Morocco gave the company considerable political clout, while the armaments industry was given full political and diplomatic support for its efforts in the Balkans and the Ottoman empire.

Tirpitz's first naval bill was debated in 1897. It was relatively modest, but it was presented as the first stage of a long-range plan to build a battle fleet. The reception in the Reichstag was mixed. Conservatives, who represented agrarian interests, detested this "ghastly fleet" since for them it represented nationalism, "world politics," industry, and export markets all to the detriment of Prussia, the army, agriculture, and the old order. The bill squeaked through largely due to the support of a majority of the Center Party, which was anxious to show its loyalty to the regime. In the following year Germany showed its determination to continue its naval building program by flatly refusing to agree to disarmament and international arbitration as proposed at the conference at The Hague, convened on the initiative of the tsar. The brusque and threatening attitude of the Germans created a most unfavorable impression in the international community, as did a repeat performance at the second peace conference in 1907.

Navalism and Imperialism

The motives behind German imperialism were many and varied. As with other complex historical phenomena it is impossible to establish a convincing causal hierarchy. Liberals such as Gustav Stresemann, Max Weber, and Friedrich Naumann hoped that imperialism would help modernize Germany society, break the stranglehold of the conservative agrarian elite, and provide the additional assets to enable a fairer distribution of wealth, thereby encouraging the integration of the working class. Social imperialists, Bülow at their head, saw imperialism as a glamorous project that would integrate the nation and marginalize the Social Democrats. A number of socialists, from Marx on down, saw a positive moment in imperialism in that it brought progressive ideas to backward areas, gave the colonized the weapons for their eventual liberation, and provided jobs for their working-class supporters. As the years went by there emerged a remarkably broad consensus on imperialism.

In 1897 the Germans used the murder of two missionaries in Kiautschou in order to establish a naval base in China. It was a suitable harbor with nearby coalmines and soon boasted a fine German brewery at Tsingtao which still produces China's best-known beer. The British, who controlled 80 percent of the trade with China, resented the German presence in Shantung, but their fears were unfounded. Germany never became a major player in China and only managed to capture a fraction of the China market. The former chief of the general staff, Waldersee, was appointed to command the international force that crushed the Boxer Rebellion in 1900, but he arrived after British and Japanese troops had taken Peking. His overbearing attitude earned him the sobriquet "World Marshal" while back at home the kaiser gave another of his unfortunate speeches to German troops who were being sent to China urging them to behave like the Huns, adding that the Chinese should henceforth not dare to look a German in the eye. The kaiser's discourse was now peppered with references to the "yellow peril." The crude racism of the "Hun speech" was widely seen as further evidence of the unpredictably aggressive nature of Wilhelmine Germany.

Criticisms of the Naval Building Program

A second naval bill was debated in 1899 that foresaw a German fleet that would be the third largest in the world, behind those of Britain and France. The proposal was sharply criticized by the agrarians on the right and by Bebel and Richter on the left. The former complained about the effects on agriculture and what they were pleased to call "the national cause"; the latter denounced the bill as a further example of the kaiser's personal rule. A number of deputies warned of a further worsening of relations with Britain, which had already been poisoned by the Boer War. In spite of such complaints the bill passed with minor revisions. It was a triumph for Tirpitz and the kaiser. There was no further talk of the need for a coup d'état. Tirpitz had hoped that his naval building program would effectively shut out the Reichstag and in his words "place the social order in quarantine." He was not fully successful in this endeavor, but there was now a consensus, however hesitant in some circles, for a large navy and the strident imperialism of "world politics."

Differences between agrarians and industrialists that were apparent in the debates over the naval bills came to a head in 1899 when a proposal to build a canal connecting the

Rhine to the Elbe was debated in the Prussian House of Representatives. The kaiser whole-heartedly supported the idea, but the conservatives were in violent opposition. For them it was a floodgate through which cheap North American grain would swamp eastern agri-culture. William II did not dare to dissolve the House, but he took the constitutionally highly dubious step of threatening to ask for the resignation of all those representatives in state employ who opposed the bill. In spite of such drastic measures the bill was rejected. It was not until 1905 that funds were approved for the construction of part of the canal. This incident clearly showed the limits of the kaiser's personal power.

The agrarians' more extreme demands were clearly unacceptable, but concessions had to be made. Trading in grain futures was forbidden, strict veterinary controls were applied to imported meat and livestock, generous subsidies were provided, and tariffs increased. On the other hand there was general agreement that Germany was now primarily an industrial country. The efforts of those like Count Hans von Kanitz, who wanted to turn the clock back with drastic measures such as a state monopoly on the sale of grain, were hopelessly unrealistic. Furthermore, the increase in the price of essential foodstuffs was causing widespread discontent and debate – all to the advantage of parties on the left. The situation was further complicated by the demands of the middle classes, who felt trapped between industrialists and agrarians on one side and by the working class on the other.

In this complex and confusing situation, where the interests of various significant groups were at odds, Miguel was inspired by Bismarck's notions of an alliance between rye and iron and of a "cartel" to propose in 1897 a policy of "solidarity" (*Sammlung*) whereby all the "productive classes" should stand together, thus overcoming the differences between agriculture and industry without harming the middle classes. Conservatives would be won over to support the naval building program by tariff increases. The interests of consumers were to be respected, the Social Democrats excluded. All ideas of integrating the industrial working class by means of social reform were abandoned, the *Sammlung* being cemented by a common struggle against the Red Menace and by collective enthusiasm for *Weltpolitik*.

This attractive vision of a society pulling together in pursuit of a common cause soon proved to be a fantasy. Industrialists complained that the agrarians were being favored. They in turn grumbled that they were getting the sharp end of the stick. It was a disaster in electoral terms. In 1898 the SPD increased its share of the vote from 23.3 percent to 27.2 percent. The two conservative parties lost 20 percent of their seats in the Reichstag. The National Liberals also lost seats. The Center Party, as the largest party, held the balance of power.

Bülow

In October 1900 Bernhard von Bülow was appointed chancellor. Secretary of state for foreign affairs since 1897, he had been groomed as Hohenlohe's successor. He was elegant, charming, vain, and superficial – the "minister of fine appearance" as one wit described him – but he was also a strong-willed and competent administrator. He brought order to government, ending the conflicts between Prussia and the Reich by pushing aside Miquel, who as vice president of Prussia had carved out a personal empire. Bülow was very skillful in manipulating the kaiser, who in turn became less involved in day-to-day politics, largely due to the fact that Tirpitz, the other strong man in the government, was successful in obtaining funding for his beloved fleet. William II frequently caused havoc with his ill-considered interventions. August Bebel claimed that each speech made by the monarch resulted in 100,000 additional votes for the Social Democrats. Bülow shielded the kaiser from mounting criticism and sycophantically calmed the monarch's irascible and unpredictable humors.

Although Bülow was at first not prepared to continue Miquel's appeasement of the conservatives by tariff concessions, he soon realized that there was no real alternative to *Sammlungspolitik*. At first he refused to increase the tariffs on grain with the result that the conservatives once again defeated the Mittelland Canal project. In 1902 the government proposed a tariff increases of up to 40 percent. This prompted an outburst of protest from the left which was matched by equally inflammatory rhetoric from sundry agrarian interest groups denouncing the proposed increases as far too modest. It took a certain amount of procedural chicanery to pass the tariff bill, which did not come into effect until 1905.

The tariffs were long overdue. Years of the low Caprivi tariff combined with the parlous state of world markets had placed the German farmers, whether East Elbian Junkers or Bavarian peasants, in a precarious position. They desperately needed the help afforded to the agricultural sector elsewhere. The effect of price increases on low-income groups was nowhere near as dire as had been predicted. Nevertheless, dissatisfaction with the new tariffs was expressed in the elections in 1903 in which the turnout was remarkably high. The Social Democrats again made substantial gains, admittedly at the cost of the left liberals. The conservatives lost votes. Once again the Center Party, as the largest party, held the balance.

The Center Party used its influential position to secure modest improvements in social policy, which were enthusiastically endorsed by the energetic and progressive secretary of state for the interior, Count Posadowsky. They were also able to remove some of the remaining traces of the *Kulturkampf*. In 1904 the Bundesrat annulled the anti-Jesuit law, occasioning howls of protest from fervent Protestants and godless liberals. Support for the new tariffs was made conditional on the introduction of an insurance scheme for widows and orphans. None of these measures were of spectacular importance, but they all showed that the Reichstag played an increasing role within the context of Bülow's plebiscitary imperialism.

Anglo-German Rivalry

When Britain reached an agreement with France in 1904 it no longer needed to consider the possibility of winning Germany's support against Russia. Germany supported Russia in its war against Britain's ally Japan, thus prompting a violent reaction in Britain. The British press blamed the Germans for an incident on the Dogger Bank in which the Russian fleet fired in error upon some British fishing vessels. In February 1905 Admiral Fisher gave a provocative speech calling for a pre-emptive strike against the German navy. The Germans now suffered from an acute "Copenhagen complex." Hotheads in the admiralty planned to invade Denmark and Sweden and blockade the Baltic, but cooler heads prevailed, including both Tirpitz and Schlieffen.

With Russia's crushing defeat and subsequent revolution Britain no longer had to worry about the Russian menace, opening the way to an understanding between the two powers. Germany was also significantly strengthened by the Russian debacle. Given that France was now allied with Russia's greatest rival, Berlin imagined that there was a strong possibility of a Russo-German understanding. The kaiser visited the tsar in the summer of 1905 and signed the Treaty of Björkö whereby the two powers agreed to cooperate in Europe for a period of one year. William II was overjoyed with the success of his personal diplomacy, but the treaty had no substance. It was in clear contradiction to the Dual Alliance, and the Russian government, which was desperately in need of French financial support, refused to renege on its commitment to its ally.

Schlieffen and Holstein now thought in terms of a preventive war against France. The situation was ideal and such a golden opportunity was unlikely to recur, but the problem remained that there was no convincing *casus belli*. The foreign office therefore sought to split the Entente Cordiale by provoking a crisis over Morocco. The French, with blissful disregard for international agreements but with the blessing of the British, set about turning Morocco into a protectorate in which they would have a trade monopoly. Germany protested vigorously and called for an open-door policy in Morocco. The kaiser, much against his will, was persuaded to pay an official visit to Tangier to proclaim his support for the sultan. Germany was unquestionably in the right, but its heavy-handed approach, far from splitting the Entente, brought the partners closer together in their determination to stand up against such browbeating. The French foreign minister Delcassé, the architect of the Entente Cordiale and advocate of France's imperialist ambitions in North Africa, was forced to resign, but Germany was left completely isolated at an international conference held in Algeçiras.

Some important concessions were made to internationalize Morocco, but they made no significant difference to France's dominant position. Germany suffered a severe diplomatic defeat. Britain was now convinced that this overbearing power with its colonial and naval ambitions represented the major threat to European stability as well as to the security of the British empire. This view was shared by Campbell-Bannerman's liberal government, which took office in December 1905.

The Bülow Bloc

The first major clash between the Center Party and the chancellor came in 1906. The Social Democrats had long been harsh critics of German colonial policy with its severity, corruption, and brutality. The rising star in the Center Party, Matthias Erzberger, took up the cause somewhat to the discomfort of the party leadership. The brutal suppression of the rebellions of the Hereros and the Hottentots in German Southwest Africa (Namibia) was both widely criticized and hideously expensive. A proposal for additional funding for Southwest Africa was rejected by a narrow margin after a fierce debate in the Reichstag in December 1906. Bülow promptly called for a fresh round of elections, even though both Posadowsky and Tirpitz felt that it was still possible to reach an understanding with the Center Party.

Relations between the kaiser and the chancellor had become increasingly strained, William II accusing Bülow of kowtowing to the Center, a party that he detested. Bülow had been sick for six months, had only just returned to work, and was anxious to show that he was a strong man who was not dependent on the Catholics. He now set about forming the "Bülow Bloc" of parties that were fervently anti-socialist and anti-clerical, devoutly patriotic, enthusiastically imperialist, and loyal to kaiser and fatherland. What Bebel labeled the "Hottentot election" was a disaster for the Social Democrats, who lost almost half their seats in the Reichstag. The Center Party made modest gains, with many Catholics fearing a fresh round of the *Kulturkampf*. The conservatives and National Liberals also increased their representation, as did the left liberals who were no longer in opposition after the death of the brilliantly adversarial Eugen Richter earlier in the year.

Bülow intended to convert the Bloc from an electoral alliance to a parliamentary coalition, thus unwittingly further enhancing the importance of the Reichstag. Bülow's opening to the left was distasteful to many on the right who saw the Center Party as the lesser evil, whereas on the left the refusal to make fundamental reforms in the Prussian electoral system meant that their allegiance was questionable. The Bloc was thus ever in danger of falling apart. Only the National Liberals were solid in their support.

Scandals and Crises

In 1907 Russia and Britain settled their differences over Tibet, Afghanistan, and Persia, leaving Germany dangerously isolated. Bülow's *Weltpolitik* was in ruins. Slavophile anti-Germans were gaining the upper hand in Russia. At the British foreign office, Eyre Crowe wrote his famous memorandum in which he argued that Germany was striving for hegemony in Europe and posed a threat to the vital interests of the empire. Inspired by the lessons of the Russo-Japanese naval war Britain had begun to build the monster vessels – the heavily armed and swift dreadnoughts – in 1906. Germany immediately took up the challenge. A fresh round of naval building began which further poisoned relations between the two countries.

The Bülow Bloc was responsible for some minor reforms of a liberal character such as the liberalization of the right of assembly, the relaxation of the absurdly stringent laws on *lèse-majesté*, as well the removal of the restrictions on futures trading; but this legislative activity was wholly overshadowed by a spectacular series of scandals that rocked the monarchy. Ever since 1906 Maximilian Harden, enthusiastically abetted by Holstein, who had been dismissed from the foreign office and was out for revenge, began to publish a series of articles exposing a number of homosexuals in the upper echelons of the military. In 1907 he began to make similar insinuations about the kaiser's favorite Prince Philipp zu Eulenburg und Hertefeld and the gay coterie that met regularly at his castle in Liebenberg, many of who were close to the kaiser. There was a series of spectacular trials since male homosexual acts were an offense under paragraph 175 of the criminal code of 1871. Eulenburg was charged with perjury, the affair was debated in the Reichstag, and Bülow made blustering denials of the existence of a gay "camarilla." The end result was that the kaiser sustained irreparable damage to his reputation.

The Eulenburg trial took place in July 1908, and in October the British paper the *Daily Telegraph* published a résumé of a number of conversations that the kaiser had had with an English officer. The tone of these remarks was typically ill considered, blustering, and tactless. He claimed that the British had won the Boer War because they had adopted a plan that he had sent to his grandmother, Queen Victoria. He insisted that he had turned down a Franco-Russian proposal to intervene in the Boer War. He further suggested that the German navy might eventually cooperate with the Royal Navy to attack Britain's ally Japan. William had quite correctly given the text to Bülow for perusal, but it passed unread from his desk to some underling in the foreign office who, failing to see the political implications of this diatribe, gave his imprimatur.

The kaiser came under ferocious attack in the press. Maximilian Harden suggested that he should abdicate. Bülow offered his resignation, while at the same time washing his hands of the whole affair, distancing himself from the views expressed in the article and placing the blame squarely on the kaiser. The leader of the conservatives begged William II to be a trifle more circumspect in future. The affair was debated in the Reichstag. Bülow refused either to defend the kaiser or to use the crisis to strengthen the relative position of the chancellor. He managed to win the support of the Reichstag majority, the Bundesrat, and the Prussian ministry of state, all of whom hoped that he would be able to curb their precocious monarch. Meanwhile the kaiser went hunting with his friend, the witty Jewish banker Carl Fürstenberg. During one evening of jollification the worthy chief of the Civil Cabinet, Count Dietrich von Hülsen-Haeseler, died of a heart attack while dancing in front of the king-emperor in a ballerina's tutu. This terpsichorean transvestism was greeted with a mixture of ribald humor and outrage. The kaiser's tottering reputation suffered yet another setback.

Surprisingly enough, the brouhaha soon subsided. The Eulenburg and *Daily Telegraph* affairs did not cause widespread public dismay, even though they were compounded by the Bosnian crisis of 1908. It was of concern to the political and the chattering classes, not to the average voter. The kaiser's wings had been modestly clipped, but Bülow no longer enjoyed his confidence, without which his power was strictly limited. The question whether it would have been possible to use the crisis to reform the system of government is open. Bülow was certainly not the man to perform such a task. Maybe it needed the profound crisis caused by a lost war for any fundamental changes to be possible.

Germany, feeling isolated and insecure, compensated by stepping up the naval building program, which now became a symbolic representation of its Great Power status, rather than a carefully considered component of the country's strategic requirements. Tirpitz now argued that the relative strength of the two navies should be three to two rather than two to one. This proved to be mere wishful thinking. With Britain's position greatly strengthened by the ententes with France and Russia, the British Liberal government took up the challenge. By 1908 it was clear that Tirpitz's plan could not possibly be realized.

In the wake of the Young Turk revolution and subsequent reorganization of the Ottoman empire, Austria-Hungary decided to annex the provinces of Bosnia and Herzegovina, which it had administered since the Congress of Berlin, even though they remained nominally under Turkish rule. Serbia, which regarded the provinces as part of a greater Serbia, saw this as a deliberate affront. Russia, in no position to give Serbia anything beyond verbal support, had to accept the Austrian move. It was left angry and humiliated. Anti-German feeling ran high, as it did in France. In an exchange of telegrams between the Prussian chief of general staff, the younger von Moltke, and his Austrian homologue Conrad von Hötzendorf, Germany promised support should Austria-Hungary attack Serbia, thereby finding itself at war with Russia. Bismarck's Dual Alliance was thus reinterpreted to be a guarantee of unconditional support for Austria-Hungary. Were Germany to go to war in support of its ally, the Schlieffen Plan would automatically go into effect. A war in the Balkans that involved Russia would thus of necessity become a European war that many prominent military minds believed would be long and inconceivably bloody, and which Germany was unlikely to be able to win.

The pressing order of the day was the long overdue reform of the Reich's finances that were strained to breaking point by the sharp increases in government expenditure, especially on armaments. It was hoped that an increase in taxes on such items as alcohol and tobacco, as well as death duties, would provide the 500 million marks needed per year to balance the books. The conservatives and their allies in the Farmers League denounced the proposed death duties as an underhand attempt to destroy agricultural property as well as a tax on widows and orphans. The Center Party, which had strong ties to agriculture, particularly in its Bavarian sister party, supported this stand. The urban middle class was determined to oppose this agrarian demagogy and the newly formed Hansa Association (Hansabund) gave its full support to Bülow's proposals. But without the support of the conservatives and the Center Party the chancellor was doomed. The proposed death duties were turned down by the Reichstag in spite of the Social Democrats voting with the government on the issue. The kaiser began to prattle about a coup d'état. Bülow once again offered his resignation. This time it was accepted. The new minister of finance, Reinhold von Sydow, then brought in a set of proposals that would cover the deficit. The death duties were dropped, to be replaced by a series of indirect taxes.

Bethmann Hollweg

The kaiser had no regrets in parting from a chancellor whom he no longer trusted and who relied on Social Democrats and left liberals for parliamentary support. The crisis that led to Bülow's fall left German society deeply divided, with the middle class indignant at the selfishness of the agrarian and clerical reactionaries. The National Liberals moved to the left, but neither they nor the Social Democrats were ready to follow the recommendation of those like Friedrich Naumann who called for a firm alliance "from Bassermann to Bebel." Most National Liberals still felt that the struggle against Social Democracy was as important as the struggle against the agrarians. Some, feeling uncomfortably close to the red revolutionaries, hoped that the party could restore its ties with the conservatives.

The new chancellor, Bethmann Hollweg, was a conservative reformer, a man of compromise who hoped to smooth the troubled waters. He came from a distinguished Frankfurt banking family, and his father was a professor. The family estate at Hohenfinow was a relatively recent acquisition. A man of melancholy and pessimistic disposition, which many regarded as evidence of a philosophical cast of mind, he avoided confrontation where possible, only moving into action when absolutely necessary.

In early 1911 the French responded to a revolt in Morocco by occupying Rabat and Fez. Although this was in clear violation of international agreements Kiderlen-Wächter suggested leaving Morocco to the French in exchange for a substantial chunk of the French Congo. In order to put pressure on the French to accept this proposal he sent the gunboat *Panther* to Agadir, ostensibly to protect German interests in the region. He turned to Heinrich Class, the leader of the Pan-German League, to provide propagandistic support for this move. Class called for the annexation of west Morocco, a suggestion that was vigorously endorsed in much of the German press, even though it was unthinkable without a war. Moltke, who felt that a war was inevitable, suggested that the moment was propitious. When France refused Germany's proposals Germany threatened to go to war. Lloyd George stood by France in a speech at the Mansion House in London, warning that Britain was ready for war. William II and Bethmann Hollweg persuaded Kiderlen-Wächter to lower the ante. The French, unwilling to risk a war without being sure of Russian support, gave way. Germany let Morocco become a French protectorate in 1912. In return Germany was given most favored nation status in Morocco, plus a substantial chunk of the French Congo, Germany ceding a frontier strip of Togo to the French.

Germany had suffered a humiliating defeated in this ill-considered and extremely risky affair. Heinrich Class held Kiderlen-Wächter hostage, while Bethmann Hollweg came under ferocious attack in the Reichstag for having threatened war and then backed down. Bassermann accused him of engaging in the "politics of illusion"; a future chancellor, Count Georg von Hertling, argued that peace had been bought at the cost of the nation's prestige. Ernst von Heydebrand, the conservative leader and "uncrowned king of Prussia," in a wild tirade against Britain and France, urged the nation to prepare for war. The Social Democratic leader August Bebel met with howls of derisive laughter when he suggested that the arms race would lead to a war on an unimaginable scale that would result in a catastrophic "*Götterdämmerung* of the bourgeois world."

With public opinion in an ugly and aggressive mood, Tirpitz could count on wide support for stepping up the naval building program. Kiderlen-Wächter and Bethmann Hollweg realized that Germany had to tread softly and try to reach a détente, but they faced powerful opposition from Tirpitz, the military, the Reichstag majority and inflamed public opinion. Support from the kaiser was barely lukewarm.

The British war minister Haldane, who had been educated at Göttingen and was fluent in German, visited Berlin in February 1912 with a proposal to slow down naval building while maintaining the two-to-one ratio. He suggested that a three-to-two ratio might be discussed at some future date. He flatly rejected the preposterous German request that Britain should promise to remain neutral in the event of a continental war. Haldane's proposals were unacceptable to the kaiser and Tirpitz, Haldane did not trust Bethmann's assurances that he was anxious to preserve the peace. The British cabinet was even more skeptical. The Haldane mission thus did nothing to improve relations between the two countries and served further to undermine the chancellor's position.

The Challenge from Social Democracy

The clamor for reform of the monstrously inequitable Prussian electoral system based on wealth could no longer be ignored. Bethmann was prepared to make some minor adjustments to the system to silence criticism without alienating the conservatives, thus making possible a renewal of the conservative–National Liberal alliance. The reform proposal was exceedingly modest. The number of voters in the first class was to be almost doubled, but was still only 7 percent of the electorate. The second class was to be 17 instead of 13.8 percent and thus 76 percent of the electorate would be represented by one-third of the delegates to the House of Representatives. Even these modest changes were opposed by the conservatives and the Center Party, and a debate in the House of Representatives had to be called off. The National Liberals were outraged. The conservatives denounced Bethmann for threatening to undermine their position in Prussia. Their discontent mounted when the government introduced universal manhood suffrage in Alsace-Lorraine, a measure wholeheartedly supported by the Social Democrats. Bethmann Hollweg was now known as Bethmann Sollweg ("must go") in respectable conservative circles.

The Reichstag election campaign of 1912 was a rally against the conservative-Center Party alliance, although some National Liberals still felt that the struggle against Social Democracy should take precedence. A rival organization to the Hansabund, the Middle Class Association (Mittelstandsverband), formed in the previous year, supported the conservatives. The fronts hardened, dashing Bethmann's hopes for a liberal–conservative compromise. He held himself aloof from the election in gloomy resignation. The results were nothing short of sensational. The number of Social Democratic mandates increased from 43 to 110. The SPD was now the largest parliamentary party with more than a quarter of the seats. The conservative Center Party bloc was the clear loser, dropping from 211 to 158 seats, but their opponents, with 197 seats, were divided amongst themselves. The Reichstag was deadlocked. The chancellor, with no grouping with which he could work comfortably, relied on making back-room deals and compromises to which he gave the pretentious title "politics of the diagonal." Conservatives denounced him for being soft on socialism. The kaiser gave him no support. The left clamored for reforms which, although modest, were effectively blocked by Prussia.

The parties reacted very differently to the election. The Center Party, having sniffed the wind, edged cautiously to the left. The National Liberals, who had lost badly at the polls, moved closer to the conservatives and stepped up their attacks on the Social Democrats, while denouncing the government for its lack of imperialist fervor and its failure to arm to the teeth. Young Turks in the party, prominent among them Gustav Stresemann, hoped to steer a middle course between the conservatives and the Social Democrats, a view that was shared by most of the Independents. On the left the radicals around Karl Liebknecht and Rosa Luxemburg, as well as Karl Kautsky and the center, wanted nothing to do with the bourgeois parties. The revisionists and reformists on the right were determined to remain in opposition. Even in Baden, where liberals and Social Democrats had worked together for a while, the two parties drifted apart. The Social Democrats were thus still pariahs, "fellows without a fatherland" in the kaiser's words. The other parties felt that any close association with them would be the kiss of death.

It was thus virtually impossible to create a working parliamentary majority. None of the proposed solutions was viable in the long term. The "Cartel of the Creative Estates" (Kartell der schaffende Stände) of 1913, made up of conservatives and the right wing of the National Liberal and Center parties, was a toothless version of *Sammlung*. A populist appeal to the mass organizations such as the Pan-German League, the Army and Navy Leagues, and the Farmers League to join together in an attack on the conservative reformers around the chancellor produced little beyond a lot of hot air and unproductive sloganeering. Those in the middle of the political spectrum were too few and too weak to offer a way out of the crisis, which was virtually impossible to find without opening up towards the Social Democrats. This in turn was impossible as long as the party persisted with its bloodcurdling revolutionary rhetoric that disguised its moderate reformist stance.

The conservative reformers aimed at further social legislation so as to counter the appeal of Social Democracy and reconcile the working class to the state, but the electoral success of the Social Democrats forced the reformers onto the defensive. The right demanded an all-out attack on the trade unions and the SPD. The government hoped to create a reserve of social peace between the ardent class warriors on the left and on the right, but ever sensitive to the criticism that it was being too conciliatory towards the socialists, made only modest efforts in this direction.

Armaments

Armaments were still the great issue of the day, with a number of pressing questions to be addressed. What armaments strategy was best suited to Germany's needs? Which should be given priority – the army or the navy? Above all, the question was how to meet the spiraling costs of armaments. Tirpitz and the navy, smarting from Germany's humiliation after bungling the Moroccan crisis of 1911, wanted to step up the naval building program that had been slowed down in 1908. Both Bethmann and Kiderlen-Wächter hoped to improve relations with Britain. They were supported by a treasury that was horrified at the cost involved. The proposed army increases of 1911 seemed to put paid to Tirpitz's plan.

Once again the role of the kaiser was critical. Regarding the Haldane mission as an insult and affront, he ordered the German ambassador in London to wave the big stick. Tirpitz leaked his proposals to the press. Bethmann protested that Germany was heading for war and offered his resignation. The kaiser, seeing no viable alternative candidate, refused to accept; but relations between the two men were further strained. The resulting naval and army bills of 1912 were relatively modest. The army was increased by a mere 29,000 men, much to the consternation of the Army League and of the proponents of a mass army such as Colonel Ludendorff. The navy was to have three new battleships by 1920. The additional cost was to be met by a prolongation of the increased tax on sugar and a tax on distilleries, the latter much to the disgust of the agrarians, many of whom produced schnapps on their estates.

The Balkan Crisis of 1912

By 1912 the Triple Alliance was in ruins due to fundamental differences between Italy and Austria-Hungary in the Balkans and the Middle East. The situation became extremely precarious with the Balkan War of 1912 when Serbia, Greece, Bulgaria, and Montenegro combined to drive the Ottomans out of Europe. Austria-Hungary, determined to stop Serbia from establishing a foothold on the Adriatic, supported the creation of an independent Albania. Russia supported Serbia, leaving Europe on the brink of war. A conference was held in London that temporarily defused the situation. Britain urged both Russia and Austria-Hungary to back down. Germany also urged moderation, but was determined that its ally should not be further weakened. An independent Albania was created, and Serbian ambitions were frustrated. The crisis appeared to have been mastered.

The Balkan crisis created an ugly atmosphere in Berlin. There had been a marked increase in demands for Germany to assert itself throughout the world and prepare for war. War was seen by some to be inevitable because of the fundamental differences between Teutons and Slavs. Others argued that a nation that was forged in Bismarck and Moltke's wars had become enfeebled and needed a war to restore its moral fiber. An alarming number of influential figures saw war as an inescapable component of the Social Darwinist struggle for existence between nations and races. Bestselling books such as Friedrich von Bernhardi's *Germany and the Next War*, published in 1912, both echoed and inflamed this dangerously bellicose spirit.

At the height of the crisis Britain warned Germany that it would not stand idly by should an Austrian war against Serbia lead to an attack on France. On December 8, 1912,

William II held a crown council attended by the military leadership. Moltke announced that Germany should go to war at the first suitable opportunity. Tirpitz wanted to wait eighteen months until the fleet was ready. Moltke sourly remarked that since the fleet would never be ready Germany should go to war "the sooner the better." The kaiser called for increased armaments and began to talk about a "racial struggle" with an "overconfident" Russia. This was a typical piece of theatrical posing and swagger, an indication of a blustering lack of direction at the top rather than of Germany's determination to go to war.

There were no immediate consequences from the crown council, from which Bethmann Hollweg had been excluded. Germany once again urged Austria-Hungary to be cautious when war broke out again in the Balkans the following year. The victors of 1912, supported by Turkey and Romania, turned on their former ally Bulgaria, which was promptly defeated. Germany now tried to improve relations with Serbia, and dynastic links with Romania and Greece were bolstered. A German general, Liman von Sanders, was made inspector general of the Turkish army in 1913 and given command over the troops around Constantinople. Russia protested vigorously. Under intense international pressure Liman had to surrender his command. Bethmann Hollweg came under further heavy attack for permitting the Reich to suffer such a humiliation.

The Balkan wars, coupled with Germany's weakened position relative to the Triple Entente, lent weight to those who argued that the Reich's armaments program was dangerously modest. In December 1912 Ludendorff presented a memorandum arguing for an army increase of 300,000 men. The war ministry was horrified at this suggestion, fearing that it would result in an influx of dubious bourgeois into the officer corps and of Social Democratic sympathizers among the troops, making the army unreliable as an instrument of repression against revolution and domestic unrest. After much debate, from which Bethmann held aloof, a compromise was reached, with the army being increased by 136,000 officers and men. Ludendorff was posted away from the general staff, soon to make a triumphant return to center stage.

Bethmann Hollweg now had to find a way to foot the bill. He did not dare reintroduce a proposal for death duties. That would have involved an opening to the left. The Reichstag demanded a number of concessions in return to voting for the increased taxation to meet the enormous costs involved. These included a reform of military law and the ending of certain outmoded privileges and offices. Three proposed new cavalry regiments were refused funding. The kaiser, regarding this as a deliberate attack on his sacred power of command, ranted and raved in a painfully familiar fashion. Bethmann threatened to dissolve the Reichstag until, much to his surprise, he was able to win a comfortable majority among the parties of the middle to the proposals, which were to be funded by a capital gains tax – a measure that was supported by the Social Democrats, thus further angering the conservatives.

Bethmann did not enjoy his success for long. In December 1913 the Reichstag passed a vote of no confidence in the chancellor of 293 to 54. He had defended the actions of the army in Alsace-Lorraine during the Zabern affair of the previous year, during which a young lieutenant had insulted the Alsatians, prompting civil unrest. The army had proclaimed martial law and acted in a singularly brutish and insensitive manner. A provocative speech in the Reichstag by the war minister Falkenhayn had further inflamed the situation. Bethmann dismissed the vote as an empty gesture that merely showed that the liberals and the Center Party had made common cause with the Social Democrats. The lieutenant was tried and acquitted to general approbation and no changes were made in the army's right to suspend civil law.

Domestic politics on the eve of the war were thus approaching stalemate. A conservative reforming chancellor could not distance himself from the court, Prussia, the military, or the conservatives. The middle parties were reluctant to seize the opportunity to strengthen their position. They could not risk refusing to pass the budget for fear of hurting their constituents, and they were not yet prepared to approach the Social Democrats. The conservatives, having been gradually pushed aside, resorted to drumming up support from the extra-parliamentary opposition, amongst whom there were calls for a counter-revolution. These were endorsed by the crown prince, who had to be called to order by his father. Others felt that a war might solve Germany's problems, however high the risks involved. Germany stood at the crossroads. Reaction to events outside its borders was to determine the road ahead.

By 1914 there were signs of improvement in the international climate. Germany and Britain reached an agreement over the Portuguese colonies in August 1913. In June the following year Britain agreed to German schemes for the Baghdad railway in return for an assurance that it would not go all the way to Basra. Germany, having abandoned its ambitions to have shipping rights on the Euphrates, joined an Anglo-Dutch consortium as a junior partner to exploit the oil resources of the Ottoman empire. German firms invested heavily in western Europe and there were many instances of fruitful cooperation between Germans and their future enemies. But the system was fundamentally unstable and proved incapable of mastering the crisis that lay ahead.

CHAPTER TEN
THE FIRST WORLD WAR

CHAPTER CONTENTS

A History of Modern Germany: 1800 to the Present, Second Edition. Martin Kitchen.
© 2012 Martin Kitchen. Published 2012 by Blackwell Publishing Ltd.

On June 28, 1914, the Serbian national day, the heir to Austro-Hungarian thrones, the Archduke Francis Ferdinand and his wife, were murdered in Sarajevo. It was the work of a Serbian secret society The Black Hand, whose head was Dragutin Dimitrievitch, a colonel in the Serbian general staff which stood opposed to the more moderate and flexible policies of the Serbian minister president Pachich. It was assumed in Vienna that the government in Belgrade was at least partially responsible, as was indeed the case. It knew of the plan, and although it did not approve was powerless to stop it. Austria-Hungary had to act, and Germany was obliged to give its ally appropriate support.

The war party in Austria-Hungary insisted that the time had come to settle accounts with Serbia. They were given wholehearted support from Berlin, where the feeling was one of now or never. Austria-Hungary was therefore given a free hand to act as it saw fit, and although it seemed highly unlikely that a war between Austria-Hungary and Serbia could be localized, even the more moderate among the leadership, headed by the chancellor, were prepared to risk a war that would involve Russia, France, and possibly Britain. The more bellicose among the military, the political elite, and the press urged unconditional support for Austria in the hope that this would indeed trigger a major European war. A number of soldiers, including Moltke, thought that a war was likely to be very long, would be unimaginably bloody, and that the outcome was uncertain. The war minister Falkenhayn made the grotesque remark that even if Germany perished, it would all have been great fun.

There were a number of arguments put forward in favor of going to war. Moltke and the army claimed that Germany would fall behind in the armaments race, and that they had to strike now before it was too late. Civilians argued that soon the pacifist Social Democrats would be so powerful that a war would be impossible, adding that a victorious campaign would put the socialists in their place. Bethmann Hollweg felt that a war could only be fought with the Social Democrats, not against them. Only if Russia could be construed as the aggressor would they forget the resolutions of the Socialist International against war and support the common effort. Continued support would depend on making concessions to the party over such matters as the Prussian electoral law. The chancellor was full of foreboding, but he uncritically accepted Moltke's argument about the arms race, thus managing to convince himself that this would be a preventive war.

Austria-Hungary waited until July 23 before sending Serbia a wide-ranging set of demands. The Serbian response came two days later. It was so conciliatory that William II, who had previously urged Austria-Hungary to take the firmest possible line against Serbia, came to the conclusion that there were now no possible grounds for war. Vienna, however, finding Belgrade's answer to the ultimatum unsatisfactory, at 11 a.m. on July 28 declared war. On the following day Russia ordered the partial mobilization of several military districts. Egged on by his generals, Nicholas II ordered a general mobilization in the night of July 30/31.

Also on July 30, Bethmann Hollweg urged Austria-Hungary to respond to the British foreign secretary Sir Edward Grey's offer of mediation. This was not part of an effort to defuse the situation, since he had repudiated the British proposal for a conference on July 27, but rather to make sure that Russia would be made to look responsible for an eventual European war. The next day Moltke, who had not yet heard that the Russians had mobilized, urged his Austrian colleague Conrad von Hötzendorf to mobilize immediately, thus prompting the famous rhetorical question by the Austro-Hungarian foreign minister Count Berchtold: "Who rules: Moltke or Bethmann?" The Austro-Hungarian army was promptly mobilized at midday on July 31. One hour later the German government announced a "state of imminent danger of war." Since Russia had not answered a German ultimatum issued on July 31, Germany mobilized on August 1, and declared war on Russia, thereby setting the Schlieffen Plan in motion. Germany officially declared war on France on August 3. On the following day, when German troops were already pouring into Belgium, Britain declared war.

Attitudes Towards the War

Thus began what George F. Kennan so judiciously called "the great seminal catastrophe of this [the twentieth] century." It was a catastrophe for which Germany must bear the main responsibility. The German military strengthened the war party in Austria-Hungary. A substantial portion of the middle class lent their full support to this aggressive stance and called for a "preventive war," in spite of the fact that none of Germany's neighbors harbored aggressive intentions towards the Reich. Waverers, including the vast majority of the Social Democratic Party, misled into believing that Russia was the aggressor, supported the government. The party had organized a number of anti-war demonstrations at the end of July, and the party press was sharply critical of the government's handling of the crisis. As the danger of war loomed larger the party leadership began to get cold feet. They argued that were they to adopt too critical a stance they would face severe repression along the lines of Bismarck's anti-socialist laws, which still traumatized the party. That this would be a war against imperial Russia, the despotic bastion of reaction and arch-enemy of all progressive forces, made it all the easier for them to cast aside considerations of proletarian solidarity and the pacifism of the Socialist International. On August 3 the SPD deputies decided by a vote of 78 to 14 to accept the government's request for war credits. Speaking for the party in the Reichstag on the following day Hugo Haase, a member of a the left-wing minority, took the kaiser's words to heart when in his throne speech he proclaimed this to be a purely defensive war in which Germany harbored no territorial ambitions. He announced that the Social Democrats would never leave the country in the lurch in such a moment of peril, but added the warning that they would never support a war of conquest.

As Lenin, fulminating in his Zurich exile, never tired of pointing out, the SPD had abandoned class warfare and proletarian internationalism, thereby beginning the process of reconciliation with the "ideas of 1914" – the new nationalist ideology that was to form the basis of National Socialism. The brainchild of the sociologist Johann Plenge and popularized by the Swedish constitutional lawyer Rudolf Kjellén, the "ideas of 1914" were a declaration of war on the "ideas of 1789." The rights of man, democracy, liberalism, and individualism were all rejected in favor of the truly German values of duty, discipline, law, and order. Order was to replace the anarchic libertarianism of the past century. Divisions along class lines were to be overcome by a feeling of ethnic solidarity (*Volksgemeinschaft*) in which the new Social Democrats of August 1914 were welcome comrades. Socialist internationalism was to be replaced by robust national egotism. All "racial comrades" (*Volksgenossen*) were now to play a role in the building of a truly socialist society, and join in the glorious struggle of "proletarian" Germany against "capitalist" Britain.

By 1915 the war, which had ostensibly begun as a defensive campaign against Russia, had become a pseudo-socialist crusade against materialist Britain, the nation of shopkeepers and imperialists. The tsarist empire posed no great threat after Hindenburg, Ludendorff, and Hoffmann's great victory over the Russians at Tannenberg at the end of August 1914. The war would be decided on the Western Front. France was the traditional enemy and the curious love-hate relationship with Britain could easily be fanned into an intense loathing. Learned scholars became intoxicated with visions of an apocalyptic struggle between manly German militarism and sordid British capitalism. The distinguished economist Werner Sombart proclaimed the war to be a struggle between "tradesmen and soldiers," in which German militarism was inspired to fight for Beethoven's "Eroica" Symphony and Egmont Overture, Goethe's *Faust*, and Nietzsche's *Thus Spoke Zarathustra* against a squalid, money-grubbing non-culture. He welcomed the war as an antidote to cultural pessimism and as a means to the regeneration of the race. The Catholic philosopher Max Scheler appealed to all Social Democrats to join in the struggle against the homeland of modern capitalism. He also called attention to the therapeutic effects of war on the German people. Thomas Mann was immensely relieved when the Treaty of Brest-Litovsk brought an end to Germany's war against the country that had produced Dostoevsky. In his *Reflections of an Unpolitical Man* he called for an all-out struggle against "les trois pays libres" that stood for "civilization" rather than "culture." There was an enthusiastic audience for such rubbish, and "God punish England!" replaced more conventional forms of address.

War Aims

Since until 1916 the war was believed to be defensive, there could be no public discussion of war aims. Behind the scenes the situation was quite different. As early as September 1914 Bethmann Hollweg called for the annexation of the ore fields of Longwy-Briey, of Belfort and Luxemburg. Belgium was to be reduced to total dependency on Germany, handing over Liège and Verviers to Prussia and given Calais, Dunkirk, and Boulogne as compensation. The frontiers of Russia were to be pushed eastwards and a central European economic zone was to be formed under German leadership. Bethmann's "September Program" soon became richly embroidered. The Pan-Germans called for the annexation of the Baltic states and White Russia, along with vast tracts of northwestern Russia and Russian Poland. Russian Jews were to be expelled to Palestine. They proposed that the Russian empire should be split apart, leaving the Crimea and the Caucasus firmly under German control. A group of prominent intellectuals put forward a plan for the ethnic cleansing of eastern Europe and its resettlement with stalwart German peasants. The steel magnate August Thyssen, seconded by his lobbyist Matthias Erzberger, called for the annexation of Belgium and the eastern departments of France, along with the Baltic states. Another group, which included Hans Delbrück, Max Weber, Albert Einstein, and Gustav von Schmoller, protested vigorously against such hair-raising fantasies; but this group, along with the Social Democrats who opposed any annexation, formed a small minority. Bethmann Hollweg's September Program was fleshed out by the liberal politician and journalist Friedrich Naumann in his book *Mitteleuropa*, published in 1915, which called for a revival of the Holy Roman Empire.

None of these schemes could be realized without a victory. This seemed remote after the costly failure of Falkenhayn's offensive against Verdun in 1916. The Pan-Germans and their allies mounted a massive campaign to appoint Hindenburg and Ludendorff, the heroes of Tannenberg, to the High Command (OHL). The kaiser, who saw this as a quasi-plebiscitary attack on his power of command, reluctantly gave way in August 1916. The decision to launch unrestricted submarine warfare was taken in January 1917 in spite of

Bethmann's protests. It soon proved to be a serious mistake. The Allies quickly overcame the submarine menace and the United States declared war in April.

German Society in Wartime

The ordinary Prussian or Bavarian, unless he had been directly involved or lost a family member, had hardly been affected by the war of German unification. Now, for the first time, what was soon to be called the "home front" played an ever more important role as the conflict began to approximate what Ludendorff was to call "total war." Aerial warfare was still in its infancy, so civilians did not have to suffer the horrors of large-scale bombing. There was still a clear distinction between the battlefield and the homeland, but the war overshadowed almost every aspect of life and led to profound social changes.

The staggering numbers of the dead, mutilated, and wounded affected almost every family. Thirteen million men served in the armed forces, representing half of those between the ages of 16 and 60. More than half of them were killed or seriously injured. The rest were traumatized by the experience of trench warfare, of artillery barrages, gas attacks and the constant sensation of the nearness of death and serious injury. The ever-increasing number of widows and orphans had not only to deal with their grief; they also confronted a remorseless increase in deprivation, hunger, and disease. But different classes experienced these horrors to different degrees. Class distinctions were thereby reinforced, tensions between them heightened. Just as the situation at the front steadily deteriorated, so society began to fall apart as class conflicts intensified, regional disparities were amplified, and town confronted country. Real incomes fell by 30 to 40 percent. Daily calorific intake fell from 3,400 in 1913 to 1,000 in the winter of 1917. There was precious little money available to provide for soldiers' wives and families. For the first two years of the war wives received 9 marks per month in summer and 12 in winter, plus 6 marks for each child. Thus a woman with three children got 30 marks in winter, but she needed 60 to live. In 1917 a wife's payment was increased to 50 marks, but this increase was lower than the rate of inflation. Welfare payments from local authorities were inadequate to meet basic needs, while at the other end of the scale industrial profits soared, particularly in the armaments sector, rising to up to eight times the 1913 levels. The gulf between the wealthy and the vast mass of the poor grew to an unpardonable extent. Distinctions that might have been tolerable in peacetime were unacceptable in wartime. The political truce of 1914 was in tatters. The proclamation of a state of siege and the imposition of martial law only served to increase tensions. Nothing could stop the mass strikes and protest demonstrations that led to revolution.

The impact of four years of war was felt with varying degrees of severity among the various groups of a highly complex society. We have already seen that the term "class" is shorthand for a group made up of many different components. Thus within the bourgeoisie there are many factions, often with conflicting interests. "Class" is an imprecise, but nevertheless useful, sociological term, from which it does not necessarily follow that those within a given class pursue identical or even similar political goals or have comparable economic interests. Thus among the bourgeoisie there were industrialists who profited enormously from the war, while others faced serious difficulties. Those in the armaments industry made staggering profits, but the producers of consumer goods lost their share of the market. The vulgar display of newfound wealth in times of brutal austerity was widely felt to be an outrage. In was not merely the left that railed against the war profiteers. The industrialist and statesman Walter Rathenau, in his widely circulated essay on 1917 entitled "On Things To Come," called for a heavy tax on war profits, which would be redistributed to overcome the ever-increasing gulf between rich and poor. It was not a suggestion that won much favor among his equals.

Industrialists initially hoped that the political truce of 1914 would put an end to working-class demands, perpetuating the freezing of welfare services that had begun in 1912, at least for the duration. Some even went as far as to hope that the war would last a long time so that social peace would be reinforced and Social Democrats would see the error of their ways and sustain "throne and altar." Almost all supported the government's social imperialist war aims, accurately predicting that a "compromise peace" would open the floodgates of reform and lead to a change in the Prussian electoral system that would spell the end to conservative dominance.

The industrialists were increasingly isolated from and antagonistic to society at large. Their accumulation of vast wealth in times of appalling suffering offended most of the middle classes. Many began to sympathize with left liberals and Social Democrats. The *Bildungsbürgertum* was particularly hard hit. Such savings as they had went into war bonds and were thereby lost. Senior civil servants' real incomes were halved. Those lower down the scale deeply resented the fact that they now earned less than industrial workers. In 1917 the military commander in Frankfurt noted that many civil servants now lived "from hand to mouth" and that the "social decline of civil servants represents a danger to the state that should not be underestimated."

This was certainly true of civil servants such as postal and railway workers, who flocked to the Social Democrats. But senior civil servants and many *Bildungsbürger* responded to their loss of status by adopting extreme reactionary ideas. Salaried employees were similarly faced with a loss of status as employers used the war as an excuse to cut costs. Their real incomes fell even more than those of industrial workers to the extent that many earned considerably less than workers in the armaments industries. This made them more deter-mined than ever to preserve their distinction from the proletariat. Small enterprises were hard hit by the war. Owners and workers alike were called up, businesses closed. The extreme right's denunciation of controls and "state socialism" found a resounding echo in these quarters. They were stuck between a resentment of big business and their opposition to social democratic cooperatives. Faced with a mounting threat from the left, they tended to side with industrialists and dropped their often excessive denunciations of the evils of capitalism.

The working classes suffered the most. They made up the bulk of the cannon fodder at the front. Women and children were obliged to work under appalling conditions for deri-sory wages. Their already dismal standard of living plummeted. Nominal wages increased, but failed to keep up with inflation, so that real wages sank dramatically. Wholesale prices rose by 415 percent during the war. Retail prices rose up to tenfold. There were exceptional disparities in incomes. A skilled worker in a Berlin armaments firm earned 7,500 marks per year – a sum inconceivable in peacetime – whereas an unskilled worker in a small-town textile factory earned a mere 1,200 marks. The composition of Lenin's "aristocracy of labor" changed dramatically. In 1914 a printer with a daily wage of 6.50 marks was at the top of the wage scale. By 1918 a skilled worker in the electrical industry earning 13.40 marks a day had replaced him. Textile workers on 3.46 marks a day were at the bottom of the pile. At the same time differences between the wages of skilled and unskilled workers began to level off. Unskilled workers in the armaments industry could earn more by piecework than skilled workers who were paid on an hourly basis.

Gross disparities remained between the remuneration of men and women. In 1914 in the metal industry women earned a mere 37 percent of men's wages, in textiles 63 percent. By the autumn of 1918 this had risen to 51 percent in the metal industry, but had only increased by three points in textiles. In the armaments industry real wages fell by 22 percent for men and 12 percent for women. In other sectors of industry the drop was even more dramatic – 44 percent for men, 39 percent for women. By contrast real wages in British industry fell by 15 percent during the war. It must also be noted that wages would have fallen even further had it not been for working days of up to fifteen hours and frequent seven-day weeks. In industrial warfare, involving mass armies, the problem of labor was acute, particularly the shortage of skilled labor. By 1916, 2 million men had to be exempted from military service to work in the armaments industry – more than had served in the entire army in 1870/71. Women made up the shortfall. In 1913, 22 percent of industrial workers were women. By 1918 this figure had risen to 34 percent. Labor was channeled into sectors of industry essential for the war effort. The number of those employed in the chemical industries rose by 170 percent, in metals by 80 percent and in the electrical and mechanical engineering industries by 50 percent. Peacetime sectors such as clothing, the building trades, and consumer goods lost up to half of their employees. The result was a strengthening of heavy industry and the decline of medium-sized and small concerns.

Declining real wages, longer hours, inadequate nourishment, an alarming increase in industrial accidents, the crass inequalities in earnings, and scandalous war profiteering resulted in the steady radicalization of the working class. The SPD's argument that this was a temporary situation caused by the war and that far-reaching reforms would soon be implemented failed to convince. For all the differences between the "aristocracy of labor" and unskilled workers there was a growing sense of class solidarity, fueled by the widening gap between owners and management at the top and the men and women on the shop floor at the bottom. Although all but the small group that had made vast profits from the war were worse off than they had been in 1913, there was an acute and growing awareness of relative deprivation. The senior civil servant might be suffering as his standard of living steadily declined, but his lot was increasingly enviable, even to the best-paid industrial worker. The result was a widespread feeling of indignation, class antagonism, and a mounting clamor for a more equitable apportioning of the hardships of war. The much-vaunted wartime community spirit, enshrined in the political truce, was shown to be a sham. Discrimination against the "fellows without a fatherland" in the SPD continued. In April 1917 additional rations for heavy labor were cut. In Berlin 200,000 workers went on strike. The SPD split in two. On the far left Rosa Luxemburg and Karl Liebknecht formed the Spartacus Association (Spartakusbund), which was the nucleus of the Communist Party. The stage was being set for major political change.

In the countryside the tensions were less between employer and employee, landowner and laborer, than between country and town. The war inevitably caused major problems. Men were called up to serve in the armed forces, resulting in a chronic shortage of labor. Fertilizers, machinery, and seeds were in ever shorter supply. There was deep resentment at the increasing number of controls and regulations, requisitions and inspections that served to heighten the feeling that agriculture, no longer the privileged sector, had now to bow to the needs of urban dwellers. The state appeared to be privileging the town at the expense of the country.

The challenge to agriculture was overwhelming. The British imposed a blockade in an attempt to starve the country into surrender. It was impossible for the agricultural sector to provide adequate nourishment for a country of 60 million inhabitants. The state responded with rationing and regulations. Farmers countered by fudging the statistics, hording, and selling on the black market. Urban dwellers resented the fact that the peasantry was well fed while they starved in the "hunger winter" of 1915/16 and the "turnip winter" of 1916/17. But the peasantry were equally resentful, claiming that they had to foot the bill for the war. But their mounting resentment did not cause them to take a sharp left turn as many arch-conservative landowners feared. The resented the bureaucratic red tape from the War Food Office (KEA) and were against a parliament that seemed to them to be only concerned with the requirements of townsfolk and the armaments industries. Urban dwellers countered by denouncing peasants for snatching potatoes from the mouths of good Germans and feeding them to their pigs, simply because the price of meat was soaring. The government hoped that the Treaty of Brest-Litovsk would bring relief, but in fact it made the situation worse. Russian prisoners of war, who had been working on the land, returned home, while food supplies from the Ukraine were barely enough to feed the German army of occupation.

The agrarians were the loudest supporters of extensive war aims, the most vehement opponents of a "feeble peace." They resisted any concessions to the left and championed the three-class Prussian electoral system. As staunch upholders of the status quo they were unable to deal with the harsh reality of defeat. They lost much of their status during the Weimar Republic, a state that they bitterly opposed, and dreamt of colonization in eastern Europe. Small wonder that they thought they had found a savior in 1933.

Women

The war had, perhaps surprisingly, little effect on women's status. The cause of female emancipation was not advanced. Women did not become more self-aware or self-reliant. Patriarchal family relationships were reinforced when the simple breadwinner was transmogrified into a heroic warrior.

The increase in the number of working women was relatively small: 17 percent between 1914 and 1917. Compared with 22 percent between 1905 and 1909 and 20 percent between 1909 and 1913 these figures show that the war had a very modest impact on women entering the workforce. It was not that women were not eager to work. With inadequate financial support from the state they were forced to seek employment, but the opportunities were not available. In the first year of the war 158,000 women applied for work in Berlin, but fewer than half were accepted. The major change was that women now worked in increasing numbers in sectors of industry from which they had hitherto been excluded: metals, mechanical engineering, and chemicals. Previously they had worked in the textile industry, in domestic service, or on the land.

There were a number of factors hindering women from working in industry. Married women with several children, loath to leave them alone, preferred to work at home. Women were miserably paid. They were lucky to earn half as much as men doing the same work. The working day was formally eight hours, but could be up to sixteen hours, with frequent night shifts and seven-day weeks. The work was often extremely arduous. In one factory women were called upon to lift shells weighing 37 kilograms up to chest level and to do so continually for eight hours. In another factory women had to carry an 80 kilogram lump of red-hot metal to a hydraulic hammer. Safety measures were largely ignored in the interest of speeding up production, which led to an alarming increase in industrial accidents. Women were given no training, so they remained permanently at the bottom of the wage scale. Then gradually the state realized that much more had to be done to support women whose husbands were fighting at the front. Payments increased to the point that unemployed female textile workers were no longer forced to seek work in the armaments industry. Employers were reluctant to employ women because they wanted to show the authorities that they could not do without their trusted skilled workers, so as to get them exempted from military service.

The War Commission (Kriegsamt) under General Groener, which was responsible for the coordination of war industry, appointed two prominent women from the bourgeois women's movement to a Women's Department (Frauenreferat), which was responsible for recruiting women workers. This resulted in the creation of an elaborate bureaucracy, involving trade unions, women's organizations, welfare agencies, and NGOs, with offices in major towns. Their view of the role of women remained anchored in tradition. They did nothing to champion women's rights and were careful not to get involved in the controversial issue of votes for women. But they did what they could to provide an adequate infrastructure for working women such as day-care centers, medical services, adequate housing, maternity homes, further education, and instruction in home economics and parenting; thereby laying the foundations for the Weimar Republic's social policies. It was an uphill struggle that eventually led the head of the Women's Department, Marie-Elizabeth Lüders, to give up in despair. Their work was hampered by inter-departmental rivalry, clashes between civil and military authorities, wounded male pride, and, not infrequently, the resistance of working-class women themselves.

The war had an alarming effect on the birth rate. With 13 million men serving in the armed forces the number of new marriages fell significantly. The fertility rate (the average number of children born to a woman over her lifetime) in 1913 was 6.1. By 1918 it had plummeted to 1. The wider use of birth-control devices, mainly condoms, provided as prophylactics against widespread venereal diseases, plus the increase in abortions, although they were strictly illegal, also contributed to this decrease.

Germany was now a country of single parents who found it increasingly difficult to make both ends meet. Malnutrition resulted in a large number of children suffering from rickets (known as the "English disease" for its prevalence in industrial regions there), tuberculosis, and anemia. Childhood morbidity increased threefold during the war. Lacking the authority of a father, many teenagers ran amok, joined gangs, engaged in petty theft, or traded on a thriving black market. Most preferred life in the streets to the tedium of school. In Cologne by 1917 an average of 48 percent of schoolchildren were failing to turn up for classes. An attempt to introduce a program of compulsory education in the years before military service failed for lack of funds. An effort to provide cadet training never got off the ground because the authorities, both civil and military, wanted adolescents to go to work rather than play soldiers.

Shortages made housework even more challenging. The scarcity of fuel made cooking, washing, heating, and lighting a constant worry. Soap was soon in very short supply. Hours were spent queuing for food. Rations were inadequate for a healthy diet, so that hours were lost looking for black-market suppliers. These problems were only partly overcome by works canteens and "people's kitchens" in the towns, but a study in 1916 showed that the average citizen had lost 20 percent of an already modest body weight since the outbreak of the war. This resulted in a lowering of energy levels and serious health problems such as gastroenteritis, amenorrhea, and famine edema.

Widows and orphans in the working class were provided with 33 marks per month if the husband and father had been a simple soldier or 50 marks if he were a sergeant. Neither sum was sufficient to provide for a family. The official propaganda that men had died a "hero's death" or a "sacrificial death for kaiser and fatherland," echoed by the churches in what the great Protestant theologian Karl Barth denounced as "bellicose Germanic theology," not only failed to provide any solace – it was seen as a cruel mockery. Working-class women became increasingly politicized and gave vent to their discontent: they demonstrated, plundered stores, and took an active part in the strikes and protest marches in 1917–18.

Planning began in late 1915 for eventual demobilization. The aim of all bodies concerned, including the trade unions, was to return to the status quo of 1914. This would involve removing women from the workforce to provide jobs for men as they returned to civilian life. Women were obliged to sign a contract that they would cease to work as soon as the war ended. The experience of near-total war thus did precious little to further the cause of women's emancipation. Paradoxically, it was during the Second World War that women made the greatest leap forward, in spite of the National Socialists' determination to stifle their demands to be freed from traditional restraints.

Mounting Opposition to the War

Germany now no longer had a realistic chance of winning the war and there was widespread discontent at home. The public had been promised a resounding victory in 1914 with the Schlieffen Plan, and again two years later at Verdun. Unrestricted submarine warfare was touted as an infallible recipe for success. The failure of the campaign was yet another bitter disappointment. The Allied blockade caused a serious food shortage. The black market thrived. The gap between the haves and the have-nots grew ever wider. Right-wing parties blamed the Jews for all Germany's miseries. They were painted as black marketeers, war profiteers, and skrimshankers who avoided the draft. In October 1916 the Prussian war ministry gave way to popular demand and called for a "Jewish census." The results were disappointing for the anti-Semites and were not published. They showed that Jews served their country every bit as loyally as Gentile Germans, not that this information would have changed anyone's mind. Bethmann Hollweg continued to be seen as the "chancellor of German Jewry."

Protests against the war from the left began as early as December 1914 when Karl Liebknecht, the son of the SPD's co-founder, voted against the war credits. A number of other prominent figures, mostly from the left of the party, followed suit. This group was expelled from the Reichstag parliamentary party in 1916 and formed the "Social Democratic Working Group": a mixed bunch of opponents to the war that included Rosa Luxemburg, Klara Zetkin, and Franz Mehring on the left, and Karl Kautsky, the leading theorist of "centrism," the economist Rudolf Hilferding, and Eduard Bernstein, the founder of revisionism, on the right. The left remained loyal to the ideals of the Second International and took part in a congress in Zimmerwald in Switzerland in September 1915, at which militant socialists from the belligerent countries met to denounce their parent parties for their treacherous support of an imperialist war. Lenin excoriated the centrists and revisionists who opposed the war as weak-kneed "social pacifists," and urged that the imperialist war be turned into a civil war. With very few delegates prepared to go quite so far, the congress ended with a unanimous called for an immediate end to the war with a peace based on the principle of the self-determination of peoples, without annexations or reparations. The group met again in Switzerland at Kienthal in the following year. The anti-war rhetoric was stepped up, but Lenin was once again left seething in vituperative isolation.

The small anti-war faction won considerable popular support in the "turnip winter" of 1916/17 when the combined effects of a poor harvest and the blockade caused widespread hunger. The situation was compounded by the Auxiliary Labor Law of December 1916 that forced all men from the ages of 17 to 60 who had not been drafted into the armed forces to do labor service. It was hoped that this measure would lead to the success of the Hindenburg Program, which called for a substantial increase in armaments production. The Auxiliary Labor Law did not go nearly far enough for Hindenburg, Ludendorff, and Colonel Bauer, the principal architect of the bill. They wanted to militarize the economy by placing workers under military law, with strikes being tantamount to desertion. They complained bitterly that too many concessions had been made to the trade unions by creating arbitration committees with equal representation from capital and labor. Most workers, resenting this attempt to regiment the workforce, felt that the unions had been co-opted. The February revolution in Russia and the formation of the Independent Social Democratic Party (USPD) in April 1917 marked a further stage in working-class radicalization. There was a wave of strikes, in which "revolutionary shop stewards" first made an appearance. Calls for an end to the war were frequent. Two sailors were executed for mutiny, a harsh measure that only served to heighten discontent below decks.

The Peace Resolution

Bethmann Hollweg, with his "politics of the diagonal," tried to defuse the situation with the kaiser's "Easter message" of April 1917, in which a reform of the monstrously inequitable Prussian electoral law was promised once the fighting was over. But this was altogether too vague, too little, and too late. Meanwhile, Austria-Hungary, Germany's principal ally, desperately wanted to end the war. Negotiations were begun with France for a separate peace but got nowhere. The new emperor Charles and his foreign minister Count Czernin now turned to the Center Party politician and perennial busybody Matthias Erzberger for help. Realizing that the unrestricted submarine warfare campaign had been a costly mistake, he had come to the conclusion that that war had to be ended. A large number of his colleagues agreed. The SPD had reached a similar verdict and adopted the Petrograd Soviet's slogan calling for a peace without annexations or indemnities. In June 1917 the SPD issued an ultimatum to the chancellor to the effect that the party would vote against the war credits if he did not produce a clear catalogue of war aims. Bethmann, anxious not to appear as hostage to the socialists, refused, thus losing the support of the parliamentary majority he had enjoyed since the onset of hostilities.

On July 6, 1917, Erzberger consulted with members of the SPD, the Progressives, and the Center Party, before being briefed by Colonel Bauer on the seriousness of the military situation. Having been informed that Pope Benedict XV was about to launch a peace initiative, he denounced the unconditional submarine warfare campaign and called upon the

Reichstag to do everything possible to end the war. Erzberger's peace initiative marks a major turning point in German politics. The very same day the Social Democrats, National Liberals, Center Party, and Progressives formed a Joint Committee (Interfraktionellen Ausschuss) that was a significant step towards the creation of responsible parliamentary government. There were still wide differences between the parties. The National Liberals refused to accept the Petrograd Soviet's peace formula. The Center Party was anxious not to press the question of Prussian electoral reform too hard. The Social Democrats and Progressives wanted to push ahead with reforms and establish a thoroughgoing parliamentary regime. Meanwhile, the OHL was demanding the dismissal of Bethmann Hollweg and his replacement by a man who would do their bidding. Gustav Stresemann and the National Liberals, along with Erzberger and his supporters in the Center Party, agreed that the chancellor should go. The rest were largely indifferent to the chancellor's fate, so his days were clearly numbered.

William II, deeply resenting the OHL's political intrigues, was furious that Bethmann's proposed successor was none other than Bülow, with whom he had become utterly disenchanted. The kaiser therefore stuck to Bethmann more out of stubbornness than conviction until July 12, when Hindenburg and Ludendorff threatened to resign unless the chancellor was dismissed. On the very same day the SPD, Center Party, and Progressives agreed on a text for the peace resolution. It called for a peace that would lead to reconciliation and understanding between the warring factions, in which there would be no annexations or excessive economic burdens. The resolution was not without its ambiguities, but was too much for the National Liberals who, never having felt comfortable in the Joint Committee, now left in protest. Bethmann also disapproved of the resolution but, powerless to stop a debate in the Reichstag, offered his resignation that evening. Hindenburg and Ludendorff travelled to Berlin the next day in an attempt to convince the "majority parties," as they were henceforth known, to withdraw the peace resolution, but to no avail. The kaiser was reluctant to give way to the OHL's blackmail tactics, but agreed with the majority of his countrymen that the war could not possibly be won without the two demigods. On July 14 he appointed a relatively obscure Prussian civil servant, Georg Michaelis, as Bethmann's successor. He thus abandoned most of his few remaining sovereign powers.

The struggle was now between the OHL and the majority parties of the Reichstag. It was an unequal struggle in that Michaelis, as the tool of the OHL, shared none of Bethmann's concern to achieve a broad consensus. He appointed a number of members of the majority parties to important positions in the civil administration, but the Reichstag still had no share in the responsibilities of government. This fact was somewhat obscured by the passing of the peace resolution on July 19 by a vote of 212 to 126, and many were deceived by Michaelis' assurance that he would respect the resolution "as I interpret it." Satisfied that they had won a significant victory, the majority parties voted a few days later for the war credits.

In September 1917 the lawyer and banker Wolfgang Kapp of the eponymous putsch founded the Fatherland Party (Deutsche Vaterlandspartei) in Königsberg to organize opposition to the peace resolution. The party, an organization that the liberal historian Friedrich Meinecke described as a "monstrous creation of an egoism blind to its true interests and of misconstrued idealism," saw itself as an interest group rather than a conventional political party. It attracted a large number of members, particularly in the eastern Prussian provinces, but also among industrialists and discontented Bildungsbürger. A number of prominent figures lent their support, including Admiral Tirpitz, who had resigned as secretary of state for the navy in 1916 when his proposal to start unrestricted submarine warfare had been rejected. The party detested parliamentary democracy, which it saw as "hypocritical" and "English," contrasting it with something it was pleased to call "German freedom," which could only be secured by means of a "Hindenburg peace." Germany had therefore to unite in an all-out struggle for final victory in which the most exotic war aims would be achieved.

Two months later a group of moderates, which included Max Weber and the historians Friedrich Meinecke and Hans Delbrück, formed the People's Association for Freedom and Fatherland (Volksbund für Freiheit und Vaterland) to counter the strident propaganda of the Fatherland Party. This group called for fundamental political reform and for a peace on the basis of the Reichstag resolution. It failed to attract the mass support enjoyed by the Fatherland Party, but with important contacts in the trade unions and left-wing parties it helped overcome the antagonisms between the moderate bourgeoisie and the working class. The lines were now more clearly drawn between the proponents of a "victorious peace" and between a "renunciatory peace": between a "Hindenburg peace" and a "Scheidemann peace," named after its prominent Social Democratic advocate.

Meanwhile, Michaelis had gone the way of his predecessor. He had dithered on all the great issues of the day: the peace resolution, foreign policy, the Auxiliary Labor Law, franchise reform in Prussia, and how to respond to the papal peace initiative. His exceptionally inept handling of a naval mutiny lost him all the remaining sympathy of the majority parties, who now seized the initiative to secure his dismissal. Acting on behalf of the OHL the crown prince once again suggested that he be replaced by Bülow. His candidature was vociferously seconded by Erzberger, whose party was beginning to have second thoughts about the peace resolution. The kaiser, predictably having none of this, appointed the Bavarian minister president Count von Hertling, a man who had more sympathy for the peace resolution than Michaelis, but who as a Bavarian patriot resisted any constitutional reforms that might strengthen the federal structure of the Reich.

Michaelis' fall was significant in that for the second time the Reichstag had played the key role in his dismissal. The OHL had used the Reichstag to get rid of Bethmann, but in doing so had greatly strengthened its powers. This time the OHL had played no part in the dismissal of the chancellor. The Reichstag had done it virtually alone. Hindenburg and Ludendorff had no time for Hertling. Not only a Catholic, he was also – even worse – a Bavarian. Although he was appointed behind their backs they were obliged to accept him. Treated with unaccustomed deference by the OHL, the chancellor caused them precious few headaches. The SPD watched him closely from the other side of the fence on which the chancellor uneasily sat, making sure that he did not stray too far from the moderate course he had promised to follow.

The Impact of Bolshevik Revolution

The Bolshevik revolution in early November 1917 sent shock waves throughout Germany. The peace resolution of the Second All-Russian Congress of Soviets was widely welcomed. The German working class showed no particular enthusiasm for communism in its Leninist form and almost all socialists, even the most radical, were disturbed by the violence and brutality of its dictatorial methods. But Lenin's passionate call for an end to the imperialist war met with an eager response, not only among war-weary workers, but particularly among disillusioned soldiers at the front who were called upon to risk their lives for the absurdly unrealistic war aims of the Fatherland Party. There was virtually unanimous disillusionment with a Bolshevik regime after the violent dissolution of the constituent assembly in January. Only a handful of radicals in the extreme left-wing Spartacus Group, which included the feisty feminist Klara Zetkin and the armchair revolutionary Franz Mehring, welcomed the move. The intellectual leader of the group, Rosa Luxemburg, was appalled, and penned the famous lines about freedom being the right to disagree, but she made it plain that she too placed strict limits on the room for disagreement. She insisted that civil war was just another name for the class struggle, and that the idea that socialism could be achieved by means of parliamentary democracy was "an absurd petit-bourgeois illusion."

A wave of spontaneous strikes that began at the end of January in Berlin was inspired by widespread strikes in Austria-Hungary. In the Dual Monarchy there were clear signs of Bolshevik influence, although the principal demands were that the peace negotiations with Russia should not become unnecessarily protracted by reason of excessive war aims and that there should be a more equitable distribution of foodstuffs. In Germany strikers were also mainly concerned with these two key issues. Although the strikes were far less damaging to the war economy than were those in Britain, the majority of socialists and the trade unions were acutely embarrassed, and did everything possible to bring them to an end for fear of being accused of undermining the war effort. The strikers denounced the military dictatorship of the OHL. The military authorities responded by declaring a state of martial law, arresting a number of prominent figures, including a Reichstag deputy. *Vorwärts,* the SPD's main newspaper, was banned. The court preacher Bruno Doehring denounced the strikers as "venal and cowardly creatures who have treacherously profaned the altar of the fatherland with their brothers' blood." The conservative leader Ernst von Heydebrand und der Lasa accused the strikers of committing treason, having been led astray by outside agitators and the SPD. Ludendorff preferred to use the soldierly demotic for his public announcement: "Anyone who strikes is a cunt!" The foundations of the powerful "stab in the back" legend were thus laid in January 1918.

Lenin knew that the Bolsheviks could only remain in power if they ended the war. On March 3, 1918, peace was eventually signed at Brest-Litovsk. It was a peace of unprecedented ferocity besides which the *Diktat* of Versailles pales in comparison. Russia was forced to give up the Ukraine, Finland, the Baltic states, and parts of Armenia. It lost the Trans-Caucasus and the Crimea, and was forced to pay colossal reparations. It lost one-third of its population and agricultural land, in addition to an even higher percentage of many key raw materials. The Treaty of Brest-Litovsk was a clear repudiation of both the letter and the spirit of the Reichstag's peace resolution, but it was ratified by the overwhelming majority of deputies. The Center Party and Progressives voted for the treaty, the SPD, chastened by official reaction to the strikes, abstained; only the USPD defiantly voted against.

The Failure of the March Offensive

The peace movement was temporarily silenced with the spectacular initial success of the "Michael" offensive across the old Somme battlefields which was launched on March 21, 1918. The Germans made a deep penetration on a broad front that destroyed General Sir Hubert Gough's Fifth Army, whereupon the OHL announced that a victory was in sight that would result in a "Hindenburg peace." The more perspicacious of the German generals, harboring serious doubts whether it would be possible to follow up these initial successes, began to have reservations about Ludendorff's operational acumen and mental stability. Subsequent offensives in Flanders, on the Chemin des Dames, on the Aisne, and in the Champagne proved them to be perfectly correct. The Entente seized the initiative with the Mangin offensive in July, which was followed by a powerful blow at Amiens in the following month. By now it was plain to all that the war was lost. By September 1918 the German army's morale was broken and the number of desertions steadily mounted.

Disillusionment was also widespread on the home front. Victory had been promised in 1914, at Verdun in 1916, and again with unrestricted submarine warfare in 1917. The propaganda machine had gone into high gear in the spring of 1918 with the result that disappointment in the summer was even greater. There was widespread disillusionment with the kaiser, the army leadership, and the government. In southern Germany Prussian militarism was blamed for the present wretched state of Germany. Particularist sentiment ran high. Discontent in certain sections of the working class was such that some began to fear that the Reich might go the way of Russia. Germany faced the dire prospect of defeat and red revolution.

At this juncture the role of the SPD was crucial. The party leader, Friedrich Ebert, was determined that Germany should not emulate Bolshevik Russia. The clear alternative was to work together with the bourgeois parties to secure moderate reforms. When faced with the alternative of revolution or reform the SPD, for all the radical Marxist rhetoric of the party program, unhesitatingly opted for reform. Those who viewed such a choice as a betrayal of the fundamental principles of socialism and class solidarity had already left the party, so that Ebert had little difficulty in persuading the parliamentary party to accept his reformist course.

It took lengthy and intense debate to get the Center Party to accept the idea of a constitutional monarchy, largely because it feared that the Catholic minority would suffer under a system based on majority rule. The party dropped its objections when the National Liberals endorsed the idea of a thoroughgoing parliamentary regime led by a more amenable chancellor. On September 28 the Joint Committee reached an agreement on fundamental reform. The following day Hindenburg and Ludendorff told the kaiser that the war was lost. They urged that negotiations for an armistice based on President Wilson's peace proposals should begin at once. The OHL was now determined that the blame for a lost war should be placed squarely on the shoulders of the majority parties in the Reichstag. On October 1 Ludendorff told a group of senior officers: "We shall now see these gentlemen enter various ministries. They can make the peace that has to be made. They can now eat the soup they have served up to us!" The changeover to a parliamentary regime was part of the "revolution from above" masterminded by Admiral Paul von Hintze, a devious, blasé, and ambitious opportunist who had been appointed secretary of state for foreign affairs in July. The "stab in the back" legend, that was to play such a critical role in the downfall of the Weimar Republic, was thus carefully constructed in late summer of 1918.

On October 3 Prince Max of Baden, heir to the grand duchy, was appointed chancellor, even though he was a man virtually without a political profile. Members of all the majority parties were given ministerial positions. As a result of the constitutional changes on October 28, Germany was now a fully fledged constitutional monarchy. The chancellor was made responsible to the Reichstag and was obliged to resign if he no longer enjoyed its confidence. War could not be declared nor peace concluded without parliamentary consent. The right was flabbergasted. Heinrich Class, the president of the Pan-German League, called for an all-out offensive on the Jews, whom he held responsible for this disastrous turn of events. The League's official newspaper the *Deutsche Zeitung* published an article by Baron von Gelbsattel blaming the Jews for this "bloodless revolution," because democracy was an essential ingredient of Jewry's "destructive potential." At a meeting of senior officials of the League in late October, Class quoted Kleist out of context by saying of the Jews: "Kill the lot; you will not be asked the reason why at the last judgement."

Armistice Negotiations

The first act of Prince Max's government was to begin, at the OHL's insistence, negotiations with the United States government for an armistice. Secretary of state Lansing spelt out the conditions on October 23. He demanded the kaiser's abdication, followed by Germany's complete surrender. The OHL, who were looking for a breathing space, pronounced these terms totally unacceptable. Prince Max wrote to the kaiser saying that if Ludendorff, whom he knew to be the driving force behind the absurd idea of continuing the war, were not dismissed he would resign. Hindenburg and Ludendorff traveled to Berlin to confront the kaiser. In a stormy scene William accepted Ludendorff's resignation. General Groener, a moderate staff officer who hailed from Württemberg, was appointed in his stead. The kaiser then left Berlin. Following Hindenburg's suggestion he traveled to headquarters at Spa in the vain hope of saving his crown.

Meanwhile, as part of the armistice negotiations the submarine campaign was stopped, whereupon the navy under Admiral Scheer, which had not ventured forth since the battle of Jutland in 1916, decided to launch a massive attack on the Royal Navy. Scheer's motives were mixed. He wanted to save the honor of the High Seas Fleet, which had stood idly by for two years, but above all he wanted to sabotage the armistice negotiations. It was thus an act of such gross insubordination as to amount to an attempted coup. Orders were issued, prompting mutinies at Wilhelmshaven that rapidly spread to Kiel, Lübeck, Hamburg, Bremen, and Cuxhaven, along with a number of lesser ports. The government tried to pacify the mutineers by sending Conrad Haußmann from the Progressive People's Party and the Social Democrat Gustav Noske with a promise of an amnesty. The offer was refused. The mutiny turned into a revolution as workers joined the sailors. On November 7 a motley crew of socialists and anarchists under Kurt Eisner seized power in Munich. The king abdicated, and a republican Free State of Bavaria was proclaimed. On the following day, revolutionary sailors and workers took over control in Brunswick. By November 8, Düsseldorf, Stuttgart, Leipzig, Halle, Osnabrück, and Cologne were in the hands of workers' and soldiers' councils. The mayor of Cologne, Konrad Adenauer, calmly announced that he fully accepted the new circumstances.

By now it was clear that the kaiser would have to go. The sailors in Kiel were the first to publicly demand his abdication. Then the prominent Social Democrat Philipp Scheidemann wrote to Prince Max at the end of October, saying that the kaiser should abdicate in order that the armistice talks could proceed smoothly. Friedrich Ebert who, unlike Scheidemann, was far from being a republican, suggested to the chancellor on November 7 that a regent should be appointed so as to avoid a revolution. According to Prince Max he then added the famous words: "I hate revolution like the plague."

Also on November 7, the commanding general in the Marches, General von Linsingen, determined to take decisive action against the radical left, banned the workers' and soldiers' councils that had mushroomed throughout Germany. He also forbade any meetings sponsored by the USPD. This ran quite contrary to the more relaxed policy of the Prussian war minister General Scheüch, who had removed a number of restrictions on the right of assembly only a few days beforehand. He also released Rosa Luxemburg and Karl Liebknecht from jail. The SPD protested vigorously at von Linsingen's high-handed action and insisted that the kaiser should abdicate. On the following day the Centre and Progressives agreed that both the kaiser and the crown prince would have to relinquish their claims to the throne. They also agreed with the SPD's demand that the franchise, both in the states and the Reich, be extended to include women. The majority of the members of the moderate parties had come to the realization that Germany was ungovernable without the SPD. The only alternative was revolution and civil war.

On the morning of November 9, Otto Wels, regional secretary of the SPD in Brandenburg, a rough-hewn populist of exceptional courage and sound instincts, called for a general strike in protest against Linsingen's decree. Shortly afterwards Scheidemann resigned his post as secretary of state without portfolio in Prince Max's government. Ebert then began negotiations with the USPD, the revolutionary shop stewards and the workers' and soldiers' councils with a view to forming a government on the Bavarian model. The pragmatist Wels knew that Ebert's efforts to co-opt the extreme left were unlikely to succeed without military support. He therefore approached the Naumburg Light Infantry (Naumburger Jäger) a traditional regiment known for its loyalty to the kaiser. Wels appealed to the other ranks to support the Social Democrats in their endeavor to create a new republican government. He met with a warm response. The news that that the Naumburger Jäger had thrown their support behind the Social Democrats was a shattering blow to Prince Max and to the OHL. At headquarters Groener had already come to the conclusion that the army would refuse to follow the kaiser in an attempt to oust the Social Democrats and that he therefore had to go. Hindenburg agreed, but refused to relay this unpleasant news to the All Highest. On the morning of November 9 Groener told the kaiser: "The army no longer stands behind Your Majesty!" whereupon William II expressed his intention to abdicate. The armistice was signed two days later.

For the next ten weeks Germany was in turmoil. The misery caused by an economy in ruins with widespread famine was compounded by violence from both left and right. Thanks to close cooperation between moderate Social Democrats and the army, as well as an agreement between industrialists and the trade unions, relative peace was restored. Elections were held on January 19, 1919. The message from the electorate was clear. It wanted a resolutely democratic form of government and moderate reform. Both Red Revolution and Black Reaction were repudiated. The people wanted parliamentary democracy based on a fruitful compromise between Social Democrats and the moderate bourgeois parties. It was a vote of confidence in the majority parties of the old Reichstag, the architects of the new republic. It was a promising beginning to a new chapter in German history.

CHAPTER ELEVEN
THE WEIMAR REPUBLIC
1919–1933

CHAPTER CONTENTS

A History of Modern Germany: 1800 to the Present, Second Edition. Martin Kitchen.
© 2012 Martin Kitchen. Published 2012 by Blackwell Publishing Ltd.

The new parliament met in peaceful Weimar, the town of Goethe and Schiller, far away from troubled Berlin. Ebert was elected temporary president, Scheidemann appointed chancellor. The German Democratic Party (DDP) insisted that it would only form a coalition with the SPD if the Center Party and its Bavarian wing, the Bavarian People's Party (BVP) were included, so that the center of gravity was shifted to the right. Deliberations over a new constitution began amid mounting unrest, and a wave of strikes by militant workers who made a number of radical demands, the principal one being the nationalization of the coal industry. Violence was widespread. The fighting in Berlin in March left 1,000 dead. The government responded to a general strike in the Ruhr by sending in the troops. Bavaria was in a state of turmoil. Munich followed the example of Béla Kun's Soviet Hungary when Ernst Niekisch proclaimed the end of the "bourgeois capitalist age" in a Soviet Bavaria. Had it not ended in a terrible bloodbath, the Bavarian Soviet Republic would have been regarded as pure operetta, the object of almost universal derision. At Noske's behest the White terror made quick work of the Republic, which had come under the dauntless control of the Communist Eugen Leviné. Munich became a hotbed of sundry right-wing extremists who blamed recent events on the machinations of world Jewry. Agitators like Adolf Hitler found a ready audience for their hateful messages.

The Treaty of Versailles

When the guns fell silent on November 11, 1918, most Germans confidently imagined that the peace settlement would be based on President Wilson's idealistic fourteen points. They had few regrets at the prospect of losing Alsace-Lorraine along with some of the Polish provinces, and even entertained the illusion that the new Austrian republic, proclaimed on November 12, would be permitted to join a greater Germany, thus completing the process of German unification. The hard-nosed realists in the OHL and their associates knew otherwise. They had negotiated the draconian peace of Brest-Litovsk on the basis of the self-determination of peoples and the rejection of indemnities and reparations. They knew full well that the fourteen points would be interpreted in such a way as to bleed Germany white. Some argued that the harsher the peace the better. The odium of ending the war had been shifted onto the majority parties in the "Hintze Action." They could now bear the blame for a harsh peace and thus be totally discredited. The German government was informed of the Allied peace terms on May 7, 1919, shortly after the bloodbath in Munich. They exceeded the worst fears of the direst of pessimists. That Germany should lose Upper Silesia, a large chunk of West Prussia, Danzig, and Memel, and that East Prussia should be separated from the rest of Germany, came as a devastating blow. Things were hardly better in the west. The Saar was to be placed under the League of Nations for fifteen years, the west bank of the Rhine permanently demilitarized, the entire Rhineland occupied for up to fifteen years. Eupen-Malmedy was to be handed over to Belgium. Union (*Anschluss*) with Austria was expressly forbidden. Germany's colonial empire was to be dissolved. The army was not to exceed 100,000 men. Military aircraft, submarines, and tanks were among a number of outlawed weapons. The fleet was to surrender, but it was scuttled before it reached the Scottish naval base at Scapa Flow. Ninety percent of the merchant navy had to be handed over, along with 10 percent of the cattle and a substantial proportion of the rolling stock in the state railway. The victors were unable to agree on a final sum for reparations, but 40 million tons of coal were demanded annually. Germans were particularly incensed by article 231, which demanded that they should make good the damage caused by a war which they and their allies had begun. A deliberate mistranslation of the article to read "sole guilt" (*Alleinschuld*) further inflamed a consternated public, setting off a wave of righteous indignation at the "war guilt lie."

The Scheidemann government was at first inclined to declare these terms unacceptable. The chancellor worked himself up into a rhetorical frenzy proclaiming: "May the hand wither that binds us in such shackles!" Other leading politicians in the coalition argued that the proposed peace was merely a continuation of the war by other means, or that it would sow the seeds of further conflict. Cooler and more realistic heads soon prevailed. Groener told the government that it would be impossible to resist an Allied invasion. Scheidemann resigned the chancellorship in favor of a nondescript Social Democrat, Gustav Bauer. The Allies made minor concessions by permitting a plebiscite in Upper Silesia, and suggesting that the occupation of the Rhineland might end somewhat sooner if Germany behaved to their satisfaction. The request for a revision of article 231 met with a point-blank refusal. After a secret ballot in which the National Assembly voted in favor of acceptance, the foreign minister Hermann Müller from the SPD and the minister of transport Johannes Bell from the Center Party signed the treaty in the Hall of Mirrors in Versailles. It was the very place where the German empire had been proclaimed less than fifty years before.

PLATE 16   The German delegation to the Versailles Peace Conference. © BPK

PLATE 17   Mass protest in Berlin against the Treaty of Versailles. © BPK

The Treaty of Versailles was harsh and unjust, but it was neither as harsh nor as unjust as the Treaty of Brest-Litovsk. It was soon recognized as such by the Allied governments, which had been driven by their electorates' lust for revenge to draft a peace they knew to be fraught with problems. The process of revision, which Germany was quick to exploit, began almost immediately. Indeed Germany was in a stronger position after Versailles than it had been in 1914. With Russia in the hands of the pariah Bolsheviks it was no longer encircled. The bordering states of Poland and Czechoslovakia were hopelessly weak. The *entente* between Britain and France had never been particularly *cordiale*, and under the strains of a coalition war and a controversial peace was now in tatters. Germany was still united, and the Ruhr was virtually a guarantee that it would once again be a major power. But the treaty had a disastrous, indeed deadly, effect on domestic politics. The majority parties were blamed for accepting the *Diktat* of Versailles along with the "war guilt lie." The wooden titan Hindenburg gave his full support to the "stab in the back legend" (*Dolchstoßlegende*), which the OHL had fabricated. He announced that the undefeated army had been betrayed by the politicians. The majority parties, and with them the entire system of Weimar democracy, were henceforth denounced from the right as the "November criminals." Everyone agreed that the Treaty of Versailles had to be revised, but opinions differed on how this was to be done and how far that revision should go. On the right it was argued that revision of the treaty should also involve the overthrow of the parties most responsible for Germany's humiliation. For them the struggle to revise the Treaty of Versailles was first and foremost a fight to the death against the Weimar Republic. That was the treaty's fatal legacy.

The Weimar Constitution

The new republic was a federal state, but was far more centralized than the old empire. The larger states lost their "reserve rights" that permitted them to have their own armies, postal services, and taxes. Prussia, still by far the largest state with 60 percent of the population, was no longer a hegemonic power. The fiercest debates were over the role of the president. Largely due to the advocacy of Max Weber, the architect of the new constitution, the left liberal Hugo Preuß, proposed a president elected by universal suffrage whose democratic legitimation would make him a powerful counterweight to parliament. This suggestion was sharply attacked by a number of Social Democrats, who saw such a strong president as a potential autocrat à la Bismarck, or as a surrogate kaiser. Ebert might well be entrusted with such powers, but what would happen if he were succeeded by a reactionary? Most members did not share this grim view. Shaken by the recent violence they welcomed a powerful head of state, who could take decisive action in difficult times. They had no objection to the president having a seven-year term of office, or to his being able to use emergency powers under article 48, the latter being subject to the Reichstag's veto. The president appointed the chancellor and could dissolve the Reichstag. In a multi-party system, with proportional representation favoring the splinter parties, this gave the president immense powers over the Reichstag.

The constitution came into effect on August 14, 1919. One week later the National Assembly left Weimar and returned to Berlin. The most pressing task of the new Reichstag was financial reform. The problems facing Matthias Erzberger as minister of finance were awesome. The war had been financed on credit, leaving the state hopelessly indebted. Excessive increases in nominal wages had been granted in order to placate a dangerously discontented working class. Inflation was running rife, with the Reichsbank finding it difficult to resist the temptation to encourage inflation to reduce the national debt. The situation was further complicated by the prospect of having to meet the excessive Allied demands for reparations. Erzberger set about reforming and centralizing the tax system, taxing war profiteers, increasing death duties, and introducing a one-shot tax on assets and a national income tax. The net result of these reforms was to further fuel inflation. Erzberger imagined that significant increases in the tax burden would reduce the amount of money in circulation and thus cut back inflation, but the cost of higher taxes was quickly offset by higher prices.

The Kapp Putsch

Erzberger, already the bête noire of the right, was subjected to a scurrilous defamation campaign. He had introduced the peace resolution in 1917 and had signed the armistice. Now he was responsible for the punitive taxation of the wealthy and propertied. In January 1920 he was seriously wounded in an assassination attempt. On March 12 he felt obliged to resign. On the same day Noske, as army minister, informed his cabinet colleagues that a plot was afoot to overthrow the government. The coup was masterminded by Wolfgang Kapp, head of the former Fatherland Party, and by Captain Waldemar Pabst, who had ordered the murders of Rosa Luxemburg and Karl Liebknecht. Military support was provided by Baron von Lüttwitz, the commanding general of Army Group I in Berlin and by

Captain Hermann Ehrhardt, whose Free Corps Marine Brigade had fought Bolsheviks in the Baltic states with the blessing of the Allied powers. He had also played a leading role in the White terror in Munich. The conspiracy was coordinated by the National Association (National Vereinigung), under Ludendorff's patronage.

Ehrhardt's troops entered Berlin on March 13, their helmets adorned with swastikas, an ancient Indian symbol that had been adopted by a number of extreme nationalist and anti-Semitic movements. President Ebert and Gustav Bauer's cabinet prudently moved to Dresden and relied on General Georg Maercker for protection. Kapp installed himself in the vacant chancellery. Lüttwitz proclaimed himself commander-in-chief of the armed forces. The Kapp putsch, which had initially been so successful, was doomed to failure because the vast majority of the ministerial bureaucracy refused to acknowledge its legitimacy. Bauer refused to negotiate with the putschists, so that after four frustrating days the military advised Kapp to throw in the towel. Ehrhardt's troops left Berlin on March 17. Kapp and Lüttwitz fled the country, and Ehrhardt was hidden by right-wing extremists in Munich, where he founded the terrorist group Organization Consul (OC) after his pseudonym "Consul Eichmann." After an eventful life spent largely on the run, he died in 1971 at the ripe old age of 90. Although responsible for a number of spectacular assassinations, including the deaths of Erzberger and Rathenau, he was never called to account in a court of law.

With Kapp in Berlin and the government paralyzed, there was unrest elsewhere in Germany. In Munich the local army commander, General von Möhl, prompted by a group a prominent figures on the extreme right, demanded of the SPD minister president, Johannes Hoffmann, that he be given full emergency powers. This led to Hoffmann's resignation and to his replacement by Gustav von Kahr at the head of a resolutely right-wing government that provided a safe haven in Bavaria for all manner of outlandish groups on the wilder shores of the radical right. In the Ruhr the Communist Party of Germany (KPD) organized a Red Army made up of "Proletarian Centuries" that attracted men of disparate political affiliations. On March 24 the Prussian minister of the interior and Reich Commissar, Carl Severing, concluded a lengthy series of negotiations with the insurgents with the Bielefeld Agreement. The KPD still refused to end the struggle, whereupon the government sent military units to the Ruhr, which only a few days before had supported Kapp. Well over 1,000 workers lost their lives in the bloodshed that followed. The brutal suppression of the Ruhr workers had a sobering effect on the labor movement. There were no more general strikes during the whole period of the Weimar Republic. The KPD's putsch attempt in the "March Action" in the following year was a damp squib that had no popular support.

Whereas those responsible for the uprising in the Ruhr were severely punished, Kapp's supporters were let off virtually scot-free. There was a general amnesty in August 1920 for Free Corps officers, who were then welcomed into the armed forces. Kapp returned to Germany in 1922 to face trial, but died before the proceedings began. Elections were held in June that marked the end of the rule of the Weimar coalition. The SPD share of the vote fell by 43 percent. The DDP dropped by 55 percent. The Center Party remained relatively stable. On the left the KPD fielded candidates for the first time, but only obtained 1.7 percent of the votes. The USPD more than doubled its share, so that it was only three points behind the SPD. On the right, votes for Gustav Stresemann's German People's Party (DVP), the successor party to the National Liberals, trebled, and the conservative German National People's Party (DNVP) improved its showing by almost 50 percent.

Reparations

Ebert found it exceedingly hard to find anyone willing to attempt to form a government, until the Center Party politician Konstantin Fehrenbach managed to tack together a minority government. He was a respected figure, known for his tact and sense of humor. He had considerable political experience, having been chairman of the Joint Committee of the Reichstag. He also had a reputation for his principled stand against the rising tide of anti-Semitism. But with an indecisive and hesitant personality he proved unequal to the weighty problems that faced his government. His task was made all the more difficult by Allied intransigence and inequity. At the beginning of May 1921 Lloyd George, on behalf of the Allies, presented the German government with an ultimatum that unless a back payment of 12 billion gold marks (which, unlike the Reichsmark, were pegged to the price of gold) in reparations was made, and war criminals brought to justice, the entire Ruhr would be occupied. One billion was to be paid by the end of the month. This was no idle threat. Düsseldorf, Duisburg, and Ruhrort had already been occupied a few weeks previously when an earlier ultimatum had been disregarded. In addition, the Allies finally reached an agreement that Germany should pay 132 billion gold marks in reparations, with an additional 6 billion for Belgium. Finding it impossible to meet these terms, Fehrenbach resigned.

The crisis was rendered all the more acute by events in Upper Silesia. The Polish government refused to accept the result of the plebiscite in March 1921, in which 60 percent of the population voted for Germany. It supported Polish insurgents who laid claim to the bulk of the province. The German government responded by arming paramilitary units determined to ensure that the vote be respected. The fighting stopped when the Allies accepted a report by the League of Nations which suggested that four-fifths of Upper Silesia should be given to Poland, including certain industrial districts that had voted overwhelmingly for Germany. Also in March the KPD, supported by the Communist International, mounted an abortive coup attempt in the Ruhr that was quickly suppressed by the Prussian police.

The Weimar coalition returned to office in a minority government under Joseph Wirth. The new chancellor was something of an *enfant terrible* on the left wing of the Center Party. He was a brilliant orator, an ardent republican, and a fervent nationalist. He was the architect of the policy, soon to be called "fulfillment," of cooperation with the Allies in the hope of being able to expose the impossibility of their demands and thus revise the Versailles treaty. The Allied demands were indeed virtually impossible to meet. The initial billion gold marks could only be raised by the sale of three-month treasury bonds that further fueled inflation. The problem could not be solved without a substantial tax on capital, but this was unacceptable to the Reichstag majority, even to those like Walther Rathenau who supported Wirth's fulfillment policy. If the capitalists were not going to pay then the consumers would have to foot the bill. Employees already hit by inflation would be made to suffer still further. The right mounted a massive hate campaign against the Wirth government and its policy of fulfillment. There were a number of political murders, including Erzberger's assassination in August 1921. His killers, who came from Ehrhardt's Organization Consul, were compared in the right-wing press to Brutus, William Tell, and Charlotte Corday. Only six murderers were brought to trial, the two most vicious of whom were sprung from jail thanks to Organization Consul. The press waxed increasingly indignant over the antics of the "Jewish swine on the Spree" and the country seemed to be heading rapidly towards civil war. At the end of August the government made use of article 48 to ban a number of extreme right-wing publications that were disseminating such filth, but the Bavarian government refused to cooperate, allowing the infant Nazi Party's *Völkischer Beobachter* to continue publication.

Wirth felt obliged to resign in October when the Reichstag majority protested at the flagrant disregard of the right to self-determination in Upper Silesia. It was a futile gesture since no government could be formed without the Center Party, so Wirth was soon back in office. The outstanding figure in the second Wirth cabinet was the new foreign secretary, Walther Rathenau, who had previously served as minister for reconstruction. He was the most remarkable and admirable personality in the Weimar Republic. As head of the family firm AEG he was an exemplary modern manager with a complete mastery of both the technical and the financial complexities of a vast corporation. In addition he was a sensitive and highly cultured intellectual, a perceptive essayist, philosopher, and cultural critic. He was a member of the DDP and an enthusiastic advocate of the policy of fulfillment. But even he was not free from the malignant prejudices of the age. Although himself a Jew with a strongly homoerotic predisposition, in 1908 he called for the "Nordification" of the German race by natural selection. He waxed eloquent over this "wonderful race," which was duty bound, along with all "truly Occidental races, to seize control over the globe, disinherit the incompetent races and exercise stewardship over them." This came from a man who also wrote: "There is a painful moment in the youth of every German Jew, which he remembers for the rest of his life: when for the first time he becomes fully aware that he has entered the world as a second-class citizen and that no amount of effort and no meritorious achievements will ever change this situation."

Rapallo

His first and only appearance on the international stage as foreign minister was at the Genoa Conference in April 1922. The conference was held at Lloyd George's request ostensibly to deal with the problem of reparations and war debts, but primarily it was a desperate attempt to save his political skin. Although it was doomed to failure from the outset, largely because the United States declined to attend, it was not without significance. For the first time the Soviet Union was invited to attend an international meeting. A number of influential figures in Germany were determined to use this opportunity to strengthen ties between the two countries. As early as 1920, even before the Polish–Soviet war, General Hans von Seeckt, the de facto head of the German general staff, an organization that had been officially outlawed by the Treaty of Versailles, and which was now known simply as the "Troops Office" (Truppenamt), argued that Germany could only regain the territory it had lost to Poland in close cooperation with the Soviet Union. Wirth enthusiastically agreed and both men dreamt of the destruction of Poland and a common frontier between Germany and the Soviet Union. Top-secret cooperation between the German army (Reichswehr) and the Red Army began in 1921, soon after the Treaty of Riga obliged the Soviet Union to accept a substantial loss of territory to the victorious Poles. A few months later the head of the eastern department of the foreign office, Ago von Maltzan, began talks with Karl Radek, the German expert in the Soviet government, with a view to working out an economic agreement that would bypass the Allied syndicate to assist Soviet economic development. Rathenau was a convinced westerner and wanted nothing to do with the

Soviet Union, but when the Soviet commissar for foreign affairs, Georgi Chicherin, stopped off in Berlin on his way to Genoa substantial progress was made towards the conclusion of a treaty. At Genoa Maltzan played up the rumor that the Allies were about to do a deal with the Soviets at Germany's expense, in order to convince Rathenau to drop his objections to an alliance with the Bolsheviks. It is something of a mystery why Rathenau was so easily persuaded against his better judgment to take this fateful step, but when told that Chicherin was ready to sign a treaty on Germany's terms he agreed to meet the Soviet delegation on Easter Sunday at the nearby resort of Rapallo. The Treaty of Rapallo was seemingly an innocuous document. The signatories agreed not to make any demands on one another for war reparations or indemnities. Diplomatic relations were resumed, most favored nation status granted.

In Berlin some conservatives objected to the acceptance of the Soviets as partners. On the left concerns were voiced that it would ruin any chances of reaching an agreement with the Allies. On the whole reactions to the treaty were positive, so that it was ratified by a comfortable majority. The Allies, in particular the French, who saw Rapallo as a repetition of crude Wilhelmine tactics and of Kiderlen-Wächter's Morocco policy, were outraged. They were now determined not to stand for any further nonsense from Germany. The French minister president, Poincaré, publicly threatened Germany with armed intervention. Prospects for an agreement over reparations thus dissolved into the dim and distant future.

Six weeks after signing the Treaty of Rapallo, Rathenau was gunned down by members of Organization Consul. He was hated by the radical right as a Jew, as a man who sought a compromise with the Allies, as a political beneficiary of the revolution of 1918 and as an immensely wealthy capitalist. The republic was shattered by the death of this fascinating and complex figure. The Communists joined in the mass demonstrations organized by the unions and the two socialist parties. Wirth gave a rousing speech in the Reichstag which contained the memorable words "The enemy is on the right" – words that were met with tumultuous applause from delegates from the left and the center. The government introduced legislation to protect the republic against right-wing terror, but it had little effect and was fiercely resisted by the Bavarian government. Offenders from the left continued to be far more harshly treated by the courts than those from the right.

Rathenau's murder was the most alarming sign of the mounting tide of anti-Semitism that was to plague the republic. "The Jew" was seen as a polyvalent evil. The fact that a number of leading figures on the left were Jewish was taken as clear evidence that the Jews were responsible for Germany's defeat. Had they not subverted loyal German workers with their Judeo-Marxist ideology, undermined the empire, overthrown the crowned heads of Germany, and accepted a humiliating peace? Had they not avoided service at the front in order to fatten themselves with war profits? Were they not the driving force behind inflation, the black market and fulfillment politics? Then there were the "eastern Jews" (*Ostjuden*). Unlike the majority of German Jews they were Orthodox and unassimilated. With their strange attire and alien habits, speaking Hebrew and Yiddish, they were seen as menacing foreign invaders and a sinister threat to the German race, culture, and identity. A number of *Ostjuden* lived and worked in Germany before the war, where they were safe from the brutal pogroms of the Pale. During the war many had been forced by the German army of occupation to work in munitions factories in the Reich. Others came as prisoners of war, or as refugees from Bolshevik terror and civil war. Most dreamt of emigrating to the United States, and many succeeded in doing so. By 1925 there were just over 100,000 *Ostjuden* left in Germany – hardly the hordes that haunted the anti-Semites' fantasies.

Anti-Semitic prejudices were widespread, but were seldom publicly voiced in respectable bourgeois circles. Student fraternities nurtured their anti-Semitic traditions, and some members of the DNVP reveled in bouts of Jew-baiting, but the party had to distance itself somewhat from these creatures after Rathenau's murder. The Prussian government banned a meeting of student fraternities in Marburg at which it was intended to sing the praises of his murderers. The DNVP thus showed some restraint in Berlin, but the party's Munich branch allied itself with the German National Association (Deutschvölkische Arbeitsgemeinschaft), an anti-Semitic party created by dissident members of the DNVP. It was very small beer compared with Hitler's National Socialist German Workers Party (NSDAP), which was rapidly becoming a political force of more than local interest.

Hyperinflation and the "Struggle for the Ruhr"

The nervousness and uncertainty caused by Rathenau's murder induced an alarming hyperinflation that provided fresh ammunition for anti-Semites, political radicals, and assorted malcontents. Tensions between capital and labor mounted when the prominent industrialist Hugo Stinnes suggested to the National Economic Council (Reichswirtschaftsrat) that German workers should work an extra two hours per day, without additional pay, for at least ten years, in order to overcome the crisis. Fortunately, cooler heads prevailed and the council, which included members of a wide range of opinion from the Marxist economist Rudolf Hilferding to a number of prominent industrialists, came up with a number of proposals acceptable to both sides in the dispute. The eight-hour day, one of the great achievements of the revolution, remained the legal norm. It was agreed that the government should cut back expenditure in an attempt to balance the budget. A serious attempt was also made to stabilize the mark by international loans and support from the Reichsbank. Agreement in the council over these measures augured well for Wirth's efforts to create a coalition from the DVP to the SPD, but all such hopes were dashed by the Social Democrats. The party had recently united with the rump of the USPD, the remainder having joined the KPD. For fear of alienating the left by a coalition with the DVP, which they saw as the bosses' party, they decided to remain aloof. Wirth resigned as chancellor, to be replaced by Wilhelm Cuno, the head of the Hamburg-America Line (Hapag). The new cabinet was largely made up of experts who, like the chancellor, had no party affiliations. Once again a government was formed without the support of the SPD, by far the most important of the parties that wholeheartedly supported the republic.

Cuno took office in November 1922 and was soon to face a crisis that almost destroyed the republic. Ever since Rapallo the French had been looking for an excuse to get back at Germany and to assert France's position as the hegemonic power in Europe. The Wirth government had been somewhat lackadaisical about reparations payments, so that Germany was seriously behindhand with deliveries of coal, wood, and telephone poles. On January 11, 1923, French and Belgian troops occupied the Ruhr. The British government, appalled at this display of hubris, adopted an attitude which one observer described as "surly neutrality." Cuno's minority government responded to this aggressive act by calling for passive resistance. This earned him the instant and enthusiastic support of the trade unions and the SPD. Even the Communists joined in the heroic struggle against French imperialism, but were hasty to add that they were equally opposed to the gang of capitalists in Berlin. The KPD's slogan was now: "Destroy Poincaré on the Rhine and Cuno on the Spree!"

Passive resistance was initially successful. Republican Germany was united as never before or since, leaving the French unable to extract any reparations. In March the French, having seized the coalmines and the railways, began the confiscation of German assets. By this time the republic was in serious financial difficulties. The Reichsbank was obliged to pay the striking workers and to grant massive credits to enterprises that had closed their doors in patriotic protest. Printing presses worked overtime, resulting in hyperinflation. The exchange rate of the dollar rose from 21,000 marks in April to 110,000 by June. The currency was soon to become utterly worthless.

As the crisis deepened there were a number of violent attacks on the invaders. Germany was soon to find a national hero in Leo Schlageter, a member of an ultra-right party who was executed in May for his part in sabotaging a French train. His praises were sung by Karl Radek on behalf of the Communist International, in a dramatic speech in which he portrayed the "fascist" Schlageter as a martyr to the national cause, who lost his life in the struggle for a better future for all humanity, by taking up the cause of the working class against the coal and iron magnates. Adolf Hitler was also persuaded to join in the chorus, but his encomium paled beside Radek's. Ten years later Heidegger was to give one of his more preposterously distasteful harangues to his students at Freiburg University, where Schlageter had studied, in which he presented this unsavory figure as a model of German manhood.

It is one of the great ironies a history that whenever a Communist party moved radically to the right and abandoned much of its ideological baggage it made spectacular gains in popular support. Radek's "national Bolshevist" line in 1923 met with an enthusiastic response among German workers. The KPD's membership had risen by 24 percent by September and the party made significant gains in local elections. The KPD could only profit as the crisis deepened and living conditions became increasingly wretched. Was this the revolutionary situation of which Lenin and the Bolsheviks had dreamt for so long? Zinoviev, the secretary general of the Communist International, along with Karl Radek and Trotsky, argued that it was. Stalin, as secretary general of the Communist Party of the Soviet Union, prudently disagreed, but the triumvirate went ahead with plans for a German revolution, to take place in November on the anniversary of the Glorious October Revolution, so as to inspire the German proletariat to greater deeds of heroism. Meanwhile, the KPD was urged to join the minority government in Saxony and then ensure that the Saxon workers formed paramilitary units that would spearhead the revolution.

At long last the left wing of the SPD overcame its repugnance towards supporting a government that included the DVP. Cuno's government had brought such misery to the average German that it could no longer be tolerated. Inflation had to be brought under control and the currency stabilized, national unity restored and the occupation ended. Unwilling to bear full responsibility for a policy that risked them being charged with a second "stab in the back," the majority of SPD delegates supported a national government under the DVP's strongman, Gustav Stresemann, which took office on August 13. After lengthy debate and soul-searching, Stresemann's government eventually ordered an end to passive resistance on September 26. The Bavarian government immediately declared a state of emergency, whereupon Berlin invoked article 48 to give the Reichswehr minister Gessler full executive powers. A struggle for power now developed between the governments in Munich and Berlin. The Nazi daily rag *Völkischer Beobachter* denounced the "Stresemann–Seeckt dictatorship" as another Jewish conspiracy, pointing out that both men were married to Jewish women and that the minister of finance Rudolf Hilferding was both a Marxist and a Jew. Otto Gessler, the DDP Reichswehr minister since the Kapp putsch, ordered the Bavarian minister president von Kahr and the local army commander, General von Lossow, to ban the paper. Both men refused in an act of defiant insubordination, leaving Berlin in an awkward quandary. Seeckt refused to take sides, just as he had done during the Kapp putsch. Stresemann was left in an impossible situation and resigned at the beginning of October; but within four days he was back in office. Most DVP deputies were reluctant to follow the confrontational line of Stinnes and the industrialists. The SPD showed a willingness to compromise lest worse befall. As a result the eight-hour day was retained in principle, but could be exceeded. Contract negotiations between capital and labor were subjected to compulsory arbitration. Hilferding celebrated the fact that wage contracts were no longer subject to market forces as an example of "organized capitalism," and thus a major step towards a socialist economy. With the government now in a much stronger position, Gessler demanded that General Otto von Lossow be dismissed. Kahr upped the ante by appointing him as commander-in-chief of an independent Bavarian contingent. Kahr now contemplated a national dictatorship, but was uncertain who was to be the German Mussolini. Maybe he should aspire to this role? Seeckt was another possibility, but certainly not Adolf Hitler, who was to play a subordinate role in this drama. While he pondered this question Kahr won considerable support throughout Bavaria by ordering the expulsion of large numbers of *Ostjuden*.

Meanwhile, Communists had been appointed to key positions in the governments of Saxony and Thuringia. The local army commander in Dresden promptly banned the Communist paramilitary wing and placed the Saxon police force under his orders. Heinrich Brandler, the leader of the KPD, acting on orders from Moscow, hoped to organize a general strike in Saxony that would trigger the "German October," but the Reichswehr was firmly in control and the enterprise was doomed to failure. Orders were issued to cancel the uprising, but they did not reach Hamburg, where there were three days of bloody fighting before the police were able to crush the revolt. There were sporadic outbreaks of violence in Saxony, which the Reichswehr had no difficulty in mastering. Article 48 was now used to reconstitute the Saxon government under a commissar from the DVP. In Thuringia the local SPD broke its alliance with the Communists and the Reichswehr marched in. The state was soon to welcome all manner of *Völkisch* movements. In 1930 Wilhelm Frick was the first National Socialist to be appointed a provincial minister.

The spotlight now turned once again on Munich where, on the evening of November 8, Adolf Hitler held the Bavarian triumvirate of Kahr, Lossow, and the police chief Hans von Seisser hostage by taking over a meeting the Bürgerbräukeller, a vast and popular watering-hole. The "Beer Hall Putsch" was a badly bungled affair. The three were set free at Ludendorff's insistence, and promptly planned their revenge. On the following day Hitler's march towards the Feldherrnhalle was halted by a brief salvo from the police. Sixteen of his followers were killed and became the first martyrs of the "National Revolution" to whom homage was rendered every year on November 9. The bloodstained swastika banner became the most sacred relic of the movement. Seeckt was now formally given the full executive powers under article 48 that he had enjoyed in practice since the end of September. Paradoxically Hitler's comic opera coup helped to save the republic in that it ruined Kahr's far more threatening schemes. Kahr remained in office as Reich commissar for Bavaria, with Lossow still in command of the local Reichswehr units. Neither was ever punished for their outrageous violations of the constitution. They quietly resigned in February 1924, having first ensured a number of additional privileges for their home state.

Having successfully met the threats from radicals on the left and the right, Stresemann's government now set about stabilizing the mark that was no longer worth the paper on which it was printed. By November it took 4,200,000,000,000 (4.2 trillion) marks to buy one dollar. In the course of an operation involving clouds of smoke and a large number of mirrors, the prominent banker Hjalmar Schacht, as special commissar for the currency who was soon to become Reichsbank president, along with Hans Luther the minister of finance, created a new currency known as the Rentenmark. Twelve zeros were struck off the mark, so that one dollar was now equal to 4.2 Rentenmarks. Once the new currency had stabilized, largely thanks to the government's careful housekeeping, the Rentenmark was converted back into marks at par in August 1924. At the initiative of the American secretary of state Charles Hughes, a commission was set up with the banker Charles G. Dawes in the chair to examine the whole question of German reparations.

The SPD was outraged by the unequal treatment of Bavaria and Saxony. In Bavaria an illegal regime from the extreme right had been left untouched, whereas a constitutionally impeccable government in Saxony had been violently suppressed. The party's demand that Bavaria should be given the same treatment as Saxony was rejected by the bourgeois parties. Stresemann called for a vote of confidence, which he lost by 231 to 156, with seven abstentions. President Ebert called on the Center Party leader Wilhelm Marx to form a new government. He was a somewhat colorless Rhinelander, a dull speaker, and lacked popular appeal, but he was a brilliant administrator, an open-minded pragmatist, and a man of absolute integrity. He was also a man of compromise, but always had the courage to face tough decisions. This underrated politician was to be the longest-serving chancellor in the history of the Weimar Republic.

The Marx government was a coalition of the Center Party, BVP, DVP, and DDP. Stresemann served as foreign minister, and was to do so in successive governments until his death in 1929 at the age of 51. Even though it was a minority government that relied on the support of the SPD, it had the courage to take some exceedingly difficult and unpopular decisions. The new mark could not be maintained on the gold standard without considerable sacrifices being made. The middle classes had lost all their savings in the inflation, but the government could not afford any compensation. Pay in the civil service was reduced to way below the pre-war levels. The vast majority of pensioners were ruined. All those who were seriously in debt profited immensely. The ranks of the unemployed swelled alarmingly. Average real wages fell to a mere 70 percent of pre-war levels. But although the state was relieved of this crippling burden of debt, it was totally discredited in the eyes of those millions who had patriotically bought war bonds and other government paper. The republicans had first stabbed the country in the back, then robbed the little man of his savings. This was fertile soil in which radical political movements could readily take root.

Hitler and his confederates were tried in April 1924. Ludendorff was acquitted, Ernst Röhm the head of the brown-shirted bully-boys in the SA (Sturmabteilung) received three months' imprisonment and a 100-mark fine. Hitler was given a five-year term, but was released by Christmas having spent the time in a comfortable minimum-security jail at Landsberg, where he whiled away the time writing *Mein Kampf*. These absurdly light sentences were seen a virtual acquittals, thus causing jubilation on the right and consternation on the left.

The results of the Dawes Commission's deliberations were published shortly after the Munich court handed down these verdicts. Germany was called upon to make annual payments of 1 billion marks in the first five years, then rising to 2.5 billion. The creditor nations were given a degree of control over the German economy, but the pill was sweetened with a loan of 800 million marks, which was designed to help stabilize the currency. The prospect of further investments, particularly from the United States, had an immediately stimulating effect on the economy. The total sum of reparations was not mentioned, but it was understood that it would be less than the 132 billion marks demanded in Lloyd George's 1921 note. Dawes was awarded the Nobel Peace Prize in 1925, but the situation in Germany was far from peaceful. The radical right and left made further significant gains in the elections of 1924. The parties in the republican center lost voters to the DNVP, whose electoral campaign was based on a repudiation of the Dawes Plan. Even the leaderless Nazis won an impressive 6.5 percent of the popular vote. The KPD, with 12.6 percent of the vote, was now a significant political factor. Marx's new minority government had great difficulty in gaining a majority for the ratification of the Dawes Plan, particularly the sections dealing with Allied control over the railways. Marx decided to go to the country after a series of defeats in the Reichstag. Fresh elections were held in December 1924.

The economy showed remarkable signs of recovery in 1924. Foreign investments poured into Germany, unemployment dropped dramatically, wages rose. In such circumstances it was hardly surprising that support for the KPD dwindled while the SPD made significant gains. The Nazis and their associates the German Nationalists lost more than half their supporters, and were now insignificant splinter parties. The DNVP managed to improve its showing somewhat, thus making the process of cabinet-building all the more difficult. After lengthy negotiations a government was formed in mid-January 1925 under Hans Luther, the energetic mayor of Essen. He was without party affiliation, and had gained a reputation as a tough and effective minister of finance. The DNVP participated in government for the first time, and soon found itself in the embarrassing situation of supporting policies it had roundly denounced during the election campaign.

Hindenburg Elected President

A few weeks after the Luther cabinet had taken office President Ebert died. Although acute appendicitis was given as the cause of death he was the victim of character assassination. Ebert was a man who stood for compromise at a time when compromise was a dirty word. He was cruelly mocked by the extremes of both left and right. He died shortly after a court in Magdeburg ruled that the charge by a journalist, whom he had sued for libel for suggesting that he had committed high treason by supporting a strike by munitions workers in 1918, was legally admissible. Ebert won the libel case and the journalist received a three-month prison sentence, but the charge of treason broke the heart of a true patriot, who had lost two sons in the war.

Among the many candidates in the ensuing presidential election were the former chancellor Marx, and the outstanding minister president of Prussia, Otto Braun, for the SPD who was known as the "Red Tsar" and "the last king of Prussia." The KPD fielded their party chairman Ernst "Teddy" Thälmann, a bone-headed Stalinist of dubious probity, and the National Socialist candidate was General Ludendorff. In the first round of the election only Otto Braun did reasonably well, with 29 percent of the vote, but he trailed behind the candidate of the DNVP and the DVP, Karl Jarres. Although an ineffective minister of the interior in Stresemann's second cabinet, Jarres polled 38.8 percent of the votes.

The SPD knew that they could only beat the right-wing parties in the final round if they backed a bourgeois candidate. They therefore agreed to support Marx, in return for which the Center Party backed Otto Braun as minister president in Prussia. Jarres clearly had no hope of winning against such a powerful coalition, so the right had to find a more appealing candidate. They agreed upon Field Marshal von Hindenburg, who for the second time was called out of retirement, in spite of opposition from the industrialists, who saw him as a dyed-in-the-wool agrarian, and from Stresemann, who feared negative reactions from abroad.

The Protestant Hindenburg's chances were greatly improved by the fact that he was supported by the Catholic BVP, which could not stomach the Center Party's alliance with the Social Democrats. Marx's chances were further reduced by Thälmann's refusal to step down, even though he had only obtained 7 percent of the vote in the first round. Hindenburg emerged as the winner thanks to the help given him by the KPD. He received 48.3 percent of the vote, Marx 45.3 percent, and Thälmann 6.4 percent. The election of the monarchist career officer Hindenburg was a vote against the republic. The old Wilhelmine elites now had ready access to the president, who might well be tempted to make liberal use of article 48. Ebert had already set an unfortunate example by using it to pass forty-two pieces of emergency legislation.

Locarno

Hindenburg's election was not proof that Weimar was a "republic without republicans," but it did show that they were very thin on the ground. This gloomy fact was all too easily overlooked thanks to the striking success of Stresemann's foreign policy at Locarno in the same year. Germany, France, and Britain agreed that Germany's western frontiers would not be changed by force. The question of Germany's eastern frontiers was left open, with Germany agreeing to arbitration treaties with Poland and Czechoslovakia, with whom France signed treaties of mutual guarantee. Stresemann made it perfectly clear that he had every intention of revising the frontiers with Poland, as the Soviets immediately recognized. Moscow was convinced that Locarno was a sinister move by the western powers to turn Germany eastwards as the spearhead of an anti-Soviet crusade. Stresemann knew full well that a revision of the eastern frontiers could not even be contemplated without assuaging these fears. The Berlin Treaty of 1926 with the Soviet Union strengthened the Treaty of Rapallo by guaranteeing mutual neutrality in the event of an unprovoked attack on either of the contracting parties. Both parties undertook not to take part in any boycott or sanctions on the other. The treaty thus aimed to put pressure on Poland, so furthering Germany's revisionist ambitions in the east. Germany scored a further victory over Poland in that it was admitted to the League of Nations with a permanent seat on the Council. Germany's prestige was further enhanced when Stresemann, along with his French homologue, Aristide Briand, was awarded the Nobel Peace Prize in 1926.

The DNVP withdrew its support from the Luther cabinet, denouncing Locarno as craven appeasement of the western powers. The treaty was only ratified thanks to enthusiastic support from the SPD, but unfortunately it refused to join the coalition. The Luther government fell a few weeks later over the highly emotional question of whether German embassies and consulates should be allowed to fly the black, white, and red flag of the merchant marine in place of the black, red, and gold flag symbolic of democracy and republicanism. A new minority government was formed under Marx, with the SPD again standing aloof. The party had moved sharply to the left by supporting a plebiscite calling for the confiscation, without compensation, of the property of the German princes. It clung to its newly won ideological purity and refused to compromise with its class enemies. Stresemann tried desperately to win the support of the SPD for a great coalition so as to stop an embarrassing debate over illegal armaments, but without success. On December 16, 1926, Philipp Scheidemann made a sensational speech in the Reichstag in which he exposed the illegal financing of armaments and the close links between the Reichswehr and right-wing paramilitary groups, which were designed to circumvent the restriction of the army to a mere 100,000 men. He also stated that the KPD was well aware that armaments forbidden by the Treaty of Versailles were being imported from the Soviet Union.

The Depression

The Marx cabinet fell as a result of these revelations, but there was no alternative to yet another minority government under Marx in which the DNVP played a prominent role. The appointment as minister of the interior of Walther von Keudell, a leading figure in the Kapp putsch who loudly professed his anti-Semitism, was an indication of a sharp right turn. But the fourth Marx cabinet was also responsible for the most important piece of social legislation in the history of the republic. The unemployment insurance bill of 1927 provided comprehensive coverage for all employees. It was financed by both employer and employee paying premiums equal to 3 percent of a worker's wages. The state was henceforth obliged to grant a bridging loan if the unemployment insurance fund fell into the red. The new system was admirably suited to deal with the problems of moderate unemployment as existed at the time, but was soon to be stretched to the limit when the depression began to be felt in following year. A substantial wage increase for civil servants was awarded in mid-December that was soon to prove a fiscal disaster, as some prudent deputies warned. With an election looming their jeremiads were ignored.

Once again the government fell over a failure to reach a compromise, this time over the financing of confessional schools. The election campaign of 1928 was overshadowed by the issue of whether or not to build a battlecruiser. The KPD demanded that the money designated for the ship should be spent on free school meals for the needy. The SPD, eager to remain in the proletarian vanguard, echoed this exhortation. They were the big winners in the election, the DNVP the losers. A great coalition was clearly indicated by the results, but Stresemann had to pull out all the stops to persuade the DVP to ally with Hermann Müller's SPD. It was not forgotten that he was the man who had signed the Treaty of Versailles.

The Müller government was immediately faced with a crisis in that the cabinet decided to go ahead with building Battlecruiser "A," even though the SPD had fought the campaign in fierce opposition to the proposal. Otto Wels, who was effectively leader of the party while Müller was chancellor, demanded that the money be spent on school meals as the party had promised. The majority of SPD deputies were united in opposition to the plan. When the bill was debated only the chancellor and the three SPD ministers voted in favor; the parliamentary party voted against. The bill was approved, but the SPD's credibility was in ruins.

The depression had already had a devastating effect on the economy by the spring of 1929, and it was obvious to the man responsible for supervising the collection of

reparations, Parker S. Gilbert, that Germany would not be able to meet to increased payments demanded by the Dawes Plan than year. With 3 million unemployed by February
1929 it was unlikely that the unemployment insurance fund would be able to meet the
demands made upon it. A new reparations commission was formed, chaired by another
American, Owen D. Young, which met in The Hague. The resulting Young Plan, published
in June 1929, reduced the annual payments. It made the German government, rather than
an agency, responsible for their collection, so that Germany regained its economic sovereignty. Furthermore, the plan was open for revision if Germany were to find it difficult to
meet its obligations. In return for German agreement to the Young Plan the Allies con-
sented to an earlier evacuation of the Rhineland. The right-wing parties mounted a massive
campaign against the Young Commission, even before the final report was published. The
DNVP under the press and film magnate Alfred Hugenberg, the Pan-Germans under
Heinrich Class, and the veterans' organization Stahlhelm (Steel Helmet) banded together
in the Reich Committee for a German national plebiscite and called for a referendum
against the "war guilt lie" that left Germany burdened with reparations until 1988. Hitler
and the NSDAP joined the campaign, much to the disgust of many on the Nazi left, who
were horrified to see their Führer hobnobbing with a bunch of reactionaries, aristocrats,
and plutocrats. Hitler's tactics paid handsome dividends. He was now in respectable
company, no longer a bohemian outsider. Rather than trying to win the working class away
from the "Marxist" parties, he began to focus his attention on the disaffected middle classes.
The response was immediate. Money began to flow into the party's coffers and spectacular
gains were made in state elections in Thuringia and Baden as well as in local elections in
Prussia, Berlin, and Lübeck. Wilhelm Frick was appointed minister of the interior in
Thuringia, and thirteen Nazis entered the Berlin city council. All this seems to have escaped
the notice of politicians in Berlin.

The Plebiscite Committee managed to get just over the 10 percent of eligible voters
needed to support the initiative, and a referendum on "The Law Against the Enslavement
of the German People" was held in December 1929. Only 5.8 million voted in favor when
21 million votes were needed for the referendum to pass, but in some districts more than
20 percent voted for the proposal.

For Communists the onset of the depression was clear indication that the contradictions
within capitalism were becoming so acute that the working masses throughout the world
would soon rise up in a revolutionary war against their capitalist exploiters. The foremost
task of Communist parties in this "Third Period" was the destruction of Social Democracy.
The SPD was denounced as the "twin brother of fascism," the party of class compromise,
the capitalists' henchmen. This ultra-left course was part of Stalin's campaign against
Bucharin and his associates, who had voiced serious reservations about collectivization and
the forced pace of industrialization in the Soviet Union, in the course of which paranoid
fears of a capitalist offensive against the homeland of the workers and peasants were
whipped up to fever pitch.

The Middle Class

For all the disastrous consequences of four years of war, there was a remarkable
continuity in the class structure of society. Within the bourgeoisie the immensely wealthy
"grands bourgeois" and the tone-setting *Bildungsbürgertum* made up about 2 percent of

the population. The comfortable and secure echelons of the middle class comprised 6 percent, below which were 10 to 11 percent of petits bourgeois. Thus the bourgeoisie – a more inclusive term than the somewhat confusing term "middle class" – made up less than one-fifth of the population. Although very little had changed in the structure of society, there was a widespread feeling that "bourgeois society" had been dealt a crippling blow in the war. It no longer seemed to be an adequate paradigm for a healthy society. There were now the tempting chiliastic visions of a Communist utopia or a National Socialist "racial community." The bourgeoisie seemed unable to defend its class interests. There was no political party that represented its common values and aspirations, merely splinter groups that furthered selfish sectional interests. The bourgeoisie had a host of critics, mostly from within its own ranks, but no champions. It was thus powerless to withstand the disaster that lay ahead. It was only after the nightmare was over that the bourgeoisie regained its confidence and set about putting its ideals into practice.

The worldwide economic crisis, which followed upon four terrible years of war and the hyperinflation of the 1920s, had a profound effect on Germany's social fabric. With the collapse of imperial Germany the last hindrances to the creation of a class society, molded by the exigencies of a market economy, were removed. It was an unfamiliar, uncertain, and pitiless world that many viewed with deep aversion. The most striking feature of this social upheaval was that it marked the end to the aristocracy's dominant role. This small group of less than 1 percent of the population had gradually lost ground politically, legally, and economically, as estate gave way to class in a modern industrial society. In the critical years from 1914 to 1930 it merely managed to hang on to a few favored positions in the military, the diplomatic service, and the administration, only to be reduced by the Nazi regime and Red Army to a somewhat absurd, if often immensely wealthy, clique that still provides ample fodder for the popular press.

The *Bildungsbürger*, another minute group that was scarcely larger than the aristocracy, were also profoundly affected by these changes. As officers and student volunteers they had paid a disproportionately high price during the war. They lost the money they had patriotically invested in war loans. What was left disappeared in the hyperinflation. The horrors of a war that had unleashed unimaginable destructive powers shattered their traditional value system, by exposing how thin was the veneer of the civilization that they valued so highly. Having identified closely with the old regime, they found it exceedingly hard to adjust to a new political reality that was dominated by the left. In a world that was becoming increasingly specialized, there was precious little room left for the broadly educated. With mass democracy antagonistic towards a self-conscious elite that had lost its faith in the civilizing value of a humanistic education, it withdrew into gloomy isolation where it wallowed in cultural pessimism. Although it had been ravaged economically, this highly educated elite still had a profound influence, due to its dominant role in the civil service and higher education. This was detrimental to the creation of a healthy democratic society. The *Bildungsbürger* extolled the superiority of German culture, seeing in their fatherland a "new Greece" that would show the lesser breeds the path to enlightenment. With such an attitude it was easy for them to be swept away with patriotic fervor in the heady days of August 1914 or when the army made its spectacular advance on the Western Front in the "Michael" offensive of 1918. Unable to accept the humiliation of defeat, they rejected the "Versailles system" out of hand. Their once hubristic nationalism grew sour, aggressive, and mean-spirited. Under a parliamentary democracy the upper echelons of the bureaucracy, used to the deference of Reichstag deputies and industrialists, had to accept the humiliation of taking orders from Social Democrats or Catholics. Some even had to cede their positions to the new "political civil servants," experts of proven republican sympathies. As the material level of this caste descended to that of the petite bourgeoisie they became acutely aware of their loss of status. Their resentment was expressed in a radical rejection of parliamentary democracy, which had brought with it mass people's parties that threatened the exclusive rights of the educated and the cultured. The old social norms no longer applied, a familiar hierarchy had vanished, but mental structures remained impervious to change. The new reality appeared unstable, threatening, and based on reprehensible values. Longing for stability, they joined the ranks of those who harbored utopian visions. Of these there were plenty, ranging from the National Socialist racial community to the Communists' dictatorship of the proletariat, but the majority of the *Bildungsbürger* opted for various versions of the extreme right. The universities, which produced the recruits for this group, were infected with extreme right-wing views. Students flocked to the radically nationalist "German University Circle," which demanded rearmament and a revisionist foreign policy. Eugenics and a thoroughgoing racial policy were widely expected to provide the means to revive the body politic. By 1929 the National Socialists seemed to offer the best means for achieving such goals. Even before the Nazis had made their breakthrough on the national stage the student governments in most universities were in the hands of the National Socialist Students Association. There were all too few republican professors who opposed this shameful denial of humanistic values. Young scholars who endorsed the new state had scant chance of obtaining an academic appointment.

The roughly 5 percent of the population in the economic elite survived this multiple crisis largely unscathed. In many cases they had benefited from wartime profiteering, and thanks to their fixed assets had weathered the storm of inflation. They were now the objects of envy and censure, denounced on the left as capitalists and on the right as plutocrats. Yet although they had thrived under these new conditions, and nothing stood in the way of their social advancement, they felt threatened by the organized working class, and looked for an authoritarian solution to the pressing social, economic, and political problems that beset the republic. For this reason Walther Rathenau, *Bildungsbürger* and capitalist, but also a principled republican, was viewed with particular revulsion as a traitor to his class and station. They found it almost impossible to adapt to the republic. The new elites had none of the sparkle and glamour, however tawdry, of the old regime. They had to come to terms not with stolid conservatives but with unstable left-of-center coalitions. They resented the power of the SPD and trade unions, which had burdened them with a higher wage bill. Even when the parliamentary coalition moved to the right in the prosperous years between 1924 and 1928, they still remained hostile to the republic. When the system collapsed in 1929 this group reacted in a manner that was to have fatal consequences.

Contrary to the vulgar Marxist legend, this "state monopoly capitalist elite" did not hire Hitler to do their dirty work for them. They spread relatively meager funds evenly between those right-of-center parties that seemed likely to further their interests. The Nazis, with their radical party program calling for the abolition of the "interest slavery," the abolition of department stores, the protection of small businesses against big business, and the denunciation of "plutocrats," were an uncertain quantity. The anti-capitalist rhetoric of the vociferous left wing of the party was highly alarming to captains of industry. Initially they saw little that was attractive in this unpredictable movement. Even its anti-communism was suspect when it joined hands with the KPD during the Berlin transport workers' strike.

The Nazi Party, far from being in the pay of the Ruhr barons, was largely self-financing, with contributions on a sliding scale according to income.

This in no sense absolves the industrialists from their complicity in the destruction of the Weimar Republic. They agreed with the Nazis' denunciation of the Treaty of Versailles, the war guilt clause, and the "serfdom" resulting from reparations, and joined with them in demonstrations against the Young Plan. They virulently opposed Stresemann's fulfill-ment policy. They supported the DNVP and the right wing of the DVP, both parties being in opposition to the republic. Then as the crisis deepened and successive administrations failed to find a means to drag the economy out of the depression, they began to think in terms of an authoritarian solution. None of them lifted a finger to save the republic. All, at least initially, were happy to accept Hitler as chancellor.

The middle classes include the traditional class of artisans, small businesses, shopkeep-ers, and workers in the service industries along with a relatively new and rapidly expanding groups of white-collar workers: schoolteachers, clerks, technicians, and craftsmen. Among these heterogeneous groups those in the craft trades suffered the worst. Their once proud businesses declined to become mere repair shops. Earnings dropped well below the level of those of skilled workers in industry. Seeing no future ahead, journeymen joined the ranks of the industrial working class. Craftsmen and tradesmen tried to protect their interests through trade organizations working together with local chambers of commerce and through a national Reich Association of German Craftsmen. They called for what amounted to a return to the old guild system, with compulsory membership, rigorous control, price fixing, and protection against competition from the chain stores and coop-eratives. It was all in vain.

Although all faced much the same problems, politically they did not act as one. Most Catholics remained faithful to the Center Party. About 25 percent felt that the SPD best represented their interests. Most of the rest supported the DVP, the DNVP, and, eventually, the NSDAP, the latter making a particular pitch for support from this group with extravagant promises to protect small businesses and destroy the "Jewish department stores," spiced with raucous denunciations of big business and "money-grubbing capitalism" – a tactic that Hitler had to tone down when he drew closer to big business during the Young Plan refer-endum of 1929. Craftsmen were attracted by the NSDAP's militant anti-Marxism as well as by its promise to create a harmonious "racial community" (*Volksgemeinschaft*), but they did not flock to the party en bloc. There were other strong contenders for their support.

There were 800,000 small family stores in Germany between the wars. They struggled desperately to stay in business, their owners working long hours in order to maintain a standard of living roughly equivalent to that of an industrial worker. A large percentage of these enterprises collapsed during the depression. Many in this group sought protection from the Nazis, but others remained skeptical. They were right to do so. Once in power the Nazis failed to honor their promise to help the small shopkeepers.

About one-third of the 2 million white-collar workers were employed in industry; the rest were in business and various departments of the civil service. There was a steady increase in the number of women in this group during the Weimar Republic. They were distinguished from the working class in that they were paid by the month rather than by the week, did no manual labor, had relative security of employment, and enjoyed longer holidays as well as better insurance. This group's self-awareness was strengthened by an increasing degree of endogamy. There was a marked decrease in the number of marriages with partners from the working class. They aspired to a bourgeois lifestyle by spending a greater share of their income on housing and their children's education than on food, tobacco, and alcohol. They planned their families, with two children as the norm. They also prudently prepared for retirement by investing in insurance schemes.

White-collar workers did not react in a unified manner politically. In the difficult years immediately after the war many were attracted to the SPD, but about half were either conservative or liberal. In the boom years between 1925 and 1929 they moved steadily to the center and right, but contrary to what has been suggested in many earlier studies they did not support the NSDAP to any significant extent. In constituencies that had a large number of white-collar voters the Nazis were noticeably unsuccessful.

The Working Class

During the war the working class, comprising some 70 percent of the population, had suffered the worst decline in living standards since the early years of the industrial revolution; but they were also the great beneficiaries of the revolution of 1918–19. They gained political power, their real wages increased substantially, they had a voice in management, and they had made significant gains by collective bargaining. These remarkable achievements soon began to erode. They suffered a severe setback with the defeat of the Weimar coalition. Management, determined to turn the clock back, mounted a vigorous counterattack. The depression and subsequent mass unemployment wiped out most of their hard-won gains, leaving them frustrated and prone to political radicalism. There were 8 million unemployed, real wages fell by one-third, and 40 percent of the workforce was dependent on government support: all this only ten years after the deprivations of the war years. It is small wonder, then, that the Hitler regime's success in putting Germany back to work won for it the loyalty of vast majority of the working class. There were also profound changes within the working class itself. The industrial working class began to shrink, whereas the number of white-collar workers increased by one-third. Opportunities for social advancement had improved greatly, so that a number of positions in the lower ranks of the civil service, in junior management, and in the primary schools were filled with the children of skilled workers.

Within the working class there were steep differentials in wages. A skilled metal worker earned 36 percent more than an unskilled worker, a qualified miner 46 percent more than his helper. Women earned on average less than half of a man's wages for the same work. Sixty-hour, six-day weeks were the norm. Holidays were an inconceivable luxury. Huge increases in nominal wages in 1919 failed fully to offset the drastic fall in real wages during the war. Taking wages in 1913 as 100, they were still only about 85. The hyperinflation of 1923 resulted in real wages falling 48 percent below the 1913 level. A skilled worker's wages were not enough to provide for a wife and two or three children. This appalling situation was rendered even worse with mass unemployment in 1923 and again in 1929. There was some improvement in the "four golden years" between the hyperinflation of 1923 and the depression of 1929, with real wages rising 20 percent above the 1913 level. German workers also enjoyed the benefits of a welfare state that by world standards was remarkably generous. Subsidized housing, rent controls, and insurance schemes for health, old age, and unemployment provided a certain degree of relief.

Social mobility remained minimal. Only 6 percent of the students in institutions of higher education came from the ranks of the working class. In law schools – which held the key to social advancement – it was a mere 1 percent. The working class was largely self-recruiting. Eighty percent of workers came from working-class families. But there were escape routes. Thirteen percent of primary school teachers and 10 percent of the lower echelons of the civil service had working-class backgrounds. Their children had some chance of moving up into the middle class. Educational programs for the working class, plus the cultural efforts of Social Democrats and Communists, did much to encourage aspirations for education and self-advancement.

The trade unions played an important role in strengthening class consciousness. The unions had 2.5 million members in 1913. Numbers dwindled during the war, but by 1920 the General German Trades Union Association (ADGB) had 8.03 million members: the highest number until the 1950s. With hyperinflation the figure fell to about 4 million in 1924 and rose to almost 5 million in 1929, soon to fall back to just over 4 million. The unions did a great deal to make sure that a fair share of gross domestic product went to wages. In fact they were so successful in this regard that they were often denounced for placing too heavy a burden on the economy and slowing down the rate of growth.

The serious divisions within the working class were political rather than structural. Before the war the bulk of the working class supported the SPD. The party split during the war, with the USPD demanding a peace without annexations or reparations. Opposition to the war was all that held the party together and in by 1922 it had dissolved. Two thirds of the USPD's former supporters flocked to the KPD. The Communists were rent apart with dissent and it took some time before Moscow managed to impose an iron discipline on the party. It remained a relatively small sect until 1929, when it seemed that its prediction of the imminent collapse of capitalism was justified. The unemployed looked admiringly at the Soviet Union, whose thriving economy appeared to be untouched by the horrors of the depression. The KPD rapidly became the equal to the SPD in membership, share of the popular vote, and number of Reichstag deputies. The working class was now split in two. One half supported the republic and a pragmatic policy of social reform; the other struggled to replace it by a Soviet-style dictatorship.

Before the war the SPD controlled every aspect of working-class life, to the point that people spoke affectionately of a "party fatherland." There was a vast Social Democratic press, a party university, night schools, football clubs, a pigeon fanciers' association, cycling clubs and philatelists' groups. Life began in a Social Democratic maternity home. It ended with a Social Democratic cremation. This separate world was the result of the suppression of Bismarck's anti-socialist laws and the discrimination of the Wilhelmine era. Now the SPD was part of the establishment, took part in government and was the staunchest supporter of the republic. But the party's cultural associations faced competition from new forms of entertainment. By 1929, 2.2 million people went to the cinema each day. Professional sports attracted vast crowds. Radio, which began in 1923, steadily attracted more listeners, mainly in public places. Until the Nazis produced the "people's receivers" (VE301) costing 76 marks and the "small German receiver" (DKE38) costing 35 marks, the latter affectionately known as "Goebbels' gob," a set was beyond the means of the average worker. The new mass media gradually destroyed a unique and homogenous proletarian culture, eroding class distinctions by offering a soothing escapism as an alternative to political engagement.

The fundamental experience of the working class during the Weimar Republic was the mass unemployment of the depression years, the horror of which matched wartime pauperization. By 1932 there were 8.5 million unemployed, 5.2 million were forced to work short-time, and only 7.6 million were fully employed. By 1933, of those registered 40 percent were out of work. In addition there were the hundreds of thousands of the unemployed who were not registered with the labor exchanges and thus do not appear in the statistics. Eighty-five percent of the unemployed were industrial workers. Only about 15 percent of white-collar workers lost their jobs. With their lower pay women were more secure than men. Young people hoping to enter the workforce were particularly severely affected. In 1931 only 20 percent of school leavers found an apprenticeship. In Berlin two-thirds of the unemployed were under 25 years old.

The republic was unable to meet even the basic needs of the unemployed. Unemployment insurance, with contributions paid equally by employer and employee, was available to those who had been in continuous employment for two years, with an average 52-hour week, but payments only lasted for twenty-six weeks. From 1927 additional relief was available when the six months were over, but they were based on a rigorous investigation of needs and household income. Those not eligible for unemployment insurance had to rely on welfare payments handled by local government. None of these payments was sufficient to raise the recipient above the level of abject poverty.

The situation was desperate, but it grew steadily worse. Economy measures by the Brüning and Papen governments were at the expense of the unemployed, with benefits cut by 52 percent. Wives and children were no longer eligible for support. Local government was called upon to augment allowances by up to 47 percent, but had insufficient funds to meet rapidly increasing demand. Those who were fortunate enough to remain employed had their wages cut. A docker in Hamburg needed 205 marks per week to feed a family of five. Even in the boom year of 1927 he never reached that level. By 1932 he was earning between 110 and 142 marks per week. Weekly wages for a miner in the Ruhr fell from 241 marks per week in 1929 to 162 marks in 1932. At the Krupp works in Essen 11 percent of the workforce lost their jobs in 1929, a third of the remainder were fired in 1930, another third in 1931 and one-fifth of the rest in 1932. An unemployed worker in Cologne with four children received 54 marks per month in August 1932.

Germany had not experienced such abject misery since the mass poverty of the pre-March. This time it affected far more people and the consequences were infinitely more severe. The working class, once the pillar on which the Weimar Republic rested, lost all faith in the state. The shattering experience of mass unemployment, with the state not only failing to relieve the misery but actually making it far worse, was the fundamental experience of an entire generation. It provides a partial answer to the question why the Nazis made such sensational gains beginning in 1929. The heroic "anti-fascist working class" has long since been exposed as a Communist myth. Forty percent of new "party comrades" in 1929 came from the working class. Two-thirds of the bully-boys in the brown-shirted SA were young workers. Relatively few workers moved from the extreme totalitarian left to the extreme totalitarian right. Hitler's determined and successful efforts to overcome unemployment earned him the gratitude and loyalty of the working class. He solved the problem within three years, nominal wages rose sharply, the working week was reduced, welfare provisions were improved, and a massive effort brought cheap holidays, recreation facilities, and cultural programs to the masses. The Nazis had no need to use terror to win the acclamation of the working class.

PLATE 18   Homeless men, December 1930. © Bundesarchiv

PLATE 19   Homeless women, December 1930. © Bundesarchiv

Rural Society

The agricultural sector resented the controls imposed upon it during the war, no longer benefited from protectionist policies, and was losing relative status as Germany became a fully industrialized society. Hyperinflation rid many farmers of their debts, while they benefited from an increased demand for foodstuffs; but they still felt aggrieved. They paid higher taxes, faced fierce foreign competition, and by 1924 were obliged to pay higher interest on bridging loans. They were reluctant to adjust, as Dutch and Danish farmers were quick to do, to a new market in which meat and dairy products took a larger share. East German farmers doubled the production of wheat between 1928 and 1932, with rye increasing by 30 percent, even though prices had fallen by about 70 percent. Those who were best able to meet market needs, such as farmers in Schleswig-Holstein who specialized in livestock and dairy products, were dependent on the highly elastic demand of the urban population, which collapsed in 1929.

In 1928 a group representing farmers' interests, the National Christian Farmers and Rural Population Party (CNBL), split off from the ultra conservative and nationalist DNVP. Usually known as the Landvolk, it organized mass rallies, halted the seizure of bankrupt farms, and, in collaboration with the extremist Organization Consul, began a terrorist campaign. Its newspaper, also called *Landvolk*, thundered on about the republic's "Jewish blood-sucking," denounced the SPD as the "party of organized treason," and yearned for a "Third Reich." The Landvolk, which was concentrated in Schleswig-Holstein, never became a national party; but there were similar rural protest movements in other parts of the country. They all soon ran out of steam, so that by 1930 there was a political vacuum in rural areas that was rapidly filled by the Nazis. In Protestant rural areas the party did not face competition from the proletarian voters for the SPD and KPD or from Catholics voting for the Center Party, so it made rapid inroads.

The Nazi Party's agricultural specialist, Walther Darré, although the high priest of a ludicrous "blood and soil" cult, was an exceptionally talented organizer. His "Agricultural Political Apparatus" set out to become the principal mouthpiece for rural interests. It infiltrated local agricultural associations, thereby winning voters for the NSDAP in local and national elections. In 1928 the National Socialists only got about 2 percent of the vote in the Reichstag elections in Schleswig-Holstein, East Prussia, Pomerania, Hanover, and Hesse. Largely due to Darré's efforts this rose to almost 23 percent in the election in July 1932. The Reich Agricultural Association (Reichslandbund – RLB), the most important agricultural interest group, ended its association with the DNVP and turned to the NSDAP. In the 1932 presidential election it called upon its members to vote for Hitler rather than Hindenburg, even though the old field marshal was the very incarnation of agricultural interests.

The Demise of Parliamentary Democracy

In spite of these profound changes in the status of the aristocracy, the *Bildungsbürger*, and the industrial working class, the structure of social hierarchy remained remarkably resilient. What had changed was people's perception of the nature of society. Class antagonisms existed in pre-war Germany, but they were partially disguised by the trappings of monarchy, the remnants of a traditional society, regional loyalties, and ingrained deference. Much of this had now disappeared in a market economy, in which selfish social and economic interests openly conflicted. These struggles were compounded by socially constructed mentalities that pitched the aristocracy against the bourgeoisie, the *Bildungsbürger* against the less educated, the traditional middle class against the proletariat. Real conflicts of interest were mixed with ritualized expressions of group identity. Such blatant antagonisms came as a great shock to all but the industrial working class, which had never doubted that this was a society riven by class resentment. Instead of seeking for ways to overcome, or at least to mitigate, these inevitable clashes of interest within the framework of a democratic society, all too many fell prey to Hitler's promises that National Socialism would supersede all conflicts of class and interest, and create a harmonious "racial community."

The SPD police chief of Berlin forbade all demonstrations on May 1, 1929, the traditional occasion for the expression of proletarian solidarity and militancy; but the KPD ignored the ban. The police were alerted, resulting in riots which left in thirty-two dead and 200 wounded. About a thousand people were arrested. After this "Bloody May" the KPD's paramilitary wing, the Red Front (Roter Frontkämpferbund) was banned nationwide. These events served as further proof to party militants that the Social Democrats were indeed "Social Fascists." Such harebrained radicalism was fueled by rapidly rising unemployment, which in turn meant that a drastic reform of the unemployment insurance system was needed if the republic's finances were not to get into serious difficulties. The SPD and the unions agreed that since the depression was causing real wages to rise, those still fortunate enough to find steady employment could be called upon to pay higher premiums. These were to be matched by the employers. The DVP, as the party of the employers, turned the proposal down flat, arguing that benefits should be reduced. After a lengthy and acrimonious debate, Stresemann managed to get his DVP to agree to abstain during the vote for a bill, to be debated in December, that called for a half-point increase in both employer and employee contributions. Stresemann did not live to witness this victory, which seemed to promise Müller's government a comfortable majority.

"Black Friday" on Wall Street, on October 24, 1929, caused investors to withdraw funds from Germany; short-term credits were not renewed, and it was virtually impossible to borrow money abroad. Hjalmar Schacht, as head of the Reichsbank, used this opportunity to finally defeat his rival Rudolph Hilferding, the Marxist minister of finance, by calling for a comprehensive tax reform. In addition to the increase of unemployment insurance premiums from 3 to 3.5 percent, it included an increase in the tax on tobacco and a reduction of income tax, coupled with massive support from the government in an attempt to rescue the country from insolvency. This was a declaration of war not only on Hilferding, who promptly resigned, but also on the entire SPD, whose gross mismanagement and largesse the power elite held responsible for the present crisis. A cabal collected around General Groener as Reichswehr minister, General Kurt von Schleicher, the head of his ministerial office, and the state secretary in the chancellery, Otto Meissner. They set about planning a government that would exclude the SPD. Hindenburg, sympathetic to the idea of an anti-parliamentary and anti-Marxist government, began talks with the DNVP leaders Hugenberg and Count Kuno von Westarp. The radical Hugenberg was in favor, the more moderate Westarp against.

The Müller government survived because agreement had to be reached over finance reform before the Reichstag could approve the Young Plan. A compromise solution, whereby the SPD ministers agreed to increase unemployment premiums to 4 percent, half a point higher than previously proposed, in return for which there was to be no refund of income taxes, was rejected by the DVP. The BVP, as good Bavarians, raised objections to an increase in the tax on beer. Hindenburg then threatened to use article 48 to secure approval of the Young Plan. The Reichstag promptly approved the Young Plan bill, thus decoupling it from finance reform. Heinrich Brüning, as leader of the Center Party's parliamentary party, suggested postponing a decision on whether to raise premiums or lower payments until a comprehensive reform of the entire system had been completed. Once again the SPD ministers agreed, but the parliamentary party objected vigorously to Brüning's compromise, which they saw as a vicious attempt to destroy the welfare state. The government was thus obliged to resign. Hilferding sadly remarked that the argument that a compromise had to be rejected because it implied that things would later be worse was the equivalent of committing suicide for fear of dying. The SPD had failed to do everything possible to save parliamentary democracy in Germany at this critical juncture and must thus share a major part of the blame for its demise.

Brüning

The man chosen to convert the Weimar Republic from a parliamentary to a presidential regime was a dour 44-year-old bachelor, a devout Catholic who had served with distinction as a front-line officer. He had a reputation for fiscal responsibility and administrative rigor. Within three months he faced a deadlock in the Reichstag over how to deal with the budgetary deficit. This was exactly what Hindenburg and his advisors had hoped would happen, for now they were able to give the chancellor emergency powers under article 48, thereby circumventing the Reichstag. The SPD objected vigorously to this misuse of an article that was designed to meet genuine emergencies, not to be used as an ersatz constitution to help the government out of awkward situations. They therefore introduced a motion to suspend the president's emergency powers, whereupon Hindenburg promptly dissolved the Reichstag, leaving article 48 still in effect. During the election campaign it was used to introduce a number of new taxes, including an increase of unemployment insurance premiums to 4.5 percent, a poll tax, and a tax on the unmarried.

The elections resulted in a victory for the extremes. The KPD, by attacking the SPD as the "agents of French and Polish imperialism," the corrupt and treacherous "hangman's assistants of the German bourgeoisie," increased the number of deputies from fifty-four to seventy-seven. The Nazis' triumph was even greater. In the last Reichstag election in 1928 they had received 800,000 votes and obtained twelve mandates. Now they got 2.6 million votes and 107 seats. Hitler's new course in 1929, combined with the political and economic crisis, thus paid handsome dividends. Some of those who voted for the NSDAP in 1930 were new voters, but most of them switched their allegiance from the bourgeois parties: the DNVP, the DVP, and the DDP. Up to 10 percent of SPD voters decided the future lay with National Socialism rather than Social Democracy. Nazi voters were predominantly Protestant, from rural areas, the self-employed, civil servants, and pensioners. The unemployed looked to the Communists for help. Women tended to be more loyal to the traditional parties than men. A substantial number of workers broke ranks with the "Marxist" parties and voted for the Nazis. Their brilliantly conducted propaganda campaign was careful to avoid emphasizing anti-Semitism, since this was not an issue that had much resonance among the working class. Similarly, the "socialism" of National Socialism was downplayed for fear of alienating the bourgeoisie. Nationalism and the creation of a "racial community" (*Volksgemeinschaft*) were the key issues. The party, by attracting support from all walks of life, was now a genuine people's party.

The elections of September 1930 mark the end of German liberalism. Stresemann's DVP made its peace with the extreme right, as did the DDP, which henceforth dropped the word "Democratic" from the party's name to become the German Party (DP). The Center Party had already moved sharply to the right under Monsignor Ludwig Kaas, who took over the party leadership after its poor showing in the polls in 1928. This situation left the "rational republicans" hopelessly at sea. Thomas Mann appealed to the responsible and cultured bourgeois to overlook the last remaining vestiges of Marxist rigmarole and support the SPD. Otto Braun responded positively, calling for a "coalition of the reasonable." With neither side in the mood for compromise, appeals for reason fell on deaf ears. The bourgeois parties wanted nothing to do with the Social Democrats, who in turn detested the chancellor and his coalition supporters. Many saw no distinction between the "fascist" Brüning and Hitler. Hindenburg, determined to go ahead with his plans for a presidential regime, refused to welcome the SPD back into the fold. The cabinet still needed a Reichstag majority. The NSDAP was far too "socialist" for the industrialists and bankers. The SA was seen as a challenge to the Reichswehr. Hitler was still a wild card. The SPD feared another round of elections that would almost certainly make the Nazis even stronger. A conflict with the central government might result in the Center Party withdrawing its support for Otto Braun's government in Prussia. The SPD therefore reluctantly agreed to support Brüning's second government.

The first debate in the new session of parliament did not bode well. The Nazi deputies arrived in SA uniforms and behaved like street rowdies. The Communists ranted on about overthrowing capitalist exploitation and establishing the dictatorship of the proletariat in a Soviet Germany. The SPD stuck to its agreement, enabling legislation covering the budgetary deficit to pass, in return for which Brüning made certain concessions over social policy. But the SPD had to stomach an increase in the unemployment insurance premiums to 6.5 percent, along with higher duties on imports of wheat and barley. Brüning continued with his rigorous deflationary policies, thereby running the risk of losing the SPD's grudging support. With the country on the verge of bankruptcy, he used presidential decrees in June 1931 to reduce unemployment benefits along with the pensions for invalids and the war-wounded. Civil servants' salaries were slashed. This placed the SPD in an intolerable position. The left could not continue to support a government bent on destroying the welfare state; the right could not risk toppling Otto Braun's government in Prussia. How could the party defend democracy against the Reichstag majority, or use constitutional means when the constitution had been suspended?

Meanwhile, the economic situation worsened dramatically. The Hoover Moratorium of 1931 suspended reparations payments, but unemployment continued to rise, while the banking system began to fall apart. Taxpayers' money was poured in as a stopgap, the bank rate hiked to such an extent that it seriously impeded any chance of recovery. The International Court of Justice in The Hague ruled that a proposed customs union between Germany and Austria was a violation of the peace treaties, and thus contrary to international law. Prompted by General Schleicher, Hindenburg urged Brüning to move still further to the right in order to keep the increasingly disaffected DVP in the coalition. The chancellor obliged, but it was too late.

A mass meeting of the extreme right was held at Bad Harzburg in October 1931 which was attended by Hugenberg's DNVP, the Stahlhelm, the Pan-German League, members of former ruling houses, Hjalmar Schacht, and General von Seeckt. The former army chief was now a Reichstag deputy for the DVP. He, along with other members of party, attended the meeting to show that they no longer supported Brüning. Hitler and the NSDAP also joined this "Harzburg Front," with the SA prominent in the march past; but the Führer demonstrably left the platform to show that he was a genuine alternative to the tired old parties, distanced from the traditional reactionaries. The Harzburg Front reconciled the SPD to Brüning, so that a vote of no confidence from the right was narrowly defeated. The chancellor was determined to persevere with his rigorously deflationary policies, using emergency legislation to cut back wages and prices. At the same time he rejected all proposals for priming the pump by investment in job creation, insisting that balancing the books was his first priority. Inevitably the standard of living of the average German rapidly declined, thus fanning political radicalism.

In 1932 the 84-year-old Hindenburg announced that he was prepared to stand for re-election. This caused the Harzburg Front to fall apart. The DNVP proposed the Stahlhelm's president, Theodor Duesterberg, as candidate. After agonizing for a long time Hitler decided to enter the race, but in order to do so he had at last to become a German citizen. This was done by securing an appointment as a humble civil servant in the surveyor's office in Brunswick. The KPD put Thälmann forward on the assumption that the SPD would support Hindenburg and that the majority of their voters would be so disgusted that they would support the "red workers' candidate." The first assumption was correct, the second totally false.

Hindenburg failed to win an absolute majority in the first round of the election in May 1932. Hitler was second with a remarkable 30.1 percent. Thälmann trailed behind with 13.2 percent, and Duesterberg, whom the Nazis denounced as "quarter-Jew," came last with 6.8 percent. Prompted by Moscow, Thälmann stayed in the race in order to expose the SPD as the moderate face of fascism. As a result he made a deservedly poor showing with only 10.2 percent. Hindenburg won with 53 percent, thanks to the undivided support of the SPD. The president, furious that he owed his re-election to the Social Democrats, blamed Brüning for putting him in this embarrassing position. Hitler got an impressive 36.8 percent of the popular vote.

A few days after the presidential election, the Brüning government banned the SS and the SA. General von Schleicher had persuaded his minister, General Groener, that this step was necessary as Germany was fast slipping into anarchy. Schleicher then changed his mind and persuaded his friend Oscar von Hindenburg, who had served in the same regiment, to point out to his father that the ban was most unpopular on the right. Hindenburg signed the emergency decree with considerable reluctance, and then tried to offset any possible damage by a ban on the SPD's paramilitary wing, the Black, Red, and Gold Standard (Reichsbanner). Groener, as minister of the interior, felt that there was no evidence to support a ban on the Reichsbanner, so the president's plan was stymied. As a result the president and his son, along with their *éminence grise* Schleicher, were furious with both Brüning and Groener. Their days were now clearly numbered.

With spectacular gains by the Nazis in a number of provincial elections, Catholic Bavaria providing a notable exception, the KPD toned down its denunciations of the SPD and called for a "united front from below" for a common struggle against the "capitalist robbers" and "fascist hordes"; but they continued to denounce the reformist leadership. The Weimar coalition lost its majority in Prussia, but since all attempts to form a new coalition failed, largely as a result of the Center Party's refusal to work with the NSDAP, Otto Braun remained in office. Schleicher was now determined to topple the Brüning cabinet and create a new government, which would include the NSDAP. To this effect he began talks with Hitler, who demanded new elections and a lifting of the ban on the SS and SA. But it was the East Elbian Junkers who brought about Brüning's downfall. Hans Schlange-Schöningen, the man in charge of the *Osthilfe*, a system of outdoor relief for the landed aristocracy, put forward a proposal that bankrupt estates in the east should be turned into settlements that would provide work for the unemployed. The Junkers were incensed at this suggestion. The president of their organization, the RLB visited Hindenburg, who was on holiday at his estate at Neudeck in East Prussia, to voice their complaints. Hindenburg's aristocratic neighbors joined in the chorus of criticism, and there was much talk of "state socialism" and "agrarian Bolshevism." The president hardly needed any persuasion to act. On his return to Berlin he immediately told Brüning that he would have to go. Brüning handed in his resignation in the course of a brief meeting with the president on May 12, 1932.

The RLB's reaction to *Osthilfe* was symptomatic of the radicalization of the aristocracy, a small caste that had lost much of its power and prestige. Article 109 of the constitution stated that "all advantages in public law due to birth or social standing are abolished"; furthermore, "noble titles are no longer considered part of one's name and will no longer be granted." The aristocracy reacted by uniting in opposition to the republic with its "Jewish constitution," "Jewish parties," and "Jewish government." The Aristocrats' Cooperative, their principal interest group, banned anyone with Jewish blood in their family from membership. The agrarians' traditional antipathy against "Jewish cattle dealers" and "urban Jewish usurers" escalated into a hysterical denunciation of "Social Democratic-Jewish controlled economy" and the "plague of eastern Jewish locusts." Berlin was denounced as a "Zionist-Jewish stronghold" intent on building the "new Jerusalem." The "Protocols of the Elders of Zion," a sickening anti-Semitic forgery by the tsarist police, found an eager readership in these circles. The Nazis' agricultural expert, Walther Darré, successfully courted the aristocracy and managed to get his deputy elected as one of the RLB's four presidents in 1931. The anti-republican, radical nationalist, and viciously anti-Semitic Nazi Party was an increasingly attractive option for the aristocracy. The informal alliance between the "barons" and the Nazis was a significant contributory factor to Hitler's rise to power.

Brüning was neither the villain who destroyed parliamentary democracy, thus paving the way for the Nazis, nor was he the conservative hero who offered a genuine alternative to a bankrupt democratic system or a brown dictatorship. His government was little more than the moderate and parliamentarily sanctioned phase of the presidential dictatorship planned by the camarilla around the 85-year-old president. Brüning's refusal to make a deal with the Nazis, whom the right wanted to engage as junior partners in an authoritarian regime, was the real reason for his downfall. The decision to dismiss Brüning, dissolve the Reichstag, and call a fresh round of elections two years before term was a disastrous decision for which Hindenburg and the clique around him must bear full responsibility. Had they waited, the worst of the economic crisis would have passed, the radical parties would have lost much of their appeal, and the world would possibly have been spared untold misery.

Papen

Brüning's successor, hand-picked by Schleicher, was Franz von Papen, a backbencher in the Prussian diet, who stood on the extreme right of the Center Party. He was an aristocratic ex-cavalry officer, a landowner, and an accomplished horseman, well known for his impeccably tailored suits and his wide circle of influential friends. He had proved a disaster as military attaché in Washington, his career proof positive of the "Peter Principle." He was little more than Schleicher's creature, the general having secured his own appointment as Reichswehr minister in place of Groener. The new government, replete with the scions of some of Germany's most illustrious families with only three commoners in subordinate posts, was soon labeled "the baron's cabinet."

At Papen's request an election was called for July 31. The ban on the SS and SA was lifted, with the predictable result of an alarming increase in violence. Fights between Communists and Nazis were particularly prevalent in the industrial areas in the Rhine and Ruhr, with the government placed the blame on the Prussian minister of the interior, Carl Severing, for discriminating against the National Socialists. On July 17 an illegal demonstration by the SA through a Communist district in Hamburg ended with seventeen deaths, many of them victims of the police. Hindenburg's response to this "Bloody Sunday in Altona" was to use article 48 to suspend the Prussian government, appointing in its place a commissar with full executive powers. The Prussian government promptly appealed for a ruling from the High Court (Reichsgericht), but the Social Democrats were in a helpless position. Having been repudiated by the general public in the recent elections, with millions of unemployed and fearing a civil war in which they were bound to be defeated, the SPD and the unions refused to consider a general strike or massed protest against the "Prussian coup." They left it to the electorate to express its disapproval of this provocative and dubiously legal act in the forthcoming national elections. Left-wing activists were disgusted at this pusillanimous response by the leadership. The KPD, once again on an ultra-left tack having abandoned the "united front from below," used the SPD's inaction as further evidence of the perfidy of these "social fascists."

On July 31, 1932, the electorate once again moved to the extremes. Support for the SPD fell by a further 2.9 points and the Communists made modest gains. The National Socialists were the big winners, with 37.4 percent of the vote, thereby increasing their representation in the Reichstag from 107 to 230 seats. Catholic Germany and the supporters of the "Marxist" parties remained relatively immune to the siren calls of the Nazis, their increased support coming from the "bourgeois" parties and from first-time voters. Buoyed by his triumph at the polls, Hitler now demanded the chancellorship, but Hindenburg still shuddered at the thought of appointing the "Bohemian corporal." Papen then proposed Hitler as vice chancellor, promising that after a while he would step down and make way for him. Hitler, furious that he had been spurned, denounced both the president and the chancellor. A few days after the election, the storm trooper perpetrators of a particularly brutal murder of a Communist in the Silesian village of Potempa were condemned to death by a special court. Hitler at once warned Papen of the dire consequences were he to soil his hands with the blood of these national heroes. Goebbels announced that the Jews were behind the sentencing of these paragons of Germanic virtue. Hindenburg decided it would be prudent to commute the death sentence to life imprisonment. He used the fact that the murders occurred immediately after the promulgation of a decree prescribing the death sentence for politically motivated murders as an excuse, feebly arguing that the guilty men could not have been aware of the consequences of their action.

The NSDAP and the KPD formed a majority in the new Reichstag, which met for the first time on August 30. Since both parties were bent on the destruction of parliamentary democracy, this meant that constitutional government was no longer possible. Klara Zetkin, an enthusiastic admirer of Joseph Stalin, was appointed president of the Reichstag for the opening session on account of her being, at 75, the oldest deputy. She announced that she hoped to live to be the president of the congress of a Soviet Germany. This pleasure was denied her. She died in exile in Moscow the following year. Hermann Göring was then elected president by a handsome majority according to the custom that the office was traditionally filled by a member of the largest party. He soon made it abundantly clear that he had no intention of making impartial rulings.

Papen, with virtually no support in the Reichstag, urged Hindenburg to dissolve parliament. With parliament no longer in session, Papen had to read his government's program over the radio. It called for the creation of a presidential and authoritarian "new state" based on the ideas of Edgar Jung, a prominent spokesman for a "conservative revolution." His reflections on democracy in his book *Rule by Inferiors* (*Herrschaft der Minderwertigen*) were much admired in right-wing circles. Papen called for a thoroughgoing reform of the constitution based on "national leadership irrespective of the political parties," with an upper house representative of the professions and trades. The franchise for the Reichstag elections would henceforth be decided by such factors as marital status and the number of children. The dualism between Prussia and the Reich would be ended. Similar views were held by the group around Hans Zehrer's magazine *Der Tat* (*Action*), but here with a distinctly populist emphasis that sought an opening to the left. This group appealed greatly to Schleicher, who began to distance himself from his creature Papen, who was in thrall to Jung and his aristocratic cronies in the ultra-conservative Herrenklub (Gentlemen's Club).

The election was held in the shadow of a strike of transport workers in Berlin in which National Socialists and Communists marched arm in arm, much to the alarm of middle-class electors. The result was a disappointment for Hitler's party, which lost the support of 2 million voters and returned thirty-four fewer deputies to the Reichstag. The SPD also did far worse than expected. The DNVP were the big winners, while both KPD and DVP made significant gains. The election was thus a modest vindication of Papen's government. The conservative parties had done well, partly because of concern about the radicalism of the National Socialists, but also because certain Keynesian measures were beginning to have a positive effect on the economy. But the "baron's cabinet" was still only actively supported by about 10 percent of the electorate. The Communists, who had reached the magic number of 100 seats in the Reichstag, once again entertained the illusion that this was the dawn of the red revolution. Other more clear-sighted observers of the political scene, Josef Goebbels among them, realized that the Communists' success was a golden opportunity for the Nazis. The respectable middle-class now imagined that they were faced with a simple choice between Communists and Nazis, and did not hesitate when deciding which to choose.

Schleicher

Hindenburg wanted to continue with a presidential regime with Papen as chancellor. Papen, who had discussed the situation with a number of influential businessmen, began to toy with the idea of a Hitler chancellorship. There was mounting support for such a move among a number of industrialists, bankers, and landowners who, on November 19, sent a letter to the president suggesting that the leader of the largest single party should take over from Papen. Among those who signed this letter were Hjalmar Schacht, the banker Kurt von Schröder, and the steel baron Fritz Thyssen. Other prominent industrialists, including Paul Reusch of the Gutehoffnungshütte, Fritz Springorum of Hoesch, and Albert Vögler of the Vereinigten Stahlwerke, let it be known that they supported the idea, but did not want their names to appear on the letter. A large number of influential figures in the Rhine and Ruhr came to share this point of view in the course of the next few weeks, in part because they feared that the KPD would appeal to a large number of younger voters in the "national" parties, including the Nazis. The NSDAP and SPD refused to talk to the chancellor. The Center Party and BVP insisted that Papen should step down and that a new government should include the Nazis. The BVP suggested that Hitler should be chancellor. Realizing that he could not possibly form an effective government, Papen recommended that the president dismiss the entire cabinet. Hindenburg agreed, but still refused to contemplate a Hitler government, hoping that Papen would somehow manage to form a new cabinet. With Papen reluctant to continue in office and Hindenburg insisting that he remain, Schleicher offered to test the political waters.

He first approached the ADGB and the SPD's parliamentary party with a promise to rescind the emergency legislation of September, which made it possible for employers to break wage contracts. The response from the union boss Theodor Leipart, whose head was full of ideas borrowed from radical conservatives like Ernst Jünger and the *Tat* circle, believing that the trade unions should detach themselves from specific political parties, was favorable. These inchoate ideas were enthusiastically endorsed by Gregor Strasser the organizational genius of the Nazi Party and the leading figure on the movement's left wing. The SPD was not impressed. Fearing that the Communists would make political hay out of any such compromise, they refused to postpone the election until the spring, on the grounds that this would be unconstitutional. Schleicher and the *Tat* circle now called for a front extending from Strasser's left-wing Nazis to the trade unions, but Strasser was unable to win Hitler over to the idea, while most trade unionists vehemently opposed Leipart's sharp turn to the right. Hindenburg was now ready for a showdown with the Reichstag. Wanting Papen to remain in office, he promised that he would use his presidential powers to support him, backed if necessary by armed force. General von Schleicher was highly alarmed at the prospect of what amounted to a military dictatorship, for which the public had absolutely no sympathy and which would undermine both the prestige and the morale of the Reichswehr. With considerable support right across the political spectrum he now prepared to oust Papen and make a bid for the chancellorship.

On December 2, 1932, Schleicher ordered Lieutenant Colonel Eugen Ott to present the results of a recent war game to the cabinet. They showed that, should there be a confrontation between the government and the Communists and National Socialists, the Poles would be tempted to invade. The Reichswehr and police would then be unable to master the situation. The cabinet was impressed by this hair-raising scenario. Hindenburg, horrified that the country seemed to be heading for a civil war, abandoned his plans for a quasi-dictatorship and appointed Schleicher chancellor on December 3. This was greeted with general relief. Plans for a hazardous constitutional experiment had been shelved. Schleicher, known to be a man who sought compromise, had far wider support than his unfortunate predecessor. The major question was how he was going to deal with the National Socialists.

Undaunted by their initial response, Schleicher set about trying to split the Nazi Party by offering Gregor Strasser the post of vice chancellor.

Hitler Appointed Chancellor

The Nazi Party now seemed on the point of collapse. Popular support was dwindling at an alarming rate, the coffers were empty, and Strasser had considerable support, particularly in northern Germany. Hitler dramatically contemplated suicide were he to lose control of the party, but unfortunately this was not to be. On December 9, it was announced that Strasser, with no stomach for a fight with Hitler, had resigned all his party offices. Schleicher took this as a sign that he was about to enter the government fold, but Hitler acted swiftly and decisively. That same day he called a meeting of the Gauleiter (district officials of the party), the NSDAP's Reichstag deputies, and other top officials, at which he won an unconditional pledge of allegiance. Schleicher's attempt to split the party had thus failed, and Strasser took off to Austria for two weeks' holiday, his political career at an end. Schleicher still clung to the illusion that it would be possible to win over the NSDAP, and even imagined that Hitler and Strasser might be reconciled under his benign tutelage. There were also encouraging signs that the trade unions were anxious to cooperate with a government that offered to put the country back to work with imaginative reflationary policies.

Such confidence was sadly misplaced. On January 4, 1933, his two arch-rivals, Papen and Hitler, met at the banker von Schröder's house in Cologne to bury the hatchet and plot their revenge. Papen agreed to plead with Hindenburg to dismiss Schleicher and accept a Hitler–Papen government; but it was still doubtful whether the president would agree to Hitler's appointment as chancellor. Papen then discussed the situation with some of the leading Ruhr barons. Most were satisfied with Schleicher's attempts to stimulate the economy and steer a moderate course between capital and labor. Few raised serious objections to another Papen government, but it would have to be one in which the NSDAP played a subordinate role. Most industrialists still had serious reservations about Hitler and his party. The chancellor now came under massive attack from the RLB, emboldened by its success in ousting Brüning. In all too familiar language the association accused Schleicher of pursuing a "Marxist" policy of plunder and expropriation, while kowtowing to the export industry, which it claimed had led to the ruination of German agriculture. Walther Darré, the Nazi's agricultural expert and author of *The Pig as a Criterion for Northern People and Semites*, *The Peasantry as the Life Source of the Nordic Race*, and *The New Aristocracy of Blood and Soil*, condemned the chancellor for "Bolshevizing the German people." He also denounced Schleicher as a second Caprivi, yet another general "without an acre or a blade of grass," who vainly imagined that a solution to the economic crisis could be found by encouraging industrial exports. Hindenburg, ever mindful of agrarian interests, found his misgivings about Schleicher confirmed.

Much now depended on the attitude of the Reichstag, which was due to reconvene. Given that the government was unlikely to survive a vote of confidence, the cabinet agreed that the next round of elections should not be held within the statutory sixty days but should be postponed until the autumn, or possibly until December. An alternative was to declare a vote of no confidence invalid and to rule by presidential decree, a solution that was constitutionally acceptable under article 54, and which was approved by such eminent constitutional experts as Carl Schmitt on the right and Ernst Fraenkel on the left.

The question remained open whether the president would agree to dissolve the Reichstag and to postpone the elections.

Schleicher's position began to erode when the DNVP parroted the RLB and condemned his "socialist" policies for opening the door to Bolshevism. Discussions continued in Berlin between Papen and Hitler, in the course of which Papen reconciled himself to the idea of Hitler as chancellor, and Oscar von Hindenburg dropped many of his objections to the Nazis. Hindenburg, warned by the Center Party and the SPD that postponing the elections would be a gross violation of the constitution, became deeply concerned that a presidential emergency regime pending the elections would plunge Germany into civil war. He was ever mindful of Colonel Ott's dire warnings of the consequences, and it soon became clear that Schleicher, by using this underhand weapon against Papen, had dug his own political grave. The Social Democrats and the Center Party, the twin pillars of Weimar democracy, now set about bringing down the Schleicher government on the grounds that he threatened to violate one article of the constitution. Since by now there was no viable alternative to a Hitler government they thus paved the way for a regime bent on destroying parliamentary democracy once and for all. For them a Hitler government appointed according to the constitution was preferable to a temporary dictatorship under Schleicher, to say nothing of a presidential government under Papen, or even Hugenberg. Schleicher, left virtually without support, came to the inevitable conclusion: on January 28, 1933, the cabinet resigned.

Faced with the imminent prospect of a Hitler cabinet, the SPD finally saw the light. The party called for a mass demonstration in Berlin against a government that was denounced as "the springboard for a fascist dictatorship." Papen busied himself persuading prominent conservatives to consider cabinet posts in a Hitler cabinet. The two outstanding problems were to get Hugenberg to serve and the question of who should be commissar for Prussia. Hugenberg's objections were largely overcome when he was offered the post of minister of finance and agriculture. Papen insisted on becoming commissar for Prussia, but accepted Hermann Göring as his deputy, responsible for the police force. Göring was also to be a minister without portfolio and commissar responsible for aviation. Wilhelm Frick, who as Nazi minister of the interior in Thuringia had earned a reputation as a ferocious reactionary with a blissful disregard for legality, was to continue the good work as minister of the interior. Hindenburg chose one minister himself. He swore in General Werner von Blomberg, one of the very few senior officers who supported Hitler, as Reichswehr minister. He did so even before Hitler became chancellor. Since it was the chancellor who appointed ministers, this was a serious breach of the constitution.

The only remaining obstacle was to get Hindenburg to agree to Hitler's demand that there should be new elections immediately. Since neither the Center Party nor the BVP would agree to support a Hitler government, and since a two-thirds Reichstag majority was needed for an enabling act, which Hitler insisted was essential if the government were to be effective, Hindenburg gave way. Thus, in the late afternoon of January 30, 1933, Chancellor Hitler swore allegiance to a constitution he was determined to destroy. On the following day he asked Hindenburg to dissolve the Reichstag. On February 1 elections were called for March 5, and in the meantime Hitler could make full use of the emergency powers permitted under article 48. The conservative elites were delighted. There were only two National Socialists in Hitler's first cabinet: Wilhelm Frick and Hermann Göring, who as yet was without a ministerial portfolio. They still controlled the civil service, the army, and the judiciary while enjoying the support of the agrarians and the industrialists.

Hitler the drummer boy provided the mass support that they had hitherto lacked. Papen spoke on their behalf when he announced: "He is now in our employ!" adding: "In two months' time we will have pushed Hitler so tightly into the corner that he will squeak!" The Stahlhelm leader, Theodor Duesterberg, who refused a position in Hitler's cabinet, claimed that Hitler would soon be seen running in his underpants through the chancellery garden to avoid arrest. It seemed to be a perfect solution: Hitler's popularity, drive, and dynamism had been harnessed by experienced and responsible conservatives.

On the left the SPD was hamstrung by its fetishistic loyalty to a constitution which it was determined to uphold whatever the cost, argued that since Hitler had been legally appointed they should not be tempted away from the narrow path of legality. The KPD, suffering from no such scruples, called for a general strike against the fascist dictatorship. With 6 million unemployed this fell on deaf ears. For most contemporaries Hitler's appointment as chancellor marked a welcome end to unseemly and unproductive party strife. It opened up the prospect of a united, powerful, and prosperous Germany. Only a few lonely visionaries realized the disastrous consequences of an appointment which was neither inevitable nor necessary and for which Hindenburg, his intimate advisors, and the old elites must bear the major share of the blame.

CHAPTER TWELVE
THE NAZI DICTATORSHIP

CHAPTER CONTENTS

A History of Modern Germany: 1800 to the Present, Second Edition. Martin Kitchen.
© 2012 Martin Kitchen. Published 2012 by Blackwell Publishing Ltd.

The DNVP leader and minister of economics Hugenberg was soon to admit that he and his associates had completely misread the situation. The conservative elite failed to realize that behind a threadbare facade the Weimar Republic was falling apart. Society was in the midst of a profound crisis, and for all his moderate assurances in the last few days, Hitler was a man with a fanatical determination to destroy the existing state and establish an iron dictatorship. His clearly stated intention to call elections as soon as possible should have been indication enough to his conservative allies that he was out to destroy them and that his assurances to the DNVP had to be taken with a truckload of salt. The Nazis had mass support and a superb propaganda machine, and the SA was more than happy to resort to violence whenever necessary. Precious little stood in their way. At the time of the Nazi "seizure of power" there were some 850,000 party members. They mounted a series of torchlight processions and heralded the "National Revolution." Skeptical intellectuals, such as the charming Count Harry Kessler, dismissed such demonstrations as a mere carnival. Others waited anxiously upon events. Most Germans were indifferent. There was no rush to join the party.

Hitler's first announcement of his long-term goals was made behind closed doors to a group of generals on February 3, 1933. He did not mince his words. He promised strict authoritarian rule that would rid Germany of the "cancer" of democracy and "exterminate" Marxism. Rearmament and the introduction of universal military service would make Germany once again ready for war. In an ominous aside, which most of his audience seem to have overheard, he spoke of "radically Germanizing" the east in order to carve out "living space" (*Lebensraum*). The generals, with their traditional anti-Semitism, their loathing of "Jewish Bolshevism," and their determination to rearm and to revise the Versailles settlement, were encouraged by these remarks. For all their snobbish disdain towards some of the more vulgar aspects of National Socialism, they were in broad agreement with Hitler's program. Most of them remained so until the bitter end.

On February 1 Hindenburg had agreed to dissolve the Reichstag, and elections were called for March 5. In the meantime Hitler could make use of the emergency presidential powers as provided in paragraph 48 of the Weimar constitution. Counting on wide support, he complacently remarked at the cabinet meeting on February 1 that this was to be the last Reichstag election, and that there would be no return to the parliamentary system.

On February 4 Hitler used the Communist appeal for a general strike as an excuse to push through an emergency decree "For the Protection of the German People." It permitted severe restrictions on the freedom of the press and of assembly should there be "an immediate danger to public safety," or in instances where "the organs, organizations and offices of the state and its employees were insulted or mocked." This gave Hitler and his minions discretion to silence the opposition parties during the election campaign. Appeals against the flagrant misuse of this decree could were made to the High Court, but by the time they could be lodged the election was long since over.

Hermann Göring used the decree to the utmost in Prussia, where he had been appointed minister of the interior in the commissarial government. Otto Braun's government had been reinstated when the State Court (Staatsgerichtshof) ruled that Papen's coup in July 1932 was unconstitutional, so that there were now two governments in Prussia. Hitler then issued another presidential decree "For the Restoration of Orderly Government in Prussia." On February 6 the Prussian parliament (*Landtag*) was once again dissolved.

Although Göring was formally subordinate to Papen as Reich commissar for Prussia, he promptly weeded out the few remaining democrats in the upper echelons of the Prussian civil service, police force, and judiciary. The Prussian secret police was reorganized into a separate Secret Police Office (Gestapa). The police were ordered to cooperate fully with the SA, the SS, and the Stahlhelm in an all-out campaign against the Communists. Meetings of the democratic parties were systematically broken up, politicians were brutally beaten to within an inch of their lives, and the opposition press was silenced. On February 17 Göring published a decree in which he ordered the police to shoot to kill if necessary.

The SA was given carte blanche to disrupt the meetings of republican parties, to beat up politicians, threaten officials, and make arbitrary arrests. Their hapless victims were flung into hastily improvised concentration camps. Thus a former minister, Adam Stegerwald of the Center Party, was brutally assaulted during a rally in Krefeld. The Social Democratic police president of Berlin, Albert Grzesinski, was made to fear for his life and was obliged to resign. The offices of a number of republican newspapers were torched. In all there were sixty-nine deaths, and hundreds were seriously wounded during the five weeks of the election campaign. There was widespread revulsion against such barbarity. Ludendorff, Hitler's brother-in-arms in 1923, wrote to his old superior Hindenburg complaining bitterly about such "unbelievable events" and claiming that this was "the blackest time in German history."

Hitler traveled tirelessly the length and breadth of Germany preaching his simple message of national redemption to vast and enthusiastic crowds. He denounced the "November criminals" who were responsible for the last fourteen years of economic misery, political bickering, and national humiliation. He promised to unite the nation into a strong-willed "racial community" (*Volksgemeinschaft*) that would transcend all divisions of class and station. The economy would be revitalized in two successive four-year plans. "National rebirth" would result from reasserting family values and Christian morality. He made no concrete proposals, but he spoke with such utter conviction and passion that the crowds believed that he could be trusted. In this highly charged emotional atmosphere what mattered was not a carefully crafted program, but a spontaneous and passionate reaction. The opposition forces were so hopelessly divided, demoralized, and cowed that they could offer precious little resistance.

On February 20 Hitler addressed a group of leading industrialists and told them that this would be positively the last election and that he intended to create a strong and independent state, regardless of the outcome of the election. First he had to gain absolute power, and then he would destroy his opponents. The industrialists were delighted, and promptly got out their checkbooks. The party was thereby relieved of all financial worries.

The Reichstag Fire

At nine o'clock in the evening of February 27 smoke was seen billowing through the roof of the Reichstag. Shortly afterwards a dim-witted Dutch anarchist, Marinus van der Lubbe, was arrested in the Bismarck Room. He promptly admitted that he had set the building on fire. The National Socialists convinced themselves that this was part of a Communist plot. Their opponents claimed that the Nazis had organized the fire in order to find an excuse to bring in further emergency legislation. The Communists soon published a "Brown Book" that purported to show Nazi complicity in the fire.

The Nazi claim that van der Lubbe was under orders from the Communists was soon shown to be utterly false. Communists later admitted that their "Brown Book" was a fabrication. In 1962 Fritz Tobias published a detailed study of the Reichstag fire and came to the conclusion that van der Lubbe acted alone. Most historians now accept this version, although some respected scholars still believe that the Nazis were implicated.

When Hitler was told of the fire he wound himself up into a passion and said that all Communist functionaries should be shot, their Reichstag deputies hanged. The Prussian ministry of the interior promptly set about drafting an emergency decree. On the following day the "Decree for the Protection of the People and the State" was promulgated. All the fundamental rights guaranteed in the constitution were suspended. The death penalty was extended to include a number of crimes, including treason and arson. Summary arrests could be made and the Nazis' opponents placed in "protective custody" in concentration camps. In an important step towards dismantling the republic's federal structure, Wilhelm Frick as minister of the interior could disregard the sovereignty of the states if he deemed that law and order were in jeopardy. This decree, which claimed to be solely directed against the Communists, was the fundamental law on which the Nazi dictatorship was based. It remained in force in spite of the fact that van der Lubbe's trial in September clearly showed that there was no evidence that the Communists were involved. The accused was executed even though arson was not a capital offense at the time he committed the crime. There was a wave of arrests throughout Germany. 100,000 people, mostly Communists, were arrested in Prussia, among them the prominent left-wing writers Egon Erwin Kisch, Erich Mühsam, Carl von Ossietsky, and Ludwig Renn.

In spite of all the intimidation, mass arrests, and harassment of the opposition parties, the results of the elections were most disappointing for the National Socialists. They only managed to obtain 43.9 percent of the popular vote, 6.5 points more than their best showing in the July elections of 1932. Their largest gains were in Bavaria and Württemberg, where they previously had little support. Since the conservatives got a meager 8 percent, the coalition parties had a very narrow majority in the Reichstag. Voters remained faithful to the Social Democrats and the Center Party, while the Communists, with 12.3 percent, did surprisingly well under the circumstances. The astonishingly high voter participation of 88.8 percent shows how important these elections were to the average German.

The ballots were hardly counted when the National Socialists set about the demolition of the republic's federal structure. A two-pronged attack on local government was launched. SA thugs and party activists stormed town halls and local government offices, hoisted the swastika flag, and chased terrified officials away. The authorities in Berlin used such lawlessness as an excuse to overthrow provincial governments by using the powers vested in them in article 2 of the Reichstag Fire Decree. Commissars, often the local party leader (Gauleiter), were appointed in each of the states, and prominent Nazis replaced the police chiefs.

In some areas the Nazis met with considerable resistance. The Bavarian minister president, Heinrich Held, adamantly refused to give way to threats from the SA, but the local army units gave him no support when ordered from Berlin to stay out of domestic politics. Hitler's wooing of the Reichswehr on February 3 thus paid a handsome dividend. Held was left without any support and Frick appointed the stalwart Nazi Lieutenant-General Franz Ritter von Epp as commissar for Bavaria. The commissar's protégé Heinrich Himmler, head of the still minute SS, was made chief of police in Munich and then took over the Bavarian secret police. Ably assisted by his ruthless and brilliant underling Reinhard Heydrich, this was the beginning of a remarkable career in law enforcement.

On March 21, the first day of spring, the regime held an impressive ceremony in Potsdam organized by Joseph Goebbels, who had recently been appointed minister of propaganda. The occasion was designed not only to mark the opening of the new parliament, but also as a symbolic gesture of reconciliation between the old and the new Germany. Representatives of all walks of life were present. Only the Communists and the Social Democrats were not invited because, as Frick remarked with obvious relish, they had a lot of important work to do in the concentration camps.

The "Potsdam Day" began with a service in the garrison church after which Hitler was presented to Hindenburg. The humble other-ranker bowed before the field marshal. Hindenburg then saluted the empty chair where the kaiser used to sit and behind which stood the crown prince. Hitler gave an anodyne speech in which he spoke of the union of past greatness with youthful vigor. National Socialism was thus presented as the apotheosis of German history in the long and glorious tradition of Luther, Frederick the Great, Bismarck, and Hindenburg.

Gleichschaltung

The atmosphere was menacing when the Reichstag met three days later in the Kroll Opera House in Berlin. The SA surrounded it, Hitler appeared in party uniform, all of the eighty-one Communist deputies were forbidden to attend and twenty-six Social Democrats had been arrested. There was only one item of business on the agenda: a constitutional amendment labeled the "Enabling Act" that would put an end to the last vestiges of parliamentary rule.

Since a constitutional amendment needed a two-thirds majority, all depended on the attitude of the Center Party. The leadership, under Monsignor Ludwig Kaas, favored an authoritarian solution to the present crisis and feared that opposition would result in further restrictions of the freedom of the Catholic Church. Others managed to convince themselves that the bill was aimed solely against the Communists. The former chancellor Heinrich Brüning had serious reservations. After lengthy discussions the party agreed to vote for the proposal. Otto Wels from the Social Democratic Party was the only member who had the courage to speak out against the bill. His measured but passionate plea for democracy, the rule of law, and the fundamental principles of his party aroused Hitler's fury, but had no influence on the outcome. There were 444 votes in favor and only 94 against. Even though the bill had been pushed through in a blatantly unconstitutional manner, it was formally renewed twice, thus providing the pseudo-legal basis for twelve years of untrammeled dictatorship.

On March 31 the government used its new powers to promulgate the Provisional Law for the Coordination (*Gleichschaltung*) of the States (*Länder*) with the Reich. This gave state governments the right to pass legislation without consulting regional parliaments. State governors (*Reichsstatthälter*), who acted on instructions from Berlin, were appointed under the terms of a second bill of April 7. Hitler appointed himself *Reichsstatthalter* of Prussia, but delegated his authority to Göring. Thus ended the long tradition of German federalism.

The new system was further confused by the fact that many of the *Reichsstatthälter* were also Gauleiter, but the state and party district boundaries did not correspond. It was typical of the Third Reich that this resulted in a confusion of state and party functions, as well as power struggles where state and district boundaries overlapped. The situation was further muddled when armaments commissars were appointed in areas that corresponded to neither the state nor the party districts. Furthermore, the Gauleiter and state governors established themselves as little Hitlers in their satrapies, paying scant attention to instructions passed down from Berlin. They considered themselves beholden to the Führer alone.

For all the talk of the unity of the National Socialist state, there was thus from the very beginning a hopeless confusion over the areas of competence of state and party, federal and state governments, and special plenipotentiaries. Hitler was in many ways a "hands off" tyrant. He preferred to let his myrmidons struggle among themselves and let the strongest and fittest emerge triumphant. This corresponded to his view of life as an endless struggle and it ensured that the Nazi movement never lost its activist dynamic by becoming bureaucratized. The end result was that the leading figures in the Third Reich were almost without exception a repulsive collection of brutish gangsters, corrupt place-seekers, and ruthless careerists. The advantage of this administrative blitzkrieg was that it was possible to cut through red tape and avoid futile paper-shuffling, but far too much time and energy were lost on interdepartmental rivalries and the struggle for power.

The regime now set about the systematic destruction of the political parties that no longer had any role to play after the passing of the Enabling Act. On May 1 Goebbels staged a "Day of National Labor." On the following day the trade unions were banned. Units of the SA and SS stormed union offices, and union leaders were arrested. Although most leading Communists had been imprisoned or had fled the country after the Reichstag fire, the party was not formally banned until the end of March in order to ensure that the working-class vote would be split in the March election. Moscow appeared curiously indifferent to the destruction of the party and the martyrdom of its members.

The Social Democratic paramilitary organization Reichsbanner, which had been involved in a series of street battles with the SA, was banned state by state. The party had been harassed since the Reichstag fire decree, its party offices raided, and its newspapers banned. The membership was demoralized and rapidly dwindled. Many of the leadership moved to Prague, whence they called for an all-out struggle against Hitler's regime. The Nazis used this as an excuse to ban the party on June 22, ordering the arrest of all those party leaders who were still in Germany.

The smaller democratic parties self-destructed, so that now only the Center Party, its Bavarian branch party (BVP), and the conservatives (DNVP) remained. Members were leaving these parties in droves, many of them joining the National Socialists in a scramble to jump on the bandwagon. These opportunists, contemptuously known as the "March fallen" (Märzgefallenen) by the old guard, were so numerous that by January 1934 party membership had almost trebled. The ironic reference was to those who had died during the revolt in Berlin in March 1848.

On March 28 the Catholic bishops, fearing that the state might interfere with the church, made a solemn pledge of allegiance to the Nazi state. Monsignor Kaas was in Rome discussing the details of a concordat with Papen and Vatican officials, so the Center Party was left leaderless. Brüning took over command on May 6, but the party had no fight left in it. Under the terms of the concordat priests were forbidden to take part in politics, and the Vatican thus clearly distanced itself from political Catholicism. A number of leading figures in the BVP were arrested and on July 4 the party dissolved itself. The Center Party followed suit the next day.

The regime made quick work of the DNVP. The party leader Hugenberg caused a scandal during the London economic conference in June by demanding the return of Germany's colonies and expansion in the east, thus providing Hitler with an excellent excuse to dismiss him from the cabinet. The Stahlhelm leader Franz Seldte pointedly joined the National Socialists on April 26, and on June 21 the Stahlhelm was amalgamated with the SA. On June 27 a "friendly agreement" was reached between the NSDAP and the DNVP. All conservative members of the Reichstag became Nazi Party members, and all party members who had been arrested were released. The demise of the DNVP passed almost unnoticed. The Nazi daily newspaper *Völkischer Beobachter* had already announced on June 10 that the "party state" was dead. On July 14, a day of particular significance to democrats, a law was promulgated which declared the NSDAP to be the only legal party in Germany. Goebbels announced that this was the final victory over the ideals of the Enlightenment and the French Revolution. But the regime made provision for plebiscites, thus showing that even dictatorships have, however fraudulent the means, to make some claim to legitimacy by securing popular consent. The spirit of 1789 was thus not quite extinguished.

All professional associations, societies, and clubs were brought under party control as part of the comprehensive program of "coordination" (*Gleichschaltung*). Walter Darré, the party's agricultural expert and a long-time friend of Himmler, took control of all Germany's farmers' associations and was given the title of "Reich Farmers' Leader." He was appointed minister of agriculture at the end of June, and thus had complete control of all aspects of agriculture.

On April 1 the offices of the Reich Association of German Industry (Reichsverband der Deutschen Industrie – RDI) had been raided by the SA and a number of officials dismissed, among them the vice president Paul Silverberg who, although a Nazi sympathizer, was Jewish. In the following month the RDI was completely reorganized. The name was slightly changed, but the initials remained the same to give the appearance of continuity. Gustav Krupp von Bohlen und Halbach was appointed president and, along with Hjalmar Schacht the former president of the Reichsbank, organized the "Adolf Hitler Fund," which collected money from industrialists for the NSDAP.

Gleichschaltung affected every walk of life. The professional organizations of doctors, lawyers, and engineers were brought under party control and henceforth there were only National Socialist beekeepers' associations and National Socialist cycle clubs. Even the village skittles teams were closely watched by the party. As a result, Germany's vigorous and varied club life withered, and people stayed at home or visited the local inn, where they learnt to keep an eye out for police informants.

The SA combed local government offices, the banks, and department stores in the search for democrats and Jews. A campaign began to drive women out of the professions, the civil service, and business, so that they could become the ideal wives and mothers that National Socialism demanded.

In May hundreds of university professors made an open declaration of their devotion to the new regime, hoping thereby to further their miserable careers. But it was not only the second-rate who supported Hitler's dictatorship. Martin Heidegger, Germany's greatest philosopher, lauded the regime in a speech given in his capacity as rector of the University of Freiburg. It was a speech that he never retracted. Carl Schmitt, a renowned expert on constitutional law, provided ingenious justification for Nazi lawlessness. But he soon fell from grace because, unlike Heidegger, he had a wide circle of Jewish friends. This, however, did not stop him from addressing a meeting of German jurists with the words: "We need to free the German spirit from all Jewish falsifications, falsifications of the concept of spirit which have made it possible for Jewish emigrants to label the great struggle of Gauleiter Julius Streicher as something un-spiritual." Streicher was the obscenely anti-Semitic editor of the repulsive weekly rag *Der Stürmer*, the circulation of which reached almost half a million by 1935. Its headline slogan was: "The Jews Are Our Misfortune."

The Law for the Restoration of a Professional Civil Service of April 7, 1933, was designed to purge the civil service of Jews and others whom the regime found undesirable. Since university professors were civil servants it was used to rid the universities of a number of prominent intellectuals, many of whom went on to make an incalculable contribution to the countries in which they found asylum. The systematic purge of the universities was carried out by Alfred Rosenberg's "Battle Group for German Culture," ably assisted by students in the National Socialist German Students' Association.

Having one Jewish grandparent was sufficient to be considered a Jew under the terms of this law, which was soon extended to include the legal profession, doctors, dentists, and dental technicians as well as accountants. At Hindenburg's insistence, "Jewish" civil servants who had been in office before August 1, 1914, who had served in the war, or who had had either fathers or sons killed in the war, were temporarily exempted.

Germany's rich and exciting cultural life was also brought under strict party control. In mid-February the socialist novelist Heinrich Mann was forced to resign as president of the Prussian Academy of the Arts. When the academy was required to make a declaration of loyalty to the regime in March, Heinrich Mann's brother Thomas, along with Ricarda Huch and Alfred Döblin, resigned in protest. Other distinguished writers such as Franz Werfel and Jakob Wassermann were also forced to leave. In April a long list was published of authors whose works were banned, among whom were Karl Marx, Albert Einstein, Sigmund Freud, and Eduard Bernstein. Heinrich Heine was also banned, but some of his poetry, such as "The Lorelei," was so popular that it was still published. The author was said to be anonymous.

In May the National Socialist German Students' Association organized an "Action Against the Un-German Spirit." Bonfires were lit throughout the country into which books and newspapers were thrown. Goebbels addressed the crowds assembled around a huge bonfire in Berlin proclaiming that the intellectual foundations of the November republic had now been destroyed. Heinrich Heine, who had witnessed similar book burnings almost a century before, uttered the prophetic words: "In the end one burns people where books are burnt."

The Persecution of the Jews: The First Phase

The persecution of the Jews, which began in the first weeks of the regime, was carried out in a manner typical of the Nazis. It was a combination of uncoordinated violence from below and control from above. Bully-boys from the SA went on the rampage vandalizing Jewish property, beating and murdering their hapless victims. Jews from all walks of life fell prey to this ever-increasing wave of violence.

The reaction from abroad was immediate and robust, but this merely provoked the regime to step up its anti-Semitic campaign. Goebbels promised that he would "teach foreign Jews a lesson" for interfering in German affairs on behalf of their "racial comrades." A "Central Defense Committee Against Jewish Atrocity and Boycott Besetment" was formed under Julius Streicher the Gauleiter of Franconia, an utterly repulsive creature even by the exceptional standards set by the National Socialists, who rejoiced in the reputation of being the movement's most brutal, scatological, and vicious anti-Semite. He was rewarded by being given the task of organizing a boycott of Jewish businesses to take place on April 1, 1933. It was not a success. The SA prevented people from shopping at their favorite stores, and there were widespread complaints about the crude excesses of the brown-shirts. Goebbels, disappointed at the lack of popular enthusiasm for his operation, promptly called it off. Party activists continued the boycott in some areas, even though both Hitler and Frick had ordered them to stop for fear of foreign reaction.

Within a year, two thousand Jewish civil servants had been dismissed and about the same number of artists were forbidden to work. Four thousand lawyers were no longer able to practice their profession, while hundreds of doctors and university professors had lost their livelihoods. For the moment Jewish businessmen were needed to help the process of economic recovery, but their days were numbered.

In the first year of the regime some 37,000 German Jews emigrated, even though Jewish agencies only recommended leaving the country if an individual was in extreme personal danger. They hoped that things would calm down, making it possible for the Jewish community to enjoy a degree of autonomy within the new state. It was almost impossible for Jews to believe that worse would befall them. Had not Rabbi Leo Baeck described Germany as witnessing the third golden age of Judaism following that of Hellenic Judaism in the period before the destruction of the second temple, and the second that of Sephardic Judaism before the expulsion from Spain? Did the fact that thirteen of the thirty-three German Nobel prizewinners were Jewish count for nothing? Could the extraordinary contribution of Jews to Germany's cultural heritage simply be ignored? Others were less confident. In 1934 a further 23,000 Jews left the country.

There was some reason for such optimism. Things began to settle down in the summer of 1933 by which time Hitler had destroyed the republic and had virtually absolute power. But the military, industry, and the bureaucracy still enjoyed a degree of autonomy. Hitler was still partially dependent on them and thus could not afford to go on too radical a course. Concerned not to alienate foreign opinion, he presented himself as a man of moderation and peace. The Nazi radicals around Ernst Röhm and the SA were deeply frustrated at such pusillanimous behavior and complained bitterly that there had been no revolutionary changes in German society.

The SA and the Röhm Putsch

Thus while the SA, with about 3 million members, was chomping at the bit, eager to begin what it called the "Second Revolution," Hitler was trying to dampen down this radicalism which threatened his fruitful alliance with the old elites. In an attempt to bring the anarchic violence of the SA under control greater powers were given to Himmler's SS, specialists in orderly, bureaucratic violence infused with ideological passion. The SS established its first concentration camp in a former munitions factory at Dachau near Munich. Here the regime's victims were systematically bullied, tortured, and murdered in a secluded camp, without offending the sensitive German public who found the open violence of the SA, to which they had been eyewitnesses, somewhat disturbing. At the end of June 1933 Himmler appointed SS-Oberführer (Brigadier) Theodor Eicke commandant. He was a sadistic brute who had recently been released from a psychiatric hospital for the criminally insane. He immediately began to organize the SS Death's Head units, which guarded the camps. He was soon to be promoted inspector general of the concentration camps, with his headquarters at a new camp near Berlin at Sachsenhausen. In October 1933 the SA lost control over its concentration camps, which were henceforth administered by the SS, even though the SS was still formally subordinate to the SA.

By the spring of 1934 the conflict between the SA and the army had become so acute as to be worrisome to Hitler. Ernst Röhm had accused the regime of "falling asleep" and announced that "It is high time that the national revolution should become the National Socialist revolution." At a series of mass meetings he demanded that "reactionaries" should be weeded out from the bureaucracy, industry, and the military. He was outraged that the military had been largely spared from the process of *Gleichschaltung*, but said that its time would come. "The grey rock of the Reichswehr," he proclaimed, "will disappear beneath the brown wave of the SA." Hitler could not tolerate such a suggestion. He needed the professionals in the Reichswehr and knew full well that he could never fulfill his territorial ambitions with gangs of street-fighting men, whatever their ideological fervor and activist élan. The Reichswehr saw Röhm and his ouvrieriste ideas as a serious danger, and suggested that the SA should form a sort of Territorial Army under its close control. Hitler felt that this solution would probably be unacceptable to Röhm, but decided to test his reactions.

The Reichswehr was more than happy to make some concessions to the new regime. The traditionally anti-Semitic officer corps was happy to purge its ranks of Jews. Admittedly this purge was far from complete, largely due to the difficulty in determining who was Jewish. Between 2,000 and 3000 "pure Jews" (*Volljuden*) served in the Wehrmacht during the war, along with 150,000–200,000 "half-Jews" and "quarter-Jews." Most served in the ranks, but there were many officers and some twenty generals among them. In February 1934 the swastika was incorporated into military emblems. In the same month Hitler called a meeting between the Reichswehr minister, General Werner von Blomberg, and Röhm. He insisted that, since the revolution was over and the Reichswehr should remain above politics, the SA should restrict its activities to political indoctrination and pre-military training. He told them that a war would have to be fought to secure *Lebensraum*, and that that war should be left to the professionals. Röhm left the meeting in a towering rage calling Hitler "an ignorant corporal" and vowing to keep up the struggle against "reactionaries." In a speech on April 18 he denounced "the incredible tolerance" of the regime towards "the supporters and associates of former and ancient regimes" and demanded that they should be "ruthlessly removed."

Although Hitler was still reluctant to act against his old comrade, Röhm had powerful enemies. It was not simply the Reichswehr that was determined to frustrate his ambitions. Göring, Goebbels, and Hess were envious of his position, while Himmler and his associate Heydrich resented the fact that the SS played second fiddle to the SA. The fact that he was a notorious homosexual in a country where homosexuality was a criminal offense left him wide open to attack. Göring put together a weighty dossier on Röhm and his numerous homosexual accomplices and catamites. Reichswehr intelligence cooperated closely with the National Socialist Security Service (SD) in the search for further material to use against Röhm. It was at this time that Himmler took over control of the Prussian Gestapo, and he promptly set them to work on the case.

On June 4, 1934, in an attempt to calm things down, Hitler ordered the entire SA to go on leave for the month of July. Röhm's "reactionaries" were emboldened by this obvious split among the National Socialists and went on the offensive. Once again Papen was to play a key and characteristically disastrous role. It was obvious that Hindenburg did not have much longer to live and the question of a successor now became a pressing concern.

The president had fallen seriously ill in April and had not made a complete recovery. Papen tried to convince Hindenburg to call for the restoration of the monarchy in his will. His aim was to establish a military dictatorship in which the conservative elites would keep the Nazi activists in check.

On June 17 Papen gave a speech at Marburg University, which had been written for him by Edgar Jung, an ultra-conservative Calvinist lawyer whose hazy notions of "revolutionary conservatism" were strongly influenced by the muddle-headed corporatist speculations of Othmar Spann. The speech was a forceful expression of the conservative opposition to Hitler. Men who had colluded with the Nazis in the vain belief that they could be tamed now realized that they had made a serious error of judgment and that Hitler had to be removed. It is doubtful whether Papen grasped the full implications of the speech that Jung had prepared for him, for it came as a bombshell. It was an outspoken attack on the regime's radicalism, violence, and lawlessness. A sharp distinction was made between conservative authoritarianism and the "unnatural totalitarian aspirations of National Socialism." Dynamism and movement could achieve nothing but chaos, and the "permanent revolution from below" had to be brought to an end. A firm structure was needed in which the rule of law was respected and state authority unchallenged.

Goebbels promptly banned the publication of this speech, and no mention was made of it on the state radio. Hitler hastened to visit Hindenburg on his estate at Neudeck in an effort at damage control, but realized that the time had come to take more drastic action. Göring, Himmler, and Blomberg decided that the SS should be let loose on the SA leadership, the weapons and logistical support to be supplied by the Reichswehr. Hitler then called a meeting of senior SA commanders at Bad Wiesee, where Röhm was taking the waters. In the early morning of June 30, Hitler arrived at Röhm's hotel in a state of great agitation, riding crop in hand, accompanied by Goebbels and SA-Obergruppenführer (General) Viktor Lutze, who was to take over command of the SA, along with an SS detachment. Röhm and his associates were arrested and taken to the Stadelheim prison in Munich. All but Röhm were executed by SS-Gruppenführer Prince Josias zu Waldeck und Pyrmont. Sepp Dietrich, commander of the SS-Leibstandarte Adolf Hitler ("SS Personal Standard Adolf Hitler"), was unable to stomach the executions and excused himself. Röhm, having turned down the offer to shoot himself, was executed the next day.

This "Röhm Putsch" or "Night of the Long Knives" was not confined to the SA. A number of old scores were settled. Schleicher, his wife, and his adjutant were gunned down in his own home. The former Bavarian minister president von Kahr was assassinated, as was the leader of a prominent Catholic laymen's group. Gregor Strasser was dragged off to the cellars of the Gestapo headquarters in the Prinz-Albrecht-Straße in Berlin, where he was shot. Edgar Jung was murdered. Othmar Spann, as an Austrian, was temporarily spared. After the *Anschluss* he was sent to Dachau, where he was brutally mishandled and left virtually blind. A music critic by the name of Dr. Wilhelm Schmidt was also murdered, having had the misfortune to be confused with the SA leader Ludwig Schmitt. There was a total of eighty-five known victims on June 30, but the real figure is almost certainly considerably higher.

The regime had taken a critical step towards a state of total lawlessness that was characteristic of the fully fledged Nazi tyranny. Although the state had now degenerated to the level of a criminal organization, there was widespread popular support for this bloodbath. A cabinet meeting was held on July 3, at which a law that justified these "emergency measures" that were needed to combat "treasonable attacks" was hastily cobbled together. These criminal acts were thus legalized after the event, and no legal action could be taken against the perpetrators. Carl Schmitt opined that "The Führer protects the law from the worst forms of abuse when he uses his position as leader to create the law in his capacity as supreme judge." He was later to extend this dubious definition of the law in the lapidary injunction that "The will of the Führer is the highest law."

Most Germans were relieved that the SA, with its brutal activism, had now been brought under control by Hitler's decisive action. They forgot that law and order could not be restored by murderous disregard for the law. Even though two prominent generals had been slaughtered in cold blood, the Reichswehr was delighted that the SA had been silenced. The generals cravenly congratulated Hitler for saving Germany from the horrors of civil war. Hitler had thus overcome all serious opposition within the Nazi movement, and his dazzling position as the omniscient and omnipotent Führer in the eyes of his countless devotees was further enhanced.

Hitler Becomes Head of State

The cabinet met as President Hindenburg lay dying and it was agreed that on his demise Hitler should combine the offices of chancellor and president. None of those present were troubled that this was blatantly unconstitutional and flouted the Enabling Act. Blomberg toadishly announced that on the field marshal's death he would order the Reichswehr to make a personal oath of allegiance to the Führer rather than to the constitution as had previously been the case. A number of soldiers were thus to suffer severe and genuine pangs of conscience when they contemplated resistance to the man to whom before Almighty God they had sworn total allegiance. Blomberg vainly imagined that the oath of allegiance would guarantee their independence. They were soon to find out that the absolute reverse was true.

Hindenburg died on August 2, 1934, and Hitler was promptly appointed "Führer and Reich Chancellor." The dictatorship was now complete. On August 19 a plebiscite was held asking the German people to approve the appointment of Hitler as head of state, chancellor, supreme commander of the armed forces, head of the judiciary, and party leader, thus giving pseudo-democratic sanction to a transparently unconstitutional move: 89.9 percent voted in favor. On the following day Hitler announced that the "fifteen-year struggle for power" was completed and that the National Socialists now controlled everything from the highest offices in the Reich to the smallest village council. This was no idle boast. All aspects of German life were now firmly under party control. At the beginning of September the sixth party rally was held in Nuremberg to celebrate this astonishing victory. Its pomp, ceremony, and menace were captured on celluloid in Leni Riefenstahl's brilliant piece of propaganda, *Triumph of the Will*.

The film's title, whether deliberately or not, is misleading. Hitler did not owe his success to his iron willpower, but to a set of fortunate circumstances that offered him opportunities that he exploited adroitly. He gambled for very high stakes and lady luck smiled upon him. The social, economic, and political crises created a situation in which a firm hand was needed. Men of power and influence imagined that they could use the little drummer boy for their own purposes, while the National Socialist movement developed an anarchic activist dynamic that swept all before it. Hitler the master tactician managed to stop the situation from getting out of hand, thereby winning the allegiance of the conservative elites,

PLATE 20   Nazi Party rally 1934. © Bundesarchiv

who felt most threatened by party radicals. This was no carefully considered plan carried out with ruthless determination, but eighteen months of breathless improvisation and nerve-racking gambling for the highest stakes.

The rule of law no longer applied. Parliamentary democracy had been destroyed, the separation of powers ended, the constitution was defunct, the federal system dismantled, and a number of new bodies created that were answerable neither to the state nor to the party, but alone to Hitler. Conservatives believed that with the destruction of the radicals in the SA the regime would now settle down to be firmly repressive yet predictably authoritarian and that the road ahead would be smooth.

Once again the conservative elites had seriously misread the situation. They failed to see that behind the facade of unity there were ferocious struggles for power, conflicts over areas of competence, and bitter rivalries. Since the system was in a constant state of flux, it possessed an inner dynamic without which it would atrophy. It was unpredictable, anarchic, and individualistic in that the little Führers called the shots and were not bound by rules, regulations, or the law. Officials tried to interpret Hitler's will, for that was the highest law and the secret of success. The resulting situation was so chaotic that during the war Hitler's closest associate, Martin Bormann, complained that whereas the republic had been far too tightly bound with red tape the present situation was so disorderly as to be dysfunctional. A highly complex modern state could not possibly operate effectively by attempts to interpret the wishes of an individual, particularly when that individual became progressively more unpredictable as the war dragged on and his will amounted to little more than wishful thinking. Hitler was indubitably the fount of all authority and the final arbiter, but his unbridled power did not rest solely on his willpower, and certainly not on his careful planning, but rather on the inner workings of the system and the willingness of so many Germans to lend him their full support and absolute devotion.

The National Socialist Dictatorship

The years from 1934 to 1938 appeared to be a time of tranquility and peace in Germany. The regime was authoritarian, but it seemed to have distanced itself from the radical activism of the "Years of Struggle." It had a number of striking successes to its credit, both at home and abroad. A comprehensive welfare state was created and the feeling of "racial community" (*Volksgemeinschaft*) was more than an empty slogan. It was not only in Germany that Hitler was seen as a man of peace who had restored Germany to its rightful place in the world.

Behind the scenes the situation was very different. Hitler was systematically laying the groundwork for the realization of his schemes for conquest, expansion, and racial purification. Many in the military, civil service, and industrial elites, to say nothing of the people at large, agreed in principle with these aims, but they feared the risks involved. Hitler needed first to bring them totally under his control and bend them to his will before he put all his chips on the table for one desperate throw of the dice. It was to be total victory or total destruction – Hitler would brook no alternative

By August 1934 he had absolute power. In the state there was no body or person who could check or control him. With the removal of Ernst Röhm he had unbridled authority over the party, which followed him blindly. Hitler as Führer was the awesome figure that bound this confusing and fissiparous movement together. Goebbels' brilliant propaganda helped make him into a figure of messianic proportions, the superbly choreographed rallies becoming quasi-religious ceremonies. This could not have been done purely with smoke and mirrors, nor could the German people's longing for a savior in their hour of need have been stilled without results. The regime overcame the unemployment problem, stimulated the economy, and had a series of foreign political successes that silenced most of Hitler's critics and reconciled the masses to the countless irritations of daily life. Hitler was credited with all the many successes; the failures were ascribed to his wretched underlings.

For an initial short period he played by the book as written by Brüning and Papen. But he quickly dropped established governmental routine. The cabinet met seventy-two times in 1933, twelve times in 1935, and not at all after 1938, so that the vast cabinet room in Hitler's magnificent new Reich chancellery was never used. At none of these cabinet meetings was a vote taken. Members of the cabinet met Hitler individually, access to the Presence controlled by his assiduous head of chancellery, Hans Heinrich Lammers. Once the Enabling Act was passed Hitler's working methods became even more haphazard. When he was not rushing around the country addressing rallies, laying foundation stones, and calling impromptu meetings with sundry officials, he paid increasingly long visits to the Berghof, his mountain fastness in Berchtesgaden. Officials scurried around after him begging for his approval. The result was inevitably chaotic. Often one minister secured his endorsement for legislation that contradicted something that had already been passed via another ministry. All this further strengthened Hitler's position as Führer, for he alone could reconcile such inevitable differences and order the implementation of laws so as to create the impression of a degree of order and consistency.

Hitler resisted all attempts to bring some method into this appalling confusion that served to exasperate the orderly minds of experienced bureaucrats. His instructions were often deliberately vague, so that many different interpretations were possible as to how they should be executed. Or he hesitated until one of his powerful subordinates took it upon himself to act. Amid this tangled situation there was plenty of room for an ambitious Gauleiter or Reichsstaathalter to carve out his own empire where he reigned supreme, virtually unhampered by considerations of the law or established practice and with a direct line of communication to Hitler. Since Hitler took little interest in domestic politics in these early years, there was ample scope for power-hungry and resourceful men to establish themselves in positions of authority and influence. They could be almost certain of the Führer's blessing. In National Socialist Germany nothing succeeded like success.

The longing for a leader who would deliver Germany from all evil was deeply rooted both ideologically and psychologically. There was the Emperor Frederick I of Hohenstaufen, who as "Barbarossa" lay buried in the Kyffhäuser mountain and who would rise again to save Germany in its hour of need. There were the Parsifals and Siegfrieds in Wagner's operas that Hitler professed to love so dearly. There was the deeply ingrained military spirit of Brandenburg-Prussia, the leadership ideology of the youth movement, plus the widespread desire to find a substitute for the monarchy as a symbolic representation of the nation. But it was Goebbels and his propaganda machine that transformed admiration for the regime's achievements into a quasi-religious cult of the Führer. "The whole Volk," he proclaimed, "is devoted to him not merely through respect, but with deep and heartfelt love, because it has the feeling that it belongs to him. It is flesh of his flesh, blood of his blood." Perhaps only someone who had been educated by Jesuits could be capable of such blasphemy. Few were able to resist enchantment by this superhuman figure. Erstwhile opponents became his devotees, and even those who remained critically distanced from him found it hard to withstand his attraction. Hitler himself succumbed totally to the myth so that this mean-spirited, cruel, and bigoted creature became convinced that he was an infallible and indispensable instrument of providence, with a world-historical mission to fulfill. Those who even today speak of the "fascination" of the Hitler phenomenon are still under the spell of this despicable megalomaniac.

In *Mein Kampf* Hitler stressed the vital importance of "religious belief" and "self-sacrifice" for the success of any political movement. He later defined National Socialism as "apodictic faith" and as a church, insisting that "We are not a movement. We are a religion." At the same time he mocked the Wotan-worshipers and armchair Siegfrieds with their runes and old Germanic names, who wanted to replace Christianity with a Germanic religion. Shortly before he was appointed chancellor he announced: "I hereby put forward for myself and my successors in the leadership of the party the claim for political infallibility. I hope the world will grow as accustomed to that claim as it has to that of the Holy Father." Goebbels insisted that National Socialism was nothing without "absolute conviction – unconditional faith." Albert Speer was in full agreement and hoped to build a "secular cathedral" that would be "basically a hall of worship" for "without cult significance Hitler's ideas would be meaningless."

Hitler as the central figure in the National Socialist religion was kept deliberately distant, to the point that there was at times a certain confusion between the earthly leader and the Heavenly Father. This was emphasized by the insistence that he always be addressed as *Mein Führer*, by the elaborate ritual of the Nuremberg party rallies in which he acted as high priest, and by presenting himself publicly as a sexless bachelor with no private life, whose energies were devoted solely to the wellbeing of his followers. For Goebbels, Hitler was first "an apostle with a mission," but by 1938 he could write: "I trust in him as I trust in God." The French ambassador, François-Poncet, spoke of the "almost mystical ecstasy, a kind of holy madness" that took hold of the participants at the annual Nuremberg party rally. They reminded the American journalist William Shirer of the ecstatic ceremonies of the Holy Rollers, adding that these cultic ceremonies "had something of the mysticism and religious fervor of an Easter or Christmas mass in a gothic cathedral." National Socialism, like the churches, had its calendar: January 30 was celebrated as the day of the so-called "seizure of power"; a Heroes' Memorial Day was held in March; Hitler's birthday on April 20 was followed by the Day of National Labor on May 1, which was also Mother's Day. The party rally was held in September, harvest festival in October, and November 9, the anniversary of the Munich putsch, was celebrated in the "movement's capital" of Munich. As a concession to the Germanic enthusiasts the solar equinoxes were also celebrated, but in a rather more subdued manner.

As early as 1940 the émigré social scientist Ernst Fraenkel described this confusion of rival power centers in the state and the party as the "Dual State," and another brilliant colleague, Franz Neumann, analyzed how the normative state apparatus gradually dissolved into an "organized anarchy" with its characteristically amorphous dynamic. The dualism was not a clear-cut distinction between party and state, but a highly complex intertwining of areas of competence that led to ever-increasing radicalization both of goals and of methods.

There were substantial changes within the power structure of this polycratic state. The SS triumphed over the SA in 1934 and began its rapid growth to become a state within the state, submitting the judiciary and the police to its whims. Walter Darré, although grossly inefficient, was made food tsar and minister of agriculture with extensive powers. The German Labor Front, (Deutsche Arbeitsfront – DAF) built on the ruins of the democratic unions under Robert Ley, a chronic alcoholic, had 25.3 million members by 1939. This gave Ley immense power, which he used to tackle questions of professional training, social problems, housing, and leisure-time activities. His empire thus infringed at many points on the competence of other ministries. Similarly, Fritz Todt was made responsible for building the highways and given special plenipotentiary powers that enabled him to tread on the toes of a number of ministers, principal among them the minister of transport. One of these was the founder of the Stahlhelm, Franz Seldte, a bone-idle creature who had been appointed minister of labor in 1933. When Goebbels suggested to Hitler that Ley should replace Seldte, on the grounds that although he was an appalling drunk he tended to get things done, Hitler refused point blank, arguing that Seldte could always be removed, whereas Ley was in a position of such power and influence that it would be extremely difficult to dislodge him. The situation was made even more absurd in that, as Ernst Jünger pointed out, under normal circumstances none of these magnates would have even been made a junior partner in a halfway decent firm.

No one accumulated so many offices as the intelligent, jovial, sadistic, morphine-addicted, and progressively deranged Göring. He was president of the Reichstag, Prussian minister of the interior, and Prussian minister president. He was a Reich minister without portfolio, air minister, minister responsible for hunting and the forests, commander-in-chief of the Luftwaffe, and commissar for raw materials and foreign exchange. When Hitler decided to push ahead with his autarchy plans in spite of the resistance of the central bank, the ministry of economics, and powerful voices in the private sector, he appointed Göring head of the Four Year Plan. As such he was a virtual dictator over all aspects of the economy.

Goebbels combined the office of minister of propaganda with that of Gauleiter of Berlin. Bernard Rust, the Gauleiter of Hanover and Brunswick, was also minister of technology and education, even though he had lost his job as a schoolteacher by sexually abusing one of his charges. He also suffered from a severe mental handicap as a result of a head wound received while serving as an infantry lieutenant during the war. Rust and Goebbels were the only Gauleiter who were also ministers.

Heinrich Himmler was both head of the SS and police chief for all of Germany. In October 1939 he was made "Reich Commissar for the Strengthening of the German Race [*Volkstums*]." As such he was responsible for the brutal deportation and murder of Jews and Poles, and the resettlement by pure-blooded Germans of the areas they had been forced to leave. This new office as a "Higher Instance of the Reich" was placed outside the law and kept secret from the regular civil service. Himmler became minister of the interior in 1943. He was given command over the reserve army in the following year.

Some were in positions of great power without holding state office. Julius Streicher, the grisly Gauleiter of Franconia, enjoyed Hitler's absolute and unconditional support for his rabidly pornographic and sadistic anti-Semitism. Baldo von Shirach, as head of the Hitler Youth (HJ) and later Reich Youth Leader, was another powerful figure, in spite of his widely rumored homosexuality and his endless struggles with Bernhard Rust.

Hitler was obsessed with architecture and had gigantomanic plans for rebuilding Berlin. When he felt that planning was not going ahead fast enough he appointed an ambitious young architect, Albert Speer, General Building Inspector for the Reich Capital, and vested him with plenipotentiary powers over building and traffic. Speer was appointed minister of munitions on Todt's death in an airplane crash in February 1942.

The traditional ministries continued to work as before, so that an impression of normalcy was created amid all this chaos. By 1937 the party had become a gigantic, bureaucratized apparatus with 700,000 well-paid employees. It nearly trebled in size during the war as the "golden pheasants," as these gold-braided officials were caustically called, found ingenious ways to avoid dying a hero's death for Führer and Fatherland.

Party officials down to the very lowest level had the means to make the lives of ordinary people miserable, and many took great delight in doing so. The party wards (*Ortsgruppen*) were obliged to provide certificates of good conduct for civil servants, for those who requested social assistance, and for students and apprentices. No business could be started without the sanction of the party. During the war it was the party that decided which workers were essential (*Unabkömmlichkeitsstellung*) and therefore exempted from military service. The block leader (*Blockleiter*) kept a close watch on the citizenry and extracted contributions from them for party membership, the National Socialist People's Welfare (Nationalsozialistische Volkswohlfahrt – NSV) as well as for "winter help" (*Winterhilfswerk*). These Nazi charitable organizations amounted to little more than state-sponsored mugging, and a large chunk of the proceeds went to build Goebbels' magnificent villa in Berlin. Money was also collected through "Casserole Sundays" whereby the proceeds of a modest one-course meal went to assist needy "racial comrades." During the war the *Blockleiter* issued ration cards. The opportunities for harassment were unlimited, and complaints were legion about these vile mini-Hitlers at the bottom of the Nazi midden.

The SS

The most spectacular change after 1934 was the rise of the SS to become the purest expression of National Socialism. Himmler began to build up his police empire in Bavaria, but the way ahead was blocked by Göring, who controlled the police in Prussia. There began a bitter personal rivalry between the two men with strong ideological overtones. Göring saw the police as an organ of the state. Himmler wanted a political police force that was completely free from any form of outside control and utterly devoted to the Führer.

Heinrich Himmler was an improbable leader of this new order of ideologically charged Aryan supermen. Born in 1900, he was a weedy and shy little man who, in spite of the permissive atmosphere of the Weimar Republic, did not lose his virginity until 1928. In gratitude for this act of mercy he promptly married his dreary Jezebel, temporarily retired from political life, and took up chicken farming. Although unsuccessful with the poultry, he channeled his agricultural expertise into an obsession with breeding and with race. His devotion to Hitler was unconditional.

The SS (Schutzstaffel – Guard Squad) was founded in 1923 under a slightly different name, and was reorganized in 1925. Himmler took over command of its 289 members in 1929 and set to work turning it into an elite formation. In 1931 he established the National Socialist Security Service (Sicherheitsdienst – SD) under the unrelentingly malevolent 25-year-old Reinhard Heydrich, a racial fanatic who had recently been dismissed from the navy for dishonorable conduct. Shortly after the March elections the first military formation was created, known as the SS-Leibstandarte Adolf Hitler under the command of Sepp Dietrich, a former butcher and bouncer whose coarseness was only partially concealed beneath a heavy layer of beer-swilling Bavarian joviality. After the SS victory over the SA in 1934, the first units of the SS-Verfügungstruppe (Emergency Troops) were formed, which were later to be reorganized into the Waffen-SS, the military wing. On June 20, 1934, the SS was made solely responsible for the concentration camps, which were guarded by the SS-Totenkopfverbände (Death's Head Units).

By the spring of 1934 Himmler had taken over the political police forces in all the German states with the exception of Prussia. Göring, who was looking for an ally in the interminable power-struggles that beset the Third Reich, decided to make his peace with Himmler and gave him control over the Prussian secret police, the Gestapo, in April 1934. Himmler was now in control of the secret police throughout the Reich and placed Heydrich in command. Heydrich was now head of the SD and the Gestapo, and thus of both the party and the state secret police forces. In 1936 the Gestapo was made independent of judicial and administrative control. Himmler was now given command over all the regular police forces in Germany and sported the pompous title of Reichsführer-SS and Chief of the German Police in the Reich Ministry of the Interior.

In a situation typical of the Third Reich, Himmler was thus subordinate to the minister of the interior in his capacity as state secretary in charge of the police, but as head of the SS he reported directly to Hitler. With immediate access to the Führer he could afford to ignore the minister of the interior, so that the entire police force was beyond state control. Himmler did not see fit to even have an office in the ministry of the interior.

He immediately began the reorganization of his all-encompassing empire. The police was divided into two sections. The Order Police (Ordnungspolizei), which dealt with minor offences, comprised the Safety Police (Schutzpolizei) and the Gendarmerie. It was

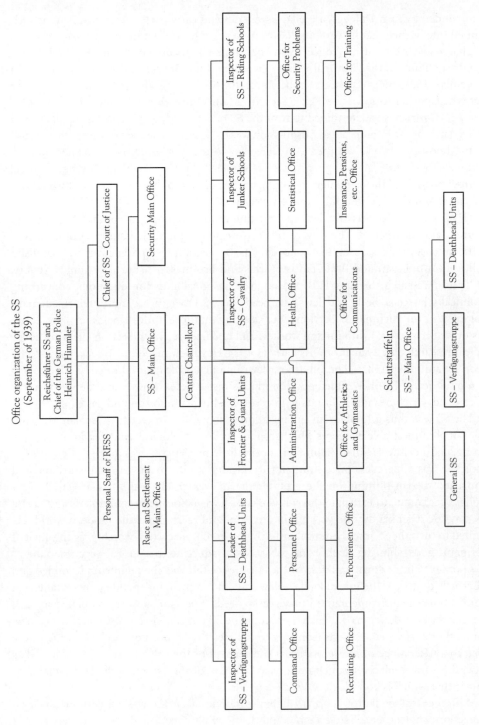

Office organization of the SS (September of 1939)

Reichsführer SS and Chief of the German Police Heinrich Himmler

Personal Staff of RFSS

Race and Settlement Main Office

Chief of SS – Court of Justice

SS – Main Office

Security Main Office

Central Chancellory

Inspector of SS – Verfügungstruppe

Leader of SS – Deathhead Units

Inspector of Frontier & Guard Units

Inspector of SS – Cavalry

Inspector of Junker Schools

Inspector of SS – Riding Schools

Command Office

Personnel Office

Administration Office

Health Office

Statistical Office

Office for Security Problems

Recruiting Office

Procurement Office

Office for Athletics and Gymnastics

Office for Communications

Insurance, Pensions, etc. Office

Office for Training

Schutzstaffeln

SS – Main Office

General SS

SS – Verfügungstruppe

SS – Deathhead Units

FIGURE I   Office organization of the SS (September 1939)

commanded by Kurt Daluege, a Freikorps veteran and early party member, a man of such limited intelligence that he was popularly known as "Dummi-Dummi." Heydrich was put in charge of the Security Police (Sicherheitspolizei), made up of the Political Police (Politische Polizei), the Criminal Police (Kripo), and the Border Police (Grenzpolizei). In September 1939 the party's secret police force, the Security Service (SD) was added to the Sicherheitspolizei to form the Reich Security Main Office (Reichssicherheitshauptamt – RSHA). Heydrich was determined to turn the SS into the "ideological storm-troopers and bodyguards of the Führer's ideas." Its mission was to "keep a close eye on the political health of the body politic [*Volkskörpers*], quickly diagnose any symptoms of sickness and to immediately destroy all malignant cells." Himmler told his men that they had to steel themselves to face "the campaign to annihilate Germany's subhuman enemies throughout the entire world" which would soon be unleashed.

Heydrich's RSHA was divided up into numerous divisions to combat the regime's enemies and ill-wishers. There were sections dealing with such issues as communism, Marxism and its allies, reactionary movements, opposition groups, legitimists, liberalism, political Catholicism and Protestantism, sects and Freemasons, abortion, homosexuality, and racial research. Section IVB 4 was given responsibility for questions concerning "Political Churches, Sects and Jews." Its head was SS-Obersturmbannführer (Lieutenant Colonel) Adolf Eichmann. Section IVC dealt with those unfortunates in "protective custody"; Section IVD with foreign workers and hostile foreigners; Section VII with "ideological research and evaluation." As early as 1934 Heydrich made his intentions perfectly clear. He announced that "The aim of our Jewish policy [*Judenpolitik*] must be the emigration of all Jews." He then added an even more sinister note: "Rowdy anti-Semitism must be rejected. One does not fight rats with revolvers, but with poison and gas."

The SS was thus a totalitarian organization designed to protect the German *Volk* and rid it of all undesirable elements whether biological or ideological, thus rendering it pure, strong, and healthy. Heinrich Himmler, a prim little bureaucrat, was a mass of contradictions. He was a merciless mass murderer who found a visit to Auschwitz disturbing, and who tried to ban hunting on the grounds that it was cruel to animals. He used every modern technique to extirpate the evil works of Jewish-Bolshevik subhumans and create his atavistic dystopia, but he was full of anxieties and fears about the modern world. He wanted to turn the SS into a mystical order, living in remote castles, worshiping the ancient Germanic gods, abjuring alcohol and tobacco, and adhering to a strictly vegetarian diet.

In order to hunt down and destroy the enemies of the *Volk* the regime undermined and eventually destroyed the rule of law. The law could not remain independent in a totalitarian regime, but was instrumentalized to serve its needs. Special courts were opened in each state, against the decisions of which there could be no appeal. There were a number of new criminal offenses, such as "Acts Contrary to the Healthy Feelings of the *Volk*," which were open to a wide range of interpretations. The concept of the rule of law was denounced as "liberal." It was replaced by such notions as "the will of the Führer is the highest law," or "law is that which is good for the *Volk*."

With the Gestapo law of February 1936 the individual citizen was left without any legal protection whatsoever. The Gestapo could define what constituted a political crime and the courts had no jurisdiction over its activities. If the Gestapo did not approve of the judgment of a court they would simply arrest the accused and fling the hapless individual into a concentration camp. Roland Freisler, state secretary in the ministry of justice and later president of the People's Court, a sadistic former Communist commissar, threatened to deliver any judge who handed down light sentences to this "police justice." The law became even more draconian during the war, with a host of new capital crimes such as "taking advantage of the state of war."

The Persecution of the Jews: The Second Phase

The persecution of the Jews provides the paradigmatic example of the lawlessness, ideological fervor, and ruthless brutality of the Nazi tyranny. It was also characteristic of the regime that it should be part of a process of gradual radicalization, and that it should be carried out in a somewhat haphazard way as various power-centers within this polycratic system vied with one another. The very notion of the "racial community" is by definition exclusive, and from the beginning the Nazis spoke of their determination to destroy everything that was deemed to be "alien to the community" (*Gemeinschaftsfremd*) in order to hasten the creation of a pure, healthy, and superior race. The National Socialist concept of law was based on the will of the Führer and on the "healthy instincts of the *Volk*," thus all who were outside the *Volk* were also outside the law. Although Jews were seen as the greatest danger to the *Volk*, other groups were also singled out for exclusion. These included the mentally. and physically handicapped, psychiatric patients, male homosexuals, Gypsies, habitual criminals, alcoholics, drug addicts, and other "asocials." This in spite of the fact that most of the leading figures in Nazi Germany fell under one or more of these categories, with the possible exception of the Gypsies. These latter were damned on three counts: they were deemed to be "asocial," "inferior," and "racially unacceptable" (*Fremdrassig*). In Berlin Goebbels declared Jews also to be "asocial," but it was difficult to charge this sinisterly powerful and deeply threatening people with "inferiority." Lesbians were only persecuted in Austria where, under paragraphs 129 and 130 of the criminal code, their proclivity was condemned as an "unnatural sexual offense." Unlike the Jews, homosexuals were not systematically hunted down and murdered. There was an extensive homosexual subculture in the Third Reich. In the early years many homosexuals were attracted by the markedly homoerotic aesthetic of the "Movement." A number of leading Nazis would have been in serious trouble had paragraph 175 of the criminal code been rigorously enforced.

Compulsory sterilization of the "hereditarily sick" began in July 1933. A total of about 360,000 such operations were performed. Initially those suffering from such disorders as schizophrenia, epilepsy, manic depression, and "idiocy" were singled out, but soon social rather than medical criteria were more often used. Habitual criminals, alcoholics, prostitutes, and tramps were also sterilized in this extensive program of "racial hygiene." The Nazis first decided what was "normal" and then set about destroying everything that did not match their criteria in a desperate attempt to build a new society.

Julius Streicher stepped up his personal anti-Semitic campaign in his obscene publication *Der Stürmer*, which was put on public display in showcases throughout Germany from the summer of 1934. He demanded that Jews should be denied all civil rights and that marriages between Jews and non-Jews should be forbidden. In a number of instances registrars refused to allow such marriages. Appeals to the courts against such illegal actions were mostly in vain.

In 1935 Jews were forbidden to serve in the armed forces. Attempts to create a special nationality law for Jews failed because there was no agreement on how to define who was Jewish. Should "half-Jews," those with only one Jewish parent, be treated the same as "full

Jews," both of whose parents were Jewish? Hitler demanded clarification so that further discrimination against Jews could be put in train and "mixed marriages" outlawed. There had been a revival of "rowdy anti-Semitism" in 1935 as a result of dissatisfaction among the ranks of the SA at the regime's refusal to carry out a National Socialist revolution. This had hurt Germany's reputation abroad and was bad for business. Consequently there was widespread disapproval of such lawlessness. Most important of all, Hitler could not tolerate such insubordination from this dissident rabble. Anti-Semitism had to become a government monopoly. To this end officials from Frick's ministry of the interior worked feverishly during the Nuremberg party rally, drafting the "Law for the Protection of German Blood and German Honor," otherwise known as the "Nuremberg laws."

The laws made marriage and sexual intercourse between Jews and non-Jews criminal offenses. Jews were forbidden to employ female non-Jews as domestic servants. Only those German citizens who had "German or similar blood" could enjoy full civil rights. The thorny question of the definition of who was a Jew was still left open. After lengthy debates it was decided that a Jew was someone who had "three grandparents who were racially full Jews," a practicing Jew with only two Jewish grandparents, or someone with two Jewish grandparents who was married to a Jew. Those who only had two Jewish grandparents were dubbed "Jewish half-breeds" but for the time being still retained their civil rights. Also in 1935 the "Law for the Protection of the Hereditary Health of the German People" made it impossible for people with hereditary diseases to marry.

Although the Nazis insisted that the Jews were a race, they were thus obliged to use religious criteria for deciding who was Jewish. A grotesque and tragic exception was in the Crimea where Otto Ohlendorf, a brilliant academic economist turned mass-murderer, ordered his Einsatzgruppe D to kill 6,000 Tartar Krimshaks, whom racial experts certified as Jewish. The Turkic Karaimen, who practiced a heterodox form of Judaism, were spared. But other factors played an important role in this bizarre episode. The Karaimen had fought with the Whites in the civil war, whereas the Krimshaks supported the Bolsheviks.

The Nuremberg laws were something of a compromise and did not satisfy the more radical anti-Semites in the party. Although the Nazis continued to insist that Jews were a race, the definition of who was Jewish was based solely on religious affiliation. It did not occur to the hordes of crackpot racial researchers and skull-measurers that there could be no other definition.

Jews had already been excluded from the civil service and the professions, and by 1938 60 percent of Jewish businesses had been confiscated. The once prosperous Jewish community was now poverty-stricken, subjected to never-ending humiliation and chicanery. In April 1938 Jews were forced to make a full disclosure of their assets. In July they were given special identity cards. In August they were obliged to add, in front of their own name, the first names Sarah or Israel, and their passports were stamped with a "J." German Jews thus lost their individual identity, a fact that was further underlined by the Nazi habit of referring to the Jews as "the Jew" (*der Jude*). In November Jewish children were forbidden to attend state schools.

The fresh wave of radical anti-Semitism in 1938 was particularly strong in Berlin, where Goebbels announced that the capital would soon be "uncontaminated by Jews" (*Judenrein*). He told a meeting of 300 policemen that "Law is not the order of the day, but harassment." In the summer, synagogues and Jewish shops were ransacked, with the appallingly corrupt police chief, Count Helldorf, proving most cooperative with the Nazi thugs. In addition to ordering his men to make life as unpleasant as possible for Berlin's Jews he amassed a vast fortune by confiscating the passports of rich Jews and selling them back for up to 250,000 marks apiece. Later he was to see the writing on the wall: he joined the conspirators of July 20, 1944, and was tortured and hanged.

The SD now decided upon a policy of "ordered harassment" (*geordneter Schikanieren*). This involved local bans on Jews from visiting public parks, theaters, cinemas, and the like. With very few exceptions Jews were banned from practicing medicine, the law, and similar professions. This placed the Nazis in a bind: they wanted the Jews to leave Germany, but they had reduced them to such a state of poverty that they were unable to bear the cost of emigration. Violence, as in Austria, now seemed an attractive alternative.

On November 7, 1938, Ernst von Rath, a diplomat serving in the German embassy in Paris, was assassinated by a young Polish-German Jew by the name of Herschel Grynszpan. It was ostensibly an act of revenge for the gross mistreatment of his parents by the Gestapo; but both men were prominent homosexuals, with Rath having contracted anal gonorrhea in China, so there may well have been another dimension to the crime. Grynszpan's parents were among the 75,000 Polish Jews expelled from Germany whom the Poles promptly refused citizenship. A few obtained passages to America; the majority were interned. Rath died on November 9, the anniversary of Hitler's putsch in Munich, where the party leadership was assembled for the yearly celebrations. A "spontaneous expression of popular outrage" was carefully organized by Goebbels on Hitler's orders, and the Gauleiter let loose the SA in a nationwide pogrom euphemistically known as Reichskristallnacht (The Night of Broken Glass). Goebbels eagerly seized this opportunity to organize this "spontaneous action" because he was in Hitler's bad books as a result of his stormy affair with the Czech starlet Lida Baarová and his mishandling of propaganda over the Sudeten German crisis.

It was a night of shattered lives and broken hopes in which some one hundred Jews were brutally murdered, several hundred synagogues burnt to the ground, and countless Jewish stores, apartments, and houses ransacked. Thirty thousand Jewish men were arrested and shipped off to concentration camps. That same night Himmler spoke in apocalyptic terms of a war to the death between Germans and Jews. The majority of Germans averted their gaze while disapproving of the SA rowdies who reminded them of the bad old days of Nazi violence. Somewhat sanctimoniously they expressed their horror at the material damage that had been done. Some were concerned about the reaction from abroad. Precious few helped the unfortunate victims of this outrage.

The 250,000 Jews who still remained in Germany were fined 1 billion marks for the 220 million marks of damages caused by SA rowdies, who claimed to have been provoked. Göring also seized the proceeds of all the insurance claims. Finally all remaining Jewish stores and businesses were "Aryanized," i.e. they were confiscated by the state and sold off to non-Jews at well below their market value. Throughout the Reich all Jews were now forbidden to go to the theater, the cinema or public swimming pools. They were thus excluded from German society and barely able to exist.

There were clear indications that even worse was to come. The official SS magazine, the *Schwarze Korps*, called for the "extinction" and the "total annihilation" of this "parasitic race." On November 12 Göring told a meeting of senior officials that in the event of a war Germany would "first of all settle accounts with the Jews." November 9, 1938 thus marked the end of the phase of pogrom anti-Semitism and the beginning of a bureaucratized and systematic approach to a "final solution." The Nazis had by now decided that "harassment" was not enough; more drastic measures were needed.

CHAPTER THIRTEEN
NAZI GERMANY
· 1933–1945 ·

CHAPTER CONTENTS

A History of Modern Germany: 1800 to the Present, Second Edition. Martin Kitchen.
© 2012 Martin Kitchen. Published 2012 by Blackwell Publishing Ltd.

Hitler had promised to put Germany back to work, and he was true to his word. Within four years unemployment had been virtually overcome. In some sectors there was even a shortage of skilled labor. He benefited from programs that had already been put in train by the Papen and Schleicher administrations, but the National Socialists set about them with exceptional energy and determination. Plans for a network of highways (*Autobahnen*) had already been laid, but Hitler gave this program top priority. He invested 1.7 billion marks in road-building, but this only provided employment for 38,000. The regime scored a major propaganda victory, but the impact on the unemployment figures was minimal. A further 1.3 billion was invested in housing and 1 billion in government buildings. But it was armaments that consumed a steadily increasing share of the budget. In September 1933 Erhard Milch, secretary of state in the air ministry and the first managing director of Lufthansa (then known as Deutsche Luft Hansa), called for 2,000 front-line aircraft, a weapon that was forbidden by the Treaty of Versailles. Milch was in a somewhat precarious position in that his father, and perhaps also his mother, were Jewish, but he was protected by Göring, who echoed the former mayor of Vienna, the impeccably anti-Semitic Karl Lueger, by saying: "I decide who is Jewish!" The army called for an increase to 300,000 men by 1937, three times the amount permitted by the treaty. This would mean that conscription would have to be introduced. The aim was the occupation of the demilitarized Rhineland, also by 1937. In October Hitler withdrew from the League of Nations as well as from the disarmament talks. In the following March Admiral Raeder, commander-in-chief of the navy, was given the go-ahead for a naval building program that was greatly in excess of the limits set in the treaty. Expenditure on weapons increased from 720 million marks in 1933 to 10.8 billion in 1937. In the six peacetime years the government spent the staggering sum of 90 billion marks on armaments. It was this sector that provided the hundreds of thousands of jobs that helped solve the unemployment crisis.

Expenditure on this scale could not be covered by revenue or offset by the six-month compulsory labor service, introduced in 1935. At first the regime used the same methods as Papen and Schleicher, who had financed their Keynesian schemes by bills of exchange. In May 1933 four large companies, Krupp, Siemens, the Gutehoffnungshütte, and Rheinmetall, pooled their resources to form the Metallurgical Research Association (Mefo) with a capital of 1 billion marks. The government paid for armaments orders with five-year promissory notes guaranteed by the government and known as Mefo Bills. The government then discounted them, so that the Mefo Bills acted as a form of currency. None of this solved the fundamental problem that the concentration on armaments meant declining exports and an increased demand for foreign currency in order to purchase raw materials. In June 1934 Hjalmar Schacht, president of the Reichsbank, made the shattering announcement that all payments in foreign currencies were to be suspended. The minister of economics, Kurt Schmidt, who argued for financial orthodoxy and business-led recovery based on increased consumer demand, which would have meant the end of the ambitious rearmament program, objected to this move by his arch-rival. Schmidt was called to Bayreuth, where Hitler was attending the Wagner festival. His resignation was announced. Schacht was appointed in his place.

German exports, which fell by 40 percent between 1932 and 1934, were also hurt by a number of other factors. Protectionism was worldwide in a misguided effort to overcome the depression. There was a strong reaction, particularly in the United States, against the anti-Semitic outrages in Germany, particularly the boycott of Jewish businesses in April 1933. The moratorium on the amortization of long-term foreign debt announced in June

1933 prompted President Roosevelt to call Schacht a "bastard." Schacht was determined to keep the mark overvalued as long as there was a heavy burden of debt. Hitler, who believed that devaluation would trigger inflation, gave him his full support. Foreign countries responded to Germany's aggressive debt diplomacy by clearing agreements designed as counter-measures.

Schacht, the "financial wizard," set about a de facto devaluation of the grossly overvalued mark by subsidizing exporters. They could buy $100 German bonds in New York, where they were valued at $50, and then sell them to the Reichsbank at par. Exports were further subsidized by a turnover tax on industry that seriously cut into profits. But these were only temporary measures. A fundamental restructuring of the economy was needed. The result was Schacht's "New Plan" of September 1934 designed to improve the balance of payments by further subsidizing exports through increased taxes on industry and by cutting back on imports. It was an extraordinary tightrope act, made possible by an improvement in world trade and by exceptional administrative skill. The Reichsbank's reserves seldom provided cover for more than the value of one week's worth of imports. Today the IMF considers less than six months' cover to be most imprudent.

"Autarchy" was now the magic formula. Darré, whose ministry had control over 25 percent of GDP, had his wings clipped by Schacht when exchange and price controls were imposed on agriculture. Darré responded with the rather feeble argument that Schacht was an agent of the Freemasons and echoed Hitler by insisting that conquest in the east was the only feasible solution to the agricultural crisis and the problem of self-sufficiency. Schacht's system, which amounted to state-subsidized dumping in order to get foreign exchange, obviously had severe limitations. As early as 1935 he realized that the rearmament program was getting out of hand and was leading to dangerous inflationary pressures. Devaluation was the obvious solution, but this would have meant the end of the rearmament program, which was totally unacceptable to Hitler.

The Nazis might have solved the problem of unemployment, but the condition of the working class was still wretched. A report in September 1935 showed that almost half of German workers earned less than 18 marks per week, which was below the poverty level. Nationwide the standard of living was still below that of 1928. Food prices were rising rapidly, placing further strain on low-income families.

Concentration on rearmament meant that Schacht's plan failed to overcome the acute shortage of foreign exchange, so that raw materials remained in short supply. The New Plan had introduced strict currency controls, but they did little to stem the persistent drain on reserves. The Four Year Plan of 1936, which was designed to overcome these problems, placed the economy under strict government control and aimed at the greatest possible degree of self-sufficiency. Synthetic rubber and substitute fuel were produced on a vast scale, while domestic ores were exploited in an attempt to lessen dependence on foreign suppliers. Huge investments were made in the production of synthetic oil by the hydrogenation of lignite at IG Farben's Leuna works. This brought windfall profits to the company, which had been unable to compete against a glut of oil resulting from the rapidly falling prices of crude. IG Farben's synthetic rubber (Buna) was also heavily subsidized. A thousand tons were produced in 1936, 22,000 in 1939, and 120,000 by 1943. The New Plan had an enormous bureaucracy that imposed rigorous price controls and organized compulsory cartels. Industrial profits rose substantially. They accumulated rather than being passed on to shareholders as dividends. Once again the party took the helm, with Göring as a virtual economic dictator setting the course. Two Gauleiters, Walter Köhler and Adolf

Wagner, were made responsible respectively for the allocation of raw materials and for setting prices. Senior officers in Göring's Luftwaffe were put in charge of oil and energy. Carl Krauch from IG Farben was given plenipotentiary powers over the chemical industries. He succeeded in keeping them firmly in private hands. Hjalmar Schacht, feeling that this approach to Germany's pressing economic problems was disastrous, ceased to be minister of economics in 1937. He left the Reichsbank two years later.

Just as Schacht had predicted, the autarchy program was an expensive failure. A vast amount of capital was invested in the Buna and Leuna works near Halle. The Reichswerke Hermann Göring's steel plant at Salzgitter was the largest in the world. But Germany was

PLATE 21   Göring and Hitler. © Bundesarchiv

still largely dependent on foreign supplies of rubber, oil, and ores. Domestic iron ore was of very inferior quality and was extremely expensive to mine and smelt, so that half of the iron ore requirement still had to be imported. Germany was also dependent on imports of manganese, chrome, and wolfram. It was still far from self-sufficient in foodstuffs.

Mefo Bills worth thousands of millions of marks fell due in 1938 and the government had recourse to highly dubious methods in order to foot the bill. Tax relief was offered in lieu of payment, banks were forced to buy government bonds, while the government dipped into savings accounts and insurance companies. By 1937 the central bank was no longer able to control the volume of money in circulation, so the government used the printing press to meet the cash shortage. Some relief was provided when Austria's gold and foreign exchange reserves were seized, but this was only temporary. Shortly after the *Anschluss* Hitler, realizing that he could not in the long run win an arms race against Britain, France, the United States, and possibly the Soviet Union, ordered the Wehrmacht to be ready for war in 1939.

German Society in the Third Reich

Although the regime was able to influence German society to an extent that bordered on the revolutionary, at first sight this transformation was scarcely noticeable. Much remained the same. Outwardly the economic system was substantially unchanged. Those radical National Socialists who demanded far-reaching anti-capitalist measures were silenced and had to make do with the destruction of "Jewish capitalism." The bourgeois elites in business and the professions were still largely self-recruiting. Yet there was now a host of new opportunities for advancement through the vast network of party organizations, the hypertrophic bureaucracy, and the rapidly expanding armed forces, criteria for selection in all of which had been drastically modified. Class barriers, already slightly more flexible in peacetime, were significantly lowered during the war.

The aristocracy, even though the vast majority loyally served the regime, with many famous names flocking to the SS, was despised by the party radicals as the degenerate remnant of a decadent past. After the attempt on Hitler's life on July 20, 1940, in which a number of aristocrats were implicated, 5,000 people were sentenced to death, a high percentage of whom were aristocrats. Hitler promised that once the war was over he would "mercilessly get rid" of the aristocracy. This provided the aristocracy with a useful alibi in the Federal Republic where, by styling themselves as staunch anti-Nazis and wholehearted supporters of Count Claus von Stauffenberg's assassination attempt, they were able to regain some of their lost prestige.

The middle class was also affected, most of all the hundreds of thousands of German Jews. They lost their jobs. Those who were not fortunate enough to emigrate suffered endless discrimination and humiliation. In the end they were murdered. There was scarcely a murmur of protest at this outrage. On the contrary, it was widely felt that this was a necessary correction against members of an assertive race who had jumped the queue and pushed their way into positions to which they did not belong. The disappearance of a Jewish business partner, professor, teacher, lawyer, or doctor opened up welcome opportunities for ambitious Aryan graduates. Similarly, there was nothing but a shrug of the shoulders when bourgeois Social Democrats were dismissed, many of them sent to concentration camps or forced to emigrate. The bourgeoisie thus assented to an end to the rule of law – the essential foundation of bourgeois society – with judges and state attorneys shamefully giving way to expressions of fanatically totalitarian "healthy racial feelings." A few bourgeois isolated themselves from the brown rabble in snobbish disdain, but the vast majority enthusiastically embraced the new ideology, even though in theory at least it threatened their status, their property as well as their cultural and educational preferences. The marketplace, formerly a free arena for individual action, came increasingly under state control. The *Bildungsbürgertum* had to accept the pseudo-science of "racial studies"; history and the social sciences were now based on "racial" criteria, as was the study of literature, art, and music. Among the fresh absurdities were "German physics," which claimed that relativity was a Jewish swindle, and "German mathematics," which dismissed Georg Cantor's set theory as "Jewish formalism." Captains of industry remained in control, but they had to meet the insatiable demands of the rearmament program, and competition from nationalized conglomerates such as the Hermann Göring Works.

This disagreeable interference with the free market was largely offset by the fact that the business elite pocketed a disproportionate share of the increased wealth created by the Nazis' reflationist policies. Although workers' wages failed to reach the 1928 level by 1939, GDP rose by 27 percent and entrepreneurs' real incomes rose by a staggering 120 percent. Upper management was still largely self-recruiting and exclusive: 86 percent of directors had university degrees, 68 percent had doctorates; only 10 percent had begun their careers on the shop floor. Fifty-three percent of top management came from the sons of entrepreneurs. There were very few recruits from the working class. Almost all were perfectly content with the new regime.

They had good reason to be so. The Social Democrats and Communists were banned. The unions had been destroyed and replaced by obediently subservient "works organizations" (NSBOs). Labor's share of national income was falling, while the real income of those in management positions was rising. The Wilhelmine ideal of the entrepreneur as "master in his own house" was perpetuated in the National Socialist ideology of the "works leader" (*Betriebsführer*). The armaments industry offered opportunities for generously subsidized research and development in addition to the prospect of healthy profits. Plunder from "Aryanization," the seizure and redistribution of Jewish property at bargain basement prices, was greatly appreciated. It was not until 1942, when Albert Speer was appointed minister of armaments, that the regime began to plant party members on boards of directors and thereby to influence decision-making. The only non-Jewish industrialist to fall foul of the regime was Fritz Thyssen, an early supporter who began to have seconds thoughts when confronted with the party's violent eradication of its critics from the right, its harassment of the Catholic Church, the pogrom of November 9, 1938, and most of all by Hitler's decision to go to war. He went into exile to Switzerland, was handed over to the Gestapo by the French in late 1940, and spent the rest of the war in various concentration camps. His industrial empire was absorbed by the Hermann Göring Works.

The *Bildungsbürgertum* fared less well. The 28,000 university-educated civil servants in the higher echelons of the bureaucracy lost status. Many were replaced by the new men from the National Socialist polycracy. Those who stayed in office had to toe the party line. With very few exceptions in the very top ranks, they were relatively poorly paid and their salaries never reached their 1928 level. They lost much of their competence to frame laws and were reduced to becoming the meek executants of the Führer's will. The SS empire formed an entirely new elite, but its officer corps was still preponderantly middle-class. One-third had university degrees and only 7.4 percent came from the working class. Fifteen percent of university professors and lecturers, including twenty-four Nobel Prize laureates, lost their jobs either because they were Jewish or for political reasons. Those that remained either submitted to or enthusiastically supported the regime. Many specialized in the new pseudo-disciplines such as "racial history,""eastern studies,""German physics," the "Jewish question,""racial biology," or "German sociology."

Class distinctions were reflected in significant disparities of income. Whereas during the Third Reich the average yearly wage of a worker was 1,375 marks, a doctor earned an average of 12,500 marks, a lawyer 10,850 marks, and a white-collar worker 2,727 marks. Comparative figures for Germany in 2006 are: a construction worker €25,792, a doctor €75,892, a lawyer €82,135, qualified office workers €41,138.

It is truly remarkable that, with the benefit of hindsight, we can see that a society that was rent apart, underwent a revolutionary change in attitudes and convictions, and was then totally destroyed, should re-emerge, at least partially, as a healthy democracy with a social structure intact, with the energy that the Nazis had unleashed now directed to positive goals. That this was possible is due to two main factors. The Third Reich lasted for only twelve years, six of which were in the extreme and exceptional conditions of total war. Secondly, deeply ingrained social structures cannot be radically changed in such a short space of time. They can be pulled, twisted, and pushed, but once the revolutionary pressure is released they snap back into place. The tectonic plates of the *longue durée* might have twitched a little, but they soon settled.

Labor

The regime's proclaimed intent was to produce both guns and butter, but armaments took precedence over consumer goods. By the summer of 1935 industrial production and employment were back at their 1928 levels and there was no longer any need to prime the pump. The problems that beset the economy were now almost solely due to excessive government expenditure on armaments. Thus in spite of the remarkable economic recovery between 1933 and 1939 life remained very austere. In 1938 meat consumption was still below the 1929 level and there was a shortage of quality consumer goods. The average German was happy to have a job, but there was an increasing number of complaints about food shortages and the paucity of the better things in life. Industrial wages did not reach their 1928 levels until 1941, and then largely because of long hours of overtime rather than increases in basic wages. In the summer of 1933 "trustees of labor" were appointed by the ministry of labor to determine wages, contracts, and working conditions. Since these officials were mostly recruited from management, they looked after the interests of the employers rather than those of the employees.

Robert Ley was obliged to purge the German Labor Front (DAF) of all those who hoped to create National Socialist unions and now concentrated on the educational programs and leisure-time activities run by "Strength Through Joy" (Kraft durch Freude – KdF). This vast organization, founded in November 1933 offered further education courses, theatrical performances, concerts, sports, holidays at home and abroad, and even cruises.

The DAF was thus rendered totally docile and workers no longer had any voice in management. In November 1933 Gustav Krupp agreed that businessmen should be included in the DAF. In the following year the DAF was reorganized with four "pillars": blue-collar workers, white-collar workers, industrialists. and small businessmen. It had

40,000 full-time staff, plus 1.3 million volunteers; 1.5 percent of workers' wages was deducted to cover costs. In 1935 the "leadership principle" (*Führerprinzip*) was applied in the business world. The "Works Führer" ruled supreme over the "Works Community." When members of various factory councils complained about this denial of all workers' rights, council members were no longer elected, but appointed by the trustees. Workers were now issued with "labor books," which drastically curtailed their freedom of movement from one place of employment to another. The concessions that had been made to labor during the Weimar Republic were all revoked.

Workers enjoyed full employment and were partially lulled by the endless repetition of the mantra "labor ennobles." Paid holidays were increased from three days a year to six, and in many cases to twelve or fifteen. Social services, especially for mothers and children were greatly improved. The DAF ensured that adequate canteens, toilets, and showers were installed in the workplace, that medical assistance was available, and that workers had access to sports facilities. By 1939, 10.3 million people had been on lengthy holidays sponsored by the KdF, and a further 54.6 million had been on shorter trips.

On the negative side wages were no longer determined by collective bargaining, but by the works leaders, who interpreted the wage scales set by the trustees. They had no unions or political parties to protect their interests, but the DAF gradually won the confidence of the majority of workers by ensuring very real improvements in working conditions and facilities. This is hardly remarkable. Workers had flocked to the NSDAP before 1933. The SPD steadily lost its working-class support, and the KPD was largely a party of the unemployed. Even before the Nazis came to power, there were considerably more workers in the Nazi NSBOs than there were in the Communist organizations on the factory floor, and membership in the Nazi cells doubled in February 1933. German workers were immensely proud of the regime's achievements both at home and abroad. Wages might still be low, but there was now full employment, job security, and greatly improved social services. When the Wehrmacht held a victory parade in Paris in June 1940, Hitler had triumphantly revised the decision of 1918 that Germany had been defeated in France. Unless people were directly affected there was virtually no objection to "stamping out" the handicapped and the asocial or the sterilization and castration of bearers of hereditary diseases. In fact many felt this to be a positive and long overdue achievement. Very few worried about the fate of the German Jews.

Hitler, Goebbels, Göring, and Ley never tired of singing the praises of the German worker. No doubt this was sheer hypocrisy, but it was in marked contrast to the hostile attitude towards labor manifested in the Wilhelmine empire and the Weimar Republic. Many workers were encouraged and flattered by such attention, which further increased their sense of self-esteem, already strengthened by the greater opportunities offered as industry was modernized and income disparities increased. German workers could also look down upon a vast army of prisoners of war, and foreign and slave laborers, all living in various degrees of depravation and squalor, thereby confirming the Nazis' crude racial stereotyping. These unfortunates at the bottom of the pile formed a new class of 8 million sub-proletarians.

Much has often been made of the astonishing number of protests and work stoppages in peacetime, but these were only brief interruptions, usually by unskilled workers complaining about low wages, or that they had been forced to live in barracks while working on the defensive emplacements on the West Wall. They were not organized, class-conscious protests against the system. Any such activity would have been instantly crushed. Severe punishments were meted out for breaches of discipline: one year's imprisonment for refusing to work overtime, two years for failing to turn up for work on two occasions, three for frequent unpunctuality. The ordinances of June 1938 and February 1939, which placed the economy on a war footing and removed the last vestiges of freedom of movement, were protested by carefully orchestrated slowdowns. The wage freeze, the canceling of overtime pay, and the reduction of holidays in the decree of September 4, 1939, caused such widespread discontent that the Nazi Party became genuinely concerned. With the victory over France these measures were rescinded and real wages increased by up to 23 percent. Hitler was absolutely determined to avoid a repetition of the social unrest of 1917/18, which he believed was the root cause of Germany's defeat. Soldiers' wives were given very generous allowances. Up until the end of 1944 consumer goods were still widely available and food supplies generous.

The Nazis destroyed the old working-class milieu, and encouraged individual initiative by means of piecework, special bonuses, steeply graded wage scales, and nationwide competitions in various trades and skills, thereby replacing a relatively homogenous class of working people – a proletariat – by the performance- and consumer-oriented workers, who were to realize their full potential in the Federal Republic.

Peasants

Although the Nazis intervened substantially in the industrial sector, their efforts in this respect pale in comparison with their attempts to restructure agriculture. The German peasants were proclaimed to be the unsullied source of Aryan blood. As such they were to be protected against the exigencies of a capitalist market economy and privileged as a new racial aristocracy named the National Corporation of Food Producers (Nährstand der Nation, or Reichsnährstand). It was an absurdly romantic and utopian vision that initially appealed to a peasantry that felt abandoned by the Weimar Republic and who had been among Hitler's most enthusiastic supporters on his way to power. The peasantry was the darling of the Nazi propagandists, the "biological kernel" of Germany's future greatness, where "blood and soil" were one. Susceptible to such flattery, they flocked to the Nazi cause; but once Hitler was in power they were treated in much the same way as industrial workers.

Hitler had little sympathy for this racist twaddle served up by Himmler and Darré, but he wanted Germany to be fully self-sufficient so that in a future war there would be no repetition of the appalling hunger of the First World War. The task was initially entrusted to Darré, a man of very modest ability, who was given the impressive title of Reich Peasants' Leader (Reichsbauernführer) in May 1933. In the following month he was appointed minister of food. This combination of party, state, and professional offices made him initially second only to Göring in the accumulation of power.

Gleichschaltung resulted in all of Germany's 17 million peasants joining the National Corporation of Food Producers, which rigorously controlled prices, production levels, and the marketing of all agricultural produce. It was a vast bureaucratic apparatus with autocratic "farmers' leaders" (*Bauernführer*) operating all the way down to the village level. These self-important officials were soon locked in battle with local Nazi party officials, who were anxious to defend their bailiwicks against all intruders. The Corporation had its own courts, which were empowered to fine farmers for violations of the complex code governing their every activity.

Plans for the future were so far-reaching as to border on the fantastic. The primary goal was to make Germany fully self-sufficient in foodstuffs. To this end smallholdings would have to disappear, their land absorbed by larger farms. Himmler, once a close associate of Walter Darré, by 1939 had become a bitter rival. Darré favored small-scale and sustainable farming, as is favored by today's ecological movement, whereas Himmler thought on a far larger scale. He planned for the "Aryanization" of Poland and the western parts of the Soviet Union so as to provide "living space" for millions of ethnic Germans (*Reichsdeutsche*). The concept of "living space" (*Lebensraum*) had been cooked up by the geographer Friedrich Ratzel, the founder of the dubious discipline of "biogeography," in an essay published in 1901. It was a crudely Social Darwinist call for territorial expansion as a mark of a nation's vitality. His ideas were refined by his Swedish pupil Rudolf Kjellén, who coined the concept of "geopolitics." This was taken up by Karl Haushofer, whose radical imperialist views profoundly influenced Hitler, whom he first met in 1921. Hitler's vision of a "war of anni-hilation to create living space" (*Lebensraumschaffender Vernichtungskrieg*) stemmed from these noxious notions. It became a nightmarish reality when enthusiastically espoused by Himmler and enforced by the Wehrmacht. As the Greater German Reich expanded east-wards 4.5 million German peasants were to be resettled, whom Himmler saw as a mixture of Teutonic knights and the pioneers of the American West, with the Volga as Germany's Mississippi. It was intended that between 30 and 45 million Slavs, considered to be an unnecessary strain on limited food resources, should be murdered. Fourteen million "racially valuable" Ukrainians and Balts would become the helots of these Aryan "armed farmers" (*Wehrbauern*). It was gigantomanic undertaking that beggars the imagination, which the Nazis in their typically idealistic manner thought could be achieved through a mental reconstitution of reality, rather than a changed reality.

Darré's more modest ideal was the "hereditary farm" (*Erbhof*). Peasants who could show that they stemmed from generations of "German or racially similar blood" were given entailed farms of between 75 and 125 hectares (185–312 acres). Inherited by the eldest son, they could not be bought or sold. They remained under stringent government control. Twenty-two percent of farms, comprising 37 percent of all agricultural land, were thus transformed into quasi-feudal estates. This amounted to a new form of serfdom in that elder sons were tied to the soil. Only those who could prove their racial purity, who were known to be honorable men as well as efficient farmers, could be addressed as "farmers" (*Bauern*), whereas those who did not meet these rigorous criteria were somewhat condescendingly labeled "agriculturalists" (*Landwirte*). Reactions to these measures were mixed. It put an end to farms being split up through inheritance into a series of uneco-nomical small units, but it meant that a great deal of agricultural land would be taken off the market. The Reich Food Department rigorously controlled the agricultural market, ignored the equation of supply and demand, tied up the peasantry in red tape, and submit-ted them to endless bureaucratic meddling. None of this did anything to stop the move-ment away from the land, and the number of those employed in agriculture dropped by about half a million between 1933 and 1939. Peasants were given a helping hand by the DAF, the Hitler Youth, and the League of German Maidens (Bund Deutscher Mädel – BDM), but this was never enough to offset the chronic lack of manpower. That agricultural production increased between 1933 and 1939 was almost solely due to the intensification of human labor. Some relief came when foreign labor and prisoners of war were put to work on the land, but that put an end to "blood and soil." Foreign blood now tilled German soil.

A still powerful lobby of landowners managed to ensure that many large estates were exempted from Darré's land reform. A further constraint was that the younger sons of hereditary farmers had to be given compensation for being excluded from their inheritance. Poor crops in 1934 and 1935, coupled with the incompetence of Darré's grossly inflated bureaucracy, resulted in serious shortages. Fats had to be rationed in 1935. The situation was somewhat improved when a trade agreement with Poland was signed later in the year that enabled rationing to be lifted. But this provided only temporary relief. By 1936 there were once again serious shortages. Darré had shown himself to be grossly incompetent and was obliged in 1942 to hand over his authority to his secretary of state, Herbert Backe, an odious "blood and soil" ideologue, but a man better versed in the infighting that prevailed in Nazi Germany. Darré's empire was absorbed by Göring's Four Year Plan, for which Backe was also an emissary. Backe was formally appointed minister of food in Darré's place in 1944. His principal contribution was the development of the "Backe Plan" for the death by starvation of tens of millions of Soviet citizens, Jews, and psychiatric patients, a ghastly project that mercifully was never fully realized. His career ended with his suicide in his prison cell in Nuremberg.

Darré hoped that by modernizing agriculture, particularly by greatly increasing the amount of machinery, he could create a new rural society that could overcome the gulf between urban and rural and thus create a genuine "racial community." Since the hereditary farms could not be sold, and others only by special permission, agricultural land could not be used as collateral for a loan. As a result there was a desperate shortage of capital that made modernization virtually impossible.

Darré made extravagant promises that farmland would be made available for those peasants who had lost their land to hereditary farms, as well as for the younger sons of hereditary farmers, but very little was achieved. Of the 7 million hectares selected for agricultural consolidation only 70,000 were converted. Although 536,000 hectares of barren land were brought under cultivation, 650,000 hectares of agricultural land were lost for building motorways and for training grounds for the military. During the Weimar Republic 57,300 new farm jobs had been opened up, but Nazi Germany only created 22,000 new positions, while the flight from the land continued unabated.

Thus in spite of all these efforts the results were somewhat disappointing. Self-sufficiency was never achieved, although Germany managed to reduce its dependence on imported foodstuffs. Prices rose sharply, causing widespread discontent. Coffee and citrus fruits were rationed in early 1939. White bread was only obtainable with a medical certificate. Very few workers in Germany's industrial heartland could afford meat more than once a week. Visitors from Britain were appalled at such austerity, a stark reminder that Germany was a relatively poor country. Taking the average per capita GDP between 1924 and 1935 in the United States as 100, the figure in Britain was 89, but in Germany a mere 63. In contemporary terms, Germany was roughly at the level of development of Iran or Tunisia. Wages in the agricultural sector were far lower than in industry, with rates based on a twelve-hour rather than an eight-hour working day. In spite of the determination to amalgamate smallholdings into large farms, the majority of German peasants lived in poverty, unable to provide sufficient income for a family without an outside job. Many small farms had neither running water nor electricity. Very few could afford a tractor.

All the efforts to overcome the yawning gap between town and country – turning ignorant peasants into valuable "racial comrades," well-trained and efficient farmers of impeccable racial stock, working on medium-sized and productive farms – came to nothing.

The most exotic of these plans was cooked up under the aegis of Konrad Meyer, an expert on regional planning and a prime example of a highly efficient and knowledgeable technocrat who was also a fanatical National Socialist, a murderous racist, and a "blood and soil" fanatic. He was the mastermind behind "General Plan East," the first draft of which dates from February 1940, when Meyer was working for the Reich Security Main Office (RSHA). He then was appointed head of planning in Himmler's Reich Commissariat for the Strengthening of the German Race (Reichskommissar für die Festigung deutschen Volkstums), where the final version was produced in 1941. It envisioned the "evacuation" of all Jews from Poland, along with 3.4 million Poles, replacing them by 3,345,000 German peasants, most of whom would come from the "Old Reich," as there were not enough pure-blooded Germans in the east. Meyer then called for the "transfer," a euphemism for murder, of 34 million Slavs to make room for these settlers and to ensure that there was more than enough food to go around. He also had ambitious plans for the "Old Reich," which involved abolishing all smallholdings in a massive land reform scheme, as well as a grisly scheme for the "racial improvement" of the rural population. It was a typically National Socialist plan that combined a perfectly justifiable desire to improve agricultural productivity by eliminating farms that were no longer viable, with perverted racist eugenics, an aggressive war, plunder, and mass murder. Meyer then worked as chief planner in Herbert Backe's agricultural ministry, where he was responsible for settlements and land reform in eastern Europe. After the war, ably supported by his defense lawyer Kurt Behling and helped by witnesses willing to commit perjury, he lied his way out of charges of crimes against humanity. He was later appointed professor for regional planning in Hanover, where he continued his distinguished career.

Small Business

Extravagant promises had also been made to small business. It was seen by party radicals as the backbone of society, unlike the selfishly greedy "plutocrats" and "capitalists" in industry and banking. Here too hopes were dashed. The National Socialists had pledged to protect small businesses against the cartels and monopolies, the insatiable bankers who held them in the "thralldom of interest," and the stranglehold of the big department stores, thus helping the struggling butchers, bakers and candlestick makers get back on their feet. At first it seemed that the Nazis would be as good as their word. A boycott was imposed on Jewish department stores. The opening of new branches of such stores was forbidden, while stringent restrictions were imposed on the founding of new enterprises. Life was made so hard for the chain stores that within a few months some were threatened with bankruptcy. By June 1933 the Hertie chain was on the brink of collapse, which would have meant 14,000 employees losing their jobs. The government, with its commitment to full employment, could not possibly afford to allow this to happen. Hitler reluctantly agreed to bale out the company.

The decision to rescue Hertie marked a critical change in policy towards what was called the "old middle class," which was tied in to the offensive against the radicals in the SA. Their interests were also furthered by the National Socialist Commercial Middle-Class Fighting Group (NS-Kampfbund für den Gewerblicher Mittelstand) under Adrian von Renteln, who was one of the key figures in organizing the boycott of Jewish stores. When the boycott was called off Renteln was reined in and the Fighting Group was absorbed by the DAF, thus rendering it totally innocuous. Renteln was bought off by being appointed head of the National Socialist Chambers of Commerce, in addition to a number of other offices that he held. In 1941 he was made general commissar in Lithuania. Some 200,000 Jews were murdered on his watch by Dr. Franz Walter Stahlecker's Einsatzgruppe A.

In fact the number of small businesses declined sharply. Many were simply closed down as the economy came under ever closer state control, a process that was stepped up markedly in the latter stages of the war. Others were starved of labor. The department stores were obliged to pay higher taxes, but their share of the market increased. Taxes were lowered in 1940. Competition from Jewish businesses was savagely ended, and many small businessmen joined the unseemly scramble to snap up Jewish property on the cheap. But even this windfall did not offset the overall losses. By the outbreak of the war 180,000 small enterprises and workshops had been closed down in the interests of rationalization and modernization. Hitler's most enthusiastic initial supporters thus paid a heavy price for the forced rearmament program.

Women

National Socialist policies towards women were also profoundly contradictory. The Third Reich was not quite the misogynist hell that some feminist historians have painted, but it was also no paradise. Women were to serve the Führer and *Volk* by raising large numbers of children, and tending the family home rather than going out to work. On the other hand, the increasing shortage of labor, particularly during the war, meant that opportunities became available to break out of the stereotypical mold.

For many women Nazi Germany was sheer hell. Jewish women suffered unimaginable horrors. Women who were unfortunate enough to fall into the hands of the eugenicists were submitted to shattering humiliation. The wives, sisters, and daughters of political prisoners were harshly punished for crimes committed by male members of the family. Women were excluded from political power, were underpaid, and were denied access to birth control, unless they were Jews or other such undesirables. Abortions, which averaged 600,000 annually during the Weimar Republic, were made illegal and ferociously punished if the mother was an "Aryan." Nevertheless, the lot of most women improved considerably. Their husbands had steady jobs, real wages, although still below the level of 1928, were steadily rising, and the future looked promising. Married couples were given a low-interest loan of 1,000 marks, on condition that the husband and wife were eugenically acceptable and that the wife stayed at home. A quarter of this loan was written off with each child born. Generous tax relief was provided for children, and child allowances were paid with the third child, with payments coming from the brimming unemployment insurance fund. Medical services for women were greatly improved. By 1944, 5 million women had visited the new maternity schools, while 10 million had consulted specialized women's advice centers. By 1941 there were 15,000 childcare centers run by the Mother and Child Charity (Hilfswerk Mutter und Kind, often shortened to Muki). Working women were given six weeks' fully paid maternity leave, both before and after birth. This generous allowance was unequaled anywhere. Free holidays were offered to women and children. Generous provisions were made for unmarried mothers, provided of course that they were of sound racial stock and were not carriers of a genetically determined disease.

Women, appreciative of these measures, were enthusiastic supporters of the regime, but in spite of the resolute efforts of the natalists there was a steady increase in illegal abortions and the birth rate never reached the level of the early 1920s. It increased from 14.7 per thousand in 1932 to 18.6 per thousand in 1936, but this was the result of improvements in the economy rather than ideological pressure.

In spite of all these efforts to help women there were many who were sharply critical of the regime's narrowly patriarchal policies. As Paula Müller-Ortfried, president of Protestant Ladies Aid, bitterly remarked in 1933: "Nowadays one talks an awful lot about the German *Volk*, but one really means German men." The National Socialist ideal was for women to be confined to their homes as dutiful wives and mothers of racially pure children, in the interests of eugenics, racial politics, and preparation for war. The Führer called upon women to provide him with the racially sound human capital he needed to achieve his ambitious goals. To this end Mother's Day, an American celebration that had been introduced to Germany during the Weimar Republic thanks to energetic lobbying by florists, was celebrated with great pomp, ceremony, and sentimentality as the annual celebration of the Nazi fertility cult. In 1934 it was made an official holiday, held on the third Sunday in May. Further to encourage fecundity, Hitler instituted the German Mother's Honor Medal in December 1938. There were three levels: bronze for women with four to five children, silver for those with six to seven, and gold for those with eight or more. The parents had to be of "German blood" and "sound heredity." The mother had to be "genetically healthy," "decent," and "morally irreproachable." Only live births counted. The medals were first awarded on Mother's Day 1939 to 3 million women by the local Nazi party leader, attended by uniformed representatives of the League of German Maidens. The award could be withdrawn were "racial ideological deficiency" detected – a nebulous and flexible misdemeanor against which there was no appeal. The medal was soon sarcastically known as Mother's Service Cross and was the object of much ribaldry. Motherhood was no longer seen as a private affair, but as a public service to improve the racial stock in order to build a genuine "racial community." A new law on marriage and divorce in 1938 further reduced women's legal rights.

The number of women workers increased sharply, particularly in low-paid and unskilled positions, and this in spite of generous loans offered to married women who left the workforce. In agriculture 65 percent of workers were female. Things were very different at the top of social scale. Women with university degrees were forced to quit their jobs, and strict limits were imposed on the number of women admitted to institutions of higher learning. In 1933 there had been 20,000 female university students, but by 1939 their number had fallen to 5,500. Married women were dismissed from the civil service. They were forbidden to practice law or medicine and were barred from senior teaching positions. In 1936 they were no longer called for jury duty on the grounds that they were constitutively "unable to think logically or reason objectively."

The regime soon found itself in an awkward quandary. They wanted women to stay at home and breed, but at the same time with the increasing shortage of labor they were desperately needed in the workforce. By 1937 women no longer had to give up their job to qualify for the 1,000-mark marriage loan. They were urgently needed to service a mushrooming bureaucracy as well as the extensive social and medical services provided by the Nazi welfare state. All this had a liberating effect. Women saw new opportunities opening up for them, felt that they were making a valuable contribution to society, and were grateful that their efforts were appreciated, however grudgingly.

The persistent myth that women in Nazi Germany, freed by a pagan regime from any obligations to the *Kirche* (church), although still obliged to worship the Führer and take part in cultic celebrations, were chained to *Kinder* (children) and *Küche* (kitchen) can be summarily dismissed. The "thee Ks," sometimes increased to four with the inclusion of *Kleider* (clothes), was an ironic expression adopted by German feminists at the turn of the century that no longer applied. By 1936 there were 600,000 more working women than there had been in 1933. By 1939 just over half of German women between the ages of 15 and 60 were in regular employment. By contrast the figure in the Britain was 45 percent, and in the US 25 percent.

Hitler repeatedly resisted attempts to force women to work during the war in part because of his highly conventional views on women's role, but also because he feared that it would have an adverse effect on morale, leading to unrest similar to that in 1918. He refused to allow women's wages to rise to the level of those of men, and soldiers' wives were given remarkably generous allowances to encourage them to stay at home and look after their children. But none of this stopped women from gradually taking on jobs that previously had been a male preserve. Female bus conductors and readers of gas and electric meters became a commonplace and they were paid the same wages as their male counterparts. The chronic shortage of doctors meant that women had to be admitted to the medical schools. In 1933 only 6.5 percent of physicians were women; by 1944 the figure had risen to 17 percent. Still faced with a chronic labor shortage, Hitler finally gave way in 1943 and 900,000 women were forced to work, the vast majority of whom came from the deprived classes. For all the talk of the "racial community," women higher up the social scale did not have to dirty their hands with manual labor and enjoyed lives of fashionable ease. Germany thus remained a two-class society in spite of all the exigencies of total war. With millions of men at the front, women had to take on a whole host of new responsibilities and with them came an increased sense of autonomy. They ran the family firm, looked after the farm, stood behind the counter, and provided a host of services for the mounting tide of refugees and those left homeless due the devastating bombing raids.

There were 3.3 million members of the National Socialist Women's Association (Nationalsozialistischen Frauenschaft – NSF) led by the formidable Gertrud Scholtz-Klink, a slender, blonde, blue-eyed mother of eleven children, six of whom were stepchildren from her third husband. She also was the head of the German Women's League (Deutsches Frauenwerk – DFW) with some 4.7 million members. In addition she was head of the women's section of the DAF. She was thus the most powerful woman in the Third Reich, but she was caught in the glaring contradiction between her vision of German women as submissive wives, mothers, and housewives, and their role as party activists in the NSF and DFW. Scholtz-Klink was unable to find a solution to this fundamental discrepancy and her remark that the wooden spoon was as powerful a weapon as the machine-gun was somewhat unconvincing. She was further troubled by the contradiction between her own prudish sexual morality and the racial theories of the party that made no distinction between legitimate and illegitimate motherhood. Although well versed in political infighting, she was unable to realize her anti-modernist revolution. Hitler had no time for plaited hair and frumpish outfits à la Scholtz-Klink, or for the uniformed maidens of the BDM. He decorated his Munich apartment with photographs of glamorous film stars and alluring dancers. He had no time for worrying about how to reconcile the National Socialist ideology of women as apolitical nurturers of the master race with the desire to mobilize them for political ends.

Women were subjected to a great deal of ideological harassment and blatant discrimination in a male-dominated and misogynist society, but they also made great gains during the Third Reich, thanks to generous social policies as well as to the opportunities that perforce opened up to them as a result of desperate shortage in the workforce. Gertrud Scholtz-Klink might denounce the women's movement as a "symbol of decay," Hitler dismiss it as a product of the Jewish intellect bent on the systematic destruction of the Aryan race, and Goebbels proclaim that women were being removed from public life in order to restore their essential dignity, but they were powerless against the pressures exerted by a society stretched to the limit. In spite of fierce political resistance, the exigencies of a terrible war were such that women gained a degree of independence that was to fuel the demand for further emancipation in the post-war years.

National Socialism and Modernity

Nazi Germany was so irredeemably awful that it took many years before serious scholars could ask the question whether there was anything positive about it. In 1965 the sociologist Ralf Dahrendorf presented the startling thesis that the twelve years of Nazi dictatorship had provided the impetus for a surprising degree of modernization. Two years later David Schoenbaum went one stage further by claiming that here had been a "brown revolution," resulting in a fundamental change of mental and social structures. These ideas were either rejected or ignored by historians for at least twenty years, to be revisited when a rather unfruitful and agitated debate began about modernization. This soon got bogged down in a theoretical muddle, caused by methodological inadequacies and the sheer impossibility of applying a theory designed to reveal long-term trends to a period of a mere twelve years.

Some questioned whether it was possible to talk meaningfully of a "society" when for half the time one-fifth of the population was at war and one-tenth were virtually slaves. Millions of "racial Germans" in the east were uprooted and resettled in the "Great German Reich." Eighteen million served in the armed forces from Narvik to North Africa, from Brest to Baku. The National Socialists did what they could to destroy the familiar class structure with their ideology of the "racial community" in which class divisions were to be replaced by racial discrimination, with the Aryans offered equal opportunities, all dutifully serving the common cause under a charismatic leader. It was a system that encouraged maximum effort and rewarded achievement, but all for murderous and ultimately self-destructive ends. The end results were surprisingly modest.

The basic question is whether the Third Reich helped to further, retard, or even reverse the process of modernization. Was this a case of what Jürgen Habermas has called a "radically uprooting modernization" that reversed the trend towards the creation of symmetrical relationships between free and equal citizens? How much of what happened was by accident, how much by design? The answers can only be found if these twelve fateful years are seen within the context of the Weimar Republic and post-war Germany and not taken in isolation, as a hideous historical accident or an abrupt break with the past. The problem is also compounded by the Janus face of modernization. The horrors of total war, industrialized mass murder, the misuse of science, a grossly inflated bureaucracy, and ubiquitous propagandistic indoctrination are all products of modernization. Furthermore, the very concept of modernization is normative and some would argue that it is manifest in various different forms.

Social mobility and relative equality of opportunity are hallmarks of a modern society. Nazi racial policy allowed little room for this democratic notion. The challenges of the modern were to be met by racial selection, not by a meritocracy open to all. Only the Aryan "racial comrade" could move up the social scale by political selection into the upper ranks of the party, or within the swollen bureaucracy and the rapidly expanding military. One of the most remarkable achievements of the Nazi regime was that, in spite of glaring evidence to the contrary, it somehow managed to create the illusion that this was a new society in which class divisions had been largely overcome and that equal opportunities were there for all with a will to succeed. This phenomenon was almost solely due to the effects of Hitler's charismatic leadership rather than to any fundamental change in the structure of society. The Nazis with their ideology of the "racial community" played skillfully on widespread yearnings for the loosening of traditional social restrictions and for greater social mobility. They made much of the phoney egalitarianism of "Casserole Sundays," held every first Sunday in the months from October to March, when stews were served that cost less than 50 pfennigs per person. The difference between that and the cost of a normal Sunday meal had to be handed over to the Nazi charitable organization Winter Help (Winterhilfswerk – WHW). This practice was described as "German socialism in action." Pictures of Hitler and Goebbels eating the same humble fare as a simple "racial comrade" were designed to drive the point home. They put as many people as possible into uniforms and held frequent mass rallies, while the persecution of minorities served further the sense of community and belonging. The remarkable social policies of the DAF and the KdF did much to improve the lot of the working class and smoothed, but did not fully overcome, the distinctions between blue-collar and white-collar workers.

For those safely within the "racial community" life was indeed better than it had been under the Weimar Republic. There was soon full employment, in part because the host of new party and state organizations provided employed for 2 million people, but mainly because of the gargantuan armaments program. The social services were greatly improved. Germany was on the move and had regained its self-esteem. But there was much that seemed to hark back to an earlier age. The neo-feudalism of Darré's "hereditary farms" could not be reconciled with modernity or any feeling of equality; nor could the godlike status of an omniscient and all-powerful Führer, not to mention the atavistic mumbojumbo of Himmler's SS. Hitler's close comrades, of whom Göring was an increasingly grotesque example, living in splendor and enjoying exceptional powers within a polycratic state, were a startling reminder that this was not an egalitarian society.

Hitler as a rudimentarily educated autodidact had an intense loathing of what he was pleased to called "hook-nosed intellectualism." Intelligence was for him an empty and sterile concept, whereas "all truth comes from belief." He was fond of saying that "feelings must push thinking aside." Words such as "intelligence," "system," and "objectivity" were banned from his vocabulary. With such an attitude it is hardly surprising that there was a dramatic reverse to the process of modernization in the field of education, which served to reinforce class distinctions. Fees for state schools were increased by 30 percent in 1935. Only families with three or more children were given free education beyond the basic level. The number of young adults entering university was reduced, from 13,000 matriculations in 1933 to 7,303 in 1939, while the social composition of the student body remained virtually unchanged. The number of university students thus sank from 121,000 in 1933 to 56,000 in 1939. The percentage of women university students fell from 15.4 to 11.6. In technical colleges the drop was even greater: from 4.6 to 1.9 percent. There were very few scholarships available for working-class students, so that their share of the student population fell from 3.9 to 3.2 percent, and that for those from farming backgrounds from 7 to 5 percent. Universities had to cut back because one-third of the teaching staff had been purged, either because they were Jewish or because they were politically undesirable. The damage done to German universities was irreparable, the gain to Germany's future adversaries incalculable. There was a marked decrease in the number of applicants for university teaching posts. Virtually none came from the working class.

The Nazis, with their profound dislike and distrust of intellectuals, were little concerned about the disastrous decline of the universities, while the vast majority of professors shamefully toed the party line, even though they were under no pressure to do so. Vital areas of research were ignored, while effort was wasted on such absurd pursuits as "racial research," or the hunt for the Holy Grail or Atlantis. The theory of relativity was condemned as being "Jewish," while two Nobel Prize laureates, Philipp Lenard (1905) and Johannes Stark (1919) asserted that time and space were absolutes. Another Nobel Prize winner, Werner Heisenberg (1932), was condemned as a "white Jew" and only survived because he had been Himmler's classmate at high school. His mother asked the Reichsführer's mother to leave him alone. Frau Himmler passed on the message and Himmler, as a dutiful son, made a generous exception for Germany's greatest physicist in spite of the "Jewish" overtones of the uncertainty principle. Doctors, badly needed for public health, set about the forcible sterilization of 360,000 women and the castration of 20,000 men whom they deemed to be genetically inferior. They measured skulls, pickled brains, and conducted sadistic research on live subjects, thus perverting medical science in the pursuit of irrational ends.

In spite of all these horrors and officially sponsored nonsense, much good work was done by German scientists. Werner Heisenberg, Max von Laue (Nobel Prize 1914), and Max Planck (Nobel Prize 1919) still managed to uphold traditional scientific values. Among the outstanding achievements of German scientists during the Third Reich were the discovery of sulfa drugs, the establishment of the link between smoking and cancer, and research into the serious health hazards presented by asbestos, certain types of food coloring, pesticides, and alcohol. Much of this important work was ignored outside Germany, partly because it ran up against powerful lobbies, but also because it could easily be dismissed as "Nazi science."

The attempt to create National Socialist elite schools, which began in 1933 with the building of the first National Socialist Political Educational Establishment (Nationalpolitischen Erziehungsanstalten, known as Napolas), was not a success. The idea was to train a carefully selected elite of impeccable racial purity for the SS and SA. Selection was based almost entirely on racial and athletic criteria. Intellect played virtually no role. In 1936 the minister of education, Bernhard Rust, handed over control of the Napolas to the head of the SS Main Office, August Heissmeyer, who in 1940 became Gertrud Scholz-Klink's third husband. He went on to become SS and police chief in Berlin and Brandenburg, succeeded Theodor Eicke as head of the concentration camps, and commanded the SS Totenkopf Division. After the war this distinguished Nazi criminal spent a short spell in prison before working for Coca-Cola. A hundred Napolas were planned, but only fifteen were built in peacetime. Thirty more were built during the war, two in Holland and one in Belgium. By this time they were little more than cadet schools for the Wehrmacht and SS. Pupils spent much of their time manning anti-aircraft guns and were hastily bundled off into the armed forces.

The first Adolf Hitler School was opened in 1937, followed by ten more. Like the Napolas they were boarding schools. The only real difference was that they were under the control of the youth minister, Baldur von Schirach, and Robert Ley's DAF. The Napolas and the Adolf Hitler Schools accepted a relatively high percentage of students from poorer families, but there were too few of them to have a significant statistical impact on the degree of social mobility. In 1938 the party's chief ideologue, Alfred Rosenberg, called for the creation of National Socialist universities, to be called "order castles" (*Ordensburgen*), but only three were built. They were a total failure. Forty percent of the places were left unfilled, students were barely qualified, the instruction was of an abysmal standard, and the majority of graduates found cushy administrative positions far from the front.

The Nazi Party offered by far the best opportunities for social advancement. The vast majority of members were from the working class, the peasantry, clerical workers, small businessmen, and artisans. Like the Communists, it was a very youthful party. Even as late as 1935, by which time many opportunists, particularly civil servants, had joined, 65 percent of party members were below the age of 40. The number of "senior officials," from the Gauleiter down to block leader (Blockwart) increased from 700,000 in 1937 to 2 million by 1943, thus offering plenty of opportunities for those of lowlier birth to throw their unaccustomed weight around and make the lives of their "racial comrades" thoroughly miserable. But mobility within this cadre was strictly limited, with the upper echelons restricted to "old warriors," many of whom had been party members before 1925. They jealously guarded their exalted positions, warded off any attempt by the younger generation to usurp their powers, and could rely on Hitler's virtually unconditional support and loyalty. He overlooked astonishing instances of ineptitude, indolence, and downright criminality among his satraps. Very few fell by the wayside. Darré was dismissed in 1942 for sheer incompetence and sought solace in the bottle. In the latter stages of the war Göring spent much of his time playing with his electric trains and fiddling with a pocket full of diamonds in his vast palace, Karinhall. Wilhelm Frick, the minister of the interior, relaxed in his villa on the Chiemsee, while his ministry was gradually absorbed by Himmler. Phillip Bouhler, who ran Hitler's private chancellery and who masterminded the mass murder of the psychiatric patients and the handicapped in "Action T4," was shunted aside by Martin Bormann and idled his time away for months on end at his country estate. Competence was not required in the National Socialist elite; all that really mattered was absolute faith in the Führer, unconditional loyalty to the party, and a determination to get things done, no matter what and regardless of cost.

Hitler's pre-war cabinets were recruited from the privileged classes, with five aristocrats among the ministers. The two exceptions were Hitler himself and Hans Kerrl, the ineffectual minister for religious affairs and also for town and country planning, hence his nickname "minister of space and eternity." Once Jews and republicans had been removed, the bureaucracy remained virtually unchanged. The Nazis thus inherited a highly efficient administrative machinery from the republic that left the more controversial "special duties," such as mass murder, to special commissions that unquestioningly and enthusiastically carried out the allotted tasks. Admission to the officer corps still required passing the university entrance examination (*Arbitur*), along with a number of other stringent requirements, so that although the army increased 28-fold between 1933 and 1939 the social profile of the officer corps remained virtually unchanged, with promotion based on time-honored criteria. It was not until 1942 that major changes were made simply because the customary source of officer cadets was drying up. Even the nerve centers of Nazi tyranny, the SD and the RSHA, were staffed largely by university graduates from comfortable middle-class backgrounds. Many in leading positions had doctorates. Had the Third Reich survived they would have formed a power elite, so that bourgeois hegemony would have been preserved within the "racial community," making a mockery of all the talk about equality.

The change from an agrarian to an industrial society is a key component of modernization. For all of Darré's half-baked "blood-and-soil" ideology, the Third Reich did not stand in the way of this process. Agriculture's share of GDP steadily declined. The flight from the land accelerated, with agriculture depending to an increasing extent on government support in the form of subsidies and protective tariffs. Industry continued to expand, largely due to rearmament and war. Government interfered with the economy, entrepreneurial initiative was curbed by governmental regulations, but the basic structure of a capitalist economy remained unaffected.

Hitler's charismatic dictatorship was the most dramatic break with the modern, which implies a growth of democratic forces and the development of what, for want of a better word, is known as civil society. The democratic constitution of the Weimar Republic was torn up, the rule of law repudiated, as Germany relapsed into a neo-feudal free-for-all, in which the Führer's close associates skirmished for power and status while dispensing patronage to their servile underlings. The "racial community," designed to overcome the latent tensions within society, was thus nothing but a cruel and derisory sham. Nevertheless, the traditional social hierarchy had been delegitimized by this ideology, and many people managed to fool themselves into believing that their longing for a social consensus, which had become acute in the latter years of the Weimar Republic, had been largely realized in the "racial community." Subjective perception, if widely shared, takes on the form of objective fact. Class, in the form of self-perception, could vanish with effective integration into a dynamic National Socialist society that had brought full employment, had spectacular successes in foreign policy, and had restored Germany's standing and prestige. A series of stunning victories, at least until the reverses at El Alamein and Stalingrad, provided further evidence that the National Socialist theory of the master race was based on objective fact. The welfare state and consumer society, which the Nazis promised would follow upon a final victory, seemed close to realization.

Progress had already been made, and what Himmler called the "socialism of good blood" was more than an empty slogan. Much had been done to improve the lot of underprivileged "racial comrades" beside which the efforts of most social democratic parties pale by comparison. Wages might have been frozen and hours of work lengthened, but workers were provided with a host of social services and welfare benefits. Protection for tenants and debtors was appreciably strengthened. The feudal remnant of entailment (*Fideikomiss*), which liberals had been trying to abolish for over a century, was ended in July 1938. Family allowances were substantially increased to double those in the United States or Britain. Taking the 1938 level as 100, they rose to 125 in 1939, 128 in 1940, 156 in 1941, and 196 in 1942. Taxes on low-income families were minimal. When the war began wives of serving men were given 85 percent of their husband's former income. The only major tax increases were between 1936 and 1938, designed to cover part of the spiraling cost of rearmament. They were remarkably evenly distributed. Tax-free allowances for families were increased according to the number of children. The rich were heavily taxed, followed by the unmarried and the childless. The tax on corporations was increased from 20 to 40 percent, so as to cream off the profits from rearmament and to help service a debt that now claimed three-fifths of total revenue. A number of tax loopholes were closed and write-offs sub-stantially reduced. Homeowners faced a heavy tax burden that was significantly increased during the war. The luxury Hotel Adlon in Berlin was called upon to pay a 40 percent turnover tax in 1941. By 1943 profits were taxed at between 80 and 90 percent. Blue- and white-collar workers paid no extra direct taxes in wartime, although much has been made of the hardship caused by the wartime increases in the taxes on tobacco, beer, hard liquor, and sparkling wine, but these were regionally adjusted so that the price of beer was sub-stantially less in beer-swilling Bavaria and there was no increase in the tax on wine in the Rhineland so as to protect the struggling vintners and local oenophiles. There were no tax increases in the agricultural sector. The attempt to stop overtime pay, with the bonus handed over to the state, caused such outrage that it had to be stopped in late 1939. Pensions for the needy were increased in 1941. In the same year universal health care was introduced with premiums of a token 1 mark per month. Widows and orphans were treated free of charge. Only "racial comrades" enjoyed such benefits. A Jewish worker at Daimler-Benz who earned 234 marks per month paid 108 marks in tax. An Aryan co-worker earning the same amount paid a mere 9.62 in tax and 20.59 marks in social benefits and WHW and DAF contributions.

By contrast Churchill's Britain of "blood, toil, tears, and sweat" increased taxation by 335 percent in a grossly inequitable way. Eighty-five percent of tax revenue was paid by those earning less than £500 per year. Unlike the British, lower-income Germans were singularly reluctant to buy war bonds, thus denying the government an important source of revenue. Hitler would not consider such austerity measures and even reversed a ban on household pets, except of course in the case of Jews. Germany's tax burden increased by only 196 percent, the additional burden falling mainly on the rich. The government behaved as if there were no tomorrow, with Hitler, as his conservative opponent Carl Goerdeler said: "going ever further along the easy path of self-delusion." The price for this profligacy was paid by the occupied countries, which were ruthlessly exploited, and by the billions in assets stolen from Jews.

Hitler was himself an embodiment of the crisis of the modern. On the one hand he loved fast cars and aeroplanes, announcing that he was "crazy about technology." He shared none of his cranky followers' dislike of industry and mastered the modern techniques of mass communication. But he was haunted by the threat posed by Jewry, which for him embodied all the negative aspects of modernity. Modern technology was placed at the service of an irrational, atavistic ideology and it was precisely the crushing defeat of these aims that removed so many barriers that stood in the way of modernity. The military was destroyed, the officer corps discredited, the East Elbian aristocracy robbed of any influence, all pretensions to the superiority of the German race reduced to an utter absurdity, and the poisonous notion that a charismatic dictator could reach the promised land by means of a war of conquest and genocide was finally revealed as a satanic delusion.

First Steps in Foreign Policy

At first the regime moved very cautiously in the field of foreign affairs. With its demands for a revision of the Treaty of Versailles it hardly distinguished itself from the other parties in Weimar Germany. Calls for the restoration of Germany's status as a Great Power and for the return of the colonies were also commonplace in conservative and nationalist circles. But from the outset Hitler was determined to create a vast empire in eastern Europe to secure "living space." He was prepared to go to any lengths to achieve this goal. His single-minded determination, his gambler's instincts, and his ruthless pursuit of long-term goals alarmed his generals. Even the most robust among his myrmidons began to waver. As Hitler played for ever higher stakes, winning every time, his prestige grew, his critics were silenced, and his charismatic status as a Führer of genius was further embellished. He was thus able to manipulate the conservative nationalists, using them to help realize his vision of *Lebensraum* and the extermination of the "racial enemies" who threatened the "racial community."

The international situation was very favorable for a forceful revisionist policy. The powers were seriously weakened by the depression. Collective security was in ruins with the Japanese invasion of Manchuria and the subsequent feeble response of the League of Nations. Reparations had effectively been ended in 1932 and Brüning had got to within an inch of removing the military restrictions placed on Germany by the Versailles Treaty.

Hitler was anxious to allay the fears of Germany's neighbors while he established his dictatorship at home. To this end he retained the aristocratic career diplomat of the old school, Konstantin von Neurath, as foreign minister along with his secretary of state Wilhelm von Bülow. Diplomats in the Wilhelmstraße, ignorant of Hitler's alarming message to his generals on February 3, 1933, did not think that the new government meant a radical change in course. They imagined that it would be possible to pursue a somewhat more aggressive policy than that of Stresemann, whereby Germany's position would be strengthened by rearmament, unification with Austria, and the restoration of the lost colonies.

Hitler's first major public address on foreign policy was made in the Reichstag on May 17, 1933: in it he promised to respect all international treaties and obligations and called for a peaceful revision of the Versailles settlement. For all his anti-Marxist rhetoric, and while he was busy murdering Communists at home, he signed a credit agreement with the Soviet Union on February 25, 1933, and a friendship and non-aggression treaty on April 4.

On October 14 the German government took the British and French proposal at Geneva that Germany should be given a four-year trial period before reaching a general agreement on disarmament as an excuse to leave the League of Nations. This was an enormously popular move in Germany, where the League was seen as little more that an instrument whereby the victorious powers upheld the *Diktat* of Versailles.

This was followed by a surprising non-aggression pact with Poland on January 16, 1934, which marked a radical departure from the pro-Soviet and anti-Polish policy of the Weimar Republic since Rapallo. The Poles had every reason to be suspicious, particularly as Hitler pointed out that the treaty did not mean that there would be no frontier changes between the two countries. Feeling abandoned by their French sponsors, they had no other choice.

Relations between Germany and Austria were extremely tense. Most Austrians had welcomed the idea of an *Anschluss*, but they had grave reservations now that Germany was in the hands of the National Socialists. The Austrian government complained bitterly about the massive financial help given to Austrian Nazis. The Germans replied by imposing a 1,000-mark tax on any German citizen traveling to Austria. This effectively closed the border, thereby ruining Austria's tourist trade. The Austrians then required visas, thus making it difficult for German Nazis to cross the border. The Austrian Nazis promptly stepped up their terror campaign, culminating in the assassination of the chancellor, Engelbert Dollfuss, on July 25, 1934. Mussolini, anxious to maintain Austria as a buffer state between Italy and Germany, moved troops to the frontier. Hitler thought it prudent to disavow any connection with his unruly followers in Austria.

In a plebiscite on January 13, 1935, 91 percent of the electorate in the Saar voted to return to Germany, in spite of massive anti-fascist propaganda in this largely working-class mining area. In February Hitler invited the British foreign secretary, Sir John Simon, and the Lord Privy Seal, Anthony Eden, to go to Berlin on March 7 to discuss an Anglo-French communiqué that proposed certain measures to avoid a renewed arms race. Then, only three days before the British delegation was due to arrive, the British government published a White Paper on defense that called for substantial increases in spending on the armed forces, said to be in direct response to Hitler's overbearingly belligerent tone. Hitler, buoyed up by his remarkable victory in the Saar, promptly postponed the visit. Feigning an indisposition, he took great delight in snubbing the British government. Six days later, on March 10, Göring announced the formation of the Luftwaffe, the German air force that was expressly forbidden under the terms of the Treaty of Versailles. On March 15 the French National Assembly approved an increase in the term for military service from one to two years. Then, on March 16, Hitler announced the introduction of universal military service in order to create an army of 550,000 men.

Simon and Eden eventually went to Berlin on March 25. They were treated to a series of monologues, most of them on Hitler's favorite topic of the menace of Bolshevism. They were scarcely able to get a word in edgeways. When they did manage to register a complaint they were shot down in flames. Sir John Simon complained of Germany's breach of the disarmament clauses of the Treaty of Versailles, whereupon Hitler archly inquired whether Wellington had raised similar objections when Blücher arrived on the field at Waterloo.

The French were particularly concerned about recent developments in Germany. In reaction to the Röhm putsch in June and the Austrian crisis in the following month they began fence-building with the countries in central and eastern Europe, while making approaches to Moscow. The result was the Franco-Soviet mutual assistance pact of May 2, 1935, whereupon the Soviet Union joined the League of Nations. For the Soviets this was a mighty anti-fascist coalition, but it was a fissiparous alliance fraught with all manner of ideological differences and conflicts of interest. Meanwhile, France's efforts to persuade Britain and Italy to stand together against German violations of the Treaty of Versailles resulted in the Stresa front of April 14, 1935, which upheld the 1925 Treaty of Locarno.

Hitler was not in the least bit concerned. Having clearly dominated the talks with Simon and Eden, he was convinced that if he kept up a bold front the British would be accommodating. Accordingly, he sent his special representative Joachim von Ribbentrop to London to follow up on the British delegation's visit to Berlin. Ribbentrop reminded Paul Schmidt, Hitler's interpreter and a keen observer of human frailty, of the dog on HMV records. He was an insufferably ill-mannered former sparkling wine salesman, whose boorish behavior soon earned him the sobriquet "von Brickendrop." He immediately demanded that Germany should be given a free hand in Europe to destroy the Soviet Union. In return Britannia could continue to rule the waves and concentrate on the empire. The British government, not taking kindly to this proposal to divide the world, threatened to cancel the talks, but eventually assented to a naval agreement on June 18, 1935, whereby the ratio of British to German surface fleets was fixed at 100 to 35. Submarines, Hitler's favored weapon, were not included.

Hitler had every reason to consider this as his "happiest day." The British had single-handedly torn up the disarmament clauses of the Versailles Treaty without even consulting their French allies. The British, whose eyes were on the very real threat posed by Japan, were relieved that an understanding had been reached and were determined to avoid any confrontation with Germany. Encouraged by the feeble response of the British and French to Italy's aggression in Ethiopia, and taking the ratification of the Franco-Soviet treaty as a excuse, Hitler ordered the remilitarization of the Rhineland on March 2, 1936, having first received assurances from Mussolini that he had no serious objections to such a move. France was in the middle of an election campaign and the government was paralyzed. The British did not feel that their vital interests were affected. On March 7, Hitler announced in the Reichstag that he had no further territorial demands. Eden told the House of Commons that there was no cause for alarm. Churchill's jeremiads were dismissed as the fulminations of an elderly politician totally out of touch with the times.

Hitler's triumph in the Rhineland helped silence those who complained about the hardships caused by the concentration on rearmament and the harassment of the churches. In the elections held on March 29, 98.8 percent voted for the "Führer's list." Hitler's descent into outright megalomania was greatly accelerated by these giddy successes. His speeches were now full of references to providential guidance, his sacred mission, and his visionary prescience, while Goebbels' propaganda machine pumped out clouds of adulatory incense in honor of this preternatural being.

After some initial hesitation Hitler, prompted by ideological and economic considerations, decided to intervene in the Spanish civil war. He now found himself fighting alongside Mussolini for General Franco's nationalists against the republicans in the "Marxist" popular front. Mussolini had already expressed his gratitude for German neutrality over Ethiopia by ceasing to support the Austrian Heimwehr against the National Socialists and making it plain that he now had no objections to an *Anschluss*. The Italian foreign minister Ciano went to Berlin in October 1936 and signed a pact of mutual cooperation. He then visited Hitler in his Bavarian mountaintop retreat where his host proposed an offensive treaty designed to crush Marxism and to bring Britain to heel. Hitler said that the German army would be ready to go to war within three to five years. On November 1 Mussolini first spoke openly of an "axis" from Rome to Berlin and invited other European states to cooperate.

Meanwhile Ribbentrop, frustrated that he had been unable to win over the British government, worked feverishly to secure an agreement with Japan so as to form a triple alliance that would leave Britain isolated. Both the German foreign office and the Wehrmacht leadership were opposed to this idea. There was also considerable resistance on the Japanese side. But Major General Hiroshi Oshima, the military attaché who was to become ambassador later in 1936, was an enthusiastic admirer of National Socialism who fought long and hard for an agreement with Germany. The result was the Anti-Comintern Pact of November 1936, a vague understanding that Hitler felt might help put pressure on Britain to reach an understanding with Germany.

Rearmament was now putting an intolerable strain on the economy. There was a chronic shortage of foreign exchange, and import prices had risen an average of 9 percent since 1933. There was a shortage of foodstuffs resulting from a series of poor harvests, so that the regime was faced with the choice of guns or butter. Hitler was determined to keep up the pace of rearmament and therefore supported those who argued that domestic sources of raw materials should be exploited and synthetic rubber and petroleum produced so as to reduce the reliance on imports. He brusquely dismissed all concerns about the horrendous cost of autarchy, imagining that it would be offset by the rich booty acquired from a war of conquest. In a secret memorandum in August 1936 Hitler said that the country had to be ready for war within four years, and that a series of short campaigns would then result in an "increase in *Lebensraum* and thus of raw materials and foodstuffs."

Hitler gave vent to increasingly frequent outbursts about the necessity of finding a solution to "Germany's space question" and of the need to settle matters by force as early as 1938. On November 5, 1937, he called a top-level meeting in the chancellery attended by von Neurath, the war minister von Blomberg, as well as the commanders-in-chief of the army, the navy, and the air force, von Fritsch, Raeder, and Göring. They were treated to a four-hour monologue, which Hitler announced should be taken as his testament in the event of his death. It began with a rambling discourse on familiar topics such as Social Darwinism, race and geopolitics, and the need to strengthen the "racial mass" (*Volksmasse*) and to secure *Lebensraum*. None of these outstanding problems could be solved without recourse to force. He then announced that in the first stage Austria would have to be annexed, and then Czechoslovakia would be attacked. Germany would have to be prepared to fight both England and France should they decide to intervene. Hitler brushed aside all objections, but realized that he would have to replace traditionally minded men like Neurath, Blomberg, and Fritsch to secure the cooperation of the foreign office and the army for his hazardous policy. Schacht, who was expressing grave concern over the inflationary pressure of forced rearmament, would also have to go.

The *Anschluss*

In January 1938 Austrian police unearthed evidence that the National Socialists were planning to cause so much disorder that the Germans would have an excuse to intervene in order to restore law and order. The Austrian chancellor, Schuschnigg, decided to visit Hitler in an attempt to ease the tension between the two countries. He arrived in Berchtesgaden on February 12, 1938, and was immediately subjected to a vituperative tirade from Hitler, who accused Austria of all manner of misdemeanors, including "racial treason." He warned the Austrian chancellor that he only had to give the order and the country would be destroyed. Ribbentrop then demanded that the National Socialist Arthur Seyß-Inquart should be put in charge of home security, that there should be a general amnesty for all Nazis, and that Austria's foreign and economic policies should be coordinated with those of the Reich. Talks between the two general staffs should also be scheduled.

Schuschnigg felt that he had no alternative but to accept; but on his return home he called for a referendum for a "free, German, independent, social, Christian and united Austria" to be held on March 13. The Nazis saw this as a provocation, the more so since younger voters who were highly susceptible to the movement were excluded. They insured that Austria descended into violent anarchy. The Austrian president, Wilhelm Miklas, courageously refused Hitler's demand that Seyß-Inquart be appointed chancellor, whereupon the Austrian Nazis seized government buildings in Vienna. Hitler then gave orders to his troops to cross the frontier.

The German army met with a rapturously enthusiastic welcome on March 12. Hitler made a triumphant return to his birthplace at Braunau before moving on to Linz where, impressed by the vast and enthusiastic crowds, he announced that Austria would be incorporated into the German Reich. From Linz he traveled to Vienna, where he addressed an even larger crowd of ecstatic devotees. On April 10 a referendum was held in which 99 percent of those eligible, including the Austrian socialist leader Karl Renner, voted in favor of the *Anschluss*. Austria promptly ceased to exist. It became a German province known as the Ostmark. The German Reichsmark replaced the Austrian Schilling. Overnight Austrians had to learn to drive on the right-hand side of the road like the Germans.

For the Austrian Jewish community these were days of horror. Austrian Nazis were even more vicious and brutal in their anti-Semitism than their German comrades, which in turn helped to radicalize the Germans immediately after the *Anschluss*. Units of the SS and police followed behind the army. Along with their Austrian colleagues they carried out a bestial pogrom in which thousands of innocent victims were brutally beaten, imprisoned, and murdered, and their property seized. Their humiliation and savage mistreatment was savored by jeering crowds. It was a gruesome foretaste of what was to happen in Germany on November 9. The RSHA sent Adolf Eichmann to Austria, where in August he established the Central Office for Jewish Emigration, which began the expulsion of the 200,000 Austrian Jews, the vast majority of whom lived in Vienna.

Munich

Boosted by his triumph in Austria, and encouraged by the supine attitude of Britain and France and by Mussolini's support, Hitler now turned his attention to Czechoslovakia. On April 21 he told the military that he would either go to war after a few preliminary diplomatic moves or would use some incident to strike a lightning blow. He had already decided on the latter alternative and had instructed the Sudeten German leader Konrad Henlein to make demands of the Czechoslovakian government that could not possibly be fulfilled.

On May 30, Hitler announced that he intended "to destroy Czechoslovakia by military means in the foreseeable future." Throughout the summer of 1938 there was widespread violence in the Sudetenland as the crisis deepened. On September 15 the British prime minister Neville Chamberlain flew to Munich to meet Hitler at Berchtesgaden, where he announced that neither Britain nor France would object to parts of the Sudetenland being handed over to Germany. Hitler, taken by surprise by Chamberlain's readiness to stab an ally in the back, decided to take a tougher line when they met again at Bad Godesberg on September 22. Having already told the Polish and Hungarian governments that he would support their claims against Czechoslovakia, he now told Chamberlain that he was prepared to use force if his wishes were not immediately granted.

War now seemed inevitable. Both Czechoslovakia and France mobilized. Britain prepared for war and the Soviet Union promised support. Hitler moved seven divisions up to the Czech border. Opposition forces in Germany went into action. General Ludwig Beck had already resigned as chief of staff in August in protest against Hitler's risky policy. Now Colonel Hans Oster from military counter-intelligence, and the former mayor of Leipzig and prince commissar, Carl Goerdeler, contacted British politicians, begging that a firm stand be taken against Hitler. Much to Hitler's disgust the majority of Germans viewed the prospect of war with sullen apprehension.

Prompted by Mussolini, and supported by Göring, the minister of finance Schwerin von Krosigk and the army's chief of staff Halder, Hitler agreed to meet with the British and French prime ministers in Munich on September 29. Without consulting either Czechoslovakia or the Soviet Union, Chamberlain and Daladier agreed that those areas in the Sudetenland where the Germans had a majority should be handed over to Germany between 1 and 10 October 1938.

In one sense Munich was a triumph for Hitler. He had gained an important industrial area, rich in natural resources and with a highly skilled labor force. Czechoslovakia was now virtually defenseless and its economy in ruins. But he had been denied the crisis that he needed were he to destroy the country and make a triumphal entry into Prague. He was furious that Chamberlain and Daladier were seen as heroes by the majority of Germans and asked: "How can I go to war with a people like this?!" On October 21, 1938, Hitler issued instructions for the destruction of Czechoslovakia and the occupation of the Memel. The Slovak president Monsignor Jozef Tiso was ordered to declare Slovak independence. On November 10, the day after the pogrom, Hitler gave a lengthy speech to representatives of the press, ordering them to desist from any talk of peace and to steel the people for war.

By the spring of 1938 the printing press had taken over the German economy, resulting in rampant inflation. The amount of money in circulation had doubled between 1937 and 1939, prompting Schacht to call the rearmament program to a halt. The Reichsbank's economics department, seeing Germany's current situation as analogous to that of Prussia after the Seven Years War or to Britain's after the Napoleonic Wars, boldly asserted that since the Führer had announced at Munich that Germany had no further territorial claims in Europe, expansion could only take place by regaining the lost colonies. This could best be accomplished through diplomatic negotiation. The other great aim, the defeat of Bolshevism, should be achieved by working towards the internal breakdown of the Soviet regime. Excess purchasing power could best be absorbed by increasing the supply of consumer goods, while the balance of payments crisis had to be addressed with an export drive. In other words the country had to reverse its priorities by returning to a peacetime economy.

War

Nazi Germany was now on a headlong course towards war. Driven forward by its inner dynamics, it was virtually out of control. Hitler was now an absolute dictator who paid no attention to the mounting crisis in the economy and was impervious to all notes of caution. He rambled on incessantly about a "battle of world-views" and "racial war." On January 30, 1939, the sixth anniversary of the "seizure of power," he told the Reichstag: "If international Jewry in Europe and elsewhere plunge the peoples once again into a world war, the result will not be the Bolshevization of the world, and thus a Jewish victory, but the destruction of the Jewish race in Europe." He promised to create a vast German empire, one that was purified of all alien racial elements. There could now be no turning back.

Monsignor Tiso slavishly obeyed his orders from Berlin and declared Slovak independence on March 14. That day the Czech president Emil Hacha traveled to Berlin in a desperate attempt to preserve the independence of his rump state. Hitler ranted and raved until the unfortunate Hacha suffered a heart attack. Having been revived by Hitler's personal physician, Dr. Theodor Morell, he was told that if he did not hand over the state to Nazi Germany it would be invaded. A shattered president then signed a document placing his unhappy and betrayed people "confidently into the hands of the Führer of the German Reich."

German troops crossed the frontier that night. Hitler traveled to Prague the following day to be met by a silent, crushed, and tearful crowd. The Czech Republic was transformed into the "Protectorate of Bohemia and Moravia," and was thereby submitted to a pitiless occupation regime.

On March 21 German troops occupied Memel (Klaipéda), German territory that had been awarded to Lithuania under the terms of the peace treaty. This strengthened Poland's resolve to resist further German demands over the Danzig question. On March 31 the British government gave a guarantee to both Poland and Romania. Hitler was furious. On April 3 he ordered plans to be drawn up for the invasion of Poland. His fiftieth birthday was celebrated on April 20 with a massive military march-past in Berlin, and one week later he rescinded the Non-Aggression Pact with Poland of 1934 and the Anglo-German Naval Agreement of 1935. The next day he rejected President Roosevelt's appeal for world peace in an unrelentingly derisive speech. Hitler had an intense loathing for Roosevelt, whom he described as "the chosen one of world Jewry," manipulated by his sinister Jewish confidant, the financier Bernard Baruch. Hitler thus saw himself about to embark on a two-front war: against "Jewish" capitalism, democracy, and liberalism embodied by Roosevelt and against Stalin's "Jewish" Bolshevism. It was an awesome undertaking for a relatively poor country like Germany. Small wonder therefore that there were many who were hesitant when they realized that this was not mere abstract speculation, but that Hitler was hell bent on a war of aggression.

Britain and France now made a half-hearted attempt to bring the Soviet Union into a European security pact, but Stalin was deeply distrustful of these two imperialist powers. Neither Poland nor Romania was at all keen to entrust their security to a power that harbored substantial claims on their territory. In May the Soviet commissar for foreign affairs, Maxim Litvinov, who still hoped that Britain and France would realize the gravity of the situation, was replaced by the boot-faced Stalinist Molotov. This move was seen as a clear signal to Berlin, and was underlined by frequent mentions of Rapallo.

Hitler decided to test the water. The "Pact of Steel" between Berlin and Rome did not amount to much, since Mussolini had made it plain that Italy would not be ready for war until 1943. Talks with Japan over a similar military alliance had come to nothing. He had set August 26 as the date for an invasion of Poland and he was virtually without an ally in this hazardous undertaking. Ribbentrop, who had replaced von Neurath as foreign minister in 1938, made the first move towards Molotov, who reacted positively. Ribbentrop flew to Moscow on August 23, 1939, and was immediately taken to see Stalin. He thus became the first minister of a foreign government to meet the Soviet dictator. Agreement was reached within a few hours once Hitler agreed that the Soviets should be given all of Latvia. The Ribbentrop–Molotov Pact, which was in fact negotiated personally by Stalin, was a non-aggression pact to last for ten years and to go into effect immediately. In a secret protocol the Soviet Union was given a free hand in eastern Poland up to the line of the Narev, Vistula, and San rivers, along with Estonia, Latvia, Finland, and Bessarabia. The future of Poland was to be settled at a later date. After the signing ceremony numerous toasts were drunk in vodka and the gangsters swapped what passed for jokes in such circles. These sordid jollifications lasted until 2 a.m.

On August 25, the eve of the planned invasion of Poland, Hitler suffered two setbacks. The British government finally sealed the pact with Poland and Mussolini let it be known that he would not join in the war. Hitler nervously inquired whether the attack could be postponed. He was assured that it could be. September 1 was set as the new date. Göring warned Hitler that the risks were too great. Hitler replied: "I have played all-or-nothing [*va banque*] my entire life!" This time there was to be no further delay. At 4.45 on the morning of September 1 the battleship *Schleswig-Holstein* opened fire on the Polish garrison on the Westerplatte near Danzig, while Stuka dive-bombers swooped down on the city. Europe was once again at war.

Poland

Britain and France reluctantly declared war on September 3, 1939. The Dominions followed suit a few days later, but they did nothing to help Poland. The "phoney war" in the west enabled the Germans to concentrate on a swift campaign in the east. Within a week they had reached the outskirts of Warsaw. One week later the city was encircled. On September 17 the Polish government left the country, and the Soviets invaded that very day. Warsaw capitulated ten days later, having been flattened by aerial and artillery bombardment. The next day Germany and the Soviet Union divided up the spoils of war. Lithuania was given to the Soviets; the Germans got Warsaw and Lublin. The fighting ended on October 6.

SS Einsatzgruppen, made up of men chosen from the SD and from the Security Police (Sipo) followed behind the victorious Wehrmacht. They were ordered to "fight all elements behind the fighting troops who are enemies of the Reich and the German people." They immediately set to work, arresting 30,000 representatives of the Polish elites, who were thrown into concentration camps where they were, in Heydrich's words, "rendered harmless." On September 21 Heydrich ordered all Jews to be herded into the larger cities. Meanwhile Himmler's order to summarily execute any "franc-tireurs" was give a generous interpretation, permitting the Einsatzgruppen to indulge in an orgy of slaughter. They were given the enthusiastic support of those Germans living in Poland who were organized in "self-defense" (*Selbstschutz*) units, and by detachments of the Wehrmacht. In the days immediately after the invasion 50,000 Poles and 7,000 Jews were killed. The army joined in this orgy of slaughter with a series of summary executions, but some senior officers such as von Bock and Blaskowitz began to get concerned about the brutalization of their men, which threatened discipline and morale. Misleadingly laying the entire blame squarely on the SS, they protested at this barbarism. Hitler dismissed their protests as the "childish" outcome of a "Salvation Army attitude."

In October about half of German-occupied Poland was incorporated into the Reich. The remainder was called the General Government, which was to become a reservoir of helots to serve the master race. Himmler, as "Reich Commissar for the Strengthening of the German Race," immediately set about expelling all Poles and Jews from areas recently annexed by Germany. By the end of 1940 325,000 Polish citizens had been deported and their property stolen, their place taken by Germans from the Baltic states and Volhynia. A roughly equal number of Poles were shipped off to work in the Reich.

The population was divided into four categories according to National Socialist racial criteria. At the top of the ladder came the "citizens of the Reich" (*Reichsbürger*), made up of ethnic Germans and Poles who were deemed to be capable of being turned into Germans (*eindeutschungsfähig*). Next came two classes of "citizens" (*Staatsangehöriger*) who were regarded as being on trial to see if they could be made into true Germans. Lastly came the 6 million Poles labeled "protected" (*Schutzangehörigen*) who were to serve their racial superiors.

Of these "Protected" Poles, 311,000 were shipped off to work in the armaments industry in Germany, some voluntarily others forcibly; 400,000 further workers were sent by 1942. In early 1940 as a result of 408,000 expulsions, the newly annexed territories were proclaimed "free of Jews" (*Judenfrei*). The Jews were forced into ghettos in Warsaw, Kraków, Lvov, Lublin, and Radom. Large numbers of them were denied this temporary respite and were murdered by the Einsatzgruppen. The Germans were equally determined to exterminate the Polish intelligentsia. Seventeen percent of those listed as "intellectuals" were promptly murdered. Also in early 1940 the SS built a vast concentration camp at Auschwitz, where Polish prisoners were treated as slave labor and executed at will. The first victims of systematic industrialized murder at Auschwitz were Soviet prisoners of war, Poles, and sick inmates.

The War in the West

On the day that fighting stopped in Poland, Hitler made a peace offer to Britain and France. It was an entirely fraudulent move for at the same time he issued orders for an invasion of Holland, Belgium, and France to take place as soon as possible, insisting that he had first to have his hands free in the west before taking on the Soviet Union. The military leadership felt that an invasion of the west was an extremely risky undertaking. The commander-in-chief, Walther von Brauchitsch, tried to convince Hitler to change his mind, but to no avail. Bad weather finally obliged Hitler to postpone the attack on the west until May 10, 1940.

Some officers close to General Ludwig Beck conspired to overthrow Hitler. Göring, feeling that the German armed forces were not sufficiently prepared, again made a half-hearted attempt to call a halt. A few menacing remarks by Hitler about "defeatists" among his generals were enough to silence the opposition. Then, on November 9, a cabinetmaker named Georg Elser planted a bomb under the podium in the Bürgerbräukeller in Munich where Hitler was to address a meeting of "old fighters" on the occasion of the anniversary of the 1923 coup. The bomb went off, but it missed Hitler by thirteen minutes: he had to leave the meeting early to catch the train back to Berlin, because bad weather made flying impossible. Sympathizers, among them the Soviet government, expressed their relief that Hitler had been saved. Anti-fascists argued that it was a put-up job, like the Reichstag fire, designed to paint Hitler as a man of destiny, protected by premonition. In fact Elser acted alone in an attempt to end the war.

In April 1940 the Germans invaded Norway to forestall an Anglo-French expeditionary force and to protect the Swedish ore fields that were vital to the war economy. Operation "Weser Exercise" (*Weserübung*) was swift, economical, and met with very little resistance, although the Royal Navy managed to sink a number of German ships. An attack on Denmark, "Weser Exercise South," was an even greater success, and the whole operation was over within twenty-four hours.

Despite Hitler's insistence to the contrary, the delay of the western offensive worked to Germany's advantage. Thanks to the Herculean efforts of Fritz Todt, armaments production had increased by 50 percent and the army now had an excellent plan based on the ideas of General Erich von Manstein. Army Group A was to drive its armor and motorized infantry through the Ardennes and then head for the Channel coast at Dunkirk in a "sweep of the sickle." Army Group B was to occupy Belgium and Holland and thus trap the bulk of the enemy's forces between the two army groups. Army Group C was to tie down the French forces in the Maginot Line without actually attacking these heavily fortified defensive positions.

The attack was launched on May 10 and went like clockwork. The French were caught off balance by the speed of the advance, and the British were forced to abandon the Continent in "Operation Dynamo," a brilliantly organized evacuation. The "spirit of Dunkirk" became part of popular mythology and a humiliating defeat was transformed into a resounding triumph of the British spirit. The French Third Republic, torn apart by political dissent, began to fall apart. Armistice negotiations began on June 21, pointedly, in the same railway carriage in which the Germans had been forced to capitulate in 1918.

Characteristically of Hitler's tactics, the conquered territories were treated differently, thus creating a hastily improvised confusion of military, state, and party administrative bodies. France was divided into the occupied northern zone and a rump state in the south with an authoritarian government in the spa town of Vichy under Marshal Pétain, the octogenarian hero of Verdun. Alsace, Lorraine, and Luxembourg were annexed and ruled by Gauleiters. Belgium was placed under military occupation. Holland was governed by a Reich Commissar. Denmark was left as a theoretically sovereign state. The government remained in office, the Germans transmitting their requests through traditional diplomatic channels. Even though it was under military occupation it retained its own armed forces. Because of its strategic significance, Belgium was placed under military command. General von Falkenhausen and his administrative assistant Eggert Reeder ruled the country in a manner that was by Nazi standards reasonably benign, but they were unable to keep Heydrich and the SD at bay. As a result some 30,000 Jews were deported to the death camps, while 43,000 non-Jewish Belgians were sent to camps in the Reich, where 13,000 died. The brutal and mean-spirited Josef Terboven was appointed Reich Commissar for Norway, where he tried unsuccessfully to form a credible government under Vidkun Quisling, a contemptible stooge whom, like the vast majority of Norwegians, he heartily detested.

Hitler now turned his attention to Britain. It was a frustrating problem for him. He could not understand why the British refused to make peace at a time when they appeared to be helpless. Even if Germany defeated Britain the problem of the empire would remain. Would it fall into the hands of the Japanese or the Americans, and thus immeasurably strengthen one or even both of Germany's future rivals? He agreed with his generals that an invasion was far too risky without first gaining absolute control in the air. To this end the Luftwaffe began massive attacks on August 5. Because Germany switched its attacks on August 24 from airstrips and radar installations to civilian targets, the "few" in RAF Fighter Command were given a respite and were thus ultimately able to win the Battle of Britain. The air offensive was called off on September 17, and Hitler thus suffered his first serious defeat, as he himself was grudgingly forced to admit. Admiral Raeder now suggested concentrating on attacking British forces in the Mediterranean and the Middle East.

On July 31 Hitler ordered his generals to prepare an attack on the Soviet Union, arguing that it was "England's last hope." Given that all experts agreed that the Red Army was in a state of disarray, victory was assured. Hitler said: "We only have to kick in the front door and the whole rotten structure will collapse." Goebbels was of the same mind: "Bolshevism will collapse like a house of cards." With virtually all of continental Europe under German control the United States would not dare to intervene. Germany would then have all the *Lebensraum* it could possibly want at its disposal.

Barbarossa

When Molotov visited Berlin on November 12 and 13, 1940, Hitler made the preposterous suggestion that their two countries should divide up the spoils of the British empire. Molotov replied that if Germany wished to maintain good relations with the Soviet Union it would have to agree that Finland, Romania, Bulgaria, and the Straits were all vital to the defense of the Soviet Union. Later he added Hungary, Yugoslavia, and eastern Poland to this impressive list. Hitler, smarting under Molotov's taunt that he was acting as if Britain were already defeated, announced that his pact with Stalin "would not even remain a marriage of convenience." On December 18 he issued "Direction Number 21 for Case Barbarossa" which stated that "The German army must be ready to crush the Soviet Union in a swift campaign once the war against England is ended."

This was to be no ordinary war. Hitler announced that it would be a "a battle between world views" in which the Einsatzgruppen would destroy the "Jewish-Bolshevik intelligentsia." No mercy was to be shown to the civilian population, Himmler and the SS were given "special tasks" within the Wehrmacht's operational area involving the "final battle between two opposing political systems." In the final version of "General Plan East," published two days after the launching of Barbarossa, this would involve the murder of 34 million Slavs. Hitler gave repeated instructions to the military not to treat the Red Army as normal soldiers, to ignore the rules of war, and to give no quarter. From the very beginning of the planning stage the Wehrmacht was deeply implicated in the criminal conduct of this unspeakably frightful campaign. Most of his generals enthusiastically endorsed Hitler's demented vision of a crusade against these Asiatic-Jewish-Bolshevik subhumans. A few remained silent. None raised any serious objections.

A decree was published on May 13, 1941 to the effect that "crimes committed by enemy civilians" did not have to go to trial. Any "suspicious elements" should be shot on the spot on an officer's orders. No German soldier was to be punished for crimes committed against enemy civilians. This was an invitation to every perverted brute and sadist to have a field day. The infamous "Commissar Order," whereby any commissar captured in battle should be instantly shot, was issued on June 6. Commissars discovered behind the German lines were to be handed over to the Einsatzgruppen for immediate dispatch. The army objected to both these orders on practical rather than moral grounds. It was frequently argued that the Commissar Order simply strengthened Soviet determination to resist, while military discipline was severely threatened by the limitation of the army's jurisdiction in the earlier decree. Such protests had no effect: 600,000 Soviet citizens, who as prisoners of war were under the army's jurisdiction, were shot as "commissars." Hundreds of thousands of others, including numerous small children, were shot either as "commissars" or as "partisans."

General Georg Thomas, head of the Military Economic and Armaments Office, consulted with a number of prominent civilian officials from various ministries in the spring of 1941, and came to the conclusion that the Wehrmacht would have to live off the land in the Soviet Union. It was agreed that "several million" Soviet citizens would starve to death as a result, but these worthy civil servants viewed such a prospect with equanimity. The Wehrmacht and the SS were thus substantially in agreement that mass murder on a staggering scale was a desirable necessity. In May Heydrich's Einsatzgruppen were ordered to kill all Jews in the occupied territories since they were the "biological root" of Bolshevism. Since the Wehrmacht was responsible for the logistical support of the Einsatzgruppen, it

PLATE 22   Hitler and Goebbels. © DIZ Munich

was once again deeply implicated in this indescribable crime. The much-vaunted honor of the German army was lost forever.

In mid-December 1940 Hitler ordered preparations to be made for a campaign in the Balkans in order to secure the flank of "Barbarossa" and to protect the Romanian oil fields from attack by the RAF. A pro-Western coup in Belgrade at the end of March 1941 enraged Hitler. He ordered an immediate attack on Yugoslavia and Greece. Yugoslavia capitulated on April 17, Greece four days later. Large numbers of German troops were now tied down in the Balkans in a brutish and bloody campaign against highly motivated and skillful partisans.

The Germans attacked the Soviet Union on June 22, 1941, with 153 divisions totaling about 3 million men. Anticipating a swift campaign lasting three months, they had precious few reserves at the ready. No preparations were made for a winter campaign. The early stages of Barbarossa seemed to indicate that such confidence was justified. Within a few months Army Group North was approaching Leningrad, Army Group South had reached Kharkov, and Army Group Center had begun its final assault on Moscow. By mid-November the Wehrmacht was within 30 kilometers of the Soviet capital.

From the outset Barbarossa was, as Hitler admitted, a gamble, but it was a risk dictated by strategic issues. The Red Army had to be destroyed before it retreated behind the Dnieper–Dvina line, which was the absolute limit for the Wehrmacht's supply lines. Beyond that line the armed forces would face a logistical nightmare. Field Marshal Fedor von Bock, commanding Army Group Center, was keenly aware of this problem and voiced his concerns to Halder. Major General Marcks, the staff officer responsible for drafting the plan, was also concerned that the Red Army might survive the initial attack and continue the fight in the winter; but he consoled himself that the resources of the Ukraine would be sufficient to supply the Wehrmacht. Others, such as General Thomas, were not so sure. They pointed out that the Ukraine had been virtually worthless to the Germans in the First World War, because the Ukraine provided just about enough to feed itself. In any case without oil from the Caucasus there would be no fuel for the tractors to bring in the harvest. Herbert Backe's suggestion in the "Hunger Plan," which was developed well before the invasion, that killing between 30 and 45 million people would release sufficient food for the Wehrmacht, was endorsed by Himmler, General Georg Thomas at High Command of the Armed Forces (Oberkommando der Wehrmacht – OKW) and most major ministries; but it was hardly a solution. It was difficult to see how this horrendous scheme could ever be put into effect, quite apart from the fact that it would leave the agricultural sector somewhat shorthanded.

On December 5 the Russian Marshal Zhukov launched a massive counter-offensive, striking north and south of Moscow. The Germans were forced back some 100 to 250 kilometers, and all hopes for a swift campaign were dashed. Having been locked in seemingly endless arguments with Hitler throughout the summer as to where the main thrust (*Schwerpunkt*) of the attack should be, Brauchitsch handed in his resignation, whereupon Hitler appointed himself commander-in-chief.

Between June 22, 1941 and March 1942 the Germans lost more than 1 million men. Only 450,000 replacements could be found. They had also lost enormous amounts of materiel and were running short of food. As early as November, General Friedrich Fromm, commander of the reserve army, felt that the situation was hopeless and urged Hitler to negotiate a peace. At the same time Fritz Todt also urged Hitler to end the war, given the relative weakness of Germany's armaments industry. Hitler would not hear of this and entertained dark apocalyptic thoughts. "If the German *Volk* is not strong enough and is not sufficiently prepared to offer its own blood for its existence," he announced portentously, "it should be destroyed by a stronger power and cease to exist."

On December 11 Hitler declared war on the United States, four days after the Japanese attack on Pearl Harbor. It was another characteristic gamble, based on the belief that he could win a victory in the Soviet Union before the Americans could engage in the European theater. Referring to a speech made by Hitler on December 12, Goebbels commented in his diary: "This is now a world war and the annihilation of the Jews must be the necessary consequence." It was an extraordinarily risky move in which the gambler made his second really serious miscalculation. Or did he already realize that all was lost and was preparing for the final *Götterdämmerung*? There is evidence to suggest that this was at the back of his mind when Barbarossa failed.

By the time the spring offensive began only 10 percent of the wheeled vehicles the Germans had lost could be made good. A mere 5 percent of the Wehrmacht's divisions were fully operational. They pushed on regardless of the fact that there was a shortage of 650,000 men, profiting from the Soviets' poor intelligence and serious operational blunders. In the summer of 1942 Army Group A of Army Group South under Hitler's direct command was ordered to head for the Black Sea and the Caucasus. The bulk of Army Group B stationed around Kursk was to push on to the Don at Voronezh and then head southeast towards Stalingrad. Paulus' Sixth Army was to break out west of Kharkov and meet up with the rest of the Army Group.

The battle of El Alamein beginning on October 23, 1942 and the subsequent American "Torch" landings on November 8 spelt an end to the North African campaign. On November 19, 1942, the Soviets launched a massive counter-offensive at Stalingrad that left Paulus' Sixth Army in a hopeless situation. Now nothing short of a miracle could bring victory. Hitler was so far removed from reality that his blind faith in destiny and his own unique genius was undiminished, and such was the nimbus that surrounded the "Greatest Commander of All Time" (sometimes disrespectfully shortened to *Gröfaz*) that precious few grasped the true gravity of the situation.

The Final Solution

With the invasion of the Soviet Union the Nazi persecution of the Jews entered its final and most terrible stage. When the General Government was created out of the remains of Poland, Heydrich hoped to create a "Jewish Reservation" in the Lublin area as a temporary measure prior to a "territorial solution" of the "Jewish problem" somewhere in the east. This proved impractical. The area was simply not large enough, so the Jews were herded into ghettos in the larger cities. Hans Frank, the governor of the protectorate, also vigorously objected to the proposal, because he wanted to make his satrapy "uncontaminated by Jews" (*Judenrein*).

After the fall of France, Franz Rademacher, head of Section III (Jewish Questions) in the foreign office, suggested that the west European Jews could be shipped off to the French colony of Madagascar. Eastern Jews were considered "more fertile, and would produce future generations versed in the Talmud and forming a Jewish intelligentsia." They should be used as hostages so as to silence American Jews and keep the United States out of the war. Adolf Eichmann enthusiastically endorsed the Madagascar plan, which had long been popular in anti-Semitic circles. It was assumed that climatic conditions on the island were such that the death rate would be exceedingly high. With Britain still determined to fight on, and with the consequent shipping problem, this scheme had to be dropped.

Meanwhile conditions in the overcrowded Polish ghettos grew steadily worse, facing the authorities with serious problems guarding and feeding their victims. Suggestions were now made by some lower-ranking SS officers that the only solution was to kill all those who were unable to work. The situation worsened still further with the invasion of the Soviet Union with its large Jewish population. There was a conflation in the Nazi mind of Jews and partisans, as well as Jews and Bolsheviks, so the Germans immediately set about their destruction with murderous intensity. Göring, who announced that "This is not the Second World War. This is the Great Racial War," gave Heydrich plenipotentiary powers on July 31, 1941 to find a "general solution [*Gesamtlösung*] to the Jewish problem in German occupied Europe."

In September Hitler decided that all German Jews should be expelled to the General Government. They were now forced to wear a yellow Star of David, their few remaining civil rights were taken away from them, and their property was seized. Preparations were now made for the mass murder of Jews and psychiatric patients in the east so as to make beds available for those wounded on the Eastern Front. Among the first victims were Jews in the ghettos of Riga and Minsk as well as the psychiatric patients in the Warthegau. The Einsatazkommandos murdered them using carbon monoxide in mobile gas chambers, or shot them in mass executions. Extermination camps were built in Belzec, Chelmno, Sobibor, and Treblinka, where gas chambers were constructed along the lines of those used to murder the handicapped in Germany in Action T4, which had begun in September 1939. The gas chambers at Chelmno were first used in December 1941.

Heydrich set December 9, 1941 as the date for a major conference on "the final solution of the Jewish question" to be held in a villa Am Großen Wannsee 56–58 in Berlin, but it had to be postponed because of the Japanese attack on Pearl Harbor. The Wannsee conference, attended by fifteen party functionaries and senior civil servants from most of the major ministries, was eventually held at noon on January 20, 1942. Heydrich chaired the meeting and Eichmann kept the minutes. Heydrich announced his intention to render all of Europe, including Britain and Sweden, as well as North Africa, "uncontaminated by Jews." He estimated that a total of 11 million Jews would be deported to the east. Those who were able to work would be subject to "natural reduction." Those that survived would be given "appropriate treatment" since they would otherwise represent an exceptionally tough "germ-cell" of a Jewish revival. An exception was made for those over the age of 65 in the "old people's ghetto" in the concentration camp in Theresienstadt. This was to serve as a model institution to counter any Allied charges of the mistreatment of Jews. Joseph Bühler, Hans Frank's deputy in the General Government, requested that the "final solution" should begin there as soon as possible, since most of the Jews were unable to work and posed a serious economic and health problem. According to Eichmann's testimony at his trial there was a frank and open discussion of the relative merits of different methods of mass killing. The question was shelved whether Jewish partners of "mixed marriages" or Jewish "half-breeds" should be deported. The meeting was brief and no objections were raised to this horrendous undertaking.

In one sense the Wannsee conference was a confirmation of what had already been done. The decision to murder large numbers of Jews had already been taken and many of the death camps built. Hundreds of thousands had already been slaughtered in an orgy of the basest savagery, but now for the first time the intention to murder every single Jew in Europe was clearly expressed. There had been a number of previous "final solutions to the Jewish question," but this was the definitive "Final Solution" by means of a cold-blooded, carefully planned, industrialized and centralized genocide, a horror unparalleled in human history.

Rudolf Höss' concentration camp at Auschwitz was now greatly expanded so as to accommodate victims from western Europe, the Balkans, and the Czech Protectorate. The original camp (*Stammlager*) was now called Auschwitz I, the extermination camp at Birkenau, Auschwitz II, and IG Farben's factory in the work camp at Monowitz, Auschwitz

III. The Monowitz plant was the largest single investment made under the auspices of the Four Year Plan. It cost 776 million marks and 30,000 men died during its construction; 40,000 workers slaved away for four years in the Buna works under the most appalling conditions, all to no avail. No synthetic rubber was ever produced. Other factories at Auschwitz III were somewhat more productive. Fifteen percent of Germany's methanol production came from the camp. It was a modest return for a huge investment and unimaginable human suffering.

Zyklon B, a gas based on prussic acid, was first used to kill Russian prisoners of war in Auschwitz I in September 1941. The first Jews were murdered by such means in February 1942. Himmler visited Auschwitz in July 1942, witnessed the entire process, from selection on the ramp to gas chamber and crematorium, and expressed his complete satisfaction with the arrangements. He ordered a major expansion of Birkenau, as a result of which up to 10,000 victims could be killed daily. Those who were not killed in the gas chambers were beaten to death, shot, or fell victim to grisly medical experiments, rampant disease, or malnutrition. Only the very strongest and most resourceful survived.

The German eastern empire was so unspeakably frightful that it beggars description. It was run, as one perceptive SS officer remarked, by a sordid bunch of "boneheads and ass-lickers." Erich Koch, as Gauleiter of East Prussia and then Reichskommissar in the Ukraine, was a murderous, corrupt, and drunken idiot, who described the Ukrainians as "niggers" and announced that in the unlikely event of finding an intelligent one, he would have him shot on the spot. He cooperated enthusiastically with Fritz Sauckel in shipping off Ukrainians and Poles for labor service in the Reich, sent hundreds of thousands of Jews to their death, plundered the countryside, and closed down schools and universities. The net result was that the partisans had no shortage of recruits. Hinrich Lohse as Reichskommissar East was hardly an improvement, although he did allow those under his rule a greater degree of independence. In spite of the fact that he was a major player in the genocide of the Jewish people, as well as in the "euthanasia" program Action T4 and a plunderer of art treasures in the Soviet Union, he got off relatively lightly after the war, although he was denied a pension for his service as president of Schleswig-Holstein. Wilhelm Kube, who lorded it over Belorussia, was so staggeringly corrupt and foul-mouthed that he had been dismissed from all party and state offices. After a brief turn of duty as an SS corporal (Rottenführer) in Dachau he was reactivated in July 1941 as Reichskommissar in Belorussia. Kube ran foul of the local SS commanders by objecting to the murder of German Jews who had served in the war, for his love of Mendelssohn and Offenbach, and for calling a policeman who had shot a Jew a "pig." He denounced the methods of SS-Gruppenführer Eduard Strauch, who "liquidated" the Minsk ghetto, as unworthy of "the Germany of Kant and Goethe." On the other hand he raised no objections to the murder of those Jews who were unable to work and helped himself generously to Jewish property. He was a quarrelsome creature, constantly locked in battle with Heydrich and Himmler. In 1943 he was killed when a partisan, acting as a chambermaid, planted a bomb under his bed.

Hans Frank ruled the General Government of Poland from the splendid castle in Kraków, which he filled with art treasures stolen from the Catholic Church and the Polish aristocracy, while his wife hoarded jewelry and furs taken from her husband's Jewish victims. He was a generous patron of the arts, counting among his friends Richard Strauss, Gerhart Hauptmann, Elisabeth Schwarzkopf, Hans Pfitzner, and Hitler's favorite, Winifred Wagner (née Williams), who had been married off to Wagner's homosexual son Siegfried as a convenient cover. But he was determined to eradicate the last traces of Polish culture and ruthlessly to exploit the country for the benefit of the Reich. Announcing that the more Jews that died the better, he ordered them to be herded into ghettos and then murdered in the concentration camps at Belzec, Sobibor, Treblinka, and Majdanek, over all of which he ruled as "king of Poland" or, as it was popularly known, of "Frankreich." Frank was soon locked in battle with Himmler over areas of competence, but managed to win Hitler's support, even though many of those close to him thought him utterly contemptible. Speer described him to Hitler as an "idiot," Goebbels called him a "grade A political criminal," and Bormann, who had engineered his dismissal before the war, was determined to remove him. Frank was Hitler's lawyer and president of the Academy of German Law. In 1942 he attacked Hitler, who had recently proclaimed himself to be the "highest judge," in a series of lectures in which he said that the law was being made subservient to the police, thus undermining the rule of law without which no state, not even a National Socialist one, could exist. Hitler responded by forbidding him to make speeches outside the General Government and stripping him once again of his functions within the Reich, but he turned down Frank's request to resign as Governor General. Hitler saw Frank as a useful restraint on Himmler, who threatened to become all-powerful as the Third Reich entered its final and horrific stages.

Alfred Rosenberg, best known as an anti-Semitic ideologue, editor of the party daily newspaper *Völkischer Beobachter*, editor of a critical edition of the "Protocols of the Elders of Zion," and author of the ineffably dreary tract *The Myth of the Twentieth Century*, which he saw as a continuation and completion of Houston Stewart Chamberlain's *The Foundations of the Nineteenth Century*, was appointed Reich Minister for the Occupied Eastern Territories immediately after the invasion of the Soviet Union. As such both Lohse and Koch were his subordinates, but since he was locked in battle with the SS his authority was minimal.

Rosenberg's case is a dramatic illustration of the fundamental contradictions within National Socialism. Although he was a murderous anti-Semite who enthusiastically endorsed the mass murder of the European Jews, he believed that for German imperial aims to be realized it would be necessary to support the national ambitions of Ukrainians and Balts. He was not without support for this view. Werner Best, head of personnel in the RSHA, later head of the civilian administration in occupied France and then plenipotentiary in Denmark, argued in favor of indirect rule, as in western Europe. He could point out that in France the ratio of Germans to French was 1 : 15,000, whereas in the protectorate it was 1 German to 790 Poles. Best thus showed that Heydrich and Himmler's racist and exterminationist policies demanded so much manpower that it seriously undermined the war effort and was bound to fail. Otto Ohlendorf, taking time out as an economist to command Einsatzgruppe D, although personally responsible for the murder of 90,000 Jews, complained of the "Bolshevik methods" of the SS and felt that encouraging national aspirations was preferable to exterminating minorities. He denounced Himmler's reign of terror in the east as "organized disorder." SS-Gruppenführer Harald Turner, the murderous head of the military administration in Serbia, agreed. He enthusiastically slaughtered Jews, Communists, and Gypsies, while insisting that it was better to submit Serbs to what he termed "supervisory administration" rather than ruthlessly suppress them at great cost. Himmler, who was appalled at this pusillanimous approach, reminded Turner that "a Serb is a Serb" who needed to be ruthlessly crushed. Other powerful satraps agreed with Best. Albert Forster, Gauleiter of Danzig-West Prussia, unlike his colleague Arthur Greiser, who was a fanatical ethnic cleanser, believed in assimilating Poles and putting them to work for the Reich. He had no sympathy for ethnic Germans who wished to settle in his fiefdom. Predictably he was locked in constant battle with Himmler, of whom he remarked: "If I looked like Himmler, I wouldn't talk about race." Most civil servants, prominent among them Dr. Wilhelm Stuckart from the ministry of the interior, were appalled at the administrative chaos caused both by Himmler's murderous campaign and by the inefficiency and corruption of the Gauleiters and Reichskommissars.

These interminable arguments point to the central problem of the National Socialist enterprise. It was impossible to achieve both imperial domination and racial purity. A relative degree of cooperation in the west, in spite of the manipulation of rates of exchange, the demand for labor, and the heavy burden of an occupation regime brought results. Mass murder and ruthless exploitation in the east did not. That those who urged a more flexible approach were ignored was due to Hitler's conviction that economics was a zero sum game, that racial purity was essential to the nation's well-being and that Germany needed "living space" for its excess population. Himmler shared these views, not only out of conviction, but also because it was the means by which his SS could be made all-powerful. The Wannsee conference of January 1942, by putting the SS in charge of the "Jewish question," endorsed the murderous approach to empire-building. But this view was not restricted to the SS. General Alexander Löhr, commander in the southeast, announced that: "It may well be necessary (in areas where the guerrillas were active in Greece) to round up all those who do not have to be shot or hanged as bandits or for supporting them. Except for those who are incapable of working; they shall be sent to prisoner collection points for transportation to the Reich." Field Marshal Alfred Kesselring took much the same view as supreme commander in Italy.

The situation was made even more grotesque by the inherent problems involved in the definition of race. Not only was it obviously impossible to find anything other than religious criteria for the definition of Jewishness, but some leading experts such as the racial theorist Otmar von Verschuer, editor of a standard text *Foundations of the Science of Human Heredity and Racial Hygiene* and under whose aegis Josef Mengele was awarded a doctorate, proclaimed that Jews were not a race at all, but mongrels who were indistinguishable from Germans. On the other hand their negative traits, which included neuroticism, a penchant for white-collar crime, loquacity, and a love of garlic, made it desirable that they should be destroyed in the interests of "racial hygiene." After the war von Verschuer pursued his scientific investigations as professor in a newly founded Institute for Human Genetics at the University of Münster, where he became dean of medicine.

Germany as a "people without space" soon turned out to be a myth. Himmler managed to move 800,000 Germans to the *Lebensraum* in the east, but precious few of them were settlers in the true sense. Soon the Germans faced the problem of dealing with 8 million refugees, who in the end made the Federal Republic into a "people without space," to the point that the Russian-American demographer Eugene Kulischer, who coined the expression "displaced persons," proposed a systematic emigration program for the excess German population as well as drastic measures to reduce the birth rate. Hjalmar Schacht, having been acquitted at Nuremberg, suggested that they should be shipped off to colonies in West Africa in the interests of national security. Exotic plans for shifting populations thus lived on, although the methods proposed were noticeably less drastic.

Eventually Himmler and his cronies came to realize that imperial powers cannot do it alone. They always have to rely on outside help. It was an insight that made a mockery of all the vile racist doctrine that lay at the heart of National Socialism. The once purely

Aryan SS became remarkably miscegenated. By the final stages of the war half of the thirty-eight SS divisions were made up of foreigners: 50,000 Dutch, 40,000 Belgians, 20,000 French, and 100,000 Ukrainians served in their ranks. Assistance was also offered by Bronislav Kaminski's "Russian National Liberation Army," a horrifying mob of some 10,000 prisoners of war, who chose to "volunteer" rather than starve to death. Militarily of dubious value, its greatest achievement was to send a detachment of 1,500 men to assist in the slaughter of Poles during the Warsaw uprising, where they indulged in an orgy of rape and plunder. Their brutality was a trifle excessive even for the SS. Kaminski was shot on Himmler's orders, having been court-martialed for looting. An equally dubious unit was the Bergmann Battalion, made up of assorted Cossacks, Armenians, Georgians, Kalmucks, and Azerbaijanis, which specialized in anti-partisan warfare, which was often simply another word for the murder of Jews. Himmler proclaimed the heterodox dogma that Muslims, regardless of race, were Aryans and as such could serve in the SS. Rosenberg added that Armenians were Indo-Europeans and thus Aryans. Hitler had no great objection to Muslims and did not question their anti-Semitic credentials, but he had serious reservations about the Armenians, whom he regarded as having distinctly Jewish characteristics. Himmler ordered the formation of an SS "Handschar" division in Sarajevo, made up of Bosnian Muslims. They went on parade smartly turned out with fezzes adorned with SS runes and scimitar badges. They specialized in mountain warfare. There were also a number of people of dubious ethnicity in the upper echelons of the SS. Prominent among them was Erich von dem Bach-Zelewski, who was of Polish origin and had a Jewish brother-in-law. He prudently added the aristocratic sounding "von dem Bach" to his name in the 1930s. He earned his spurs by deporting Poles, having seized their property and by murdering hundreds of thousands of "partisans" in the Soviet Union. It was under his command that 200,000 Poles were killed in the Warsaw uprising, for which heroic deed he was awarded the Knight's Cross.

None of these opportunistic adjustments modified in any way Himmler's determination utterly to destroy European Jewry. This was his sacred mission, ordained from on high. It was the basis of his enormous and ever-increasing power. Nothing could be allowed to stand in the way. Military prerequisites, economic necessities, and political exigencies were all of secondary importance. He did, however, make one concession to those who insisted on the need for labor. He agreed that Jews who were capable of work should be given a temporary reprieve from the gas chambers, but the emphasis was on the word "temporary." He imagined that he could reconcile the necessity of ridding Europe of all Jews with the need for labor by simply working them to death. Inevitably, the work camps at Auschwitz III and Albert Speer's slave labor battalions were hopelessly unproductive. Moving skilled workers from productive factories, starving them almost to death, and forcing them to work inhumanly long hours in indescribably dreadful conditions is hardly the best way to optimize productivity.

Well over 5 million Jews were murdered in the Shoah, but they were not the only victims of the Nazis' dystopian mania. Up to 3 million Polish gentiles were slaughtered and at least as many Soviet civilians in addition to the 2.1 million Soviet Jews. 3.3 million Soviet prisoners of war were also killed, most of them by starvation. In addition about half a million Gypsies were murdered. The precise number of those who died in this horrific massacre will probably never be known. Precision hardly matters with figures such as these, except to counter wicked people who deny that it ever happened, or that the number of victims was insignificant. Up to 15 million died as a result of the National Socialists'"Racial New Order." Had they won the war the number would have been infinitely higher.

The path to Auschwitz was twisted. There is no single document, verbal order, or single cause that can explain these terrible events. Every attempt to explain hardly brings us closer to an understanding and we are mindful of Primo Levi's fellow Auschwitz inmate Iss Clausner, who scratched the following words on the bottom of his soup bowl: "Ne chercher pas à comprendre." It needed a highly complex multiplicity of causes and actors for virulent, repulsive, but still conventional anti-Semitism and racialism to result in mass murder on such an unthinkable scale. Food shortages were such that it was possible for desk-bound experts to contemplate the removal of 30 million "useless eaters" and "ballast material." Housing shortages as a result of Allied bombing led to demands that Jews should be expelled from the Reich. Financial experts cast greedy eyes on Jewish property. Exotic plans were drawn up for the resettlement of eastern Europe. Half-crazed racial fanatics were free to indulge in their wildest fantasies, while grim specialists in economic rationalization played with statistics and cooked up equally inhuman schemes.

The initiative did not always come from the SS. The foreign office objected to the Madagascar plan because it was "too slow" and would "only" apply to Jews in occupied Europe. Thousands of anonymous accomplices were involved in a highly developed modern society in which the rule of law had broken down. Partial knowledge hardly troubled the consciences of these desktop murders as they drew up their railway timetables, wrote their memoranda, gave their lectures on racial theory, made their films, studied the accounts, and interpreted the Führer's will. As the regime grew progressively radical, all restraint was cast aside. As Goebbels said: "Whoever says A must also say B. ... After a certain moment Jewish politics [*Judenpolitik*] takes on a momentum of its own."

The Turn of the Tide

The Red Army seized the initiative in the summer of 1943 and kept it for the rest of the war. Meanwhile the Allied landing in Sicily meant that Germany's ally was likely to be lost. Hitler was obliged to pull troops out of the Eastern Front to defend Italy, this at a time when the Wehrmacht was reeling after its defeat at Kursk. It was all in vain. Mussolini was deposed on July 25, 1943, and the Italians switched sides. By the summer of the following year the Germans had been pushed back to their starting positions on the Eastern Front in June 1941. The successful Allied landing in Normandy on June 6, 1944 meant that Hitler's days were numbered.

The nimbus around the Führer began to fade as disaster followed disaster. The great gambler now held a series of losing hands. Nothing but a miracle could save him from ruin. For an increasing number of Germans an end to the horror now seemed preferable to what was becoming a horror without end. A small group of mostly aristocratic soldiers and civil servants decided that the time had come to act to save Germany from total destruction and from sinking further into moral turpitude. They were brave men who had virtually no support from the population at large, even though the regime had become savagely repressive at home and the tentacles of Himmler's SS reached into every corner. Hitler became increasingly remote and isolated. Entry to the Presence was jealously guarded by his brutish secretary Martin Bormann. He was surrounded by sycophants, court jesters, and mindless agitators. A failed assassination attempt on July 20, 1944 gave this isolated despot with his warring barony a renewed popularity. Expressions of sympathy came from throughout the Reich. How could these wicked men attempt to kill the Führer at this moment of national peril? There was widespread approval of the bestial treatment of the conspirators, their associates, and their families, who were denounced as "reactionaries," "toffs," and "plutocrats," then executed or subjected to various forms of degradation.

The Shortage of Labor

The absurd proposition that Germany was a "people without space," the premise on which a war to achieve *Lebensraum* had been unleashed, was soon shown to be utter nonsense. Germany was in fact a space without people, totally dependent on foreign workers. This in turn was most disturbing to strict upholders of National Socialist racial policy. They had serious racial-political objections to such a policy, while also harboring ideological reservations about the employment of women.

Walter Darré and his "blood and soil" disciples were deeply disturbed that by as early as 1938 a shortage of a quarter of a million agricultural workers meant that German soil was increasingly tilled by workers from the "lesser breeds." By the autumn of 1944 there were about 8.5 million foreign workers in Germany, amounting to more than a quarter of the workforce. The armaments industry was now dependent on foreign workers and prisoners of war. Of these about 2 million were prisoners of war, 2.8 million workers came from the Soviet Union, 1.7 million from Poland, 1.3 million from France, and 600,000 from Italy. In addition there were 650,000 concentration camp inmates engaged in some form of labor, most of whom were Jews.

It was easy enough to put prisoners of war to work, but few of them had the skills required in the armaments industry. The recruitment of foreigners proved exceptionally difficult, and party functionaries feared that workers from the east would weaken the "racial basis of the biological strength of Germany," especially as there were an alarming number of instances of sexual relations between Aryan Germans and Slav subhumans. This problem was partly overcome by moving a number of factories from Germany to the General Government. Workers from western Europe posed less of a biological threat, but it was feared that they might be prone to indulge in acts of sabotage.

In March 1942 Fritz Sauckel, the Gauleiter of Thuringia, was appointed General Plenipotentiary for Labor. His remit was "to ensure the ordered employment of labor in the German war economy by taking all the measures he deems necessary in the Greater German Reich, the Protectorate, the General Government and the occupied territories." As a good National Socialist, Sauckel refused to be bound by any legal norms. He adopted the Pauline principle of "he who does not work shall not eat" by taking away ration books and clothing coupons from anyone who refused to work. He called this total disregard for the law "active legitimization." His attempts to find volunteers by offering pay equal to that of German workers was not a success. Of 5 million foreign workers, only 200,000 came of their own accord.

Primitive living conditions, malnutrition, and long working hours resulted in a noticeable decrease in productivity. Sauckel tried to overcome this by increasing wages, introducing piecework, and giving foreign workers a great deal more freedom. The result was a significant increase in productivity. Prisoners of war were not so easily bribed, and proved exceedingly reluctant to work for the benefit of the Greater German Reich. In spite of Sauckel's energetic and ruthless approach there was still a desperate shortage of labor. In

October 1942, for example, pedantically thorough statisticians calculated that there was a shortage of precisely 107,417 miners in the coal industry.

All foreign workers, apart from those from Poland and the Soviet Union, were given the same wages and working conditions as Germans. They thus had paid holidays, child allowances, pension contributions, and special bonuses for birthdays, marriages, and deaths. Polish and Soviet workers were given the same gross wages as the others, but they were subject to special taxes, which left them between 10 and 17 marks per week. Since they had to pay 1.5 marks a day for board and lodging this left precious little over at the end of the week. Progressive taxation was so steep that no amount of overtime made any significant difference to net wages.

Sauckel significantly reduced the burden of taxation on Soviet and Polish workers. He also allowed Polish workers to travel home until shortage of transportation made this impossible. Soviet workers were not permitted to travel, but were given a few days' rest provided they could be spared from work. Sauckel soon found himself in direct conflict not only with the SS but also with Robert Ley, the head of the DAF, and Robert Pleiger, director of the Hermann Göring Works and Reich Commissar for the Eastern Economy. He was anxious to find as many able-bodied workers as possible, and therefore insisted that they should be properly fed, housed, and clothed, and given adequate incentives to work. Ley and Pleiger complained that Sauckel was far too lenient with this scum and objected vigorously when he tried to ban corporal punishment. Hitler basically agreed with Sauckel, but pointed out that there simply was not enough food to go round. The SS aimed to kill all the millions of Soviet prisoners of war along with the hundreds of thousands of Jews who were working for the Germans. The SS won the struggle, and millions of Soviet prisoners of war worked until they dropped or starved to death. As a consequence at least 800,000 Jews, 170,000 Soviet citizens, 130,000 Poles, and 32,000 Italian prisoners of war died while working in the Reich.

In the final stages of the war the situation of foreign workers and prisoners of war became desperate. They wandered among the rubble of the ruined cities in search of food and shelter. Many organized themselves into armed bands and had pitched battles with the security forces. Those caught plundering, in other words those who actually found something to eat, were shot on the spot.

The End

On December 16, 1944 the last German offensive was launched in the Ardennes against the American forces in Luxembourg and Belgium. It was a pale imitation of "Plan Yellow" of 1940 that further weakened the hard-pressed Eastern Front. The Americans were at first caught completely by surprise, but reserves were rushed in to halt the German advance. Brigadier General McAuliffe stopped von Manteuffel's Fifth Panzer Army at Bastogne, and to the south Patton's Third Army made a brilliant 90-degree shift north to hit the southern flank of the "Bulge." The ill-equipped and exhausted Germans fought tenaciously with inadequate air cover; relying solely on Allied fuel depots for replenishments. The odds against them were overwhelming. The Allies launched their counter-offensive on January 3, 1945. Within a few days it was clear that Hitler's final gamble had failed. He had expended the slender reserves that were badly needed to meet the Soviet winter offensive, which began on January 12. The Luftwaffe had virtually ceased to exist.

Hitler returned to Berlin on January 16, spending the rest of his days huddled with his cronies in the bunker under the chancellery where the atmosphere was claustrophobic, divorced from reality, and nightmarishly apocalyptic. Meanwhile, millions of half-starved refugees trudged westwards to escape the Red Army, which indulged in a disgusting orgy of murder, rape, plunder, and mass deportations to the Gulag. Poles and Czechs joined in this appalling debauch, taking terrible revenge on their oppressors. Hundreds of thousands of Germans who suffered from this barbaric treatment must also be counted among the millions of Hitler's innocent victims.

Hitler took to the airwaves for the last time on January 30 to give his traditional address on the anniversary of the "seizure of power." It was a poor performance full of talk of fighting to the death against "Asiatic Bolshevism," but it was clear to all around him that the war was lost. On March 15, 1945 Speer pointed out that the war could not last more than four to eight weeks because of the loss of essential sources of raw materials, particularly Romanian oil, and because of the destruction of the transportation network. He did not want to stop the fighting, but rather to let it continue as long as possible, so that the "moral shame" for its prolongation should fall on the Allies. Furthermore, the population loss in these last few weeks would be a form of "tough selection" that would preserve the "healthy kernel" of this "unique people." Three days later he wrote another memorandum for Hitler in which he argued in favor of a last-ditch stand on the Rhine and the Oder in order to "win the enemy's respect" and bring the war to a "favorable" conclusion. Speer's main concern was to ensure that the production of armaments was maintained at the highest possible level so that the war might be prolonged. His efforts to style himself as a man of conscience, who realized the error of his ways in the final stages of the war, managed to fool the judges at Nuremberg and several journalists who chronicled his career, but the archival record proves them to be without any basis in fact. His attempts after the war to show that his skills as an organizer were greater than the destructive power of Allied bombers also managed to hoodwink a surprising number of scholars and provided ammunition, just as he had hoped, to those critical of the bombing campaign. Speer knew full well that strategic bombing played a significant part in the defeat of Nazi Germany.

Allied bombing resulted in about 600,000 deaths and destroyed 3.37 million homes in Germany. It obliged the Germans to employ 800,000 people in air defense; other fronts were thus denuded of artillery, aircraft, and manpower. 88s that were needed against Soviet tanks had to be transferred to the Reich for use as anti-aircraft guns, while air support for the *Ostheer* had to be drastically reduced. There was a desperate shortage of aluminum resulting from its use in fuses for anti-aircraft shells. Constant air raids clearly had a devastating effect on civilian morale, and there was widespread disillusionment with a leadership that failed so spectacularly to defend the Fatherland. RAF Bomber Command's great mistake was to end the "Battle of the Ruhr" in 1943 and concentrate on the destruction of Berlin. Had they kept at it they would have brought the German armaments industry to a standstill. But Allied bombers had effectively disrupted Germany's transport network by September 1944. They then concentrated on the destruction of oil refineries, bridges, canals, and chemical plants.

The cost of this success was terribly high. Without long-range fighter support the bombers were easy targets for the night fighters. Four thousand crew went missing, either killed or shot down and taken prisoner; 640 bombers were lost. It was not until the American B-17 Flying Fortresses flying by day were supported by long-range P-51 Mustangs

PLATE 23   Dresden after the raid. © Bundesarchiv

with detachable reserve fuel tanks that "Fortress Germany" was left without a roof. The morality of strategic bombing is questionable, but attempts by some to make men like "Bomber" Harris the moral equivalent of Heinrich Himmler are clearly grotesque. Strategic bombing made a major contribution to the defeat of Nazi Germany, and Albert Speer's self-serving arguments to the contrary are further evidence of his mendacity and his slippery efforts to absolve himself from his heavy burden of guilt for his complicity in the crimes of the regime he so slavishly served.

In his final weeks Hitler argued that a people which had shown itself so weak and feeble deserved to be destroyed. To his dismay Germany's performance in this titanic clash between the races had demonstrated that his lunatic vision of the biological-racial superiority of the German *Volk* was woefully deficient. On March 19 he issued his "Nero Order" calling for the total destruction of Germany's economic infrastructure. Mercifully this insane command was only obeyed in rare instances. There were no explosives left to carry it out. Communications with the front had broken down. The enemy advance was far too rapid, the fighting too intense for elaborate demolition jobs. Some began to think of the tasks ahead when the war was over. The Führer's wish was no longer law, his voluntarism an expression of impotence.

Hitler's fifty-sixth birthday on April 20 was a gloomy affair during which he decided he would stay in Berlin to the last. On April 29 he married his long-term and long-suffering mistress, Eva Braun. He then dictated his political testament. Even his devoted secretary, Traudl Junge, was appalled by this mean-spirited and repulsive document. Hitler and his young bride committed suicide the following day at 3.30 p.m.

PLATE 24   Red Army troops hoisting the Soviet flag on the Reichstag, May 5, 1945. © BPK

Meanwhile, on April 23, Göring, who had removed himself to Berchtesgaden, asked whether he could take over command, as Hitler no longer had any freedom of action. Hitler's reply was to dismiss him from the party. Himmler sent out some peace feelers, whereupon Hitler ordered his arrest. The Reichsführer-SS ended his wretched life with a cyanide pill on May 23. Goebbels failed in an attempt to sign a separate peace with the Soviets and committed suicide along with his wife on May 1, having first murdered their six children.

On May 7 Jodl signed an act of surrender at Reims. The laconic General Eisenhower reported to the Combined Chiefs that the Allied mission was over. On May 8, Field Marshal Keitel signed a second act of surrender along with Marshal Zhukov and Air Marshal Tedder in Berlin. Hitler's war was thus formally ended at midnight.

It was also the end of National Socialism. The Third Reich left nothing behind it but horror. The horror of tens of millions of dead, of a continent laid waste, the horror of a great nation reduced to barbarism, moral squalor, and mass murder, and soon to be crippled by guilt. It is a horror that will not go away, that refuses to distance itself by becoming history. It is the horror of the unfathomable.

CHAPTER FOURTEEN
THE ADENAUER ERA
1945–1963

CHAPTER CONTENTS

A History of Modern Germany: 1800 to the Present, Second Edition. Martin Kitchen.
© 2012 Martin Kitchen. Published 2012 by Blackwell Publishing Ltd.

Hitler's war left Germany bankrupt and starving amidst a pile of rubble. More than 9 million had been killed. Twelve million refugees, and 5 million homeless joined millions of prisoners of war returning home and "displaced persons" wandering in search of their loved ones and for a safe place to stay, bartering their few remaining belongings for a scrap of food. Defeat was palpable and surrender unconditional. There could be no renewed talk of a "stab in the back." There was no doubt as to who was responsible for the war and there was little possibility of another "war guilt lie." Germany's second bid for hegemony in Europe had failed utterly, leaving the country under Four Power control. One-third of German territory was lost. The Polish frontier was moved westwards to the Oder and the western Neisse, while the Soviet Union laid claim to a large part of East Prussia and to Königsberg, the town of Immanuel Kant. These arrangements were subject to revision in a peace treaty that was not to be signed for decades, by which time there could be no serious consideration of a revision.

A terrible revenge was wreaked on the Germans in the east, even though it was agreed at the Potsdam Conference that they should be permitted to return to the rump Germany in a proper and humane manner. Particularly harsh treatment was meted out on the Sudeten Germans who were not covered by this agreement. Appalling acts of willful brutality were committed by people who had suffered under the Nazis' brutal occupation regime. Many got their just deserts, the vast majority were further innocent victims of Hitler's war.

Germany was now divided into four occupation zones as agreed during the war. The Soviet zone extended as far west as the rivers Elbe, Werra, and Fulda. In the west the British occupied the northern half, the Americans the south, and the French areas contiguous to their frontier with Germany. All political power was now in the hands of the Allied Control Council, and the twenty-two most prominent leaders of the Third Reich who were still alive were called upon to answer for their crimes in front of the International Military Tribunal in Nuremberg. Some were concerned that these people were being tried for crimes that did not exist at the time they were committed, such as "crimes against humanity," "crimes against peace," or the crime of belonging to a criminal organization. Others felt that the Allies, particularly the Soviet Union, should also be tried for similar crimes of which they were clearly guilty. There were murmurings of "victors' justice"; but the enormity of the crimes committed in the name of the German people and their Führer was so great that such cavils were soon forgotten. Only twelve of the main criminals were condemned to death, including Göring, Ribbentrop, and Rosenberg. Keitel and Jodl were the only leading soldiers to be hanged for their part in planning and executing an aggressive war. The odious Albert Speer was lucky to be spared, largely because of his slippery admission of guilt and his refusal to admit the full extent of his complicity with the regime's crimes. He and Rudolf Hess, who gave the impression of having lost his mind, were given lengthy prison sentences. Schacht and Papen were set free.

Between 1946 and 1949 the western allies conducted 5,025 further trials: 4,000 were sentenced, 806 were condemned to death, and 486 were executed. In the so-called Nuremberg Successor Trials 184 prominent Nazis were brought to trial, most of them doctors and officials from concentration camps: 147 were found guilty, and twenty-four were executed. A further 200,000 persons with dubious pasts were interned, many of whom were released after a few weeks; others were held for up to three years. By 1947, 40,000 of these people were still detained. The vast majority of those who were given prison sentences were soon set free by the Federal Republic, where calls for an amnesty were loudly proclaimed by the churches, which were heavily compromised by their silence during the Third Reich. Soldiers who were guilty of the most appalling crimes were released on the grounds that they were simply obeying orders. The army was absolved of all crimes, until historians began to uncover the full extent of its complicity with a criminal regime.

All four occupation powers made use of Nazis with desirable skills, whether as scientists, administrators, or publicists. Many opportunistic Nazis in the Soviet zone found the transition from one dictatorial regime to another easy to make, whereas in the Western zones the difficulty of finding competent anti-fascists was such that a blind eye was all too often turned. This was particularly true of the legal profession, where a large number of singularly unsavory characters remained in office. Some of the more egregious of the Nazi university professors, including Martin Heidegger and Carl Schmitt, lost their chairs in spite of their stellar international standing, but many who were equally guilty but less prominent were soon reinstalled. The French were the most lenient in dealing with their Nazis, the Americans the most stringent, although they quickly lowered their standards as tensions with the Soviet Union began to worsen. All in all the denazification program was an expensive and time-consuming failure. There were precious few devout Nazis left by 1945, degrees of complicity were hard to establish, and the need to rebuild the country was such that even those with a heavy burden of guilt were forgiven after a few years. Many serious criminals managed to avoid prosecution for several years. A few still live in secure anonymity.

The Federal Republic was anxious to stop agonizing about the past and start afresh. The old elites needed to be reintegrated into the new state. The theory of collective guilt had to be energetically rejected. The judicial authorities were increasingly reluctant to pursue their investigations into the past. But at the same time it would be a mistake to imagine that the country had been smitten with collective amnesia. Anxious to escape from a disreputable past, people looked eagerly to the future. Meanwhile artists and intellectuals began to wrestle with the fundamental moral and political issues raised by National Socialism and Germany's recent history. As early as 1946 the minister presidents in the western zones began discussion of laws on the compensation for "Aryanized Jewish property." In September 1952 it was agreed that a provisional sum of 35 billion marks should be set aside for indemnification (*Widergutmachung*), to be administered by a Jewish Material Claims Commission.

The Occupation Zones

The British Labour Party, which won the general election in 1945, wanted to nationalize the larger concerns in the British zone, but this was vehemently opposed by Lucius D. Clay, the American military governor. He argued that such a far-reaching measure should be left to a future German government to decide. Some large firms, such as IG Farben, the Dresdner and Kommerz banks, and a number iron and steel works that had had particularly dubious dealings with the Nazi regime, were placed under trusteeship.

Whereas in 1919 Germany had been left with greatly reduced armed forces and certain types of weaponry were forbidden, in 1945 the country was completely demilitarized. In the Soviet zone the baronial estates of the Junkers were parceled out, while heavy industry was nationalized. Thus the military, the Junkers, and the industrialists lost most of their power and influence in this fundamental change in the social structure of the country brought about by total defeat rather than by the twelve years of the National Socialist "revolution."

In spite of these radical changes 1945 was hardly "zero hour." Germany did not start from scratch. There were inevitably strong elements of continuity. Nevertheless, for contemporaries this was a period of profound anxiety about a future that was largely beyond their control. Having hit rock bottom they longed for a normal life with a steady job, food on the table, and a roof over their heads. Most had through bitter experience learnt to mistrust the ideologues and pied pipers who had reduced them to this pitiful state. They wanted pragmatic answers to practical questions.

In 1945 the democratic forces were determined not to repeat the mistakes of the Weimar Republic. There could be no place for the multiplicity of small parties that had bedeviled the republic and no room for confessional politics. The Christian Democratic Union (CDU) with the former mayor of Cologne, Konrad Adenauer, as its dominant figure, was founded shortly after the war's end. Based on the former Catholic Center Party it was soon to become a non-denominational people's party of moderate conservatives.

Much of the leadership of the Social Democratic Party (SPD), the great historic party of the left, had been martyred during the Third Reich, but it was revived two days before Germany's capitulation at a meeting in Hanover called by Kurt Schumacher. This remarkable man had been severely wounded in the First World War and had spent ten of the Third Reich's twelve years as a prisoner in Dachau. He was an almost frighteningly charismatic figure, even though his health was broken. A fervent nationalist and virulent anti-Communist, he was determined that the SPD should also become a people's party by reaching out to the middle-class voter.

Between the still distinctly clerical CDU and the still theoretically Marxist SPD were a number a local liberal parties which united in December 1948 to form the Free Democratic Party (FDP) under the leadership of a genial Württemberger, Theodor Heuss. He was an archetypical grand bourgeois: an honest, open, highly intelligent *homme de lettres*, but also a man who had made some serious errors of judgment in the turmoil of 1933. The split between left and right liberals that characterized German politics from Bismarck to Hitler was largely overcome, although as in any large party there were differences of emphasis and disagreements over the details of policy. The liberals were opposed to the clericalism of the CDU and the socialism of the SPD; but as the CDU became less clerical, and the SPD less socialist, the FDP found it increasingly difficult to offer a serious alternative to the two main parties. Its importance resided largely in its ability to tip the scales and decide which way to turn in a coalition government.

The first party to be formally reconstituted was the Communist Party (KPD). Its leading cadre, the "Ulbricht Group," having been carefully selected and trained in Moscow, was flown to Germany in April. On June 11, 1945, the party published a moderate reformist program that proclaimed its determination to uphold the rights of private property, private enterprise, and free trade. Proclaiming that it would be a serious mistake to force a Soviet system of government upon the German people, it called for an anti-fascist, democratic, and parliamentary regime that would guarantee freedom for all.

This was nothing more than a cynical attempt to win over Social Democrats in support of a united front, thus creating the impression that the Potsdam formula for a democratic Germany was being respected, after which Walter Ulbricht and his minions would take over control and establish a Communist dictatorship. Many Social Democrats in the Soviet zone were understandably suspicious of the Communists, but massive pressure by the

Soviet authorities resulted in a shotgun wedding between the KPD and SPD in April 1946 resulting in the formation of the Socialist Unity Party (SED). Henceforth it became a criminal offense in the Soviet zone to proclaim one's allegiance to the principles of Social Democracy. Social Democrats were once again "social fascists." Two other parties, the Liberal Democratic Party of Germany (LDPD) and the CDU, were permitted, but the leadership was purged and bullied by the Soviet occupation authorities (SMAD) to the point that they obediently followed the directions of the SED.

That the KPD failed to persuade the SPD in the western zones to work towards the "unity of the working class" was due in no small part to Kurt Schumacher's unyielding opposition. A free vote among SPD members in the western sectors of Berlin resulted in 82 percent opposed to union, but 62 percent were in favor of cooperation with the KPD. Schumacher's attacks on the CDU were equally virulent. He denounced it as a party of clerical obscurantists and rapacious capitalists. He condemned Adenauer as a Rhineland separatist who did not care a fig for the unity of the nation. As a Prussian Protestant he was committed to the Germany of Bismarck, whereas Adenauer, as a devoutly Catholic Rhinelander, harbored deep suspicions of Prussia and is said to have asked for divine protection when crossing the Elbe since he felt himself then to be in Asia. Adenauer the realist knew from the very beginning that the Soviet zone was lost to the German nation for the foreseeable future. Schumacher the romantic nationalist, refusing to accept this unpleasant fact, stepped up his attacks on his rival for his betrayal of the national cause.

The center of gravity in German politics in the years immediately after the war was well to the left. The Social Democrats called for widespread nationalization and a planned economy. The CDU in the British zone endorsed these ideas. When Josef Kaiser, a union leader and prominent member of the resistance, called for "Christian Socialism" that would enable Germany to bridge the gap between Soviet communism and American capitalism he met with a warm response among party members.

The CDU moved steadily to the right, partly because of the mounting tensions between East and West, but also because of the influence of another of the dominant figures in these post-war years. Ludwig Erhard was an economist with valuable connections in industry and banking who had kept his hands clean during the Nazi years. He was a convincing advocate of what his associate Alfred Müller-Armack called a "social market economy." Although committed to the market and the free play of supply and demand, he insisted that the state had to intervene to make sure that free competition was not unduly hindered by monopolies and cartels and that an extensive welfare state should provide assistance to the less fortunate and overcome marked social differences, thereby easing the tensions they created.

From Bizonia to Trizonia

For the time being Erhard had to wait on the sidelines. Amid the ruins of 1945 there could be no question of a social market economy. With a flourishing black market and a starving population, this was purely visionary talk. The Soviet insistence on milking Germany dry obliged the British and Americans heavily to subsidize their occupation zones. Bread was rationed in Britain for the first time so that yesterday's enemies could be fed. Millions of Americans sent CARE (Cooperative for American Remittances to Europe) parcels to save Germans from starvation. Such measures could only bring temporary relief, and the refusal of both the Soviets and the French to implement the Potsdam agreement that Germany be treated as an economic whole obliged the British and Americans to rethink the situation.

The Big Four foreign ministers met in Paris in early 1946 for a lengthy series of frustrating meetings. Ernest Bevin, Britain's foreign secretary, used his remarkable persuasive skills to convince James F. Byrnes, the American secretary of state, that the two Anglo-Saxon powers should stand up to the Soviet Union and not allow French objections to German unity to stop them from going ahead to save what could be saved. On September 6, 1946, Byrnes gave an epoch-making speech in Stuttgart in which he announced that American troops would remain in Germany as long as other countries left theirs. He also made it clear that the United States would no longer respect the Soviet Union's demand that industrial production in Germany for domestic use should be drastically limited. He further called for the unification of all the occupation zones. Knowing full well that the Soviets would not accept, he was thus proposing the division of Germany.

In January 1947 the British and American zones were joined economically to form "Bizonia," the French still objecting to the idea of a West German state. On June 12 of that year the American president proclaimed the "Truman Doctrine" whereby the United States promised economic and military assistance to all peoples in their struggle against communism. On June 5 the new American secretary of state, General George C. Marshall, gave a speech at Harvard University in which he promised massive economic aid to Europe. The resulting Marshall Plan was accepted by Congress in April 1948. The allocation of $17 billion of aid to western Europe was a dramatic demonstration of the United States leadership of the "Free World" as well as establishing American domination of European markets. The Soviets responded by forming the Kominform, in which the states in the "anti-imperialist and democratic" camp banded together to combat the United States and its "imperialist and anti-democratic" allies.

In March 1948 Britain, France, and the Benelux countries formed the Western European Union (WEU), a military alliance clearly aimed against the Soviets, who responded by promptly withdrawing from the Allied Control Council, thus ending four-power control over Germany. The French now dropped most of their objections to the Anglo-American plan for the unification of the western zones, and in April "Bizonia" became "Trizonia."

The currency reform in Trizonia on June 20 introduced the German mark (Deutschmark – DM) and ended price controls and food rationing, thereby putting the black market out of business. The currency reform was a drastic measure: everyone was given a one-off payment of 40 DM, with a further 20 DM a month later. Wages, salaries, and rents were at parity. Savings were exchanged at the rate of 10 Reichsmarks to 1 Deutschmark. Those with material assets, such as real estate, were the big winners from these measures. The immediate results were disappointing. Between June and December 1948 prices rose by 15 percent, while unemployment rose from 447,000 in June to 2 million a year later. By February 1950 unemployment had risen to 13.5 percent. With prices rising far more rapidly than wages, combined with mass unemployment, the SPD had a field day attacking this unpopular measure, but the economy stabilized within a relatively short space of time and the critics were soon silenced with the onset of the boom caused by the Korean War.

The Soviets responded to currency reform in the western zones by introducing a new currency in the Soviet zone and in Berlin two days later. The feisty Social Democratic mayor of Berlin, Ernst Reuter, protested vigorously, insisting that the Deutschmark should be circulated in the three western sectors of the city. The three western commandants agreed, whereupon the SMAD made it a criminal offence for East Berliners to possess Deutschmarks.

PLATE 25   Ludwig Ehrhard. © Friedrich Ebert Stiftung

Then, on August 4, the Soviets blocked all road, water, and rail routes to the western sectors of Berlin. In November the transport of goods from the eastern to the western sectors of Berlin was stopped. Two million Germans were now threatened with starvation. It would seem that Stalin hoped that the western allies would abandon Berlin, get rid of the Deutschmark and drop their plans for a West German state. The western powers took up the challenge in a remarkable display of solidarity and American efficiency. The Berlin airlift supplied the western sectors for eleven tense months. A plane landed at Tempelhof airfield almost every minute, bringing more than 6,000 tons of supplies every

PLATE 26　The Berlin airlift. © BPK

day. The Berlin blockade strengthened America's commitment to Europe and the West's resolve to resist communism.

The Berlin blockade was a propaganda disaster for the Soviets that severely hurt the economy in their occupation zone. It was ended on May 12, 1949, a month after the United States, Canada, and the five states of the western European Union, along with Iceland, Norway, Denmark, Italy, and Portugal, had joined together to form the North Atlantic Treaty Organization (NATO). The United States, the sole possessor of atomic weapons, was now firmly committed to the defense of western Europe. The victory of Communist forces in China did little to console the Soviets when their bluff was called.

The Formation of the Federal Republic of Germany

During the tense months of the Berlin blockade there were heated discussions about the constitution of a West German state. A "Parliamentary Council," elected by the provincial governments, was entrusted with the task of working out the details of a "Fundamental Law" (*Grundgesetz*). This was designed to underline the provisional nature of the future state. The details of the Fundamental Law were hammered out by a group of experts who met in a convent in the idyllic Bavarian setting of Herrenchiemsee in August 1948. Their conclusions were presented to the Parliamentary Council in September for further discussion, with Konrad Adenauer in the chair. Carlo Schmid, a genial and brilliant constitutional lawyer, Social Democrat, and bon vivant, who was born in France of a French mother, dominated the proceedings. He insisted that a democracy should always have the courage to be intolerant towards those who set out to destroy it. In other words the new republic should not repeat the fatal mistakes of Weimar, which had such a democratic constitution that its enemies had at least as many, if not more, rights than its supporters.

The first twenty paragraphs of the Fundamental Law, which guaranteed essential freedoms, were made unalterable under article 79, clause 3, so that there could be no more Enabling Acts or similar constitutional changes that would undermine democratic rule and civil rights. Similarly, a constitutional court was empowered to ban parties that were deemed to be undemocratic. A government could only be toppled by means of a "constructive vote of no confidence" whereby the removal of one chancellor depended on the election of a successor. Backroom intrigues and the decisions of a president elected by popular vote that had helped bring Hitler to power were thus no longer possible. Henceforth parliament alone bore the responsibility for appointing a chancellor. The president was not elected by popular vote, but by an assembly of parliamentarians. The office was almost entirely representational, but the president alone had the right to dissolve parliament under carefully designed provisions.

The issue that was most fiercely debated was over the relative powers of the states (*Länder*) and the federal government (Bund), and how the finances should be apportioned between the two levels of government. The Allies and the CDU/CSU (Christian Social Union, the Bavarian wing of the Christian Democrats) were in favor of states' rights; the SPD and FDP wanted a strong central government. Kurt Schumacher openly defied the Allies over the issue of the financial sovereignty of the federal government and won major concessions on this issue, much to the surprise and amazement of his supporters and to Adenauer's disgust.

The Parliamentary Council concluded its deliberations on May 8, 1949, four years to the day after Germany's unconditional surrender. The Fundamental Law was accepted by an overwhelming majority, with a handful of disgruntled Bavarians and Communists voting against. All the provincial state governments voted in favor of the new law with the exception of Bavaria. A face-saving formula was found, special arrangements were made for West Berlin, the military governors gave their seal of approval, and the Fundamental Law was formally proclaimed on May 23. Bonn was chosen as a suitable capital for a provisional state with a provisional constitution. According to the final paragraph (146), the Fundamental Law would cease to be in effect once a united Germany freely decided upon a constitution.

The election campaign for the first parliament (Bundestag) was fought over the issue of the Social Democrats' version of a planned economy versus Erhard's "social market economy." The election was held on August 14, 1949 and resulted in the CDU/CSU winning 31 percent of the vote, the SPD 29.2 percent, and the FDP 11.9 percent. The remaining 27.9 percent was divided up among five smaller parties, the Communists winning 5.7 percent and thus meeting the requirement of getting at least 5 percent of the popular vote in order to get a seat in the Bundestag.

On September 12 Theodor Heuss, the leader of the FDP, was elected President of the Federal Republic of Germany by the members of the Bundestag and an equal number of representatives of the state governments. Three days later Adenauer was elected chancellor by a majority of one (his own) vote in the Bundestag. His government, made up of the CDU/CSU, the FDP, and the German Party (DP), had 208 of the 402 seats.

In a final act on September 20, 1949, the Allies formally recognized the new state, but required that all laws be countersigned by the three high commissioners. The Federal Republic was thus far from being a sovereign state. A major problem that had to be confronted was how to reconcile the efficiency of the new state's bureaucracy with the dubious pasts of many of its most experienced members. Adenauer had no doubts whatsoever that know-how was of paramount concern. In 1950 one-quarter of department heads in Bonn were former Nazi Party members. By 1953, 60 percent of heads of new departments had this dubious distinction. In the foreign office 78 percent of the senior officials had served under Hitler. There were more party members in the foreign office than there had been in 1938. The most shocking case of all was that of Hans Globke. Although he had helped draft Papen's law dissolving the Prussian state government, as well as Hitler's emergency law, and had written a commentary on the infamous Nuremberg Laws, for twelve years he was head of Adenauer's chancellery. Criticism of this willingness to give people of proven ability a second chance was muted by the astonishing success of the Federal Republic in the "economic miracle," but it still left a nasty taste in the mouths of those who put their ideals above immediate material advantage.

A second wave of rehabilitations began in 1952, whereby under paragraph 131 of the Fundamental Law civil servants who had lost their jobs had a right to be rehabilitated. Although the vast majority of these people had failed to pass through the denazification process, only 0.4 percent were rejected. An exception was made for members of the SS and Waffen-SS, but ways were soon found round this hurdle, so that a number of members of the Reich Security Main Office RSHA found employment in the police and security forces. In a further retrograde step a large number of women who had worked in the civil service during the war were weeded out of the bureaucracy. Use was made of the Brüning government's law of 1932 and the Nazi law of 1937 whereby married women could be dismissed because they were "double earners," so as to make way for the unemployed. Thus married women with an impeccable employment history lost their jobs so that former Nazis could earn a living. Ninety percent of women in the postal service were unmarried; a change in marital status involved a considerable risk of losing one's job. Things began to improve in the 1960s with men gradually leaving the civil service to work in the private sector where remuneration was considerably more generous. But even then only 23 percent of civil servants were women, a far lower percentage than in the Weimar Republic. On the other hand, rising prosperity made it possible for many women to remain at home as housewives and mothers. There were as yet no ideological objections to this option.

Allied experts had estimated that it would take at least thirty years for West Germany to be back on its feet. It was therefore truly astonishing that within ten years the country had largely recovered from the ghastly consequences of death, destruction, and the poisonous ideology of National Socialism. This was a stable, efficient, and democratic society that looked confidently towards the future. There were a number of reasons for this remarkable recovery. The opportunities offered by the boom fueled by the Korean War were exploited to the full. The contrast between the steadily rising level of prosperity in the West contrasted sharply with the misery in the East, thus acting as a powerful antidote

2. Parteitag der SED VOM 20.–24. SEPT. 1947 IN BERLIN

Für die einheitliche demokratische deutsche Republik.

PLATE 27   East German Communist poster. © Landesarchiv/N.N

to the lure of communism. The Fundamental Law provided the constitutional framework for a functioning democracy in which the three main party groupings attracted 94 percent of the electorate. The splintering into a number of smaller parties, which had bedeviled the Weimar Republic, was not yet a problem. The CDU/CSU's social policies greatly ameliorated the condition of the poor, the dispossessed, refugees, and the elderly. Harmonious relations between capital and labor, in a system known as "Rhineland capitalism," encouraged a spectacular rate of economic growth. This in turn meant that those who mourned the Third Reich and its charismatic Führer remained a tiny, disillusioned, and impotent minority.

It was a striking characteristic of the new Germany that nationalism was now a left-wing cause. It is hardly surprising that the SED should call for a united Germany that was "democratic" and "anti-fascist," in other words Communist; but it was truly remarkable that the SPD that had once been the leading light in the Socialist International should now under Kurt Schumacher and Erich Ollenhauer be fervently nationalist. By contrast the moderate conservatives under Konrad Adenauer, committed to a policy of integration with the western powers, refused to pay the high price in the loss of freedom and security that a policy of national integration was bound to involve. Schumacher, unable to untangle the problem of reconciling his desire for national unification with his robust democratic principles and his passionate anti-communism, gave vent to his frustration by denouncing Adenauer as "the chancellor of the Allies." But such outbursts brought him little credit.

Adenauer's concern to remain in good standing with the western allies and the concessions he was obliged to make over such issues as reparations, the allocation of coal and steel in Rhineland-Westphalia, and the status of the Saar met with opposition even within the ranks of the coalition. After a long struggle he was able to overcome all obstacles and remained deaf to protests that he was throwing away what little remained of the country's sovereignty. The Federal Republic took part in the Council of Europe, the Schuman Plan, and, in January 1952, the European Coal and Steel Community.

Rearmament

All these issues were highly technical and secondary. The fundamental political issue was rearmament. Adenauer knew right from the outset that were the Federal Republic to play an equal role in the western alliance it would have to make a major contribution to its defense. Both the Americans and the British agreed, but the French were still deeply suspicious. The invasion of South Korea by the Communist North in 1950, combined with Ulbricht's pointed comparison of the Federal Republic to South Korea, prompted the chancellor to propose the formation of a 150,000-man West German army.

The debate over rearmament was to dominate German politics for years to come. In August 1945 the Allied Control Commission had called for the complete disarmament and demilitarization of Germany. On November 12, 1949, in its first international treaty, the Federal Republic expressed its "full determination to stick by the demilitarization of the Federal Republic and to oppose by every possible means the recreation of any type of military force." The SPD was predictably opposed to rearmament. It was supported by a number of influential figures in the Evangelical Church whose fervent nationalism led them to adopt a pacifist stance. The most outspoken of these was Martin Niemöller, a former U-boat commander and Free Corps mercenary, who as a Protestant minister had fallen foul of the Nazis and had been imprisoned. A rigid and humorless authoritarian, he denounced the Bonn republic as being begotten in Rome and born in the United States.

With the Korean War in the headlines and the memories of the horrors of the last war all too painfully vivid, pacifist sentiment ran high. "Leave me out" (*ohne mich*) was the prevailing sentiment among those likely to be called upon to serve. There was also the problem of how a future German army was to be integrated into a European defense structure. The French premier, René Plevin, proposed a European Defense Community (EDC) in which national contingents would be integrated at the battalion level and later, after German protests and American support, at the corps level. Plans for a new German army went ahead with a de facto ministry of defense under Theodor Blank.

The Soviets, highly alarmed by these developments, decided to intervene. In November 1950 Otto Grotewohl wrote to Adenauer proposing the formation of an All-German Council to work out the details for elections in both Germanys. After lengthy debate the Federal Republic responded by calling for free elections in East and West to be supervised by the United Nations. On March 10, 1952 the Soviets released a bombshell by proposing to the western allies that a peace treaty with Germany should be concluded that would result in a free, democratic, united, and neutral Germany. There was no mention of free elections in this note.

Adenauer saw this proposal as an artful attempt to torpedo his policy of western integration, thereby ruining plans for a western European defense community. The nationalists, both Social Democrat and Protestant, called for a careful examination of the Soviet proposal, but the western allies had already decided that it was unacceptable. The Americans and the British considered that a neutral Germany would mean Soviet hegemony over Europe. For the French the mere thought of a united Germany, in whatever form, was a horror that did not bear contemplation. For years to come the opposition continued to accuse Adenauer of having missed a golden opportunity for national unification in 1952, but history was to prove them wrong. The eventual unification of Germany met Adenauer's requirement for freedom to be combined with security. Furthermore, the formal loss of Silesia, East Prussia, and Pomerania, which was required under the Soviet conditions, was by 1989 no longer a burning issue. The majority of West German electors would have found such terms unacceptable in 1952.

If anything the Soviet note hastened the process of western integration. Under the terms of a treaty, on May 26 the occupation was formally ended. A few days later the treaty creating the European Defense Community was also signed. The Federal Republic was still not fully sovereign, but Adenauer was comforted by the undertaking of the western powers to work towards the creation of a united Germany that was integrated into the European community. All this was anathema to the opposition. Schumacher proclaimed that "whoever signs this treaty ceases to be a German." He was to die shortly afterwards at the age of 57, but his spirit lived on in the lively debates over the treaty, which was not formally ratified until May 1953, by which time Stalin had died, the Soviet threat seemed to have diminished and opposition to German involvement in a European defense community was growing apace in France.

The expellees' party, the Association of Those Who Had Lost Their Homes and Their Rights (Bund der Heimatentrechteten – BHE), won considerable support by clamoring for the release of those who had been given prison sentences by the Allies as a result of the crimes they had committed during the Nazi era. They were supported by the nationalist DP and by the liberals (the FDP). The latter had a number of prominent Nazis in their ranks. There was general agreement that those who had been sentenced at Nuremberg had got their just deserts, but others were deemed simply to have done their duty as soldiers or civil servants. There were loud calls for a general amnesty that would include such noisome characters as SS General Kurt "Panzer" Meyer. The SPD jumped on the bandwagon by subscribing to the myth that the army and the Waffen-SS had fought a clean war, unlike the other SS departments who alone were responsible for all the crimes of the Nazi era. The Jewish Bund protested against this preposterous assertion, but Kurt Schumacher replied that it was inhuman to treat the 900,000 former members of the Waffen-SS as pariahs. According to a public opinion poll in 1952 an amazing 24 percent of the population still thought highly of Adolf Hitler; 30 percent condemned the July 20 resistance movement.

In West Germany 1953 was an election year, and Adenauer was in a particularly strong position which he bolstered by holding well-publicized interviews with such recently released war criminals as generals Kesselring, Mackensen, and Manstein and by visiting "Panzer" Meyer in prison. The brutal suppression of the June uprising in the German Democratic Republic (GDR) confirmed to many voters that his firm anti-Communist stand was fully justified. The "economic miracle" (*Wirtschaftswunder*) helped to integrate the expellees and silence radical critics from the extremes of left and right. West Germany seized the opportunities offered during the golden age of industrial capitalism from the 1950s to the oil crisis of 1973 to reach a level of material prosperity unrivaled in Europe.

The CDU/CSU won a convincing victory, gaining 45.2 percent of the popular vote, 14.2 points more than in 1949. The SPD's share of the vote remained virtually unchanged at 28.8 percent. This was largely due to the uninspiring leadership of Erich Ollenhauer, a conventional and doctrinaire party functionary. The FDP, with 9.5 percent, gave Adenauer a majority, even though they had lost 20 percent of their supporters since 1949, many of whom were disgusted with a party that harbored so many former Nazis. A number of smaller parties, including the Communists, failed to reach the 5 percent minimum, although the expellees' party, with its unsavory leadership of old Nazis, just squeaked in.

An abortive meeting of the Big Four foreign ministers in Berlin beginning in January 1954 made it clear that neither side was prepared to make any concessions over the German question. Shortly afterwards the Bundestag voted in favor of rearmament, but this was of little consequence owing to the attitude of the French. In May the French forces in Indochina met with a crushing defeat at Dien-Bien-Phu, the Laniel government fell, and his successor Pierre Mendès-France negotiated an armistice with Ho Chi Minh's Vietnamese Communists. After such a humiliation the French were in no mood to accept any diminution of their sovereignty. The National Assembly rejected the European Defense Community by an overwhelming majority.

This was a shattering blow to Adenauer, who had set great store by the EDC, but France's NATO partners were determined to get the West Germans on board. Italy and the Federal Republic were invited to join the Western European Union, and discussions began as to the nature of Bonn's future contribution to NATO. Adenauer readily agreed that Germany would not produce ABC weapons, battleships, or strategic bombers. Much to the fury of his nationalist critics, he also agreed to an autonomous Saar that would be economically linked to France, pending a final peace conference and subject to a referendum to be held the following year. The western allies in return ceded a number of their rights over the Federal Republic, whose sovereignty nevertheless still remained restricted.

The Soviet Union responded to these negotiations in Paris by making a half-hearted offer of free elections in all of Germany, but when the treaties were signed Molotov announced that there could now be no question of reunification. A number of leading Protestants, supported by the SPD and the trade unions, mounted a massive campaign against the Paris treaties, but the public response was muted. The treaties were ratified with a convincing majority. French objections to German rearmament were overcome thanks to some skillful diplomacy by the British foreign secretary Anthony Eden, so that the Federal Republic joined the Western European Union on June 7, 1955. Two days later it became a member of NATO.

The Soviet Union responded to German membership of NATO by forming the Warsaw Pact five days later, which placed the armed forces of all the satellite states, including the GDR, under direct Soviet command. At the same time Molotov and the three western allies signed a treaty that ended the occupation of Austria. The new state was neutral, an *Anschluss* was forbidden, but it was in all other respects fully sovereign. At Molotov's suggestion a summit meeting of the Big Four was held in Geneva in the summer of 1955, at which the German question was discussed at length. Much to Adenauer's alarm the western powers proposed disarmament talks as a means of lessening tension in Europe. This implied an acceptance of the division of Germany. Adenauer's belief that western integration was the most effective way of achieving reunification on acceptable terms began to fade. His fears were largely confirmed when the first secretary of the Communist Party and the coming man in the Soviet Union, Nikita Khrushchev, gave an inflammatory speech in East Berlin in which he said that the GDR should never give up its "socialist achievements." He pointedly made no mention of German unity. It was clear from the tame assurances of the western powers to the contrary that the division of Germany was now accepted by both sides in the Cold War. Adenauer traveled to Moscow in September in order to establish diplomatic relations with the Soviet Union. He had to accept that there would henceforth be two German ambassadors in Moscow, which was a bitter pill to swallow, but he did succeed in securing the release of thousands of wartime prisoners, which greatly enhanced his popularity at home.

On his return to Bonn, Adenauer adumbrated what came to be known as the "Hallstein Doctrine," named after the permanent secretary in the foreign office, Walter Hallstein. The Federal Republic henceforth considered itself to be the sole representative body of the German people. Were any third state to establish diplomatic relations with the GDR it would be considered in Bonn as an "unfriendly act." For this reason Bonn refused to establish diplomatic relations with any of the Soviet satellite states, but relations with the Soviet Union were not affected. The Hallstein Doctrine was first put into effect in 1957 when diplomatic relations with Yugoslavia were severed upon Belgrade opening an embassy in East Berlin.

Somewhat to Adenauer's surprise the people of the Saar rejected the "Europeanization" of the region in a referendum, thus opening the way for the return of the Saar to Germany, a process that was finally concluded in 1959. None of this undermined the Federal Republic's relations with western Europe as the chancellor had feared. In 1957 the Treaty of Rome created the European Economic Community (EEC), in which the Federal Republic was to play a key role. It was a milestone along the road to European integration.

From the "Economic Miracle" to "Eurosclerosis"

There were many reasons why the West German economy thrived to such a spectacular extent that it was hardly an exaggeration to talk of a "miracle." The country was in ruins, but it still had virtually unlimited reserves of human capital in the form of a skilled labor force, augmented by a stream of refugees from eastern Europe and the GDR. It had industrial expertise and know-how that rivaled those of the United States. It thus had its own resources on which to build, so that it was able to exploit to the full the opportunities offered in the neo-liberal post-war world. Ludwig Erhard's model of a social market economy was perfectly tailored to meet the challenge. The exchange system established at Bretton Woods, the lowering of tariff barriers in the General Agreement on Tariffs and Trade (GATT), the International Monetary Fund (IMF), the European Payments Union (EPU), the European Recovery Program (ERP), the Organization for Economic Cooperation and Development (OECD), the European Union (EU), and the European Economic Community (EEC) were all institutions which provided excellent incentives for Germany's export industries. Exports as a percentage of GNP were 9 percent in 1950, 19 percent in 1960, and 25 percent in 1970. All this was within the context of the boom years from 1950 to 1973, which resulted in what some economists have called a "worldwide economic miracle." In 1971 the United States unilaterally tore up the Bretton Woods Agreement, forcing an increase in the exchange rate of the Deutschmark to the dollar of 13.7 percent. Then in 1973 oil prices rose by 400 percent, causing a worldwide economic crisis that put an end to the European economic miracle and ushered in years of stagflation.

The Federal Republic seized the opportunities and the results were impressive. Between 1950 and 1973 GNP grew at an average yearly rate of 6.5 percent, twice the rate in the USA. The economy expanded threefold in these years, an aggregate higher than that between 1800 and 1950. In large part this was due to an exceptionally high rate of investment. By 1960 one-quarter of gross national income (GNI) was invested, much of it by plowing back profits, a practice encouraged by generous tax allowances. The part played by American capital in enterprise resource planning (ERP) has often been exaggerated. It did so only indirectly. The bulk of the capital went to Britain and France, enabling them to reduce their demands for reparations from their former enemy. Payments to Germany were more of symbolic value, in that they showed that Germany was welcome back as an economic partner. The export sector was particularly strong without as yet any competition from Asia. The West produced 93 percent of all industrial goods and West Germany's portion thereof steadily grew, in spite of the fact that the Allies had taken the patents of a number of leading firms estimated to be worth $10 billion. In 1950 West Germany's net material product (NMP) was 40 percent of that of the USA; by 1980 it had risen to 80 percent. By 1960 per capita real income had doubled; by 1973 it had trebled. There was a brief sobering moment in 1966/7 when the economy was hit by a recession. Industrial production was reduced. GNP remained stagnant. Radical voices on the extreme right and extreme left were raised, but the crisis soon blew over due to the stimulating effects of the Vietnam War.

The flight from the land increased with a booming industrial sector offering far higher wages. Two-thirds of the agricultural workforce left the land between 1949 and 1969. Agriculture's share of GNP fell from 25 percent in 1949 to 13.3 percent in 1960; it went down to 5.3 percent in 1980, and by 2000 it had dropped to 2 percent. The negative effects of this social revolution were offset by huge subsidies that in turn helped increase productivity to an astonishing degree. Between 1949 and 1978 a massive program of land consolidation led to the redistribution of 4 million hectares of farmland, equal to one-third of all agricultural land. A million smallholdings disappeared. The productivity of these larger farms increased rapidly, due to mechanization, the use of chemicals, and the application of innovative techniques. Between 1950 and 1990 the production of wheat rose from 2.58 to 6.58 tonnes per hectare, of potatoes from 24.49 to 39.25 tonnes per hectare, and of sugar beet from 36.10 to 54.92 tonnes per hectare. Meat production rose by 50 percent.

The decline in the agricultural sector to become a minute and insignificant part of the economy occurred without any serious consequences. West Germany was spared the enormous social and political problems created by this upheaval that still bedevil France. But one major issue remained unresolved. The extraordinary, one is tempted to say revolutionary, leap forward in agricultural production meant that Germany could meet three-quarters of its demand for foodstuffs, even in times of exceptional prosperity. But in some sectors there was the serious problem of overproduction. This was addressed with colossal subventions, the burden of which to both the state and the consumer became increasingly difficult to bear. Prices were rigidly controlled, markets guaranteed, exports heavily subsidized, discrepancies between production costs and prices promptly addressed. Echoes of "blood and soil" were to be found in the government's determination to preserve a "healthy rural middle class." It was a situation that benefited the larger enterprises, which were favored by the government because they could offer economies of scale. When they were situated near large towns they readily sold off land as building sites at a handsome profit. Farms of less than 20 hectares gradually fell by the wayside. By the 1990s two-thirds of net value added in the agricultural sector came in the form of subventions from the state and the EEC. Maintaining this ludicrously inequitable system today consumes half of the EEC's annual budget. Excess production is stored in butter mountains and wine lakes, or simply destroyed to maintain prices. Agricultural products from Third World countries are excluded by high tariff barriers, so that consumers have to pay well above the world price for their food, as well as having to foot the bill for these massive subsidies. The farmer is thus protected against the contingencies of the market, but his social and functional status is reduced, leaving him dependent on what amounts to welfare payments. A person in charge of a large farm might still enjoy a substantial income, but he is selfishly profiting from the successful lobbying of special interest groups and is the beneficiary of funds that should have been invested in endeavors that are in the general interest.

Prosperity enabled the state to meet the needs of those who fell by the wayside with generous welfare provisions, but this was done at a cost. National debt rose from 17 percent of GNI in 1950, to 32 percent in 1970, to 49 percent in 1982. It has continued to grow, placing a heavy burden on further generations. The Federal Republic also had to pay off pre- and post-war debts. In 1953 the German delegation to the London Debt Conference, led by the banker Josef Abs, negotiated a favorable deal in which it was agreed that the total debt amounted to 14.5 billion Deutschmarks. The Germans repaid this sum with relative ease, so that by 1957 the Deutschmark was fully convertible, and foreign investors began to put their money into a booming economy. The transformation of the European Community into the European Economic Community (EEC) offered German exports further opportunities, which were eagerly seized.

By 1970, with 48.5 percent of its employees in the industrial sector, Germany was the most heavily industrialized country in the world. But then began a steady movement of workers to the service industries, a characteristic of the "post-industrial age." Gradually the number of industrial workers sank by one-third. By 2000 the service industries employed 63 percent of the total workforce. This was due to the rapid expansion of the welfare state with its huge bureaucracy, the vast investment in education at all levels, the growing importance of banking and insurance, increased employment in the maintenance and repair of consumer goods, and the growth of the media.

Prosperity was also due to the maintenance of a degree of industrial peace that was exceptional in Europe. On the one side there were the immensely powerful pressure groups of industrialists and agrarians, successors to those behind the protectionism of the 1870s and which played such a vital role in domestic politics until the *Gleichschaltung* in 1933. Chief among them were the Federal Association of German Industry (Bundesverband der Deutschen Industrie – BDI), modeled on the former Reich Association of German Industry and the powerful Central Association of German Industrialists (Zentralverband). In addition there was the German Industry and Trade Association (Deutscher Industrie- und Handelskammertag), an umbrella organization for eighty-three regional chambers of commerce, with a compulsory membership of 2.7 million. Farming was represented by the German Farmers' Association (Deutscher Bauernbund), heir to the legendary Farmers' League and to the Nazi Reichsnährstand. It was able to secure staggering levels of subsidies for the declining agricultural sector.

On the other side of the equation were seventeen trade unions, organized under the German Trades Union Association (DGB), but fully independent. By 1980, 7.9 million of 23.5 million wage-earners were union members: 68 percent were industrial workers, 20 percent women. Trade unions alone had the right to make wage agreements, but they were anxious to avoid industrial action, preferring reasoned argument to strikes. Workers' representatives on the boards of major firms also helped maintain industrial peace by giving workers a voice in management. The result of this pragmatic approach was that German workers were the highest paid in Europe. The SPD was the political arm of the union movement. In 1980, 218 of the 238 SPD members of the Bundestag were trade union members. Similarly, 82 percent of the DGB's top officials were members of the SPD.

On the whole the two sides cooperated, in conjunction with the government and political parties, to achieve an exceptional degree of corporate solidarity so that most major problems were squarely addressed and appropriately settled. It is perhaps curious that a system that was neither anchored in the constitution nor legitimized by democratic consent, and that smacks of Fascist corporatism, should continue to play such a positive role within a liberal democratic state.

Social peace was also reinforced by the "burden-sharing" (*Lastenausgleich*) law of 1952, which affected one-third of the population. Compensation was paid for property lost by expulsion from the East, by seizure in the GDR, by bomb damage, or by inequalities caused by the currency reform. The colossal sum of 140 billion Deutschmarks was spent over the years on this remarkable project

The dramatic expansion of the economy caused a profound change in the social structure. The flight from the land continued apace and blue collars were exchanged for white. West Germany became a society of office workers and government employees, of unpretentiously comfortable petty bourgeois families with a Volkswagen and a television set, a modest home and a secure pension. A class-conscious proletariat ceased to exist, the all-powerful captains of industry had mostly disappeared, divisions along confessional and regional lines became blurred. Gross inequalities still existed and were to become more pronounced, but the Adenauer era was one in which the somewhat philistine and narrow values of the modestly situated middle classes set the tone.

The immigration of skilled workers from East Germany, which saved the Federal Republic vast sums of money in the cost of education and training, abruptly stopped in 1961 with the building of the Berlin Wall. Foreign workers were now recruited, mainly from Italy, Spain, Turkey, and Yugoslavia. By 1973 there were 2.6 million "guest workers," making up 12 percent of the total workforce. With the onset of the oil crisis the government put a stop to the influx of foreign workers, but those who had taken up permanent residence were able to obtain visas for family members.

The economy now slowed down. The rate of growth between 1973 and 1989 averaged 2 percent. This was a respectable amount, equivalent to that in the boom years from 1896 to 1913, but compared to the previous twenty-three years it seemed miserable. The major problem was that it became increasingly difficult to pay for the generous welfare provisions as greater demands were placed upon them, resources dwindled, and debt mounted at an alarming rate. "Stagflation" meant slow rates of growth, inflated prices, and rising unemployment. The OECD began to talk of "Eurosclerosis." Problems were compounded from 1976 when OPEC again increased the price of oil, and in 1979 with the fundamentalist Islamic revolution in Iran. This led to a further oil price hike of 130 percent. Things began to steady by 1981, and by 1990 prices had fallen.

Far more serious than the oil crisis of 1976–9 was the challenge from Asia. Not only were Japan and China now serious players in the world economy, the "little tigers" in Singapore, Taiwan, Malaysia, and Thailand were also thriving, thanks to extremely low rates of pay for a compliant workforce, coupled with exceptionally low rates of taxation. With the United States dominating the world in electronics, Germany was in serious danger of slipping behind. Above all the process of de-industrialization was gaining momentum, with a failure to keep up in research and development, the ever-mounting fiscal burden of the welfare state, the reluctance of the trade unions to adjust to a new reality, outsourcing to countries offering lower wages and lower rates of taxation, the growing challenge from Asia, as well as large enterprises gobbling up smaller ones thereby pruning the workforce. The spectacular successes of the years from 1950 to 1973 created the illusion that the economic miracle was the norm, that the glory days would come again, so that there seemed to be no reason for any fundamental changes in order to meet future challenges.

The Heyday of Adenauer's Germany

The year 1957 was election year, and Adenauer was once again in an almost invincible position. The brutal suppression of the Hungarian uprising in November of the previous year lent credence to his anti-Communist stand. The index-linked pensions that were introduced early in the year were enormously beneficial to millions of pensioners and were extremely popular. The SPD had been obliged to vote for the measure, but the credit went to the CDU/CSU. Pensions were set at 60 percent of average wages for those who had worked for forty years. The previous rate had been 34 percent. Since pensions were also index-linked this meant that the average pension increased by 110.5 percent. The long-term problem was that, with lower rates of growth, a dwindling birth rate, increased life expectation, and rising unemployment, within forty years it was no longer possible to finance such a generous pension scheme. For the moment, however, the Christian Democrats had found a powerful election slogan that was pasted all over the country: "NO EXPERIMENTS!" The SPD's call for more housing was very small beer by comparison with the government's pension boost. A grateful electorate gave Adenauer's Christian Democrats an absolute majority.

Elections were held in West Berlin in December 1958, and resulted in a victory for Willy Brandt's SPD. He and Adenauer were the two towering figures in the history of the Federal Republic. Born in Lübeck as Herbert Frahm in 1913 to a single mother, he emigrated to Norway in 1933 and joined the Norwegian army in order to escape the clutches of the Gestapo. Later he worked as a journalist in Sweden. He regained his German citizenship in 1948, adopting his nom de plume as his official name. He endorsed the Federal Republic's membership of NATO and rejected his own party's plan for the future of Germany that bore a certain resemblance to Ulbricht's proposals. They had been drawn up by Herbert Wehner, a brilliant and sourly ironic former Communist. Shortly after his election Brandt addressed the NATO council in Paris in his inimitable English. He impressed his audience with his absolute determination to stand up to Soviet pressure to ensure that West Berlin remained an island of freedom in the heart of the GDR.

Brandt was the outstanding example of the new type of Social Democrat. He was pro-western, flexible, ready to compromise while remaining true to his principles, a brilliant speaker, and a thoroughgoing democrat. Although born in the humblest of circumstances

PLATE 28   No experiments! © Konrad Adenauer Stiftung

he enjoyed a solidly bourgeois lifestyle, while never losing the common touch. No politician was less corrupted by power, none more widely loved and respected. His modernizing ideas were reflected in the SPD's new party program adopted at Godesberg in 1959. The last vestiges of the Marxism that remained in the Heidelberg program of 1925 and the Dortmund program of 1952 were cast aside. The party endorsed the free market economy by announcing that it was no longer a party of the working class, but an open-ended people's party.

In 1960 Herbert Wehner gave a brilliant speech in the Bundestag in which he said that the SPD fully endorsed NATO and the western alliance as the basis of the Federal Republic's foreign policy. He insisted that "a divided Germany cannot tolerate a situation in which Christian Democrats and Social Democrats are in a permanent state of mutual enmity." Wehner thus turned his back on his Plan for Germany (Deutschlandplan) of March 1959, thereby showing that the Godesberg program, which he had played a key role in writing, marked a genuine new beginning for the SPD. Wehner was every inch a power politician who realized that the SPD would remain without influence as long as it stood in principled opposition to the CDU/CSU. The party would have to become an acceptable coalition partner for it to have any share of political power. In such circumstances there was no serious alternative for the SPD but to make Willy Brandt its chancellor candidate in 1960. As mayor of Berlin he was a popular national figure, a youthful and even glamorous alternative to the octogenarian chancellor, a man much respected in the West, and who could appeal to all sectors of German society except those who could not stomach the fact that he was both illegitimate and an émigré.

The next round of Big Four talks was held in Paris in May 1960, but when the American pilot Gary Powers was shot down over the Soviet Union in his U2 reconnaissance plane Khrushchev walked out, announcing that he would not attend another such meeting for several months to come. He promised that in the meantime he would not raise the issue of Berlin. He clearly intended to await the outcome of the US presidential elections in which John F. Kennedy faced Richard Nixon.

The Berlin Wall

Adenauer breathed a sigh of relief when the Paris talks were thus abruptly ended, but he was soon to be alarmed by the diplomatic ineptitude of the young and inexperienced American president. After the abortive invasion of the Bay of Pigs in April 1961 there followed a disastrous meeting between Kennedy and Khrushchev in Vienna in June. Kennedy was sent reeling by Khrushchev's renewed threat to sign a peace treaty with the GDR and to seal off all routes to West Berlin. He returned to Washington in a highly agitated state. In the following month he gave a radio address announcing a substantial increase in America's conventional forces and his absolute resolve to stand by West Berlin.

Tension over Berlin was such that refugees flooded to the West to the point that the East German economy was on the verge of collapse. In the early morning of August 13, 1961, work was begun to seal off West Berlin with an "anti-fascist defensive wall" which made it virtually impossible for anyone to leave the GDR. Planners no longer had to face the disastrous economic effects of the mass flight of what was often the best and the brightest. Snow White, as one cabaret artist in East Berlin remarked, now only had three dwarves since the other four were in the West. But at least she was not totally bereft of help.

The West contented itself with verbal protests and was relieved that West Berlin had been left untouched. August 13 was a shattering blow for Germans in both East and West. Both sides of the wall felt abandoned by their allies and well-wishers. Reunification now seemed nothing but a pipe dream. The two societies grew steadily apart, each taking on a distinctive identity. On the personal level families and loved ones were separated by barbed wire, minefields, and machine-gun posts. The idea of a united Germany that was free, peaceful, and secure seemed little more than an empty formula. The way ahead seemed more uncertain than ever.

PLATE 29   Adenauer and De Gaulle. © PA

The End of the Adenauer Era

The Berlin Wall was built in the middle of an election campaign in the Federal Republic in which Adenauer showed signs of losing his grip. He did not allow for a pause in the campaign when the wall was built and concentrated on scurrilous attacks on the opposition, at one point referring to his rival Willy Brandt as "Herr Brandt alias Frahm." Brandt, as mayor of West Berlin, used his position in these crisis days to the utmost and overnight became a figure of international stature.

When the votes were counted on September 17, the CDU/CSU had lost almost 5 points compared with 1957, the SPD gained 4.4 points, and the FDP, with 12.8 percent, had increased its share of the popular vote by a remarkable 66.2 percent. Coalition discussions were protracted and acrimonious. The FDP wanted to maintain the alliance with the CDU/CSU but insisted on getting rid of Adenauer, who was now 85 years old and stubbornly refused to resign. Eventually a compromise solution was found when Adenauer agreed to step down mid-term in the new parliament, thus enabling the coalition between the CDU/CSU and the FDP to be renewed. The SPD, which had hoped for a national government to deal with the Berlin crisis, remained in opposition.

In April 1962 President de Gaulle successfully brought the ugly Algerian war to an end and thus avoided what could have become a civil war in France. He then turned to Adenauer and proposed close cooperation between the two countries, particularly with respect to European defense. Adenauer made an official visit to France in July that culminated in a Franco-German military parade, and the two old men celebrated Mass in Reims cathedral. De Gaulle then paid a return visit to the Federal Republic in September in which he was given a heartfelt welcome.

Relations with France became a major debating point in Germany, particularly within the ranks of the CDU/CSU. The division was between the "Atlanticists" like the foreign minister Gerhard Schroeder, who wanted the closest possible ties with the United States, and the "Gaullists" such as Franz-Josef Strauss, who wanted Europe to be less dependent on America. The debate between the two factions intensified when de Gaulle proposed an alliance between the two countries shortly after his visit to Germany.

Meanwhile the crisis over Berlin continued, as the Soviets harassed the air corridors. Then an 18-year-old construction worker was left by American soldiers to bleed to death on the frontier strip, having been shot trying to cross the border into West Berlin. The public outrage was such that a serious incident was only narrowly avoided thanks to Willy Brandt's skillful handling of the situation. Adenauer got no support from Kennedy, and Khrushchev exploited the president's weakness to step up the pressure by stationing middle-range missiles in Cuba. Kennedy forced Khrushchev to back down in an extremely hazardous poker game that brought the world perilously close to nuclear war. The building of the Berlin Wall and the Cuban missile crisis forced both sides to rethink their positions. The Americans and the Soviets realized that it would clearly be madness to continue along this dangerous path, and the way was open for a gradual détente.

At the height of the Cuban missile crisis Germany was rocked by the most serious domestic political crisis in the history of the Bonn republic. The popular news magazine *Der Spiegel* published an article on the recent NATO exercise "Fallex 62" which had shown up some disastrous deficiencies in West Germany's defenses and a number of serious differences between the US and the Federal Republic over the deployment of atomic weapons. All of this was in the public domain, but the impetuous minister of defense and chairman of the CSU, Franz-Josef Strauss, a man of dubious political morality and one of the magazine's favorite targets, was convinced that top secret documents had been leaked that endangered the republic's security. The magazine's offices were searched and sealed. A number of journalists were arrested with total disregard for due legal procedure in a scandalous attempt to muzzle the free press. Strauss blatantly lied to the Bundestag about his role in the affair and when caught out refused to resign. Adenauer made a fool of himself by accusing *Der Spiegel* of committing high treason simply to make money. The minister of the interior admitted that he had "acted somewhat outside the law"; the minister of justice confessed that he had not been informed that the arrests were to be made, as was required by the law. The five FDP ministers resigned in protest and the party leader, Erich Mende, made it clear that the coalition could not continue if Strauss were to remain in office. A number of CDU ministers followed suit. Massive protests were held throughout the country in expressions of solidarity with the *Spiegel* journalists and for the freedom of the press. In the end the journalists were acquitted by the High Court of all charges and the constitutional court had a tied vote on whether or not the action against *Der Spiegel* was unconstitutional. Rudolf Augstein, the paper's editor, emerged from 103 days in jail to be feted as a national hero. Strauss eventually bowed to the inevitable and resigned, his parting marked by a ceremonial parade and an effusive panegyric from Adenauer. The *Spiegel* affair marked a turning point in the history of the Bonn republic. The old authoritarian tradition of the *Obrigkeitsstaat*, whose obedient citizens meekly followed orders from above, was totally discredited. A younger generation called for a more open, liberal, and free society of autonomous subjects.

In December 1962 British prime minister Harold Macmillan met President Kennedy in the Bahamas, where an agreement was reached to arm British submarines with American nuclear warheads. This was designed as the first stage of the creation of a multi-national atomic force (MLF) under American command within the framework of NATO. De Gaulle, taking this as a personal affront, announced that France would now join the nuclear club and would veto Britain's entry to the EEC. Shortly afterwards, on January 22, 1963, the Franco-German Agreement was signed in Paris which called for regular meetings between the two heads of government and consultations over all key issues of foreign policy, along with an extensive program of cultural and educational exchanges.

At first it appeared that the Federal Republic was now on an anti-American course, but Adenauer made it plain that the republic would live up to its NATO obligations and was interested in joining the proposed MLF. The Bonn government also supported British entry to the EEC – an empty gesture since the French veto was already in effect. The Elysée Treaty as ratified by the Bundestag removed all traces of anti-Americanism, thus frustrating de Gaulle's intentions. The general suffered a further setback when the CDU/CSU decided upon Ludwig Erhard, a prominent Atlanticist, as Adenauer's successor.

The Atlanticists were given a further boost when Kennedy paid a state visit to the Federal Republic in June 1963. He was given a rapturous welcome when he underlined the United States' commitment to the Federal Republic. In Berlin he announced: "ich bin ein Berliner!" At the same time, in accordance with his recently expressed determination to "make the world safe for diversity," he urged the Germans to be patient, warning that national unification would be an extremely lengthy process. Willy Brandt was in total accord with Kennedy. He had told his audience in Harvard in October 1962 that coexistence, détente, and communication were the keys to any progress. In July the following year he told a German audience that "a solution to the German problem can only be found with the Soviet Union, not against it." Here were the clear outlines of his future *Ostpolitik*. His close associate Egon Bahr had already spoken of "change through convergence" (*Wandel durch Annäherung*) which was soon to become a popular slogan. Brandt and Bahr agreed with Kennedy that the Soviet regime could not be overthrown, but it could be subject to change. As a consequence the Hallstein Doctrine, plus the still persisting claim on land to the east of the Oder and Neisse, had to be called into serious question.

Adenauer, refusing to accept these arguments, fell increasingly out of step with the times. A new crisis erupted when all nations were invited to sign a treaty banning the testing of atomic weapons, which had been concluded between the Soviet Union, the United States, and Britain in Moscow in August 1963. Since the GDR was invited to append its signature, the chancellor considered this to be a form of recognition of the East German regime. His foreign minister Gerhard Schröder strongly disagreed. With the support of the FDP and the opposition SPD he won the day. The Federal Republic signed the treaty in August, while formally declaring that this should not be seen as granting recognition to any regime with which it did not already have diplomatic relations. This position was endorsed by the US government.

Finally, after fourteen years in office, Adenauer ceded his place with singular ill grace to Ludwig Erhard on October 15, 1963. The 87-year-old remained as party chairman and set out to make life as difficult as possible for his successor, whom he considered to be a political lightweight. Adenauer regarded the corpulent, cigar-smoking and incurably optimistic Erhard with deep suspicion. He was a dyed-in-the-wool liberal, he did not share the old man's profound mistrust of his countrymen, and he did not seem to be concerned about the decline of Christian values that in his view threatened to undermine European civilization; worst of all, he was a Protestant.

For all Adenauer's authoritarian style, which led many to draw a parallel with Bismarck, he left behind him a well-functioning democracy. He was a devoutly Catholic patriarch and democratic Rhinelander, with a deep distrust of the Protestant Prussian tradition, particularly with respect to its emphasis on the military. He thus acted as a bridge-builder, who enabled many of those who were nurtured within the old authoritarian culture and the Nazi dictatorship to reconcile themselves to a pluralistic parliamentary democracy. His other great achievement was that he had integrated the Federal Republic into the western alliance against fierce opposition, and that this was no longer challenged except by a handful on the lunatic fringes of left and right. At the same time he forged a close alliance with Germany's "hereditary enemy" France which was to become the cornerstone of a new European order. He always feared that, were Germany not fully committed to the Atlantic Alliance and to Europe, it would once again be a loose cannon on deck, thus threatening peace and stability in Europe.

The Federal Republic had come a long way, but there was still a great deal to be done. A serious debate over the Nazi past was still confined to a handful of historians and journalists. Perhaps that dreadful time was too close and too traumatic for this to happen so soon, and it was not until the 1990s that a united Germany really came to grips with these intractable problems. Although article 3 of the Fundamental Law accorded equal rights to men and women, this bore no resemblance to reality and German women were expected to be content with being dutiful wives, hard-working home-makers, and diligent mothers. The educational system had still not recovered from the damage done by the Nazis and the law was in need of fundamental reform. Most serious of all, Adenauer's rhetoric about reunification in peace and in freedom rang hollow. In the midst of the Cold War this was clearly an impossibility. The time had come for a completely new approach to the German question.

CHAPTER FIFTEEN
THE GERMAN DEMOCRATIC REPUBLIC

CHAPTER CONTENTS

A History of Modern Germany: 1800 to the Present, Second Edition. Martin Kitchen.
© 2012 Martin Kitchen. Published 2012 by Blackwell Publishing Ltd.

The Soviet Military Government (Sowjetische Militäradministration in Deutschland – SMAD) ensured that 520,000 former members of the Nazi Party lost their jobs; 150,000 were thrown into former Nazi concentration camps at Sachsenhausen, and Buchenwald or Gestapo prisons like Bautzen; 70,000 died. Countless others were deported to labor camps in the Soviet Union. The Soviet authorities were anxious to show respect for the Yalta agreements, so SMAD's order number 2 of June 10, 1945, permitted "the creation and operation of all anti-fascist parties" that were devoted to "the irrevocable destruction of the remains of fascism and the strengthening of the foundations of democracy and bourgeois liberties" in the Soviet occupation zone. The Communist Party was the first party to be organized. It studiously avoided using the word "socialism" in its propaganda, insisted that it was not intent on establishing a Soviet-style regime in Germany, and styled itself as heir to the bourgeois revolution of 1848. It announced that it stood for "a parliamentary-democratic republic, where the people enjoyed all rights and freedoms." Its economic program called for the "development of free trade and private entrepreneurial initiative on the basis of private property." Few people were fooled by this maneuver. For most Germans the KPD was the "Russian party," backed by an army of rapists and plunderers. By contrast the Social Democrats in their manifesto of June 15 announced that their aims were "democracy in state and local government, socialism in the economy and society." The party, mindful that the rivalry between the SPD and KPD in the Weimar Republic had helped bring Hitler to power, called for the "organizational unity of the working class," but the SPD turned down the offer for the moment. On June 26 the Christian Democratic Union (CDU) styled itself as a bourgeois party, but called for the nationalization of heavy industry and the redistribution of large landed estates. The Liberal Democratic Party (LDPD), constituted on July 5, stood for the inalienable right to private property and guarantees for the independence of the civil service and judges.

These parties (KPD, SPD, CDU, and LDPD) formed the United Front of Anti-Fascist Democratic Parties (Antifa-Bloc), which guaranteed that no coalition could be formed against the KPD. It was also hoped that this political model, with the Communists appearing as models of moderation, would find resonance in the western zones. This was after all in marked contrast to the fatal divisions between the parties during the Weimar Republic: its moderate left-leaning program had considerable appeal and seemed to be broadly similar to the program of the British Labour Party that had won the election in 1945, a victory that many Germans enthusiastically welcomed.

The reality was very different. The KPD leadership had been carefully groomed in Moscow to take over power in the Soviet zone. As Walter Ulbricht put it: "It must appear to be democratic, but we must have everything under our control." Furthermore, the SMAD gave the KPD material support that was denied to other parties. It set out to become a mass party that would fill the middle ground between "progressives" and "reactionaries." To this end it would welcome new members "even if they had not completely broken with petit-bourgeois, social-democratic and even fascist-imperialist ideologies." There was no room here for talk of the dictatorship of the proletariat or of the socialist revolution. The KPD wolf was disguised as an SPD lamb.

By the winter of 1945 it was all too apparent that the Communists were losing ground to the Social Democrats in terms of popular support. They tightened their organizational structure and enjoyed the backing of the SMAD, but their message was not getting across. The only solution seemed to be an amalgamation with the SPD. Otto Grotewohl and the SPD leadership were opposed to the idea, as was the fiery anti-Communist Social

Democratic leader in the west, Kurt Schumacher, who denounced the Communists as "red fascists." But there was widespread support for the idea among the rank and file, as well as some provincial leaders. They took the Communists' avowal of democracy at face value and argued that as allies in the anti-fascist struggle past antagonisms had been overcome. The SMAD put massive pressure on reluctant Social Democrats and arrested the stubbornly recalcitrant. At a Christmas peace rally the Communists sugared the pill by proposing a uniquely German and democratic way to socialism. In April 1946 a joint conference was held with delegates from the KPD and the SPD, which resulted in the formation of the Socialist Unity Party (SED).

The new party was not yet a typical Stalinist party. Key positions were shared equally between the two parties, while the SPD initially had slightly more members; but the Social Democrats had precious little with which to withstand pressure from their partners and the SMAD. Social Democrats were gradually weeded out. In 1946, 52 percent came from the SPD; by 1951 this had been reduced to a mere 6.5 percent. In the elections in the autumn of 1946 the SED won narrow majorities in Mecklenburg, Saxony, and Thuringia. In Brandenburg and Saxony-Anhalt the CDU and LDPD won by a neck. But any hopes that the election marked a step towards a united, democratic Germany were soon to be dashed.

Daily life in the Soviet occupation zone was still grim. The black market was thriving, but things were improving slightly and conditions in the west were not yet noticeably better. In one respect the East was ahead of the West. The SMAD set to work immediately reviving cultural life, particularly in Berlin. Two months after the end of the war there were a dozen theaters, several cabarets, two opera houses, five major symphony orchestras, and several smaller ones in the Soviet sector of Berlin. But there was a menacingly shady side to the Soviet zone that presaged ill. An indiscriminate wave of arrests swept through the it to the point that an internal review by the Soviet authorities showed that 35,000 people had been wrongfully arrested. These unfortunates were mostly released in 1948 along with a number of others, but thousands remained who were handed over to the East German authorities in 1949 to complete their sentences in equally appalling conditions.

The Soviets responded to the amalgamation of the American and British zones in Bizonia, the Truman Doctrine, the Marshall Plan, and the policy of "containment" by creating the Communist Information Bureau (Cominform), a revival of the Communist International (Comintern), in September 1947 at a meeting in Poland at which Andrei Zhdanov promulgated the "two camps theory." This claimed that the world was divided into two blocs: an imperialist and anti-democratic camp under the USA and an anti-imperialist and democratic one under the Soviet Union. The duty of all Communist parties and "truly patriotic" elements was now to struggle against "American expansionist plans for the enslavement of Europe." This marked the end of any discussion of a uniquely German and democratic way to socialism, thus marking an important step towards the division of Germany. The SED was not invited to the conference and had to meekly swallow its resolutions.

The creation of Bizonia meant that the Soviets were denied reparations from the industrial zones in the west and they began to fear that the potentially wealthy western zones would be absorbed into the "imperialist camp." The Soviet Union's paramount concern for security was now seriously challenged. In July 1947 the SMAD responded by urging the SED to show a more militant spirit and to express its ideological solidarity with the Soviet Union. Colonel Tulpanov, the SMAD's political advisor, told the party to adopt a

"Leninist-Stalinist course," acknowledging that Germany was effectively divided and that East Germany should therefore become a "people's democracy." This was also an attempt to overcome ideological differences within the SED. A large number of former Social Democrats in the party, denounced as "Schumacher ideologues," could not understand why the Soviets had not accepted the Marshall Plan. Others, condemned as "left-wing sectarians" denounced the concessions made by the party to "petit-bourgeois interests." At the same time the CDU and the LDPD began to resist the encroachments of the SED. The CDU leader, Jakob Kaiser, called upon the party to act as a "breakwater against dogmatic Marxism." The LDPD echoed these sentiments and threatened to leave the Antifa-Bloc.

By early 1948 the division of Germany seemed almost inevitable. In January Otto Grotewohl said that Germany would soon be "torn apart." The following month Stalin prophesied: "The West will make West Germany its own, and we shall make our own state in East Germany." The six-power conference of the three western allies and the Benelux countries, held in London that month, confirmed the Soviet leader's prophecy by concluding that a West German government should be formed. The SMAD had taken off the gloves after the failure of the foreign ministers' conference in London in December 1947. Jakob Kaiser and his deputy lost their positions in the CDU, and the leading role of the SED was further emphasized. "Progressive" forces in the Soviet zone were privileged and "reactionaries" hounded out. In June the German Economic Commission (Deutsche Wirtschaftskommission – DWK) was formed to coordinate the administration of the zone, which was the nucleus of an East German state. As in the West, work began on drafting a constitution for a German Democratic Republic in the zone.

Two new parties were formed to counteract the CDU and LDPD. The German National Democratic Party (NDPD) recruited members from former officers, Nazis, and bourgeois. The German Democratic Farmers' Party (DBD) appealed to farmers and agricultural workers, particularly those who had profited from the land reform. The leadership of both parties was firmly in the control of Communists, who made sure that that they did not wander too far from the SED's line. In the summer of 1948 these new parties were admitted to the Antifa-Bloc, as was the Free German Trades Union Association (Freie Deutsche Gewerkschaftsbund – FDGB).

The FDGB was just one of the Leninist "organizations of the masses" designed as instruments of social control, mobilization, and indoctrination: in party jargon the "transmission belts" of the SED. Other similar organizations were the Free German Youth (Freie Deutsche Jugend – FDJ), the German Democratic Women's Association (Demokratische Frauenbund Deutschlands – DFD), the Cultural Association (Kulturbund der DDR – KB), and the Society for German–Soviet Friendship (Gesellschaft für Deutsch-Sowjetische Freundschaft – DSF). As the SED tightened its grip on these associations they steadily lost members. Those who objected, such as the Leipzig student activist Wolfgang Natonek, were arrested. He was condemned to twenty-five years' penal servitude, but was released in 1956.

The transformation of the SED into an orthodox Marxist-Leninist party was in lockstep with developments in the Soviet Union. Stalin's break with Tito in June 1948 led to the denunciation of the Yugoslav heresy of belief in different roads to socialism, a notion that Stalin had at first approved and which had been adopted by the SED. Tito's defiance of Soviet aspirations to hegemony in eastern Europe meant that such heterodoxy could no longer be tolerated. The SED was now a carbon copy of the Communist Party of the Soviet

Union (CPSU). This did not significantly reduce the attractions of membership. Amid the deprivations and hardships of the immediate post-war years and the ruins of Nazi tyranny, the party seemed to be genuinely concerned with rooting out fascism, committed to social justice, and offering a way out of current misery. That joining the party meant loss of individual freedom seemed to be a modest price to pay in such exceptional circumstances. There were also less idealistic motives for joining the party. It was the key to social and professional advancement. The old doctrine of a "German way to socialism" was now condemned as a "false, rotten and dangerous theory." Social Democratic notions were denounced as "adverse to the party." Any opposition to the new course was construed as anti-Soviet propaganda and resulted in automatic expulsion from the party.

Parallel to the sovietization of the SED was the gradual transformation of the economy and society along Soviet lines. The first priority was to significantly increase productivity, which had fallen to 56 percent of the pre-war norm. The SMAD's order number 234 called for wages to be linked to productivity – in other words, piecework, a practice which in a capitalist economy was denounced as the vilest form of exploitation. The Soviet Stakhanovite movement was copied when a carefully chosen and well-prepared miner, Adolf Hennecke, exceeded his daily norm by 387 percent. A reluctant workforce was urged to following this shining example of socialist labor. Hennecke was initially reluctant to play this role, accurately predicting that he would be ostracized by his colleagues, but he was richly rewarded. He was appointed to the Central Planning Commission, became a deputy in the People's Chamber (Volkskammer), and a member of the Central Committee of the SED.

The SED staged a series of spectacular trials of "saboteurs, speculators, and grafters," who threatened the party's two-year plan of June 1948. The enterprises of businessmen who fled to the West were promptly converted into "People's Own Enterprises" (VEBs). At the same time the Soviets ceased their practice of dismantling such industrial plant as had survived the Allied bombing and now extracted reparations via Soviet public limited companies (SAGs), whose products and profits went directly to the Soviet Union. About 60 percent of all industrial enterprises were SAGs, so that East Germans profited little from the increased production resulting from the two-year plan. These companies were handed over to the GDR in 1949 with the exception of the uranium mines run by Wismut SAG in Saxony and Thuringia that were essential to the Soviet atomic program. Initially there were 130,000 workers in Wismut, many of them slave laborers. There was a high incidence of lung cancer among these unfortunates. All mass organizations were now transmission belts for the SED's policy for the "ideological and political education of party members and particularly functionaries in the spirit of Marxism-Leninism." The aim was to increase productivity and to punish "slackers." Rewards in the form of food packages, clothing, tobacco, and free holidays were allotted for productivity and for loyalty. An effort was made to stop the exodus of scientists, engineers, and technicians, as well as "cultural workers" in the arts, but the steady encroachment of Stalinist methods and the proclamation of "socialist realism" in 1948 left many nervously uncertain of the future, and scores of these experts prudently left for the West.

In March 1948 the Soviet representatives left the Allied Control Commission. The currency reform in the western zones on June 20 and the creation of the Deutschmark, followed a few days later by the creation of a separate East German currency (MDN) resulted in the economic division of Germany. The economic disparity between East and West now began dramatically to increase. The Soviets responded by blockading Berlin in an attempt to drive the western allies out of their sectors in the former capital. The allies responded with the Berlin airlift, which in turn strengthened their determination to create a separate West German state.

The SED and SMAD labored under the illusion of the superiority of a Soviet-style planned economy, based on the primacy of heavy industry, the success of which would convince the West Germans that their vision of a social market economy was sadly misguided. The very reverse was true. The already insurmountable problems of reaching the planning goals were compounded by the cost of the occupation, the heavy burden of reparations, and the mass departure of skilled workers to the West. The enormous cost of rearmament was an additional problem. It soon accounted for one-fifth of the national budget. Another fifth was later allotted to subsidies for food, housing, and transport to stifle discontent and maintain the party's hold over the masses. Further problems were caused by the "right to work," which resulted in a large number of employees having virtually nothing to do. Planning did not take such factors as profitability, productivity, reduction of costs, maintenance of quality, or demand into consideration. Under the "tonnage ideology" norms were set in weight so that, for example, massively heavy furniture that could hardly be moved was produced simply to meet the tonnage set by the planning staff. Economists who criticized such idiocy were condemned as "revisionists" and lost their jobs. The East German economy was firmly linked to that of the Soviet Union so that it never opened up to thriving western markets. Industry refused to adopt the internationally recognized German industrial norms (DIN). They were stuck with the wretched standards of the Soviet norms (GOST).

The SMAD now got to work restructuring society. In September, the land belonging to 7,000 owners of more than 100 hectares (247 acres) and former National Socialists was expropriated without any compensation. It was provisionally given briefly to 250,000 "new farmers." The CDU called for some form of recompense, whereupon the SMAD removed the party leader and his deputy. That autumn the process of expropriating the assets of the firms of "war and Nazi criminals" began. After a series of plebiscites, these were nationalized in 1946 without any form of restitution or compensation. By 1948, 10,000 such enterprises were in the hands of the state and formed the basis of a future planned economy.

The situation of the "New Farmers" was particularly wretched. They were allotted minuscule patches of land. Only 14 percent were given somewhere to live; 25 percent had a plow, and 20 percent a harrow. In a second round of expropriation, beginning in 1952, almost all farmers were forced into "agricultural productive cooperatives" (LPGs). The widespread resentment in the countryside at the destruction of the old estates, the demolition of many of the fine manor houses, and the expropriation of the peasantry was shrugged off by the SED as further evidence of their backwardness and reactionary nature. An entire class of proud, independent farmers had been destroyed. Fifteen thousand fled to the West. Those that remained were demoralized, unmotivated, and resentful of close government control.

The Soviets plundered East Germany to such an extent that the economy was bled white. Production of automobiles dropped by 80 percent. Output in the world-famous optical industry, centered in Jena, dropped by 50 percent, as did that in chemicals, fine mechanics, artificial fibers, and electrical engineering. Half the railway lines and 40 percent of locomotives were confiscated. The entire production of 200 firms, which accounted for 30 percent of East Germany's industrial production, was sent to the Soviet Union as reparations.

"The First Workers' and Peasants' State on German Soil"

On December 12, 1948, Stalin called Wilhelm Pieck, Otto Grotewohl, and Walter Ulbricht to Moscow to give them their marching orders. The SED leadership hoped that they would be granted permission to go ahead with the formation of a people's democracy in the Soviet occupation zone, but Stalin urged caution. Loath to admit that his hopes for a united and neutral Germany would not be fulfilled, he called for an "opportunistic" policy that would pave a "zig-zag road to socialism." Only when a separate West German state had been formed would he consider granting the Germans' request.

On May 8, 1949, the West German parliamentary council accepted the Fundamental Law. On September 16 Wilhelm Pieck, Walter Ulbricht, and Fred Oelssner, along with the Social Democrat Otto Grotewohl, were called to Moscow. Their welcome was far from warm. They spent several days in a government dacha anxiously wondering what was going on. Stalin did not even bother to meet his distinguished German comrades. The reason for this uncertainty was that Stalin was still loath to concede that his policy of keeping Germany weak by bleeding the country white through reparations from the industrial zones of the west had failed. He still felt that the only way for the Soviet Union to protect itself against any renewed threat from Germany was to create a unified, neutral state with a bourgeois democratic regime that would include Communists. It was an admission that a united Communist Germany could not be achieved in the foreseeable future.

The East German delegation was finally given the go-ahead on September 27 and rushed back to Berlin. The SED leadership set to work organizing a "workers' and peasants' state" run by the party. Gerhard Eisler, the head of East German radio and the brother of the composer Hans, who had been the de facto leader of the American Communist Party until he was arrested for failing to answer questions from the House Committee on Un-American Activities, boldly announced that "once we have formed a government we will never relinquish power due to elections or other methods." On October 7 a People's Council (Volksrat) was formed from members of a People's Congress, elected from a "unity list" – in other words, without any choice. The People's Council converted itself into a People's Chamber (Volkskammer), which in turn appointed Otto Grotewohl minister president with Walter Ulbricht (SED), Hermann Kastner (LDPD), and Otto Nuschke (CDU) as his deputies. Wilhelm Pieck was appointed president of the German Democratic Republic.

The constitution of the new republic, like the Soviet constitution of 1936, was on the surface a very liberal document that guaranteed traditional civil rights, including property rights, as well as the right to strike, but a clause outlawing "rabble-rousing," "anti-democratic propaganda," "warmongering," and the like made all such guarantees worthless. Article 6 gave the SED the right to prosecute "all opponents and all forms of opposition." Similarly, the marginal preponderance of the "bourgeois" parties was a charade, which did not disguise the fact that the GDR was a one-party dictatorship based on the Leninist principle of "democratic centralism" in which Ulbricht was the key figure, behind whom stood the Soviet Union. The new regime marched under the banner of "anti-fascism," the most powerful weapon in the Communists' propaganda arsenal. The establishment of a Stalinist dictatorship was thus presented as "anti-fascist social transformation" – the continuation of the glorious struggle of the Soviet peoples against Nazi tyranny. The GDR, like the Federal Republic, was seen as a provisional state pending the unification of Germany as an "indivisible democratic republic."

The "people's democracy" was quickly transformed into a one-party dictatorship. In February 1950 a ministry of state security (the Stasi) was created under veteran Communist Wilhelm Zaisser, a former NKVD operative who had served as chief of staff to the International Brigade in the Spanish Civil War under the pseudonym "General Gomez." Show trials of 3,300 Nazis, war criminals, and political prisoners, including fifty-five members of the KPD, began in April. The SED was purged of some 150,000 unreliable elements among whom, in accordance with Stalin's anti-Semitic obsessions, were a number of "Zionists" and "cosmopolitans." A hunt began for "imperialists" and "American agents," which culminated in the show trials of a number of prominent figures in the SED in 1953 which were soon to become entwined with the struggle for power after Stalin's death.

Walter Ulbricht, who was elected secretary general of the party, announced the details of a five-year plan at the Third Congress of the SED in 1950. Since Stalin wanted to keep the option of a united Germany open, the GDR was deemed to still be in the midst of an "anti-fascist and democratic transformation" and the five-year plan was concerned with doubling industrial production, not with the creation of a socialist society. In February 1952, in response to efforts to integrate the Federal Republic into a western military alliance, Stalin launched another diplomatic initiative to create a united Germany. He called for the creation of a united neutral Germany, with its own armed forces, within the 1945 borders. The four powers would withdraw their forces within one year of the signing of a peace treaty. The western powers rejected the "Stalin Note" out of hand. The troika of Pieck, Ulbricht, and Grotewohl returned to Moscow, where they were informed that the "pacifist period was over." The GDR was to be remilitarized, "productive cooperatives" were to be created in the villages, the class war intensified, and enemies of the party hunted down and eradicated. On July 9, 1952, Ulbricht announced in the name of the Central Committee of the SED that: "Socialism will be built according to plan in the German Democratic Republic." The second party conference voted for the creation of collective farms (LPGs). The old federal structure was replaced by administrative districts, thus creating a rigidly centralized system.

By 1952 almost 80 percent of industry had been nationalized. "Socialism" now meant a concentration on heavy industry, regardless of the cost, the lack of raw materials, and economic feasibility. East German planners blindly followed the outmoded and inefficient Stalinist model of industrialization. As a result the GDR's economy was hamstrung from the start. Consumer goods were scarce, prohibitively expensive, and of extremely poor quality.

The "class struggle" in the agricultural sector was intensified. Farmers who failed to meet their increased quotas were accused of being "speculators" and "grafters." By January 1953, 1,200 farmers had been arrested. Similarly, in the trades the slightest irregularity was construed as sabotage and subject to draconian punishment. At the political level the ranks of the CDU and LPD were combed to remove any elements that deviated from the SED's line. Thousands were charged with being American agents or for being in contact with West German politicians. The Antifa-Bloc parties now simply parroted the party line so that the pretense that the German Democratic Republic was a multi-party state became an empty farce.

"Smashing the bourgeois educational monopoly" was considered a prerequisite to building socialism. "Bourgeois" children were barred from all forms of higher education. New faculties for Marxism-Leninism and "scientific atheism" were founded. In spite of compulsory courses in historical and dialectical materialism (*Histomat* and *Diamat*), 80 percent of the citizenry remained at least nominally members of the Evangelical Church, on which the Stasi kept an ever-watchful eye. A number of prominent churchmen were arrested in 1953, and hundreds of young people who were active in the church were forbidden to continue their studies. Within the Communist state the churches were centers of relative freedom in which dissent and resistance steadily grew.

The "intensification of the class struggle" in 1952 was not only aimed against the bourgeois and petit bourgeois but also affected the working class. The middle class was taxed to the limits of the possible, while workers were forced to increase productivity. Where exhortations for sacrifice failed, terror was used to ensure that planning goals were met. In the autumn of 1952 an investigation was launched to discover those responsible for the shortfall from the plan's hopelessly unrealistic norms. The party rid itself of "boozers," "womanizers," and anyone who hinted that the SED was not omniscient; but some courageous souls in the administrations of nationalized industry ignored the party's strictures, refused to cut corners, and increased wages. The vast majority of East German workers, unwilling to make any special sacrifices for the creation of socialism, were deaf to the party's propaganda. When 900 building workers from Magdeburg were driven to Berlin to admire the glories of socialist architecture in the Stalinallee, 700 of them took the opportunity to visit West Berlin's department stores and cinemas.

With only 38 percent of its members from the working class, the SED was not a proletarian party. There was no longer any pretense that the party stood for "democracy in the state, society and economy," for emancipation in all fields of endeavor, for human rights and relief for the underprivileged. Reconciliation between Communists and Social Democrats was no longer the order of the day. The party was rapidly becoming little more than a collection of self-seeking functionaries, solely concerned with exercising and hanging on to power. It was thus hardly surprising that it was resented and even loathed by the vast majority of the population.

In November 1952 the trial began in Czechoslovakia of those involved in "an anti-state conspiracy centered around Rudolf Slansky," the party secretary charged with Titoism. Of the thirteen other prominent party officials charged, eleven were Jews. Eleven were executed, and three sentenced to life imprisonment. Jewish party functionaries and officers in Hungary and Poland were also arrested, tried, and executed. In Romania Ana Pauker, "a Jewess of bourgeois origin" in the prosecution's words, former foreign minister and de facto leader of the party, was charged with "cosmopolitanism" and "factional intrigue." She managed to survive by outliving Stalin.

Initially the Soviet Union had been supportive of the young state of Israel, hoping to use it as a weapon against British imperialism and as a bridgehead for Soviet interests in the Middle East. This policy failed and the magisterial authority of Lenin was used to condemn Zionism as a form of "bourgeois nationalism" that was "socially regressive" in that it overlooked the class struggle. Zionism was henceforth condemned as "racist imperialism" and latent anti-Semitism was instrumentalized in the struggle against Titoism and fractionalism to insure that the people's democracies closely followed the Soviet model. Ulbricht, heedless of Germany's shameful recent past, did not hesitate to join in this witch hunt. The German Democratic Republic was after all a state based on the heroic anti-fascist struggle of the German Communist Party. The mass murder of the European Jews was the work of West German fascists. For this reason it was never deemed necessary to go through the painful confrontation with Germany's recent horrific past. The few Jewish communities left in eastern Germany were searched for Zionist literature and a number of prominent

Jews were arrested. One former Politbüro member, who had been number six in the party hierarchy, Paul Merker, was charged with the crime of suggesting that compensation should be paid to Jews whose property had been seized by the Nazis. Although not a Jew, he was accused of "having adopted the defense of the interests of Zionist monopoly capitalists," furthering the interests of the "Zionist agency," and attempting to "win over SED comrades of Jewish descent." At that time Merker was already in prison, charged with having collaborated with a Noel H. Field, an American Communist accused of being an "imperialist agent," as well as of offering "extensive help to the class enemy." He managed to survive and lived to work as a journalist. Some of his Jewish comrades arrested at the same time were less fortunate.

This anti-Jewish purge reached its apogee with the "doctors' plot" in the Soviet Union, when it seemed that Stalin was about to launch another massive purge. The dictator died on March 5, 1953, but in the GDR Ulbricht kept up the pressure. Franz Dahlem, Ulbricht's rival and number two in the party hierarchy was charged, like Merker, with being a "Zionist agent" in league with Noel H. Field. In May the Central Committee ordered that the "lessons of the Slansky trial" should be implemented in the GDR, and a thoroughgoing purge of party and state should result in the elimination of the "class enemy." Dahlem, along with a number of other prominent figures, was relieved of all offices. The consequences were no quite so dire for most of those affected by the purge in the more tolerant atmosphere of "the thaw" after Stalin's death, and a somewhat chastened Dahlem went on to enjoy a privileged career in the GDR until his death in 1981.

Although "anti-Zionism" remained the GDR's official policy until the bitter end, hanging like a sword of Damocles over East German Jews, anti-Semitism was never as blatant in the GDR as it was in the Soviet Union. Indeed Soviet visitors were shocked at the number of Jews in prominent positions: Albert Norden, Kurt Hager, and Hermann Axen in the Politbüro, Hilde Benjamin the fanatical minister of justice, Hanna Wolf the director of the SED University, Margarete Wittkowski the president of the State Bank, Konrad Wolf the president of the Academy of Arts, and Markus Wolf the deputy head of the Stasi. Many of the GDR's leading literary figures were Jewish, but they were mostly careful not to mention their Jewish origins and refused to be identified as Jewish writers. Those Jewish writers, such as Stefan Heym and Jurek Becker, who addressed Jewish questions were closely watched by the Stasi. Viktor Klemperer's profoundly moving diaries that chronicle his persecution as a middle-class Jew in the Third Reich could not be published until after the collapse of the GDR. On the other hand Anne Frank's diary was a bestseller, as was Bruno Apitz's novel *Naked Among Wolves* (*Nackt unter Wölfen*), with its moving portraits of Jewish inmates of the Buchenwald concentration camp, which was made into one of the GDR's best films. On the other hand there was not a single rabbi or mohel in the GDR until 1987. It was exceedingly difficult to learn Hebrew, although it was never forbidden as it was in the Soviet Union. It was thus virtually impossible to live as a practicing Jew in the GDR.

June 17, 1953

The citizenry voted with their feet against the "intensification of the class struggle." In 1952, 181,000 left the GDR, thus contributing to and benefiting from the rapid economic growth in the Federal Republic. A further 180,000 followed in the first five months of 1953. The Central Committee of the SED imagined that economic misery could be relieved by a 10 percent increase in industrial norms – in other words by making people work harder for the same pay. This resulted in widespread protests and an alarming increase in the number of refugees. The party leadership was then called to Moscow, given a severe dressing-down, and ordered to take a more lenient approach. Ulbricht, Grotewohl, and the economist Fred Oelssner were ordered to desist from "forcing the pace of building socialism in the GDR." The struggle against tradesmen and Christians was to cease; expenditure on armaments was to be drastically reduced.

The Politbüro of the SED now proclaimed a "New Course." Somewhat lame apologies were offered for past mistakes, and promises were made to improve the consumer industries and to lessen restrictions on travel to the West. Recent price increases were rescinded, but the 10 percent norm increase remained in place. For the working class this was an intolerable slap in the face. Protests and strikes began on June 11, 1953. Two days later 5,000–6,000 workers at the site of the Friedrichshain hospital in Berlin, who were on a Saturday outing at one of the city's many lakeside beer gardens, became spontaneously politicized and voted for strike action. On Monday June 16 news of this strike spread throughout the land. When the People's Police surrounded the hospital site, construction workers on East Berlin's showpiece, the Stalinallee, downed tools and marched in protest, demanding not only a reduction of industrial norms but also the release of all political prisoners, freedom to travel, the resignation of the entire government, and free elections. The Politbüro promptly rescinded the increased norms, but it was too late. On June 17 hundreds of thousands demonstrated in the major cities throughout the GDR demanding free elections and reunification.

This was the first mass protest against a Communist regime and it left the Politbüro helpless. The People's Police tried to control the crowds, but were beaten back by a hail of stones. Soviet tanks rolled into Berlin, at least fifty demonstrators were killed, and thousands were arrested. Crowds, estimated at 60,000 in Halle and 40,000 in Leipzig, robbed the regime of any claim to legitimacy. Soviet military might and emergency decrees were its only resort against what it claimed was "fascist provocation" orchestrated by West German agents. The Stasi then made 13,000 arrests, but smaller strikes and protests by workers continued for months in a remarkably courageous protest against an inhuman regime that cynically claimed to be a government of and for the workers and peasants. In the last six months of 1953, 86,000 refugees fled to the West. As Bertolt Brecht wrote at the time: "The people have lost the confidence of the government. The government has decided to dissolve the people, and to appoint another one."

At first it seemed that Ulbricht, the main proponent of a tough line, was bound to topple, but at the end of July Beria, Stalin's bloodstained executioner turned reformer, was executed so that the moderates in the SED lost their patron. Ulbricht promptly purged the SED and the trade unions of his opponents, while Stasi informers worked overtime hunting down dissidents. He announced a series of administrative and disciplinary reforms that would, in his jargon, "make the German Democratic Republic into a hell for enemy agents." The number of "unofficial colleagues" in the Stasi was doubled to 30,000, whose task was to keep a watchful eye for any signs of a repeat performance of June 17.

In the end the "New Course" meant that the SED leadership could no longer totally ignore public opinion and was obliged to secure modest improvements in the consumer sector; but the GDR was more than ever a police state with refugees still pouring out to the West. Norms were reduced to the previous level. Old-age and widows' pensions were increased by about 12 percent. Housing starts were greatly increased and repairs to the existing stock given priority. Sanitation facilities in the VEBs were improved. Substantial sums were allotted for building kindergartens and holiday homes. The price of gasoline was reduced from 3 DM to 1.80, but Soviet soldiers still undercut the market by offering stolen petrol at 1 DM for a 5-liter canister. The Soviet Union greatly increased the export of foodstuffs to the GDR, but fears that this was only a temporary measure led to hamstering, leaving shelves in the state stores empty.

Given that the new American president, Dwight D. Eisenhower, and his secretary of state John Foster Dulles did nothing to help the protesters in the GDR, there was little that the Federal Republic could do beyond expressing solidarity by making June 17 into a national holiday as "The Day of German Unity." Since there was general agreement among the political parties, with the exception of the KPD, which denounced the uprising as a putsch organized by the imperialist powers, a Committee for an Indivisible Germany was formed to orchestrate the ceremonies on June 17. Much to Adenauer's horror and disgust, this fiercely nationalist body called for the restitution of the frontiers of 1937, a demand that threatened to undermine his policy of western integration. He distanced himself from the committee whose "revanchist" policies provided rich material for the GDR's propagandists; but for years to come the maps of Germany that were prominently displayed in the corridors of West German trains clearly showed the German frontiers as those of 1937. The powerful lobby of expellees could not be ignored.

The GDR after Stalin

In 1955 the Soviet leader, Nikita Khrushchev, promulgated the "Two-State Theory" whereby a reunification of Germany would only be possible were it to preserve the "socialist achievements" of the GDR. In September the Treaty on the Relationship between the GDR and the USSR granted the GDR "full sovereign rights." In January 1956 the National People's Army (Nationale Volksarmee – NVA) was formed by simply renaming the shadow army in the Armed People's Police (Kasernierte Volkspolizei). It was then integrated into the Warsaw Pact. Fears of a deal over Germany that would topple the SED were thus assuaged, but the country was soon rocked by the crisis triggered by Khrushchev's speech to the Twentieth Congress of the CPSU, in which he denounced Stalin's crimes. Ulbricht and his fellow Stalinists were at something of a loss as to what to do. For a while it seemed once again that he might be toppled. His attempt to distance himself from his former idol by writing in the party's daily newspaper *Neues Deutschland* that Stalin was not "a Marxist classic" was little comfort to the countless victims of Stalinist oppression. Clearly more had to be done. A number of prominent dissidents were pardoned and some 21,000 political prisoners were released, but functionaries who had been critical of Ulbricht were not restored to their former prominence. In this brief period of uncertainty after Khrushchev's speech some brave souls spoke out for fundamental reforms in state and society; but the thaw was all too brief.

Widespread protests in Poland led to the release of Władysław Gomułka, who had been jailed as a "Titoite" in 1951. He was then appointed first secretary of the party. The Hungarian uprising in October led to the formation of a new government under the reforming Communist Imre Nagy which called for withdrawal from the Warsaw Pact, whereupon Soviet tanks rolled in. Two thousand death sentences were handed down and some quarter of a million Hungarians fled to the West. With Britain and France engaged in their futile invasion of Egypt, the West was in no position to give the Hungarians any effective support. Khrushchev could pose as the Egyptian's champion against western imperialism, and celebrated his victory over the counter-revolutionaries in Hungary. Many Communists in the West, finding the revelations of Stalin's crimes and the brutality of the Soviets in Hungary impossible to stomach, tore up their party cards. Those who remained in the party began the gradual process of loosening ties with Moscow, thereby laying the foundations of a distinctive form of Eurocommunism.

In the GDR the suppression of Imre Nagy's regime was used as an excuse for an abrupt change of course. A number of prominent "revisionists" were arrested, including Ernst Wollweber, the minister of state security. He was replaced by Erich Mielke, a particularly odious creature whose principal claim to the office was that he had murdered two police-men in 1931 on orders from the party. He was to remain in charge until the state's inglori-ous demise. Karl Schirdewan and the economist Fred Oelßner were dismissed from the Politbüro. The Central Committee's specialist for economics, Gerhart Ziller, committed suicide. The philosopher Wolfgang Harich and the publisher Walter Jankas, who had called for a "third way" and "humane socialism" that would avoid the injustices of capitalism, Stalinist terror, and the rigidity of Communist economic planning, who influenced a number of key figures in the SED, were given ten-year prison sentences. Their ideas lived on in the Prague Spring of 1968 and in the heady last days of the GDR.

Ulbricht had weathered the de-Stalinization storm and was now in full command. The economy was steadily improving and the majority of people had come to terms with a regime which, although grim, did not quite match the stereotype of a Communist hell that prevailed in the West. Ration cards for food were abolished, health and welfare amenities were greatly improved, and the standard of living rose to the point that the citizens of the GDR were viewed with envy by those of the other socialist states. The stream of refugees was still immense, but was diminishing: from 260,000 in 1957 to 144,000 in 1959.

Subsequent to the Berlin crisis of November 1958, caused by the Soviet proposal that the city be demilitarized and independent, for the first time the GDR sent a delegation to an international conference held in Geneva. Although it was there only in an advisory capacity, it was given equal status to the delegation from the Federal Republic. Encouraged by these developments, Ulbricht announced at the Fifth Party Congress in 1958 that a socialist society was in the making in which the quantity of consumer goods per capita would overtake that of West Germany. The process of "catch up and overtake" was to be completed by 1961. This was to be made possible in part by heavy investment in "socialist education" in which science, mathematics, and economics would be privileged. But there were sticks as well as carrots in this program for "building socialism." Ulbricht, who had very nearly been deposed in 1956, was determined to solidify his hold over party and state. A thoroughgoing program of ideological indoctrination in the principles of Marxism-Leninism, which included courses in "socialist morality," was launched. The emphasis was on the "collective," to the point that one of the worst insults was to describe someone as "an individual." As the party's *Guidelines for the Education of Youth* put it: "The aim of re-education in a youth camp is to overcome the peculiarities of personal development, to eradicate unique thoughts and behavior in children and young adults, so as to create the foundations for a normal development." The GDR's educational ideal was thus the exact reverse of that of Wilhelm von Humboldt, after whom, along with his brother Alexander, East Berlin's university was cynically named. He had written that the aim of education was "to turn children into people," autonomous subjects free from tutelage, whether self-imposed or imposed by the state.

The attempt to make socialism into an ersatz religion had begun in the mid-1950s with the institution of the "Consecration of Youth" (*Jugendwiehe*), as an alternative to confirmation as a rite of passage. Similar ceremonies had been common among secular societies from the mid-nineteenth century and were instituted in the GDR at Soviet insistence to counteract the influence of the churches. First, 14-year-olds had to complete a year-long course in which they learnt about the dignity of labor by visiting various enterprises, were given sex instruction, and were taught how to dance. They then made a solemn oath of allegiance to peace, socialism, and solidarity with the victims of imperialism, after which they were presented with a bouquet and an improving book of impeccably orthodox socialist content. They were also presented with an identity card and thenceforth were addressed by the formal *Sie* rather than the familiar *Du*. Consecration was carried out at a time when a youth left the Young Pioneers and joined the Free German Youth. The FDJ's remit was to "help overcome the remaining vestiges of capitalism such as rowdyism, drunkenness, loutish behavior towards old people, the reading of pornography etc." This was not a particularly attractive program for adolescents, who objected strongly to being controlled and censored by the killjoys in the SED. It was therefore hardly surprising that the membership of the FDJ slowly dwindled in the late 1950s.

The Berlin Wall

When Wilhelm Pieck died in 1960, Walter Ulbricht became chairman of a newly created Council of State (Staatsrat). He was also secretary general of the SED and chairman of the Council of National Defense, thus holding all the key positions in the state. He faced a difficult situation. Within a year it was plain that the economic goals of the plan were all pie in the sky. The five-year plan became a seven-year plan. At the same time it was decided to complete the process of collectivization. Forty percent of farmland had been collectivized by 1959. By 1961 almost 90 percent was in the hands of the agricultural production cooperatives. The result was a severe food shortage and the mass exodus of peasantry to the West. The nationalization of a large number of small enterprises had a similar result. The SED's ideologues calculated that, were the capitalist "basis" of the economy destroyed, the "superstructure" would automatically become socialist. With a chaotic basis the superstructure collapsed: 200,000 people left in 1960, most of them via West Berlin. The exodus became even greater in 1961, with 30,415 people leaving in July and 47,433 in the first two weeks of August. By now, 3.1 million people had demonstrated their opposition to the regime. West Germany thereby gained 7,500 doctors, 1,200 dentists, one-third of the GDR's academics, and hundreds of thousands of skilled workers, thus saving an estimated 30 billion Deutschmarks in education and training. Others found an even more drastic way out. The GDR's suicide rate was the second highest in Europe, just below that of Finland; 12.5 percent of East Germans were alcoholics. Whether to stay or leave was now the main existential question facing every citizen. Would things improve, or had one to cut one's losses and start afresh in the West? Perhaps things were not so bad. Berliners could always travel to the western sectors, where GDR currency was accepted. Every day 500,000 crossed the border between East and West Berlin; 12,000 West Berliners worked in the East, and 50,000 East Berliners in the West. On August 12, 1961, the GDR's national television proudly announced the sale of the millionth television set, but that same night everything changed.

At two o'clock in the morning work began to close off the eastern sector of Berlin. Three hours later forty-five of the sixty crossing points to the western sectors were barricaded. Within hours the eastern sector was hermetically sealed and work began to build an "anti-fascist protective wall." The SED was mobilized in a campaign to weed out "whiners," "laggards," and "enemies of the state." Special "order groups" of the FDJ combed bars and cinemas for "provocateurs and jackasses," who were to be beaten up and then handed over to the police. Commando groups from the FDJ in "Operation Blitz on NATO Transmitters" climbed on to roofs and turned television aerials so that they could no longer receive western television. Anyone who dared criticize the building of the wall was liable to be beaten up by party activists to within an inch of their life. There were four times more prosecutions for political offenses from August to December than in the previous seven months, an indication of widespread discontent with the new course.

There was a certain relaxation of tension in the GDR after this grim period of repression immediately after the building of the Berlin Wall. At least people were now no longer faced with the agonizing choice between staying and leaving. They had now to make the best of existing conditions. Taking the cue from Khrushchev's speech at the Twenty-Second Congress of the CPSU in October 1961 which revealed further horrors committed during the Stalin era, Ulbricht at last began to speak of "crimes" committed in the name of communism. The town of Stalinstadt on the Oder was given the robustly socialist name of Eisenhüttenstadt (Iron Works Town). The foremost showpiece of socialist architecture, Berlin's Stalinallee, was renamed Marx-Engels Allee. Statues of the Soviet dictator were hastily dismantled. His works were removed from libraries. In January 1962 universal military service was introduced, but remarkably in 1964 the GDR became the first socialist country to accept conscientious objectors.

By 1962 the GDR was rapidly becoming a society divided into two classes – those who had Deutschmarks and those who only had the East German currency (MDN). Special stores, known as Intershop, sold western goods for Deutschmarks. The even more exclusive Exquisit and Delikat shops were similarly only for those with the prized West German currency. Later, attempts were made to overcome this gross injustice by importing goods from the West for the general public; but there was a strict limit to this, due to the chronic lack of hard currency and an already alarmingly high level of indebtedness.

The New Economic System

In 1963 the New Economic System for Planning and Direction (NÖSPL), based on the ideas of the Soviet economist Evsei Liberman, was introduced. It permitted the use of "economic levers" such as prices, wages, and even profit to bring a degree of flexibility into the fossilized planned economy. In the same spirit a degree of decentralization was permitted. It was hoped that a dose of capitalism would revive a moribund economy. The results were encouraging. Productivity and gross national product rose substantially, to the point that it seemed that a totalitarian society was gradually becoming what the West German political scientist Peter Christian Ludz was soon to call a system of "consultative authoritarianism." As western scholars moved steadily to the left there was much talk of the "convergence" of the two systems. According to this theory communism and capitalism were gradually being transformed into technocracies that recognized the importance of input from society at large and which had to take individual needs and aspirations into account. This was altogether too rosy a view of developments in the GDR, where the people were still left without a voice, but at least it was no longer a totalitarian Stalinist police state.

The SED adopted a more liberal policy towards youth. In September 1963 the Politbüro announced that "spoon-feeding, finger-pointing, and admonishment" were no longer appropriate. The ban on "dancing apart," previously considered to be a sign of Western depravity, was lifted. It was now permitted to dance as one wished, provided that one remained "discreet." The FDJ leader, Horst Schumann, danced the twist in public, even though this popular style had recently been denounced as "NATO music," an "outgrowth of capitalist decadence," an anti-Communist weapon "disseminated by the American secret service." It proved impossible to immunize East German youth against Beatlemania, and there was a brisk black market trade in the group's albums. "Beat concerts" were a popular expression of a new sense of self-confidence and the state radio instigated youthful programs, such as DT64, named after the All-German Youth Meeting (Deutschlandtreffen) in 1964, which attracted a wide audience. But this period of liberalization soon ended.

Khrushchev fell from power in 1964 and was replaced by a "collective leadership" under the dreary Leonid Brezhnev, who presided over the inexorable economic decline of the Soviet system, hastened by excessive expenditure on the military and by neo-Stalinist ideological sclerosis. Ulbricht's crown prince, Erich Honecker, promptly mounted a campaign against "long-haired beat fans" and "rowdies," who "undermined socialist morality." FDJ activists were encouraged to get to work with scissors and chop off the locks of such "layabouts" and "mangy deadbeats." Students who copied "reactionary West German fraternity brothers" by binge drinking were severely punished. A campaign was launched against "manifestations of American immorality," and "beat music" was no longer permitted in DT64.

The new Soviet leadership ordered Ulbricht to distance himself from the New Economic System that had failed to meet its target and had put the economy above politics. Ulbricht promptly made the chief planner, Erich Appel, responsible for all deficiencies in the plan, which were in large part due to the failure of the Soviet Union to supply the raw materials they had promised. Appel was found shot dead in his office in December 1965. It remains uncertain whether this was murder or suicide.

The Central Committee of the SED drew up a long list of past mistakes and returned to a system of rigidly centralized planning. At the same time Erich Honecker as secretary for state security clamped down on the arts, which had become infected by the "lack of moral inhibitions and the brutality of capitalist West Germany." The highly talented folk singer Wolf Biermann was forbidden to perform in public and his friend the physicist Robert Havemann, also a prominent critic of a procrustean Marxism, was expelled from the SED and lost his professorship at the Humboldt University in Berlin. Honecker was a uncompromising anti-intellectual. Until his dying day he was convinced socialism could only be built by the working class, under the leadership of a Marxist-Leninist party. Intellectuals, artists, and academics were at best secondary, often positively harmful. Parallel to this cultural clear-cutting, an educational reform added a heavier dose of Marxism-Leninism to the curriculum and emphasized mathematics and science in the vain hope that East German youth would overtake their western counterparts in both ideological fervor and scientific attainment.

Throughout the 1960s the SED confronted the problem of meeting the challenges of the "scientific and technical revolution." The educational system was again reformed in

1965, with greater emphasis on practical skills. A universal ten-year polytechnic school system provided practical instruction in such things as carpentry, vehicle maintenance, cooking, and gardening in the first six years. In the next four years pupils were given courses on "an introduction to socialist production," technical drawing, and "productive work." Those who remained in school for the next two years concentrated on "scientific and practical work."

The first article of the new constitution of 1968 guaranteed the leading role of the SED, and the articles guaranteeing freedom for religion, the press, radio, and television were still meaningless, but the pressing need to modernize the state demanded a degree of flexibility that gave the much-maligned "individual" slightly more space for self-development. A new version of the New Economic System was announced, called the Socialist Economic System (ÖSS), but it was a change more in name than in substance. Ulbricht announced that the aim was to "overtake without catching up." This meant overtaking West Germany in technology, without reaching the same standard of living, productivity, or rate of growth. It was once again a totally fantastic and unattainable goal. There was a marked increase in the production of consumer goods that resulted in vacuum cleaners, refrigerators, washing machines, and television sets becoming available, but they were ludicrously expensive. Average monthly wages were 491 MDN. A television set cost 2,050 MDN, refrigerators and washing machines 1,350 MDN. The ecologically disastrous Trabant automobile, with its evil-smelling two-stroke engine that produced nine times the amount of hydrocarbons of the average European car and which had a plastic body made of recycled material, won iconic status in the GDR. It was an object of both affection and derision. It was unbelievably expensive, originally costing 7,500 MDN, rising to 14,000 MDN, with the waiting time for delivery between five and fifteen years. Delivery time could be speeded up with a bribe of 20,000 MDN. It was technically backward, unreliable, and its production was hopelessly labor-intensive; but it was also a symbol of freedom, consumerism, and better times to come. It was soon to become a cult object of "ostalgia," but was condemned to extinction in an ecologically conscious united Germany.

The GDR and Willy Brandt's *Ostpolitik*

In 1966 the newly installed Great Coalition government in Bonn began a policy of détente towards the GDR. Previously the East Germans had called for the two Germanys to sit down at the same table. Now they announced that they wished to have nothing to do with a country run by "monopoly capitalists," and that its change of course was nothing less than "aggression in slippers." The GDR stated that it would make no further concessions on this issue unless Bonn formally recognized the East German regime. The GDR was "a socialist state of workers and peasants," eternally allied to the Soviet Union, whereas the Federal Republic was "not only a foreign country, but a capitalist country."

The Soviets were concerned that Brandt's *Ostpolitik* might well lead to a blurring of distinctions between East and West Germany, eventually leading to the collapse of the GDR. Ulbricht soon began to respond by making some remarkably flattering remarks about the SPD in the hope of persuading Bonn to help finance high-technology industries in a renewed bid to overtake the West. It was both politically and economically a disaster. The GDR lacked the infrastructure and the expertise to make such a leap ahead. Capital was urgently needed for investment in less utopian schemes. A lowering of living standards

PLATE 30   Willy Brandt in Warsaw. © BPK

was a necessary corollary, for all the high-flown rhetoric about the "socialist human community." Ulbricht, locked in an arcane ideological struggle with the Soviets over the precise nature of socialism, had the impertinence to remind them that the GDR was an independent state and not a Soviet state like Belarus. The Soviets were alarmed at the spectacle of Ulbricht hobnobbing with the SPD and thought that his notion that the GDR would be able to outstrip the Federal Republic economically, then uniting Germany "on the basis of democracy and socialism," was dangerous nonsense. Brezhnev loathed Ulbricht, who arrogantly lectured him on the errors in Soviet policy. The Soviet leader did not mince his words: "There is, there cannot and should not be, the slightest hint of rapprochement between the GDR and the Federal Republic." The time had come to replace Ulbricht with Erich Honecker, a man who was utterly subservient to Moscow and who wanted no truck with the infidels in the West. In August 1970 Brezhnev reminded Honecker that "without us there would be no GDR." The truth of this became abundantly clear nineteen years later, when Gorbachev refused to prop up the regime with Soviet tanks.

The Honecker Era

Crown prince Honecker had to wait for some time until the green light came from Moscow. In the meantime he continually intrigued against the 77-year-old first secretary. As Moscow's elect he gained increasing support in the upper echelons of the SED. By January 1971 the vast majority of the Politbüro felt that the time had come for Ulbricht to relinquish power. All that was now needed was Moscow's approval. Finally, in April 1971 Brezhnev ordered Ulbricht, whose health was rapidly deteriorating, to resign as first secretary but graciously permitted him to stay on as chairman of the council of state. He died two years later.

Erich Honecker was born in the Saar, and was a roofer by trade and a life-long Communist. He had been arrested by the Nazis in 1937 and sentenced to ten years' imprisonment for conspiracy to commit treason. He was made head of the Free German Youth in 1946. He was a dreary, unimaginative paper-pusher whose speeches were even duller than the ineffably boring tirades of Ulbricht. His tastes were impeccably petit bourgeois and he was unquestioningly loyal to Moscow. He immediately dropped Ulbricht's madcap Socialist Economic System, replacing it with a five-year plan concentrating on consumer goods and the improvement of living standards. Ulbricht's heterodox notions of a "socialist human community" and of socialism as being something other than a mere phase in the development towards a Communist society were also denounced.

The system of government remained unchanged under Honecker. The SED maintained discipline under the old slogan "The Party Is Always Right." The party trained an elite from which new members of the *nomenklatura* were admitted. Its Marxist-Leninist theory was held to afford a scientific understanding of the world. Real power was held by Honecker and two of his closest advisors – Erich Mielke and Günter Mittag. It was a dictatorship that was totally without the charismatic aura of a Stalin, a Hitler, or a Mussolini. Unable to mobilize enthusiastic popular support, it was widely seen as a collaborationist regime, maintained by the brute force of the Red Army. It was a dogmatic and self-opinionated sultanate that imagined that it held the key to a perfect understanding of the world-historical process. The net result was a society ridden with corruption, willfulness, irresponsibility, favoritism, and lawlessness. Far from creating the socialist Adam, with a deep concern for the welfare of the community, the typical product of this society was a self-serving and servile egoist. The ossified bureaucratic planning system disregarded market exigencies with fatal consequences. Honecker's attempt to catch up with the modern world resulted in hundreds of millions being invested in microchip production. The cost of production per chip was 536 MDN. The sale price was 16 MDN, well above the market price in the West. The state thus subsidized each chip to the tune of 520 MDN.

Without open discussion, the free exchange of ideas, and a willingness to accept error, this wretched state of affairs could not be ameliorated. The Central Committee and Politbüro simply rubber-stamped the decisions made by the gerontocratic clique around Ulbricht and Honecker. There was no discussion, even at the highest level, no hint of collective responsibility, no place for innovative or critical ideas. When a degree of transparency was reached in the crisis of 1989/90 the appalling mediocrity and political incompetence of the leadership around the gawkily smirking Egon Krenz were all too apparent.

Honecker's reign began with a proclamation that the Federal Republic was an "imperialist foreign country," so that Johannes R. Becker's words to Hans Eisler's national anthem, which spoke of a united German nation, were no longer allowed to be sung. True to the Soviet's "two nation" theory, Honecker countered the SPD's assertion that Germany was one nation consisting of two states by proclaiming the GDR to be a "socialist state of the German nation." A fresh round in the class struggle was begun by an all-out attack on the remaining vestiges of private enterprise. Small independent business were nationalized, resulting in a disastrous drop in productivity.

With the signing of the Treaty on General Principles with the Soviet Union in August 1970 the GDR was ordered to draw a sharp ideological line between East and West Germany. Kurt Hager, the SED's chief ideologue, preached the somewhat perplexing doctrine of "socialism as it really exists" whereby the unbridgeable differences between the "socialist state of workers and peasants" and the "continuously existing capitalist nation" in the West were emphasized. The "socialist brotherhood" between the GDR and the Soviet Union and with the other states in the "socialist community" was another leitmotif of Hager's propaganda offensive. The GDR also provided a safe haven and technical advice to West German terrorists. Yet in spite of this rigidity towards the West the regime became marginally more tolerant at home. In November 1971 a delivery of 150,000 pairs of Levi's jeans, previously denounced as a symbolic representation of western decadence, sold out within hours. Citizens were now permitted to watch western television and listen to western radio. Young people were inspired by glamorized versions of people's liberation movements: Castro's Cuba, Allende's Chile, the heroic struggle of the Vietnamese against American imperialism. Ernesto Che Guevara became an iconic figure. Socialism under palm trees was a romantic vision that contrasted with the dreary everyday reality of "socialism as it really exists."

Meanwhile, Willy Brandt's *Ostpolitik* began to bear fruit. In December 1971 an agreement was reached on transport through the GDR to West Berlin. This was followed shortly afterwards by a general agreement on transport. In June 1972 discussions began on normalizing relations between the two Germanys. The GDR wanted full diplomatic recognition, the Federal Republic refused. Further discussion resulted in an agreement in December 1972 recognizing that the sovereign rights of both countries were restricted to their respective territories. This meant that the Federal Republic did not give up its aim for eventual unification, nor did it settle the question of nationality. But it had thereby abandoned the Hallstein doctrine, its attempt to isolate the GDR diplomatically, thus provoking the ire of right-wing elements in the West. In 1974 the two Germanys became full members of the United Nations and were equal partners in the Conference on Security and Cooperation in Europe (CSCE). In June 1974 a West German diplomatic mission was opened in East Berlin.

Although the GDR became more tolerant, it remained a rigidly controlled society. Erich Mielke's Stasi expanded exponentially. Its 91,000 employees were assisted by "unofficial associates," the number of which increased from 100,000 in 1968 to 180,000 by 1975. Society was further militarized under Honecker's aegis. In 1978 schools were obliged to give pupils military training. Students of both sexes were made to take part in several weeks of training in small arms and infantry tactics. Those who failed to take part in these exercises, or who showed little enthusiasm, were severely punished, often by losing the opportunity to go to university.

Social Structure of the GDR

The "workers' and peasants' state," with its hypocritical egalitarian ideology, rapidly developed into a hierarchically divided society with precious little room for social mobility. Karl Marx's ruling classes had been decimated. The estates of the landowning aristocracy had been seized, the bourgeoisie destroyed. In their place was an gerontocratic clique that jealously guarded its hold over the SED, below which was a self-perpetuating class of bureaucrats and "socialist intellectuals" with exclusive rights to a university education. These groups had undivided power over society, state, and economy. They decided what should be produced and how it should be distributed. The only limitation to their power was that they controlled a Soviet satrapy and therefore were bound to obey their masters in Moscow.

The power elite consisted of a mere twenty-four men and two women in the secretariat of the Central Committee of the SED and the Politbüro. In the 1980s their average age was 66. For almost twenty years this group was effectively controlled by three men: Honecker, Mittag, and Mielke. A second echelon was made up of the members of and candidates for the Central Committee, the leadership of its various mass organizations such as the Free German Youth and local party bosses. Most of this elite lived in the isolated petit bourgeois splendor of a heavily guarded enclave in Wandlitz, a few kilometers north of Berlin.

Below this minuscule elite was a larger group made up of the Council of State, the Council of Ministers, the People's Chamber, the Planning Commission, the Associations of People's Own Enterprises, the leadership of the SED and the Antifa-Bloc parties, the mass organizations, the Central Committee's scientific and economic institutes, and the universities. Broadly speaking admission to this group was based on a Soviet-style *nomenklatura* system of patronage, whereby the followers of leading figures formed families, analogous to those in the Mafia, so that one's fortune depended upon that of one's patron. In later years the number of those recruited directly from the universities and technical colleges increased.

A third caste was made up of middle-level officials in the state and party, the People's Own Enterprises and collective farms as well a professionals such as doctors, engineers, university professors, and teachers. Membership in this group of some 250,000 was reserved exclusively for those who belonged to the SED. Due to the fact that a large number of these highly qualified people fled to the West, there were exceptional opportunities open to those with talent to better their lot. Although government statistics are notoriously unreliable and the definition of "working-class" highly flexible, it would seem that about half of this group was recruited from the working class, so that there was an exceptional degree of social mobility in the early years of the GDR. This process of rapid social mobility was of relatively short duration. By the 1960s the elites began to close their ranks and became self-recruiting. Their children were over-represented among university students to such a degree that statistics on the social composition of the student body were no longer published after 1967. Working-class children in the Federal Republic had a far greater chance of gaining a place in a university than did those in the GDR.

Membership of this privileged group thus depended on status and political reliability, rather than qualifications and skills. The staggering inefficiency of the economy was due in large part to incompetent management and poor research. Only those enterprises that managed to keep personnel who had had leading positions before 1945, irrespective of their past histories, were able to maintain standards. An educational system that placed such emphasis on parroting the platitudes of Marxism-Leninism was incapable of producing qualified personnel for leading positions in a modern industrial state. With top management taking home only about 50 percent more than workers, there was no great material incentive to succeed. Within a rigidly conformist society there was no place for originality, creativity, or contrariness.

Although SED's ideology gave the industrial working class a privileged status as a historical subject, the heroic architects of a Communist paradise, the reality was grimly otherwise. Although East Germans, with their average of a 43.75-hour working week, toiled 5.25 hours longer than the "viciously exploited" West Germans, they earned about half as much. Their pensions were a mere 30 percent of those in the West. On the other hand the gap between rich and poor, which rapidly widened in the West, was relatively small. Incomes were leveled, consumer goods were scarce, travel to the West was denied to all. But it is doubtful whether a relative equality based on scarcity and deprivation was of much comfort to those at the bottom of the heap.

The FDGB as an executive organ of the SED in no sense acted as an active proponent of the interests of the working class and there was no equivalent to West Germany's system of workers' representation in management. Workers' interests were represented at the shop-floor level by "brigades," which were concerned with such things as medical coverage, day-care centers, holidays, leisure-time activities, and housing; but also with political indoctrination and social control. Denied the right to strike, the only means of protest was to slow down, thereby threatening not to meet the targets set by the current plan. The SED, anxious to avoid open confrontation with the working class after the traumatic events of 1953, often gave way.

Rural society was radically transformed in East Germany. The complex hierarchical culture was destroyed. The estates of the landed aristocracy were seized, independent farmers were transformed into laborers on collective farms; then, in fit of megalomania, in the 1970s the collective farms were bundled together into gigantic agribusinesses, each with more than 4,000 workers. The net result of these efforts was to transform an efficient and productive agricultural economy into one that was motiveless, incompetent, and resentful. It is hardly surprising that in the crisis of 1989/90 the vast majority of both workers and peasants, who were touted as the twin pillars of a socialist society, voted for its dissolution. By contrast 90 percent of university students and 80 percent of professors hoped that the GDR would survive.

The chronic shortage of labor resulting from the mass exodus to the West could only be offset by the employment of women. Whereas in 1950 a mere 44 percent of employable women were in the workforce, by 1989 the percentage had risen to 91 percent, making the GDR the European state with the highest percentage of women employed. Although the SED styled this process as emancipatory along lines adumbrated by August Bebel, the founder of German social democracy, in his book *Women and Socialism*, it was nothing more than an effort to plug the gaps in the workforce.

Although the regime eased the burden on women by providing a large number of day-care centers, their lot was far from enviable. Chronic shortages resulted in hours spent queuing in what were ironically called "socialist waiting collectives." In one regard East German women exercised more agency than their western sisters. There were 50 percent more divorces than in the West, most of them instigated by women. In most respects, however, the GDR was a traditional male-dominated society. The SED has been described as an "authoritarian male association." Although 52 percent of doctors and 54 percent of students were women, they were under-represented in the higher ranks of the medical and academic professions. Only 12.8 percent of chief physicians and 4.3 percent of university professors were women. They were virtually excluded from the centers of political power. There was not a single woman in the Politbüro. Only eighteen of the 165 members of the Central Committee were female. Honecker's wife Margret was the only woman among the forty-two members of the Council of Ministers. Of the 169 ministers, deputy ministers, and secretaries of state, four were women.

Dissent

Honecker's efforts to improve living standards were only partially successful. Subsidized housing, free medicine, family allowances, improved pensions, and the like meant that capital had to be found in the West and the interest paid by new loans, thus creating a spiraling debt.

The oil crisis of 1973 also had a shattering effect on Honecker's dogma of the "unity of economic and social policy." It could only be partially realized by deficit financing. Imports of raw materials increased by 170 percent, exports by a mere 65 percent. Debt mounted at an alarming rate. The Soviet Union, with its grossly mismanaged economy and shortage of capital, was unable to help out the socialist countries by exploiting its huge reserves of natural resources. Mounting economic problems led to increasing criticism of the regime's ossified ideology and resulted in an attempt to stifle all critical voices. A wave of repression dashed all hopes for a gradual democratization and independence from Moscow, for "socialism with a human face" and a "third way." Dissident artists and intellectuals were harassed, bullied, and tormented in an attempt to make them change their ways. When all failed they were forced to leave for the West. East Germany thereby lost its cultural and intellectual elite and relapsed into dreary mediocrity.

In August 1976 a Protestant minister, Oskar Brüsewitz, set fire to himself in protest against the persecution of his church. In October 1977 members of the FDJ attacked the police during a demonstration in East Berlin. A steady flow of visitors from West Germany did much to fuel discontent. An increasing number of GDR citizens were permitted to travel to the West for pressing compassionate reasons. Rudolf Bahro, a leading dissident whose vision of a reformed communism earned widespread assent, comparing the Politbüro to the Inquisition denounced the SED as a political police force. He was given an eight-year prison sentence in 1978, but was deported to West Germany in the following year. On the positive side, the promises made in the CSCE agreement enabled an increasing number of GDR citizens to leave for the West. The regime was eager to get rid of pensioners, who were regarded as a tiresome burden, a large number of dissidents were ransomed, and others found legal ways of escape. Those who remained lived wretchedly at the poverty level. Between 1962 and 1988, 625,000 East Germans moved to the West, two-thirds with official sanction, the rest by various devious routes, mainly through Yugoslavia. With the benefit of hindsight it is possible to see the cracks in the system caused by Brandt's *Ostpolitik* and by the GDR's internal contradictions, but they were hardly visible amid a dreary, Stasi-ridden daily routine.

By the end of the 1970s the GDR enjoyed a standard of living that matched those of countries such as Portugal or Greece. One-third of households owned a car, 80 percent a washing machine, 90 percent a television set. Virtually all had a refrigerator. Housing, power, water, and food were heavily subsidized. Vast sums of money were invested in education and health. Generous family allowances and day-care centers relieved the burden on young families. But all these achievements did not alter the fact that most citizens compared their lot not to that of other socialist states, but to the incredibly prosperous Federal Republic that enjoyed the luscious fruits of the "Economic Miracle." With 85 percent of the population regularly watching West German television, the promises of planners and the party rang hollow. Not only was life on the other side of the wall obviously better, the GDR was lagging ever further behind the Federal Republic.

The statistics only told half the story. By the early 1980s major consumer goods were hopelessly obsolete. Motor cars, such as the Trabant and the Wartburg, could not compare with West German models. The last two-stroke car in the Federal Republic, the DKW, had left the assembly line in 1965. The company then changed its name to Audi. East German roads were in such an appalling state of repair that 18 percent of them were classified as impassable. Color televisions were of lamentable quality. Only hideously expensive refrigerators had freezer compartments, and automatic washing machines were out of the price range of the ordinary consumer. The GDR ranked sixty-fifth among states as regards the number of private telephones owned, and 62 percent of these were more than thirty years old. Pollution on a horrendous level destroyed the ecology and presented a major health hazard. There were three main reasons for this misery. First, industry lacked capital for research and development, was shackled by the planning bureaucracy, and was forced to accept the priority of full employment over productivity. Second, with more money in people's pay packets consumer demand increased, but could not be met by an inefficient system. Third, the attempt to offset the lack of high-quality consumer goods by importing them from the West simply resulted in a crippling debt. By 1981 the GDR owed the Federal Republic 23 billion Deutschmarks and the debt was steadily mounting. The SED's hopes that the import of technology from the West could be offset by increased exports were soon dashed. Hard currency was used to import food and consumer goods to keep the citizenry happy. What was left over was used to service the debt. The problem of the undercapitalization of industry thus grew steadily worse.

A further blow came in 1981 when the Soviet Union, desperately short of the hard currency needed to buy foodstuffs, decided to send oil destined for the GDR to the Federal Republic. The price of Soviet oil sent to the GDR was by now thirteen times that of 1970. Honecker was outraged. He complained that the "revanchist West" bombarded the GDR with five television and thirty-five radio channels. The Poles were plotting a "counter-revolution" behind the East Germans' backs, the reference being to the Solidarność (Solidarity) movement among the Polish trade unions. The Central Committee of the SED was about to announce the new five-year plan, aimed at improving consumer choice, and thus dampening discontent, with an injection of Hungarian-style "goulash communism." This was now made impossible by lack of oil: the GDR risked being destabilized for want of 2 million tons of Soviet crude. None of this made the slightest impression on Brezhnev, who was on the best of terms with the West German chancellor, Helmut Schmidt.

The GDR felt that the only way out of the crisis was to rely increasingly on lignite as a source of energy. Open-cast mining, mainly in the Lausitz, caused a social and ecological disaster. Over 300 million tons of coal were dug up every year. Whole villages were displaced, soil erosion became chronic, air pollution unimaginable. Sulfur dioxide emissions increased by 30 percent between 1974 and 1985, creating a major health hazard.

Relations between the Two Germanys

The GDR was now effectively bankrupt, only to be saved by a shadowy Stasi officer, Alexander Schalck-Golodkowski, who with the Bavarian minister president Franz Josef Strauß and his bosom pal Josef "Sepp" März brokered a $3 billion loan. This helped keep the ship of state afloat, but it was leaking badly. The dubious manipulations of

Schalck-Golodkowski's economic empire, Commercial Coordination (KoKo), which indulged in such activities as the confiscation of works of art to sell them abroad, the export of blood plasma and weapons, dealing in drugs and pornography, the ransoming of political prisoners, and the import of waste materials for disposal in the GDR, all designed to get hold of hard currency, were mere drops in a bucket.

The Federal Republic might have bailed out the GDR, but tensions between East and West were worsening with the crisis over medium-range ballistic missiles. Within this grim context neither the GDR nor the Federal Republic enjoyed full sovereignty, but Helmut Kohl's conservative government of 1982 continued the social-liberal *Ostpolitik*, in the conviction that this was the only possible way to improve the lot of Germans in the East. The GDR's leadership knew that the economic survival of the country depended on help from the West, but suddenly in October 1980 Honecker, acting on instructions from Moscow, demanded full diplomatic recognition by Bonn. The SED Politbüro was divided on this issue. Honecker and Mittag realized that good relations with the Federal Republic were imperative for the GDR to survive; whereas the prime minister, Willi Stoph, and Werner Krolikowski, who was responsible of oversight of the balance of payments with the Federal Republic, argued that their two colleagues had fallen into a trap set by Helmut Schmidt, designed to separate the GDR from the Soviet Union. Honecker, who had engineered Ulbricht's fall by bringing exactly the same charge against him, knew exactly what was a stake. Without Moscow's support he was finished.

Relations between the two Germanys were nevertheless cemented during the early 1980s. The two rogue elephants Schalck-Golodkowski and Franz Josef Strauß formed a close macho partnership. The SPD began discussions with the SED on "ideological differences and mutual security." The Liberal Democratic Party's leader and foreign minister, Hans-Dietrich Genscher, maintained close ties with Otto Reinhold, head of the SED's Academy for Social Sciences, who argued that the GDR had to remain "an anti-fascist, socialist alternative to the Federal Republic." These efforts were given fresh impetus with the appointment of Mikhail Gorbachev in 1985. Moscow finally permitted Honecker to accept Helmut Kohl's invitation to visit the Federal Republic in September 1987. This was a triumph for Honecker in that he was received as the head of a sovereign state, but he had serious misgivings about the trajectory of the young Soviet leader's new course. He felt that the policies of glasnost (openness) and perestroika (restructuring) threatened the leadership role of the SED and would lead to an end to the clear distinctions between the GDR and the Federal Republic.

Great was Honecker's alarm when the Soviet Union's star poet, Yevgeny Yevtushenko, announced on West German television that there was only one kind of German literature. He denounced this remark to Gorbachev as "counter-revolutionary." In 1987 the GDR's chief ideologue, Kurt Hager, dismissed perestroika in an interview with the West German magazine *Stern* by saying that "one doesn't have to change the wallpaper in one's apartment just because one's neighbor has done so." For almost forty years the SED had faithfully followed Moscow's instructions in order to stay in power, now it was losing the support without which it could not hope to survive. In November 1986 Gorbachev emphasized the "independence of every party, its sovereign right to make decisions, and its responsibility towards its own people." Reform movements in the socialist states would no longer provoke military intervention from the Soviet Union. The Brezhnev doctrine had been replaced by the "Sinatra doctrine." Socialist states could do it "their way."

The Collapse of the GDR

The SED leadership, refusing to accept the challenge, remained set in their ways. No longer able to rely on Soviet tanks, they had to fall back on the Stasi and their own "armed organizations" to resist glasnost and perestroika and remain in power. But there were opposition forces at work within the party. Calls for more democracy, for a relaxation of press censorship, and for a serious discussion of economic problems were heard at the Eleventh Party Congress in April 1986. The leadership responded with denunciations of "grumbling" and "bitching." A number of these petulant comrades were dismissed from the party, but this only served to increase the level of discontent as reformers looked to Gorbachev for leadership. The Soviet Union, once a threat and a menace, was now the hope for the future.

The SED leadership tried desperately to stem the tide of reform initiated in the Soviet Union. Speeches of Soviet leaders were carefully censored, publications vetted. Things came to a head when the Soviet magazine *Sputnik*, which contained an article criticizing the Hitler–Stalin Pact, was banned in the GDR. Honecker told the Central Committee of the SED that it should not be influenced by "the babbling of rabid petit-bourgeois, who are trying to rewrite the history of the CPSU and the Soviet Union in a bourgeois sense." The Stasi reported that there was widespread criticism of the decision to ban *Sputnik*, even among "long-term members and party functionaries." Dissatisfaction with the existing state of affairs was particularly strong among young people, but the leadership had nothing to offer that might counter this dangerously mounting level of discontent. They had neither the political imagination nor the material resources to meet the challenge. The State Planning Commission suggested ending the system of extensive subventions, cutting back on military expenditure, and putting a stop to investments in the hopelessly inefficient microelectronics sector. Honecker would hear nothing of this. With the social services accounting for half of total state expenditure and as the sole means whereby the SED could legitimize its power monopoly, it was an impossible situation. All he could offer were empty words of encouragement and the threat of repression.

In the communal elections in May 1989 a number of informal political groupings, categorized by the Stasi as "inimical, negative forces," used the Helsinki accords (that called for human rights to be respected) to insert themselves into the political process. Whereas the GDR heavily subsidized the peace movement in West Germany, it clamped down on similar groupings at home. The slogan "Swords into Ploughshares" was forbidden. The Stasi could no longer indulge in Stalinist methods to destroy the movement, but it was able to do considerable damage by undermining it by infiltrating "informal colleagues," by imposing short-term prison sentences, and by expulsion to the West. The opposition groups wanted improvements at home, not reunification. Human rights, disarmament, pluralism, and the development of a civil society were their principal concerns. The elections were rigged, with the "Unity List" gaining 99 percent of the votes, but the opposition groups mounted a series of effective protests against such shameless manipulation.

One popular form of protest was to apply for a visa to leave the country. By the end of 1988, 110,000 applications were pending. In January 1989 the Soviet Union forced the GDR to sign on to the CSCE, which guaranteed the right of all citizens to travel as they wished. The SED did not honor this commitment. In February two young men tried to escape over the Berlin Wall. One was shot dead, the other wounded and condemned to a three-year prison sentence. Chris Gueffroy was the last person to die on this shameful frontier. Nearly

700 people before him had died in the attempt. Then the situation began to slip out of the SED's control. In May 1989 the Hungarians began to open up their frontier with Austria. Hundreds of East Germans went to Budapest, where they waited in the West German embassy for permission to travel to Austria. Others sought asylum in West German embassies in Prague and Warsaw. Without prior discussion with the GDR, the Hungarians opened the frontier with Austria during the night of September 10. Within a few days 25,000 GDR citizens had seized this opportunity to escape.

Honecker was left stubborn but powerless. In August he announced that "neither ox nor donkey could hold up the advance of socialism" and that as far as the refugees were concerned it was a case of good riddance to bad rubbish. At the beginning of October he ordered the frontier to Czechoslovakia to be closed. Opposition groups changed their slogan from "We Want To Leave!" to "We're Staying Here!" The SED countered this threat with praise for the Chinese government's massacre in Tiananmen Square in June, but civil rights groups ignored the threat. In September New Forum, Democracy Now, and Democratic New Beginning applied for recognition as official parties. Mass rallies in Leipzig were broken up by baton-wielding police, followed by numerous arrests. Regardless of this repression they continued every Monday. When the SED organized mass demonstrations to celebrate the GDR's fortieth anniversary, the opposition groups organized counter-demonstrations demanding fundamental democratic reforms. Those who chanted the new slogan "We Are the People!" were brutally assaulted by the "People's Police."

The SED no longer had the support of the Soviet leadership. Gorbachev was openly critical of Honecker's mulish refusal to see that times had changed. Within the party there was a growing realization of the need to find a way out of economic misery and political bankruptcy. Honecker, the Stasi boss Mielke, and the economics expert Mittag were an isolated troika. Honecker's crown prince and head of the FDJ, the toothily grinning Egon Krenz, began to wonder whether it might be time to abandon ship, but he too could not count on Soviet support. The "Sinatra doctrine" meant that he would have to do it his way. The country was by now hopelessly in hock to the Federal Republic, with the debt mounting by 500 million Deutschmarks every month. At this rate by 1991 the GDR would be bankrupt. In this hopeless situation all the old guard could offer was repression, while the young Turks yearned for major changes. Most simply waited upon events in silent resignation. The number of those who called for a "Chinese solution" steadily dwindled, while the Soviet Union made it clear that it would not countenance a repeat performance of 1952. During the fortieth anniversary celebrations in East Berlin Gorbachev made this perfectly clear when he said: "Life punishes those who come too late."

On the evening of Monday, October 9, 70,000 people assembled in Leipzig. The heavily armed security forces stood ready. Kurt Masur, the conductor of the famed Gewandhaus Orchestra, was joined by three district SED functionaries in a radio address calling for a peaceful solution. Violence was avoided. On October 17 a crowd of 100,000 in Leipzig called for democratic reforms. Egon Krenz, Willi Stoph, the Berlin party boss Günter Schabowski, the trade union leader Harry Tisch, and other leading SED functionaries at last realized that the time had come to remove Honecker. Tisch had kept Gorbachev well informed of these plans. The Soviet leader wished him the best of luck. That same October 17 the Politbüro met, as it did every Tuesday. By a unanimous vote Honecker was toppled and replaced by Egon Krenz. The most prominent of the rats that abandoned the rapidly sinking ship was Erich Mielke, the Stasi chief, formerly Honecker's closest associate. Krenz blandly announced that there would be a "change of course," that a "political solution"

PLATE 31   Monday demonstration in Leipzig in 1989. © Gerhard Gabler

could be found to all present problems, and that force would not be used against the demonstrators. The security forces' main concern now was to save their own skins, as they braced themselves for an inevitable collapse of the entire system.

On November 4 a vast crowd assembled in Berlin's Alexanderplatz demanding freedom of speech, assembly, and the press, as well as the unrestricted right to travel wherever and whenever one wished. Two days later Alexander Schalck-Golodkowski went cap in hand to Bonn, requesting a 12–13 billion DM loan. The West German government was prepared to foot the bill, but demanded in return that the SED abandon its monopoly of political power, permit opposition parties, and conduct free elections. Could the SED live with this arrangement? There was no alternative.

Once again the situation got completely out of control. At a press conference on the evening of November 9 designed to report on the SED Central Committee's meeting, Günter Schabowski announced new regulations governing exit permits: "Private travel abroad can be requested without preconditions (such as sufficient reasons for travel and family problems). Permission will be speedily granted. Only in exceptional cases will permission be denied." Citizens, however, needed to have a passport and only 4 million people had one. The rest had to wait several weeks before one was issued. The Central Committee hoped thereby to stop a mass flight to the West. But when Schabowski was asked when these new regulations would come into force he replied, on the spur of the moment and without due authorization: "At once, immediately!" The news that the border had been opened went like wildfire through East Berlin. The border police had no orders, but were helpless against the masses. At 23:20 hours the commander of the border police on the

PLATE 32   The Berlin Wall, November 10, 1989. © BPK

Bornholmer Bridge, between Prenzlauer Berg and Wedding, said: "We're swamped!" and ordered the barrier to be lifted. The dam was broken and East Berliners flooded into the West. As one East Berliner said: "Anyone who sleeps tonight is already dead!"

The wall fell down without permission from either the Soviet Union or the SED. It was a spontaneous act of a people that had had enough both of the SED and the GDR. The SED began rapidly to fall apart. Within a few days most of the leading figures at every level of government were replaced in a frantic rescue attempt. On November 13 the Antifa-Bloc parties – CDU, NDPD, and DBD – announced that they no longer accepted the "leading role" of the SED. They further demanded that the constitution be changed to this effect and that free elections be held. In a scene of bitter farce, the 81-year-old Stasi chief announced before the television cameras: "But I love you, all of you!" This was met with a chorus of derisive laughter from the deputies in the People's Chamber. A leading reformer, the Dresden party boss Hans Modrow, was appointed head of the government.

The constitution was changed on December 1 so that the SED lost its "leading role." Of the 2.3 million party members, 600,000 had already torn up their party cards. The entire party leadership was dismissed, there were mass expulsions from the party, and several party functionaries were arrested for corruption and misuse of power. At a conference on December 8–9 the rump party changed its name to the Party of Democratic Socialism (PDS). Its new leader was a relatively unknown but highly intelligent and eloquent lawyer, Gregor Gysi. The reformed party set out to find "a third way beyond Stalinist socialism and the domination of trans-national monopolies." It was not at all clear what this meant, but the party remained a power in the land. It could still call the shots as the country adjusted to living in unfamiliar territory. The opposition parties were determined not to be left out of the process of restructuring the state. Agreements had already been reached that all political parties and groups should meet in Berlin for "round table" discussions. Similar "round tables" were held at various levels of local government. This was a classic repeat of the revolutionary experiences of the Soviets in 1917, the German Soldiers' and Workers' Councils of 1918–19, or the Turin Workers' Council of 1920–21. It was an expression, however inchoate, of direct democracy in a moment of crisis. The opposition groupings found it exceedingly difficult to challenge the monopoly position of the SED/PDS, but they scored a major triumph when the party tried to transform the Stasi into an Office of National Security. On December 4 demonstrators stormed a local Stasi office. On January 15, 1990, crowds occupied the Stasi's central office in the Normannenstraße, thereby delivering a deadly blow to this hideous organization. The Stasi had already seen the writing on the wall after December 4 and had begun to destroy incriminating evidence, but 170 kilometers of documents remained as a monument to its perfidious efforts. According to the Reunification Treaty, it was intended that the Stasi archives should be placed in the West German archives in Coblenz, thereby cordoning off the unpleasant past, but fortunately civil rights groups in East Berlin ensured that all these documents were to be held in the public domain. A special archive was created under the skillful management of Joachim Gauck, a Protestant minister and the co-founder of the New Forum movement. It has proved to be a mine of information about the history of the GDR, much to the embarrassment of those that were coopted by the Stasi state, in both East and West.

The more familiar East Germans became with life in the West the less enthusiastic they were about the idea of a reformed GDR. The slogan "We Are The People!" soon changed into "We Are One People!" All now depended on Moscow's attitude. The Russians had refused to send in the tanks when the Berlin Wall was breached, and the 500,000 Red Army men in the GDR had remained in their barracks. Officially the Kremlin refused to accept any discussion of a change in the status quo, but unofficial talks began about a possible confederation between two sovereign states. Chancellor Kohl took this up, proposing a "Ten Point Program," whereby after five to ten years of confederation the two states should reunite.

The USA favored Kohl's plan, but the Soviet Union, France, and Britain were opposed. Opposition groups in the GDR argued that they should first set their own house in order along democratic socialist lines. They were supported by left-wingers in West Germany, while some argued that Germany should atone for its past crimes by remaining divided. The ecstatic welcome accorded Helmut Kohl when he visited Dresden in December 1989 had indicated that the opponents of reunification in Germany formed a small minority.

The mass flight to the West substantially worsened the economic crisis in the East to the point that by January 1990 the Soviets realized that there was no viable alternative to reunification. Anxious to keep the initiative they proposed a conference attended by the four victorious powers and the two Germanys. Gorbachev also began to consider the eventual withdrawal of Soviet troops from the GDR. Kohl and his foreign minister, Hans-Dietrich Genscher, went to Moscow in February, where Gorbachev gave the green light to reunification, in return for which the West Germans agreed to give the Soviets' ailing economy a massive injection of capital. They thus trumped Gregor Gysi's attempts to stop the process of reunification and maintain the privileged position of the new version of the SED, as well as Hans Modrow's efforts to get substantial economic aid to revive the East German economy.

Free elections were held in the East in March 1990. The West German CDU supported the East German party of the same name; the FDP backed the LDPD. The CDU, allied with

Democratic Renewal (DA) and the German Social Union (DSU) in the "Alliance For Germany" were the victors, with just over 48 percent. The Liberals obtained a mere 5 percent, the SPD 22 percent, and the PDS just over 16 percent. The electorate thus soundly rejected the idea of a reformed, socialist GDR. Local elections in May reaffirmed this judgment. The new government was a coalition between the Alliance for Germany, the Liberals, and the SPD. It faced a host of seemingly intractable problems. The constitution had to be substantially amended, the economic situation was chronic, the country was shattered as information was released about the machinations of the Stasi which compromised almost everyone in public life, including a number of prominent opposition figures, including the chairmen of Alliance For Germany and the SPD. The new minister president, Lothar de Maizière, was also soon to be disgraced.

The question now was whether the fears of a united Germany that might dominate Europe which were voiced in London, Paris, and Rome could be assuaged. The steady stream from East the West, under the slogan "If We Don't Get the German Mark, We'll Come and Get It!" was gradually creating an intolerable situation. Agreement was reached to exchange East marks for West marks at a rate of 2:1, thus grossly overvaluing the East German "aluminum chips." Wages, pensions, and a certain percentage of savings were converted at par. The Economic and Social Union came into force on July 1, 1990. The Federal Bank wrung its hands in despair at such profligacy.

Meanwhile the "Two Plus Four" talks continued. The two German parliaments partially reassured Margaret Thatcher and François Mitterrand by passing resolutions on the "inviolacy" of Poland's western frontier and the territorial integrity of Germany's eastern neighbors. The major issue now was whether a united Germany should be a member of the NATO alliance. Given that the Warsaw Pact was in the process of dissolution, the Soviets were naturally concerned, but Kohl managed to convince Gorbachev that he need not fear for his security. He agreed that the German army would be reduced, and that Germany would undertake never to make, own, or seek the use of ABC weapons. Further massive financial support sweetened the pill.

Everything now moved with breathtaking speed. In August 1990 the Volkskammer voted by a large majority for unification, accepting the Fundamental Law as the constitution, as permitted under article 23. The two Germanys signed a complex Unification Treaty on August 31. A number of controversial issues such as the site of the future capital and the legalization of abortion were shelved. In September the treaty was ratified by a vote of 442 to 50 in the Bundestag and of 299 to 81 in the Volkskammer. The German Democratic Republic ceased to exist at 0:00 hours on October 3, 1990. The novelist Stefan Heym had once asked whether the GDR would be merely "a historical footnote." The question was now answered. Few bemoaned its demise, but for many East Germans the future was grim. The economy had collapsed, unemployment was rife, and many were ill prepared to adjust to the exigencies life in a modern capitalist environment. Those who had held privileged positions in the GDR lost status and nourished grudges against the new Germany. Freedom, democracy, and the rule of law sounded fine in principle; but they demanded dedication, responsibility, initiative, and hard work. It was difficult to adjust to becoming an individual rather than part of a collective, a cog in the machine. Many *Ossis* (Easterners) felt that they were regarded as second-class citizens by the *Wessis* (Westerners). More often than not it was true. Even today the process of unification is far from complete.

CHAPTER SIXTEEN
THE FEDERAL REPUBLIC
1963–1982

CHAPTER CONTENTS

A History of Modern Germany: 1800 to the Present, Second Edition. Martin Kitchen.
© 2012 Martin Kitchen. Published 2012 by Blackwell Publishing Ltd.

Konrad Adenauer's successors inherited a precarious situation. The Brezhnev administration showed no interest in improving relations with the Federal Republic. In 1965 the majority of Arab states broke off diplomatic relations with Bonn when West Germany exchanged ambassadors with Israel. The struggle between "Atlanticists" and "Gaullists" in Germany grew all the more intense when President Johnson finally dropped the idea of a multilateral atomic force, thus further weakening West Germany's diplomatic effectiveness. Then de Gaulle withdrew France's delegation from the ministerial council of the EEC in protest against a German-sponsored plan for a thoroughgoing reform of the community's agricultural policy, which featherbedded the French peasantry. The way for further European integration, which the German government enthusiastically supported, was thus blocked. But for all these diplomatic setbacks the economy continued to flourish. Although there had been serious deficiencies in the labor market since the Berlin Wall was built, they had largely been made good by over a million "guest workers," mostly from Italy, Spain, Yugoslavia, and Turkey.

Willy Brandt entered the election campaign of 1965 with an outstanding team, but they were no match for Ludwig Erhard, the man so closely associated with the "economic miracle" from which almost all were profiting. The CDU/CSU were the clear winners with 47.6 percent of the popular vote. Willy Brandt, the object of a scandalous press campaign that was even more vicious than in 1961, announced that he would stay on both as mayor of Berlin and party chairman, but would not stand again as a candidate for the chancellorship.

Many thorny issues had to be resolved before a coalition could be formed, principal among them relations with the GDR and whether Franz-Josef Strauß should be allowed back into the cabinet after the *Spiegel* debacle. The new government did not get off to a good start. A proposed exchange of top-level speakers with the GDR did not come to fruition thanks to the intervention of the USSR. De Gaulle continued to refuse to accept changes in the common European agricultural policy. In June 1966, having announced that France would withdraw its forces from NATO, he went on a dramatically staged state visit to the Soviet Union. Erhard felt it prudent to go to Washington to reassure the Americans that Bonn was still a faithful ally, hoping thereby to win some concessions over such issues as access to atomic weapons, the offset payments for US troops stationed in Germany, and currency exchange. President Johnson refused to give way on any of these points.

Bonn's finances were now in dire straits. The FDP refused to accept tax increases to cover the substantial deficit, with all four FDP ministers resigning in protest. Erhard, who had never had close ties with his party, was now clearly a man of the past. The extreme right-wing National Democratic Party of Germany (Nationaldemokratische Partei Deutschlands – NPD) won 7.9 percent of the vote in local elections in Hesse and with Erhard as a seriously weakened chancellor in a minority government there was much wild talk of a resurgence of the radical right and of Bonn going the way of Weimar.

The Great Coalition: 1966–1969

Erhard refused to step down until he was forced out by a "constructive" vote of no confidence that appointed the minister president of Baden-Württemberg, Kurt Georg Kiesinger, as his successor. He was a smoothly charming man, an experienced politician who was always well briefed and was widely admired as an effective administrator. There was, however, a major blot on his escutcheon. He was one of the "March fallen," who had joined the Nazi Party after the March elections of 1933, and there was much talk on the left of his appointment being further evidence of an alarming swing to the extreme right. All suspicions to this effect were dispersed when *Der Spiegel* published Gestapo documents that charged him with "hindering anti-Jewish actions" and supporting "political tendencies" which "ran counter to the Führer's foreign policy."

After lengthy negotiations a new coalition was formed between the CDU/CSU and the SPD. There had been considerable resistance to the idea of a coalition with the CDU/CSU among the Social Democrats' rank and file, by the Young Socialists (JUSOs) in the party, and by left-wing intellectuals, but Herbert Wehner and the rising star of the party, Helmut Schmidt, were determined that the Social Democrats should at last take an active part in government. In many ways it was an unsatisfactory solution; at best it was a temporary measure to deal with the immediate budgetary crisis. With only the tiny FDP in opposition the extreme right and left were both greatly strengthened.

Meanwhile the new government had to deal with the major problem of a deep recession. The key post was now that of the minister of trade and commerce, Karl Schiller. A professor of economics, a member of the SPD, and a former member of the NSDAP, he was a convinced Keynesian. He called for economic expansion, globalization (which had not yet become a dirty word), and the reduction of unemployment, which was fast becoming a major problem. Franz-Josef Strauß as minister of finance was fully in accord with Schiller and the result was a reduction in the prime rate from 5 to 3 percent and the release of vast sums of money for investment. Management, labor, and the state were brought together in a "concentrated action" to achieve "measured growth" while maintaining "social symmetry." To the radical left "concentrated action" smacked of Mussolini's corporatism and was denounced as a fascistoid form of bourgeois domination in the era of late capitalism. The remarkable growth of the economy in 1968 served to disguise the fact that Schiller's much-vaunted plan was actually little more than smoke and mirrors. The new boom triggered a fresh round of inflation and the prime rate was back at 5 percent by June 1969, and was raised to 6 percent in September.

The Great Coalition passed a considerable amount of important legislation. A finance reform act was followed by a major overhaul of criminal law along more liberal lines. Adultery, homosexuality among adults, and blasphemy ceased to be criminal offenses. The statute of limitations on major Nazi crimes and on murder was lifted; in the case of lesser crimes it was extended from twenty to thirty years.

There was considerable resistance in the ranks of the CDU/CSU to the SPD's call for a more flexible approach to the GDR; but Kiesinger kept an open mind on the issue. When he became party chairman on Adenauer's death at the age of 91 in April 1967, he gradually convinced the party to drop its hard-line approach. In his view East and West Germany could only come closer together within the context of a lessening of the tensions between East and West in Europe. His avowed aim was to find areas in which progress could be made in an effort to reduce tension. These included economic cooperation, easing of movement between the two states, and cultural exchanges.

The new approach to policy towards the Soviet bloc got off to an uneasy start when diplomatic recognition was afforded to Romania, thus for the first time breaching the Hallstein Doctrine. With the megalomaniac dictator Nicolae Ceauşescu pursuing an nationalist foreign policy independent of Moscow, which ensured him a warm welcome in the West in spite of his ferociously Stalinist policies at home, the Soviet Union was far from pleased with Bonn's initiative. At a meeting of the Warsaw Pact all member states were warned not to open diplomatic relations with the Federal Republic. The Great Coalition was not deterred. Diplomatic relations were established with Yugoslavia, even though Belgrade recognized the GDR.

The Nuclear Non-Proliferation Treaty proposed by the USA and the USSR presented another major difficulty. Adenauer had denounced the treaty – which forbade non-nuclear countries to build their own nuclear weapons and banned countries possessing nuclear weapons from transferring the capability to produce them – as "the Morgenthau Plan squared," a reference to the US secretary of the treasury's plan in 1944 to convert Germany into an agrarian country. Franz-Josef Strauß, in equally dramatic tones, claimed that it was a "Versailles of cosmic dimensions." Kiesinger complained bitterly that the US government had failed to consult the Federal Republic over the treaty, and accused Washington and Moscow of conniving against western Europe's interests. This hard-nosed approach, which left some observers amazed at Bonn's audacity, paid handsome dividends. The US became much more mindful of Bonn's legitimate concerns, particularly over the peaceful use of atomic energy, and relations between the two countries were greatly improved. At the same time Willy Brandt as foreign minister played a key role in convincing NATO to adopt a more flexible policy towards the Warsaw Pact and to work towards a gradual reduction of armed forces on both sides of the Berlin Wall. This did nothing to ease tensions with Moscow, which continued to lambaste the Federal Republic as "revanchist" and claimed the right under the United Nations Charter to intervene in its affairs as an "enemy state." With the Soviet intervention in Czechoslovakia in 1968, Bonn's *Ostpolitik* ground to a standstill. Willy Brandt and the SPD continued to insist that this was merely a temporary setback, and they were soon to be proven correct.

A series of events in 1969 opened the way for a fresh round of détente. Richard Nixon, a master of *Realpolitik*, was elected US president. The Soviet Union, engaged in armed conflict with China, was anxious to improve relations with the West. Much to Bonn's relief, de Gaulle staged his own fall from power in April. The Federal Republic refused to give way to pressure from the US, Britain, and France to revalue the Deutschmark to offset the weakness of their own currencies.

The Great Coalition had a host of critics in spite of its many achievements. Many agreed with the philosopher Karl Jaspers that it was symptomatic of a drastic decline in democracy. With virtually no opposition there was an alarming lack of transparency and precious little control of the executive by the legislature. The proposal to abolish proportional representation was seen by some as an indication that the coalition was out to annihilate the opposition. But at the same time there were signs that the Great Coalition was only a temporary expedient. The SPD wanted to push ahead with its *Ostpolitik* while the CDU/CSU had serious reservations. The opposition FDP sympathized with the SPD and formed an alliance in March 1969 which secured the election of the Social Democrat Gustav Heinemann as president by a margin of only six votes in the third round. With a general election soon to be held it seemed that the Great Coalition's days were numbered.

In the September elections the CDU/CSU dropped 1.5 points but still won the largest share of the vote with 46.1 percent. The SPD had its best ever showing with 42.7 percent. The FDP did very poorly, and with 5.8 percent only just squeaked back into the Bundestag. No other party managed to clear the 5 percent hurdle.

Thanks to the energetic intervention of Willy Brandt and Karl Schiller, the SPD formed a new coalition with Walter Scheel's FDP. Scheel, who was on the left wing of the party, had as much difficulty in convincing his right-wing colleagues to ally with the SPD. Willy Brandt presented his government's program to the Bundestag in October 1969. It called for major reforms in education which, very much in the spirit of the times, included the "removal of outmoded hierarchical structures" in the universities. The goal of Schiller's economic policy was "stabilization without stagnation." An overhaul of criminal law and the penal system was promised. In foreign policy Brandt expressed his determination to continue trying to improve relations with the East and to reach an accommodation with the GDR.

Confrontations with the Past

The Great Coalition marked a major turning point in the history of the Bonn republic, but it raised more questions than it answered. A serious debate took place about the nature of the state. Was it merely a provisional structure as the Fundamental Law asserted? Should it be regarded as permanent, with all talk of reunification struck from the agenda? What were the obligations, if any, of West Germans to their fellow Germans in the East? Where were the boundaries of "Germany"? How was the distinction to be drawn between "state" and "nation"?

These questions were intertwined with the fierce debates triggered by discussions of Germany's past. Fritz Fischer's book, *Germany's Aims in the First World War* (1961), challenged the conservative historical establishment's comfortable belief that Germany bore no particular share in the blame for the outbreak of war in 1914. After a lengthy and ferocious debate Fischer and his young assistants emerged victorious. Ralf Dahrendorf's *Society and Democracy in Germany* (1965) suggested that the failed coup attempt on July 20, 1944, and the subsequent terror resulted in the destruction of the old German elite thus opening the "brutal path to modernity." Alexander and Margarete Mitcherlich's *The Inability to Mourn* (1967) used a Freudian approach to argue that the "brutal path to modernity" had in fact been blocked by Germany's inability to go through the painful process of dealing with collective responsibility for the crimes of the Nazi era. The "culprit generation" suffered from a collective amnesia and remained, in the Mitcherlichs' terms, "infantile." The younger generation, which had played no active role in events between 1933 and 1945, was to a large extent plagued by a feeling of guilt for crimes that had been committed in the name of a people with whom they had an uncomfortable relationship. They felt bitter towards their smug, self-satisfied, and morally dubious elders. The trial of Adolf Eichmann in Jerusalem in 1960–61 was an uncomfortable reminder of a past that many hoped would go away. Thanks to Fritz Bauer, the courageous and steadfast chief prosecutor of the state of Hesse, a trial began of those accused of crimes committed at Auschwitz. After four years of preparation, during which statements from 1,300 witnesses were taken, the "Auschwitz trial" began in Frankfurt in December 1963. It lasted for twenty months. Six of the accused were imprisoned for life, eleven were given prison sentences of between three and fourteen years, and three were acquitted. Many felt that these sentences were too lenient, triggering a stormy debate over quite what the trial was supposed to achieve; but it served as a shocking reminder of the appalling crimes of the Nazi era, memories of which had been suppressed. It was also an uncomfortable reminder of the active complicity of ordinary Germans in Hitler's crimes. The Auschwitz trial and the Majdanek trial between 1975 and 1980 fueled a fierce intergenerational clash. The scandalous inactivity of the heavily compromised German judicial system during the 1950s was fully exposed. The Center for the Pursuit of Nazi Criminals was established in Ludwigsburg in 1958 and did a superb job helping young and eager state attorneys and historians to uncover the sordid truths of Germany's past. The result was that by the end of the century 106,000 trials had been conducted; 6,000 of them ended in convictions. Yet in spite of all these efforts the scandal remained that of the at least 300,000 people directly involved in the mass murder of the European Jews, Slavs, psychiatric patients, and other minority groups, only 500 were convicted. In the atmosphere of the Cold War, with its militant anti-communism, it was easy for those with a Nazi past to remain in the shade, to continue in virtually the same posts they had held in the Third Reich and not to feel the slightest feeling of shame or remorse.

The Extra-Parliamentary Opposition (Apo)

Students were in the vanguard of the left-wing opposition. They were organized in the Socialist German Students' Association (SDS), which had been strongly opposed to the right turn the SPD had taken in the Godesberg program. Their theoretical journal *Das Argument* took up some of the basic notions of the "critical theory" of Theodor W. Adorno and Max Horkheimer, who had returned from exile in America and now held court at the Institute for Social Research in Frankfurt. Their rarefied reworkings of Marx and Hegel provided them with an opaque language with which they imagined they could influence the structure of society from comfortable positions within it.

The protest culture of the 1960s was the product of a saturated society. The material rubble had been cleared, and although much of the moral detritus remained, the economic miracle had brought a degree of prosperity to almost all. Jean-Luc Godard's "children of Marx and Coca-Cola" escaped this bloated and philistine world by going "underground." In a world of sex, drugs, and rock and roll, of eastern meditation and western Marxism, young people imagined that they were living the revolution. In fact the underground was very much above ground and, as the outstanding Marxist philosopher Ernst Bloch was shrewd enough to fear, was soon packaged and sold to the general public, as wily capitalists made huge profits from "alternative" culture.

Solidarity with Ho Chi Minh's anti-imperialist struggle for national liberation against the United States, and identification with the glamorous figure of Che Guevara, soon to become the most prominent of martyrs in the anti-colonialist cause, gave the movement an international dimension and a revolutionary flavor. Radical students in Berlin were one with their colleagues in Berkeley, Paris, and Rome. In June 1967 a mass demonstration was held in Berlin protesting the visit of the shah of Iran, during which a student, Benno Ohnesorg, was shot in the head by a policeman, who was later unmasked as a Stasi agent. The assassination was a vile attempt to show that West Germany was indeed a fascist state.

The student movement accused the older generation of refusing to face the Nazi past. They denounced the government for supporting the United States in its brutal war against the Vietcong in which chemical weapons such as napalm and Agent Orange were used on a vast scale, and for allying with such tyrants as the shah of Iran. When the Great Coalition government proposed legislation which would remove judicial and parliamentary control over the government in a state of emergency (rights which the Allies had reserved in the German Treaty of 1955) they denounced the measure as a "Nazi law" comparable to Hitler's Enabling Act. Their protest was joined by a number of prominent artists, churchmen, and intellectuals who in turn were denounced in inflammatory tones by the gutter press, in particular by Axel Springer's mass circulation *Bild-Zeitung*. In April 1968 the principal spokesman of this Extra-Parliamentary Opposition (APO), Rudi Dutschke, was gunned down on the Kurfürstendamm in Berlin by a house painter with a criminal record, who was an assiduous reader of the *Bild-Zeitung*. Dutschke suffered severe brain injuries, from which he died in 1979.

The widespread protests at the attempt on Rudi Dutschke's life gave renewed momentum to the struggle against the emergency laws, but this was all to no avail. The alliance with the proletariat for which the protestors yearned came to nothing. Stolid trade unionists refused to be associated with what they saw as a bunch of rowdies. The emergency law was passed in the Bundestag by an overwhelming majority in May 1968, in part as a response to the unruliness of the student protestors, whereupon the SDS began to fall apart. The protest movement became even more strident. Sit-ins, teach-ins, strikes, and riots were now the order of the day. Dress and behavior became increasingly provocative. A new vocabulary made up of concepts taken from psychoanalysis, Marxism, and existentialism, with a large admixture of the scatological, was used to attack what Adorno was pleased to call the "jargon of the literal" (*Jargon der Eigentlichkeit*) used by those in power. A new violent phase began shortly after the shots were fired at Rudi Dutschke when Andreas Baader and Gudrun Ensslin set two Frankfurt department stores on fire in protest against the "tyranny of consumption."

Before long the philosophers of the Frankfurt School realized that the protest movement was getting out of hand as raucous demands were made that "critical theory" be put into practice. A younger sorcerer, Jürgen Habermas, issued a frenzied warning about the "left-wing fascism" of his unruly apprentices. Almost none of their mentors accepted any responsibility for having produced the intellectual justification for much of the activity that took place in these years. Only Herbert Marcuse continued to lend his support to the empirically unjustified and morally dubious struggle against "one-dimensionality" and "repressive tolerance" from the agreeable distance of Orange County, California. Not that it really mattered. The students' "long march through the institutions" achieved very little beyond giving them a greater say in the running of universities which established the right to sit on a number of immensely tedious and time-consuming committees. Those whose hearts were on the left were soon reminded that their wallets were on the right and pursued careers in the professions, the media, and business to become in turn pillars of the establishment. With comfortable bank balances, they preached the virtues of their simple lives in Tuscan villas and Spanish fincas, expressing their deep concerns about an ecosystem which, in their working lives, they did so much to endanger. Those who failed to jump on the capitalist bandwagon opted out. Protest ceased to be political and became a mere matter of what was to become known as "lifestyle." They had to wait a while until the postmodernists comforted them with the preposterous notion that their very passivity was a form of political activism.

The Chancellorship of Willy Brandt

The Great Coalition's schemes for economic reform were soon shelved when the new government faced an alarming increase in the rate of inflation. The Deutschmark was allowed to float, and all levels of government were obliged to reduce expenditure. This led

to a fierce struggle between the Keynesian Schiller and the deflationist minister of finance
Alex Möller, the former head of a major life insurance company. Möller resigned when
ministers objected vigorously to his cutting back the budgets of their departments. Karl
Schiller, who was popular with the voters, was now given a new "super ministry" which
combined those of trade, industry, and finance. Never a man to hide his talents, Professor
Schiller's penchant for self-promotion now knew no bounds as he obstinately clung to an
economic theory that no longer commanded the undivided respect of either his academic
colleagues or the business world.

In 1971 the USA unilaterally tore up the Bretton Woods Agreement by taking the dollar
off the gold standard. At a conference of the ten richest countries in December it was agreed
that the dollar exchange rate of the Deutschmark should be revalued by 13.7 percent, a
measure that was supported by the Bundesbank president Karl Klasen. In March the following year the EEC member states agreed to the "snake," whereby the exchange rates of
members' currencies could only change by a maximum of 2.5 percent in an attempt to give
a degree of stability to the money market and to discourage the flood of speculative capital
into Europe. Schiller, who vehemently opposed these measures, handed in his resignation.
It was accepted with sighs of relief from his cabinet colleagues. Helmut Schmidt, his bitterest
critic, succeeded him in the super ministry, a major step forward in his meteoric career.

Willy Brandt, who had neither interest nor expertise in economics, had an exaggerated
faith in Karl Schiller, but he showed true mastery in foreign affairs. First he managed to
persuade de Gaulle's successor, Georges Pompidou, to accept British membership of the
EEC along with that of Ireland, Denmark, and Norway. In January 1970 he proposed
opening discussions on a joint declaration on peaceful coexistence to Willy Stoph, the
chairman of the GDR's Council of State (Staatsrat). Stoph took three weeks to consider his
reply, but eventually agreed.

Brandt was welcomed in Erfurt by an enthusiastic crowd, much to the annoyance of the
East German leadership. It was resolved that this should never be allowed to happen again,
and the next meeting between the two heads of government took place in Kassel in May.
Once again nothing concrete was achieved. Brandt offered the normalization of relations
between the "two German states"; Stoph insisted on full diplomatic recognition of the
GDR. The significance of these meetings can hardly be overestimated. No formal agreement
was reached, but at the same time each state accepted the existence of the other. The
remaining problem was to agree on the precise terms of that acceptance. It was a major
achievement, made possible by the full support given to Willy Brandt by President Nixon
and his national security advisor, Henry Kissinger.

Meanwhile, Brandt's close associate Egon Bahr began talks with the Soviet foreign minister Andrei Gromyko. The two sides could not agree on a common formula for Germany,
but the Soviets took note of the Federal Republic's position, leaving the door open for
further discussion. Bahr, a past master of secret diplomacy, pursued every opening. In May
1970 Gromyko accepted his memorandum laying out the Federal Republic's position on
the German people's right to self-determination. The details of this confidential meeting
were leaked to the popular weekly Quick by a foreign office official set on torpedoing
Brandt's Ostpolitik, but this scandalous act of treachery did nothing to damage relations
between Bonn and Moscow. A treaty outlawing the use of force in any revision of the
Federal Republic's frontier with the GDR was signed in Moscow in August 1970 when
foreign minister Walter Scheel managed to get the Soviets to agree that this frontier was
not absolutely immutable.

The next major step in Brandt's *Ostpolitik* was to reach an agreement with Poland. Acceptance of the Oder–Neisse frontier in perpetuity was extremely unpopular in the Federal Republic, because the refugee organizations still had a powerful voice and about one-quarter of the population was opposed to the idea. Ignoring these objections, Brandt and Scheel signed a treaty in Warsaw in December 1970. For Willy Brandt the renunciation of any claims to German territory lost to Poland in 1945 was the price that had to be paid for the monstrous crimes of the Nazi regime. In a remarkable and spontaneous gesture during a wreath-laying ceremony in the Warsaw ghetto he knelt in silence, his hands crossed, his head bowed, as he later wrote, "before the abyss of German history and under the burden of the murdered millions." This deeply moving act of contrition was a milestone along the difficult path of Germany's confrontation with its criminal past. Willy Brandt was awarded the Nobel Peace Prize in 1971. No one has been more worthy of this high honor.

In September 1971 a four-power agreement on Berlin was signed which guaranteed unhindered passage between the Federal Republic and West Berlin, but the three western powers continued to insist that West Berlin was not to be considered as an integral part of the Federal Republic. Brezhnev was now playing a curious double game. While urging Honecker to distance himself from the Federal Republic, he was growing ever closer to Brandt, with whom he developed a close personal relationship. Brandt used his influence over the Soviet leader to further détente. This enabled him to play an important role in the negotiation of the Mutual Balanced Force Reduction (MBFR) Treaty. Indeed, relations between Brezhnev and Brandt became so cordial that there was much concerned talk in the West of another Rapallo. President Nixon harbored deep suspicions of Brandt; Kissinger saw him as a dangerous nationalist and even as a neutralist.

Debates over the ratification of these three "Eastern" treaties began in April 1972. It looked as if Brandt would not find the necessary majority. A number of members of the Bundestag from the FDP and SPD had jumped ship, while the CDU under its chairman Rainer Barzel (who was also the CDU/CSU candidate for the chancellorship) mounted a vigorous campaign against the treaties. On April 27 Barzel proposed a motion of constructive no confidence in a bid to unseat Brandt and become chancellor. At first it looked as if he would succeed, but when the votes were counted Barzel was two votes short of victory. It would seem that the Stasi had bribed a senior member of the CSU to vote against the motion, thus saving Brandt. The SPD in turn bribed a CDU deputy who was also a double agent, almost certainly using funds provided for this purpose by the GDR. In both cases the 30 pieces of silver were worth 50,000 Deutschmarks. Brandt and his *Ostpolitik* were saved, but the democratic system was severely damaged.

The treaties were eventually ratified after certain revisions were made with the CDU/CSU abstaining from a key vote. At the same time the USA, the Soviet Union, Britain, and France signed the final version of the four-power agreements that facilitated inter-German travel. While East–West relations were thus greatly improved, the Federal Republic moved in the opposite direction in domestic politics. A law was passed in January 1972 that banned members of and sympathizers with radical groups from becoming civil servants. The state had every right to make sure that people who did not accept its "fundamental free and democratic system" did not become teachers or senior administrators, but the heavy-handed approach taken to the implementation of the law caused widespread and justified criticism of what was dubbed a "ban on the professions" (*Berufsverbot*).

Terrorism

In part this measure was an excessive response to the growth of radical Marxism, particularly in the universities. The Young Socialists in the SPD were trying to move the party sharply to the left, thus scaring off middle-of-the-road voters. On the wilder shores of the left Andreas Baader and Gudrun Ensslin, having served a time in jail for arson, set about organizing the Red Army Faction in 1969. Baader was once again arrested and then sprung from jail by the left-wing journalist turned terrorist, Ulrike Meinhof. The group fled to Syria in the summer of 1970 where they were given expert training in terrorist methods by the PLO.

A number of people were killed in a series of terrorist attacks in 1972 at American army headquarters in Germany, and the Springer building in Hamburg was set on fire. Andreas Baader was once again arrested in June, along with two other ringleaders of the Red Army Faction: Holger Meins and Jan-Carl Raspe. Shortly afterwards Ulrike Meinhof and Gudrun Ensslin were also placed in custody. Black September, a group with direct links to the Yasser Arafat's Fatah, attacked the quarters of the Israeli team at the Munich Olympic Games in September, killing two athletes and taking nine hostages. They demanded the release of Baader and Meinhof, along with 234 prisoners held in Israeli jails. The Bavarian police badly bungled an attempt to free the hostages, all of whom were killed, along with five terrorists. Three surviving terrorists were captured, then freed and flown to Syria when a Lufthansa flight was hijacked by Black September and the passengers held to ransom. There is no evidence that any Germans were involved in this terrorist attack, but in an atmosphere of horror, fear, and uncertainty it was easy to imagine that such links existed. Israel responded by killing a large number of Palestinians whom they claimed had been involved in the Munich massacre.

Willy Brandt's Second Term: 1972–1974

Meanwhile Brandt had lost his majority in the Bundestag due to defections from the FDP and the resignation of Karl Schiller. During the election campaign Walter Scheel traveled to China and Egon Bahr visited Brezhnev before negotiating the "Treaty on the General Principles of Relations Between the Federal Republic of Germany and the German Democratic Republic" with the GDR. This amounted to a de facto recognition of the GDR. Instead of an exchange of ambassadors, "permanent representations" were established in Bonn and East Berlin. Thorny issues, such as that of reunification, were left open with a reference to differences of opinion. Both states agreed that they should be represented in the United Nations. The GDR was now free to establish diplomatic relations with any country without fear of reprisals from the Federal Republic.

The election campaign soon turned into a plebiscite over the treaty. Rainer Barzel as the CDU/CSU candidate for the chancellorship said that he would not support ratification of the treaty as long as the National People's Army continued to kill refugees attempting to cross the border, but this met with little response from the electorate. A group of prominent historians, including Karl Dietrich Bracher, Fritz Fischer, and Thomas Nipperdy, signed a declaration of support for Brandt's *Ostpolitik*. Support also came from artists, intellectuals, and the soccer star Paul Breitner, while the novelist Günter Grass campaigned tirelessly for the SPD. Young Socialists, forgetting their ideological differences with the party leadership for the moment, lent their wholehearted support. Amid general prosperity Karl Schiller's spiteful attacks on the coalition's economic policy fell on deaf ears. What was soon to be called the "Willy election" (*Willy Wahl*) was a personal triumph for the chancellor, but it was soon to prove the beginning of the end.

Willy Brandt was sadly unable to exploit his triumph. He had to undergo surgery on his vocal cords, which were seriously damaged by heavy smoking. He was forbidden to speak during the critical negotiations for the new coalition. The treaty was the coping-stone of his *Ostpolitik*, so there was nothing exciting left to do in foreign policy and he was loath to devote all his attention to the drudgery of domestic politics. His rival, Rainer Barzel, resigned as chairman of the CDU and of the CDU/CSU parliamentary group when the caucus voted in favor of membership of the United Nations, even though it meant that the GDR would also be admitted. He was replaced by Helmut Kohl, the minister president of Rhineland-Palatinate.

It was widely believed that the economic miracle would continue, but within a year it came to an abrupt halt with the oil crisis and subsequent stock market crash. The cost of transfer payments such as pensions, children's allowances, student grants, and subsidized housing rose alarmingly. In 1970 they amounted to 174.7 million Deutschmarks; five years later they consumed 334.1 million. It was not until 1990 that Kohl's government began to trim the budget, with the Social Democrats denouncing this as "social demolition."

The chancellor's star began to wane as the economic crisis deepened. He failed to persuade Brezhnev to use his influence to get the GDR to make further concessions, including agreeing to accept a federal ministry of the environment having its offices in West Berlin. His prestige took a serious blow when a parliamentary investigation committee took a close look at the bribing of opposition members in 1972, which had enabled him to remain in office. Relations with the United States became very tense when Bonn and the rest of the European Community called upon Israel to end the Yom Kippur War and to respect the United Nations resolutions on the occupied territories. A wave of strikes was taken as further evidence of the government's lack of authority. The Young Socialists were once again becoming restless. Then in April 1974 a bombshell exploded when it was revealed that Günter Guillaume, a close advisor of Brandt's in the chancellery, was a Stasi agent. In 1973 he had accompanied Brandt on his annual holiday to Norway, during which time he had access to top-secret NATO documents. He was so close to Brandt that he was also privy to this notorious ladies' man's amorous escapades.

Suspicions were first aroused in May 1973 that Guillaume was a Stasi plant, but the authorities were singularly lax and did not trouble to keep a close watch on him. Brandt at first wanted to resign, but he was persuaded to fight back. Then Herbert Wehner, who had been informed of his numerous affairs, suggested that resignation was the most prudent way out of the crisis. Brandt tendered his resignation on May 6 and appointed Helmut Schmidt as his successor. It was a typically courageous and honorable move and he took full blame for the fiasco. He refused to name any of those who bore a far greater share of the blame, principal among them the FDP minister of the interior, Hans-Dietrich Genscher.

In his five years as chancellor, Brandt had brought about a revolution in the Federal Republic's foreign policy. He had normalized relations with the Soviet Union and the GDR while remaining firmly committed to Europe and the Atlantic alliance. The Federal Republic had been in serious danger of isolation, but was now a respected ally and a daunting opponent, led by a statesman of international stature. In domestic affairs he had been less successful. The coalition's ambitious policies for reform mostly remained on the drawing board, but the balance of his chancellorship was positive, and he stands with Adenauer as a founding father of a vibrant democracy.

Helmut Schmidt's First Term: 1974–1976

The Federal Republic's new chancellor, Helmut Schmidt, was the leading light on the right wing of the party. His often overbearingly arrogant style earned him the title "big-mouth Schmidt" (*Schmidt-Schnauze*) and he was the bête noire of the party left, of the Young Socialists, and of the extra-parliamentary opposition. Unable to suffer fools gladly, he never let an opportunity pass to demonstrate his intellectual superiority over lesser mortals. There was little that was inspiring in his resolutely pragmatic approach to politics, but none could deny that he was a man of quite exceptional intelligence, a devastatingly effective debater who, unlike Brandt, never flinched from taking on his adversaries both inside and outside the party. He was a thoroughgoing professional, who had a complete mastery of all aspects of both foreign and domestic policy. He stands head and shoulders above all other proponents of a non-dogmatic approach to social democracy that was later to be dubbed the "New Middle" or "New Labour." On the debit side he was the first of a line of chancellors from Kohl to Schroeder to avoid tackling serious social issues and structural deficiencies. They all failed to address the overriding problem of a general disillusionment and dissatisfaction with politicians, the political process, and democracy itself. Willy Brandt had dared the people to "risk more democracy" but they had failed to take up the challenge. His successors did nothing to encourage them to have another go.

Schmidt was fully committed to the Atlantic alliance and knew that West Germany's security depended on the United States, but at the same time he sent a clear message to the GDR that he was determined to improve relations between the two countries, provided both respected the spirit and the letter of all existing treaties. This was a difficult hand to play. The United States suffered a devastating loss of prestige in the Vietnam War, which was rapidly drawing to a humiliating close. The Federal Republic was going through a severe economic crisis owing to the oil embargo. The Soviet Union was bent on exploiting America's weakness to improve its strategic position in Europe by building up its arsenal of intermediate-range missiles, having failed to reach an agreement with the USA on their limitation.

The Mutual and Balanced Force Reduction talks in Vienna between NATO and the Warsaw Pact had become bogged down, with intermediate-range missiles not subject to discussion. Nixon and Brezhnev had signed the Strategic Arms Limitation Treaty (SALT) in May 1972, but it only covered long-range missiles. Schmidt did everything possible to ensure that intermediate-range missiles were included in the SALT-II discussions, which began soon after SALT-I was signed. Nixon's successor, Gerald Ford, gave Schmidt a verbal assurance that he would do so, but gave no formal written confirmation of this intention.

In the summer of 1975 Schmidt attended the concluding Conference on Security and Cooperation in Europe in Helsinki, where he laid the groundwork for a treaty with Poland as a result of which 125,000 Poles of German origin were permitted to settle in the Federal Republic. In return Poland received substantial financial assistance. An agreement was also reached with Honecker not to rock the boat in Berlin. In a wider perspective the Soviets were pleased with the Helsinki accords in that they guaranteed the inviolability (but not the permanence) of existing frontiers in Europe; but the West had secured guarantees for human rights and fundamental freedoms, which gave great encouragement to dissidents within the Soviet bloc.

The GDR found a lucrative way to avoid some of the more embarrassing consequences of the Helsinki Accords. Tiresome dissidents like Rudolf Bahro could be shipped out to the West; others were allowed to go to West Germany on receipt of handsome payment from the Federal Republic. Between 1964 and 1989 Bonn paid 3.4 billion DM and secured the release of 33,755 political prisoners, an average of about 100,000 DM per head. The GDR had access to huge interest-free loans from West Germany based on aggregate inner-German trade. Much to the alarm of hardliners in the SED, the GDR was thus becoming increasingly dependent on the Federal Republic.

Schmidt was a close ally of Valéry Giscard d'Estaing, who had been elected president of France in 1974. He gave his wholehearted support to the French initiative for calling an economic summit of six leading industrial nations which was held in Rambouillet in November 1975. The G-6 was to become G-7 when Canada was included at the London summit in 1976. With the US smarting after its humiliation in Vietnam and under the lackluster leadership of Gerald Ford, the Schmidt–Giscard tandem played a leading role in international politics, greatly enhancing the Federal Republic's prestige.

The coalition was much less successful in domestic politics. A comprehensive reform of the universities made little progress. The Constitutional Court blocked a reform of the law on abortion. A new law on codetermination in the workplace satisfied neither management nor labor. Labor had a greater say in management than in any other country, but workers did not have the parity on boards of directors they demanded.

A fresh wave of terrorist attacks began in November 1974 when a court official in Berlin was assassinated. In February 1975 the chairman of the CDU in Berlin was kidnapped, only to be released when the government agreed to set five convicted terrorists free and fly them to Yemen. Two months later the "June 2 Movement" seized twelve hostages in the German embassy in Stockholm. They demanded the release of twenty-six terrorists, including Andreas Baader and Ulrike Meinhof. Having shot the military attaché and the economic advisor, they announced that they would kill a member of the staff every hour until the German government conceded their demands. This time the government refused to back down. Swedish police stormed the embassy, killing two of the terrorists.

German terrorists were involved in an attack on the OPEC ministers in Vienna in December 1975 masterminded by the Venezuelan terrorist "Carlos." They were also complicit in the hijacking of an Air France plane en route from Athens to Uganda in June 1976. A special Israeli anti-terrorist unit freed the hostages at Entebbe, a brilliant action in which two German terrorists were killed.

The terrorists suffered under the curious delusion that their efforts to undermine the state would meet with considerable sympathy, particularly among the working class. In spite of the fulminations of some deluded intellectuals about the even worse threat to civil rights posed by the Schmidt government, quite the reverse was true. In an atmosphere of disillusionment Ulrike Meinhof committed suicide in her cell at Stammheim prison in Stuttgart in May 1976.

Helmut Schmidt's Second Term: 1976–1980

The year 1976 was an election year and the issue of terrorism played an important role in the campaign. The CDU/CSU chose Helmut Kohl as their candidate for the chancellorship largely because he was not the temperamental and unpredictable Franz-Josef Strauß, who had let loose a tirade against the SPD, painting them as closet Communists bent on establishing the dictatorship of the proletariat. The suggestion that the resolutely anti-Communist, fervently pro-Western, and thoroughly centrist Helmut Schmidt was Moscow's marionette might have been accepted by the more delusional of the denizens of Strauß's Bavarian fastness, but it was altogether too absurd for the average voter.

Kohl was a right-winger who had opposed signing the Helsinki Accords, but he had excellent personal contacts with key figures in the SED. His supporters saw him as a pragmatist, his opponents as an opportunist. He fought the campaign under the slogan "Freedom Instead of Socialism" whereas Strauß's CSU preferred the more aggressive form of "Freedom or Socialism." Although some CDU politicians felt that the attempt to paint Schmidt as a socialist would misfire, the CDU/CSU made substantial gains at the polls, but it was not quite enough to defeat the coalition. Strauß, blaming Kohl and the CDU for failing to win an absolute majority, announced that his CSU would henceforth fight a separate election campaign. Shortly afterwards he publicly denounced Kohl as an incompetent politician who would never become chancellor. The CDU responded to this extraordinarily crass attack by threatening to found a Bavarian branch of the party, whereupon the CSU got cold feet and reluctantly returned to the fold. The animosity between the stolid Kohl and the mercurial Strauß was to continue until Strauß's sudden death in 1988.

Terrorism and the Changing Nature of Dissent

A fresh wave of terror was unleashed in April 1977, when a senior state prosecutor, his driver, and a court guard were murdered by the Ulrike Meinhof Commando of the Red Army Faction. In July that year the chairman of the board of directors of the Dresdner Bank, Erich Ponto, was killed in a kidnapping attempt. In September the head of the Employers' Association and the Association of Germany Industry, Hanns Martin Schleyer, was kidnapped, and his driver and three policemen were shot. The Faction, styling the murders of prominent representatives of the "capitalist-fascist system" as "Germany's autumn," demanded the release of eleven prisoners and a large ransom. The government responded by banning all contact between the terrorists in prison and the outside world, including their lawyers.

In October four Arab terrorists hijacked a Lufthansa aircraft flying from Mallorca to Frankfurt, demanding the release of eleven prisoners. The aircraft flew to Rome, Cyprus, Dubai, and then Athens, before eventually landing in Mogadishu, where the hijackers murdered the pilot. After agonizing debates Helmut Schmidt's government decided to send in GSG9, an elite anti-terrorist group formed after the Munich Olympics massacre. The mission was brilliantly accomplished. Three kidnappers were killed, one seriously wounded, and all the hostages were released unharmed. The good news from Mogadishu was closely followed by the announcement that Andreas Baader, Gudrun Ensslin, and Jan-Carl Raspe had committed suicide in their cells at Stammheim. After forty-three days in the hands of his kidnappers Hanns Martin Schleyer was murdered. His body was discovered in the trunk of a car parked in Mulhouse in Alsace.

Many in the extra-parliamentary opposition sympathized with the terrorists. They could point to the fact that Schleyer had been a senior official in the SS responsible for the exploitation of Czechoslovakia during the war. They were convinced that the Stammheim trio had been murdered. Some imagined that the terrorists were part of a continuing anti-fascist struggle. Many felt that the anti-terrorist laws undermined the rule of law. There was some justified fear that the terrorists' attempts to reveal the Federal Republic as fundamentally "fascist" would, by such extreme measures, prove successful.

The extra-parliamentary opposition was in the process of transformation. The apolitical and selfish hedonism of late 1960s youth led to the casting off of restraints first on sex and then on greed as flower children metamorphosed into yuppies. Openly communicative and social forces were reduced to a restrictive and oppressive intimacy that put an intolerable pressure on couples, reflected in a rapidly escalating divorce rate. On the left highly theoretical neo-Marxism was giving way to a fundamentally reactionary, naively romantic anti-modernism. Nature was seen as the ultimate good, history gruesome and unpredictable, progress an all-consuming Moloch, a cruel delusion. The fruits of nature were pure, generous, and immediate; those of history the dubious, close-fisted promises of a distant future. Some thoroughgoing reactionaries argued that industrial society was one huge mistake. They dreamt of a return to an Arcadian paradise of cavorting nymphs and sturdy shepherds. Mother earth was to be protected from rapine and plunder. The prime evil was now no longer "fascism" or "imperialism," although these were still used as generic terms of abuse, but atomic energy, which became symbolic of all that was evil in a technological, profit-oriented, ecologically irresponsible society.

The question of atomic energy split the SPD. Schmidt was solidly in favor. Willy Brandt as party chairman, anxious not to lose the support of younger voters, hoped to integrate the fundamentalist ecologists into the party. Just as Brandt had feared, in January 1980 a Green Party was formed at the federal level that threatened to take voters away from the SPD. From the outset the Greens were an odd bunch. Some were former Communists or linked to various heretical Trotskyite, Marxist, or Maoist or Communist groups. Others, like Joschka Fischer who was later to become foreign minister and the most respected politician in a united Germany, were "spontaneous" (*Spontis*), stone-hurling crypto-anarchists. They were joined by sundry peaceniks, eco-friendly farmers, conservationists, and apostles of alternative lifestyles. There were Greens on the left and Greens on the right, but in the early years the weight was on the left. They insisted on "basis democracy" by which party offices rotated, no member of any legislative assembly could hold party office, and party members were to have a real and effective control over the leadership as well as the elected delegates. There was general agreement that the environment mattered, that peace should be given a chance, and that women should be given full and equal opportunities. The emancipation of women, the one important and lasting consequence of the upheavals of the 1960s, was already on the political agenda, but had been largely ignored by the main parties. It had become somewhat sidetracked by the thorny issue of abortion, to the detriment of other important issues.

In 1977 the delightfully brash, exuberant, and quick-witted Alice Schwarzer founded *Emma*, a feminist magazine that provided an intelligent and accessible forum for women's issues. The more strident forms of feminism led by an inevitable dialectic from liberation to a new form of dependence and intolerance. A form of sexual apartheid was propagated, with women's rock groups, women's theater, women's bars and cafés, women's centers, and the new discipline of women's studies, which provided a congenial male-free environment within the universities. Lesbians took advantage of the women's movement to live openly in ways of their choice and the Federal Republic, particularly in West Berlin, soon had a rich and vibrant gay culture. When the first shock waves were over, gays and lesbians were readily accepted in public life, and those on the far right were far too busy fighting immigration, desecrating Jewish cemeteries, and marching in celebration of Rudolph Hess' birthday to turn their undivided attention to the challenge of homosexuality.

The Debate on Atomic Weapons

Helmut Schmidt's relationship with President Carter, who took office in 1977, was far from harmonious. It would be hard to imagine two more different temperaments than the tough-minded pragmatist Schmidt and the dreamy idealist Carter. The German chancellor had ill-concealed contempt for the new president's woeful ignorance of foreign affairs. It was exacerbated by Carter's national security advisor Zbigniew Brzezinski's naive campaign for civil rights in the Soviet Union and his imprudent belief that the Soviets' enemies were necessarily the West's friends.

In January 1979 Carter, Giscard d'Estaing, the British prime minister James Callaghan, and Helmut Schmidt met in Guadeloupe to discuss a wide range of foreign political and security issues. Schmidt, who was accepted as an equal partner of the three atomic powers, played a significant role in reaching an agreement whereby the US would threaten to station intermediate-range missiles in Europe if the Soviets did not agree to withdraw their SS-20s. Back in Germany Schmidt found, as he had predicted, considerable resistance to the proposal. Within the government the opposition was led by Egon Bahr, who argued that it would put an end to *Ostpolitik*, to say nothing of his exotic plans for a European security system that would replace both NATO and the Warsaw Pact. The Young Socialists under the future chancellor Gerhard Schröder put forward a motion at the SPD party conference in 1979 that no intermediate-range missiles should be stationed in Germany which, had it been accepted, would have spelt the end of Schmidt's chances in the forthcoming general election.

In December 1979 NATO agreed to the US proposal to replace their Pershing Ia missiles in Europe with 108 Pershing IIs and to station 464 ground-based Cruise missiles by 1983. A thousand obsolete atomic warheads were to be withdrawn. As part of a twin-track program, negotiations with the USSR over nuclear arms reduction in Europe were to be put in train as soon as possible.

The Soviet Union invaded Afghanistan only a few days after this NATO meeting, thus causing a serious crisis not only in East–West relations, but also between the US and its European allies. Carter and Brzezinski set out to punish the Soviets, much to the alarm of Schmidt and his close ally Giscard d'Estaing. As Schmidt pointed out to US secretary of state Cyrus Vance, punishment of the Soviet Union would also involve punishing 16 million Germans in the GDR and 2 million in West Berlin. The German chancellor launched an unprecedented attack on the Carter administration's policy towards the Soviet Union, calling on both sides to halt the deployment of intermediate-range missiles. This triggered a bitter exchange of notes in which Schmidt forced the president to accept his views on the missile question.

Schmidt flew to Moscow in June 1980 with US blessing and managed finally to persuade Brezhnev to agree to bilateral talks with the United States over intermediate-range missiles. It was a diplomatic triumph, which Carter generously acknowledged, greatly strengthening the chancellor's position in the 1980 elections. Helmut Schmidt was now unquestionably a statesman of world stature, who showed a complete mastery of foreign policy while playing the leading role in the G7 summits; but this was only a short-term victory. As predicted, Carter lost to Ronald Reagan in the November presidential elections. The new hard-line administration put the talks on hold for one year.

A wave of strikes in Poland in 1980 coordinated by Lech Wałesa's Solidarność (Solidarity) movement, and supported by the former bishop of Kraków, Karol Wojtyla, who had become Pope as John Paul II in the previous year, raised the specter of Soviet intervention which would have spelt an end to Schmidt and Giscard's policy of détente. Franz-Josef Strauß, as the the CDU/CSU's candidate for the chancellorship, had little success in once again trying to paint Schmidt as a dangerous socialist and even stooped as low as to suggest that there were certain similarities between the SPD and the National Socialists. Voters who were not particularly sympathetic to the SPD often admired Schmidt for his tough stand on nuclear parity in Europe, whereas the volatile and capricious Strauß, who was acknowledged as a forceful and energetic demagogue, inspired little confidence. The election resulted in a clear majority for the SPD/FDP coalition.

Helmut Schmidt's Third Term: 1980–1982

Helmut Schmidt's new government in Bonn faced a serious economic crisis and concomitant social problems. Unemployment rose within one year from 400,000 to 1,370,000, with inflation running at 7 percent and output falling. The right found an easy scapegoat in the 4.6 million foreigners living in Germany and the 100,000 asylum-seekers. Politicians fulminated against "phoney asylum-seekers"; the less sophisticated gave vent to their frustrations by beating up Turks. The extra-parliamentary opposition and their fellow-travelers also took to violence in protest against atomic reactors, the visits of prominent American politicians, and extensions to Frankfurt airport, or in support of squatters' rights. The election of Ronald Reagan triggered off a fresh round of anti-Americanism in Germany, even though the president invited the Soviets to Strategic Arms Limitation Talks (START) in Geneva and said that the US would not station Pershing and Cruise missiles in Europe if the Soviets withdrew their SS-20s. Reagan's rhetoric about the "evil empire" and his enthusiastic support of the Strategic Defense Initiative (SDI) further convinced the German pacifists that he had no interest whatsoever in disarmament. The peace movement was skillfully manipulated by Markus Wolf, head of the Stasi's propaganda bureau, who financed the German Peace Union (Deutsche Friedensunion – DFU), a barely disguised Communist organization which included two prominent Greens, the German American Petra Kelly and her lover, Gerd Bastian, a retired general. Markus Wolf's DFU collected some 4.7 million signatures to the "Krefeld Appeal" against nuclear weapons, among them a number of mainly Protestant churchmen who were unable to reconcile NATO's policies with the sermon on the mount.

This was a matter of great concern to the Protestant Schmidt, who was also facing increasing criticism for his wholehearted support for the twin-track policy. Like Brandt before him he was in danger of losing the support of his parliamentary caucus. He was opposed within his own ranks not only by young Turks like the mayor of Saarbrücken, Oskar Lafontaine, but also by Willy Brandt as party chairman, who remained convinced that the Soviets posed no real threat and that his friend Brezhnev was seriously interested in disarmament talks. Schmidt's problems were compounded by fundamental differences with the FDP over how to deal with the budgetary crisis. He wanted increases in the income tax; the FDP wanted drastic cuts in expenditure on the social services. At the same time Bonn was hit by a major scandal over illegal contributions to the political parties in which all parties in the Bundestag were involved. The proposal for a general amnesty was rejected by the SPD caucus and by the SPD minister of justice. The FDP, which had the most to gain by such an amnesty, was incensed. The coalition was falling apart.

Schmidt began to show signs that he was losing touch when, in spite of the mounting crisis in Poland, he agreed to talks with Honecker at the SED chief's hunting lodge. Martial law was declared in Poland while the chancellor was still in the GDR. Schmidt and Honecker went to Güstrow to admire Ernst Barlach's sculptures and to visit the cathedral. To the outside world it seemed that both men were indifferent to events in Poland. Franz-Josef Strauß took great relish in denouncing his rival for having been so easily led by the nose.

There was precious little sympathy for Solidarność in government circles in Bonn. It was a fiercely nationalist and Catholic movement and Wałesa was known to be something of a lightweight. Their protests threatened the peace and stability of the Communist bloc and thus that of Western Europe. The Federal Republic was in the front line and was therefore more concerned about the preservation of peace than of the self-determination of peoples. Herbert Wehner even went as far as to let the GDR know that he favored a tough line in Poland. Some of the more perspicacious observers argued that events in Poland showed that hopes for a peaceful and gradual reform of the Communist system were illusory. In such a situation the vituperative denunciation of events in Poland coming from Ronald Reagan's America made Bonn's position even more precarious. All Schmidt could do was to try and persuade Honecker of the need for General Jaruzelski to be as forbearing as possible in the exercise of martial law.

Schmidt's visit to the United States in January 1982 was not a success. He refused to go along with the US demand for a trade embargo on Poland and was subject to such scurrilous attacks in the *New York Times* and *Washington Post* that the president felt obliged to offer an apology. Schmidt by now had also lost the confidence of those members of the SPD caucus who were sharply critical of his endorsement of American policy on intermediate-range missiles. Relations with the FDP had also been badly damaged by the handling of the party finance scandals and by differences over how to deal with the budgetary crisis. In February 1982 he called for a vote of confidence in order to clear the air. He won by a comfortable margin. At the party conference in April two-thirds of the delegates supported his position on nuclear weapons, and his commitment to NATO and the Western alliance.

At first it seemed that the Conference on Intermediate-Range Nuclear Forces (INF) in Geneva might reach a workable compromise when the US and Soviet chief negotiators took their famous "walk in the woods" and agreed to reciprocal reductions of these weapons in Europe. Then both Washington and Moscow promptly rejected this promising formula. With his policy on nuclear deployment in ruins, Schmidt now faced a serious revolt in his own ranks led by Oskar Lafontaine, who called for the SPD to abandon the coalition, go into opposition, and begin a drastic rethinking of basic Social Democratic principles. The chancellor was outraged when there was precious little protest within the party over an inflammatory interview given by Lafontaine to the weekly magazine *Stern* in July 1983. The attack was a direct response to Schmidt's plans for a budget in which he had made a number of significant concessions to the neo-liberals in the FDP. The trade unions supported Lafontaine's position and threatened to take action against the budgetary compromise. Noises were also coming from the FDP that it was considering abandoning the coalition.

Schmidt brought matters to a head in September 1982 when he challenged Helmut Kohl to introduce a motion of constructive no confidence to be followed by a fresh round of elections. Kohl hesitated while the FDP minister of trade and commerce, Count Otto Lambsdorff, presented a position paper with which Margaret Thatcher would have been in broad agreement. It was clearly irreconcilable with even Schmidt's moderate Social Democratic views, and was diametrically opposed to the radical program passed at the SPD's recent party conference. The chancellor was growing increasingly impatient and eager for a fight. Having got word that they were soon to be fired, the four FDP ministers resigned from the cabinet. Schmidt continued as head of a minority government, his popularity scarcely diminished and the FDP widely regarded as traitors who had stabbed him in the back. On October 1 a lengthy and lively debate on a motion of constructive no confidence was held. It was carried by 256 to 235 votes with four abstentions. Helmut Kohl thus became the first chancellor to be appointed as a result of such a motion.

There was a great deal of unfinished business for the new coalition between the CDU/CSU and FDP to tackle. The scandals of party financing had to be investigated, the welfare system was in desperate need of an overhaul, and fundamental changes in the tax law were long overdue. It remained to be seen whether the new chancellor, who was so obviously the intellectual inferior of his glittering predecessor, would be equal to the job.

The Transformation of West German Society

West German society was transformed in these years to become a satiated consumer society. Between 1960 and 1989 the percentage of households with automobiles rose from 25 to 65 percent, of telephones from 15 to 93 percent, of washing machines from 35 to 85 percent, of television sets from 38 to 99 percent, of video recorders from 4 to 99 percent, and of dishwashers from 2 to 24 percent. This period was the golden age of the department store, while speciality shops struggled for survival. Supermarkets took an increasing share of the market for provisions, but they were not able to establish the dominant share of the market that they enjoyed in the United States. Germans still preferred the baker, butcher, greengrocer, and marketplace to the cellophane-wrapped anonymity of the supermarket. In 1990 supermarkets accounted for only 13.1 percent of retail trade. In the USA they accounted for one-quarter as early as 1960. The net result of this transformation was a certain leveling of taste. Clothing was no longer strongly class-specific. Class differences were expressed in more subtle ways – in speech, education, leisure-time amusements, food, fashion, housing, and car ownership.

People not only had greater disposable incomes due to a rapidly expanding economy and to the larger number of women entering the workforce; they also had far more free time in which to spend their money. Until 1955 the average working week was 49 to 56 hours. By 1973 it had dropped to 40 hours for a five-day week. Annual holiday entitlement was increased from fifteen days in 1956 to thirty in 1982, by which time the German worker had 150 days free every year. This was more generous than in any other highly industrialized country. By 1980 five weeks of paid annual holidays was the norm. By the end of the 1960s a three-week holiday abroad was a commonplace. Skiing became a mass sport. Companies organized cheap tours to the Caribbean and South-East Asia. By the 1980s many were taking two such holidays every year.

Tastes were also leveled and attitudes influenced by the pervasive influence of television. By the late 1970s cinema visits had halved, and newspapers had drastically declined in quality and importance, with only a small handful able to maintain standards against enormous odds. Family life changed to integrate this fascinating device into the daily routine. Public opinion was molded, tastes changed, and political choices influenced by the affective power of this new mass medium. Combined with consumerism and mass tourism, analyzed by market researchers and exploited by ingenious entrepreneurs, choices of fashion, holiday travel, and purchasing patterns became almost automatic, self-evident and a matter of course.

All this delivered ammunition to those who argued that talk of class and social stratification, usually with a vulgar Marxist approach, was no longer relevant. A paradigm change had revealed the essential importance of individualization, pluralism, milieu, and lifestyle. In other words an analysis of the rich diversity of modern society could be addressed with a postmodernist normative disregard for such issues as social justice and equality of opportunity. Only a few sociologists argued that the older concepts of class and social stratification, based on considerations of income, property, and power, as well as inequalities of gender, age, and ethnicity, could be enriched by taking the cultural dimension into account. The baby did not have to be thrown out with the bathwater.

Pierre Bourdieu, preferring Max Weber's concept of "life management" (*Lebensführung*) to the nebulous notion of "lifestyle," argued that it could not be seen as the result of intentional action. All the talk of the essential classlessness of modern society was empty rhetoric that overlooked fundamental inequalities at every level.

All societies are to some degree hierarchical, and the Federal Republic was no exception. Social disparities today might not be so crass as they were in the Wilhelmine era. Most have benefited to some degree from the opportunities offered in the years of prosperity; but a large number have been left behind to stagnate in an underclass. Plutocracies may find fresh recruits, but they remain plutocracies. In recent years the disparities between rich and poor have grown ever wider, with disastrous social, political, and moral consequences. Gradually these inequalities can no longer be disguised behind a glittering facade of prosperity, and they are reappearing in their familiar and increasingly unacceptable form. This has transformed the marketplace. The middle-of-the-road department stores are in serious difficulties, while luxury goods, cheap speciality, and discount stores are thriving. Online shopping has also taken over an increasing portion of the department stores' share of the market.

Max Weber described income distribution as "the fundamental economic fact" upon which so much else depends; but it is almost impossible to give accurate figures for the Federal Republic because the Federal Statistics Office is not permitted to publish its data due to stringent laws on respect for confidentiality. Those at the top of the pile in Germany have a larger share of total national wealth than those in the United States, Britain, or Sweden. In 1960 it was estimated that 1.7 percent of all German households owned 74 percent of productive wealth and 35 percent of total wealth. The 0.0784 percent at the very top of the pyramid owned an amazing 13 percent of total wealth. There is no evidence that there was any significant change in this distribution over the next forty years. This inequality is further reinforced by inheritance, with Germany's inheritance taxes lower than in the USA or Britain. By 1996, 28 percent of Germans over the age of 40 had inherited an average of 13,000 DM and 9 percent expected to inherit an equivalent amount; 14 percent had inherited an average of 51,000 DM, while 7 percent expected to do so. One percent expected to inherit 1 million DM, while 0.5 percent inherited wealth beyond the dreams of avarice.

Up until the 1980s disparities in wages remained relatively unchanged. In 1950 the top fifth earned 45.2 percent of total incomes; in 1985 they earned 43.6 percent. In 1950 the bottom fifth received 5.4 percent of the total; in 1985 this increased to 7.5 percent. The three-fifths in the middle continued to receive roughly half of total incomes.

In the early years of the Federal Republic overall prosperity and the redistributive effects of the welfare state helped close the income gap between rich and poor. The gap widened rapidly in Britain and the United States as a result of Thatcherism and Reaganism's blind faith in market forces. By the 1980s successive German governments were affected by this ideology, with similar results. The consequences were not quite so dire as in Britain or the USA because the medicine was not prescribed in such toxic doses. The vast majority still enjoyed a relatively high standard of living and there were few instances of chronic deprivation.

In 1995 in Germany, the richest 10 percent took home 30.5 percent of salaries and wages, thereby earning twenty-eight times the amount of the 10 percent at the bottom of the pile; 6.6 percent earned one-quarter of the total. The number of income millionaires increased threefold between 1983 and 1997. Those in the highest two-fifths enjoy the "elevator effect" of overall prosperity, the next two-fifths remain relatively stable, while those in the bottom fifth trail ever further behind, with an alarming number falling below the poverty level. The plutocratic elite has been edging ahead ever since 1949, but in recent years they have begun to outpace the rest at a breathtaking rate, while at the same time the social problems associated with deprivation, particularly in the field of child poverty, have increased alarmingly. The political parties have yet seriously to address these pressing problems. They are either ignored or met with the shopworn slogans of a bygone era.

The oligarchy is to an astonishing degree a homogenous, self-recruiting elite. This is not in the vulgar Marxist sense of a ruling class looking after its own while co-opting fresh talent from outside. Nor are qualifications such as a university degree, a doctorate, or experience working abroad sufficient for admission. An increasing number meet such qualifications. Far more important are old-fashioned considerations of class-specific behavior transmitted in the nursery and family milieu that are the hidden foundations of temporal power. Capital, as Pierre Bourdieu reminded us, is not merely monetary. It also reproduces itself as social, cultural, and symbolic capital. Self-possession, correct manners, a broadly cultured mind, a secure sense of taste, and social graces are what count. Affable charm, a certain nonchalance and elegance, combined with a strong personality are mostly denied to the ambitious social climber, even if armed with all the necessary educational qualifications and professional experience. It was essential to go to the right schools and universities, join the appropriate tennis and golf clubs, and choose a spouse from the correct class. The same is true of other elites, whether administrative or political, although greater chances for upward mobility exist within the SPD and the trade unions. The judiciary is every bit as much a closed shop as the plutocracy. The one striking exception is the officer corps. Once a cozy elite in which the aristocracy played a dominant role, it has opened its ranks to the point that, by the end of the 1970s, 17 percent came from the working class. Much of this is due to the fact that the officer corps has lost its former prestige and is obliged to open up recruitment to those who can meet its demanding entry requirements, irrespective of social background.

The death of the German bourgeoisie has been often announced. In 1901 Thomas Mann's *Buddenbrooks* chronicled the decline of a powerful merchant family, a pessimistic parable of the decline of bourgeois society. After the First World War the satirist Kurt Tucholsky announced that "bourgeois society is finished." With the collapse of the Third Reich it was widely believed that the German bourgeoisie was buried under the rubble. Such threnodies were soon proved premature. The middle class, particularly its elite, survived inflation, depression, economic crisis, total war, and total defeat. Only one significant bourgeois group was destroyed: the Jewish middle class that had provided key entrepreneurs, bankers, and jurists. "Aryans" did not lose their jobs on boards of directors or in the courtroom. Even Albert Speer's "young men" in the armaments industry were mostly recruited from this elite group. Two-thirds of those on boards of directors and supervisory boards were interned, but only a quarter failed to get their old jobs back.

The middle class changed over the course of the twentieth century. A super-rich plutocracy had already begun to detach itself from the commercial bourgeoisie in the course of the previous century. The university-educated middle class, the *Bildungsbürger* for whom academic historians not unnaturally have a particular propensity, lost their power, influence, wealth, and prestige. The gap between the bourgeoisie and less privileged classes grew narrower. The Third Reich was a regime that was fundamentally anti-bourgeois, but had to make use of bourgeois know-how for its own nefarious ends. Efficiency and performance were all that mattered, an attitude that persisted into the post-war economy. A bourgeoisie that formerly had a snobbish distaste for "trade" and for vulgar displays of wealth now eagerly pursued affluence and material comfort. The bourgeoisie also lost two points of reference that had determined its worldview. The aristocracy was no longer of much consequence. They might enjoy certain privileges in the foreign office, the military, and banking, but they had been effectively destroyed, first by the aftermath of the war and then by land reform in East Germany. Although many were still exceedingly wealthy, they no longer posed a challenge to the middles class. Similarly, the working class no longer posed a threat to the hegemonic status of the bourgeoisie. Prosperity put an end to a self-conscious proletariat by leveling off material differences, and the collapse of the Soviet Union was the final blow to Marxism as an attractive political ideology. For more than two centuries the bourgeoisie had wrestled with the challenges from the aristocracy above as well as from the working class below. Now it concentrated on pursuing its own self-interest in a pluralist society, thereby losing its cohesion and its sense of identity. The old class struggle was a thing of the past; but the bourgeoisie remained a specific class, with its own lifestyle and habits contributing to an elaborately constructed symbolic representation of its social power. The bourgeoisie was also quick to adapt to a new situation. It eagerly adopted the French concept of the citizen and American liberalism's individualism. The notion of an open society enabled it to maintain its dominance, without risk of serious confrontation.

A whole new sub-class of white-collar workers grew exponentially during the last century. In 1882 only 2 percent of the workforce was classified as office workers. By 1930 this rose to 13 percent. The heavily bureaucratized Nazi dictatorship caused it to rise to 16 percent. By 1973 the "economic miracle" resulted in one-third of the workforce being in this category. By 1990 the ratio of white-collar to blue-collar workers was 42 to 38.5. White-collar workers earned considerably more than their blue-collar comrades. Then the balance began to tilt the other way. Rationalization and computerization revolutionized conditions on the shop floor. Unions negotiated similar pension schemes, health insurance, paid holidays, and statutory periods of notice to white-collar workers. In 1950 a white-collar worker earned a monthly average of 425 DM, a blue-collar worker 331 DM. By 1960 the ratio was 972:781, and in 1970 1,842:1,519. Patterns of consumption also began to level off, with blue-collar workers rapidly closing the gap. One key distinction remains. Children of white-collar workers have better educational opportunities. There are also far greater distinctions within the white-collar group than among blue-collar workers.

The economic miracle resulted in a drastic reduction in the number of small enterprises of artisans and craftsmen. In 1949 there were 863,000 such workshops – by 1958 only 460,000. At the same time the number of artisans and craftsmen greatly increased to meet a growing demand. As a result most enterprises became larger, the average size rising from 3.5 to 8.5 workers, thus swallowing the small fry. They also became increasingly profitable, with average turnover outpacing that of industrial enterprises. Some branches, such as motor mechanics, thrived, while others, such as tailoring, declined. The building trades profited from the housing boom as Germany rose again from the ashes. There were also sharp differences in pay: in the 1960s a motor mechanic earned on average five times more than a hairdresser.

The Nazi years witnessed the destruction of a self-conscious proletariat. Demoralized by years of mass unemployment, their trade unions and political parties destroyed, the neighborhoods reduced to a pile of rubble, they lost the coordinates of their identity. The Communists perpetrated the myth of the proletariat's heroic struggle against fascist dictatorship, but the reality was very different. The Nazis stressed the dignity of manual labor and programs such as "Strength Through Joy" and "The Beauty of Labor" were widely popular. Having been co-opted by the Third Reich they were left totally lost in the utter misery of the immediate post-war years. Then the economic miracle brought years of unprecedented growth, with average real wages rising fourfold between 1950 and 1973, while the working week was gradually reduced from forty-eight to forty hours. Disposable income on non-essentials rose from 20 to 40 percent. By the end of the 1970s, 43 percent of workers owned their own home, and 50 percent of skilled workers now considered themselves to be middle-class.

It would be a grave mistake, however, to imagine that working-class life had been magically transformed. For all too many, working conditions were still appalling. Many were still manual workers. The shop floor was a dangerous, unhealthy, noisy, and filthy place. Incomes rose spectacularly, but they still limped far behind those of clerical workers, civil servants, and the self-employed. The working class, like the aristocracy, was still largely self-perpetuating. Some daughters of skilled workers managed to marry above their station, just as some bourgeois married into the aristocracy, but homogeneity was maintained to a remarkable degree. At the same time the gap between skilled and unskilled workers grew ever wider and there was a high degree of discrimination against the 12 million refugees who entered the West German workforce, not to mention the millions of "guest workers," who led a wretched existence as a sub-class. The refugees' experience of "socialism as it really exists" immunized them against communism and contributed significantly to a total rejection of Marxism as the guiding ideology of the SPD, while reducing the Communist Party to insignificance.

West Germany witnessed a decline in the working class that would have surprised both Karl Marx and Max Weber. In 1949 industrial workers comprised half the workforce; by

1990 they had declined to one-third. In the heyday of the economic miracle the number of industrial workers declined from 13.1 to 9.4 million. The number of agricultural workers dropped from 1.1 million to 219,000. In industry the proportion of skilled workers steadily increased. Their children took advantage of increased educational opportunities to improve their lot, while the children of unskilled workers were unlikely to get out of the rut.

There were 70,000 aristocrats in the Federal Republic, determined to maintain their status. That they were able to do so was due to a number of factors. The overriding ideology of anti-communism meant that they were not submitted to discriminating egalitarianism. They were compensated for the estates they had lost in the East. Thanks in large part to the energetic and self-serving efforts of Countess Dönhoff, the editor of the influential weekly *Die Zeit*, the aristocracy was represented as the backbone of the resistance against the Nazi dictatorship. It was many years before historians began to expose this version of the recent past as a myth. A number of them were still incredibly rich. The Prince of Thurn and Taxis owned 32,000 hectares (80,000 acres), the Fürstenbergs 23,000 hectares (57,000 acres), the Hohenzollern-Sigmaringen, Württembergs, and Waldburg-Zeils more than 10,000 hectares (25,000 acres). Others had prestigious positions in banking, the diplomatic service, industry, and the military. The aristocracy's exclusiveness was strengthened by the fact that no one was ennobled after 1919 and they did all they could to make sure that they did not marry outside their caste. Although organized in an umbrella organization, the League of German Aristocratic Associations, they have precious little lobbying power and concentrate on preserving their exclusivity and their status as recorded in the Almanac de Gotha.

The principal source of inequality in the Federal Republic was not so much that between classes, but in gender. Thanks to the determined efforts of the women's movement, supported by the constitutional right to equality upheld in paragraph 3 of the Fundamental Law, enormous advances have been achieved in terms of formal rights, if not always in everyday life. Inequalities still exist. Equal pay for equal work has still to be fully achieved. Problems resulting from difficulties of reconciling motherhood and career remain to be solved. Women are mainly employed in sectors that are particularly sensitive to fluctuations in the economy: 90 percent are employed as secretarial staff, sales assistants, in the textile industry, and in nursing. Only 1.7 percent are employed in male roles, such as motor mechanics, fitters, and electricians.

Discrimination also exists in pension schemes. In the 1980s males retired with an average state pension of 1,459 DM; women only received 688 DM. A widow without her own pension received only 60 percent of her husband's pension, even though expenses only dropped by an average of 27 percent. Women are more likely than men to be unemployed and are more prone to fall below the poverty level. At the other end of the scale, the more prestigious the job the more it becomes a male monopoly. Thus in the 1990s in the upper echelons of the 626 largest corporations there were 2,286 men and only twelve women. The situation is slightly less grotesque among judges and state attorneys. In 1978, 10 percent were women. Twenty years later the percentage increased to 28 percent. Inequalities in opportunities are still glaring in education. Females make up 59 percent of the teaching staff in schools, but only 12.8 percent of school principals are women. There has been a remarkable increase in the number of female doctors, but very few reach the top ranks of the profession.

Much of this discrimination is based on early socialization that encourages women to be less outgoing, less self-aware, less confident, less determined, less certain of their own abilities than men, but more emotional, considerate, and socially adept. This disability is reinforced by the patriarchal belief, for which there is not the slightest empirical evidence, that women are simply not equipped to stand the strains of life at the top. Admittedly the price that women have to pay for success is extremely high: 45 percent of the women in leading positions in the economy are unmarried, while less than 4 percent of men are bachelors; 80 percent of the women in such leading positions are childless, and their divorce rate is three times higher than that of men. Women have made substantial advances in education. In 1965 they comprised only 27 percent of university students. By 1994 the percentage had risen to 52. This remarkable change is not reflected in the teaching staff. In 1988 women made up a mere 2.6 percent of professors, 7 percent of associate professors and 9 percent of instructors. The percentage of women in politics is also remarkably low, even though the parties have felt obliged to move a number of women up into leading positions to counter criticism from voters. By 1988 of the 172 ministerial positions at the provincial level 27 percent were held by women.

The effects of this blatant discrimination are disastrous. Women are faced with a bitter choice between family and career. More often than not the choice is for a career, justified by the hollow ideology of "self-realization," until the biological clock begins to tick. The choice then has to be made between remaining childless or starting a family at an age that is far from ideal. The net result has been a steady decline of the birth rate to a point where German society is no longer replacing itself. With better day-care facilities, all-day schools, and tax incentives, professional women would be better able to reconcile family life and career. German men are also exceedingly reluctant to help with the housework. Cooking, washing, ironing, and cleaning are, in 90 percent of cases, women's exclusive preserve. This is a heavy burden that stands in the way of women's emancipation.

For all the widely reproduced illusion of the blind power of romantic love, social inequalities are reproduced by the choice of a marriage partner. The higher a person's social status, the more likely that the partner chosen will come from the same milieu. Somewhat lower down the social scale the net is cast wider, whereas at the bottom the ranks are once again closed. The aristocracy show the highest degree of homogeneity, followed closely by landowners. In the upper classes 58 percent marry their own. Two-thirds of the working classes marry within their station. This high degree of homogamy – of marrying into the same group – is surprising in a society that imagines itself to be open, socially mobile, and modern. Even the enormous expansion of educational opportunities has made precious little difference. The degree to which social class determines social behavior, including such affective faculties as the choice of a partner, is a reminder of the barriers that block the way to a genuinely open society.

Family life was severely disrupted by the war, and the process of readjustment was long and painful. Millions of women who had taken over men's civilian jobs were pushed aside once the men returned from the front. A survey in the Federal Republic in 1955 showed that 59 percent supported a law banning women with small children from working. One-quarter of German children were brought up without a father. Although many women remarried, in 1950 there were still 1.7 million young widows. This was hardly surprising given the disparity in the numbers of men and women. In Bavaria in 1946, in the 20–35 age group there were 162 women for every 100 men; it was not until the late 1950s that a balance was gradually restored. A high proportion of marriages, often hastily made in the war years, ended in divorce, with two-thirds of the petitions served by women. In 75 percent of marriages the bride was either pregnant or the baby had already been born. In the larger cities almost one-third of all newborn children were illegitimate. In one-sixth of these cases the father was a member of the occupying forces. In 1950, 3,200 pregnancies were the result of rape. By 1970 there was a total of 68,000 children fathered by occupation troops; the mothers of these "occupation children" were finally given custody, although the children were effectively wards of the state. The occupying powers refused to accept any responsibility for them, the fathers having disappeared.

With one-third of the West German population, over 20 million people, comprising refugees, evacuees, the seriously injured, those who had lost their homes in the bombing raids, and returning prisoners of war, a large proportion of families were registered as "incomplete." It was not until the late 1960s that adequate housing was available for virtually all. The lack of sanitary facilities, cramped living conditions, and food shortages imposed further burdens on these demoralized and broken families. But the family as an institution showed a remarkable resilience. It was a space, at least in theory, of solidarity, stability, and intimacy. It survived the criticisms of the libertarian generation of 1968, but began to crumble in the 1980s. The rapid increase in the divorce rate, and the larger number of unmarried couples and single mothers, was combined with an alarming fall in the birth rate. The 1960s saw 250 children for every 100 women. By 1985 it was only 128 per 100. For German society to reproduce itself the figure would have to increase to 208.

There are a number of reasons for the erosion of the family as a fundamental social institution. An increasing number of women opt for a career rather playing the traditional role of wife and mother. The hedonism of a consumer society results in an emphasis on material possessions rather than the costly investment in human beings. The grossly unjust laws governing divorce make many think twice before entering into a long-term relationship, while at the same time divorce is no longer stigmatized. In 1900 the percentage of divorces relative to the number of marriages was 1.9. By 1950 it rose to 14.6 percent. In 1990 it was 36 percent and in 2004 it reached 53.9 percent. Thanks to the pill and the easy availability of abortions, the shotgun wedding, once the norm, is now a quaint relic of the past. Rising unemployment and uncertainty about the future also weigh heavily on the decision to start a family. The decision whether to marry or not is also governed by class. A survey indicates that 41 percent of those men with a school-leaving certificate remain single, while a mere 26 percent of men with only elementary schooling are unmarried. A serious problem is looming on the horizon with an ever smaller number of young people having to provide for an increasing number of old people, who have not made any sacrifices for or investment in the succeeding generation.

Social inequality is reflected in almost every aspect of life. In spite of huge investments in education the number of working-class university students remains deplorably small. In the 1950 about 6 percent of students came from the working class. This had risen to 16.9 percent by 1971, but rapidly declined from this peak. By 1990 it was back to a mere 7 percent. Since a university education has become the essential key to a well-paid job and to social advancement, class distinctions are thus reinforced by the educational system. Health is also determined by social status. University professors enjoy nine more years of life than industrial workers and do so in incomparably more pleasant style. The death rate in the working-class district of Berlin-Kreuzberg is 50 percent higher than in middle-class Berlin-Zehlendorf. Child mortality is linked to social class to a shocking degree. The two-class health insurance scheme gives private patients access to far better treatment than those in the compulsory plan, thus reinforcing the tendency for the poor to die young. The law comes down more heavily on crimes committed by those at the bottom of the social scale.

Two-thirds of prison inmates come from the bottom one-tenth. Complex and considerably more harmful white-collar crimes are far less harshly treated. Politics are also dominated by the upper classes. Even in the Social Democratic Party the percentage of working-class politicians in leading positions has halved from 31 to 16 percent. In the trade unions skilled workers made up 62 percent of the leadership in 1976. This figure has since fallen to 47 percent.

The Federal Republic is no longer a class society with the deeply ingrained social antagonisms of the Germany of a hundred years ago. But neither is it a patchwork of different milieus and lifestyles in which the concept of class has no heuristic value. An objective analysis of the social structure reveals the continued existence of classes, but the high degree of leveling out of these distinctions is achieved by the subjective perception that such differences no longer count for much. In a market economy such as this, distinctions of income are the clearest indication of relative status. The degree to which such differences lead to a reproduction of social inequality remains obfuscated by an individualistic ideology combined with dominant notions of an open and pluralistic society. Crass class antagonisms have disappeared so that the left can no longer rally the troops under the flag of class warfare. Even blanket denunciations of "the rich" have little emotional appeal. The discriminatory term "proletariat" only remains in the vocabulary of a few remaining Marxists. Social conflicts are resolved by compromise, almost all have benefited from increased prosperity and from the many amenities available in a consumer society. Social distinctions are more subtle and complex, expressed in taste and culture, in Pierre Bourdieu's concepts of "distinction" and the reproduction of cultural capital. A great deal still needs to be done to provide greater opportunities for social advancement, but it has also to be remembered that absolute equality of opportunity is an unrealizable goal.

CHAPTER SEVENTEEN
THE REUNIFICATION OF GERMANY

CHAPTER CONTENTS

A History of Modern Germany: 1800 to the Present, Second Edition. Martin Kitchen.
© 2012 Martin Kitchen. Published 2012 by Blackwell Publishing Ltd.

The 52-year-old Helmut Kohl was the first chancellor from the post-war generation who enjoyed, as he later put it in a characteristic phrase, "the favor of a later birth." He saw himself as the heir to Konrad Adenauer, in that he was a whole-hearted supporter of European integration and the Western alliance, as well as sharing his precursor's awareness of the implicit dangers were Germany to harbor any great power pretensions. Like Adenauer he was a provincial, in his case from the Palatinate, for whose wines and stuffed pig's bellies he had a great affection that was reflected in his gigantic frame. Unlike Adenauer he had no particular resentments against Prussia or Berlin. He focused all his attention on power at the expense of any ethical concerns, to the point of violating the constitution, his oath of office, sworn before Almighty God, and laws to which he had appended his signature. This was to lead to a disgraceful end to a distinguished and remarkable career.

After a constitutionally somewhat dubious procedure, elections were called for March 6, 1983. Schmidt was no longer the SPD's front runner. He had lost the confidence of the party caucus and his health was seriously impaired, in large part because of very heavy smoking. He had had to rely on a pacemaker since 1981. The SPD's candidate for the chancellorship was Hans-Jochen Vogel, the highly respected, moderate, and somewhat uninspiring mayor of Berlin. The Kohl–Genscher coalition was denounced by the left as being run by American stooges, but Kohl somewhat surprisingly won the backing of the French president, the socialist François Mitterrand, who gave a rousing speech in the Bundestag in support of the twin-track solution. The result was a resounding victory for the CDU/CSU, which received 4.3 points more than in 1980, the SPD dropping by 4.7 points and the FDP by 3.6 points. The Greens just managed to clear the 5 percent hurdle by 0.6 points and thus were represented in the Bundestag for the first time.

The new parliament was at first exclusively absorbed by a major scandal involving the largesse of the Flick industrial empire, which made use of a money-laundering outfit conveniently situated near Bonn to channel 26 million DM into the pockets of the political parties between 1960 and 1980. The state prosecutor's office had begun trying to unravel this highly complicated affair in 1983 but the task was made even more difficult when one of the main suspects, the treasurer of the FDP Heinz Herbert Karry, was murdered by terrorists and another, the SPD's treasurer Alfred Nau, died.

Although both men took a number of secrets to the grave, survivors' heads began to roll. Count Otto Lambsdorff from the FDP felt obliged to resign as minister of trade and commerce. Rainer Barzel, president of the Bundestag, also resigned when it transpired that he had received a substantial sum from the Flick empire in 1973 disguised as a fee for services rendered in his capacity as a partner in a prominent Frankfurt law firm. Helmut Kohl also came under attack for receiving 55,000 DM in cash from Flick. His skin was only saved when three leading witnesses committed perjury, as was revealed when Kohl was disgraced in a subsequent financial scandal.

Long debates were held over proposals to change the law on financing political parties, challenges were made to the Constitutional Court, and eventually a new set of rules was passed. None of this made much difference. The parties found new ways to circumvent the law and, as was later to be revealed, Helmut Kohl continued to receive illegal payments, even though he had come dangerously close to ending his political career through engaging in such dubious activities. But the higher he climbed, the further he had to fall. Climb he did, the arrogance of power rendering him impervious to the law, as illegal millions were stashed away in secret accounts in Switzerland and Liechtenstein.

Debates over Germany's Past

In the GDR there was a growing feeling of pride in the state's achievements, particularly in the remarkable performance of their athletes, resulting in a distinct national identity – though overlooking the fact that they had been skillfully doped. In the Federal Republic the left argued that the nation-state was a thing of the past, whereas on the right there was constant criticism of the Eastern treaties as a betrayal of the national ideal. In a sense things were back to normal after the aberration of the Adenauer years. The right was nationalistic once again, the left anti-national; but both left and right had serious problems with the question of German national identity. Most were inoculated against the more virulent forms of nationalism after the ghastly experience of National Socialism, and the concept of "constitutional patriotism," made popular by the journalist Dolf Sternberger, found wide acceptance. This tended to overlook the problem that the founding fathers of the Federal Republic defined nationality in terms of blood (*jus sanguinis*) rather than place of birth (*jus soli*). A German was someone born of German parents, not someone born in Germany. A person born in Alma Ata who could claim to be of German descent had an automatic right to German citizenship; a person born of Turkish parents in the Federal Republic did not. The fierce debates over a change in the citizenship laws in 1999 showed that this issue still remained extremely sensitive, even after reunification. Meanwhile, much ink was spilt on the difference between nations and nation-states, on whether Germany was "bi-national" or "post-national," and on whether or not a "cultural nation" could encompass two German states.

These rarefied and abstract debates inevitably brought up the question of the Nazi era, and it was not until the 1980s that a serious debate began as the Federal Republic at last confronted Germany's sordid past. It was then that the word "Holocaust" entered everyday speech when a like-named American television serial attracted huge audiences in 1979. In 1985 Kohl showed typical lack of sensitivity when he invited Ronald Reagan to visit a Second World War military cemetery at Bitberg where 2,000 German soldiers lay buried. What was designed as an act of reconciliation misfired when it was revealed that forty of the dead had been members of the Waffen-SS. Some of the damage was undone by a remarkable speech given three days later by Richard von Weizäcker, who had been elected president the previous year. He stressed that May 8, 1945, should be regarded as a day of liberation, "the end of a wrong track in German history," and that the horrors suffered by Germans in the final days of the war were the direct result of January 30, 1933. The president further stressed that the mass murder of the European Jews was a unique historical event and insisted that every single German "could witness what their Jewish fellow-citizens had to suffer."

Weizäcker's speech was on the whole very favorably received, although there were a number of protests from those who insisted that ordinary Germans were wholly ignorant of what had happened to the Jews, or who suggested that the past was being dug up simply in order to further the national interests of the state of Israel. It was an article by Ernst Nolte written in the convoluted language of a Heidegger pupil and devotee, published in the *Frankfurter Allgemeine Zeitung* in June 1986, that finally triggered a fierce debate among historians over the Nazi past. Nolte suggested that there was a causal link between the Gulag and Auschwitz, that the Nazis were primarily anti-Bolsheviks. He complained that Stalinist murders were consistently ignored, while Nazi crimes were discussed ad nauseam. Hitler, the "bourgeois anti-Lenin," merely acted in self-defense against an "Asiatic" threat. Therefore the burden of guilt should be lifted from Germany's collective shoulders. The mass murder of the European Jews played little role in this analysis. Largely styled as the elimination of "Jewish Bolsheviks," it was only distinguished from Soviet mass murder by "the technical procedure of poison gas."

At much the same time the distinguished historian Andreas Hillgrüber sang the praises of the Wehrmacht, whose heroic struggle in the final stages of the war enabled millions of Germans to escape from Bolshevik terror, rape, and murder. He thereby upheld the myth of the distinction between the brave and decent army and the brutal SS. He prudently overlooked the Wehrmacht's murderous policies in the East. Nolte and Hillgrüber's revisionist work was reinforced by the historian turned speech-writer for Chancellor Kohl, Michael Stürmer, who called for a more positive version of Germany's past that would give the Federal Republic a proud sense of identity.

Jürgen Habermas, Germany's most influential philosopher, spearheaded the counterattack on Nolte and his ultra-nationalist henchmen in the historical profession in a spirited article in the liberal weekly *Die Zeit*. He accused Nolte of removing all moral issues from Germany's historical past, of reducing Auschwitz to "a mere technical innovation," and of undermining the opening to the West based on "universal constitutional principles" of which post-war Germany could be justly proud.

No new insights resulted from the subsequent *Historikerstreit* in which the majority of the historical guild lined up against Nolte and his nationalist supporters, but at least the attempt to rewrite German history had been stopped in its tracks. The approach taken by Michel Foucault and Zygmunt Bauman, which stressed that the Shoah resulted from the pathology of the modern rather than from the concrete forces in German history, was energetically countered by historians who refused to accept such a pessimistic view of the modern world. But the problem remained that insistence on the unique nature of Nazi crimes left the Habermas camp open to the charge that they overlooked the crimes committed in the name of communism, and the threadbare theory of totalitarianism was taken out of the mothballs in which it had been packed since the heyday of the Cold War. Recognition of responsibility for the terrible crimes of the Nazi era could also lead to a perverse form of nationalism. German crimes were unparalleled and German atonement equally unique.

The United States, the Soviet Union, and the German Question

Fundamental changes were taking place in the relationship between the United States and the Soviet Union. Mikhail Gorbachev knew that something had to be done to stop the Soviet Union's rapid decline. Talk of glasnost and perestroika, coupled with insistence on the need for democracy was singularly vague, but was at least indication of a certain loosening of the stranglehold of dictatorship. Ronald Reagan, who had been re-elected in 1984, was also in difficulties arising from the Iran-Contra affair. The two men almost reached an agreement to withdraw all nuclear weapons from Europe during their meeting in Reykjavik in October 1986, but this came to nothing when Reagan refused to abandon his beloved "Star Wars" project. Four months later the Soviet Union announced that it no longer linked the removal of intermediate-range missiles to the Strategic Defense Initiative (SDI) and the Intermediate-Range Nuclear Forces Treaty was signed in Washington in December 1987.

The course of relations between the Soviet Union and the Federal Republic was far bumpier. Gorbachev did not react kindly when Kohl compared him to Goebbels in an interview given to *Newsweek*, and Genscher had to use all his redoubtable diplomatic skills to smooth the severely troubled waters. Indeed he went so far in his efforts to appease the Soviet Union that he was severely criticized in Washington and London for harboring dangerous illusions about the new Russia.

The Bundestag elections, which were held in January 1987, were a disappointment for the CDU/CSU. Kohl remained in office but the two parties dropped 4.7 points and booked their worst result since 1949. The SPD under the leadership of the estimable but lackluster Johannes Rau also lost votes. The FDP and Greens both made substantial gains. In his address to the new Bundestag, Kohl expressed his determination to further the dialogue with the GDR, but added that he could never reconcile himself to "the Wall, the shoot-to-kill order and barbed wire" on the inner-German border. He called for the drastic reduction of intermediate-range nuclear missiles in Europe and for parity in defensive weapons between East and West.

The strained relations between Moscow and Bonn were greatly improved thanks to the sterling efforts of Weizäcker and Genscher during a state visit to the Soviet Union in July 1987. Shortly afterwards the SPD and SED produced a joint paper on "Arguments over Ideology and Mutual Security," in which the parties agreed to disagree within a framework of open discussion and avoiding reciprocal recriminations. The SED thus opened the door to discussion, admittedly within strict limits, of the "failures and disadvantages" of "socialism as it really exists." On the other side the SPD allowed that the dictatorial regime in the GDR was a legitimate form of government, but it was one that was definitely open to criticism.

In September 1987 Honecker made a historic visit to the Federal Republic during which he was accorded full honors. Nothing concrete came from the visit, other than an agreement on environmental control that had been negotiated before Honecker arrived. Kohl's masterly speech at a banquet in Bad Godesberg offered encouragement to those who hoped that closer relations with the GDR would bring concessions without alienating those who felt that he had already gone too far in appeasing the Evil Empire's satrapy. As for Honecker, even Oskar Lafontaine, a fellow Saarlander and his most influential supporter in the SPD, could only bring himself to express "respect" for this prissy little man. Given that the GDR had recently abolished the death penalty and had become much more generous in allowing its citizens to visit the West for compassionate reasons, there was a general feeling that, although Honecker was not even remotely likeable, the devil was perhaps not quite as black as he had often been painted. On the other side of the Wall the Stasi reported that Kohl's speech and remarks by other politicians in the host country had raised unrealistic hopes, and that the restrictions on travel to capitalist countries was causing mounting discontent.

Willy Brandt and a number of leading figures in the SPD, among them Oskar Lafontaine and the mayor of Hamburg, Klaus von Dohnanyi, hoped that the historic division between Communists and Social Democrats would gradually be overcome. The Italian and Spanish Communist parties had jettisoned their Leninist baggage, and as "Eurocommunists" were virtually indistinguishable from Social Democrats. Gorbachev, with his glasnost and perestroika, seemed to be moving in the same direction. But the belief that the SED would metamorphose to this extent was an illusion. Gorbachev was intent on reforming rather than transforming the CPSU, and Honecker was convinced that even this was going too far. The GDR was to remain a bastion of orthodoxy as the Communist world gradually became more receptive to new ideas.

The CDU/CSU was far more concerned with nuclear weapons than with the finer shades of Marxist dogma. Franz Josef Strauß and Manfred Wörner, who served as minister of defense between 1982 and 1988 before becoming secretary general of NATO, agreed with Ronald Reagan and Margaret Thatcher, prime minister since 1979, that the obsolete US "Lance" missiles needed to be replaced immediately. Hans-Dietrich Genscher, on the contrary, argued that disarmament talks should begin before the new missiles were deployed. Kohl remained undecided for a long time, but even though the hawkish George Bush was inaugurated in January 1989 fielding a team that included the hard-line James Baker as secretary of state and the uncompromisingly combative Dick Cheney at defense, he felt it prudent to support his foreign minister so as not to endanger the coalition.

Genscher, who instantly became one of the leading bêtes noires of the Bush administration, had a number of allies. Although the French were not involved in the military side of NATO they were always ready to cock a snook at the Americans. A number of NATO allies, mindful that détente was as much their concern as defense, lent their support. These included Italy, Spain, Greece, Belgium, Luxembourg, and Denmark. The leading proponent of "Genscherism," as the dove-like position was contemptuously dubbed on the other side of the Atlantic, was the Norwegian foreign minister Thorvald Stoltenberg. He played an important role in assisting Genscher in negotiating an uneasy compromise at the NATO meeting in May 1989 when it was agreed to postpone deployment of the new missiles until 1992.

The doves in Bonn having forced the hawks in Washington to back down, NATO announced its determination to work towards the creation of a new peaceful environment in Europe. Although Gorbachev was still justifiably suspicious of the US administration and appeared unwilling to take up the challenge, dramatic changes were taking place in eastern Europe, particularly in Hungary and Poland, as the Soviet Union gradually loosened its grip. The GDR remained stubbornly resilient to the winds of change.

The SED's intransigent attitude to these changes prompted a fresh round of discussions of the German problem. A group of moderates in the CDU under the chairmanship of the secretary general of the party, Heiner Geissler, produced a document for the 1988 party congress which spoke of one German nation that was divided into two states. It insisted that freedom was the precondition for unity, not the price that had to be paid. For the right wing and its mouthpiece the *Frankfurter Allgemeine Zeitung*, this was an outrageous watering down of the concept of "nation," which overlooked the absolute priority of reunification. For Willy Brandt and most of the SPD, renewed talk of reunification was little more than the revival of the dangerous illusions harbored at the height of the Cold War. He warned that behind the idea of "reunification" was the pernicious belief that it would be possible to restore the German frontiers of 1937. The most that could be hoped for was that the Federal Republic and the GDR would gradually develop closer relations. Egon Bahr was somewhat more optimistic and envisioned the two superpowers withdrawing from central Europe, thus creating the preconditions for the unification of the two German states. These discussions ended abruptly with the dramatic collapse of the GDR, but soon began again, as we have seen, when the two Germanys deliberated their future.

The New Germany

The Unification Treaty having been signed in August 1990, elections were held on October 14 for the parliaments (*Landtage*) in the five new provinces in the former GDR. They were a triumph for the CDU. Brandenburg was the only state that was won by the SPD. Kohl and the CDU/CSU could now look forward confidently to the elections on December 2. There followed a series of treaties between the new Germany and the Soviet Union, Czechoslovakia, and Poland. At a CSCE summit in Paris on November 19, NATO and Warsaw Pact leaders signed a treaty on Conventional Forces in Europe (CFE) in which both sides agreed to a substantial reduction of their non-nuclear weaponry. A covenant was also signed by all concerned outlawing the use of force, except in self-defense or when otherwise sanctioned by the United Nations Charter. Gorbachev, who was under fierce attack from Boris Yeltsin and Eduard Shevardnadze for accumulating too much power, wooed Bush in Paris by assuring him of his support in the Gulf, Iraq having invaded Kuwait on August 2.

As expected, the election results on December 2 were a triumph for the Bonn coalition. The CDU/CSU obtained 43.8 percent of the popular vote. Buoyed by Genscher's enormous popularity the FDP secured 11 percent. Oskar Lafontaine, having totally misread the mood of the country, got 33.5 percent for his SPD. The Greens in the West received less than the mandatory 5 percent, but in the East their alliance with the dissidents in Association 90 (Bündnis 90) got them just over the 5 percent hurdle. Nationwide the PDS received only 2.4 percent of the popular vote, but in the East, with 11.1 percent, they obtained seventeen seats as a special concession in this first all-German election.

There were bitter recriminations in the SPD over the party's disastrous showing at the polls. The party split along broadly generational lines, with the nationalist older age group led by Willy Brandt pitched against Lafontaine and the post-nationalists. Lafontaine charged his critics with having a racial (*völkisch*) vision of nationhood, which he contrasted with Ernst Renan's French republican definition of the nation as a "daily plebiscite." He still believed that a German confederation could have been the first step towards the creation of a European confederation. This mixture of wishful thinking and muddled logic met with precious little resonance in the party at large, so that the brilliant maverick Lafontaine was left isolated, wounded, and resentful.

A decision still had to be reached as to the capital of the new Germany. Many argued that it should remain in Bonn, the capital of the first successful democracy in Germany, a town that looked to the West. Supporters of Bonn regarded Berlin as symbolic of Prussian militarism and of Great Power illusions. They could also point to the enormous expense of moving. Those who argued for Berlin, remembering the Blockade, the Wall, and November 9, 1989, insisted that it was here that the two German states should come together. Bonn was far too remote from the five new provinces. Germany's wealth was in the West so that at least the East should enjoy the political and economic benefits of a capital city. After an intensely emotional debate in June 1991 Berlin got 338 votes to Bonn's 320. The move from Bonn to Berlin was subject to numerous delays and was not made until 1999. The idea that some of the ministries could remain in Bonn soon proved unworkable. Fears that, with Berlin as its capital, the new Germany would turn its back on the European Community proved unfounded. The ghosts of the old Berlin had long since been exorcised.

The reunification of Germany took place in a remarkably calm and level-headed atmosphere given the momentous consequences of the fall of the Wall and the collapse of communism. There was not a hint of the triumphalism of 1871, no new Treitschke to proclaim that this was the end result of an inevitable teleological process. The new Germany knew that it had to tread softly so as to make sure that fears of a renewed nationalism were assuaged. Euphoria over the demise of an unattractive dictatorship and the division between East and West was soon tempered by a realization that the cost of rebuilding the bankrupt economy of the "new provinces" would be horrendous and that overcoming the psycho-logical barriers between *Ossis* and *Wessis* would present exceptional difficulties. Existing problems were exacerbated, new ones loomed large.

The new Germany was no loose cannon on deck as some had feared. Chancellor Kohl announced that the European Union was "at the heart of united Germany's foreign policy." It was an integral part of the European Community and with the Treaty of Maastricht, which was negotiated in December 1991 and signed in the following February, Germany's sovereign powers were further reduced. Monetary union meant that mighty Deutschmark would be replaced by the euro and the all-powerful Bundesbank by a European central bank. Europe was to have a common foreign and defense policy. Henceforth the frontiers between the member states of the European Community were open. Some concerns had been expressed that the choice of Berlin as a capital would lead to a centralization of power and that provincial rights would be weakened. In fact the provinces were given increased powers under the Maastricht Treaty, and Bavaria, North Rhine-Westphalia, and Baden-Württemberg were now able to make direct representations to Brussels.

Some changes to the Fundamental Law were necessitated by unification and the oppor-tunity was taken to make a few changes. Provision was made for the federal government to hand over certain sovereign rights to the European Union Community, the provinces were given further powers, the Bundesrat was strengthened, and the role of the Bundesbank had to be modified. At the same time the rights of the handicapped were added to article 3 and the state was constitutionally bound to protect the environment. These reforms were very modest and did not go far enough for the left, who had hoped that a raft of questions such full employment, minority and animal rights, and the nature of civil society should be addressed. Fortunately the argument prevailed that a constitution should not be stuffed full of rights and aims, for that would lead to an interpretative nightmare and place an intolerable burden on the Constitutional Court. One long-overdue piece of reform failed because of resistance from the CDU/CSU. It was still not possible for the Bundestag to dissolve itself by a vote of simple no confidence and the jiggery-pokery of a manipulated vote of "constructive" no confidence remained the only way for a government to call new elections.

One of the most hotly disputed provisions of the Fundamental Law was article 16 section 2, which stated that "right of asylum is to be given to the politically persecuted." This admirable clause was written when memories of the horrors of Nazi oppression were all too vivid, but now times had changed. With the collapse of communism and the removal of western European frontier posts Germany became a haven for refugees. There were 438,191 requests for asylum in 1992, along with tens of thousands of illegal immigrants. According to very generous criteria only 4.5 percent qualified as "politically persecuted." Clearly something had to be done, but it proved impossible to uphold article 16.2 in a pristine form while trying to relieve the intolerable strain occasioned by the fact that 78 percent of asylum-seekers in the European Community landed up in Germany. An uneasy answer was found by designating certain countries as "safe": from these, refugees could not claim asylum.

Another emotionally charged issue was that of abortion. Article 31 of the Unification Treaty called for a common law on this contentious issue. It took five years to reach another uneasy compromise, between the rights of the unborn and the freedoms of individual women. The issue was resolved by the Constitutional Court, which ruled the draft law to be unconstitutional. In the court's view the termination of a pregnancy in the first twelve weeks remained illegal but should not be subject to prosecution. Medical insurance schemes should not be required to pay for abortions except in case of rape, or when either mother or child was liable to suffer undue harm. Before an abortion could be performed the woman had to undergo a medical consultation, at least three days before the operation, the aim of which should be to preserve life. An attempt by the Catholic Church, under the energetic and inspired leadership of Archbishop Lehmann of Mainz, to take part in this consultative process was frustrated by orders from the Vatican and the good bishop was pointedly kept waiting before his long-overdue elevation to the college of cardinals.

Rancorous debates over such emotional issues only served to make the severe hangover after the first euphoric rapture over unification infinitely worse. The economic desolation in the East was far grimmer than even the most pessimistic of experts had imagined. There was virtually nothing that could be saved from a hopelessly backward industry, decrepit infrastructure, and ravaged environment. A completely fresh start had to be made. The expense was astronomical. The situation was made worse by the unions demanding huge wage increases that the eastern economy could not possibly sustain and by greedy speculators who invested billions in what soon turned out to be worthless projects. East Germans were glad that the regime had collapsed, but they found it impossible to identify with West Germany. A survey in the summer of 1990 revealed that 75 percent of East Germans regarded themselves as second-class citizens. Five years later two-thirds said that they were proud of their lives in the GDR. The two states were not integrated. East Germans were obliged to adapt to life in the West. Those who failed to do so became prey to "Ostalgia" in which the problems of the present were contrasted with a romanticized vision of the past.

Chancellor Kohl spoke optimistically of the future prosperity of the five new provinces. The reality was sadly different. By the autumn of 1990 industrial production had fallen by one half, GDP by 30 percent. By 1998 per capita GDP in the eastern provinces was 56.1 percent of that in the West, while unit labor costs were 124.1 percent higher. The reasons for this were manifold. East German industry had been geared for export to the Communist bloc and had virtually nothing to offer on the world market. The conversion of the East German mark at par meant that labor costs were impossibly high, and goods even more uncompetitive. East German factories had machinery in operation that was hopelessly out of date, so that higher wages could not possibly be offset by increased productivity. Eastern Germany could not inflate its way out of some of these problems as did Poland with a 70.3 percent increase in the consumer price index, Bulgaria with 338.5 percent, or Russia with 148.9 percent. The ruble lost a quarter of its value between 1990 and the end of 1992, whereas the Deutschmark rose by 5.2 percent. State property in the East was held in trust, not handed out to a rapacious *nomenklatura* as in Russia. Privatization was a complicated, lengthy, and costly process, the resulting revenue from which was disappointingly modest. Only 40 percent of concerns in the former GDR were classified as capable of making a profit; 30 percent needed massive investments; a further 30 percent were worthless. It had been estimated that the process would turn a profit of 350 billion DM. In fact the Trust Institute (Treuhandanstalt) ended up with a deficit of 204.4 billion DM. Billions more were lost due to criminal activities involving the Trust and its employees. Although the vast majority of those working for the Trust were Easterners, there was a widespread sentiment in the former GDR that the whole process was little more than the colonization of the "Wild East" by a gang of speculators, yuppies, and carpetbaggers from the rapacious West. Detlev Karsten Rohwedder, the exceptionally capable president of the Trust, was denounced as "the Grim Reaper's skeletal hand" and as a "desktop murderer." He was assassinated by the Red Army Faction in 1991. His successor, Birgit Breuel, was soon dubbed "The Iron Lady" and "Jobkiller," who set about "the creative destruction of the former socialist economy." Among the jobs she killed were those of 500 members of her organization for criminal offenses, a Stasi past, or sheer incompetence.

The government, which was now faced with the enormous additional expense of financing its contribution to the Gulf War amounting to 18 billion DM, borrowed vast amounts and increased taxation, including a "solidarity tax" of an additional 7.5 percent on incomes in the former Federal Republic. Resentment at having to pay for ungrateful Easterners was matched by the bitterness over what seemed to be the arrogance and condescension of Westerners. The social structure and mentalities of the two Germanys were so very different that misunderstanding between *Ossis* and *Wessis* was inevitable. A few enterprising souls seized the opportunities offered by a free market economy and prospered, but most found it extremely difficult to adjust to the dramatically changed circumstances. Many gave vent to their frustration by beating up foreigners and joining right-wing extremist groups. Members of the old *nomenklatura* who had enjoyed many privileges and who owed their position more to political reliability than to their skills and abilities had no place in the new Germany and were deeply resentful at their loss of status. The gap between East and West became ever wider and it soon became a journalistic cliché to remark that the Wall had been replaced by a wall in people's minds. In April 1993 a survey showed that 85 percent of the inhabitants of the former GDR and 71 percent of those in the West felt that the two Germanys still had conflicting interests. Only 11 percent of Easterners and 22 percent of Westerners saw themselves as part of one Germany.

Most of the East German leadership escaped punishment for the crimes committed by the regime. Honecker was arrested and charged with authorizing the shoot-to-kill order on the frontier, but he was suffering from cancer of the liver and was deemed unfit to stand trial. He left for Chile, where he enjoyed a certain popularity for having offered asylum to victims of Pinochet's unmerciful dictatorship. He died there in 1995 at the age of 81. Willi Stoph's state of health was also such that proceedings against him were halted. Erich Mielke was charged with murdering two policemen in 1931 and was given a six-year prison sentence. He served less than two years and died in 2000. Three members of the Politbüro, including Egon Krenz, were given prison sentences of up to six and a half years for their part in passing the shoot-to-kill order. Two border guards were given suspended sentences for killing people trying to escape. Hardest hit were people who lost their jobs in the civil service, the judiciary, and the universities. They were mostly replaced by *Wessis*, thus providing further grist to the PDS's propaganda mill according to which unification was an *Anschluss*, the East a mere colony of the West. The PDS campaign against the "Westernization" of the five new provinces found considerable resonance among these embittered and disillusioned losers. Since there was no dramatic improvement in living standards in the East after unification, in spite of the extravagant and irresponsible promises of some Western politicians, many began to look back on the good old days of the GDR. *Ossis* relapsed into familiar mental structures; *Wessis* indulged in what Jürgen Habermas dubbed "the chauvinism of prosperity."

The GDR was a secular society in which less than 30 percent of the population belonged to the two major Christian denominations. In the West more than three-quarters were at least nominally either Protestant or Catholic. This difference was reflected in widely different moral standards and cultural practices in the two Germanys. There were also profound differences in an understanding of the German past. The Federal Republic looked back to the liberal democracy of the Frankfurt parliament and to the conspiracy to assassinate Hitler on July 20, 1944. The GDR's ideological premise was anti-fascism and the SED was in the direct line of descent from Marx's Communist League and Lenin's Bolsheviks. In the West there was an intensive debate over the Nazi past, and the burden of guilt for Auschwitz weighed heavy. For the East the only victims of Nazism who counted were members of the Communist Party. Nazism was a problem for the West, not for the sturdy anti-fascist workers and peasants in the GDR. Whereas historians in the West examined the roots of National Socialism and asked where Germany had gone wrong, their colleagues in the GDR painted a positive picture of the German past whose heroes were Luther, Frederick the Great, and even Bismarck. The principal villains were the SPD, who had betrayed the revolution in 1918, misled the working class, and left the way open for monopoly capitalists to put Hitler in command.

In 1992 the Bundestag established a commission to examine the history and nature of the SED regime. The report was published two years later on July 17, 1994, the anniversary of the uprising in East Germany in 1953. The conclusions from this lengthy document were mostly unexceptional. The GDR was described as a dictatorship which had changed considerably over the years, but which remained a totalitarian regime under the firm control of the SED. Strong objections were raised on the left to the use of the term "totalitarian," which had so often been used in the past to lump communism and National Socialism together and thus overlook the profound differences between the two dictatorial systems. The charge that a triumphant liberalism was reverting to the crude rhetoric of the worst phases of the Cold War was somewhat lamely countered by the assertion that "totalitarianism" only referred to both regimes' claim on the whole individual. On the other hand, however absurd the suggestion that the GDR was similar to the Third Reich, there was still the awesome problem of undoing the harmful results of more than forty years of Communist dictatorship, which had a far greater impact on those who lived under it than twelve years of National Socialism.

Euphoria over newly won freedoms and the prospect of a glittering future soon turned into sour resentment. East Germany was rapidly de-industrialized, its economic, social, and cultural environment destroyed. The people were faced with mass unemployment and the need rapidly to adapt to a radically different environment. Most *Ossis* felt excluded, traumatized, and unable to adjust to a new reality. Precious few faced the challenges and grasped the opportunities offered in a dynamic democratic society. This led to a widespread rejection of a market economy and of parliamentary democracy. Some hankered for the good old days of a welfare dictatorship, others turned to the radical right. As late as 1998, when asked the question: "Do you think that democracy, such as we have in the Federal Republic, is the best form of government, or are there others that are better?" only 30 percent of Easterners replied in the affirmative, compared with 80 percent of Westerners. But it was often forgotten that it took many years for the Westerners to build a viable society after the war, when conditions were much more favorable. They did so in the boom years after 1950; now the Easterners lived in a society facing mass unemployment, the challenges of globalization, competition from Asia, outsourcing, and rapid technological change. In such a situation disparities between East and West grew greater. Between 1989 and 1994, in the East unemployment rose by 3.5 million, in the West by only 1.2 million.

The new and fully sovereign Germany was soon faced with some exceedingly difficult decisions that made many hanker after a return to the time when the Federal Republic was subject to a degree of four-power control and restraint. According to the constitution the Bundeswehr could only be used to counter a direct attack on the Federal Republic or in certain instances of internal emergency. What part, if any, should Germany play in Operation "Desert Shield" in Iraq? Dick Cheney, the US secretary of defense, urged the Germans to join in the thirty-four-nation coalition, but article 87a of the Fundamental Law only permitted the armed forces to act in a defensive capacity. Genscher decided that material help should be offered to the United States, Britain, and Israel, but that German troops should not be involved, thus leaving the Federal Republic open to the charge that it was trying to buy its way out of its military obligations by indulging in checkbook diplomacy. Resentment, particularly in the United States and Israel, at Germany's reluctance to become involved was heightened by massive demonstrations against a war that was denounced as further proof of American imperialism. A number of prominent voices on the left denounced the facile comparison of Saddam Hussein to Hitler as a glib excuse to go to war on behalf of the major oil companies. Oskar Lafontaine claimed that Germany bore the mark of Cain after the crimes of the Nazi era and should never be the cause of further bloodshed. Others argued that with the end of the Cold War Europe should sever its ties to the United States and that NATO, which was rapidly becoming little more than America's unpaid Foreign Legion, should be dissolved.

The debate over Germany's participation in the Gulf War was still raging when Yugoslavia began to fall apart and NATO became actively involved in the area. Although both the United States and the European Community called for the preservation of Yugoslavian unity, foreign minister Hans-Dieter Genscher, in an exceptionally ham-fisted piece of personal diplomacy, recognized Croatia and Slovenia as independent states. A senior official in the British Foreign Office described this move as "downright stupid." How, he asked, could pressure be placed on the Serbian leader Slobodan Milosevic by recognizing Franjo Tudjman as president of Croatia and how could pressure be placed on Tudjman by granting him his every wish? Lord Carrington, NATO's secretary general, laconically condemned Genscher's move as "unhelpful." Carrington and the US envoy to Yugoslavia, Cyrus Vance, later told Richard Holbrooke, President Clinton's representative in the region, that Genscher's ill-considered move set off a chain reaction that led to the brutal war in Bosnia. Civil war in former Yugoslavia triggered a vigorous debate over the constitutionality of the use of German forces abroad in a coalition. It was generally agreed that with the end of the Cold War a new definition of the concept of security was needed. Article 24 section 2 of the Fundamental Law permitted such an engagement in order to secure "the peaceful and lasting order in Europe and between the peoples of the world." An attempt to change the constitution so as to avoid any ambiguity failed, owing to the lack of a two-thirds majority in the Bundestag. The Constitutional Court ruled that it was permissible for German-manned AWACs to patrol the airspace over Bosnia-Herzegovina in 1993 in accordance with a UN Security Council resolution. Thus for the first time the Federal Republic's armed forces were on active duty; 2,420 service personnel also took part in the humanitarian action UNOSOM II in Somalia and Kenya in 1993–4. The SPD and the FDP argued that these actions were unconstitutional and appealed to the Constitutional Court. The court rejected this argument and in 1994 ruled that the Bundeswehr could take part in humanitarian or military missions out of area provided that a simple majority in the Bundestag supported such action. The court thus ruled that both the UN and NATO were part of a "system of mutual collective security as defined in article 24 of the Fundamental Law."

In 1995 the Bundestag debated whether German troops should participate in a special NATO force that was to be on the alert for rapid deployment in Bosnia-Herzegovina. The CDU/CSU and FDP were in favor; the majority of the SPD, most of the Greens, and all the PDS were opposed. Once again the familiar argument was trundled out that after Auschwitz Germany was obliged to eschew the use of force. Four years later the left stood this argument on its head when Auschwitz was used to justify participation in the badly bungled intervention in Kosovo in an attempt to stop the genocide there. Only a small minority clung to the argument in favor of a German foreign political *Sonderweg*. The Federal Republic was at last in tune with its allies, but once again it fell seriously out of line over the invasion of Iraq in 2002.

It was hardly surprising that Helmut Kohl's coalition government between the CDU/CSU and FDP was widely unpopular. It only just managed to win the election in 1994, with a majority of a mere two votes, because the SPD made the exceptionally poor choice of appointing the colorless Rudolf Scharping as its candidate for the chancellorship. Kohl's new government set about strengthening market forces by a draconian program of what was denounced on the left as "social demolition." Short-term notice could now be given to staff in small enterprises, the age of retirement was increased, and unemployment and sickness benefits were reduced. Widespread protests culminated in a rally by the trade unions in 1996 in Bonn, which attracted 350,000 demonstrators. The opposition began to flex its muscles when the hapless Scharping was replaced by his rival Oskar Lafontaine as head of the SPD in 1995. Lafontaine in his capacity as president of the upper chamber (Bundesrat), where the opposition had a majority, managed to stop a number of bills passed by the Bundestag, including Kohl's ambitious tax reform. The result was a political stalemate in which it was no longer possible to address the many pressing problems that urgently needed to be answered.

Helmut Kohl managed to stay in office because of a fierce rivalry within the opposition SPD between the left-wing party chairman, Oskar Lafontaine, and his arch-rival the right-wing minister president of North Rhine-Westphalia, Gerhard Schröder, who sat comfortably on the boards of a number of major companies, including Volkswagen, and who was a champion of private industry. But economic stagnation and rising unemployment worked in the SPD's favor, helped by the fact that Kohl had never shown any particular interest in the economic matters that were now top of the political agenda. The question that now faced the Social Democrats was who to field as their candidate for the chancellorship in the 1998 election: Lafontaine, who had the loyalty of the party stalwarts, or Schröder, who was more widely popular? Schröder's impressive victory in the state election in 1998, which gave the SPD the absolute majority in North Rhine-Westphalia, acted as a surrogate plebiscite, thus securing his selection as candidate for the election in the same year.

Schröder appealed to small businessmen, artisans, craftsmen, and skilled workers, distancing himself from the Greens, who in an orgy of self-destruction were running their election campaign on a demand for a massive increase in the tax on petrol. Lafontaine loyally supported Schröder, in spite of personal animosity, by concentrating on attacking Kohl's "social demolition," while Schröder took a less confrontational approach, presenting himself as the champion of the average German in the "new middle." The opportunist Schröder realized that the electorate wanted to see the end of Helmut Kohl after sixteen years as chancellor, but did not want to see a change of course. He therefore thought in terms of a coalition with the CDU/CSU, which had the added attraction that it would enable him to get rid of the principled Lafontaine. But the Greens, although losing 0.6

points compared with 1994, did better than expected, with the "realist" Joschka Fischer gaining the upper hand over the "fundamentalist" ecologists within the party, obliging Schröder regretfully to opt for a Red/Green coalition. It was an alliance that left Schröder under attack on two fronts. The Greens called for an end to the use of atomic energy and a refusal to allow the armed forces to engage "out of area." Lafontaine, as finance minister, had the support of the unions and a sizeable section of public opinion for a left-wing approach to an economic and fiscal policy that was anathema to the new chancellor.

The coalition government, with Joschka Fischer as foreign minister, the traditional office of the junior partner, and another Green, Jürgen Trittin, as environment minister, agreed on a moderate plan entitled "Alliance for Work and Training." It called for cooperation between government, trade unions, and employers, a major tax reform, an "ecology tax," and an emphasis on education and research, as well as a clear plan to stop the use of atomic energy. The Greens also agreed that the armed forces could be used to support actions of the UN, provided that they were in accordance with the Fundamental Law.

Even before Schröder was sworn in as chancellor he faced the serious problem of whether or not to take part in a likely war with Serbia over Kosovo. In August the UN Security Council called for an end to the fighting between Serbian forces and Kosovo rebels, which was rapidly becoming a humanitarian disaster, so as to enable some 250,000 refugees to return home. Richard Holbrooke told the German government that the Serbian leader Milosevic was banking on the new coalition refusing to join in NATO operations in Kosovo, whereupon other NATO countries would opt out. The leadership of the new coalition met with Helmut Kohl, who was still in office, along with his foreign minister, Klaus Kinkel, and minister of defense, Volker Rühe, to discuss Holbrooke's urgent request for Germany to make a declaration of solidarity with NATO. The CDU politician Rühe had hoped that the Fischer would refuse, thus putting an end to the SPD/Green coalition and paving the way for a grand coalition in which Schröder would be chancellor and he would be foreign minister. Fischer agreed that it would be disastrous to break up the NATO alliance, thus committing his party, with which he had not had time to discuss this hotly debated issue, to a coalition with the SPD. The question was then put before the old Bundestag and the motion passed. For many this was merely a diplomatic threat to put pressure on Milosevic to accept a ceasefire. This was brokered a few days after the Bundestag vote, and a Kosovo Verification Mission made up of Organization for Security and Cooperation in Europe (OSCE) monitors was sent to the region. They were soon known as "the clockwork oranges," because of their brightly colored vehicles and because they soon proved to be utterly ineffective.

Fighting broke out again in January 1999, when forty Kosovo Albanians were massacred in Racak, prompting fears that there might soon be a repeat performance of the Srebrenica massacre of 1995 when Serbian forces under General Ratko Mladic slaughtered 8,000 Bosnian men and boys and forced some 30,000 to flee their homes while Dutch troops stood idly by. Peace discussions in Rambouillet broke down, and on March 23 four of the Luftwaffe's Tornado jets set off from an airfield in Piacenza on a mission over Serbia. This was the first time since the war that German forces had been on active service. Soon it seemed likely that ground troops would also be needed.

The Kosovo mission put the SPD/Green coalition in danger of falling apart. Foreign minister Fischer was denounced as a murderer, warmonger, and criminal at a special meeting of his party in May, and was hit on the ear with a pot of paint. Fortunately the fighting soon stopped, thanks to Boris Yeltsin making it clear that Russia no longer stood behind Serbia. A "Kosovo troika" comprising the Russian Victor Chernomyrdin, who was temporarily out of office as prime minister, Strobe Talbott the US deputy secretary of state, and the Finnish president Maartti Ahtisaari, who represented the European Union, negotiated a peace accord that was signed in Bonn at the beginning of June. A NATO-led peacekeeping force, KFOR, was sent to Kosovo. Ahtisaari, a past master in conflict resolution, was to be awarded the Nobel Peace Prize in 2008. The war was over, but not the debate. Germany had gone to war without UN sanction, because any vote in the Security Council would have been vetoed by Russia. One side argued that the Security Council was not the only source of international law. The UN Charter, previous resolutions of the Security Council, and the imperative to give aid to those in need were sufficient to legitimize the deployment of German forces. Others argued that taking action without UN sanction meant that the USA could condemn a state as rogue and call for NATO action, thus bypassing the European Union and the OSCE.

Oscar Lafontaine remained remarkably silent during the debates over Kosovo. Then, on March 11, 1999, he suddenly resigned. The day before Schröder had mounted a massive attack on Jürgen Trittin for constantly harping on about atomic energy, smog control, and the regulation of older motor cars, all of which amounted to what he called "pinprick politics" harmful to the economy. He made it plain that he would not tolerate any measures that were not in the interests of the economy as a whole. This attack was also aimed at Lafontaine, who, along with his state secretaries Heiner Flassbeck and Claus Noé, was calling for Keynesian fiscal policies, higher wages, improved social services, and lower rates of interest. All this was anathema to Schröder, the business-friendly Erhardian. Lafontaine had the continued support of the unions and the left wing of his party, but had little elsewhere, either at home or in the European Union, with the exception of the French finance minister, Dominique Strauss-Kahn. Failing to distinguish between the desirable and the feasible, he was on a collision course with the chancellor, much to the delight of the media. Verbatim excerpts from Schröder's cabinet tirade appeared in *Bild*, Germany's principal tabloid, in a carefully managed plant. The article was headed "Schröder Threatens To Resign," but it was Lafontaine who folded his hand.

It was not only the SPD that was beset with problems. In November 1999 an order was issued for the arrest of Walther Leisler Kiep, the treasurer of the CDU from 1971 to 1992. He was charged with having failed to pay tax on 1 million Deutschmarks given as a contribution to the party by an arms dealer, Karlheinz Schreiber. The affair soon began to snowball. Helmut Kohl admitted to having accepted between 1.5 and 2 million DM in party contributions between 1993 and 1998, but he refused to name the source. Further investigation revealed that the CDU had a number of shady accounts including the "Norfolk Foundation" in Liechtenstein. Shortly before Christmas the party secretary, Angela Merkel, a talented East German chosen by Kohl, told the *Frankfurter Allgemeine Zeitung* that her patron had harmed the party and should resign all his offices. It was a sad end to a remarkable career, underlined when an elaborate party to celebrate his seventieth birthday was cancelled. He was fined 300,000 DM for this misdemeanor, but still refused to name the donor. Other heads rolled. The minister of the interior, Manfred Kanther, the party treasurer, Prince zu Sayn-Wittgenstein, the minister president of Hesse, Roland Koch, and the party chairman Wolfgang Schäuble were all implicated. Only Koch managed to survive relatively unscathed. The Bundestag ordered the CDU to pay a fine of 41.3 million DM, and the law governing contributions to political parties was changed. Henceforth no such payments could exceed 1,000 euros, and anonymous contributions were set at a maximum of 500 euros. The net result of this shabby affair was that the electorate's trust in politics and politicians was shattered, while the entire political process was widely viewed with surly petulance. It was not a healthy atmosphere in which to confront a dramatically new set of problems.

9/11

When foreign minister Joschka Fischer heard the news of the destruction of the World Trade Center he expressed his confusion with a well worn cliché: a Pandora's box had been opened. Having touched base with Jacques Chirac, Tony Blair, and Vladimir Putin and having promised George W. Bush his "unconditional solidarity" he made a public statement to the effect that this was "a declaration of war against the entire civilized world." Schröder assumed that the USA would strike back and that NATO would support any such military action. But NATO had first to be convinced that the attack on the USA had been orchestrated from abroad. It soon became apparent that it was the work of Osama bin Laden's Al-Qaida network, based in Afghanistan, where it was protected by the radical Islamist Taliban, who had seized power in 1996. On October 1, NATO was placed on a war footing and the nineteen member states soon agreed upon a set of measures to support the American attack on the Taliban and Al-Qaida.

In Germany the interior minister, Otto Schily, introduced a series of measures to combat terrorism, soon to be known as the "Otto Catalogue" after the well-known mail-order company. Schily was a man who first sprang to prominence as a defense lawyer for terrorists and who was a founding member of the Greens. He then moved steadily to the right, joining the SPD in 1989. Now he was proposing a set of measures that were an unacceptable attack on civil liberties in the eyes of many in the Greens, the PDS, the libertarian FDP, and even within his own party. Unconditional support came only from the CDU/CSU. Some objections to these measures were lifted in April 2002 when Al-Qaida murdered fourteen German tourists who were visiting the El-Ghriba synagogue on the island of Djerba in Tunisia. The fact that leading figures in 9/11 came from a terrorist cell in Hamburg gave the matter added urgency.

On October 7, 2001, Operation Enduring Freedom began, with American and British bombing raids on Afghanistan. Seventy nations were soon involved directly or indirectly in operations in Afghanistan, the Horn of Africa, the Philippines, and the Trans-Sahara. They were sanctioned by UN Security Council resolutions 1368 and 1373 and article 51 of the UN Charter. On November 7 the Bundestag voted in favor of committing troops to the conflict. The debate placed the Greens in an awkward quandary. They were styled as a peace party and had already found it exceedingly difficult to accept the Kosovo mission. As one deputy put it: "If we once again agree to military operations, who will then vote for us?" A number on the SPD's left wing had similar misgivings. Schröder made the vote one of confidence, so that the CDU/CSU voted against. The vote passed by a mere majority of two, with seventy-seven Greens and Social Democrats issuing statements that although they were against sending troops, they had voted for the motion in order to save the coalition.

At the UN conference held at Petersburg near Bonn, Germany played an important role in bringing the initial phase of the fighting to an end. The conference concluded on December 5, 2001, with a resolution on an interim government and provisional administration. Germany was also one of the thirty-six nations in the International Security Assistance Force (ISAF) sent to Afghanistan to support the provisional government. Almost 4,000 service personnel, mostly stationed in the north, made up the third largest national contingent. The Bundestag's mandate does not permit these troops to go on active service against Taliban insurgents in the south and east, save in exceptional circumstances, but they have been engaged in combat operations in Regional Command North. The forces are under attack both from the Americans and the British for not taking their fair share of the fighting in the south, and at home because of the alarming number of civilian casualties that they have caused, particularly in a badly bungled air strike near Kunduz in September 2009, when a cover-up attempt caused a major rift in the alliance and serious political repercussions at home, leading to the resignations of the chief of staff as well as the defense minister and his deputy.

The Iraq War

For the neo-conservative advisors to George W. Bush, 9/11 was clear proof that their apoca-lyptic worldview was amply justified. In December 2001 the influential liberal weekly *Die Zeit* published an article describing the views of Richard Perle, chairman of the Defense Policy Board Advisory Committee, on the War on Terror. He insisted that the problem now was not individual terrorists, but states. He claimed that there were "eight or nine" states that harbored terrorists. Although the US need not go to war against all of them, they should do so against the one that posed the greatest danger: Iraq. Perle stated categorically that the Iraqi president, Saddam Hussein, offered terrorists sanctuary, and had weapons of mass destruction, which he had already used against Iran as well as against the Kurds. Furthermore, he had expelled the UN inspectors, who monitored the agreement on weapons production reached after the 1991 Gulf War. This, said Perle, was proof positive that he had something to hide. It was soon apparent that Perle was outlining official policy. In Bush's first State of the Nation address on January 29, 2002, the president spoke of an "axis of evil," comprising states that harbored terrorists. Principal among them were Iraq, Iran, and North Korea. He accused Iraq of developing anthrax, nerve gas, and atomic weapons.

The German government's defense cabinet met immediately to discuss Bush's alarming speech, at which it was agreed that there was no evidence for a connection between Iraq and Al-Qaida. Schröder flew to Washington on January 31, where he told Bush that "the same must apply in Iraq as in Afghanistan." In other words there must be absolute proof that Saddam Hussein was host to the terrorists and that any operation against Iraq must first have the sanction of the UN Security Council. Bush made some vague assurances that he would act in consultation with America's allies, but the German delegation had the impression that there was a new aggressive spirit in Washington and that the administration was determined to go ahead regardless of allied opinion.

This impression was confirmed a few days later when two prominent hawks, the deputy secretary of defense Paul Wolfowitz and Senator John McCain, flew to Germany and made it plain that the United States would not make its decision to go to war against Iraq depend-ent on the attitude of its allies. The Germans were informed that in the new world order there was not one alliance, but a series of alliances for specific purposes. McCain stated clearly that Afghanistan was merely the first round in a global war on terror. The next would be against a "terrorist residing in Baghdad."

The Germans hoped that the Americans were merely upping the ante in the hope that Saddam Hussein would permit the UN inspectors to return. This impression was confirmed when Bush visited Germany in May, where he gave a decidedly moderate speech to the Bundestag. The president hoped thereby to assuage German reservations about his policy towards Iraq. That he failed was largely due to German domestic political considerations.

Ever since the Kosovo war in the spring of 1999 the SPD had done poorly at the polls, dropping several points in the European, state, and communal elections. In the summer of 2002 the party's fortunes began to improve until July 18, when the defense minister, Rudolf Scharping, was dismissed, in part for his enthusiastic involvement in an embarrassingly widely publicized and tasteless love affair. The party leadership met in August to discuss how best to improve its chances in a forthcoming election. The party chairman Franz Münterfering insisted that the emphasis should be on the "German way": the model for a welfare state. Schröder argued that the Iraq question should be made central. Opinion polls showed that there was widespread opposition to any involvement in a war against Iraq. Foreign minister Fischer had for weeks been urging him to made his position clear. Schröder left the meeting briefly to give a television interview, in which he was asked whether he had "any rabbits to pull out of his hat" for the election campaign, to which he replied that there was "disturbing news out of the Near East, including the danger of war." He added that although Germany would stand by its allies "we are not available for adventures." Ignorant of these remarks, the meeting sided with Münterfering, who when asked by journalists what he thought of Schröder's performance on television replied that you cannot win elections with foreign policy issues.

Schröder ignored Münterfering's stricture. During the election campaign he warned against "playing with war" and repeated that "we are not available for adventures." He took up Münterfering's concept of the "German way," but applied it to foreign policy. The CDU/CSU accused Schröder of anti-Americanism and of "instrumentalizing" the Iraq question, but this met with little response. Schröder's election rival, the conservative, cultured, traditionalist Bavarian Edmund Stoiber, was stiff and distant, with none of Schröder's mastery in handling the media. The CDU/CSU was so confident of winning that this hardly seemed to matter. Schröder seized the opportunity offered by the "flood of the century" in August, when the Elbe and its tributaries broke their banks and caused widespread damage, ruining the lives of thousands. He immediately put on his gumboots and oilskins and went to the site of the catastrophe to express his solidarity with the people. 385 million euros were released for immediate assistance and a bill was rapidly passed allotting 7.1 billion euros for relief and reconstruction. Stoiber waited one week before visiting the flooded area. The chancellor had stolen the show.

The election was still closely run, with the SPD and the CDU/CSU both gaining 38.5 percent of the vote. That the Red/Green coalition could continue depended on two main factors. Schröder had concentrated on the flooded areas in East Germany, thereby winning considerable sympathy. Many former PDS supporters voted for the SPD, resulting in the party winning a mere 4 percent of vote, below the 5 percent needed for a party to send deputies to the Bundestag. On the right the FDP's leading candidate, Jürgen Möllemann, had argued in favor of the admitting Jamal Karsli, formerly deputy for the Greens in North Rhine-Westphalia, into the FDP *Landtag* faction. Karsli accused the Israeli prime minister Ariel Sharon of fighting a "war of annihilation" against the Palestinians by using "Nazi methods," and complained that all discussion was muzzled by a "Zionist lobby." Such remarks prompted widespread criticism, also in the FDP, so that Karsli left the party. Möllemann came under attack from the vice president of the Central Committee of German Jews and president of the European Jewish Congress, Michel Friedman, for his support for Karsli. Möllemann replied in a television interview that the behavior of people such as Friedman was a major cause of anti-Semitism. He then distributed pamphlets in North Rhine-Westphalia that contained scurrilous attacks on Sharon and Friedman. Möllemann's shocking behavior and the failure of the party chairman, Guido Westerwelle, to keep him in line, resulted in them gaining merely 7.4 percent of the vote, which was not enough to form a coalition government with the CDU/CSU.

Gerhard Schröder's Second Term

The United States assumed that Schröder and Fischer's anti-war stand was simply election-eering rhetoric and that the new government, having supported the US in Afghanistan and Kosovo, would do so again in Iraq. This was soon shown to be a mistake. In Schröder's official statement of intent of October 29 he called for "a consequential policy of disarmament and international control" in Iraq and made it absolutely clear that Germany would not participate in a war.

The German government, not wishing to stand alone in defiance of the United States, began to look for allies in Europe. The French, sharing Germany's concerns, together with Russia and China, managed to secure the passing of UN Security Council resolution 1441 on November 8, 2002, that called for a UN inspection team under the Swedish diplomat Hans Blix and Mohamed ElBaradei, head of the International Atomic Energy Agency, to see whether the American and British claim that Saddam Hussein had weapons of mass destruction was justified. This frustrated Bush's hopes for a resolution sanctioning military action against Iraq. In a series of talks with the French president Jacques Chirac, the British prime minister Tony Blair, and the Russian president Vladimir Putin, Schröder made it quite clear that regardless of what the UN inspectors found, Germany would not support a resolution calling for military action against Iraq. On February 25 the United States, Britain, and Spain presented a resolution to the UN Security Council stating that Iraq "has failed to take the final opportunity" to disarm, but which did not include deadlines or an explicit threat of military force. France, Germany, and Russia offered a counter-proposal calling for peaceful disarmament and a continuation of Blix and ElBaradei's inspection efforts. The alliance of Germany, France, Russia, and China was in an awkward position. They could not get Saddam Hussein to cooperate with the UN inspectors, nor could they restrain the Bush administration's determination to go to war. Troops from the US, Britain, Australia, Spain, Denmark, and Poland landed in Basra on March 20, 2003, marking the beginning of the Gulf War. On May 1, 2003 President Bush landed in full combat gear on the aircraft carrier *Abraham Lincoln*, where he made the astonishingly premature statement that the mission was accomplished.

It took time for US–German relations to unfreeze. The minister of defense traveled to Washington on May 5, and the US secretary of state Colin Powell visited Germany shortly afterwards. On June 7 Bush telephoned Schröder to express his sympathy over the death of four German soldiers in Kabul, but the president never forgave what his secretary of defense, Donald Rumsfeld, dismissed as "old Europe" for opposing the invasion of Iraq.

On the domestic front the Red/Green coalition's main problem was the mounting cost of welfare payments. The coalition had won the 1998 election mainly because of its largely unjust attacks on Kohl's lack of commitment to the welfare state and the SPD's promise that welfare would be its first priority. The problems were due not to the CDU's neglect, but rather to the immense cost of reunification and Germany's massive contribution to the European Union, compounded with the economic consequences of globalization. The coalition made good its promises to increase child support and long-term care insurance payments, but sluggish growth and rising unemployment made it imperative that cuts be made. Schröder agreed with Tony Blair's "New Labour" that massive cuts were required in a process that was camouflaged as "modernization."

A commission was set up in February 2002 under the chairmanship of Volkswagen's personnel manager, Peter Hartz, to investigate the problems of the labor market. The report, published in August with an immense flourish in the middle of the election campaign, promised "an end to maudlin sentimentality and low spirits." Hartz made the extravagant claim that his proposals would put 2 million unemployed back to work. Although many experts felt this was pie in the sky, optimism engendered by skillful public relations and energetic spin doctoring helped Schröder to victory. Then in his declaration of the new government's intent he made it clear that drastic cuts were required. The spirit of optimism soon evaporated. With public discontent growing apace Schröder was reluctant to act, but in January 2003 the EU Commission began procedures against Germany for having exceeded the 3 percent limit for fresh debt. Local elections in Hesse in February resulted in a catastrophic defeat for the SPD. Schröder reacted with a leap in the dark, turning his back on Social Democracy with his "Agenda 2010". He announced: "We will ensure that the state reduces the provision of services. We shall encourage personal responsibility and effort from each individual. All sections of society must make their contribution: management and labor, the self-employed and even pensioners." With the amalgamation of unemployment and welfare benefits as outlined in the fourth and last set of proposals from the Hartz commission that were turned into law, known as Hartz IV, it appeared to many that in Schröder's version of the "social market economy" the social element was rapidly disappearing. A hundred thousand people left the SPD, many moving to the Labor and Justice Party (WASG) and the PDS (the successor party to the Communist SED). Nevertheless Schröder had little difficulty in getting his proposals, subject to some minor compromises, signed into law.

Dissatisfaction was mounting within the SPD ranks. In February 2004 Schröder felt obliged to hand over the chairmanship of the party to Franz Münterfering, a highly respected middle-of-the-road figure. Meanwhile the trade unions mounted a massive attack on the government's "clear cutting" and welfare programs under the slogan: "Get rid of Hartz IV and Agenda 2010!" In spite of Hartz's optimistic assessments unemployment continued to rise at an alarming rate, while the economy showed no signs of recovery. The left wing of the SPD, led by the minister of finance Oskar Lafontaine, denounced the new course as a neo-liberal betrayal of the traditions of Social Democracy. Lafontaine eventually resigned in 2005 to become, with Gregor Gysi, leader of The Left (Die Linke), a coalition of the PDS and the WASG, in June 2007.

The SPD lost ground in a series of local elections. In July 2005, faced with a steadily worsening situation, Schröder decided to call for a vote of confidence. The result was that new elections were to be held in September.

Angela Merkel's Two Coalition Governments

Meanwhile CDU and CSU had decided that Angela Merkel should be their candidate for chancellor. The FDP offered its support in a coalition. The SPD made no promise to continue in alliance with the Greens. The election result made any such government impossible. The CDU/CSU, with 35.2 percent, and the SPD, with a surprising 34.2 percent of the vote, were obliged to form a "great coalition." No other possible constellation would have had a majority. Angela Merkel, who had expected a landslide victory, put on a brave face and announced that she had "a clear duty to form a government."

The coalition discussions soon made in clear that the SPD had moved so far to the right and that Merkel was far enough to the left of her party that there were no fundamental differences between the two parties. Agenda 2010 was to continue in broad outline, taxes increased, services reduced, and the EU's Stability and Growth Pact (SGP) respected. The results were impressive. The number of unemployed was reduced from 4.9 million in 2005 at the beginning of the coalition to 2.9 million by 2008, the lowest figure since 1992.

In foreign policy the coalition remained on the same course as its predecessor. Merkel was able to use the fact that she had been critical of Schröder's opposition to the Iraq war to improve relations with the USA. Germany's obligation towards Israel's security was emphasized. Her commitment to Europe was staunch. But the greatest difference from her predecessor was one of style. The flamboyant Schröder was publicity hungry and a media star, whereas Merkel concentrated on mastering the details of government while guarding her privacy. This has not endeared her to the media, which all too often take her concern for consensus and mediation for lack of leadership, but it is much appreciated by the public, as well as by leading personalities at home and abroad, who value her exceptional intelligence, competence, openness, and determination.

The fundamental weakness of the coalition was that with its overwhelming majority there was little room for opposition and debate. Politics was reduced to dull administrative routine. Disillusionment with politics and politicians was widespread. This was reflected in the election in September 2009. The campaign was exceedingly lackluster. Although Merkel expressed her preference for a coalition with the FDP, it was generally assumed that the grand coalition would continue, so that the partners were unwilling to fight openly and preferred to defend their record in government. The result was a catastrophe for the SPD, which obtained only 23 percent of the vote, its worst showing since 1949. The CDU/CSU also did poorly, losing 1.4 percentage points with 33.9 percent, with the Bavarian CSU doing particularly badly. The neo-liberal FDP was the big winner with 14.6 percent of the vote, up by 4.8 points. The Left won an astonishing 11.9 percent, thereby overtaking the Greens with their 10.7 percent. The result was a center–right coalition between the CDU/CSU and Guido Westerwelle's FDP.

From the outset the new coalition has been beset with problems. Many middle-of-the-road Christian Democrats, true to their vision of a social market economy, are sharply critical of Merkel's shift to the right with an austerity program that hurts the poor and leaves the rich unburdened. They have called for increased taxation of the wealthy, while Westerwelle has demanded tax cuts. The CSU is especially critical of the FDP, particularly of the liberals' proposals for health-care reform. Merkel continues to muddle through, giving the impression of weak leadership while keeping any possible challengers to her leadership at bay. The result has been the resignation of a number of leading figures in the

CDU, including the powerful minister president of Hesse, Roland Koch, the president, Horst Köhler, and the popular mayor of Hamburg, Ole von Beust.

On the positive side, Germany has recovered quickly from the recession. A weaker euro has helped exports, and pent-up demand on the domestic market coupled with a positive employment trend and government stimulus measures have all contributed to an unexpectedly high rate of growth. Low interest rates have benefited the building trades. The core inflation rate has remained remarkably low, in spite of increased costs for industrial raw materials and energy. Nevertheless, Germany, as a leading exporting nation, is susceptible to the global economy, even with strong endogenous forces for growth. Furthermore, much of this success is due to austerity measures that have placed the concept of a social market economy in question, which in turn has encouraged extremism on both the left and the right. Serious shortcomings in the government's economic and social policies, particularly in the increasingly difficult areas of health and pensions caused by an aging population, remain to be tackled.

Problems and Perspectives

The problems that beset the newly reunited Germany were already inherent in the old Federal Republic. An ever-widening gap between rich and poor, an increasingly inflexible class system, high levels of unemployment, seemingly insoluble problems with the welfare state, and serious environmental challenges were combined with the hedonistic culture of a consumer society, increased pressure to perform, and a widespread feeling of anomie to fuel a sullen rejection of the political system, a post-materialist pessimism, and fashionable chatter of a grim disciplinary society à la Foucault. Some commentators have suggested that present discontents are the symptoms typical of a capitalist society moving from the extremes of blind faith in technological progress to neo-Malthusian gloom.

Much to the sorrow of those who dreamed of a post-national Europe, Germany has become a nation-state but one integrated into the European Union and a responsible partner in world affairs. It is a worthy heir to the admirable liberal, constitutional, democratic, social, and federal traditions of German history. In spite of appalling scandals involving party financing which, among other things, resulted in Helmut Kohl's career ending in disgrace, and the gross feather-bedding of self-serving and unprincipled politicians, the old Federal Republic was a decent and functioning democracy that was viewed by its citizens not with overwhelming pride, but with a healthy skepticism. It was a state that scrupulously guarded the fundamental rights of its citizens, but it was not until a new law on citizenship came into effect on January 1, 2000 that an element of the democratic *jus soli* (which grants the right to citizenship to anyone born in the country) was introduced that watered down the exclusive and highly dubious *jus sanguinis* (citizenship granted by parentage), with Germany thus moving closer to the Western democracies. Thanks to Adenauer's insistence on firm ties to the West and Willy Brandt's pragmatic approach to an opening to the East in his *Ostpolitik*, Germany was able to combine national unity with democratic freedoms, unlike Bismarck's Germany of 1871. The old Federal Republic, which the historian Karl Dietrich Bracher had justifiably called a "post-national democracy among nation-states" became with unification, to the alarm of many on the left, a nation-state among nation-states with the absorption of the "international" GDR. It remains to be seen how the new Germany will wrestle with the myths, heroes, and villains of its past and whether it will be able to find a positive sense of national identity. Much is still to be done, for the nation-state will long remain with us, in however changed and weakened a form. The force of circumstances was such that Germany was unable to undertake the mission, hoped for by many in 1990, to lead Europe forward to a post-national utopia. This version of a German *Sonderweg* was not to be, and the country was left with the daunting task of facing up to the same responsibilities and obligations as its allies. None of the old excuses will wash, and the self-satisfied comforts offered by a bad conscience over a criminal past no longer offer protection against the need to face up to the burdens and vexations of normalcy.

Bibliography

General Works

Berghahn, V.R. *Imperial Germany 1871–1914* (Oxford, 1994).

Berghahn, V.R. *Modern Germany: Society, Economy, and Politics in the Twentieth Century* (Cambridge, 1987).

Blackbourn, D. *History of Germany 1780–1918: The Long Nineteenth Century* (Oxford, 2002).

Carr, W. *A History of Germany 1815–1945* (London, 1987).

Clark, C. *Iron Kingdom: The Rise and Downfall of Prussia 1600–1947* (London, 2006).

Craig, G.A. *The Germans* (Harmondsworth, 1978).

Craig, G.A. *Germany 1866–1945* (Oxford, 1981).

Fulbrook, M. *German History since 1800* (London, 1997).

Fulbrook, M. *A History of Germany 1918–2008: The Divided Nation* (Oxford, 2008).

Macartney, C.A. *The Habsburg Empire 1790–1918* (London, 1968).

Mann, G. *A History of Germany since 1789* (London, 1968).

Nipperdey, T. *German History from Napoleon to Bismarck, 1800–1866* (Dublin, 1996).

Orlow, D. *A History of Modern Germany 1871 to the Present* (Englewood Cliffs, NJ, 1987).

Ramm, A. *Germany 1789–1919* (London, 1968).

Schulze, H. *The Course of German Nationalism: From Frederick the Great to Bismarck 1763–1867* (Cambridge, 1991).

Sheehan, J.J. *German History, 1770–1866* (Oxford, 1989).

Sked, A. *The Decline and Fall of the Habsburg Empire 1815–1918* (London, 1989).

Wehler, H.-U. *The German Empire 1871–1918* (Leamington Spa, 1985).

1800–1919

Albisetti, J.C. *Secondary School Reform in Wilhelmine Germany* (Princeton, 1983).

Allen, A.T. *Feminism and Motherhood in Germany 1800–1914* (New Brunswick, NJ, 1991).

Allen, A.T. *Satire and Society in Wilhelmine Germany* (Louisville, 1985).

Angress, W.T. *Stillborn Revolution* (Princeton, 1963).

Applegate, C. *A Nation of Provincials: The German Idea of Heimat* (Berkeley, 1990).

Augustine, D.L. *Patricians and Parvenus: Wealth and High Society in Wilhelmine Germany* (Oxford, 1984).

Bade, K.J. (ed.). *Population, Labour and Migration in 19th and 20th Century Germany* (Oxford, 1987).

Barclay, D. *Frederick William IV and the Prussian Monarchy 1840–1861* (Oxford, 1995).

Barkin, K.D. *The Controversy over German Industrialization 1890–1902* (Chicago, 1970).

Berghahn, V.R. *Germany and the Approach of War in 1914* (London, 1973).

Best, G. *War and Society in Revolutionary Europe 1770–1870* (London, 1982).

A History of Modern Germany: 1800 to the Present, Second Edition. Martin Kitchen.
© 2012 Martin Kitchen. Published 2012 by Blackwell Publishing Ltd.

Billinger, W.D. *Metternich and the German Question: State Rights and Federal Duties, 1820–1834* (Newark, 1992).

Birnbaum, K. *Peace Moves and U-Boat Warfare* (Hampden, CT, 1870).

Blackbourn, D. *Class, Religion and Politics in Wilhelmine Germany: The Centre Party in Württemberg before 1914* (London, 1984).

Blackbourn, D. *Populists and Patricians* (London, 1987).

Blackbourn, D. and G. Eley. *The Peculiarities of German History* (Oxford, 1984).

Blackbourn, D. and R. Evans (eds.). *The German Bourgeoisie* (London, 1991).

Blanning, T.C.W. *The French Revolution in Germany* (Cambridge, 1983).

Breuer, M. *Modernity Within Tradition: The Social History of Orthodox Jewry in Imperial Germany* (New York, 1992).

Brose, E.D. *The Kaiser's Army: The Politics of Military Technology in Germany during the Machine Age, 1870–1918* (Oxford, 2001).

Bry, G. *Wages in Germany, 1871–1914* (Princeton, 1960).

Bucholz, A. *Moltke, Schlieffen, and Prussian War Planning* (Oxford, 1991).

Campbell, J. *The German Werkbund: The Politics of Reform in the Applied Arts* (Princeton, 1978).

Carsten, F.L. *Revolution in Central Europe, 1918–1919* (London, 1972).

Carsten, F.L. *War against War: British and German Radical Movements in the First World War* (Berkeley, 1982).

Cecil, L. *The German Diplomatic Service, 1871–1914* (Princeton, 1979).

Chapple, G. and H. Schulte (eds.). *The Turn of the Century: German Literature and Art, 1890–1915* (Bonn, 1981).

Chickering, R. *Imperial Germany and the Great War* (Cambridge, 1998).

Chickering, R. *"We Men Who Feel Most German": A Cultural Study of the Pan-German League* (London, 1984).

Coetzee, M.S. *The German Army League* (Oxford, 1990).

Comfort, R.A. *Revolutionary Hamburg* (Stanford, CA, 1966).

Craig, G.A. *The Politics of the Prussian Army 1640–1945* (Oxford, 1955).

Craig, G.A. *The Politics of the Unpolitical: German Writers and the Problem of Power, 1770–1871* (Oxford, 1995).

Crampton, R.J. *The Hollow Détente: Anglo-German Relations in the Balkans* (London, 1979).

Dahrendorf, R. *Society and Democracy in Germany* (London, 1968).

Desai, A.V. *Real Wages in Germany, 1871–1914* (Oxford, 1968).

Dube, W.-D. *The Expressionists* (London, 1972).

Eley, G. *Reshaping the German Right* (London, 1980).

Epstein, K. *The Genesis of German Conservatism* (Princeton, 1966).

Epstein, K. *Matthias Erzberger and the Dilemma of German Democracy* (Princeton, 1959).

Evans, R.J. *Death in Hamburg: Society and Politics in the Cholera Years, 1830–1910* (Oxford, 1987).

Evans, R.J. *The Feminist Movement in Germany, 1894–1933* (London, 1976).

Evans, R.J. (ed.). *The German Underworld* (London, 1988).

Evans, R.J. (ed.). *The German Working Class* (London, 1968).

Evans, R.J. *Rethinking German History* (London, 1987).

Evans, R.J. (ed.). *Society and Politics in Wilhelmine Germany* (London, 1978).

Evans, R.J. and W.R. Lee (eds.). *The German Family* (London, 1980).

Evans, R.J. and W.R. Lee (eds.). *The German Peasantry* (London, 1986).

Eyck, F. *The Frankfurt Parliament 1848–1849* (London, 1968).

Feldman, G.D. *Army, Industry, and Labor in Germany, 1914–1918* (Princeton, 1966).

Feldman, G.D. *The Great Disorder: Politics, Economics and Society in the German Inflation, 1914–1924* (New York, 1993).

Ferro, M. *The Great War 1914–1918* (London, 1973).

Fischer, F. *Germany's War Aims in the First World War* (London, 1967).

Fischer, F. *War of Illusions: German Policies from 1911 to 1914* (London, 1975).

Franzoi, B. *At the Very Least She Pays the Rent: Women and German Industrialization* (Westport, CT, 1985).

Frevert, U. *Women in German History* (Oxford, 1990).

Gall, L. *Bismarck: The White Revolutionary* (London, 1986).

Gatzke, H. *Germany's Drive to the West* (Baltimore, 1950).

Gay, P. *Freud, Jews, and Other Germans* (Oxford, 1978).

Gay, R. *The Jews of Germany* (New Haven, 1992).

Geiss, I. *German Foreign Policy, 1871–1914* (London, 1976).

Geiss, I. *July 1914: The Outbreak of the First World War. Selected Documents* (New York, 1967).

Gellately, R. *The Politics of Economic Despair: Shopkeepers and German Politics 1890–1914* (London, 1974).

Gerschenkron, A. *Bread and Democracy in Germany* (Ithaca, 1989).

Gerth, H.H. and C.W. Mills. *From Max Weber* (London, 1974).

Gray, M. *Prussia in Transition: Society and Politics under the Stein Reform Ministry of 1808* (Philadelphia, 1986).

Grebing, H. *The History of the German Labour Movement* (Leamington Spa, 1985).

Guttsmans, W. *The German Social Democratic Party 1875–1933* (London, 1981).

Hackett, A. *The Politics of Feminism in Wilhelmine Germany, 1890–1918* (New York, 1979).

Hamerow, T.S. *Restoration, Revolution, Reaction: Economics and Politics in Central Europe 1815–1871* (Princeton, 1958).

Hamilton, N. *The Brothers Mann* (London, 1978).

Hardach, K.W. *The First World War* (Berkeley, 1977).

Heckart, B. *From Bassermann to Bebel* (New Haven, 1974).

Henderson, W.O. *The Rise of Germany Industrial Power, 1834–1914* (Berkeley, 1975).

Henderson, W.O. *The State and the Industrial Revolution in Prussia 1740–1870* (Liverpool, 1958).

Henderson, W.O. *The Zollverein* (London, 1939).

Herwig, H.H. *The First World War: Germany and Austria-Hungary, 1914–1918* (London, 1997).

Herwig, H.H. *The German Naval Officer Corps* (Oxford, 1973).

Herwig, H.H. *"Luxury Fleet": The Imperial German Navy, 1888–1918* (London, 1980).

Hickey, S. *Workers in Imperial Germany: Miners in the Ruhr* (Oxford, 1985).

Horn, D. *The German Naval Mutinies of World War I* (New Brunswick, NJ, 1969).

Hull, I. *The Entourage of Kaiser Wilhelm II* (Cambridge, 1982).

Jarausch, K.H. *The Enigmatic Chancellor: Bethmann Hollweg and the Hubris of Imperial Germany* (New Haven, 1973).

Jevalich, P. *Munich and Theatrical Modernism* (Cambridge, MA, 1985).

Joll, J. *The Origins of the First World War* (London, 1984).

Jones, L.E. and J. Retallack (eds.). *Elections, Mass Politics, and Social Change in Modern Germany* (Cambridge, 1992).

Kaplan, M.A. *The Making of the Jewish Middle Class: Women, Family, and Identity in Imperial Germany* (New York, 1991).

Kehr, E. *Battleship Building and Party Politics in Germany, 1894–1901* (Chicago, 1973).

Kehr, E. *Economic Interest, Militarism, and Foreign Policy* (Berkeley, 1977).

Kennedy, P.M. *The Rise of Anglo-German Antagonism, 1860–1914* (London, 1980).

Kennedy, P.M. (ed.). *The War Plans of the Great Powers, 1880–1914* (London, 1979).

Kitchen, M. *The German Offensives of 1918* (Stroud, 2001).

Kitchen, M. *The German Officer Corps, 1890–1914* (Oxford, 1968).

Kitchen, M. *The Political Economy of Germany 1815–1914* (London, 1978).

Kitchen, M. *The Silent Dictatorship: The Politics of the German High Command under Hindenburg and Ludendorff, 1916–1918* (London, 1976).

Knodel, J. *The Decline of Fertility in Germany, 1871–1939* (Princeton, 1974).

Kocka, J. *Facing Total War: German Society 1914–1918* (Leamington Spa, 1984).

Kraehe, E.E. *Metternich's German Policy*, 2 vols. (Princeton, 1963, 1984).

Krieger, L. *The German Idea of Freedom* (Boston, 1957).

Lambi, I.N. *The Navy and German Power Politics* (London, 1984).

Laqueur, W. *Young Germany* (London, 1962).

LaVopa, A. *Prussian Schoolteachers: Profession and Office, 1763–1848* (Chapel Hill, 1980).

Lerman, K.A. *The Chancellor as Courtier: Bernhard von Bülow and the Governance of Germany, 1900–1909* (Cambridge, 1990).

Levy, R.S. *The Downfall of the Anti-Semitic Political Parties in Imperial Germany* (New Haven, 1975).

Lidtke, V.L. *The Alternative Culture* (Oxford, 1985).

Lidtke, V.L. *The Outlawed Party* (Princeton, 1966).

Makela, M. *The Munich Succession: Art and Artists in Turn-of-the-Century Munich* (Princeton, 1990).

Mann, T. *Reflections of a Nonpolitical Man* (New York, 1983).

Masur, G. *Imperial Berlin* (London, 1971).

Mayer, A.J. *The Politics and Diplomacy of Peacemaking* (London, 1968).

McClelland, C. *State, Society, and University in Germany, 1700–1914* (Cambridge, 1980).

McLellan, D. *Karl Marx* (New York, 1973).

Meyer, H.C. *Mitteleuropa in German Thought and Action* (The Hague, 1955).

Mitchell, A. *Revolution in Bavaria* (Princeton, 1965).

Mombauer, A. *Helmuth von Moltke and the Origins of the First World War* (Cambridge, 2001).

Mombauer, A. *The Origins of the First World War: Controversies and Consensus* (London, 2002).

Mommsen, W.J. *Imperial Germany 1867–1918: Politics, Culture and Society in an Authoritarian State* (London, 1995).

Mommsen, W.J. *Max Weber and German Politics* (Chicago, 1984).

Moses, J.A. *The Fischer Controversy in German Historiography* (New York, 1975).

Moses, J.A. *The Politics of Illusion* (London, 1975).

Moses, J.A. *Trade Unionism in Germany from Bismarck to Hitler*, 2 vols. (Totowa, NJ, 1982).

Mosse, G. *The Crisis of German Ideology* (London, 1966).

Mosse, G. *The Nationalization of the Masses* (New York, 1975).

Mosse, W. *Jews in the German Economy* (Oxford, 1987).

Nettl, J.P. *Rosa Luxemburg*, 2 vols. (Oxford, 1966).

Neuberger, H. *German Banks and German Economic Growth, 1871–1914* (New York, 1977).

Nichols, J.A. *Germany after Bismarck: The Caprivi Era, 1890–1894* (Cambridge, MA, 1958).

Nipperdey, T. *The Rise of the Arts in Modern Society* (London, 1990).

Noyes, P.H. *Organization and Revolution: Working-Class Associations in the German Revolutions of 1848–49* (Princeton, 1966).

Paret, P. *The Berlin Secession* (Cambridge, MA, 1980).

Paret, P. *Yorck and the Era of Prussian Reform, 1807–1815* (Princeton, 1966).

Pascal, R. *From Naturalism to Expressionism: German Literature and Society 1880–1918* (London, 1973).

Pflanze, O. *Bismarck and the Development of Germany* (Princeton, 1990).

Pinkard, T. *Hegel: A Biography* (Cambridge, 2000).

Pulzer, P.G.J. *The Rise of Political Anti-Semitism in Germany and Austria* (New York, 1964).

Retallack, J.N. *Notables of the Right* (London, 1988).

Ringer, A. (ed.). *The Early Romantic Era. Between Revolutions: 1789 and 1848* (London, 1990).

Ringer, F. *The Decline of the German Mandarins* (Cambridge, MA, 1969).

Ritter, G. *The Schlieffen Plan* (London, 1958).

Ritter, G.A. *Social Welfare in Germany and Britain* (Leamington Spa, 1983).

Rogoff, I. (ed.). *The Divided Heritage: Themes and Problems in German Modernism* (Cambridge, 1991).

Röhl, J.C.G. *1914: Destiny of Design? The Testimony of Two German Diplomats* (New York, 1973).

Röhl, J.C.G. *From Bismarck to Hitler: The Problem of Continuity in Germany History* (London, 1970).

Röhl, J.C.G. *Germany Without Bismarck: The Crisis of Government in the Second Reich, 1890–1900* (Berkeley, 1967).

Röhl, J.C.G. *The Kaiser and his Court: William II and the Government of Germany* (Cambridge, 1994).

Röhl, J.C.G. *Kaiser William II, New Interpretations: The Corfu Papers* (Cambridge, 1982).

Röhl, J.C.G. *Wilhelm II: The Kaiser's Early Life, 1859–1888* (Cambridge, 1998).

Röhl, J.C.G. *Wilhelm II: The Kaiser's Personal Monarchy, 1888–1900* (New York, 2004).

Röhl, J.C.G. and N. Sombart (eds.). *Kaiser Wilhelm II: New Interpretations* (Cambridge, 1982).

Rosenberg, H. *Imperial Germany* (Boston, 1964).

Roth, G. *The Social Democrats in Imperial Germany* (Totowa, NJ, 1963).

Ryder, A.J. *The German Revolution of 1918* (Cambridge, 1967).

Sackett, R.E. *Popular Entertainment, Class, and Politics in Imperial Germany* (London, 1982).

Sagarra, E. *A Social History of Germany 1648–1914* (London, 1977).

Sagarra, E. *Tradition and Revolution: German Literature and Society, 1830–1890* (London, 1971).

Schoenbaum, D. *Zabern* (Garden City, 1982).

Schorske, C.E. *German Social Democracy, 1905–1917* (Cambridge, MA, 1955).

Schulze, H. *The Course of German Nationalism: From Frederick the Great to Bismarck, 1763–1867* (Cambridge, 1991).

Sheehan, J.J. *German Liberalism in the Nineteenth Century* (Chicago, 1978).

Sheehan, J.J. *The Career of Lujo Brentano* (Chicago, 1966).

Showalter, D.E. *The Wars of German Unification* (New York, 2004).

Smith, W.D. *The German Colonial Empire* (Chapel Hill, 1978).

Smith, W.D. *The Ideological Origins of Nazi Imperialism* (New York, 1986).

Smith, W.D. *Politics and the Sciences of Culture in Germany, 1840–1920* (New York, 1991).

Sperber, J. *The European Revolutions, 1848–1851* (Cambridge, 1994).

Sperber, J. *Popular Catholicism in Nineteenth-Century Germany* (Princeton, 1984).

Sperber, J. *Rhineland Radicals: The Democratic Movement and the Revolution of 1848* (Princeton, 1991).

Spree, R. *Health and Social Class in Imperial Germany: A Social History of Mortality, Morbidity, and Inequality* (Oxford, 1987).

Stachura, P.D. *The German Youth Movement, 1900–1945* (London, 1981).

Steinmetz, G. *Regulating the Social: The Welfare State and Local Politics in Imperial Germany* (Princeton, 1973).

Stern, F. *The Politics of Cultural Despair* (Berkeley, 1961).

Stevenson, D. *French War Aims against Germany, 1914–1919* (Oxford, 1982).

Strachan, H. *The First World War*, vol. 1 (Oxford, 2001).

Struve, W. *Elites against Democracy* (Princeton, 1973).

Tal, U. *Christians and Jews in Germany, 1870–1915* (Ithaca, 1974).

Tampke, J. *The Ruhr and Revolution* (London, 1979).

Teich, M. and R. Porter (eds.). *Fin de Siècle and its Legacy* (Cambridge, 1990).

Veblen, T. *Imperial Germany and the Industrial Revolution* (London, 1915).

Vick, B.E. *Defining Germany: The 1848 Frankfurt Parliamentarians and National Identity* (Boston, 2002).

Vincent, C.P. *The Politics of Hunger: The Allied Blockade of Germany, 1915–1919* (Athens, Ohio, 1985).

Voegelin, E. *Science, Politics and Gnosticism* (Chicago, 1968).

Volkov, S. *The Rise of Popular Antimodernism in Germany: The Urban Master Artisans, 1873–1896* (Princeton, 1978).

Watt, R.M. *The Kings Depart* (London, 1969).

Weiss, P.J. *Race, Hygiene, and National Efficiency* (Berkeley, 1987).

Whalen, R.W. *Bitter Wounds: German Victims of the Great War, 1914–1939* (Ithaca, 1984).

Williamson, J.G. *Karl Helfferich, 1872–1924: Economist, Financier, Politician* (Princeton, 1971).

Winter, J.M. *The Experience of World War I* (London, 1988).

Wohl, R. *The Generation of 1914* (Cambridge, MA, 1979).

Woycke, J. *Birth Control in Germany, 1871–1933* (London, 1988).

1919–1933

Abrams, D. *The Collapse of the Weimar Republic: Political Economy and Crisis* (Princeton, 1981).

Balderston, T. *Economics and Politics in the Weimar Republic* (Cambridge, 2002).

Balderston, T. *The Origins and Course of the German Economic Crisis, November 1923–May 1932* (Berlin, 1993).

Bessel, R. *Germany after the First World War* (Oxford, 1993).

Carsten, F.L. *The Reichswehr and Politics 1918–1933* (Oxford, 1966).

Childers, T.(ed.). *The Formation of the Nazi Constituency, 1918–1933* (Totowa, NJ, 1986).

Eichengreen, B. *Golden Fetters: The Gold Standard and the Great Depression, 1919–1939* (New York, 1992).

Evans, R.J. and D. Geary (eds.). *The German Unemployed: Experiences and Consequences of Mass Unemployment from the Weimar Republic to the Third Reich* (New York, 1987).

Feldman, G.D. *The Great Disorder: Economics, Politics, and Society in the German Inflation, 1914–1924* (Oxford, 1983).

Fergusson, N. *Paper and Iron: Hamburg Business and German Politics in the Era of Inflation, 1897–1927* (Cambridge, 1995).

Feuchtwanger, E.J. *From Weimar to Hitler: Germany 1918–1933* (Basingstoke, 1993).

Fritzsche, P. *Rehearsals for Fascism: Populism and Political Mobilization in Weimar Germany* (New York, 1990).

Gay, P. *Weimar Culture: The Outsider as Insider* (London, 1974).

Harsch, D. *German Social Democracy and the Rise of Nazism* (Chapel Hill, 1993).

Haxthausen, C.W. and G. Suhr (eds.). *Berlin: Culture and Metropolis* (Minneapolis, 1990).

Heiber, H. *The Weimar Republic* (Oxford, 1993).

Herf, J. *Reactionary Modernism: Technology, Culture and Politics in Weimar and the Third Reich* (Cambridge, 1984).

Holtfrerich, C.-L. *German Inflation, 1914–1923: Causes and Effects in International Perspective* (New York, 1986).

James, H. *The German Slump: Politics and Economics 1924–1936* (Oxford, 1986).

Jones, L.E. *German Liberalism and the Dissolution of the Weimar Party System, 1918–1933* (Chapel Hill, 1988).

Kershaw, I. *Weimar: Why Did German Democracy Fail?* (London, 1990).

Keynes, J.M. *The Economic Consequences of the Peace* (London, 1919).

Kneische, T.W. and S. Brockmann. *Dancing of the Volcano: Essays on the Culture of the Weimar Republic* (Columbia, SC, 1994).

Kolb, E. *The Weimar Republic* (London, 1988).

Kunz, A. *Civil Servants and the Politics of Inflation in Germany, 1914–1924* (Berlin, 1986).

Lane, B.M. *Architecture and Politics in Germany 1918–1945* (Boston, 1985).

Laqueur, W. *Weimar: A Cultural History 1918–1933* (London, 1974).

Lee, M. and W. Michalka. *German Foreign Policy 1917–1933: Continuity or Break?* (New York, 1987).

Lee, S.J. *The Weimar Republic* (London, 1998).

Michalski, S. *New Objectivity: Painting, Graphic Art and Photography in Weimar Germany, 1919–1933* (Cologne, 1994).

Mombauer, A. and W. Deist. *The Kaiser: Promise and Tragedy* (Cambridge, 2003).

Mommsen, H. *The Rise and Fall of Weimar Democracy* (Chapel Hill, 1996).

Nichols, A.J. *Weimar and the Rise of Hitler* (Basingstoke, 1991).

Nolan, M. *Visions of Modernity: American Business and the Modernization of Germany* (New York, 1994).

Peukert, D.J.K. *The Weimar Republic: The Crisis of Classical Modernity* (London, 1991).

Plummer, T.G. *Film and Politics in the Weimar Republic* (New York, 1982).

Roth, J. *What I Saw: Reports From Berlin 1920–1933* (New York, 2004).

Schuker, S.A. *American "Reparations" to Germany, 1919–33: Implications for the Third World Debt Crisis* (Princeton, 1988).

Stachura, P.D. *Unemployment and the Great Depression in Weimar Germany* (Basingstoke, 1986).

Stark, G. *Entrepreneurs of Ideology: Neoconservative Publishers in Weimar Germany* (Chapel Hill, 1981).

Webb, S.B. *Hyperinflation and Stabilisation in Weimar Germany* (New York, 1989).

Weitz, E.D. *Weimar Germany: Promise and Tragedy* (Princeton, 2007).

Whalen, R.W. *Bitter Wounds: German Victims of the Great War, 1914–1939* (Ithaca, 1984).

1933–1945

Arad, Y., Y. Gutman, and A. Margaliot (eds.). *Documents of the Holocaust* (Jerusalem, 1981).

Arad, Y., S. Krakowski, and S. Spector (eds.). *The Einsatzgruppen Reports* (New York, 1989).

Balfour, M. *Withstanding Hitler in Germany 1933–1945* (London, 1988).

Barkai, A. *From Boycott to Annihilation: The Economic Struggle of German Jews 1933–1945* (Waltham, MA, 1989).

Barkai, A. *Nazi Economics: Ideology, Theory and Policy* (Oxford, 1990).

Bauer, Y. *The Holocaust in Historical Perspective* (London, 1978).

Benz, W. *The Holocaust* (New York, 1999).

Bergen, D.L. *Twisted Cross: The German Christian Movement in the Third Reich* (Chapel Hill, 1996).

Bracher, K.-D. *The German Dictatorship* (London, 1970).

Breitmann, R. *The Architect of Genocide: Heinrich Himmler and the Final Solution* (London, 1991).

Browning, C. *Ordinary Men: Reserve Battalion 101 and the Final Solution in Poland* (New York, 1993).

Browning, C. *Paths to Genocide* (Cambridge, 1994).

Bullock, A. *Hitler: A Study in Tyranny* (London, 1964).

Burleigh, M. *Death and Deliverance: Euthanasia in Germany c.1900–1945* (Cambridge, 1994).

Burleigh, M. *The Third Reich* (New York, 2000).

Burleigh M. and W. Wippermann. *The Racial State: Germany 1933–1945* (Cambridge, 1991).

Conway, J.S. *The Nazi Persecution of the Churches 1933–1945* (London, 1968).

Deist, W. *The Wehrmacht and German Rearmament* (London, 1981).

Evans, R.J. *The Coming of the Third Reich* (New York, 2005).

Evans, R.J. *The Third Reich in Power* (New York, 2006).

Evans, R.J. *The Third Reich at War* (New York, 2009).

Farquharson, J.E. *The Plough and the Swastika: The NSDAP and Agriculture in Germany 1928–1945* (London, 1976).

Fest, J. *Hitler* (London, 1974).

Friedländer, S. *Nazi Germany and the Jews: The Years of Persecution 1933–1939* (London, 1998).

Friedländer, S. *Nazi Germany and the Jews: The Years of Extermination: 1939–1945* (London, 2007).

Gellately, R. *The Gestapo and German Society* (Oxford, 1988).

Glantz, D.M. *Barbarossa: Hitler's Invasion of Russia 1941* (Stroud, 2001).

Gorodetsky, G. *Grand Delusion: Stalin and the German Invasion of Russia* (New Haven, 1999).

Graml, H. *Anti-Semitism in the Third Reich* (Oxford, 1992).

Grossmann, V. *Life and Fate* (London, 1985).

Herbert, U. *Hitler's Foreign Workers: Enforced Foreign Labour in Germany under the Third Reich* (Cambridge, 1997).

Herbert, U. *National Socialist Extermination Policies* (Oxford, 2000).

Hiden, J. and J. Farquharson. *Explaining Hitler's Germany* (London, 1989).

Hilberg, R. *The Destruction of the European Jews* (New York, 1983).

Hildebrand, K. *The Third Reich* (London, 1984).

Hoffmann, P. *The History of German Resistance to Hitler 1933–1945* (Montreal, 1996).

Huener, J. and F.R. Nicosia. *The Arts in Nazi Germany: Continuity, Conformity, Change* (Oxford, 2007).

Kershaw, I. *Hitler 1889–1936: Hubris* (London, 1998).

Kershaw, I. *Hitler 1936–1945: Nemesis* (London, 2000).

Kershaw, I. *The "Hitler Myth": Image and Reality in the Third Reich* (Oxford, 1987).

Kershaw, I. *The Nazi Dictatorship* (London, 1995).

Kitchen, M. *Nazi Germany at War* (New York, 1995).

Kitchen, M. *The Third Reich: Charisma and Community* (Harlow, 2008).

Klemperer, V. *The Diaries of Victor Klemperer*, 2 vols. (London, 1998, 1999).

Koonz, C. *Mothers in the Fatherland: Women, the Family, and Nazi Politics* (New York, 1987).

Longerich, P. *The Unwritten Order: Hitler's Role in the Final Solution* (Stroud, 2001).

Marrus, M. *The Holocaust in History* (Jerusalem, 1981).

Marrus, M. and R. Paxton. *Vichy France and the Jews* (New York, 1983).

Mazower, M. *Hitler's Empire: How the Nazis Ruled Europe* (New York, 2008).

Müller, K.-J. *The Army, Politics and Society in Germany 1933–1939* (Manchester, 1987).

Mulligan, T. *The Politics of Illusion and Empire: German Occupation Policy in the Soviet Union 1942–43* (New York, 1988).

Nekrich, A.M. *Pariahs, Partners, Predators: German–Soviet Relations 1922–1941* (New York, 1997).

Noakes, J. and G. Pridham (eds.). *Nazism, 1919–1945: A Documentary Reader* (Exeter, 1983/98).

Overy, R.J. *The Air War, 1939–1945* (London, 1980).

Overy, R.J. *Göring: The Iron Man* (London, 1983).

Overy, R.J. *The Nazi Economic Recovery, 1932–1938* (Cambridge, 1996).

Overy, R.J. *Russia's War* (London, 1997).

Overy, R.J. *Why the Allies Won* (London, 1995).

Paucker, A. *Jewish Resistance in Germany: The Facts and the Problems* (Berlin, 1991).

Tooze, A. *The Wages of Destruction: The Making and Breaking of the Nazi Economy* (London, 2006).

Trunk, I. *Judenrat: The Jewish Councils in Eastern Europe under Nazi Occupation* (New York, 1972).

Wolf, H. *Pope and Devil: The Vatican's Archives and the Third Reich* (Boston, 2010).

1945–2000

Balfour, M. *Germany: The Tides of Power* (London, 1992).

Baring, A. *Uprising in East Germany* (New York, 1972).

Berghahn, V.R. *The Americanisation of West German Industry, 1945–1973* (Leamington Spa, 1986).

Burns, R. *German Cultural Studies: An Introduction* (Oxford, 1995).

Carter, E. *How German Is She? Postwar West German Reconstruction and the Consuming Woman* (Ann Arbor, 1997).

Childs, D. *The GDR: Moscow's German Ally* (London, 1988).

Childs, D. (ed.). *Honecker's Germany* (London, 1985).

Dahrendorf, R. *Society and Democracy in Germany* (London, 1968).

Dennis, M. *German Democratic Republic: Politics, Economics and Society* (London, 1988).

Dennis, M. *Social and Economic Modernization in Eastern Germany from Honecker to Kohl* (London, 1993).

Elsaesser, T. *New German Cinema: A History* (London, 1989).

Frei, N. *Adenauer's Germany and the Nazi Past* (New York, 2002).

Fulbrook, M. *Anatomy of a Dictatorship: Inside the GDR 1949–1989* (Oxford, 1995).

Fulbrook, M. *The Two Germanies 1945–1990: Problems of Interpretation* (London, 1992).

Glaessner, G.-J. *The Unification Process in Germany: From Dictatorship to Democracy* (London, 1992).

Glaessner, G.-J. and I. Wallace (eds.). *The German Revolution of 1989: Causes and Consequences* (Oxford, 1992).

Goodbody, A. and D. Tate (eds.). *Geist und Macht: Writers and the State in the GDR* (Amsterdam, 1992).

Hallberg, R. von *Literary Intellectuals and the Dissolution of the State: Professionalism and Conformity in the GDR* (Chicago, 1996).

Humphreys, P.J. *Media and Media Policy in Germany: The Press and Broadcasting since 1945* (Oxford, 1989).

James, H. and M. Stone (eds.). *When the Wall Came Down: Reaction to German Unification* (New York, 1992).

Jarausch, K.H. *The Rush to German Unity* (Oxford, 1994).

Jarausch, K.H. and V. Gransow (eds.). *Uniting Germany: Documents and Debates, 1944–1993* (Providence, RI, 1994).

Kaes, A. *From Hitler to Heimat: The Return of History as Film* (Cambridge, 1989).

Kolinsky, E. (ed.). *Between Hope and Fear: Everyday Life in Post-Unification East Germany: A Case Study of Leipzig* (Keele, 1995).

Kolinsky, E. *Women in West Germany: Life, Work and Politics* (Oxford, 1989).

Kramer, A. *The West German Economy* (Oxford, 1991).

Larres, K. and P. Panayi (eds.). *The Federal Republic of Germany since 1949: Politics, Society and Economy before and after Unification* (Longman, 1996).

Lewis, D. and J.R.P. McKenzie (eds.). *The New Germany: Social, Political and Cultural Challenges of Unification* (Exeter, 1995).

Maaz, H.-J. *Behind the Wall: The Inner Life of Communist Germany* (New York, 1995).

McAdams, A.J. *Germany Divided: From the Wall to Unification* (Princeton, 1993).

McCauley, M. *The GDR since 1945* (London, 1983).

Merkl, P.H. (ed.). *The Federal Republic of Germany at Forty-Five: Union without Unity* (London, 1995).

Nicholls, A.J. *Freedom with Responsibility* (Oxford, 1995).

Osmond, J. (ed.). *German Reunification: A Reference Guide and Commentary* (Harlow, 1992).

Philipson, D. *We Were the People: Voices from East Germany's Revolutionary Autumn of 1989* (Durham, NC, 1993).

Pommerin, R. (ed.). *The American Impact on Post-War Germany* (Providence, RI, 1995).

Pond, E. *Beyond the Wall: Germany's Road to Unification* (Washington, 1993).

Pulzer, P. *German Politics: 1945–1995* (Oxford, 1995).

Rogers, D. Politics *After Hitler: The Western Allies and the German Party System* (London, 1995).

Scharf, C.B. *Politics and Change in East Germany* (Boulder, CO, 1984).

Schwarz, H.P. *Adenauer: From the German Empire to the Federal Republic* (Oxford, 1995).

Sinn, G. and H.-W. Sinn. *Jumpstart: The Economic Unification of Germany* (Cambridge, MA, 1992).

Smith, E.O. *The German Economy* (London, 1994).

Smith, G. *Democracy in Western Germany: Parties and Politics in the Federal Republic* (Aldershot, 1986).

Sontheimer, K. and W. Bleek. *The Government and Politics of East Germany* (London, 1975).

Thomanek, J.K.A. and J. Mellis (eds.). *Politics, Society and Government in the German Democratic Republic: Basis Documents* (Oxford, 1988).

Turner, H.O. *The Two Germanies* (New Haven, 1987).

Turner, I. *Reconstruction in Post-War Germany: British Occupation Policy and the Western Zones, 1945–1955* (Oxford, 1989).

Woods, R. *Opposition in the GDR under Honecker, 1971–85* (London, 1986).

Zelikow, P. and C. Rice. *Germany Unified and Europe Transformed: A Study in Statecraft* (Cambridge, 1995).

INDEX